From New Zion to Old Zion

AMERICA - HOLY LAND MONOGRAPHS

EDITORS

Jonathan D. Sarna
Brandeis University
Moshe Davis, 1916–96
The Hebrew University of Jerusalem

BOOKS IN THIS SERIES

The Israeli-American Connection: Its Roots in the Yishuv, 1914–1945,
by Michael Brown, 1996
*From New Zion to Old Zion: American Jewish Immigration and
Settlement in Palestine, 1917–1939,*
by Joseph B. Glass, 2002

From New Zion to Old Zion

American Jewish Immigration and Settlement in Palestine 1917–1939

Joseph B. Glass

WAYNE STATE UNIVERSITY PRESS   DETROIT

Copyright © 2002 by Wayne State University Press,
Detroit, Michigan 48201. All rights are reserved.
No part of this book may be reproduced without formal permission.
Manufactured in the United States of America.
06 05 04 03 02   5 4 3 2 1

Library of Congress Cataloging-in-Publication Data

Glass, Joseph B.
From new Zion to old Zion : American Jewish immigration and settlement
 in Palestine, 1917–1939 / Joesph B. Glass.
   —(America-Holy Land monographs)
   Includes bibliographical references (p.   ) and index.
   ISBN 0-8143-2842-3 (alk. paper)
   1. Jews, American—Palestine—History—20th century.   2. Jews—
United States—Migrations—History—20th century.   3. Jews—
Colonization—Palestine—History—20th century.   4. Palestine—
Emigration and immigration.   5. United States—Emigration and
immigration.   I. Title. II. Series.
DS113.8.A4   G52   2002
956.94004'924073—dc21
                                                            00-009470

CONTENTS

List of Illustrations / 7

List of Tables / 9

List of Maps / 11

Preface / 13

Introduction / 17

1. Attitudes toward American Jewish Migration to Palestine / 36
2. Information and Assistance / 68
3. Motivations for American Immigration to Palestine / 88
4. The Screening Process: Immigration Policies and Regulations / 118
5. The Spatial Distribution of American *Olim* / 133
6. American *Ahuza* Colonies / 156
7. The American Zion Commonwealth (1914–1928) / 181
8. Private Development in the Rural Sector / 234

CONTENTS

9. AMERICAN JEWISH SETTLEMENT ON JEWISH NATIONAL FUND LANDS / 251
10. AMERICANS IN THE URBAN ENVIRONMENT / 272

Conclusion / 326

Notes / 341

Bibliography / 393

Index / 411

ILLUSTRATIONS

1. Letter regarding decrease in need for capitalist certificates   24
2. Members of Kollel America Tiffereth Yerushalaim praying at
   the Western Wall   28
3. American *halutzim* playing volleyball at Kibbutz Ein Hashofet   32
4. Three generations of pioneers   33
5. Judah and Beatrice Magnes in front of their Jerusalem home   34
6. Cover of memorandum to Zionist Society of Engineers and
   Agriculturists   55
7. American Jewish Legionnaires   59
8. Poster for "What the American Commonwealth Is Doing
   in Palestine"   78
9a. Gan Hadar Corporation letterhead   79
9b. Scenes of moving pictures in Ganey Hadar   79
10. Simcha Reisen of New York   83
11. Gershon Agronsky in Jewish Legionnaire uniform   86
12. Jewish battalions in Palestine   94
13. Members of Kollel America Tiffereth Yerushalaim   99

LIST OF ILLUSTRATIONS

14.	American students at the Hebrew University of Jerusalem	110
15.	Page 1 of the Register of the Palestine Immigration Bureau	128
16.	Income of the Jewish National Fund according to country	144
17.	The "Aliya" to Poria	158
18.	View of the main street of Raanana	172
19.	American-style house in Raanana	173
20.	Tobacco drying at Raanana	174
21.	American Zion Commonwealth landownership certificate	184
22.	Road in the Moshav Balfouria	202
23.	Jewish pioneers lay drainage pipe	208
24.	Middle-class settlement at Herzlia	209
25.	Water tower at Gan Haim	237
26.	Orchards at Ramot Meir	242
27.	Aerial view of Netanya	246
28.	American Banir group leaving Kibbutz Mishmar Haemek	266
29.	American couple at Kibbutz Ein Hashofet	267
30.	Aerial view of Ein Hashofet	268
31.	Kibbutz America-Krit celebrating settlement	269
32.	Straus Medical Center	290
33.	Advertisements for American Tooth Manufacturing Company and Judea Insurance Company	300
34.	American Porcelain Tooth Manufacturing Company	301
35.	Panorama of Afula	312–13
36.	Aerial view of Afula	316

Tables

1. American and Jewish immigration to Palestine, 1919–39	19
2. Emigration from the United States by future country of residence, 1917–24	22
3. Emigration of "Hebrews" from the United States, 1917–24	22
4. Length of residence of American citizens in Jerusalem, 1939	27
5. Age-gender distribution of American Jewish nationals in Palestine, 1931	30
6. North American professionals in various cities, 1922	31
7. Capital reported by prospective immigrants to Palestine, 1919–20	45
8. Zionist Organization of America membership, 1918–29	73
9. Age-gender distribution of North American registrants for immigration to Palestine, 1919–20	95
10. Capitalist immigration to Palestine from the United States, May 1925–December 1942	103
11. Applicants for immigration to Palestine from the United States, July–September 1932	103
12. Distribution of immigration according to categories for selected countries, May 1925–December 1942	124

LIST OF TABLES

13. Distribution of American Jewish citizens in Palestine according to district, 1931	135
14. Distribution for rural settlements and selected urban centers of American Jewish citizens compared to the general Jewish population, 1931	135
15. Net income of the Jewish National Fund by region and selected countries, 1919–38	148
16. Summary of American land purchases up to 1939	149
17. Agricultural land purchased by the American Zion Commonwealth, 1919–26	196
18. Country of origin of family heads in Balfouria, 1926	204
19. Country of origin of family heads in Herzlia, 1926	217
20. Lands purchased in Jerusalem by the American Zion Commonwealth and the Palestine Land Development Company to 1929	275
21. Number of persons supported by Kollel America Tiffereth Yerushalaim for various years	284
22. Age of family heads of Kollel America, 1932	285
23. Floor area of new buildings in Tel Aviv, selected years from 1923–40	292
24. Palestinian exports of artificial teeth and industrial products, selected years from 1930–38	302
25. American Jewish emigration versus American Jewish immigration to Palestine, 1915–37	327
26. Relative rates of Jewish immigration to Palestine for selected countries, 1919–39	332

Maps

1a.	U.S. and Canadian applicants for immigration to Palestine, 1919–20	113
1b.	Ratio of U.S. and Canadian applicants relative to the total Jewish population, 1919–20	113
2a.	Land purchases from the American Zion Commonwealth and the Migdal Company, 1927–31	115
2b.	Ratio of land purchasers to the Jewish population, 1927–31	115
3a.	Raanana and its vicinity, 1938	170
3b.	Plan of Raanana	170
4.	Gan Yavne, 1933	177
5.	American land purchases in Palestine to 1939	195
6a.	Balfouria, plan of settlement and various structures, 1923	198
6b.	Balfouria and Rub-El-Nazra purchases, 1926	199
7a.	Plan and location of Herzlia, 1924, zones 1, 2, and 3	212
7b.	Plan and location of Herzlia, 1924, zone 4	213
8a.	Plan of Afula, 1925	220
8b.	Afula in 1939	221
9.	Purchases in Haifa Bay and the Jezreel Valley, 1926	228

LIST OF MAPS

10. Rosoff settlements, 1935	241
11. Settlement of American *Halutzim,* 1918–39	261
12. Development of Jerusalem to 1937	276
13. American activities in Tel Aviv to 1939	295
14. American activities in Haifa to 1927	304
15. Migdal garden city and estate plans, ca. 1925	320
16. Nahalat Itzhak, 1933	324

Preface

Over the past century, the aliyah (immigration to Israel) of American Jews has piqued the curiosity of both the residents of Israel and American Jewry. Why, it has often been asked, would one want to leave America, the land of opportunity and promise? Misconceptions and generalizations have tainted the image of American *olim* (immigrants). The absorbing population has often viewed them as wealthy, lacking a genuine commitment to remain, and not entirely cognizant of the challenges of life in their new homeland. While some American *olim* fit this description, for most the reality has been much different. A diverse population, they have chosen to relocate for a variety of reasons, with Zionist ideology as well as Jewish identification and commitment factoring into this decision. During the period covered by this study, American *olim* played a significant role—far beyond their actual numbers—in shaping the landscape and society of Palestine.

The purpose of this study is to understand and analyze the migration of American Jews to Palestine between the two World Wars and their contribution to the up-building of the land and its people. It follows a slightly different approach than is typically used in geographical writing. Its focus is strongly geographic in terms of migration and landscape transformation. Stories of the immigrants have been included as a humanizing factor and to supplement the quantitative information.

The research drew upon a variety of primary and secondary sources, including institutional and personal archives located in the United States, Israel, and Canada. Special attention was given to primary sources, such as correspondence and contemporary accounts in newspapers. These were combined with analysis of maps, plans, and photographs, as well as fieldwork

PREFACE

at sites connected to American Jewish settlement in Palestine. The study is augmented by tables, maps, and illustrations that provide the reader with some of the raw data used in the study.

In the introduction, general demographic information lays the foundation for what follows, first by detailing the scope and scale of the migration, and then by outlining the characteristics of the immigrants. These parameters allowed the construction of four distinct group profiles. Chapter 1 examines the environment in which the immigrants made their decisions to migrate. Chapter 2 looks into the information available to the potential immigrants which was utilized to varying degrees in their decision-making processes. Chapter 3 categorizes the motivational factors and supplements the discussion through the use of contemporary examples. Chapter 4 explores technical and political barriers to migration. Chapter 5 describes immigrants' encounters with the new environment and then outlines the processes of selecting a location for settlement. Chapter 6 tells of the "estate" or *ahuza* societies that were founded in the decade before World War I for the purpose of establishing American Jewish colonies in Palestine; it focuses on those that continued to operate during and after the war. Chapter 7 details the activities of the Zion Commonwealth (later the American Zion Commonwealth), an organization established in 1914 to purchase and develop land in Palestine. Chapter 8 portrays private initiatives for land purchase and settlement. Chapter 9 examines American Jewish settlement on Jewish National Fund land. Chapter 10 moves to the urban landscape, describing the contributions of American companies, organizations, and individuals to the development of cities and towns, and highlighting the professional activities of American settlers. The conclusion evaluates the migrational movement as a whole, placing it within the context of other ideological emigrations from the United States and the immigration of other Diaspora communities to Palestine. Further, it assesses the contribution of American Jews to the development of Palestine between the two World Wars.

This project began as a dissertation titled "American and Canadian Jews in Eretz Israel: Settlement and Initiatives for the Development of the Landscape during the Beginning of British Rule (1917–1932)." My doctoral work was supervised by Professor Ruth Kark of the Hebrew University of Jerusalem's Department of Geography and Professor Allon Gal of Ben-Gurion University of the Negev's Department of History. I am greatly indebted to them for their guidance and support in this project.

In addition, I would like to acknowledge the important contribution of the late Professor Moshe Davis, the founder of the America-Holy Land project at the Hebrew University of Jerusalem's Avraham Harman Institute of Contemporary Jewry. He introduced me to this field of research and emphasized its importance as a way to understand the history of American

Jewry. My personal connection with him and his wife, Lottie, nurtured a deep appreciation for this academic pursuit. The infrastructure that he laid down facilitated work in this field, particularly the four volumes of the *Guide to America-Holy Land Studies, 1620–1948,* and the five collections of articles, *With Eyes toward Zion.*

I would also like to acknowledge the support rendered by Professor Ruth Kark and Professor Yehoshua Ben-Arieh during my years in Israel. Both offered continual encouragement to my research and fostered my growing love of Eretz Israel, its people, and its history.

I also want to thank Professor Michael Brown of York University, Professor Jonathan Sarna of Brandeis University, Professor Deborah Dash Moore of Vassar College, Dr. Menahem Kaufman of the Hebrew University of Jerusalem, Dr. Irit Amit of Bar-Ilan University, and Professor Yossi Ben-Artzi of Haifa University for their comments and suggestions. The late professor Aaron Antonovsky graciously assisted by providing some of the material he used in his earlier study.

I gratefully acknowledge the institutional support afforded by the Department of Geography, the Halbert Centre for Canadian Studies, and the Institute of Contemporary Jewry of the Hebrew University of Jerusalem. Moreover, important funding was provided by the Finesold-Sukenik Grant for Gender Studies, the Israel Association for Canadian Studies Research Grant, Morris M. Pulver Scholarship Fund, the Baruch Tal Scholarship, the Levi Eshkol Institute Research Fellowship, and the Theodor Herzl Fellowship.

In addition, I would like to thank the staffs of the Central Zionist Archives, Jerusalem; the Archives and Museum of the Jewish Labor Movement, Tel Aviv; Central Archives for the History of the Jewish People, Jerusalem; Canadian Jewish Congress National Archives, Montreal; Glenbow-Alberta Institute, Archives Department, Calgary; Haifa Municipal Archives; Hebrew University of Jerusalem Archives, Jerusalem; Jewish Historical Society of Western Canada, Winnipeg; Jerusalem Municipal Archives; Kibbutz Kfar Menachen Archives; National Archives of Canada, Ottawa; National and University Library Archives, Jerusalem; Shomer Hatzair Archives, Givat Haviva; Tel Aviv-Jaffa Municipal Archives; Tel Aviv University Archives, Institute for the Study of the Diaspora; the Yad Itzhak Ben-Zvi Archives, Jerusalem; and the Map Library of the Hebrew University of Jerusalem.

At various stages of the project, assistance was also provided by friends and relatives. Thank you to my mother, Lucy, and my siblings Samuel, Tova, Berl, Rebecca, and Jonathan. Thank you to Tamar Helfand, the late Avram Greenbaum, Luba Greenbaum, Ruth Rischall, Dave and Essie Guttman, Oodee Eilat, Michal Link, Edit Luzia-Meidan, Julie Rabinowitz, Beverley Rubin, Amos Ron, Mark Staitman, Paula Philbin, Cathy Gurrertiez, Shoshana Migdal, and Sasha Yegorov.

The maps were adeptly prepared by the staff of the Cartography Laboratory of the Department of Geography of the Hebrew University of Jerusalem, Tamar Soffer, and Michal Kidron. Likewise, the editorial skills and invaluable suggestions of Alifa Saadya are very much appreciated. A final thank-you goes to the staff at Wayne State University Press for their efforts in bringing this book to press.

INTRODUCTION

American Aliyah: Scope and Scale

How many American Jews made aliyah? How does one characterize the American *olim*? These and other questions have not been fully addressed by researchers. A number of attempts have been made to determine the exact number of American Jewish immigrants to Palestine, but these have been hindered by the lack of comprehensive and exact statistical information.[1] Some answers to these queries are merely conjectural, while others represent estimates based on assumptions not founded on any concrete information. Calvin Goldscheider was among the few researchers who took a critical view of the available figures, and he found no definitive answer to these questions.[2] For the purposes of this study, almost every available piece of statistical information has been compiled and compared in order to create a more complete portrait of the American *olim* and their migration.

American aliyah began in the mid-nineteenth century, motivated by traditional desires to study Torah in the Holy Land and eventually to be interred in its sacred soil. The movement was at first only a trickle, reflecting both the difficulties of moving halfway around the globe and the relatively small American Jewish population prior to the large-scale migration to America that began in the 1880s. Prior to World War I, the United States consulate in Jerusalem and the American Consular Agency in Haifa, under the jurisdiction of the consulate general in Beirut, reported on their nationals within these sections of the Ottoman Empire. In 1878 there were 119 Americans registered at the Jerusalem consulate. As of 1899 there were some 800 American protégés in the Jerusalem district. These figures include both Jews and non-Jews. Most of these Jews had never been in the United States, but they were extended protection by the American consul. In 1913 there were eight Americans in Haifa and ten in the Jewish colony of Zichron Yaakov.[3] It should be noted that under United States law, effective 2 March 1907, "naturalized American citizens who remove to other countries and reside there for five years are presumed to have abandoned their American nationality." Accordingly, some American citizens were obliged to relinquish their citizenship, and thus not all those considered American in this study—i.e., persons having resided in the United States for more than five years and having the right to register for citizenship—were registered by American consular representatives. In 1911, for example, of the twenty-seven Jews residing at Jaffa with registration of their citizenship approved by the U.S. Department of State, fifteen were subject to losing their citizenship on 2 March 1912.[4]

More exact figures are available from the *Census of the Jews of Eretz Israel,* conducted in Judaea between spring 1916 (Adar 5676) and spring 1918 (Adar 5678) in the midst of the war. The numbers are smaller than might be anticipated, since some American citizens had fled Palestine as refugees or had been forced to migrate; others had starved or perished from various plagues. The census listed approximately 700 American Jewish nationals, of whom the majority—546—resided in Jerusalem; the remainder lived in Jaffa and the moshavot. The census also provided information on the immigration of 138 American nationals to the moshavot (including exiles from Jaffa): fifteen up to 1900, thirty-six between 1901–10, seventy-seven between 1911–14, and ten whose immigration dates were unknown. Of course, these figures did not take into account the deceased and emigrants, but they did point to an increasing rate of migration in the years leading up to World War I.[5]

Between the summer of 1917 (Av 5677) and the summer of 1919 (Tammuz 5679), the Jewish census was extended to northern Palestine. In 1919 the American Jewish population there totaled only forty-seven. This figure does not, however, reflect the actual number of Americans who resided in this area before the war. The United States entered the war in 1917, and some of its nationals were expelled from Turkish territory or were forced to relocate to other Turkish controlled areas. In northern Palestine, too, the rate of American Jewish migration increased before World War I: two up to 1900, eleven between 1901–10, twenty-two between 1911–14, nine between 1915–18, and three of undetermined dates.[6]

Statistics regarding the immigration of American Jews during the period of British rule in Palestine were compiled by two bodies, the Mandatory government of Palestine and the Palestine Zionist Executive (later the Jewish Agency for Palestine). The total immigration to Palestine recorded by the two is almost identical, but the breakdown into countries of origin shows great discrepancies.

Eric Mills, in charge of the 1931 census of Palestine, was critical of the figures presented by the government of Palestine immigration officer: "It is

TABLE 1
American and Jewish immigration to Palestine, 1919–39, according to the Jewish Agency for Palestine and the government of Palestine

Year	(1)	(2)	(3)	(4)	(5)	(6)	(7)	(8)
1919	—	—	1,806	—	—	1,806	0.00	0.00
1920	163	—	8,223	—	—	8,223	1.98	0.00
1921[a]	1,501	—	8,294	—	—	8,294	1.81	0.00
1922	199	166	8,685	—	—	8,685	2.29	1.91
1923	89	125	8,093	—	82	8,175	1.10	1.53
1924	162	324	12,905	—	987	13,892	1.26	2.33
1925	331	570	33,135	—	1,251	34,386	1.00	1.66
1926	184	374	13,244	—	611	13,855	1.39	2.70
1927[b]	27	130	2,320	—	714	3,034	1.16	4.28
1928[c]	71	229	784	107	1,287	2,178	9.06	10.51
1929	80	253	3,915	140	1,194	5,249	2.04	4.82
1930	132	260	4,134	115	695	4,944	3.19	5.26
1931	171	332	2,998	138	939	4,075	5.70	8.15
1932	491	864	5,480	343	3,730	9,553	8.96	9.04
1933	1,063	1,169	27,289	573	2,465	30,327	3.90	3.85
1934	1,028	1,171	36,619	1,625	4,115	42,359	2.81	2.76
1935	1,602	1,826	55,407	2,643	3,804	61,854	2.89	2.95
1936	245	357	26,976	934	1,817	29,727	0.91	1.20
1937	103	167	9,441	414	681	10,536	1.09	1.59
1938	61	94	11,222	219	1,427	12,868	0.54	0.73
1939	28	29	13,663	251	2,491	27,561	0.20	0.11
1919–39	6,379	8,438	294,630	7,498	28,285	341,575	2.17	2.47

Note: Column headings are as follows: (1) American Jews registered by the Jewish Agency Immigration Offices; (2) American Jews listed by the government of Palestine Immigration Offices; (3) Jews registered by the Jewish Agency Immigration Offices; (4) immigrants registered by the government of Palestine Immigration Offices; (5) authorized travelers registered by the government of Palestine Immigration Offices; (6) total Jewish migration according to government of Palestine Immigration Offices; (7) American Jews registered by the Jewish Agency Immigration Offices as percent of Jews registered by the Jewish Agency Immigration Offices [(1)/(3) X 100]; and (8) American Jews listed by the government of Palestine Immigration Offices as percent of total Jewish migration [(2)/(6) X 100].
Sources: Jewish Agency Records of Jewish Immigration according to citizenship, in David Gurevich, "Fifteen Years of Aliya to Ertz Israel" (in Hebrew), in *Aliya:*

Collection on Aliya Matters (Jerusalem: Jewish Agency for Palestine, 1935), 2:xiv–xv; Report by His Majesty's Government in the United Kingdom of Great Britain and Northern Ireland to the Council of the League of Nations on the Administration of Palestine and Trans-Jordan for the years 1922–1939.

[a]Figures provided for 1921 in the *Bulletin of the Palestine Economic Society* 1, no. 1 (May 1924): 13, 25 differ upward. Six American immigrants arrived in Haifa during January–April 1921. Thirty-five American immigrants, exclusive of children, arrived in Jaffa in the same period. From May–December 1921, 152 American immigrants arrived at Jaffa and Haifa (see also: CZA S6/275). Altogether at least 193 American immigrants arrived in Palestine in 1921.

[b]The report of the Joint Palestine Survey Commission, 46, provides much higher figures for Jewish immigration betwen 1922–27; it listed 2,528 originating in the United States—as compared to 1,789 listed by the government and 992 by the Jewish Agency—and a total of 88,873—as compared to 82,027 by the government and 78,382 by the Jewish Agency. It is unclear why this commission, headed by Lord Melchet, Lee K. Frankel, Felix M. Warburg, and Oscar Wasserman included such exagerated figures.

[c]The Report of the Commission on the Disturbances of August 1929, p. 102, related to Jewish immigration form 1919 to 1928. of the total 101,400 Jewish immigrants, 1,400 originated from the United States. The Jewish Agency figures differ slightly, with 1,375 Americans of the total 97,486; the government figures listed 1,916 Americans and a total of 102,522.

---

only to be expected, in the circumstances of Palestine, that the records of migration should be defective. On the one hand, there is an intense pressure among Jews to enter Palestine; and on the other hand, the country is landlocked in three directions and the frontiers are therefore difficult to control. An additional complication [is that] . . . incoming persons are exclusively classified as immigrants, returning residents and travellers."[7] Furthermore, the figures provided by Zionist bodies in their various publications are dissimilar, at least partly because the Jewish Agency for Palestine, for example, used a variety of collection methods over this period. There were inconsistencies regarding the numbers in different publications, and it is difficult to determine which figures are accurate.[8]

As explained in one of the reports from the Jewish Agency's Department of Statistics, one reason for the discrepancies was that some Americans changed their status from tourist to immigrant after they had been in Palestine for awhile. For example, for January 1932, the Jewish Agency's Department of Immigration registered eight American immigrants, while the Mandatory government's Department of Migration registered twenty individuals; the difference of twelve represents tourists who entered the country in 1930 and 1931 and changed their status to resident in January. This explanation may account for some of the discrepancies, but it does not sufficiently clarify larger deviations in the numbers. Another reason for the inconsistencies results from the unclear distinction made between country of origin and nationality. One finds individuals classified as Americans who resided in the United States for over five years but did not possess American passports. Often such persons retained their Eastern European passports or possessed no documents at all. When immigrants arrived in Palestine, government authorities registered them according to their country of origin—that is, where their visas had been issued by British consular authorities. By contrast, the Palestine Zionist Executive registered immigrants according to their citizenship. Thus the number of American immigrants cited by the British authorities was usually higher than that furnished by the Palestine Zionist Executive or the Jewish Agency for Palestine. Jewish Agency statistician David Gurevich pointed out that for the years 1926–34 there was a 5 percent discrepancy between citizenship and country of last residence for emigrants from the United States. This deviation is relatively low when compared to figures for Russia and Germany, where the discrepancies were 25 and 20 percent respectively.[9]

Neither of these sources provides complete statistics for the period of 1918 to 1939. For the years 1919 and 1920, no data is available at all. Yet evidence exists of a number of Jewish Legionnaires from America who were demobilized in Palestine and settled there. According to records of the Beit Hagdudim Museum at Avihail, at least twenty-five Americans remained in Palestine after the end of the war.[10] Sam Friedlander, chairman of the Jewish Legionnaire's Association, claimed in 1929 that over 200 American Jewish Legionnaires were living in Palestine, some of whom were demobilized in the United States and subsequently immigrated to Palestine.[11]

In an attempt to verify immigration statistics, figures for emigration of Jews from the United States were examined for this study. Information on emigration—with no distinction made for race or religion—to Turkey or to Syria, Palestine, and Iraq is available for 1917–24. The American government also listed emigrants according to race or people, providing a grouping called "Hebrew." Neither of these two listings of emigration from the United States corresponds with those of the American Jewish immigration to Palestine. For example, in 1924 the government of Palestine registered 324 American Jews as having settled in Palestine. Yet this exceeds the 260 "Hebrews" that left the United States that year.

Between 1920–39, an average of some 400 American Jews immigrated annually. A general trend can be seen during 1922–31, when an average of 277 Americans—between 125 to 570 in any given year—immigrated to Palestine. For 1932–35, immigration increased dramatically to an annual average of 1,258 (ranging between 864 and 1,826). From 1936 to the beginning of World War II, the number of immigrants steadily decreased from 357 to 29, for an annual average of 162.

The ratio of American Jews to the total Jewish immigration to Palestine

INTRODUCTION

TABLE 2
Emigration from the United States by future country of residence, 1917–24

Year	1917	1918	1919	1920	1921	1922	1923	1924
Syria, Palestine, and Iraq	—	—	—	—	—	—	—	492
Turkey in Asia	8	5	26	1,731	2,534	1,731	773	211

Source: United States Table XV—Emigration of Aliens, by Country of Future Residence, 1908–1924, in *International Migrations,* ed. Walter F. Wilcox, vol. 1: Statistics (New York, London, Paris: Gordon and Breach, 1969), 473.

TABLE 3
Emigration of "Hebrews" from the United States, 1917–24

Year	1917	1918	1919	1920	1921	1922	1923	1924
Total	329	687	373	358	483	830	413	260
To Austria, Hungary, Rumania, and the United Kingdom	205	286	169	107	162	139	72	58
Unknown Destination[1]	114	401	204	251	321	691	341	202

Source: United States Table XV—Emigration of Aliens Departed, by Sex and Race or People, 1908–1924, 477, and United States, Table XX—Distribution of Emigrant Aliens Departed, by Race or People and Country of Future Residence, 1908–1924, 480, in *International Migrations,* ed. Walter F. Wilcox, vol. 1: Statistics (New York, London, Paris: Gordon and Breach, 1969), 473.
[1]Palestine and Turkey in Asia are included in this number.

also varied during this period. From 1920 to 1939, American Jews comprised approximately 2.5 percent of the total Jewish immigration. According to Mandatory government figures, immigration ranged from a low of less than 0.5 percent in 1923 to a high of over 10 percent in 1928. There was a different rhythm for the migration of American Jews. During the years of particular economic hardship in Palestine (1927 and 1928), American immigrants continued to come to Palestine, thus increasing their overall proportion. During the Great Depression, Palestine drew more Americans.

In the first years of the period of this study, 1920–25, the percentage was below average; from 1926 to 1933 it was above average; 1934–35 was also slightly above average; and 1936–39 was again below average.

American immigration figures were exceptional in 1926–27, when the general immigration was relatively low and there was high Jewish emigration from Palestine. The flow from America was against the tide of general migration. Although these two years stand out as years of economic difficulty or crisis in Palestine, Americans possessed the necessary funds to allow them to settle there despite the adversities. Other unusual years were 1932–35, a period of hardship in America as a result of the Great Depression. Changes in the American social climate, together with relative economic prosperity in Palestine, motivated many Americans. The drastic decline in immigration toward the end of the period of study was the result of two factors. First, fewer *halutz* certificates were allotted to Americans. In addition, the 1936–39 disturbances in Palestine deterred the migration of Americans, particularly those who were middle-aged and older as well as those who had sufficient resources to obtain capitalist certificates. This trend worried the Zionist establishment in the United States. The 1938 Convention of the Zionist Organization of America, held in Detroit, addressed the issue:

> Since June, 1936, approximately 2,500 persons have applied to the Palestine Department for information and consular assistance. The majority of these applicants consists of persons ranging in age from 45 to 60 years, each of whom is in possession of an average capital from $5,000 to $15,000. The bulk of the applicants comprise middle class elements who plan to invest their capital in building enterprises, in mortgages, orange plantations or in smaller domestic enterprises.
>
> Would the situation in Palestine have followed its normal course and enabled these elements to fulfill their life-long dream, the capital brought into Palestine during the last two years by these applicants would have amounted to many millions of dollars. Under the present conditions these applicants are inclined to postpone their departure for a later date, when order and security will have been restored in the country.[12]

Within a smaller section of the population, the immigration patterns of the membership of Kollel America Tiffereth Yerushalaim (an organization established to provide assistance to Orthodox American and Canadian Jews in Palestine) are noteworthy; it appears that their immigration did not fluctuate greatly over time. Although the data is not conclusive in this regard, apparently there was a constant flow of this group into Palestine, for it was not dependent upon the variation of American or Palestine economies, the social environment, or other factors. Though allowance must be made for the higher death rate of this generally elderly population, American Kollel members'

ZIONIST ORGANIZATION OF AMERICA

החסתדרות הציונית של ארצות חברית

111 FIFTH AVENUE
NEW YORK

PALESTINE DEPARTMENT
DR. S. BERNSTEIN, Director

STEPHEN S. WISE
President

ISRAEL GOLDSTEIN
JOSEPH KRAEMER
WILLIAM M. LEWIS
ABBA HILLEL SILVER
ELIHU D. STONE
NATHAN STRAUS
Vice-Presidents

MORRIS ROTHENBERG
Chairman, Admin. Committee

LUDWIG LEWISOHN
Honorary Secretary

MORRIS MARGULIES
Secretary

EXECUTIVE
LOUIS LIPSKY
CHARLES A. COWEN
M. MALDWIN FERTIG
ABRAHAM GOLDBERG
ABRAHAM GOLDSTEIN
EDWARD L. ISRAEL
ISRAEL H. LEVINTHAL
SAMUEL MARKEWICH
IRVING MILLER
CHARLES RESS
A. J. RONGY
CARL SHERMAN
WILLIAM I. SIEGEL
ROBERT SZOLD

Associate Members
ISAAC IMBER
ADRIAN SCHWARTZ

FINANCE COMMITTEE
LOUIS P. ROCKER
Chairman

MORRIS WEINBERG
HARRY P. FIERST
Treasurers

ABRAHAM KRUMBEIN
ABRAHAM LIEBOVITZ
ELIAS PREISS
LOUIS RIMSKY
SIGMUND THAU

ISRAEL MALTIN
Auditor

June 28, 1938

Jewish Agency for Palestine
Jerusalem, Palestine

Att: Mr. A. Dobkin

Dear Friends:-

        Referring to your letter of June 16th with regard to "capitalist" certificates now at the disposal of the British Consul in New York, I beg to inform you that up 'till now about ten certificates have been utilized. I do not expect that during the month of July more than another ten certificates will be taken out by applicants.

        While the number of tourists from America at present is very large, we have from 5 - 10 tourists daily, the number of "capitalist" applicants is almost nil, since they all declare that in view of the uncertain conditions in Palestine they have decided to postpone their departure for a later date.

        All in all, I doubt whether the fifty "capitalist" certificates will be utilized until the end of August. They expire at the end of September.

Very truly yours,

Dr. S. Bernstein,
Director, Palestine Dept.

SB:f

Fig. 1. Letter regarding the decrease in need for capitalist certificates in 1938.
Dr. S. Berstein, Director, Palestine Department, Zionist Organization of America,
New York, to the Jewish Agency for Palestine, Jerusalem, 28 June 1938. (CZA S6/3,216)

responses to a 1932 questionnaire are instructive. According to the 137 respondents, forty-eight heads of families arrived in Palestine between 1927–31, forty heads between 1922–26, and thirty-two heads between 1912–21.[13]

So how many American Jews immigrated to Palestine between the two World Wars? The Jewish Agency for Palestine figures indicate a total of 6,379 American Jewish immigrants from 1920 to 1939. The government of Palestine immigration authorities reached a higher figure of 8,438 for the shorter period of 1922–39. The 1931 census of Palestine, in fact, suggested that the government of Palestine's figures were incorrect and attempted to adjust the defects in the migration records. It asserted that the annual balance of migration recorded between the censuses of 1922 and 1931 should be increased by a ratio of 1.23 to 1. Records for the period before 1925 were considered even more defective. For the years following the census, the coefficient suggested in the census was 1.1. Using these adjustments, American immigration for 1922 to 1939 would have been 9,654.[14] Another form of adjustment may be made by comparing these two totals to information from other sources (see notes to table 1). If adjusted for the maximum difference, Jewish Agency figures would reach 8,958 and government figures might drop to 7,897 or rise to 9,177. A safe estimate for American aliyah for the period of study would be *9,000*—slightly above government figures because it does not include those who did not register as immigrants. This figure would adjust the percent of total Jewish immigration slightly upward—from 2.55 percent according to government sources and 2.61 percent according to Jewish Agency sources, to 2.63 percent and 3.05 percent respectively.

However, not all Americans remained in Palestine. Determining the number of emigrants or the rate of emigration is extremely complicated. Almost no records were kept regarding the citizenship or nationality of emigrants. Thus no concrete conclusions can be drawn for the emigration of American Jews from Palestine. The limited information available is presented below to provide at best an extremely general picture.

One Palestine Zionist Executive Department of Immigration report deals with emigration for the period of May 1922 to May 1923. During this period, 1,170 Jews departed Palestine, 185 were residents of Palestine, 906 were new immigrants, and 76 were tourists. These categories are not well defined and are therefore unclear. Of new immigrants leaving the territory, 2.9 percent or 26 individuals were Americans. The ratio of American emigrés to immigrants was 5 percent. When compared to other national groups, this figure is low, with higher figures for Latvia, at 24.6 percent; Austria, 13.1; Ukraine, 10.7; and Poland, 9. The figures are lower for Romania, 2.9; Russia, 1.8; and Lithuania, 0.4.[15]

Yet Americans were stigmatized as having a high rate of reverse migration. Numbers, not based on any statistical information, were freely thrown out that suggested a return rate of one in three.[16]

INTRODUCTION
CHARACTERISTICS OF THE AMERICAN IMMIGRANTS

The main source of information on the characteristics of American Jewish emigrés is the 1931 census of Palestine. It lists 672 persons born in the United States and 2,222 American citizens.[17] The ratio of American-born to American citizenship is 1:3.10. At least two-thirds of the immigrants had lived part of their lives somewhere other than the United States. Keeping in mind that many of those born in America were children of immigrants strengthens the hypothesis that much of American aliyah was really a process of re-emigration.

Figures regarding American citizenship do not provide an accurate portrait of the American population in Palestine at this time. Some immigrants relinquished their citizenship, although there is no way to calculate the exact number who did so. On the one hand, it appears that American citizens were in no hurry to give up their citizenship for that of Palestine; a 1926 report mentions 2,000 Americans who did not opt for Palestinian papers. However, over time, a growing number of Americans forfeited their passports. The 1931 census lists 36 Americans who were granted Palestinian citizenship between 1 January 1929, and 31 December 1931—a rate of 4 per 1,000. If this rate is applied to the naturalization of 27,509 Jews between 1925 and 1931, the estimated number of Americans who relinquished U.S. citizenship for Palestinian citizenship would be 130.[18] American consular records from May 1924, however, list 216 individuals who up to that date had obtained provisional certificates of Palestinian citizenship.[19] Taking this into account, the ratio of American-born to citizenship would be even higher, at least 1:3.43.

The implication of naturalization in Palestine for an American citizen was that "under section 2 of the United States Citizenship Act of March 2, 1907 any American shall be deemed to have expatriated himself when he has been naturalized in any foreign State in conformity with the laws of that State, or when he has taken an oath of allegiance to a foreign state."[20]

The Palestine census provides no information as to the date of the arrival of Jewish immigrants, i.e., before or after World War I, as illustrated by information in the *Census of the Jewish Population in Haifa* of 1938. Residing in Haifa that year were 272 persons who had emigrated from the United States, representing 0.5 percent of the city's Jewish population. Five persons had arrived from the United States before World War I, 50 persons between 1918 and 1931, and the remainder between 1931–38.[21] If these figures are compared to the population recorded for Haifa in the 1931 census, a great variation is evident. There were 52 persons born in the United States and 94 American citizens.[22] This points to a decline in the number of Americans resident in Haifa in 1931: 96 in all, with 59 remaining in

TABLE 4
Length of residence in Palestine of American citizens in Jerusalem, 1939

Age and family status	Years of residence in Palestine							
	0–2.9	3–3.9	4–4.9	5–9	10–19	20+	Unknown	Total
Individuals 18 years and over	14	9	12	27	31	9	6	108
Heads of families 18 years and over	8	4	26	85	44	43	7	217
Adult members of families 18 years and over	15	7	31	116	61	63	6	299
Children under 17.9 years	35	16	33	58	52	—	6	200
Total	72	36	102	286	188	115	25	824

Source: David Gurevich, *The Jewish Population of Jerusalem: A Demographic and Sociological Study of the Jewish Population and Its Component Communities, Based on the Jerusalem Jewish Census, September 1939* (Jerusalem: Department of Statistics of the Jewish Agency for Palestine, 1940), 27–29.

Haifa until 1938. Reasons for the decrease might include emigration, internal migration, or death.

The 1939 Jerusalem Jewish Census also details the length of residence of that city's 824 American citizens, 115 of whom had arrived in Palestine before World War I. The years of their immigration are listed in table 4. In addition, the 1939 census lists the years of residence in Palestine of 730 individuals who had formerly resided in the United States. These figures are not analogous with the citizenship numbers, but their division into categories provides greater detail with regard to the years of residence during the pre–World War I period: 166, 0–4.9 years; 293, 5–9.9 years; 110, 10–14 years; 77, 15–19 years; 33, 20–29 years; 7, 30–39 years; 9, 40–49 years; 5, 50+ years; 30, unknown.[23]

Fig. 2. Members of Kollel America Tiffereth Yerushalaim praying at the Western Wall. (Central Zionist Archives pamphlet 50,398)

More precise information has been found for one subgroup, persons affiliated with Kollel America Tiffereth Yerushalaim, which provides some insight into the characteristics of this segment of the American population. This subgroup was generally elderly; of the 148 heads of families surveyed in 1932, 73 percent were over 51 years old.[24] This was disproportionate to the general American Jewish population, raising the average age cited in the 1931 census. This subgroup is indicative of the motivation of an elderly religious population in America to spend their last years in the Holy Land and be buried there.

In 1941–42 the Jewish Agency surveyed the resident rural Jewish population. Since American Jewish immigration in 1940 and 1941 was insignificant—only two American citizens immigrated in those years according to Jewish Agency records—this information provides a portrait of the situation at the end of the period of study. Originating from the United States were 848 persons, with 5.1 percent immigrating before 1915, 25.5 percent between 1915–29, and 69.4 percent between 1930–41. Those originating in America made up only 0.6 of the Jewish rural sector.[25]

With regard to gender, one figure stands out: in 1931, 20.41 percent of the total population were females in the age group 25–40, where 11.70 percent were males of the same age group. This weighs heavily on the general male to female ratio, skewing an otherwise normal ratio to 1 to 1.226. No explanation has been found for this disproportion. American women did not demonstrate a tendency to search for opportunities in Palestine, nor was there a high proportion of widows among the immigrants.

In his study of the demographic structure and natural growth of the Jewish population of Palestine, Roberto Bachi attempted to estimate the average number of children women gave birth to according to their country of birth. His calculations for the years 1938–40 point to a rate of 1.83 children for women from the Americas (the United States was the dominant component of this group); this figure is below the national average of 2.16. Austrian and German women had the lowest rates, at 1.32 and 1.37 respectively. The rate for Palestinian-born Jewish women stood at 3.40. Yemenite and Moroccan women had the highest rates, at 7.28 and 7.04 respectively.[26]

There is insufficient data regarding the professions of American emigrés to categorize them properly into groups or to evaluate them numerically. However, one clue can be found in the census of Jewish professionals from 1922 and a second one in the applications for immigration in 1919–20. In the early years of the British Mandate, there were thirty-nine North American professionals in Palestine—approximately 3 percent of the total Jewish professionals enumerated.[27] These 1922 figures include immigrants before the war and those who arrived during the first years of British rule. In 1919–20 a large number of American Jews applied for immigration to Palestine. As detailed and grouped by the Palestine Service and Information Bureau, the primary occupations of the 1,803 family heads were: 385 in agriculture, 368 in commerce, 124 in education, 62 in engineering, 159 in the medical professions, 21 in social work, and 684 listed as general or miscellaneous. This last group included 131 tailors, 67 laborers, 56 carpenters, 48 machinists, 43 clerical workers, 33 students, 28 painters, 24 stenographers, 17 bookkeepers, 17 insurance agents, 16 electricians, 15 rabbis, 14 bakers, 14 *shochetim* (ritual slaughterers), and others in 62 different vocations. Very few of these applicants actually immigrated to Palestine, but their vocations point to the large cross section of professions of the American Jewish population intent on immigrating.[28]

The lists of persons who received labor schedule certificates, compiled by the Palestine Bureau in New York for the Jewish Agency's Immigration Department, include details of the occupations for some of the American immigrants. The lists of capitalist visa recipients, on the other hand, only

TABLE 5
Age-gender distribution of American Jewish nationals in Palestine, 1931

Age	Number			Percent		
	Male	Female	Total	Male	Female	Total
0–10	154	185	339	6.78	8.14	14.91
10–20	209	223	432	9.19	9.81	19.01
20–45	266	464	730	11.70	20.41	32.12
45>	392	380	772	17.25	16.72	33.96
Total	1,021	1,252	2,273	44.92	55.08	100.00

Source: Eric Molls, *Census of Palestine 1931* (Alexandria: Whitehead Morris, 1933), 2:266–68.

provide their declared capital, not their vocations. Thus the occupations of only a small sector of the immigrant population are available. One example furnishes insight into the vocational training of the *halutzim* (pioneers). During the period of January to March 1933, sixty certificates were granted to Americans, who had twenty-one dependents (wives and children). Classified by their occupations, there were twenty-one laborers, nine farmers and agriculturalists, nineteen craftsmen and tradesmen, five white collar professionals, three bookkeepers, one merchant, and two with unspecified occupations. This reflects the growing number of young American Jews who prepared themselves for migration by training in various vocations deemed necessary to receive a certificate and partake in the Zionist endeavor in Palestine. Unfortunately, similar lists for all the years of this study are not available.[29]

Although not conclusive because of their incomplete, inconsistent, and inexact nature, the statistics presented above point to a number of characteristics of the American Jewish population that migrated to Palestine. The immigrant population may be subdivided into four distinct groups: the Orthodox population, *halutzim* (pioneers), middle-class agriculturalists, and urban professionals.

For the most part, the Orthodox population was older. It included families, elderly couples, widows, and widowers. Exceptional within this generally aging population were yeshiva students—unmarried young adult men. The incomes of this Orthodox group varied from the lower percentiles—those who needed financial assistance while they lived in Palestine—to a handful of the wealthy. Most of them were not American-born, but originally from Eastern Europe.

TABLE 6
North American (NA) professionals in various cities, 1922

Profession	Tel-Aviv Jaffa NA	Tel-Aviv Jaffa Total	Jerusalem NA	Jerusalem Total	Haifa NA	Haifa Total	Safed NA	Safed Total
agronomist	—	17	—	7	—	4	—	—
architect and civil engineer	1	15	2	27	1	19	—	—
artist	1	19	1	18	—	1	—	—
bacteriologist	—	3	—	—	—	—	—	—
chemist	—	7	—	3	—	—	—	—
dentist	2	26	1	24	—	8	—	3
doctor	—	47	2	35	2	16	1	5
engineer	2	32	—	24	1	20	—	—
kindergarten teacher	—	19	—	43	—	6	—	5
lawyer	—	21	1	21	—	6	—	—
midwife and nurse	—	16	4	30	1	10	1	9
official (graduated)	—	2	2	26	—	3	—	1
pharmacist	1	16	—	12	—	6	—	2
rabbi	—	4	—	9	—	2	—	5
teacher	5	125	4	290	—	31	1	35
veterinary surgeon	—	1	—	—	—	1	—	—
writer and journalist	—	13	2	16	—	—	—	—
Total	12	383	19	585	5	133	3	65

Source: "A Statistical Survey of Jewish Trades, Industries and Liberal Professions in Palestine," *Bulletin of the Palestine Economic Society* no. 2 (October 1922): 77; no. 3 (July 1923): 91; nos. 4/5 (May 1924): 71, 96, 116.

Note: The census was conducted in Tel Aviv-Jaffa during March 1922; in Jerusalem during March to May 1922; in Haifa, Tiberias, and Safed during July and August 1922. No North American professionals were listed in the census for Tiberias. The information for Tel Aviv-Jaffa includes professionals from Argentina.

The *halutzim* represented a much younger population, and the majority of them were single. Most of the couples in this group were at the beginning of the productive stage of their lives; they usually had very little capital and no children. The majority had graduated from high school, and some had

Fig. 3. American *halutzim* playing volleyball at Kibbutz Ein Hashofet, December 1938. (CZA photograph collection 6,005/57)

attended university. Many had been trained in agriculture or in skilled professions. The majority were American-born, and some even had American-born parents. Ideologically, they were affiliated with socialism and communism, as indicated by their desire to join cooperative settlements in Palestine.

The middle-class agriculturalists consisted mainly of families. More often than not, they lacked agricultural experience but dreamed of owning farms in the Holy Land. They came from urban centers in the United States and had worked as merchants, professionals, or craftsmen. Married couples in this group were in their middle years, and their children ranged in age from infancy to adolescence. Some couples had children over the age of eighteen. These families usually possessed sufficient capital to maintain themselves during their first years in Palestine, to purchase land, and to plant and maintain it until it became productive. For some, the realities of agricultural life were too hard to overcome or the limited amenities did not

Fig. 4. Three generations of pioneers: (*top*) Lifting a heavy stone with a light heart: An old Jew helping in the construction of his home in the new settlement of Kfar Ivri situated on the Jerusalem-Shechem Road; (*middle*) Springtime has come in Palestine: American Jews in Kfar Ivri planting seed in their garden. Every year sees an increasing number of well-to-do Jews from America settling in Palestine; (*bottom*) Two little farmers sitting in a row: Jewish children of Kfar Ivri working in their garden. This work inculcates in them a love for the healthy and vigorous life on the soil. (*Palestine Pictorial* 1 [April 1927])

Fig. 5. Judah and Beatrice Magnes in front of their Jerusalem home, ca. 1930. (Courtesy of the Hebrew University photo archive)

suit their needs, so they resided and worked in urban areas and occasionally visited their rural properties.

The fourth group—urban professionals—were characterized both by their vocations and their new place of residence. They had received post-secondary education and were trained as doctors, lawyers, accountants, nurses, educators, engineers, social workers, bankers, journalists, rabbis, administrators, and as other professional workers. They included single males and females as well as couples with children. Most were American-born or had been raised in the United States from an early age. They possessed the tools to integrate into mainstream American society but decided to uproot themselves to Palestine.

In summary, the absolute number of American Jewish immigrants to Palestine was approximately 9,000 in the years 1919–39. This represents just under 3 percent of the total Jewish immigration for the period. The rate of immigration of American Jews was not consistent with other immigrant groups. Their agenda differed from the others, and it was dependent upon economic and political conditions in America and in Palestine. Particular events affected American immigration: the Balfour Declaration, the liberation of Palestine, the 1929 riots, and the Great Depression. The majority of American Jewish immigrants to Palestine were first-generation Americans. Only in the very late 1920s did the proportion of second-generation Americans increase. The immigrant population comprised a disproportionate number of the elderly and consisted mainly of families. The former fact reflects the traditional motivation to spend one's last years in the Holy Land, either for religious or secular reasons, and the latter form of relocation was termed retirement. The large number of families points to a middle-class migration to both urban and rural environments. There was indeed some re-immigration. Although no conclusive figures about this can be determined, re-immigration reflected a gap between expectations and realities of Palestine, and the difficulties some Americans found in trying to integrate into the local society and economy.

In all, although it appears that this migration was numerically insignificant from the American perspective and small from the *Yishuv*'s (Jewish community in Palestine) perspective, it is asserted that this migration contributed to the development of Palestine in proportions well beyond their numbers. These emigrés comprised a relatively well-educated, professional population, possessing comparatively greater capital than other Jewish immigrants. Furthermore, since it was a free migration, as opposed to the German Jewish immigration from 1933 onward, these emigrés were likely more ideologically motivated to the goal of building the *Yishuv*.

1

Attitudes toward American Jewish Migration to Palestine

> Gabriel shoved his plate away with his sandwich still on it. "I've always assumed that Palestine was to serve as a haven for the suffering Jew," said Gabriel. "American Jews should contribute their money to build up Palestine so that their oppressed brothers in Europe can go there. So that Jews living in Nazi Germany, where anti-semitism is now running rampant and unrestrained, may have an asylum to flee to.
>
> "But why should we, from our democratic U.S.A. go to Palestine?" Gabriel continued. "I won't say that at times one doesn't encounter anti-semitic manifestations here, but it certainly is not government policy. Why, we Jews in the U.S.A. are well off, as well off as most other minorities and even better than some. You'll agree with me on that, I hope."
>
> Hillel was becoming annoyed. "Good arguments for bourgeois materialists. My dear fellow, we are not building a homeland only for others, but also for ourselves. We must strike root anew. In Palestine we'll establish a free, independent, working socialist society and I, Hillel Brenner, am going to have the satisfaction of taking part in creating it. It will provide for me that sense of accomplishment that you are craving for."
>
> Ruhama Morahg and Mordecai Morahg, *Towards Joy Profound*

In this passage from their semi-fictional novel with an autobiographical undertone, Ruhama and Mordecai Morahg recreate a discussion dealing with attitudes toward American Jewish migration to Palestine. Gabriel, a friend of the protagonist Hillel, expounds one of the prevalent attitudes of American Jewish society regarding migration to Palestine: Life is satisfactory, if not agreeable, for Jews in America, so why leave? Implicit in Hillel's words is the outlook of a fringe group in American Jewish society, the Labor Zionists—Poale Zion. These two perspectives constitute only part of the spectrum of opinions held by American Jewry with regard to migration to Palestine. A review of this broad variety of opinions will help us understand the scope and scale of the American Jewish migrational movement to Palestine; moreover, it also will afford insight into questions of Jewish identity in American society.

Jews residing in the United States faced a dilemma when deciding whether to migrate to Palestine. For most, it was a nonissue, and easily resolved. They saw no need to remove themselves from their permanent place of residence. For others, it was a pertinent issue with which they would grapple, and then ultimately decide to remain in America. A limited number chose migration to Palestine. The decision making process about migration to Palestine was complicated, based upon a number of factors and various levels of consciousness. Despite the difficulties in fully comprehending all the components in this process, a number of components can be discerned and described. These factors are recorded in written and oral statements made by individuals either at the time they migrated or in the years following their arrival in Palestine.

The potential American Jewish migrant heard many messages, articulated by different individuals and organizations, expressing support, opposition, or neutrality. The potential migrant was often drawn to the option that best suited his personal needs, and he would adopt a particular attitude as a personal credo. In certain cases, the various stances on American Jewish migration to Palestine caused some vacillation, reevaluation, and even a sense of personal conflict.

The first determinant of opinion on migration to be discussed here is American Jewish society—the environment in which most potential immigrants resided and interacted. The sentiments of members of the international Zionist organizations represented the second group of determinants. These organizations often facilitated the migrational process, and their encouragement and patronage—or lack thereof—greatly influenced the movement of American Jews to Palestine. The third and fourth groups represent the viewpoints of the two communities in Palestine: Jews (the *Yishuv*) and Arabs—the absorbing societies for the American Jewish immigrants. Their attitudes significantly affected the process of integration of immigrants into the new environment.

AMERICAN JEWISH ATTITUDES

The American Jewish community was divided along religious, ideological, and ethnic lines, with different groups holding varying opinions about migration. Indeed, it was not uncommon for members or leaders of the same group or organization to adopt opposing positions. Furthermore, many groups believed such a population movement would affect the present and future situation of Jews in America. The following overview expresses some of the points of view vis-à-vis the question of American Jewish migration to Palestine. The discussion does not attempt to illustrate all opinions but rather to illuminate general perspectives: denominational, nationalistic, ideological, and practical.

CHAPTER 1

During the years between the wars, American Jewry was subdivided into three major denominations—Orthodox, Conservative, and Reform—and each group formulated its own tenets with regard to immigration to Palestine. It is important to keep in mind, however, that not all American Jews were affiliated with an organized religious group.

The American Orthodox sector held no single, clear-cut attitude toward immigration to Palestine, though certain elements opposed Jewish immigration. Like their Eastern European counterparts, many American Orthodox Jews feared that in the process of developing Palestine, establishing settlements, and creating a Jewish political entity, migration would also prematurely bring about messianic redemption. For example, in the late nineteenth century, Abraham J. G. Lesser, an Eastern European rabbi who held different pulpits in the United States, argued that God alone could bring about the redemption. A clear message was disseminated explaining the underlying halachic restrictions.[1] American Jewish immigrant Dovid Ben Nachum explained in his memoirs that "Grandpa said he would come later, rolling underground when the Messiah blew his horn," and not before.[2] Following the Balfour Declaration, American Rabbi Baruch M. Klein clearly expressed the view that the Zionist movement violated Jewish theology. Secular Zionism, he asserted, would distance the people from the Torah. Indeed, he believed that the Zionists in Palestine would be punished: "God would have the Land repel them as a prince vomiting rotten food."[3]

Nevertheless, the Orthodox population in America provided a disproportionately large number of immigrants to Palestine. Provisions within their theological framework allowed individuals to study Torah and spend their final days in the Holy Land so as to die and be buried there. This traditional viewpoint was based on age-old beliefs in *gilgul* (the rolling of the soul underground until it reaches the Holy Land after the arrival of the Messiah). Added to this tradition was *hibbut hakever* (the belief that bodies buried outside the Holy Land would be beaten by heavenly spirits on their way to their final resting place). From the mid-nineteenth century onward, Orthodox American Jews had migrated to Palestine for these reasons, and they continued to do so during the British Mandate period. They also were among the members of Kollel America Tiffereth Yerushalaim, an organization founded in Jerusalem in 1896 that extended financial support to American and Canadian Jews residing in Palestine. Orthodox opposition to the up-building of the Land of Israel frequently confined their constituents' activities and place of settlement. Most Orthodox immigrants were not engaged in the productive sectors of agriculture or industry; instead they survived on philanthropic support or by engaging in commerce. This group mainly settled in Jerusalem, in the other three holy cities—Safed, Tiberias, and Hebron—and in Jaffa.[4]

The Orthodox community included some groups that supported aliyah.

Agudath Israel, an Orthodox and ideologically anti-Zionist group, objected strongly to the efforts of mortal men to "force the hand of God." Members of this group did not object to aliyah itself, which, according to their interpretation of the halacha, was meritorious but not obligatory. Instead, they opposed secular Zionist aliyah and what they regarded as its negative effects on Jewish society in Palestine. They strove to counterbalance Zionist efforts by developing a religious society in Palestine to offset Zionist efforts. For example, Agudath Israel established its own settlement fund, Keren Hayishuv (Jewish Settlement Fund) as well as Habayit (the Home)—an American-based land and building corporation operating in Palestine. Additionally, certain Agudath Israel leaders in Europe called for aliyah. And the Orthodox labor movement, Poale Agudath Israel, dedicated itself to developing a society in Palestine based on the spirit of Torah and social justice.[5]

The Mizrachi Organization of America, another Orthodox group, found a different way to resolve halachic issues connected to aliyah and settlement in Palestine. Mizrachi was a religious Zionist movement founded in 1911 but which already had local societies in existence in 1904. The aims and purposes of Mizrachi, as expressed in the *Jewish Communal Register of New York City, 1917–1918,* did not include Jewish immigration to Palestine in general or from the United States in particular.[6] Although certain constituents of the organization wanted to settle in Palestine and some actually did, they still had to grapple with the halachic question. Rabbi Charles B. Chavel's article "The Fostering of the Settlement and Cultivation of Palestine in the Halaka" opened with the basic question of whether a Jew had a legal obligation, based on biblical sources, to dwell in the Holy Land. Finding no clear answer in the Bible or in Talmudic sources, Chavel called attention to the writings on this controversy by two renowned scholars from the Middle Ages, Maimonides and Nahmonides. The latter had ruled that there was indeed an obligation to settle in the Holy Land, and Chavel explained that "it would be reasonable . . . to assume that the majority of scholars, basing their decision on indirect Talmudic sources, did come to the conclusion that even during the Dispersion there still exists a biblical obligation on [the] part of the Jew to reside in Palestine."[7] However, the American Mizrachi movement did not adopt this conclusion as part of its ideological tenets.

Indeed, a kind of laissez-faire attitude characterized the Mizrachi movement. It lent its approval and supported certain settlement projects in Palestine for its members.[8] Additionally, individual members and some of the movement's leadership set personal examples and migrated to Palestine. The immigration of the organization's leader, Rabbi Meir Berlin (Bar-Ilan)—who left the United States in 1926—is especially noteworthy.

Conservative Judaism expounded coexistence between the Diaspora and the Jewish spiritual center in Palestine. This perspective is expressed in the writings of two of Conservative Judaism's most influential early twentieth-century pedagogues, Professors Solomon Schechter and Israel Friedlander. It is also in line with the views of the Zionist ideologue Ahad Haam, who termed this perspective "Cultural Zionism." These men did not, however, call for a mass migration. "Palestine, the land of our fathers," explained Schechter, then president of the Jewish Theological Seminary of America, "should be recovered with the purpose of forming a home for at least a *portion* of the Jews, who would lead there an independent national life" (emphasis added). In his 1906 statement on Zionism, Schechter further asserted that this ideology would prove "a tower of strength and of unity not only for the remnant gathered within the borders of the Holy Land, but also for those [who], *by choice* or necessity, prefer what now constitutes the Galuth" (emphasis added).[9] Thus the individual was left to make a personal choice regarding immigration to Palestine, though he would more likely be lauded than criticized by Conservative Judaism if he were to migrate.[10]

Rabbi Mordecai M. Kaplan, in formulating the Reconstructionist movement's program, drew upon traditional Jewish sources, Zionist thought, and American philosophical pragmatism. The objective of this movement was the creative survival of Judaism within the intellectual, political, and social realities of the twentieth century. As with cultural Zionism, the Reconstructionist movement found Ahad Haam's spiritual approach persuasive. Two of the three points in Kaplan's 1920 program included "the fostering of the social solidarity of the Jewish people through the upbuilding of Palestine, and the establishment of Kehillahs and communal centers in Diaspora."[11] Although it did not explicitly propose American Jewish immigration to Palestine, Kaplan's program did not exclude this alternative. From his perspective of Judaism as a civilization, he saw the division of world Jewry into three zones.

> The first zone of Jewish life is Palestine, where the Jews are to be given an opportunity to develop their own civilization on the same terms as any other nation. In Palestine only will it be possible for the Jew, *if he so chooses,* to live entirely within his people's civilization. There the Jew will be able to lead a normal life, as a member of a community which functions as an integrated entity, and evolves the institutions and the arts organically related to its needs (emphasis added).[12]

Though Kaplan's devotees in American Jewish society were numerically insignificant, his ideas gained wide acceptance and were integrated into various facet of American Jewish life.

By contrast with other denominational groups, the American Reform movement raised articulate and forceful religious objections to the migration of American Jews to Palestine. In its 1885 Pittsburgh Platform, the Conference of American Reform Rabbis defined the basic principles of the American Reform movement and stated:

> We recognize in the modern era of universal culture of heart and intellect the approach of the realization of Israel's great Messianic hope for the establishment of the kingdom of truth, justice and peace among all men. We consider ourselves no longer a nation but a religious community, and therefore expect neither a return to Palestine, nor sacrificial worship under the administration of the sons of Aaron, nor the restoration of any of the laws concerning the Jewish state.[13]

Reform movement thinkers found other reasons to reject the notion of return to Zion. They believed that migration violated the concept of the universality of Jewish life, and that it was neither practical nor desirable for the modern Jew. Not only would it not put an end to antisemitism, they argued, America would pressure Jews to go to Palestine if a state were established there. Zionism, they claimed, was an ancient world phenomena that would result in a religious regression to something localized and nationalistic.[14]

However, exceptions to this stance existed within the Reform movement. In the late 1890s, for example, Bernhard Felsenthal supported the principles of Zionism, believing that if this endeavor failed Judaism would eventually disappear.[15] And at the 1917 Buffalo convention of the Central Conference of American Rabbis, Rabbi Maximilian Heller presented a report vis-à-vis Zionism that was endorsed by a minority of rabbis.

> Inasmuch as reform Judaism does not dogmatize on the geographical habitat or political status of the Jew; Inasmuch as reform Judaism does not insist on the dispersion of the Jews as an indispensable condition for the welfare and progress of Judaism; Be it Resolved, that there is nothing in the effort to secure a publicly and legally safe-guarded home for Jews in Palestine which is not in accord with the principles and aims of reform Judaism.[16]

At its convention in Chicago the following year, the conference modified its position when it responded to the Balfour Declaration and its implications. On the one hand, the conference noted "with grateful appreciation the declaration of the British Government by Mr. Balfour as evidence [of] good-will toward the Jews." The conference also sanctioned the policy of facilitating the migration to Palestine of persecuted Jews or those in economic need. However, it objected to the phrase in the declaration that "Palestine is to be a national home-land for the Jewish people." This, the conference felt, implied that Jews were not a religious group but a national group, and the creation of a Jewish homeland in Palestine would leave no place for Jews in the nations of the world." The policy developed at the conference concluded by expounding the basic tenet of Reform Judaism: "The mission of the Jew is to witness to God all over the world."[17] A year later, in 1919, a number of Reform rabbis refused to affix their signatures to the anti-Zionist petition presented to President Woodrow Wilson before he attended the Paris Peace Conference. (This petition supported assisting Jews in finding a place of refuge but opposed political aspirations of the Zionist movement for a sovereign state for Jews in Palestine).[18]

In the years following World War I, the Reform movement slowly moved away from its anti-Zionist attitude, particularly in the practical and cultural realms. In a 1932 treatise, Reform Rabbi Michael Alper, who served as the director of Jewish education of New York's Hebrew Orphan Asylum, described the variations between the two wings of American Reform Judaism with regard to Zionism. In his opinion, the right wing, or "Orthodox Re-Formed Judaism," was guilty of adhering to views of Zionism that dated back a century or more. Cosmopolitanism and universalism were not ideals that prevented a solution to "the Jewish Question" through Zionism. The right wing had not adapted to changing times, Alper declared; it had failed to recognize the movement from the "melting pot" to "cultural pluralism" or from "universalism" to "internationalism." By contrast, the left wing, which in Alper's opinion was the liberal version of "Reformed Judaism," saw an important role for Zionism.[19] The prevailing liberal attitude is expressed in the following statement by Rabbi Stephen S. Wise, a prominent Reform rabbi and ardent Zionist supporter and leader.

> It may be a tragedy to some to see the great facts of Jewish life amend or repeal the utterances of German-speaking rabbis three-quarters of a century ago. But that tragedy is not quite as woeful as is the tragedy of a leadership in our own day, which laments the passing of long-superseded theological and dogmatic shibboleths, instead of welcoming joyously the revitalization of all that is truly Jewish by the blessed and saving influence of Zionism.[20]

By 1932 the transformation of American Reform Judaism and its growing acceptance of Zionism became more noticeable. An increasing number of students attending its seminary, Hebrew Union College, showed support for Zionism. Armond Emanuel Cohen reported on the sentiment of ninety-one students there: "twenty-one are active Zionists, nine have Zionist inclinations (they may pull through); fifty-two are good traditionally Reform Rabbinical material (they are indifferent or undecided in attitude), seven are definitely anti-Zionists (their definiteness indicating that they hardly belong in the Rabbinate), and two are actively propagandistic against Zionism."[21]

A more concrete example of the Reform movement's growing recognition of Zionism was the inclusion of *Hatikvah,* the anthem of the Zionist movement and later the State of Israel, in the 1932 revised edition of the *Union Hymnal,* the official prayer book of the American Reform movement. Moreover, within the movement some individuals posited an active role for Reform Judaism in the spiritual molding of the *Yishuv.* Rabbi Samuel Schulman of New York's Temple Emanuel, in a paper presented to the 1935 Central Conference of American Rabbis convention for the formation of a platform on Palestine, went so far as to suggest that the conference "send a dozen young men or more to Palestine to bring the message of Progressive Judaism."[22] This should not be seen as a general endorsement of Zionism or of immigration, but rather as a proposal to expand the mission of the Reform movement to include Jewry in Palestine. Schulman's statement providing both clergy and laity with the choice to immigrate was actually after the fact. From 1929 onward, a number of students and graduates of Hebrew Union College attended the Hebrew University of Jerusalem.[23] No information has been found, however, as to whether these students disseminated the message of Progressive Judaism in the *Yishuv*.

The Reform movement's Columbus Platform of 1937 faced up to the reality of changes in the modern world and its membership's attitude toward Zionism, and redefined its teachings. While still believing in the principles of full loyalty to the United States and the necessity of upholding the duties and responsibilities of American citizenship, Reform leaders found a place for Palestine in the movement's dogma. "In the rehabilitation of Palestine . . . we behold the promise of renewed life for many of our brethren. We affirm the obligation of all Jewry to aid in its upbuilding as a Jewish homeland by endeavoring to make it not only a haven of refuge for the oppressed but also a center of Jewish culture and spiritual life."[24] It is important to note here that although in 1930 the Reform movement accounted for only about 6 percent of the American Jewish population, its membership included many of the German-Jewish elite, an influential and wealthy part of the community. Reform movement ideas would also have had a strong influence on the educated, Americanized Jewish population.[25]

As has been demonstrated, each of the Jewish religious denominations in the United States constructed its attitudes toward Jewish migration based on interpretation of the Scriptures and rabbinic literature. Various current events also affected their respective attitudes. The question of dual loyalty was dealt with at great length and was sometimes an issue in the different denominations' formulations of their viewpoints. Were Jews really Americans or could they ever be so if they supported Zionism? Was there a place for Jews in American society or was America simply a stopping or resting point on their journey to Palestine?

Within the American context, economic realities affected this question of dual loyalty. On the mind of the Jewish establishment was the growing American hostility toward return migration and its implications for American Jewry. From the 1890s onward, there was increasing animosity toward immigrants who, it was believed, did not assimilate into American society but intentionally "looted" the country, unfairly competing with American workers and depriving the nation of skilled farmers when they returned to their homelands. Southern and Eastern Europeans were singled out for reprobation, and the Jewish establishment feared that analogous reactions would halt Jewish immigration to the United States. If Palestine was or was to become the Jewish homeland, the logical conclusion would be that Jews had no place in America. This would contradict the carefully constructed notion that Jews were unable to return to the place from whence they had come.[26]

Much to the chagrin of the American Jewish establishment, Nachman Syrkin, in advocating his Achva plan for the settlement of Palestine, openly suggested re-immigration as a means of advancing his scheme. In 1914 he wrote that "hundreds of thousands of Italians, Poles, and Hungarians are coming each year to the U.S.A. for the sole purpose of saving money and then returning to their native lands to invest in agricultural pursuits . . . [and] the Jews [of Eastern Europe] could do the same for Palestinian settlement."[27] In fact, some American Jewish immigrants to Palestine did follow this practice.

Proponents of immigration restriction speculated in 1919 that each returnee would diminish the American economy by at least $1,500, while some would take as much as $7,500 when they left the country. Thus an estimated 2,000,000 emigrés in the early 1920s would result in the exodus of around $6 billion in capital from the American economy. An antagonism similar to that expressed toward Southern and Eastern Europeans would be aimed at the American Jewish community if some of its members were to re-immigrate to Palestine. In fact, following World War I, applicants for immigration to Palestine possessed on average much more capital than proponents of immigration restriction had predicted.[28]

From the 1880s onward, the mass Jewish immigration from Eastern Europe to the shores of America led to fears of a negative appraisal of the American Jewish population, specifically to fears of increased antisemitism. In an 1882 statement, poet Emma Lazarus clearly distinguished between Jews already in America and the suffering Jews in Eastern Europe:

> There is not the slightest necessity, for an American Jew, the free citizen of a republic, to rest his hopes upon the foundation of any other nationality soever, or to decide whether he individually would or would not be in favor of residing in Palestine. All that would be claimed from him would be a patriotic and unselfish interest in the suffering of his oppressed brethren of less fortunate countries, sufficient to make him promote by every means in his power the establishment of a secure asylum.[29]

Lazarus's opinion illustrates the belief that Jews already resident in the United States were Americans and there was no need for them to immigrate to Palestine. However, to insure their continued freedom, other Jews destined for America should be turned away.

Similar views were held by non-Zionists.[30] While they rejected the philosophy of Zionism, particularly its nationalist ideology, they encouraged its practical work: the settlement and development of Palestine. Heading this group was Judge Louis Marshall, president of the American Jewish

TABLE 7
Capital reported by prospective immigrants (family heads) to Palestine, 1919–20

Capital ($)	Number of family heads	Percent
not reported	374	19.46
less than 500	586	30.49
501 to 1,000	173	9.00
1,001 to 2,500	349	18.16
2,501 to 5,000	155	8.06
5,001 to 10,000	150	7.80
10,001 to 25,000	112	5.83
25,001 to 50,000	13	0.68
50,001 to 100,000	3	0.16
over 100,000	3	0.16
Total	1,922	100.00

Source: "Statistical Report on Applicants and Registrants for Palestine from America," Palestine Service and Information Bureau, Zionist Organization of America, New York, 31 May 1920, CZA F25/33.

Committee. In 1918 and again in a speech as the chairman of the Non-Partisan Conference to Consider Palestinian Problems in 1924, Marshall stressed that Jews in the United States had established a permanent home for themselves and their descendants. They had acquired the rights and thus the duties of citizenship. Not only did they owe their unqualified allegiance to America, they regarded themselves as an integral part of the nation. With regard to Palestine, Louis Marshall and the American Jewish Committee were not "unmindful that there are Jews everywhere who, moved by traditional sentiment, yearn for a home in the Holy Land for the Jewish people. This hope, nurtured for centuries, has our wholehearted sympathy. We recognize, however, that but a part of the Jewish people would take up their domicile in Palestine. The greater number will continue to live in the lands of whose citizenship they now form a component part."[31] Marshall, in cooperation with world Zionist leader Chaim Weizmann, played an instrumental role in founding the expanded Jewish Agency for Palestine in the late 1920s. The agency would "give adequate representation to non-Zionists to enable them, jointly with the Zionist organization, to participate in the privileges and responsibilities of the Jewish Agency."

Marshall died only days after the Sixteenth Zionist Congress in Zurich approved the expansion of the agency in 1929.

Edward M. Warburg, son of Felix Warburg—a prominent American non-Zionist of the 1920s and 1930s—recollected that his father's views on the status of Palestine were in agreement with the concept of cultural Zionism: "It was Father's non-Zionist idea that (Israel) Palestine should become a university state and be a place where the Jews of the world would go to rededicate themselves to the concepts of Judaism. It would be a place where people would have the possibility of recharging their batteries; for example, American rabbis would be able to go there and return home and be better rabbis in America."[32]

With the establishment of Zionism as a political entity, through the convening of the First Zionist Congress in Basel in 1897 by Theodor Herzl, a small assemblage within American Jewry lent its unequivocal support. Again, among various other groups of American Jews a distinction was made between support for a Jewish homeland and the actual immigration of American Jews. The Federation of American Zionists felt it necessary to deal with the interpretation of Herzlian Zionism in their American environment. Faced with opposition from various Jewish groups and organizations, particularly the Reform movement, federation president Richard J. H. Gottheil constructed in 1898 an American Zionist platform in his essay "The Aims of Zionism." The essence of Gottheil's position paper is found in his summation: "We believe that such a home can only naturally, and without violence to their whole past, be found in the land of their fathers—in Palestine. We believe that such a return must have the guarantee of the great powers of the world, in order to secure for the Jews a stable future. And we hold that this does not mean that all Jews must return to Palestine."[33]

Attempting to further clarify the American Zionist position—particularly when the issue spilled over into the purview of the American public—Gottheil wrote in a 1902 letter to the editor of the *New York Times:* "First it is our objective to find a new home for Jews who cannot live in their adopted countries, and second we work towards finding such a home for those who do not want to live in their adopted countries. We have no idea of trying to send to Palestine those who do not want to go there, but only those who desire to go from the bottom of their hearts."[34] But this was not the conclusion of the issue. Gottheil turned to international Zionist leader Theodor Herzl for advice regarding the dilemma of dual loyalty. In a letter dated 30 November 1903, he solicited advice regarding "how to square Zionism with the duties and obligations of a patriotic American citizen of the strenuous stamp of Theodore Roosevelt."[35] Herzl provided Gottheil with a response which apparently answered the needs of the American Zionist movement. His answer was published in the Zionist organ, the *Maccabean.*

> Participation in the Zionist movement means nothing which is not in the clearest and highest form in unison with patriotism of a true American. He who labors for the creation of a home assured by the public law and recognized by all the nations of the earth, will perform his duties as an American citizen with pleasure. . . . [T]he American Jews aid their beloved fatherland when they aid an unhappy people from whom they spring. This is not disloyalty, in no way, but a double measure of loyalty.[36]

The Orthodox Jewish Congregational Union of America also addressed the question of dual loyalty. In 1898 it adopted the stand that Zionism and American patriotism were not incompatible. It urged its membership to support the Zionist movement but asserted that American Jews were not obligated to immigrate to Palestine. The union's resolution declared: "The desirability and the necessity of offering to those of our brethren dwelling under the rigor of oppressive laws a refuge legally assured to them cannot be questioned. . . . Furthermore, that the restoration of Zion is the legitimate aspiration of scattered Israel, in no way conflicts with our loyalty to the land in which we dwell or may dwell at any time."[37]

These were the basic foundations of the attitudes of American Jews toward Zionism and migration to Palestine laid down in the late nineteenth and early twentieth centuries. These perspectives are best summarized in Israel Friedlander's assessment of American Jewry, written on the eve of World War I.

> [German Jewry in the United States] discarded, more radically than in Europe, the national elements still clinging to Judaism, and it solemnly proclaimed that Judaism was wholly and exclusively a religious faith, and that America was the Zion and Washington the Jerusalem of American Israel. On the other hand, the emigrants from Russia brought the antithesis on the scene. They quickly perceived the decomposing effect of American life upon Jewish doctrine and practice, and they became convinced more firmly than ever that Diaspora Judaism was a failure, and that the only antidote was Palestine, nothing but Palestine.[38]

A distinct change in attitudes began to develop when Louis D. Brandeis assumed the chairmanship of the Provisional Zionist Executive Committee on Zionist Affairs in 1914 and effectively became the leader of American Zionism. The movement received legitimization under the leadership of this successful business lawyer, the renowned advocate of individual rights and social change, and progressive civic leader from the German-Jewish elite. In 1916 Brandeis's own status was enhanced when President Woodrow Wilson appointed him to the United States Supreme Court.[39]

For a short period, and mainly as a result of wartime alliances, a sense of unity existed in Zionist circles between American Jews of German and Russian origin, though opinions regarding immigration to Palestine continued to diverge. Brandeis held a clear position on the subject, believing that migration should be embraced by the Zionist movement. He noted that "efforts are being directed towards establishing a publicly recognized, legally secured home for Jews in Palestine. Such a home will serve both as a haven for persecuted Jews from European countries, and also a center for Jewish ideas and Jewish culture."[40] If American Jews were to immigrate to Palestine, Brandeis suggested, it would be because of their connection to Jewish ideas and culture; however, their number and the scope of their activity would be limited. He explained that Zionists did not believe it was compulsory to emigrate to Palestine: "Every American Jew who aids in advancing the Jewish settlements in Palestine, though he feels that neither he nor his descendants will ever live there, will likewise be a better man and a better American for doing so."[41] Similar sentiments were expressed by Jewish philanthropist Jacob Schiff, New York Supreme Court Justice Irving Lehman, and Professor Felix Frankfurter.[42]

On the opposite side of the dual loyalty argument, certain adherents surmised that no matter how hard or how long Jews attempted to integrate into American society, they would never become full citizens. Their only real option was Palestine. In October 1899, Theodor Herzl sent Joseph Zeff to conduct propaganda work on New York City's East Side and in other Orthodox communities where it was considered imperative that an integrated organization be brought into being. However, Zeff became involved in the growing rivalry between the German elite and the Eastern European proletariat. Siding with the latter, he supported the socialists in their strike against the Sarasohn publishing house. Its owner was a member of the national executive of the Federation of American Zionists. To the dismay of many American Zionists, Zeff proposed that even American Jews should settle in Palestine.[43] "Don't fool yourselves that you are American. You are, presently, not counted as Americans and you never will be regarded as Americans. . . . [The Jew] must therefore provide himself with a place on which to rest his feet. In his land he will be able to develop and to be like all nations. . . . Only in Palestine will the Jew learn to stand erect and to be a guide to all the nations."[44] For Zionists in the United States, the question of dual loyalty was one of the most formidable issues requiring resolution. Although responses were supplied by the American Zionist leadership, these responses did not answer the arguments of those who believed that a person could be loyal to only one nation at a time.

Ideologically, American Jewry developed its own vision of Zionism, distinct from the two other traditions that had emerged, one in Eastern Europe and the other in Central Europe. At the same time, it embraced certain components of both these traditions. Over the years, within the framework of defining and redefining its meaning of Zionism, differing attitudes to one of its most pressing questions—Should American Jews immigrate and settle in Palestine?—likewise developed. Various political, economic, and social factors affected the formulation of responses to this question.[45] One response was to avoid the question altogether. The place allotted for aliyah was peripheral, it was argued. American Jewish historian Henry L. Finegold explained that "aliyah is not so much opposed by American Jewry as it is so distant from any reality they know in their lives as to be truly irrelevant."[46] American Jewry was too involved in the process of assimilation into a new society to consider an alternative locale. Melvin I. Urofsky went further and claimed that aliyah "was never an important item on the American Zionist agenda, despite the vast amount of lip service paid to emigration as an ideal."[47]

These views reflect the mainstream American Zionist attitude toward its own immigration and settlement in Palestine. However, they fall short of expressing the true complexity of American Jewry's response to the issue. Different schools of thought grew within the community, mirroring the wide spectrum of American Zionism. In the following section, a discussion of mainstream attitudes is followed by an exploration of the stances held by various branches of American Zionism.

From the 1880s onward, some Eastern European Jewish immigrants to America brought with them the hopes of the Hovevei Zion movement. Unlike their fellow American Jews of German descent who were connected to the Reform movement, these immigrants intended to settle in Palestine one day, after a period of preparation in America. There were few followers of this ideology; membership in Hovevei Zion and Shavei Zion societies was limited, as was the scope and period of their activity. Early Zionist leader and founder of the Hovevei Zion movement Rabbi Samuel Mohilever expressed his disappointment in the failure of the American movement and its adherents. "Only in the new land, in America," wrote Mohilever, "is the voice of Zion hiding, silent and the ringing sound of dollars and cents is drowning out the voice of our old mother calling her sons."[48]

In June 1918, after publication of the Balfour Declaration and the cessation of hostilities in Palestine, the twenty-first American Zionist Convention held in Pittsburgh reaffirmed the principles of the American Zionist movement: political and civil equality for all inhabitants of Palestine; equal opportunity through public ownership of resources; the utilization of public land for its fullest development; the application of the cooperative principle; free public education; and Hebrew as the national Jewish language.[49] No mention was made regarding immigration to Palestine in general or of American Jewish immigration in particular. Under the leadership of Louis Brandeis and Julian Mack, this question was regarded as potentially divisive and therefore to be avoided—particularly in the context of the search for compromise among various American Zionist groups, as well as in light of the attempt to placate non-Zionists. Some Yiddish journalists interpreted this avoidance of deeper doctrinal matters as an expression of the alienation of the leadership from the Jewish masses. The press believed the leaders lacked a genuine ideology and did not understand the true meaning of Zionism.[50]

The Mizrachi Organization of America, discussed above in the context of religious attitudes to immigration, tacitly approved the immigration of American Jews to Palestine. In a series of articles published as part of the celebrations of Mizrachi's twenty-fifth anniversary, the organization's activities and contributions are described, and its future directions outlined. Mizrachi accepted the precepts of the Basel platform, including its first point: the settlement of Palestine by agriculturalists, craftsmen, and industrial workers. The organization neither prevailed upon its members to immigrate nor prevented them from doing so, but it held in high esteem the personal example of immigration made by its leader Rabbi Meir Berlin. The organization also attempted to use its leverage to facilitate the immigration of some of its constituent—for example, by granting approval to certain settlement schemes, including Nahalat Itzhak outside Jerusalem. Mizrachi envisioned its principal work in America as supporting Jewish settlement in Palestine and Jewish religious life there, but there was no desire to upset a certain balance among its constituents.[51]

For members of revisionist groups a dilemma existed as to whether aliyah was obligatory. On various occasions the revisionist leader Vladmir Jabotinsky called on Americans to settle in Palestine and urged former Jewish Legionnaires to defend Palestine's borders. However, revisionists never formally spelled out immigration as an obligation, either to their general membership or to members of their youth organization, Betar.[52]

Within the spectrum of potential American immigrants, a unique group stands out—the *halutzim* (pioneers). Unlike others, they were involved in a process of preparation in America before their immigration. The organization of the various *halutzim*, their educational programs, and their training are of special interest. Their emphasis was on agriculture, although they believed that other vocations that would be useful for the up-building of Palestine should also be developed. Prior to World War I, a fringe group of limited scope, Hechalutz and its offshoot Haikar Hatzair (the Young Farmer), adopted the pioneering principles. Their adherents would eventually settle in Palestine and strive to rebuild it in the collective way. For example, four Haikar Hatzair members settled on the Kinneret farm on the shores of the Sea of Galilee in 1912.[53]

Halutzim were mainly drawn from the ranks of American Jewish youth and young adults, many of whom were affiliated with Zionist organizations, including Young Judaea, the Intercollegiate Zionist Association, Avukah (the Torch), Junior Hadassah, Mizrachi Youth, Poale Zion Youth (later Habonim) and Hashomer Hatzair (the Young Guard). The latter two groups had a greater orientation than the others to personal fulfillment through pioneer training and aliyah.[54]

Young Judaea, with its beginnings in 1904, never strongly supported the concept of fulfillment, in Zionist terms, through aliyah. Instead it advocated Zionist education programs and assistance to various Palestinian causes, particularly the Jewish National Fund. The organization's Zionist activities were the object of visiting Palestinian Zionist leader Chaim Arlosoroff's criticism in the late 1920s. In his assessment of Zionism in general, he asserted that this youth movement jumbled concepts and created confusion between religion and nationalism.[55] Not until the organization's 1933 national convention in Sharon, Massachusetts, was there a resolution that called for the spirit of *halutziut* (pioneering) to be incorporated into the ideology of Young Judaea. This resolution urged its membership to join the Hechalutz organization with a view to ultimately settling in Palestine.[56]

The Intercollegiate Zionist Association, founded in 1915, sponsored Zionist educational programs that emphasized intellectual aspects—conferences, educational literature, and visiting lecturers—at American universities. It did not foster aliyah. Ideologically, the association believed that Zionism would make better Americans of its members, and that politically they were part of only one nation, the United States of America. By 1922 the organization's membership had steeply declined.[57]

An offshoot, Avukah, was founded in 1925 to participate in the "study of Jewish life and literature from a creative national standpoint . . . and in practical service for Palestine."[58] Immigration to Palestine was not part of its credo, but "practical service" could easily be interpreted as such. At its first convention in 1926, an announcement proclaimed that five members from the University of Wisconsin chapter were to leave shortly for Palestine, intent on pursuing agricultural careers there. Within the Avukah organization there were some who were connected to the Labor Zionist movement and who supported the pioneering idea. Rebecca Schmuckler of the Hunter College chapter was principally responsible for the publication of the 1928 anthology *Hechalutz,* and after the riots in Palestine in 1929, she pleaded in favor of preparation for pioneering. During the years of the Great Depression, when there was growing support for pioneering in Palestine, Avukah became closely associated with the League for Palestine Labor and Hashomer Hatzair. In 1934 an annual fellowship was created to allow travel to Palestine and maintenance in a *kevutzah* (commune) for two Avukah members.[59]

Junior Hadassah, the dutiful daughter of the Hadassah organization, originated in 1916 and eventually became the largest Zionist youth organization in the United States. Its chief activities were in the spheres of Zionist and Jewish education, and involved supporting certain social and medical projects in Palestine. Junior Hadassah did not emphasize immigration to Palestine.[60]

Another organization that sprouted in the United States was Masada. It had informal antecedents in 1928, but was officially founded in 1933 at its first national convention at Niagara Falls, New York. This organization, for men aged twenty to thirty, was formally recognized by the Zionist Organization of America. Although it did not promote *halutziut* in its aims and principles, during its first year six of its members settled in Palestine as *halutzim*.[61]

Of all these youth and young adult groups, the American Hashomer Hatzair had the strongest orientation toward immigration to Palestine. This youth movement was organized by Eastern European emigrés in 1927. The single most powerful element in its educational program was the expected aliyah of every young adult member of the movement. In reality, not all of them were able to migrate; one factor that restricted them was the limited number of immigration certificates available.[62]

Outside the Zionist camps, other ideological groups also addressed the question of American Jewish immigration to Palestine. Vocal in their disapproval were Jewish trade unionists, socialists, and communists. In 1912 pro-Zionist socialists established a splinter group, the Jewish Socialist Labor Party, known as Poale Zion. The Zionist fraternal order, the Jewish National Workers' Alliance (Farband), was established that same year to rival the Workmen's Circle (Arbeiter Ring). The Workmen's Circle, which was Bundist controlled and anti-Zionist, viewed Zionism as a bourgeois religious movement that obscured basic social issues. From this organization's perspective, Zionism was attempting to force a Jewish national homeland on a hostile Arab majority. Furthermore, the Workmen's Circle regarded Poale Zion as hypocritical because it showed indifference to the international proletarian struggle. Even after a slight shifting of attitude during the late 1930s, the Workmen's Circle continued to be skeptical of Jewish immigrants who were not of the "right" type—specifically, Yiddish-speaking Marxists who would be concerned about their Arab fellows.[63]

The views of Jewish communists, numbering only a few thousand, shifted radically over the years, usually in response to changing policies of the regime in the Soviet Union. However, until the outbreak of World War II, they generally condemned migration to Palestine. Among the declarations published in the *New Masses* from 1935 was the assertion that "no nation can solve its problems by emigrating to another country, even if Palestine were not so small and so thickly populated."[64]

Some advocates of American Jewish immigration to Palestine responded to the claim that Palestine was not large enough to accommodate the intended Jewish immigration and settlement. They focused on practical considerations rather than religious or ideological credos, and without regard to the consequences of migration on American Jewish society. They considered such questions as: (1) whether Palestine was large enough to accommodate a mass migration; (2) whether the situation there was suitable for migration at the present time; (3) whether only immigrants with special skills or certain attitudes were needed; and (4) whether Palestine was the only locale for personal fulfillment. The question of the "absorptive capacity" of Palestine for immigration was an important issue in the Zionist dialogue. Polemical and scholarly discussions grappled with the question of how large a population Palestine could sustain, since the answer was integral to plans for settlement. If the country reached or neared its potential, then despite its attractiveness as the historical homeland, Palestine could not be considered the place for resolution of "the Jewish Question." If the country could support a much larger population than the estimated 650,000 to 800,000 living there at the end of World War I, then there was a question of priorities: most of all, the provision of a place of refuge for displaced Jews and those suffering from persecution.

Responding to these issues, Louis Brandeis asserted at the June 1915 Conference of the Eastern Council of Reform Rabbis in New York that Palestine could not accommodate all World Jewry. "In the first place there are 14,000,000 Jews, and Palestine would not accommodate more than one-third of that number. In the second place, it is not a movement to compel anyone to go to Palestine."[65] Thus if a choice were to be made, preference should be given to Jews in danger, not to American Jews. This position did not, however, exclude American Jewry. Indeed, those who would be useful in the development of Palestine would be welcomed and encouraged.

Economic and historical factors profoundly affected the debate—as well as Zionism itself. Before the outbreak of World War I, the Federation of American Zionists was weak, in financial distress, and with very little influence in the Jewish community. A spirit of gloom and defeat engulfed the few dedicated leaders. There seemed to be no future for Zionism in America, and several leaders thought of immigrating to Palestine, the one place where Zionism was active and had a future. The outbreak of the war, however, prevented any such migration.[66]

By 1919 Brandeis supported the closure of immigration to Palestine altogether until better and healthier conditions could be established. It seemed clear that malaria would have to be eradicated as a precondition to mass immigration. To this end, the Zionist Organization of America used most of its financial resources in support of the American Zionist Medical Unit already in Palestine. This unit had been organized and sponsored by American Hadassah to bring health practitioners and technicians to Palestine to assist the people who had suffered the ravages of war.

From within the ranks of the Zionist Organization of America rose the Zionist Society of Engineers and Agriculturalists. This group utilized the technical training of American Jewish engineers, agronomists, and scientists for the agricultural, industrial, and economic development of Palestine. It was intended that their activities would precede any mass immigration to

Palestine. Although this was never stated forthrightly in society publications, its members should feel obliged to take up temporary or even permanent settlement in Palestine. Boris Katzmann, an agricultural chemist by profession, headed this society. Katzmann held that the settlement of Palestine must be carefully planned, with all the pertinent scientific information collected in advance. Accordingly, American engineers and other experts should play an integral part in this preparation process.[67]

An additional precondition for mass immigration recognized by Brandeis and his followers was the establishment of an economic infrastructure, especially small industries. Brandeis expected small businessmen to immigrate to Palestine from the United States and Europe for this purpose. American businessmen would inject the economy with needed capital and share their experience, know-how, and business acumen.[68] Brandeis explicitly expressed this sentiment when he decided to encourage such individuals as Robert Kesselman, Emanuel Mohl, and Robert Szold to undertake various duties in Palestine. Great value was seen in encouraging "high class Americans to settle in Palestine."[69]

This same idea was affirmed by Gershon Agronsky, an American journalist and former Jewish Legionnaire. "Palestine needs Jews who have lived in America," he wrote in 1925. "It has need of their confidence and enthusiasm, their buoyancy and initiative, their system and orderliness."[70] Similarly, Dr. Israel J. Biskind, formerly of Cleveland and later chief surgeon of Palestine, stated in 1923: "I believe that there should be a larger influx of Jews from America. I believe that they are just as badly needed in Palestine as are the Chalutzim."[71]

Former Hadassah president Irma L. Lindheim, only a month after her arrival in Jerusalem, expressed her opinion of the situation in Palestine to Rabbi Stephen S. Wise. Her conviction was strongly affected by the 1929 riots that had occurred only three months earlier. She saw American Jewry's role as twofold. First she wanted American Jews to raise their voices in protest regarding Britain's capacity in Palestine. Second, she was convinced of the need for "a group who will come to Palestine *now* and who are fitted by training and experience to evolve with those here a new form of political administration" (emphasis in the original).[72]

Another point of view was that Americans and their cultural baggage were not only needed, they were essential for the development of Palestine. Samuel M. Melamed, a member of the Zionist Organization of America national executive, argued in 1928 that American civilization had to be transplanted to Palestine. He further asserted that Europeans transported an inferior "Jewish ghetto culture," to Palestine, and he deemed this unsatisfactory for the new country.[73]

Poale Zion of America, the United Labor Zionist Organization of America, did not directly endorse the immigration of American Jews to Palestine

Fig. 6. Cover of memorandum to the members of the Zionist Society of Engineers and Agriculturists, New York, September 1919. (CZA F25/298)

in its 1918 program. Its platform instead supported the creation of a "Labor Army"—Jewish workers for national service, ready to answer the call of Palestine. The primary objective was "to supply willing workers of all kinds of national purposes and to reduce the problem of successful colonization to capital raising and efficient planning and management. All the great enterprises for bringing Palestine into a state of advanced civilization could be carried through with the least possible friction."[74] The recommended period of service was two to five years, depending upon the type and quality of work done and the training attained during this national service. The service could, however, be indefinitely prolonged if so desired by the members of the "labor army."[75]

On a practical level it was quite evident that not all American Jews could or would settle in Palestine. The founder of the American Zion Commonwealth, Judge Bernard Rosenblatt, believed that most American Jewry, even those committed to the Zionist idea, would not leave America. His organization had noted the disappointing experience of the pre–World War I *ahuza* societies. Accordingly, the directors of the company decided not to emphasize any commitment to personal settlement when they marketed land to the American Jewish public. Rosenblatt reckoned that only about 10 percent of American Zion Commonwealth certificate holders would eventually settle in Palestine.[76]

In the end, most American Jewish organizations either supported or were neutral about immigration to Palestine. At one extreme, certain groups opposed any such migration, while at the other end of the spectrum some required it. Aliyah was certainly on the mind of American Jewry in the years immediately following World War I. But except for a small number, migration was not part of their personal reality but rather a question that resounded in their religious lives, and in the formulation of their national and ideological identities. This evaluation accords with Yonathan Shapiro's conclusion that the essence of American Zionist ideology after World War I was "Palestinianism"—the up-building of Palestine as a Jewish national home. According to Shapiro, this ideological tenet resulted from the fact that as an increasing number of American Jews were becoming upwardly mobile, they were beginning to encounter antisemitism. Palestinianism, with its nationalistic leanings, became a suitable ideology or point of reference for various Jewish groups, imbuing them with a sense of self-respect and pride. In many ways, it was a reaction to the wounds inflicted by antisemitism.[77]

Palestinianism, on the other hand, did not strongly support the sense of personal fulfillment through individual participation in the actual process of developing Palestine. It was only fringe groups in American Jewish society that incorporated aliyah into their platforms. The vast majority of Zionists and non-Zionists accepted and even lauded individual decisions to immigrate to Palestine, but they never espoused such actions for the Jewish population at large. The pluralism of the greater society, coupled with the concept of freedom of individual decision, facilitated diverse action among American Jewry's component members.

ATTITUDES OF THE INTERNATIONAL ZIONIST LEADERSHIP

The World Zionist Organization concerned itself with three practical issues regarding Palestine: its up-building, the growth and development of its population, and how to finance these two. Focusing on the Jewish peopling of Palestine, it attempted to provide assistance to those it deemed most suited for the venture. Until the rise of Adolph Hitler to power in Germany in 1933, the principal criteria were ideological orientation, physical and social adaptability to a new environment, and possession of the necessary skills or traits for the Zionist endeavor. After 1933 the concern turned to providing a safe haven for those in Central Europe who were in danger of economic or physical persecution.[78]

An expression of the World Zionist Organization's selection process was the distribution of labor schedule certificates, among Zionist representatives in different countries, which afforded entry into Palestine. Of the 122,135 immigrants entering Palestine with labor certificates between May 1925 and December 1934, the last previous residence of only 784 was the United States. This clearly indicates discrimination against the American Jewish community. The reasons for this discrimination are related to the general policy of preferring Eastern European Zionist groups both because this seemed more appropriate and because they were in greater need. Furthermore, it was erroneously believed that Americans who expressed an interest in settling in Palestine already possessed the necessary capital to receive a visa under other sections of the immigration ordinances.[79]

By examining the writings and utterances of prominent figures in the Zionist movement, we can gain a deeper understanding of their bias. Within the ranks of the World Zionist Organization leadership there existed a variety of opinions regarding the place of American Jewry in the immigration movement to Palestine and the country's advancement. These, in turn, reflect certain nuances and underlying feelings toward American Zionists and American Jewry at large. The prevailing attitude was that American money and political influence, not its manpower, were needed.[80]

A survey of Chaim Weizmann's attitude over the years—Weizmann was president of the World Zionist Organization from 1920–31 and from 1935–46—reveals that his opinion changed according to his perception of the Zionist enterprise's needs, the ideological tensions with the Brandeis-Mack group of American Zionists, and his encounters and interactions with American Jewry. In 1919 he addressed the question of the disbandment and repatriation of soldiers from the Jewish Legion stationed in Palestine, including a large number of American Jews who were willing to settle in Palestine. Weizmann explained to Eric Forbes-Adam that "it is not our desire to increase the Jewish population by means of an undue proportion of soldiers or ex-soldiers."[81] However, Weizmann followed this up by suggesting that thousands of Jewish men—Caucasians and Galician prisoners of war in Russia—be allowed to immigrate to Palestine. In his opinion, these men were appropriate for pioneer work and would be suitable human material for a militia. A similar attitude was expressed in Zionist Commission for Palestine member David Eder's statement—which also reflected Zeev Jabotinsky's thoughts—"these young men who want to settle can wait—after all, there are hundreds of thousands of good youth from Poland and Galicia waiting to come.... [I]t's better for them to wait in America than for others to remain in Poland."[82]

By contrast, David Ben-Gurion, a Legionnaire himself, viewed the settling of American Legionnaires in Palestine as a heavy and responsible task for Poale Zion. He pointed out that the bulk of these men were members of the organization in America, and he could not envision the party abandoning its members who, for ideological reasons, had joined the military and yearned to settle in Palestine. For Ben-Gurion this was a personal commitment, since he had traveled the length and breadth of the continent with Yitzhak Ben-Zvi recruiting young Jews for the Jewish Legion. Ben-Gurion hoped to do everything in his power to assist these Americans, regarding them as a special contribution to future progress in Palestine.[83] Zeev Tzahor, in his essay on Ben-Gurion's attitude to the Diaspora, has explained that "Ben Gurion arrived at the total negation of the Diaspora and, in effect, of everything that was not connected with 'life in the homeland.'" Tzahor further argued that Ben-Gurion's "first encounter with the United States served to confirm the convictions that Ben-Gurion had held since childhood: life in the Diaspora corrupted the Jew and warped his way of life and his beliefs, while Palestine could create new, healthy and balanced individuals. Therefore, nothing was more important than immigration to Palestine."[84]

Ben-Gurion believed that the American contribution of skilled manpower was consequential and important. On the agenda for Poale Zion was the induction of competent and experienced workers who would help promote the success of the organization's cooperative project. America could provide builders, metal-workers, carpenters, mechanics, cobblers, tailors, and sailors. If there were none of the latter, Ben-Gurion suggested that some Americans enlist in the United States Navy or Merchant Marine to acquire experience before their eventual immigration. These men would not only strengthen the position of Poale Zion in Palestine, he felt, but also contribute to the development of the land.[85]

Following the establishment of the Civil Administration in Palestine in 1920, there became a need for skilled and unskilled English-speaking

Fig. 7. American Jewish Legionnaires en route back to the United States, in front of the American Red Cross building, Winchester, England, 21 November 1919. (CZA photograph collection 21,635)

workers in various positions. Weizmann hoped that such individuals could be attracted from North America. In November 1920, he telegraphed both the Zionist Organization of America and the Zionist Organization of Canada: "Confidential: Zionist Commission reports opportunity Government employment [in] Palestine [for] two hundred skilled, one hundred unskilled, English-speaking, medically fit, unmarried labourers [in] building trade. No promise definite job or privileged treatment. Please cable how many desirous emigrating [under] those conditions. Repeat [to] Zionists Montreal our expenses."[86] Since the total number of Jewish-American immigrants to Palestine in 1921 was only 150, the plan apparently never materialized. It is probable that the former Legionnaires were not willing to be caught up in another game of uncertainty and false promises. Some had waited to settle in Palestine only to find no opportunity or assistance and, in the end, they returned to America.

In a letter from December 1921 to Sir Wyndham Deedes, the executive secretary of the Mandatory government, Weizmann protested against the negative British attitude toward Zionist endeavors in Palestine. Questioning why Jews from English-speaking countries would come to Palestine, he expressed his low expectations of American Jewish immigration to Palestine under existing conditions: "It seems to require the tenacity and devotion of Jews to go on working under such conditions. Of course work will be slow. What inducement has any Canadian or American or South African Jew at all to come to Palestine at present and at best be treated as a 'native' belonging to a minority group?"[87]

As Weizmann became more familiar with the American Jewish population, however, his opinion about whether American Jews should come to Palestine changed. In 1921 he was enlightened by the British Ambassador to the United States Sir Auckland Geddes as to American methods, politics, and state of mind, which Weizmann reiterated to British Zionist Sir Alfred Mond. Weizmann apparently adopted this position.

> [Geddes] foretold that I am going to have great difficulties and explained their nature. In his opinion, the attitude of B[randeis] and his colleagues to the International Z[ionist] O[rganization] is similar to the attitude of America to the League of Nations and to Europe. The Americans have done it all, and have won the War (have made the Zionist movement and Palestine), have done it all altruistically as they have no interest (American Jews won't go to Palestine in masses), therefore they are not anxious to take any responsibility but they would like to control it, to show us how it has to be run.[88]

Weizmann subsequently developed the opinion that Americans were in fact not suited for the demanding task ahead in Palestine. In a letter to his wife written aboard the S.S. Paris en route to New York in 1923, he communicated that he had observed "many [American] Jews with the faces and manners of shop assistants, well-fed—not halutzim!"[89]

Another facet of Weizmann's attitude toward American Jewish immigration to Palestine found expression in an address he delivered in Boston in 1923. The tone of the speech is similar to the viewpoint espoused in Brandeis's writings. Weizmann emphasized that there were many Jews, mainly outside the United States, who were interested in immigrating to Palestine. If Americans were desirous of doing so, they could, but it was not necessary. There appears to have been no attempt whatsoever to encourage at least some of the audience to ponder the possibility of immigration.

> We do not wish to interfere with the positions of the Jewish communities outside of Palestine[.] Whatever will be the status of the Jew in Palestine, it will have nothing to do, either politically or otherwise, with the status of those Jews who have made their homes outside Palestine. And this idea which is usually spread by our anti-Zionist Jewish friends that the Zionists

wish to take away all Jews into Palestine, is as stupid as it is preposterous. There are plenty of Jews whom we would like to leave here. Palestine will be built up by those who will go there voluntarily. We have no wish, we have no possibility, and we have no desire to force anybody to go there. And there are plenty who will go voluntarily.[90]

The negative attitudes toward American Jewish immigration to Palestine expressed by Weizmann in the early 1920s were transformed over the following two decades. The new reality after World War II and the loss of six million Jews in the Holocaust apparently affected Weizmann's perspective. In a speech delivered in 1946 he expressed a definite need for American *halutzim*.[91]

Another point of view found among the Zionist leadership was that American immigration was not important to the development of Palestine. One proponent of this position was Chaim Arlosoroff, who represented the World Zionist Organization and the Histadrut (General Federation of Labor in Palestine) in the United States between 1927–29. In a 1929 open letter, *Surveying American Zionism,* Arlosoroff strongly criticized the organization and its membership in the United States on many accounts—save for one. He made no reference to the lack of participation of American Jews in the actual settlement of Palestine. Even in an earlier address to American Jewish youth, he expressed no plea or request that they prepare for life in the new Jewish homeland or indicated that their participation was needed.[92]

It appears that by the early 1920s David Ben-Gurion had reached a similar conclusion. He laid out a specific agenda for Poale Zion of America, whose task was to assist in the financial support of Poale Zion's activities in Palestine as well as influence the Jewish establishment in America. He made no mention, however, of persuading American Jews, or Poale Zion members in particular, to immigrate to Palestine and join in the endeavor.[93] During his 1930 visit to North America, Ben-Gurion was criticized for exhibiting no concern about the settlement of American Jews in Palestine. With regard to Zionist youth movements, Ben-Gurion questioned the practicality of soliciting American Jewish immigration. He asked, "would it not fall upon deaf ears?" The answer was most probably yes, but in the end Ben-Gurion concluded that American Jewish immigration to Palestine—and the subsequent publicity about that experience—would facilitate the expansion of fund-raising activities in America.[94]

Another school of thought posited the special contribution that American immigration had made and could make in the future. British Zionist Sir Alfred Mond was quoted as saying that

> he was gratified with the great influx of Jews from America, an element that was bringing money and energy into the country. The most outstanding feature of Palestine was the variety of people from all over the world,—

peasants hailing from Transylvania to Jewish Legion men from New York who are running a very successful dairy farm at Merchavia. . . . The American Jews whom I have seen here are happy and they hope that more will join them and share this happiness. They will find work to do while helping to develop the country.[95]

A more concrete expression of the attempt to encourage American immigration to Palestine was the dispatching of *shlichim* (emissaries; singular: *shaliach*) from Palestine to America. In contrast to leaders from Palestine who solicited support from Zionism and asked for financial assistance, these *shlichim* arrived in the United States in order to assist in founding and expanding aliyah-oriented youth groups. *Shlichim* who reached America in the 1930s conducted seminars, ran conferences, and assisted in activities connected to the youth movements. This investment of manpower by the *Yishuv* was meant to advance the needs of the youth movements and promote aliyah. For example, the Hashomer Hatzair sent Mordechai Bentov in 1931. Ben-Zion Ilan (Applebaum) of Afikim and Enzo Sereni were *shlichim* to the Habonim and Hechalutz movements, respectively, in 1938.[96]

In summary, those in key positions in the international Zionist movement either posited that Americans had little interest in uprooting themselves so as to settle in Palestine or that the Americans were not of the same stock as their European counterparts and thus were less desirable. Often these leaders started their encounters with the United States hoping to draw American immigrants, but they frequently came to believe that such efforts were futile. American political and financial support was more important than trying to encourage immigration.

ATTITUDES OF THE ABSORBING SOCIETIES TO JEWISH IMMIGRATION

Coupled with the voices they heard in America, potential immigrants heard a voice from a distant land—Palestine. There too, different sectors expressed different opinions. Jewry in Palestine had a distinctive perception of American immigrants—both those whom it had encountered and those who would eventually arrive. Opinions were sometimes based on actual meetings with Americans, but often they were biased by speculation and conjecture. According to American Yiddish journalist Abraham Revusky, Jews in Palestine "frequently ridicule American Jews, deriding them as ignoramuses so profoundly convinced of the superiority of everything American that they cannot appreciate any accomplishment of Palestine's pioneers." Revusky continued by relating a frequently told anecdote of an individual who arrived in Palestine from New York and "immediately began to teach the Kvutza member[s] of Degania how poultry should be raised in a civilized manner."[97]

Golda Meir, although not American by birth, was subject to similar prejudice at the hands of immigrants who came to Palestine directly from

Eastern Europe. One biographer described such a confrontation at the kibbutz she had attempted to join in 1921: "The eight single women at Merhavia also objected to Golda because 'they had all heard about American girls.' All eight had come from Eastern Europe; most of them had been in Palestine for at least eight years. They pointed to the fact that almost a third of American immigrants returned to the United States. American women particularly were too soft for tough physical work, they said, and wouldn't last long."[98]

Americans in other social environments underwent similar experiences. They were not readily accepted; they had different attitudes and dissimilar lifestyles. Often disparities were the cause of tension. William Berman, an American student at the Knesset Israel Yeshiva at Hebron, succeeded in rising above these tensions. The following description tells of his triumph and provides insight into the strained relations between American immigrants and Jews of European origin:

> Berman was so well liked that he won the friendship in Hebron of the European young men. This was no easy thing for an American. The student from Europe and the student from America were unequal elements; they were as wide apart in most things as might be people from different original planets. Yet William Berman overcame this terrific distance, so hard for other[s] to span, and associated with European students as one of them, as a pal.[99]

Some older pioneers viewed American *halutzim* with admiration for their idealism and sincerity; others regarded them with apprehension. Their fear was that the Americans had been raised in comfortable surroundings and had a choice between remaining in Palestine or retracing their steps back to America. By contrast, this same choice was not available to Eastern European Jews.[100]

Arthur Ruppin's viewpoint was more pragmatic. Ruppin, a lawyer and economist by profession, immigrated to Palestine in 1908, and he was a central figure in settlement activities during the following decades. His 1919 article in *Der Jude,* "The Selection of the Fittest," articulates his viewpoint toward immigration in general. Offering no details, Ruppin expressed the general idea that before World War I, instead of a selection process for immigration there was a policy of "*laisser aller.*" "Every Jew who immigrated into Palestine was welcome; let him be old, sick, incapable of work, or even possessed of an anti-social character, public opinion in Palestine was not interested." Instead, Ruppin believed a more vigorous policy was needed to create a good social structure. First preference, he suggested, should be given to agriculturalist, secondly to artisans and workers, and then to merchants and professionals. In more practical terms, he assigned first priority to Eastern European Jews who had experience in agriculture. Since these potential emigrés were limited in number, he suggested that group immigration, organized abroad, was the best form of preparation and selection. Furthermore, Ruppin advocated physical selection and the elimination of antisocial types. His article mainly refers to European Jewry, but he also called for adolescents destined for agriculture in Palestine to be trained in California. It would appear that American Jewry was not on his agenda.[101]

Ruppin's evaluation of American immigrants was apparently influenced by his concerns over their integration into a rural environment. In 1922 he explained to Harry Goldman of Chicago under what conditions, if any, American immigrants should settle in Poria, the faltering American *ahuza* settlement.

> The settlers to be settled on the land must have a thorough knowledge of agriculture, must be able to work themselves every kind of agricultural work and must be accustomed to the climate and to the conditions of Palestine. . . . I think that the reorganization of Poriah is possible only when the actual owners of Poriah are willing to turn over the whole property to a group of Palestinian workmen which will be selected among the best Palestinian agricultural workers.[102]

Examples of praise and admiration for certain well-known American personalities—such as Henrietta Szold, Judah L. Magnes, Robert Kesselman, and Israel Kligler—run counter to the prevailing view of American Jewish emigrés. Nonetheless the usual impression of Americans was that they were spoiled and generally unsuited for the difficult task that lay before them. Often Americans were required to prove themselves before they would be seen as at least equals.

Most vocal in their opposition to Jewish immigration to Palestine was the country's Arab population. It is uncertain whether Arab inhabitants of Palestine made any distinction among the Jews who immigrated to Palestine from different countries. Canadian immigrant Goldie Hoffman sensed that North American Jewish immigration had special meaning for the Arab population, for it showed the serious intent of Zionists vis-à-vis the development of Palestine. In 1921 she wrote, "We Americans and Canadians [Jews] are hated by the Arabs—they are afraid of us. They feel that if we come then the Jews really mean business."[103] In general, the Arab population in Palestine opposed all Jewish immigration. This attitude found expression both vocally and physically. The Arab press and representatives appearing before various commissions all condemned Jewish immigration. Their objection also took on physical manifestations, including attacks on the Jewish population in 1920, 1921, 1929, and between the years 1936–39. These assaults greatly influenced the American Jew's decision about whether to immigrate.

The April 1920 attacks left five Jews dead and 211 injured. A British military commission of enquiry determined that among the Arab motivations for the hostilities were their "belief that the Balfour Declaration implied a denial of self-determination and their fear that the establishment of a National Home would mean a great increase in Jewish immigration and would lead to their economic and political subjection to the Jews."[104]

The Commission of Enquiry into the riots of 1 May 1921 also pointed to Arab anxiety over the consequences of the steady increase in Jewish immigration. That year violence first broke out in Jaffa, followed by attacks on Rehovot, Petah Tikvah, Hadera, and other Jewish settlements, leaving 47 Jews dead and 140 wounded. Americans were not spared in the violence. Moshe Strelsin a former Legionnaire, was stoned to death while trying to defend Jewish inhabitants of Jaffa. Two American merchants, Nissel Shapiro and Julius Skupsky, were attacked in their shops. The commission concluded that continuing Jewish immigration to Palestine would lead to political and economic subjection of Arabs; furthermore, it judged this immigration to be the immediate cause of high Arab unemployment.[105]

In 1926, when the net Jewish immigration to Palestine was negative, the Arab press reacted. An editorial comment in the Haifa newspaper *El Carmel* pointed to the failure of British policy based on the Balfour Declaration. The editor believed the best thing the British could do was change its policy before whatever remained of Arab confidence was irrevocably lost.[106]

The 1929 riots had a profound effect on American immigration, for among the victims were American Jews. These insurgencies rekindled memories of pogroms, strengthening the conviction that Palestine was not the solution to "the Jewish Problem." American Jews also realized that the potential peril would not pass over them because of their national origin. The riots sent a clear message that the local Arab population vehemently opposed the immigration of Jews—including American Jews—to Palestine. Paradoxically, the riots also reinforced the position that only Jewish immigration on a massive scale would build up a population large enough to withstand future assaults. Resolutions were passed at mass meetings of Jewish citizens in many American cities, calling on Jews to devote themselves with renewed energy and unlimited sacrifice to the formation of a new army of *halutzim* for the immediate and peaceful rebuilding of a Jewish homeland in Palestine.[107] A fervent reaction was seen at the 1929 Young Poale Zion convention, where the entire body took an oath to leave for Palestine within a year. However, it appears that only one person kept this pledge.[108]

In August 1933 a campaign against Jewish immigration was launched in the Palestinian Arab press, and it developed in intensity over the following months. In September, at the festival of Nebi Rubin, Musa Kasem Pasha el Husseini, president of the Arab Executive, made a violent speech against Jewish immigration. Subsequent press articles and public meetings fostered Arab agitation. Repeatedly over the following years, calls came from the

Arab sector, demanding the cessation of—if not limitations on—Jewish immigration.[109]

On 19 April 1936, riots broke out in Jaffa. These initiated a three-year period of intermittent attacks on Jews in Palestine. Immediately following two days of rioting in April 1936, the Arab High Committee called a strike that would continue until three demands were met: a halt to Jewish immigration, prohibition of the transfer of land to Jewish ownership, and the establishment of a national representative government. None of these demands was met at the time. In May 1939, the MacDonald White Paper partially accommodated Arab demands by restricting annual Jewish immigration to 10,000 over the next five years. And in 1940 Land Transfer Regulations were enacted restricting the sale and transfer of land to Jews.

Despite this hostile atmosphere, some Americans gained the respect and admiration of the Arab residents of Palestine. Dr. Olga Pickman-Feinberg, the only Jew residing in Jericho, provided health services for the locals. Almost single-handedly, she eradicated trachoma in the district. "The Arabs loved her and called her the *Jeddah* (the Courageous One)."[110]

But overall, the Arab attitude was clear and single-minded: vehement opposition to Jewish immigration, with no distinction regarding national origin. This was perhaps best summarized in a comment conveyed to the U.S. secretary of state in a report from the consulate in Jerusalem: "Had the immigrants been angels the Arabs would complain of their wings." The newspaper *Ibn Philistine* expanded on this theme: "Yes the Arabs refuse to have the doors of their country open to strangers who wish to force it from them even if they were angels." The article continued, "The Jews should understand that the overbearingness and lack of taste of the immigrants, their bad and unkempt actions, are only secondary motives for our rejecting them. The primary and most important motive is that we see in them a whirlwind which will envelop and chuck us out of our country. It is *immaterial to us* whether the immigrants are devils or angels" (emphasis in the original).[111] Reactions to this message were varied. Some took the form of acquiescence to Arab demands, with individuals in America deciding against immigration to Palestine. Other responses demonstrated a certain adamancy: far from giving in to Arab ultimatums, there should be increased immigration.

On the whole, though, American Jewry was not encouraged to immigrate to Palestine. There were few individuals and organizations in America that required immigration as a form of personal or ideological fulfillment. Indeed, apathy was the dominant attitude. This was coupled with the prevailing view among Zionist leaders and Jews in Palestine: American Jews had no special role to play in the development of the new national homeland. In general, Zionists and Jews in Palestine believed that the Palestinian endeavor could succeed without the physical presence of Jews from the United States.

This lack of moral support placed potential immigrants in a tenuous position. To counteract indifference and antagonism, a stronger sense of motivation and a more ardent belief in the virtues of their own migration were needed. The absence of an important psychological element—the whole-hearted backing of the community's leadership—inhibited American immigration to Palestine, keeping it from becoming a mass population movement. Instead American Jewish immigration to Palestine became the innovative choice of a select few.[112] To prepare for the move to Palestine, potential migrants needed to collect information that gave them a deeper understanding of their new country.

2
Information and Assistance

> Despite the daily struggle for existence, Dad never stopped dreaming. He kept a scrap book of famous Jews connected with Zionism and continued to read to us from the Yiddish paper about Palestine. During the riots of 1929, he took us to hear Menachem Ussishkin in a protest meeting in downtown Detroit. I was only 8 years old, but I remember clearly the dynamic little man, with the beard, on the platform. Itamar Ben Avi, the son of Eliezer Ben Yehuda, also spoke to us at another time.
>
> Dovid Ben Nachum, "100 Years of Dreaming"

This Detroit family had decided to migrate to Palestine; it was just a question of time. The father only awaited the day when his sons would be grown. Until that time, he continued collecting information, going to meetings, and absorbing all the material he could find regarding conditions in Palestine.

Information is the most basic need for any potential immigrant in a free migrational process.[1] The availability of information influences the construction of a notion of "place utility," an important element in the decision making procedure. Generally, in any free migrational process the variable of place may include an unlimited number of possibilities. However, in the case of possible Jewish emigration from the United States to Palestine, the individual weighed the sense of actual and perceived satisfaction between only these two places. Some naturalized American Jews did consider returning to their countries of origin, but in general going back to Europe, particularly Eastern Europe, was not a viable option. The individual resident in the United States had firsthand experience of the advantages and disadvantages of America. By contrast, Palestine was a far and distant land. Few prospective immigrants had experienced life there, even temporarily, before their actual immigration. Thus they constructed their sense of place utility on the basis of various sources of information. This flow of information was vital to the process of developing a motivation for immigration and finally deciding to migrate. Furthermore, the collection of information allowed for more practical decisions connected to preparations—the choice of vocation, training, amassing of capital, the selection of belongings to be transported, and so forth. Information also assisted in choosing a location prior to migration, i.e., whether to buy a house or tract of land in Palestine while still in the United States. Sources of information available to potential immigrants included their own recollections of personal visits, letters from previous immigrants, conversations with those who had visited Palestine, books, newspapers, and films.[2]

Information was not always accurate, however. Often underlying the decision to migrate was a cultural tradition passed on through generations. For the population with a religious upbringing, there was the message that redemption was attainable in the Holy Land. This perspective was grounded in the text of the Bible and the words of the prophets, cherished over centuries in the Diaspora. This viewpoint also included images of the Holy Land based on biblical depictions, "a land flowing with milk and honey" (Exodus 3:8).[3] The assimilating or secular population held similar feelings—not on the same level of consciousness, but as a memory ingrained in the recesses of their very being, having been passed down from generation to generation. This type of information is difficult for researchers to trace, but hints are scattered throughout the writings of most American Jews who considered migrating to Palestine. There was no special need to propagate these themes, for they were preexistent. However, these motifs were drawn upon in campaigns to enlist support for the Zionist cause and to create a common denominator for the acceptance of Zionist information. Thus, in the propagation of official and unofficial information, there were strong undercurrents of biblical or messianic allusions. For example, the American Zion Commonwealth, in its brochure for the sale of land at Afula, drew upon the biblical passage "every man under his vine and every man under his fig tree" (I Kings 4:25) to sway American Jewry to purchase property in Palestine.[4] This idyllic picture of Palestine hardly reflected the actual situation. However, the company was formed to market land, and to facilitate this endeavor it also marketed an image.

Not all groups fabricated an image of Palestine for the American Jewish public. For example, one of the express purposes of the Zionist Organization of America was to disseminate accurate and realistic information about Palestine. This was considered an important first phase in the proper development of Palestine, leading to investment in its up-building and possibly to immigration. Furthermore, the organization recognized that reliable facts would prevent undue disappointment for investors and immigrants alike.

Louis D. Brandeis also understood the importance of providing a clear picture of life in Palestine to potential American Jewish immigrants. With this in mind, Brandeis wrote in 1931 to Jacob Ettinger of the Jewish National Fund regarding plans for settling middle-class Americans in Palestine: "I think you are wise in calling the attention of possible settlers to the low standard of living which they must expect if they conclude to settle on the land. But I think it would be wise to send with the statement one of the published descriptions of life on the small plantations with its worthy social joys, so that those middle-class Jews may realize that they are not being relegated to [the] dreary, barren life common on isolated, small American farms."[5]

American author Dorothy Ruth Kahn—in her lengthy description of fellow American immigrant Rachel—aptly explained the gap between the true picture of Palestine and misconceptions about life there. Rachel had been raised as an ardent Zionist. "She had wept for Palestine. Suffered for Palestine. Contributed money for Palestine. Prayed for Palestine. Hoped for Palestine. Dreamed for Palestine. But she could not face Palestine." After eight months of living in Jerusalem, Rachel returned to the United States. Kahn presented her interpretation of Rachel's drama.

> If Rachel were an exception, her story would hardly [be] worth recording. Unfortunately her experiences, with variations, are those of numberless Zionists who face the reality of Palestine. One doubts neither the sincerity nor the zeal of these people. The bare fact is that unless one comes with complete knowledge or complete ignorance of the undertaking, one cannot succeed in brushing aside the discrepancies between what Palestine was supposed to have been and what it actually is.[6]

Information about Palestine was distributed through various channels—official and semiofficial organs of the Zionist organizations and their affiliates, as well as unofficial ones. The information varied in type, detail, and, more importantly, in point of view. There were channels at various levels—international, national, regional, and local—and potential immigrants usually passed through two stages of information accession.

The first stage was passive information collection. This usually occurred before individuals were actually contemplating immigration. At this stage, potential immigrants did not have to be affiliated with any Jewish or Zionist group. They could easily obtain information from the local press—Jewish and non-Jewish—which described news events in Palestine in varying degrees of detail and offered feature articles and editorial comment. Photographs, films, and newsreels provided visual accounts.

The second stage was active information collection, although the delineation between this and passive collection may be neither distinct nor clear. Active information collection was accomplished through personal correspondence with relatives, friends, and acquaintances residing in Palestine, and through communication with Americans who had visited there. In addition, potential immigrants could participate in various groups, read publications, and hear the orations of noted Zionist personalities.

The Fishman family of St. Albans, Vermont, represents potential immigrants who were deeply involved in this second stage of information gathering. The Fishmans created an environment in their home in which Zionist information played a key role. Family life and education were clearly oriented toward migration to Palestine. In his article, "A Zionist Childhood in St. Albans, Vt.," Hertzel Fishman described this milieu.

> My younger siblings and I spent our childhood in a profoundly Jewish home atmosphere where the daily language was Yiddish; the apartment was studded with Jewish cultural, religious and Land-of-Israel artifacts . . . our parents put us to bed each night with Yiddish and Hebrew melodies, and as we grew older their bedtime stories revolved around the heroes of the Jewish People and great moments in Jewish history—biblical, Talmudic, chasidic, and especially of the era of the modern idealistic pioneers (*halutzim*) in Palestine. . . . [O]ur parents placed an ad in the American Hebrew weekly *Hadoar.* It asked for a young Palestinian Jewess who happened to be in the United States to live with the family during the summer vacation months. The ad paid off: a lovely lady from Eretz Israel who was studying in New York City became part of our family each summer. She taught us the most recent songs and dances of the *halutzim,* played games with us (in Hebrew), read us stories.[7]

The Fishman family also subscribed to Yiddish, Hebrew, and Zionist newspapers (*Der Tog, Morgen Journal, New Palestine,* and *Hadoar*). Moreover, the head of the family was a member of the Zionist Organization of America, and during a period of residence in New York City, he was among the founders of *Beit Haknesset Hazioni* (the Zionist Synagogue).[8]

Sometimes individuals or families interested in making aliyah organized themselves into groups. Jacob Katzman detailed his parents' aliyah group in Chelsea, Massachusetts, which consisted of some twelve to twenty families. Attempting to develop the collective spirit, they organized a joint fund and met at least twice a month for a communal meal, with the purpose of getting to know each other more intimately. They hoped to send one or two families ahead to Palestine to establish a collective settlement. The rest would gradually join the colony at a rate that their joint fund would allow. In America, they had "hopeful discussions about the future life; and the not-infrequent arguments about details of what was still only a vision." Although Katzman doesn't specifically allude to this, it can be inferred that these families also collected information from various sources as part of their preparation for Palestine.[9]

Zionist and other Jewish groups generally organized lectures and discussion circles, and distributed material about conditions in Palestine. Louis Brandeis viewed lectures as an important tool for disseminating Zionist information and augmenting support for the endeavor. In 1930 he wrote:

> Our crying need is for a body of competent and willing speakers and writers. Competence implies mastery of the available material, as well as

educated brains and some talent for speaking and for writing—such as are possessed by, or are capable of development in, many young lawyers, sociologists, economists and political scientists. . . . [A] discriminating, penetrating speaker can reach the heart, the head and ultimately the pocket of almost any category of Jew who may be exposed, so numerous are the facets of the crystal.[10]

Lecturers from Palestine, Europe, and the United States traveled from coast to coast. Their purpose was to propagate information and enlist support for activities in Palestine. Michael Brown, in his study *The Israeli-American Connection,* provides a detailed narrative of the experiences in America of six major *Yishuv* leaders. Brown focuses on Vladmir Jabotinsky, Chaim Nahman Bialik, Berl Katznelson, Henrietta Szold, Golda Meir, and David Ben-Gurion's involvement with—and notions of—America, as well as the impact of America on their lives and careers; his study also details the extent, intent, and some of the results of their American speaking tours.[11] These were just six of the many lecturers who served as conduits of information and, to some extent, promoted American Jewish immigration to Palestine.

Official information about Palestine was disseminated by the World Zionist Organization and the Zionist Organization of America. Members of the latter group regularly received copies of its official publications, *New Palestine,* in English, or *Dos Yiddishe Folk,* in Yiddish.[12] These two periodicals carried various types of articles providing specific information as well as opinion on Zionist issues. For example, the 1 May 1925, issue of *New Palestine* published an official communiqué issued by the Palestine Bureau that offered information and instructions for persons desiring to emigrate to Palestine, and detailed the new immigration ordinances promulgated by the government of Palestine.[13]

Gershon Agronsky's *New Palestine* article, "American Zionists and Their Palestinian Luggage," is an excellent example of an opinion expressed within this information system. Agronsky, a journalist with his finger on the pulse of the situation both in the United States and in Palestine, voiced a need for American immigration to Palestine, yet he also warned those contemplating this step to carefully consider such action. He explained: "Zionists in America are the best judges of whether or not they are prepared for life in Palestine. Part of the preparation is knowledge of conditions, which is becoming more and more accessible and widespread."[14] Agronsky supplied concrete examples of the trials and tribulations of various Americans, and provided illustrations of the physical, cultural, economic, and social differences—all in terms that would be easily understood by his American audience.

Despite the careful balance of articles such as Agronsky's, some people were critical of these official Zionist periodicals. Chaim Arlosoroff, for

TABLE 8
Zionist Organization of America membership, 1918–29

Year	Number	Year	Number	Year	Number	Year	Number
1918	149,235	1921	30,597	1924	25,934	1927	21,806
1919	56,838	1922	18,481	1925	27,144	1928	21,539
1920	21,000	1923	24,303	1926	23,784	1929	18,031

Source: Samuel Halperin, *The Political World of American Zionism* (Detroit: Wayne State University Press, 1961), Appendix 5, 327–29.

example, during his 1929 tour of North America, questioned the effectiveness of these publications in propagating Zionist ideas. Relying on his observations and interactions with both the *New Palestine* and *Dos Yiddishe Folk,* he claimed that they exhibited "a perpetual absence of any editorial policy built upon convictions, ideas or well-informed reasoning." As a result of distortions in the Zionist press, asserted Arlosoroff, American Zionists "lose confidence . . . they become indifferent to every Zionist issue of importance, they necessarily tend to become themselves cynical in matters of Zionist policy."[15]

In addition to *New Palestine* and *Dos Yiddishe Folk,* several semiofficial organs were published by various Zionist groups. Most of these, however, failed to attain the circulation of the publications of the Zionist Organization of America. Some groups, sponsored by or affiliated with the Zionist Organization of America, produced their own publications, aimed at specific subgroups defined by special interest, ideology, gender, or age. Of these, the *Hadassah Newsletter* had the largest distribution; it was sent to every Hadassah member—10,000 in 1921, and 35,000 in 1930.[16] From 1939 to 1946, over fifteen periodicals were issued by various semiofficial groups.

Potential immigrants could obtain a third kind of material on Palestine, unofficial information, from publications with no direct connection to any Zionist body. Dailies, weeklies, and monthlies, for example, occasionally featured reports or articles relating to Palestine. These included both Jewish and general publications, such as the *New York Times,* the *New York Herald Tribune,* and the *Jewish Daily Forward.*

The American Economic Committee for Palestine sought to disseminate information on the economic situation in Palestine through this kind of publication. The acting executive committee found, however, that there was "a definite unwillingness in the general press, including general magazines, to print such specialized articles." It understood that "editors were unwilling to publish articles which did not interest their entire reading public." On the other hand, the committee pointed out the "frequency with which Palestine photographs are printed in the *New York Times* rotogravure section." Nevertheless, the committee continued to try to make use of the general press.[17]

The foremost Yiddish newspaper in America was the *Jewish Daily Forward,* the organ of the American Jewish socialist movement. By the early 1930s, its circulation had reached a quarter of a million. Its policy toward Zionism evolved over the years from indifference, criticism, and even antagonism to acceptance and sometimes support of Zionist endeavors. The turning point, according to Louis Lipsky (Zionist Organization of America president 1921–30) was a 1925 visit to Palestine by Abraham Cahan, the newspaper's editor. Cahan was impressed by the achievement of Jewish labor in Palestine and was "grateful to all Zionists in Palestine who aided him in attaining the moral satisfaction derived from contact with a throbbing, idealistic life in a Jewish land."[18] Lipsky wrote: "He is not a Zionist, but he says to his co-workers in the labor field: Give the Jewish ideal a chance; don't kill it with cynicism. What is important in his changed attitude is the fact that he will help break down prejudices and pave the way for a union of all classes of American Jewry in the establishment of the Jewish National Home."[19]

Following Cahan's visit, the pages of the *Jewish Daily Forward* regularly contained articles and editorials about Zionism and conditions in Palestine. Letters to the editor published in the popular column "A Bintel Brief" expressed readers' interest and need for information. One such inquiry was forwarded by the concerned wife of an American Jewish janitor. Her husband had purchased a plantation in Palestine, and she wondered whether the capital her husband had amassed was sufficient and if the plantation could support their family of six children. The editor referred the disquieted woman to the American Economic Committee for Palestine for further information.[20]

Other types of Jewish publications that described conditions in Palestine were not sponsored by any Zionist group. For example, *Palestine and Near East Economic Magazine*—a fortnightly for trade, industry, and agriculture—was published by the Mischar w'Taasia (Trade and Industry) Company. First issued in July 1926, it featured detailed information on the situation in Palestine, particularly focusing on economic conditions. "This Magazine is read by Importers and Exporters, Manufacturers and Merchants, and all interested in Palestine and the Near East. It is circulated to Chambers of Commerce, Trade Commissioners, Consuls, Commercial Houses, Hotels, Clubs, etc. It is also available in reading rooms of the liners sailing between the ports of the Near East and Europe and America."[21] The Zionist Organization of America president Louis Lipsky wrote to its publisher:

> I regard the magazine . . . as an important contribution to an understanding of economic conditions in Palestine. Its wide circulation will create an

intelligent appreciation of the economic problems of Palestine. It will help a great deal in removing exaggeration and unfounded expectation which prevails in every consideration of Palestine economic problems on the part of those who have in mind giving assistance to Palestine. There can be no intelligent investment in Palestine, without understanding of the conditions, and in this direction your magazine is the most valuable agency.[22]

Thus there was no lack of information available both to those who had no interest in immigrating and those who did. In addition to the periodicals discussed above, a number of books were published by Zionist groups in America that not only provided extensive information but appear to have had a strong influence on the opinions of both Zionists and other American Jews. Early examples include Jessie E. Sampter's *Guide to Zionism,* published in New York in 1920 by the Zionist Organization of America; Benjamin L. Gordon's *New Judea,* published in Philadelphia in 1919; David Ben-Gurion and Yitzhak Ben-Zvi's *Eretz Israel—Land of Our Future,* published in New York in 1918 (in Yiddish) by Poale Zion; and the *Yizkor Book*. The first edition (1916) of the *Yizkor Book* was edited by Itzhak Ben-Zvi, and the second (1918) by David Ben-Gurion; both editions were published in New York by Poale Zion.

Sampter's *Guide to Zionism* outlined the history and activities of Zionism as well as conditions in Palestine. In her preface, Sampter expressed the underlying importance of this collection. "Facts, facts, and more facts alone will prepare us for our pioneering here or in Palestine."[23]

Gordon's *New Judea* was first published as a series of articles in the *Maccabean* and the *Jewish Exponent* in Philadelphia. His aim, as he explained in the foreword to the volume, was "to describe the new Jewish life in Palestine as exemplified in the Jewish agricultural colonies and in educational institutions. I have, therefore, chosen the name for this volume, 'New Judea,' because I saw before me wherever I turned a real New Judea transformed from an old land by the will of young pioneers."[24] Gordon's work provided the potential immigrant with vignettes of life in various agricultural colonies. Particularly interesting is the description of an American family from Chicago living in Rehovot.

> Palestine . . . is in great need of capital, and cannot be considered at present an ideal land for poor immigrants. In order to make way for general immigration, our capitalists must come first and make their investments here, create industries, develop its resources, and prepare work for the less fortunate newcomers. There are great opportunities for good business men to make profitable investments. The East is rapidly awakening and the markets are growing larger daily. I would not advise Americans to come here unless they possess $5000. Of course, there may be exceptions to this rule, here as anywhere else; one may do more with a smaller sum than

another with a larger sum. It takes six years before plantations will yield fruit, and in the meantime one must live six years without any income. A smaller capital will do if suitable land can be gotten for agricultural purposes and especially if one is a trained farmer.[25]

Another important source of information was *Eretz Israel,* which ran to twenty-five thousand copies. Jacob Katzman of Chelsea explained, in his memoir of labor Zionist life in America, that "for a time, a most popular book for study was that on Eretz Israel, compiled by the two *Bonim* (literally, sons) Ben Gurion and Ben Zvi, during their more than two years of exile in America. It presented an unusual combination of the history, geography and political-economy of Palestine—truly a pioneering work of its kind."[26]

The *Yizkor Book* was a collection of biographies and eulogies of *halutzim* and members of Hashomer (the Guard; a self-defense organization of Jewish pioneers) who had lost their lives in Palestine. This work glorified their activities and sought to inspire others to partake in the up-building of Palestine.[27]

Visual images could be as informative as written words. Many of the newspapers, journals, magazines, and books described above included photographs and illustrations that provided vivid representations of Palestine and its peoples. During the 1920s, *Palestine Pictorial* specialized in propagating images of Palestine as both the Holy Land and the land of renewal.

Similarly, motion pictures disseminated a variety of images of Palestine. In fact, the Holy Land was among the first places to be depicted on film. Zionist ideals and achievements were also propagated through film. From the early 1920s, the Jewish National Fund and the Keren Hayesod commissioned and distributed films that concentrated on the growth and development of the *Yishuv.* These films were an effective tool for fund-raising campaigns, but they also offered potential immigrants impressions of Palestine undergoing renewal—the very endeavor they were considering joining. The 1935 film *Land of Promise* was "arguably the most influential Zionist propaganda film ever made."[28] Many American Jews viewed this film, which played for five weeks at the New York Astor. (Three weeks at a first-run theater was a success by Hollywood standards.) Problems connected with the distribution of *Land of Promise* eventually resulted in its becoming used mainly for Zionist fund-raising and education.

A number of other films were also intended to draw American Jewish investment and even settlement in Palestine. In 1926 the American Zion Commonwealth (see chapter 7) produced *What the American Zion Commonwealth Is Doing in Palestine,* which depicted a tour of inspection by one of its American Jewish investors. This film focused on the recent accomplishments as well as the latent possibilities awaiting investors and immigrants. The Gan Hadar group (see chapter 9) likewise sought to explain to potential investors how citrus plantations were developed, in order to draw capital to this project.[29]

ORGANIZATIONS IN AMERICA

A more active means of obtaining information about Palestine was through direct contact with organizations interested in propagating such information and assisting potential immigrants. Individuals would approach various Zionist and other organizations in an attempt to get reliable information regarding immigration, land acquisition, settlement, and life in Palestine. The Zionist Organization of America established one such bureau, the Palestine Service and Information Department, to answer inquires and facilitate the process of immigration.

The Palestine Service and Information Department had its offices in New York. Its aim was "to collect all statistical data bearing on the impending immigration to Palestine from the United States . . . [and] to give all possible information to prospective settlers."[30] Many questions from potential immigrants dealt with farming—crops, machinery, irrigation, and land prices. Others focused on industry (raw material, potential markets), commerce (demand for products, fuel, and raw material), and general information. This department received more requests for information and assistance from American Jews than did any similar organization. A few entries from its daily register illustrate the bureau's activities, which included active assistance as well as information.

1. Saw off today a few Palestine passengers sailing on the s.s.Brittanic [*sic*]. There were 30 Jewish passengers on board, all of whom have been assisted by this bureau. 12 of them were Capitalist-settlers. I published the names in the Jewish press.
2. Received settlers' permits for Dr. Solomon Kerr (capital: $12,000) of Somerset, Pa.; and for Issy Press (capital: $6000) of New York.
3. Samuel Shifman of Newark, N.J. submitted to us a statement of a bank that $5000 has been transferred to Barclays Bank in Palestine in [*sic*] behalf of his niece Lize Lieberman, 19 years old, of Riga, Latvia, for the purpose of obtaining settler's visa for her. I have made an application although I am doubtful whether the Government will recognize the applicant as a person who will engage in trade and industry. In similar cases of similar nature we had a great deal of trouble.
4. Obtained entrance-permit for Samuel Rothbort (capital: $5000) of Bronx, N.Y.
5. Application for settler's visa for Abraham Climer, his mother, wife, and three children. Has $11,000. Consider very desirable settlers. Both husband and wife are hard working and simple living people. He is leaving

Fig. 8. Views from the Land [of Israel]! In order to give the Haifa audience the opportunity to enjoy the Land of Israel movie of the American Zion Commonwealth, the movie will be presented for a second (and last) time in "Eden" Hall on Wednesday, the fourth of Kislev (10.11.1926) at 9:00 P.M. Regularly priced tickets. On the same day, at 3:00 P.M., there will be a special showing for children. The price is two Egyptian piastres.
Poster for "What the American Commonwealth Is Doing in Palestine," 1926. (CZA L65/295)

| GAN HADAR CORPORATION | GAN HADAR BETH, INC. | PRI HADAR, INC. | TEL HADAR, INC. |

RAMOTH MEYER

אמעריקאנער געזעלשאפט פאר
לאנדווירטשאפטליכער באזעצונג אין ארץ ישראל

47 WEST 34th STREET
ROOM 1116
NEW YORK

Dr. MEYER L. ROSOFF
President

WIsconsin 7-6353

Fig. 9a. Gan Hadar Corporation letterhead. (CZA J88/25)

Moving Pictures in Ganey Hadar.

1) The beginning of a citrus tree: The seed as sown in the seedbed. A seedling pulled out of the seedbed ready for transplanting in the nursery 4 months after sowing.
2) Same seedling in the nursery 6 months after transplanting.
3) The budding operation in the nursery.
4) The head of the seedling is cut off, after the bud has taken.
5) The twig developing from the bud tied and trained.
6) A general view of unbudded seedlings in the nursery.
7) A tree in the nursery one year after budding ready for transplanting in the grove.
8) A general view of a budded nursery ready for transplanting.
9) The Railroad Station "Niana".
10) The operation of planting a tree together with the ball of earth.
11) The irrigation right after planting.
12) The tree one year after planting.
13) General view of the grove, one year after planting.
14) Two years old tree.
15) Three years old tree.
16) A 3 years old grapefruit trees in blossom.
17) Plowing before planting.
18) Leveling
19) Birds eye view from the roof of the house in Gan Hadar A.

April 1934.

Fig. 9b. List of scenes of moving pictures in Ganey Hadar, April 1934. (CZA J88/25)

for Palestine simply out of fear of losing here his money and having no prospects in this country.
6. British Consul just informed me over telephone that Noe [sic] Braun, now in New York, has been granted a prolongation of his return-visa for a whole year. First time that a prolongation of visa is given for such extensive period.[31]

Another organization that responded to direct inquiries about Palestine was the American Economic Committee for Palestine. The declared purpose of the committee was to

> encourage and give guidance to a continuous and increasing flow of investors and of well-managed investments into Palestine, to the end that the constant growth of the capital resources and of the experienced manpower of the Yishub may afford greater and greater opportunity for employment and may, thereby, become the basis for the self-maintenance of that strong, steady flow of Jewish immigration which is indispensable to the solution of the Jewish problem.[32]

The committee was founded in 1932, with Judge Julian W. Mack as honorary president, Israel B. Brodie as president, Robert Szold as chairman of the board of directors, and Rehabiah Lewin-Epstein serving as director of the Tel Aviv bureau. Among its various goals was "to encourage and facilitate the immigration into Palestine of persons who, by reason of experience or capital, may contribute to the economic building of the Yishub." To this end, the activities of the New York bureau included:

> Securing from the Tel Aviv Bureau, whenever necessary, complete independently prepared reports required by prospective immigrants and investors; Searching the record of the experience of prospective settlers for practical bases of settlement and facilitating thereby the sound building of Palestine; Encouragement of the most thorough and deliberate investigation of their plans and projects by prospective investors and immigrants; and Facilitation of immigration of those families whose settlement gives promise of being successful.[33]

In its 1933 report, the New York bureau detailed fourteen typical examples of personal services to American applicants who asked for information about settling in Palestine. Some individuals were encouraged, but the committee also made an effort to dissuade those who were deemed inappropriate for the endeavor. Those who eventually arrived in Palestine were interviewed and given guidance by the Tel Aviv branch, which also investigated specific situations and opportunities for them. The Tel Aviv bureau's 1933 report described thirty-nine cases of services rendered to newly arrived American immigrants, each of whom possessed capital of £P1,000 or more, in accordance with the immigration ordinances.[34]

In addition, the American Economic Committee for Palestine amassed a large collection of reference material in its New York office and made this available to everyone. It also arranged for the release of this information to both the Jewish and the general press. Its services were much in demand; the New York office was frequently overtaxed with requests from potential immigrants.[35]

Unlike the organizations discussed so far, various Zionist youth movements gave their members a practical, indispensable preparation for a future in Palestine, as well as furnishing them with information. In comparison with other possible immigrants, those who were connected to the youth movements were firmly resolved to settle in Palestine. The movements with which they were affiliated provided an environment in which they could find others of similar ideological leanings and resolve, but it was also a setting in which they could acquire the necessary skills for successful settlement.

Before World War I, a small group of young Jews at the Baron de Hirsch Agricultural School at Woodbine, New Jersey, organized the Haikar Hatzair group. The group focused on the acquisition of agricultural skills, and eventually four individuals affiliated with this group immigrated to Palestine. The school was established in 1894 and continued to operate until 1917. "Its orchards, gardens, nurseries, apiaries, laboratories, dairy farm and machine shop served as a brilliant model—if not always attainable—for the entire area."[36] Some of this knowledge was transported to Palestine by the Haikar Hatzair *halutzim,* including a California-trained agriculturalist, Berl Klei, who introduced Jews in Palestine to systematic methods of farming. The Haikar Hatzair concept of combining agricultural education with practical experience significantly influenced groups that formed after them and also established training farms.

During World War I, Poale Zion activists from Palestine attempted to recruit American Jews to their ranks, either through enlisting in the Jewish Legion or through pioneering endeavors. In 1921 a group of twenty-two American Poale Zion members departed for Palestine; one member of the cadre was Golda Meir (Meyersohn). Most of them were in their early twenties, several were past thirty, three had small children, and one was visibly pregnant. "We were a small group, young, full of hope and zeal, ready for anything," Meir later characterized them.[37] During the years prior to their migration, these Poale Zion members had educated themselves in ideology and the Hebrew language, and had learned about conditions in Palestine. However, they possessed no special skills, nor had they undergone any particular training process before departure.

Following the implementation of more stringent immigration controls in 1925 and 1926, and again in 1932, it became necessary for emigrants to meet special qualifications before settling in Palestine. Options open to would-be settlers included American-based education at an agricultural school or university; apprenticeship or training on a private farm; training on special *hachshara* (training) farms belonging to *halutz* organizations; or training in Palestine itself, although this became the most difficult program to enter.

Formal agricultural education varied from short courses to degree programs at universities. Some potential *halutzim* attended programs at Michigan State College of Agriculture and others at Rutgers University.[38] However, the Hashomer Hatzair Organization of North America did not believe that these university programs were tailored to conditions in Palestine. At a meeting of its Kibbutz Aliya (group preparing for immigration), the organization resolved that since state colleges of agriculture required three years to complete programs that were mainly theoretical, they were impractical and thus undesirable places for *hachshara*. National farm schools were also found inappropriate "due to the demoralizing influence that the social life there exerts upon one who wishes to prepare himself for the life in a Kibutz [*sic*]."[39] The alternatives were *hachshara bodedet* (solitary training)—if the farm where the training was conducted was operated on a modern scientific basis—or a *hachshara* farm. The latter was preferred since it allowed for *hachshara chevratit* (social and ideological training), an integral part of the individual's development as part of the larger community. Similar standards were adopted by the Convention of the American Halutz, on 31 December 1933, and formalized in a resolution. The period of training would last from eighteen to twenty-four months and consist of two stages, cultural and practical. The second stage would comprise:

1. Preparation on agricultural farms of the Hechalutz, or of hired agricultural work on private farms with a collective form of life, or in similar branches of work (lumber camps, quarries, etc.) with collective forms of life.
2. Continuation of physical training and fitness.
3. Continuation of cultural development, especially during winter months, stressing use of Hebrew as [the] common medium of expression.[40]

Each of these options added to the vocational baggage of the *halutzim,* giving them knowledge of agriculture in general and, in particular, of the crops and methods of cultivation most suitable to Palestine's climate and geographic zones. Their acquired knowledge and experience would then be transferred to Palestine and applied to its up-building.

Also taken into account in the educational process of the potential *halutzim* were the perceived needs of Jewish settlement in Palestine. While serving as an emissary of the labor movement in America, Yosef Baratz of Kibbutz Degania A suggested to the Philadelphia Kvutzat Gordonia that they specialize in poultry farming. Seven members ultimately left Philadelphia for Petaluma, California, a center for this kind of agricultural activity. Each member specialized in one of the stages of poultry farming and brought their knowledge to Palestine when they emigrated.[41]

Fig. 10. Simcha Reisen of New York specializes in chicken breeding, Ein Hashofet, 1942. (CZA Keren Hayesod photograph collection)

The history of the American Halutz movement dates from the beginning of organized training farms as early as 1919. In that year the Intercollegiate Zionist Association introduced a six-week summer program—following the precepts of American educator Alexander M. Dushkin and under his direction—that combined a study course with agricultural work at the National Farm School in Bucks County, Pennsylvania. The curriculum included classes in Hebrew, Jewish history, animal husbandry, poultry raising, and horticulture. This program was repeated in 1920, and has been described as the forerunner of *hachshara*.[42]

In the summer of 1925, members of Hashomer Hatzair who were committed to the ideal of preparing for their eventual immigration went to work as agriculture laborers on farms at Flaggtown and North Branch, New Jersey. These attempts, however, bore no definite results. Researcher Samuel Grand explained that "since there is no record of successful achievement on the part of this group, which might serve as a desirable precedent or as an example for other shomrim to follow, we may assume that the rigors of farm life caused disillusionment and shattered youthful dreams."[43]

Another attempt from the ranks of the Hashomer Hatzair in 1927 consisted of a group which hired their members out as laborers on farms in the Ellington and Rockville, Connecticut, areas. Their earnings were pooled into a common treasury, which they hoped to use to pay for their passage to Palestine. This too, ended in failure, apparently because of disillusionment resulting from poor preparation for the collective experience coupled with the physical strain of manual labor.[44]

During the following years, various suggestions were forwarded for creating a permanent training farm. In 1928 Chaim Arlosoroff, then visiting the United States, tried to establish a training farm in California. This farm was not intended solely for the local pioneers; the site was chosen because agriculture in California was highly advanced and the state enjoyed similar climatic conditions to those of Palestine. However, Arlosoroff's plan was never realized.[45]

The first successful training farm was developed at Plainfield, New Jersey, in 1930. Hashomer Hatzair was unable to afford to rent a farm with the needed installations and equipment, let alone purchase one, but through the good offices of Z. Roochwarg, Judah Lapson was persuaded to convert part of his farm at Plainfield into a training center to be maintained through the sale of its produce. In 1932 this training farm was relocated to Earlton, New York, where Elias A. Cohen, a wealthy realtor and philanthropist, allowed a section of his large farm to be used for the purpose. During the 1930s and 1940s, additional training farms were developed in Liberty and Swan Lake, New York; Creamridge and Hightstown, New Jersey; and Anoka, Minnesota.[46] Those who passed through these *hachshara* farms appear to have been the best prepared for their new life, although their education, training, and ideological fervor did not necessarily guarantee their successful integration and acculturation in Palestine nor insure that they would remain there permanently.

The preparation of *halutzim* was not limited to agricultural training. Certain other vocations—such as mechanics, tool and die making, and carpentry—were also considered useful and even necessary for Palestine's development. Some young American Jews intent on immigration to Palestine selected vocations for the benefit of the greater good rather than for their personal fulfillment.

Inquiries about the possibility of immigrating to Palestine were often addressed to sources outside the boundaries of the United States. For instance, American individuals and groups approached members of the World Zionist movement, from its upper echelons to the lower ranks, with questions. Likewise, organizations and well-known personalities in Palestine received letters from potential settlers who hoped to gain correct and accurate information as to the actual conditions for immigration. This information, it was believed, would facilitate the potential immigrant's decision. Often these persons solicited advice; in other instances, they simply wanted the encouragement of a well-known authority.

Information and Assistance

The Palestine Zionist Executive Department of Agriculture and Settlement received inquiries from all over the world, including the United States. The department's files contain letters from individuals across the United States. A typical inquiry is that of L. Wilson of the Dr. Leon Pinsker Camp No. 41, Order Sons of Zion, New York, who asked "What is the amount needed in order to settle a family in Palestine?" The head of the department, Jacob Ettinger, responded that Wilson should contact the American Zion Commonwealth.[47] This answer reflects Ettinger's support for the American Zion Commonwealth as well as his confidence that the American company would provide an appropriate and prompt answer to the query in a suitable language and style. Furthermore, Ettinger's referral to the American land purchasing agent reflects the hope that Wilson would use the company's services.

A personally directed request for advice came from Gershon Agronsky, who approached Arthur Ruppin in 1914 to ask for guidance as to which career, agriculture or engineering, would better benefit the Zionist enterprise. Ruppin was an appropriate address for such an inquiry; he had lived in Palestine since 1908, serving as the director of the Palestine Office and later as director of the Palestine Land Development Company. Ruppin grappled with the question but was unable to give a clear-cut answer, although he leaned toward engineering.[48]

In another instance, A. H. Friedland of Cleveland was in a state of indecision regarding his immigration to Palestine in 1926. On the one hand, he regarded "a call from Palestine as a call to duty which no loyal Zionist is free to evade," but he had quite a number of serious problems to consider before emigrating. He decided to postpone any decision until he could meet with the renowned Hebrew poet Haim Nahman Bialik and the Zionist leader Schmaryahu Levin on their forthcoming visit to Cleveland.[49] It appears he was seeking encouragement or endorsement from these two distinguished figures. These are just a few examples of how American Jews solicited information from Zionist bodies and prominent personalities. Such information was sometimes perceived as more reliable and authoritative. Not in every instance did prominent figures recommend the option of settling in Palestine.

The most detailed, and perhaps the most opinionated, information received by potential immigrants came through private communications. These provided stronger feelings of identification with persons who had already immigrated and were thus experienced. An intimate relationship could be forged, in which an honest dialogue could reasonably be expected. Often persons in Palestine would run errands or facilitate the settlement of the immigrants before they arrived. In 1930, for example, Jessie Sampter wrote her family in the United States: "I am expecting almost any moment a young American couple with their baby who were supposed to arrive at Haifa

CHAPTER 2

Fig. 11. Gershon Agronsky in his Jewish Legionnaire uniform, ca. 1918. (CZA photograph collection)

yesterday on the Mauritania. They are *Halutzim,* which means they intend to go on the land here, and I have arranged for them to enter a cooperative group near Rehoboth [*sic*].... I don't know them at all, only by mail" (emphasis in the original).[50]

The most striking examples of these private communications appear in correspondence between relatives, whose letters were generally exchanged with greater frequency and which are more intimate in content. Often enough there was genuine interest in the well-being of the prospective immigrant, hence the evaluation of the situation and the ensuing counseling was more candid and did not deal solely with objective conditions. Subjective issues connected to potential acculturation and assimilation into local society could be better understood by those of similar background. Friends and relatives in Palestine familiar with their American counterparts often possessed the sensitivity to advise others on these subjective matters. In the semi-fictional novel *Towards Joy Profound,* cousin Shmarye, an American-born relative visiting Cleveland from Palestine, frankly answers all his family's queries. Shmarye is able to express his personal doubts and qualms, as well as his hopes and satisfactions. Eventually Hillel, the novel's protagonist, moves to Palestine. His encounter with Shmarye apparently has a profound effect, inspiring him while providing a trustworthy account of the realities of life in Palestine.[51] This type of informant was often the spearhead for the settlement of a larger group of family, friends, or a community, and provided practical assistance as well. The experienced resident's impressions and his success in being absorbed into the new society markedly affected the flow of migrants who followed.

In summary, unlike the situation with most immigrants, American Jews had opportunities to receive a great amount of information from many possible sources before they migrated to Palestine. Various American Zionist groups and organizations believed that providing this information was an important function of their groups. Their efforts were not, however, always meant to serve the prospective immigrant; such activities were also viewed as important means of acquiring new members and additional financial support.

Admittedly, some information was inaccurate, and other pieces were colored by misconceptions, yet all in all, potential immigrants were able to make their decisions on the basis of a wide spectrum of facts. Although no definite correlation can be drawn, the widespread availability of accurate information seems to have led to a decrease in the actual number of immigrants. Frank and truthful data gave potential immigrants a clear understanding of the consequences of their decision, filtering out the hesitant and those who realized that the fulfillment of their dream or fantasy was too difficult. Another possible correlation is that an American Jewish immigrant who was well-informed beforehand was less likely to re-emigrate. With more knowledge available about life in Palestine—the drawbacks as well as the advantages—the potential for disappointment was greatly decreased.

3

Motivations for American Immigration to Palestine

> Golda was one of those to whom questions present themselves in their clear essence, not in their befuddling complexities. Having decided that she was a Zionist, she had no doubts about the next step. She would go to Palestine as soon as possible, without heart-searching or breast-beating; a self-respecting person could not live vicariously.
>
> Marie Syrkin, *Golda Meir: Woman with a Cause*

According to her biographer, Golda Meir made her decision to migrate to Palestine on the basis of ideological reasons. Her example was unique in its clarity and determination, for most American Jewish migrants to Palestine were not single-minded in their decision making process. Theirs was a complex decision with many variables.

Distinct from most other Jewish migrational movements between the two World Wars, the migration of American Jews to Palestine during this period was characterized by a wide variety of motivating factors. Most waves of Jewish migration resulted from political and economic pressures and from antisemitism; these were forced migrations. During the first years following World War I, Eastern European Jews from the Black Sea to the Baltic suffered the ravages of famine, disease, and civil war. Their condition was further aggravated by the outbreak of pogroms in the Ukraine, White Russia, and Poland. Together these factors led to a mass migration out of this region. In the early 1920s, Polish, Rumanian, Lithuanian, and Latvian Jewries encountered economic and occupational restrictions and rising antisemitism that served as driving forces toward emigration. German Jews from 1933 onward left in growing numbers because of the sharp increase in discrimination that occurred with Adolf Hitler's rise to power.[1] American Jews, by contrast, were not subject to any large-scale occurrences of antisemitism; nor did they suffer greater economic hardship than did the general population. Instead of being acted on by external forces, individual Jews in the United States created their own evaluations and constructed personal credos as they decided whether to emigrate from America to Palestine.

A number of previous studies have outlined and analyzed, to varying degrees, the motivations of American Jews that led to their migration to Palestine. Particularly noteworthy are the studies conducted by Aaron Antonovsky and Abraham David Katz, Chaim Waxman, and Calvin Goldscheider.[2] Although these three studies focus mainly on the period following the establishment of the State of Israel, they also give some attention to immigration during the British Mandatory period.

Antonovsky and Katz based their conclusions on a survey of 1,649 American and Canadian Jews resident in Israel in the mid-1960s. A medical sociologist, Antonovsky originally intended to study the role of sociocultural and psychological factors in the occurrence of coronary heart disease in Israeli Jews. The North American Jewish migration offered an opportunity to investigate one facet: the effect of migration from an industrialized and more developed environment to a less industrialized and less developed one. (This type of population movement ran counter to general trends in the twentieth century.) Medical examinations were conducted to compare the health of siblings in North America and Israel.[3] The Antonovsky and Katz study was later expanded to include an analysis of the reasons why North American Jews chose to migrate to the Land of Israel and the success of their integration into this new culture. The survey population of 1,649 does not represent all North Americans in Israel at the time of the study. A larger group of 2,004 was identified, but Antonovsky and Katz excluded individuals from their study who were either younger than 22 or over 65 years of age. Antonovsky acknowledged that the subject group did not reflect the whole North American population and that it was not a representative cross section of North American Jews in Israel; for instance, apparently the study did not include most of the urban Orthodox population.[4] Antonovsky divided respondents into three groups, according to period of immigration: pre-1948, 1948–56, and 1957–66. Results with regard to the first group, although not reflecting the whole migratory population, provide insights into understanding immigrant motivation during the Mandatory period and its unique character. The number of respondents who had immigrated before 1948 tallied only 312—less than 2 percent of North American immigration during the period of British rule. This low figure may reflect the fact that those who had died or left Palestine were not part of the survey; neither were immigrants who could not be located or who were unwilling to be interviewed. Another salient factor is that the answers provided by the respondents were assessments of decisions they had made at least twenty years earlier. Instead of representing the actual decision making process, their responses constitute an after-the-fact reevaluation, likely affected by their post-migration experience.[5]

Goldscheider tried to ascertain the actual number of American Jews who migrated to Palestine during British rule, but he noted the lack of consistency in the statistics provided by various sources and the difficulties in coming up with an exact figure for the number of immigrants. His study identified some of the reasons for this migration, but his conclusions about this issue are general and do not reflect the whole phenomenon. He contended that the economic situation in the United States during the Great Depression was a central migrational factor. Although this was an important determinant, it was only one of a variety of factors leading to migration.[6]

Of the three studies, Waxman's attempted to deal in greatest depth with the period of British rule in Palestine. His discussion, however, focused more on the Zionist idea in the United States, and its origins and development through the nineteenth and twentieth centuries, than on immigration during this period. In all, he devoted only five pages of discussion to immigration before 1948, and it appears that most of his conclusions are unfounded.[7] Waxman assumed that American immigrants during the period of British rule "were active in the movement of agricultural settlement" and "the bulk of them during this period belonged to the Hashomer Hatzair movement."[8] The vast majority of American immigrants, in fact, lived in urban environments in Palestine. Of those who did settle on the land, the majority were found in agricultural colonies not belonging to the Hashomer Hatzair movement. Furthermore, Waxman furnished inadequate explanations for the motivation of American immigrants and only dealt with a small subgroup, the Hashomer Hatzair. Although he alluded to the sense of persecution, he was unable to produce any concrete evidence of it. The perception of antisemitism was indeed a genuine factor motivating American immigrants, as will be explained below. Waxman also reached erroneous conclusions because of his reliance on what he described as "one of the only available empirical studies of pre-state American immigrants," i.e., Antonovsky and Katz; as indicated earlier, there are limitations to what can be deduced from their study.

Thus it is clearly necessary to return to primary sources for an accurate appraisal of the motivating factors for American Jewish immigration to Palestine. Since models of immigration cannot be verified through any statistical data, as in contemporary studies, more general motivating trends or themes will be discussed. In reality, an individual's motivation was almost always a composite of a number of factors, with boundaries between them blurred. In the majority of cases, it is almost impossible to ascertain exact reasons for migration, and it is impractical to attempt to determine their relative weight. Furthermore, motivations were both conscious and subconscious, and the latter cannot be ascertained in a historical study. Nevertheless, these motivations collectively created the notion of place utility, which reflects an individual's sense of satisfaction or dissatisfaction with specific locations. The aggregate of reasons weighed by an individual led to his final decision to immigrate to Palestine or not.

Researcher Yohai Goell, in his study "Aliya in the Zionism of an American Oleh: Judah L. Magnes," provides an in-depth description and analysis of the motivation and decision making process of one American Jewish immigrant to Palestine during the British Mandate. His article is based on a wealth of primary material, including private journals, letters, and other writings. Magnes, a Reform rabbi, ardent Zionist, and important American Jewish community leader, moved with his family to Palestine in 1923. During their first years in the country, they experienced strong pulls to return to the United States. Goell summarized Magnes's vacillating attitude toward immigration.

> Magnes' permanent settlement in Palestine was not the result of a premeditated decision, though it was by no means contrary to his wishes. Neither did it entail a negation of American Jewry's role in the development of Judaism. It was a result of the interplay and the fortunate timing of several events in his life and in the development of the Jewish National Home in Palestine. Frustrated by his work in New York and feeling the need for spiritual rejuvenation, he fulfilled his long-cherished dream of spending a year or two at the spiritual source of Judaism exactly during that period of time which coincided with evolution of the Hebrew University, an institution that would enable him to give to Jewish education the contribution that he so greatly desired to make.[9]

The story of Judah Magnes is unique because of his background and his subsequent activities in Palestine. Nonetheless, similar studies of other immigrants would deepen our understanding of the whole migrational movement. Unfortunately, there are few cases where the information necessary to carry this out is available. Thus in the following section, elements that contributed to immigration decisions will be discussed and documented, and examples given to illustrate each factor in these decisions.

Basic analysis of any population migration divides the motivating reasons into two major categories: "push" (going away from) and "pull" (coming toward). Both of these may exist simultaneously as part of an individual's decision. The examples provided below, drawn from the experiences of American Jews, illuminate the "push" and "pull" factors. Typically there is no well-defined boundary between them. Some reasons many appear to be almost identical, but certain nuances justify their separation into distinct categories.

PULL FACTORS TOWARD MIGRATION

Antonovsky and Katz categorized the reasons for attraction to Palestine of American Jews into four type—Zionism, Jewishness, attraction to Eretz

Israel, and religious reasons. These categories were sufficient for their study, which included pre-statehood immigration, but since they are very generalized, they have been expanded.[10] Furthermore, other reasons have been found that are unique to the British Mandate period. In addition, Antonovsky and Katz's four reasons have been subdivided in an attempt to further distinguish specific motivations. Two other forms of motivation, return to the soil and economic opportunity, are discussed below as well.

The first factor, "Zionism," is difficult to define or pin down. Adopting Antonovsky and Katz's criteria, the term Zionism is used here in its broadest sense. Thus it includes any mention of Zionism or elements of the Zionist movement or ideology, e.g., membership in a youth movement or a reference by the immigrant. It also embraces various nuances of rebuilding the Jewish nation, of being part of the historical process of a people returning to its land, the solution of "the Jewish problem," and responses that can be subsumed under the general headings of nationalism and patriotism. In the Antonovsky and Katz study, 48 percent of the respondents who immigrated to Palestine prior to 1948 included Zionism as a motivating factor. Thus it would appear that during the British Mandate this was a dominant factor. During this period, many of the immigrants were affiliated with Zionist groups in the United States, as members and even as leaders.

Many emigrés cited Zionism in its general sense as a motivation for migration. For example, Hertzel Fishman asserted that "Our family life was oriented to eventual migration to Eretz Israel." Migrating to the United States in 1923, the family head, Shmuel Fishman, spent the following eleven years preparing himself and his family for migration to Palestine. This preparation was both educational and material. The family lived in an entirely Jewish environment of Hebrew, Yiddish, and Zionist culture. Shmuel Fishman eventually amassed sufficient funds for migration and purchased land at Gan Yavne through the New York Achooza Aleph. In 1934, when his eldest son Hertzel reached the age of thirteen, it was time to leave for Palestine.[11]

Under the heading of Zionist motivation there are a number of nuances—enthusiasm or euphoria for the "National Home," a sense of having a Zionist calling, the pioneer spirit, and social pioneering to develop a new type of society. These deserve separate attention, and they are examined more closely below.

A number of events greatly inspired and motivated certain sectors of Jewish society in America, particularly those events that would lead to the creation of a "National Home." Moved by the special nature of the historic times they were living in, many Jews were eager to leave for Palestine. Events that took place during World War I—including the opening of the front in Palestine, followed by the Balfour Declaration and then the conquest of Jerusalem by British forces—excited American Jews. As a result, a number of American men enlisted in the Jewish Legion. Many of them hoped to not only partake in the liberation of Palestine from Turkish rule but also to settle in the soon-to-be-established "National Home."

Until the United States entered World War I, only resident American aliens were allowed to enlist in the Jewish Legion; American citizens were excluded. Between 1,200 and 1,300 men from the United States enlisted in the Legion. Samuel Rodman outlined the type of men who joined up: "At first nine men out of ten were Zionists. At present the proportions are reversed. At first, again, enlistment was largely from the professional classes—artists, lawyers, teachers, students. Later on service in the Legion appealed more and more to the masses, and we find among the Legionnaires clerks, shopkeepers, small manufacturers and trades-unionists."[12]

Many American Jews awaited the end of the war, pondering and planning their imminent immigration. When it was finally over, those who had thought of migrating began their final preparations and applied for visas to Palestine. From the beginning of 1919 to 31 May 1920, the Palestine Service and Information Bureau in New York reported that over 5,300 persons (applicants, wives, and children) currently residing in the United States had registered for immigration to Palestine.[13] The actual immigration of American Jews to Palestine during the following years, however, fell far below this number; between 1919–23, it totaled only 601. The high proportion of young adult males among the applicants for immigration is noteworthy. Of these applicants, 10.2 percent were males aged 14 to 30, as compared to 5.23 for females in the same age range. For other age groupings the gender ratio was within normal parameters. This further demonstrates that the excitement of the period particularly attracted young single males, a relatively mobile group, to try their luck in Palestine.

Menachem Mendel Freidman, an active Zionist in Norfolk, saw the Balfour Declaration and the liberation of Jerusalem as signs that this was the right time to translate his Zionism into practical terms—immigration. For years he had been engaged in collecting funds for Palestine and developing a Hebrew school within the local community. But the time for migration had come—he wanted to serve as an example, and he called on other Zionists in Norfolk to follow suit and migrate too. Three Norfolk Jewish families were similarly moved by contemporary events in Palestine and apparently followed Freidman's lead. Despite the objections of his extended family, Freidman, together with his wife and children, left for Palestine in 1921.[14]

The appointment of Sir Herbert Samuel, a British Jew and Zionist, to the position of high commissioner for Palestine heightened the level of excitement. Samuel accepted the position on 24 April 1920, and took office in Jerusalem on July 1st. However, the outbreak of riots on 1 May 1921, weakened enthusiasm for immigration.[15] In October 1921 the American consulate in Jerusalem reported: "The officer in charge of this consulate frequently receives visits from American citizens who have rushed to Palestine

CHAPTER 3

Fig. 12. Jewish battalions in Palestine. (author's collection)

in a fervor to do something for the 'National Home' who desire visas to take them on the journey back to the U.S. disillusioned but much wiser Jewish Americans who were originally lured here by the glitter of Zionist propaganda."[16]

No subsequent event during the interwar years rekindled the earlier strong enthusiasm. To the contrary, the profound—and negative—impact of the 1929 riots is evident. Nonetheless, following the period of civil disorder, former members of the Jewish Legion living in the United States heard a calling. The sense of being needed by the Zionist enterprise also had a strong attraction for many Americans. A demand was placed upon certain individuals. They, in turn, created an atmosphere in which their contribution was considered essential for the future of Palestine. Jacob Goell, treasurer of the newly formed American Palestine Settlers Association appealed to former Jewish Legionnaires to attend a conference on settlement in Palestine. In an open letter, he explained, "Until now we American Jews have been called upon to contribute money to Palestine, now some of us feel that the present conditions demand that we give men to Palestine—especially those young men, the American Legionnaires, who went there thirteen years ago to fight and now want to return to settle."[17] Former Legionnaires believed they

TABLE 9
Age-gender distribution of North American registrants for immigration to Palestine, 1919–20

Age groups	Number			Percent		
	Male	Female	Total	Male	Female	Total
0–13	339	295	634	5.67	4.93	10.60
14–30	610	313	923	10.20	5.23	15.43
31–44	770	698	1,468	12.87	11.67	24.54
45–59	389	323	712	6.50	5.40	11.90
60>	44	30	74	0.74	0.50	1.24
Total	3,245	2,738	5,983	54.24	45.76	100.00

Source: "Statistical Report on Applicants and Registrants for Immigration to Palestine from America," Palestine Service and Information Bureau, Zionist Organization of America, New York, 31 May 1920, CZA F25/33.
Note: These figures also include registrants from other countries: 708 from Canada, 1 from Austria, 10 from South America, and 14 countries not reported.

were wanted for both rapid settlement and defense of the Jewish colonies from the Arab inhabitants of Palestine and Arabs in neighboring countries. The America-Palestine Jewish Legion was founded with a specific intent: "The prime object of our organization is to establish a net of colonies in Palestine populated by Jewish men who during the world war served in Palestine in the Jewish Legion. Such colonies if situated along the Jordan and on the Syrian frontier would serve a double purpose: They would be a bulwark against Arab invasion from Transjordania and Syria and would simultaneously give the country a number of Jewish American pioneers engaged in constructive work."[18]

Former Legionnaires in America recognized the benefits of their settlement. They believed their expectations were more realistic than others', and they thought they would produce the fewest failures and emigrants from Palestine. They felt that their participation could make the difference between the success and failure of the Jewish "National Home." Evidence of the sense of a Zionist calling can be found in responses to a questionnaire circulated in 1930 by the American Palestine Settlers Association: seventy-two individuals wanted to settle in Palestine within that year, twenty-two the following year, and fifteen in 1932.[19] As in most cases, the actual number of individuals who migrated fell well below the number of those who had declared their intention to do so.

CHAPTER 3

A variation on the Zionist motivation, linked with the urge to return to the soil, can be found in the pioneer spirit or *halutziut*. Ideologists Ber Borchov, Nachman Syrkin, and Aaron David Gordon provided the theoretical basis for this school of thought. Their writings, mainly in Hebrew and Yiddish but also later translated into English, reached the shores of America in the early twentieth century and were diffused among elements of the Jewish population. Syrkin himself lived in New York from 1907 until his death in 1924, serving as an official of the Labor Zionist movement in America. An adaptation of the doctrines of Labor Zionism, the pioneer spirit was expressed through the Hechalutz movement founded in the United States in 1905. Yitzhak Ben-Zvi and David Ben-Gurion were active as emissaries for the propagation of Labor Zionism in America during World War I. One aim of the movement was mobilizing Jewish youth to immigration to Palestine. The movement was realized through the development of scouting organizations in the Diaspora—Hashomer Hatzair, Gordonia, Dror, Hechalutz Hatzair, Hapoel Hamizrachi, and others. These groups were interested in preparing their members in the Diaspora for the up-building of the Jewish Labor community in Palestine. The majority of Americans who immigrated to Palestine under the banner of pioneering were members of at least one of these movements.[20]

Assessments and reevaluations of the pioneer ideology were made in the American context. Moshe Furmansky, an American Jew who settled on Kibbutz Mishmar Haemek, grappled with the meaning of pioneering. He felt it was not only the act of aliyah that determines the *halutziut* of an individual, nor even his decision to alter the course of his life by becoming a worker in Palestine. *Halutziut,* he posited, demanded a great deal more of the individual. *Halutziut* expressed itself in the psychological readiness of the individual to live and engage at all times in the great struggle for the rebuilding of Palestine—to be prepared at any time to travel to the most difficult fronts, the conquest of which might entail the greatest dangers.[21]

The spirit of the period is vividly described by Dorothy Ruth Kahn. Her contemporaneous account of the battle to transform the landscape illuminates the pioneering atmosphere.

> There is high adventure in Palestine. Adventure of the soul. Of the spirit. The Jew has come home. The Jew is trying to fashion that home after a pattern that would shut out this stench. Perhaps he would succeed. More than likely he would fail. What matter? He is trying. Throwing his life into that trying. The Jew has come home! You can smell orange trees pushing through parched soil! . . . Jews work and sweat in Palestine. And their sweat dampens the soil. Hard soil. Arid soil. Now dampened by their toil. Dampened until the smell of orange trees intoxicates you.[22]

Pioneering was not, of course, a concept unique to American Jews. Quite often efforts in Palestine were translated into terms of the American pioneering ethos, either that of the Puritans of New England or the opening of the American West.

For some individuals, Jewish Palestine offered opportunities to contribute to the construction of a new society. Varying from individual to individual, there were different agendas for navigating toward a progressive and enlightened Jewish society. Zionist leader Bernard Rosenblatt, in his treatise *Social Zionism,* explained his worldview of a new society in Palestine: "A Social Zionist is one whose idealism is not satisfied merely with the creation of a Jewish state, but who is determined to build a model state in the Holy Land—freed from economic wrongs, the social injustices and the greed of modern-day industrialism. While he may not be prepared to endorse the full program of any particular radical school, yet he purposes to utilize the truths of all schools in building the new Commonwealth in Zion."[23] Through his work with the American Zion Commonwealth land purchasing and development company as well as other economic activities, Rosenblatt attempted to direct his activities according to his perception of the kind of society that should be created in Palestine. Eventually he settled in Haifa in 1930, yet his activities on behalf of social engineering were more influential during the period when he was active in the United States.

Deborah Kallen, the renowned educator who settled in Palestine in 1920, expressed her vision in a 1950s interview. "I saw an opportunity for creative work. The fact that people thought the Jews were not an artistic people aroused me. I did not support the religious restriction against portraits. In fact I thought it my holy duty to start something which would refute that concept."[24] She introduced this and other ideas through her work at the School of the Parents Education Association in Jerusalem, better known as the "Kallen School."

Thus Zionism assumed different meanings for American Jewish immigrants to Palestine. While it ranged across the spectrum from obligation to fulfillment, it frequently reflected the desire to create a new and better society in Palestine.

Not unrelated to the Zionist motivation was that of "Jewishness," including any expression of living a Jewish life in a Jewish society, homeland, or state. This concept encompasses ideas such as that a Jew should live in the Holy Land, the desire to be with Jews, and the realization of the goal of living in Eretz Israel ("life-long dream," "parent instilled the idea," and so on). In the Antonovsky and Katz study, 21 percent of the respondents who immigrated to Palestine prior to 1948 cited Jewishness as one of their reasons. This is also characteristic of the immigration of the Orthodox Jewish community, especially those who joined Kollel America Tiffereth Yerushalaim in Palestine. For instance, Rabbi Shapiro, dressed in a blue satin coat and a great fur *streimal,* decided to leave "his little flock somewhere in South Jersey to spend his last days splitting Talmudic hairs in the old city of Jerusalem." After four or five decades in the American rabbinate, he was relinquishing his position of authority as the leader of his community. "The old women he knew waited for words to fall from his lips like pearls and the small boys kissed his hand in awe and reverence mingled not a little with fear."[25] It was a difficult transition but one that had profound religious significance. He would fulfill the dream, common among many religious Jews, of living out his last days in the Holy Land and being buried in its sacred soil.

Others who were not affiliated with any group or organization also perceived Palestine as a place for the expression of their Jewishness. One individual from Alabama City explained his desire to immigrate to Palestine: "I am a sabbath keeper and have bin [sic] for about 16 years and we dont [sic] eat the Swine flesh nor any of the unclean, and we are hated by the gentiles, so I have made up my mind to try to leave America and come to the land of Palestine."[26] Note that two factors—Jewishness and antisemitism—entered into his decision.

As pointed out earlier, one of the traditional reasons to immigrate to Palestine was to die and be buried there. Respondents giving this as a reason were almost always associated with Kollel America Tiffereth Yerushalaim. Information on 148 heads of families in this group shows an elderly population, with 73 percent over the age of fifty.[27] One example illustrating this motivation is found in correspondence between the Palestine Information and Service Bureau in New York and the Palestine Zionist Executive in Jerusalem. Benjamin Farkas, an American citizen aged seventy-three from Astoria, Long Island, wanted to live out his last days in Palestine. The bureau explained that his son had been killed in World War I. The father received a United States government monthly pension of $57.50 and would receive it for another fourteen years. In most cases, such requests were approved if individuals either possessed the necessary capital or could satisfy the immigration authorities that they would receive a steady income for their continued maintenance.[28]

Another religious motif was the desire to pursue religious studies in the Holy Land. For example, William Berman had studied for seven or eight years in Rabbi Isaac Elchanan's yeshiva in New York (later to be known as Yeshiva University). Berman was born in America and was "American in character." He would have had no difficulty obtaining a rabbinic position in the United States, for he possessed thorough training, fine wit, and talented oratory. Leo Gottesman recounted an occasion when Berman discussed his decision to move to Palestine:

> [W]hen I met him one day, he announced to me that he was going to Eretz Israel—to study in the Yeshivah at Hebron. Why was he giving up his splendid position? He explained to me that he desired to perfect himself.

Fig. 13. Members of Kollel America Tiffereth Yerushalaim. (CZA pamphlet 50,398)

He was not content with that learning he had already acquired. He wished to devote a few years, while he was still young, to learning Torah for the sake of learning—to study *Torah Lishmoh*. And particularly he desired to study in "the cradle where Jacob was raised." That was why he had elected to go to Hebron [emphasis in the original]. [29]

Berman fell victim to the Arab massacre of Hebron's Jews in August 1929. His martyrdom was interpreted as an expression of his true Jewishness. He was killed by an Arab sword while earnestly endeavoring to bring Torah culture to the land and rehabilitate it with a stronger sense of Judaism.

A motivating factor more difficult to explain than pursuing religious studies is "attraction to Palestine" other than Zionism or Jewishness. Immigrants frequently cited the appeal of some part of Palestine society—e.g., kibbutz life, or social, cultural, general political, or professional reasons. Palestine also offered an opportunity to do something fulfilling.

Some elderly Americans perceived Palestine, with its cultural amenities and Mediterranean climate, as an attractive place to retire. This is a variation of the traditional motivation of spending one's last days there, not necessarily to study Torah but to be buried in its ground. In addition, Palestine also had economic advantages for older immigrants. Funds set aside for retirement had greater buying power in Palestine than in America, particularly after 1929.[30]

Palestine also offered certain career opportunities to younger immigrants. A number of professions were not filled to capacity in Palestine, though they might be overcrowded in America. In many cases, American Jews proficient in English and trained in the United States were in great demand. Palestine also became an avenue for personal ambitions, including but not limited to social pioneering. Arieh Goren, in his lecture "A Two Way Street: Visitors, Sojourners and Settlers from America to the Land of Israel," focused on the idea of satisfying personal ambitions. He pointed out that there was an unusually large number of single women in the pioneering group, such as Henrietta Szold, Jessie Sampter, Alice Seligsburg, Bertha Landsman, Julia Aronson-Dushkin, and Irma Lindheim. Many of these women were connected to the Hadassah organization in the United States.[31]

Bertha Landsman had an ambition to be a nurse, and she was even willing to leave her native New York City and study in Washington if she encountered opposition from her father. However, he acquiesced, and she pursued her studies and vocation in New York. Landsman also dreamt of living in Palestine. She looked forward to the challenge of working there and contributing to the health and well-being of its inhabitants. She immigrated in 1921, becoming a prominent figure in the development of health services. She was among the initiators of *Tipat Halav* (lit., drop of milk), a welfare program for infants and mothers.[32]

Certain skills were in demand in Palestine, and many of them were connected to proficiency in English. Other vocations were better developed in America. In 1920, in a letter to Lotta Levensohn, Jessie Sampter explained that "there is such a demand for stenographers and secretaries here, that a woman like you, an executive and secretary with the additional advantage of understanding Hebrew would quickly find a well-paying job. . . . I don't think there are two first rate English stenographers in Jerusalem, to say nothing of secretaries with that accomplishment!"[33]

Levensohn indeed settled in Palestine three years later. She had strong Zionist connections in America, having worked as secretary to Federation of American Zionists secretaries Jacob DeHaas and Judah L. Magnes. She continued working as Magnes's secretary when he became president of the New York City Kehillah in 1910, remaining in this position until her migration. Her years in Palestine "ran the gamut from work on the land, to translator, lecturer, author, publicity director and organizer in association with Hadassah, the Jewish Agency, the Hebrew University and others."[34]

Another form of motivation was the view that life on the land represented personal fulfillment. The notion of returning to a simpler, pastoral life played a significant part in developing the new society in Palestine. This attitude assumed various guises. It was partly derived from a religious belief in messianic redemption, as described in the biblical passage, "Each man will sit under his vine and his fig tree" (Micah 4:4). It also reflected the longing to return to the natural life. The majority of American Jews lived in highly industrialized urban centers, and the desire to become closer to nature was a growing motif in American society generally. One American farmer in Palestine who had left behind an urban life related:

> The moment I decided, for one reason or another, to become a farmer, I found the advantages of America over other countries more doubtful. The farmer has to work just as hard in the States as in Palestine, after all, he does not get more than the world prices for his products. Furthermore, I do not want to live all isolated on a farm, as farmers do in America. I am ready to be a farmer, but I want to live with other people, preferabl[y] of my own blood and race. That is why I came to Palestine.[35]

Returning to the soil afforded a deep sense of satisfaction and pride. An American rabbi declared, "I would like to have a picture taken of myself milking a cow. I would like to send a copy to each of my former parishioners in the Bronx: let them see how a *real* man should live" (emphasis in the original).[36]

A few American Jews viewed Palestine as having equal or greater economic potential than they would find in America. Certain professions, industries, or crafts were not yet fully developed in Palestine. In other cases, opportunities in America were limited, whereas possibilities were still open in Palestine. A description of the potential for developing certain kinds of small businesses was forwarded to America by Robert Kesselman. He had became the chief accountant of the Mandatory Department of Public Works, and later he opened a private firm, Kesselman and Kesselman. With his finger on the pulse of economic developments in Palestine, Kesselman could realistically advise others. For example, he explained to his New York haberdasher that the few hat shops in Palestine were doing well and that there was potential for success for others.[37]

Palestine had certain economic advantages that attracted Americans to the eastern Mediterranean shore. Its position as part of the British Empire provided an enormous world market. And in 1929 Palestine gained the additional benefit of an enlarged regional market through the free trade accord reached with French mandated Syria—a market of four million.[38]

The sense of economic opportunity was particularly strong after 1929, with the onset of the Great Depression in America. Palestine at that time was experiencing a minor boom. In fact, capital flowed into Palestine to take advantage of the opportunities offered by undervalued prices. In 1932 David Horovitz explained that "3½ dollars will to-day buy a pound's worth of goods, and land, houses or immovables are valued in pounds. The results are obvious. A smaller capital in foreign currency is required for investment and the investor earns automatically the difference between the undervalued price in pounds and the gold value of property to which it must return."[39]

Thus in the late 1920s and early 1930s there was a significant growth in the number of capitalist immigrants to Palestine, particularly Americans. Abraham Revusky described one man's economically based decision to come to Palestine. " 'There is no future for people of our kind in America, where a small business man is crushed by chain stores,' " this American settler in Raanana told Revusky. " 'Had I remained in the states I would sooner or later have been compelled to give up my dry-goods store and look for some other occupation. If such a change is inevitable, then why not try it in Palestine?' "[40] Another example is that of Abraham Climer, who applied for a settler's visa in 1931 for himself as well as his mother, wife, and three children. Climer had $11,000 and was considered a desirable settler. Officials interpreted his migration as "He is leaving for Palestine simply out of fear of losing here his money and having no prospects in this country."[41]

Another indication of the economic pressures brought on by the Depression was the desire of some industrialists to immigrate with their factories to Palestine. A. M. Hillman, owner of the Mercantile Silk Corporation, Ltd. of San Francisco, declared: "As a man whose chief desire and aim in life is to settle in Palestine, and contribute what little my limited abilities empower me to, to the upbuilding of our father land, I am most anxious to transfer our plants to Palestine, if such a possibility should present itself." His correspondence appears to suggest that he lacked liquid capital and his business was suffering; indeed, he hoped to find investors in Palestine with $30,000, but in the end, Hillman's business was not transferred.[42] Other industrialists, like Isaac Sacks, pulled by economic opportunity in Palestine and pushed by difficult times in America, successfully reestablished their factories in Palestine.

PUSH FACTORS TOWARD MIGRATION

Push factors seem to have had less effect on the American migrational movement than did pull factors. Most Americans Jews were satisfied with life there, but some were dissatisfied enough to choose Palestine over the United States. Antonovsky and Katz surveyed the push factors cited by American Jewish immigrants to Palestine who became disenchanted with life in the United States. They discerned five kinds of responses concerning the reasons these people had come to Palestine: the decision was made for them by someone else, they were dissatisfied with America, they wanted to try living in Palestine on a trial basis, they did it for the sake of their children, and a host of idiosyncratic reasons. (The fifth type of response was largely unique, personal, or vague, and it is not addressed in the following discussion.)

Incidentally, Palestine provided a solution to some of the problems experienced by American Jewish immigrants, but their migration specifically to Palestine needs to be viewed within a larger context. The message

TABLE 10
Capitalist immigration to Palestine from the United States, May 1925–December 1942

Period	Immigrants	A-1 category	Percent
May 1925–28	670	485	72
1929	85	58	68
1930	132	120	91
1931	171	121	71
January–July 1932	120	115	96
May 1925–December 1942	5,861	4,398	75

Source: Memorandum from the Department of Statistics, Jewish Agency for Palestine to the Economic Department, Jewish Agency for Palestine, Jerusalem, 25 October 1932, CZA S6/1183; David Gurevich, Aaon Gertz, and Roberto Bachi, *The Jewish Population of Palestine: Immigration, Demographic Structure and Natural Growth* (In Hebrew) (Jerusalem: Jewish Agency for Palestine, 1944), 155.

TABLE 11
Applicants for immigration to Palestine from the United States, July–September 1932

Months	Applicants	Persons	Capital ($)
July–August 1932	66	N.A.	345,905
August 1932	35	78	367,900
September 1932	27	61	190,400

Source: Register of applicants for whom the Palestine Immigration Bureau has secured capitalist permits for various months, Palestine Immigration Bureau, New York, CZA S17/162.

propagated by American Jewish leadership was that Jewish immigrants to the United States could not return to their countries of origin. When they left their homes in Eastern Europe, for example, many had "burnt all their bridges behind them." No matter what disappointment befell them in America, or what culture shock they suffered, they were not motivated to return to Europe. Return migration rates for Jews in America were extremely low in comparison with the general immigrant population, even when adjusted upward as suggested by current research. American Jewish immigrants to Palestine, although small in number, are part of this low Jewish re-emigration.[43]

Returning to the issue of push factors, some immigrants did not make their decision to migrate independently but rather moved to Palestine on someone else's account. Some migrated to marry a Jew from Palestine; in other cases the husband wanted to immigrate and he took his family with him; others moved to be with children already in Palestine. For some members of this cohort, usually women and children, this was virtually a form of forced migration. The decision was made by the head of the family, and they often had little or nothing to say about the matter. In Antonovsky and Katz's survey, dependency was the most important push factor among North American Jews, cited by 11 percent of respondents from the group of pre-1948 immigrants.[44]

Usually the first member of the family came for reasons already mentioned in the pull factors or for those mentioned below as other push factors. As the spearhead for the remaining family members, the first family member would investigate the situation in Palestine and decide if it would be suitable for the others. This decision making process was usually contingent upon procuring some livelihood in Palestine. Immigration authorities required that a person seeking to sponsor family members have sufficient means to support them. The first immigrant, when applying for subsequent ones, would need references from a local Jewish representative body—the Jewish Community Council of Jaffa, for example—which in turn would forward the letter of reference to the district governor. The reference assured the authorities of the individual's ability to support himself and the prospective immigrants in his family. For instance, an American Jew who had immigrated in February 1922 and was working as a carpenter in Tel Aviv applied within a period of nine months for the immigration of his brother and his fiancée from New York City.[45]

The difficulties faced by some of those who immigrated only because of their spouses or parents are illustrated in the following two examples. Mrs. Sternberg, one of New York's foremost advertising women, was married to a Zionist of many years. He had immigrated to Palestine before her and opened a shop on Allenby Road in Tel Aviv. She followed him to Palestine and was willing to try life there, although she had certain worries. She related her trepidation to Dorothy Ruth Kahn en route to Palestine. Mrs. Steinberg "had heard that there was no steam heat in winter and no hot water on tap. The food was a poor grade and good maids were difficult to secure." The decision to immigrate was not her own, and her life would be changed radically as a result of her husband's resolution to settle in Palestine.[46] Another case in point is that of the Pearlman daughters. It was their father's cherished hope to settle permanently in Palestine, but he had misgivings about his daughters' ability to adapt to their new environment. As he explained to journalist Dorothy Ruth Kahn, "I'm not sure of the girls. You know how young women are to-day. They like clothes. And there aren't many shops in Palestine. And they like to have a good time. They're accustomed to New York. Perhaps we'll all return to America."[47]

The lack of independent motivation usually implied that immigration was not a question of choice but rather of being dragged to Palestine. The sense of confusion was felt not only by the dependents but also by their parents. Olga Rubinow Lurie recalled the anxiety and perplexity she sensed beneath her father's decision to take his family to Palestine. After spending more than six months in Palestine as director of the American Zionist Medical Unit, Isaac Max Rubinow returned to the United States to collect his family:

> Poor Dad! How pressured he must have felt! But he *did* return, in the summer of 1920, to take us back with him. It was a strenuous time. Should the furniture be sold or stored? Would we need clothes for all seasons? There were visits to doctors and dentists, shots, transcripts to get from our schools, passports and visas to obtain, trunks to pack, friends and relatives to visit before leaving. We ate numerous chicken dinners with the aunts and uncles, who fed us well, since they doubted whether they would see us soon (or ever) again. It was crazy, *meshugah,* for my father to take "the children" to a foreign country, so unhealthy and dangerous. It would be a miracle if we survived it. I think Mother had grave doubts herself [emphasis in the original].[48]

Parents suffered intense anxiety over whether they had made the correct decision for the family. For children and spouses, such moves often resulted in feelings of disorientation and dissatisfaction with the new environment; sometimes these led to a return to America.

A more common push factor was a sense of dissatisfaction with America. This operated on two levels. In terms of having to deal with a larger society, there was, for example, the desire not to live in the Diaspora; people were concerned about assimilation and about antisemitism in general or the fear of being the object of it. The second level was a more personal one; it included the wish to leave a job one disliked, to get away from family, or just to be independent. As with all push factors, the emphasis here is on the negative, whether with regard to the immigrant's personal situation or with how he perceived American society. Six percent of respondents to the Antonovsky and Katz survey mentioned dissatisfaction with America.[49] This figure appears to be quite low, particularly when compared to much written evidence that emphasizes unhappiness with America. It should be noted, however, that responses to Antonovsky and Katz's survey were solicited many years after the migration, when many of the respondents had resolved their personal conflicts with American society and were able to view that country in a gentler light.

The Mirsky family of Minneapolis did not adjust well to life in America, but they were comfortable in its Jewish subculture. They arrived in the United States in 1905, only to immigrate to Palestine a short time later. After spending less than a year there, they returned to Minneapolis to await a more propitious time to immigrate once again to Palestine. The Mirskys were among the founders of the local Poale Zion club and heavily involved in cultural and charitable activities. In 1921 they left for Palestine permanently, settling in Herzlia in 1925.[50]

One aspect of expressed dissatisfaction with the United States was specifically connected to a sense of alienation. As sociologist Samuel N. Eisenstadt explained, the out-migration from Eastern Europe was not merely prompted by economic and internal needs but also by the fear that children and the elderly were at great personal risk. As a result, this wave of Jewish immigration to the United States had a larger proportion of those under the age of fifteen and over forty-five. In addition, the percentage of those re-emigrating from American to their country of origin averaged about 5 percent among Jews as compared to 30 to 35 percent among non-Jews.[51] This does not necessarily indicate a lower dissatisfaction rate in the Jewish immigrant population, but it does reflect the reality that Jews could not return to Eastern Europe. The dissatisfied Jewish immigrant in the United States looked for other alternatives, and one such was Palestine. However, the time lag between immigration to America and emigration from it varied greatly: from a few months to a few decades.

Alienation and persecution, or the perception thereof, are two of the stronger themes connected to dissatisfaction with America. A lack of connection with other Americans was reported by author Myriam Harry in a meeting with an American woman probably living at Merchavia. In response to Harry's questioning—"What brought you to Palestine? The Jews are not persecuted, are they, in America?"—the respondent articulated an answer that conveyed a sense of alienation. She began by agreeing that Jews were not persecuted and stating that on a personal level, she and her family were materially better off there. But then she continued: "America is too new a country for us. We don't take root there: we are never really 'at home.' We were popular there, but aliens, goyim, while here, as soon as we landed, we felt ourselves in our own land, and it is the non-Jews who are goyim."[52] This response is open to many interpretations, but the strong sense of alienation or being foreign stands out.

Antisemitism was a more distinctive factor. Researcher Ben Halpern pointed out that the American form of antisemitism is different from its European counterpart."American anti-semitism," he noted, "has never reached the level of an historic, politically effective movement. It has remained, so to speak, a merely sociological or 'cultural' phenomenon."[53] Yet this "sociological or 'cultural' " form of antisemitism deeply affected the activities of Jews in America and served as an impetus for many of those who chose immigration to Palestine.

In the late nineteenth and early twentieth centuries, antisemitism in America was principally expressed through quotas and restrictions in education, employment, and social activities. Robert Kesselman, after grappling with the question of American antisemitism, in the end made his permanent home in Palestine.

> At University, Robert had come to see leaflets with such phrases as: "Don't vote for Klein! We have enough Jews on this team!" This stung him all the more deeply because he had for years done his best to believe that American Jews were on the same footing as other immigrants who became Americans. In the first years in America, whenever he had met with unfair and partial treatment, he had put it down to his being a stranger and a greenhorn and not to his being a Jew.[54]

Another result of being subject to antisemitism was an inability to assimilate into the larger society. Many individuals, born in America, believed that they were like all other citizens. They threw off the symbols of their Jewish heritage but were subject to antisemitism despite all their efforts to assimilate. In 1932 a reader of the *Jewish Daily Forward*'s popular advice column, "A Bintel Brief," wrote: "I am an immigrant from Russia, my wife is American-born and we are both freethinkers. We have two grown children . . . who know they are Jews but never saw any signs of religion or holidays in our home. Even Yom Kippur is another day to us." He further explained that "For the last twenty years we've lived among Christians and we socialize with them. Our children also go around with Gentiles." He had assumed that they had succeeded in assimilating. However, he related, his son, while attending a party, felt insulted when he heard other guests telling jokes about Jews. When the young man informed his hostess, a Gentile whom he had been dating, of his Jewish identity and how offended he felt, her reaction was one of surprise. Deeply affected by this experience, he began a search for his Jewish heritage that eventually drew him to a Zionist club. In the end, the son demanded that his family put their lives in America behind them and move with him to Palestine. Though the family was unwilling to do so, the son was determined to immigrate to Palestine himself. The father then turned to the editor of the *Jewish Daily Forward* with a request for guidance.[55]

In comparison to generalized disappointment with American society, certain individuals experienced discontent within their own lives—in family or personal relations, or in employment—and believed that another milieu, possibly Palestine, would be more conducive to personal happiness. For example, during her first year in Palestine, poet Jessie Sampter expressed her sense of fulfillment there in contrast to her life in the United States.

> My feeling now is that I want to, that I must, stay here indefinitely. To go back after this year, which has been really a year of difficult adjustment and preparation, would be to leave a job I had just begun. I feel at home here, as I have never felt anywhere since I was twelve years old. My childish home-feelings are associated with places that no longer exist, except in caricature. I mean Long Lake and 131 Street. Since then I have never loved any place—and I love this place; I feel planted here. If I ever return to the States, it will be to visit, not to go home. Of course I shall always love the ideal America—but not as much as I love the real Palestine and the living Jewish people, real and ideal. That is the truth. I do not know whether it is possible for you to understand it, there are personal reasons, too. Life has been too hard for me, and I have lived at too high a tension of spiritual endeavor. Here I can drop all that, and be natural. Mrs. [Edith Low] Eder agreed with me—I think Miss Szold does, too—that I ought to stay here for at least a few years to free myself from the past and myself. It seems curious to write so much more than I would ever have told you. Will you answer it fully, if you can? You see, this is a letter about myself, and not about Palestine.[56]

Sampter remained in Palestine for the rest of her life. She apparently found personal satisfaction there, involving herself in social and educational projects, and even building a family through the adoption of a Yemenite orphan whom she named Tamar Sheleg.

In certain situations, American Jews stopped short of making an explicit decision to settle in Palestine. Instead they migrated temporarily or sojourned as visitors or students. Some sought adventure; others wanted to satisfy their curiosity or merely see the country. After spending some time in Palestine, many found themselves attracted to life there, felt comfortable in this new environment, or for some other reason decided to remain or return at a later date. Often their sojourn underscored the differences between America and Palestine, further emphasizing the push and pull factors connected to the question of their personal immigration.

The vicissitudes of life in Palestine and the probationary living situation of some Americans are adeptly described in Molly Lyons Bar-David's account of an American named Harry.

> Harry had a roadster and was [a] pampered American to the finger tips. He had been four times to Palestine; each time he had come to stay, but was unable to give up the temptations of the easier life and had returned home. He became the symbol of those Americans whose life is a constant tug of war between idealistic yearnings and materialistic realities. In New York he dreamed *halutziut,* and to Palestine he brought a sports roadster and was, consequently, a misfit in both ways of life. Years later, on his sixth return, he left his car behind and came with a bulldozer to break the boulders in the Negev. Then he stayed.[57]

In some cases, a visit to Palestine raised questions in the tourist's mind of whether Palestine was the place where he should take up permanent residence. Irving Fineman, an engineer by profession and later a biographer of Henrietta Szold, described his own visit to Palestine and the attempts by persons there to convince him to remain. An encounter with entrepreneur and engineer Pinhas Rutenberg at the Naharaim power plant led him to understand that there was a need for well-trained and competent engineers. Rutenberg facilitated a meeting between Fineman and Emanuel Mohl in Jerusalem. Mohl, an American-trained engineer who held several positions connected to construction work in Palestine, was in need of appropriate personnel. So Mohl took Fineman

> to see Miss [Henrietta] Szold, hoping that her undaunted spirit would persuade the young engineer to join them in the great work for which he would be invaluable. . . . Mr. Fineman was certainly enchanted with what he had seen, and was certainly excited about the possibility of working for the Jewish National Home; but he first had to report back to his university in Illinois. . . . The Promised Land, for all its fascination, did not exert on some Americans the undeniable hold it had on her [Henrietta Szold].[58]

Educational institutions—including the Haifa Technion, the Hebrew University of Jerusalem, the American School of Oriental Research, and many yeshivot—offered an opportunity for a trial period in Palestine. Researcher Simon N. Herman, in his study *American Students in Israel,* found that temporary enrollment in the School for Overseas Students at the Hebrew University of Jerusalem during the 1969–70 academic year heightened students' motivation to settle in Israel.[59]

A similar effect apparently operated during the period of British rule in Palestine, as can be seen in Isidore B. Hoffman's account. He and an unknown number of American Jews had arrived in Jerusalem in September 1924 with the intention of attending the university. He explained: "Across two oceans and four continents, on a journey 7,000 miles long, we came hither that we might be the first students at the great Hebrew University. We traveled from New York to Jerusalem to sit at the feet of great masters who had been called from the four corners of the world to impart the accumulated wisdom of our four-thousand-year-old culture. We would be the American contingent in this greatest spiritual enterprise of the reawakened Jewish People."[60]

The drawing power of the university is also apparent from Moshe Davis's account of his student days at the Hebrew University of Jerusalem during the 1937–38 academic year. In retrospect, he considered this period—which included a visit to Europe on the eve of the Holocaust—as his "formative year." Davis returned to settle in Israel in 1959, joining the faculty of the Hebrew University of Jerusalem and founding its Institute of Contemporary Jewry.[61]

Fig. 14. American students at the Hebrew University of Jerusalem, 1929. *Left to right:* Edward Gelber, Joseph Warren, Sydney Luria, Rose Halpern, Isabelle Kitay Hyman, Isadore Goodman, George M. Hyman, Meir Lasker. (Courtesy of the Hebrew University of Jerusalem photo archive)

Between 1926 and 1938, sixty-nine Americans attended the Hebrew University of Jerusalem. Among this group were students or graduates of American rabbinical schools—Jewish Theological Seminary, 12; Hebrew Union College, 5; Jewish Institute of Religion, 3; and Yeshiva College, 2.[62] This appears to be in keeping with the changing attitudes of American Jewry, particularly Reform Judaism, toward Zionism, and the similarly changing attitudes of individual institutions—as pointed out by Armond Emanuel Cohen in 1932: "When recently there was a change in the Zionist Administration, it was said that the money-raising phase in American Zionism was past. It was also said that we were now to embark upon a campaign to educate the masses in Zionism. The latter is the task of the American Rabbi today. Yet how he educates his congregation and his community in Zionism depends in a large measure upon his own training in this matter."[63] It is not known exactly how many of those who were students between 1926 and 1938 eventually settled in Palestine, though that was clearly the hope of persons who promoted the idea of American student enrollment. In the mid-

1930s, for example, the American Alumni of Hebrew University attempted to encourage American students to travel to Palestine by helping subsidize their trip. The alumni hoped that after experiencing life there, at least some of these students would remain.[64]

Other Americans who experimented with temporary residence in Palestine include Emanuel Labes and Irma L. Lindheim. Labes went to Palestine in the mid-1930s to study with prominent archaeologists Nelson Gluck and Sir Flinders Petrie at the American School of Oriental Research in Jerusalem. This institute, founded in 1900 for the purpose of conducting research and giving instruction in the archaeology, geography, and history of Palestine during the biblical periods, was affiliated with and funded by numerous academic institutions in the United States and Canada. By 1939 Emanuel Labes was among the settlers at Kfar Vitkin, a moshav in Emek Hefer.[65] Lindheim, the second president of Hadassah, asked herself if she wanted to reside permanently in Palestine following the death of her husband, Norvin. As a result of her March 1929 visit, she decided to live temporarily in Jerusalem. She explained her strong attraction to Rabbi Stephen S. Wise: "I went to Palestine in March because I could not keep away, [and] I am going back in October for the same reason." Lindheim further elaborated: "Since I have made the big decision I have found my inner peace again. I can no longer be cut off from the source of my life's meaning." She planned a year's experiment for herself and her children. She hoped that after that period, she would find her personal answer. In 1933 Lindheim settled permanently in Palestine on Kibbutz Mishmar Haemek, having been unanimously accepted as a member of the kibbutz. Going by her adopted Hebrew name Rama, she became a well-known figure, participating in many aspects of kibbutz life.[66]

A different push factor that influenced the decision to immigrate to Palestine was the well-being of children—both born and unborn. Many parents were willing to forego their own needs in order to make a better life for their offspring. In the Antonovsky and Katz survey, only 1 percent of respondents cited this as a significant factor, but it seems unlikely that this figure expresses the actual situation.[67] City life was seen by many Jews as detrimental to the growth of children, and a rural setting was a viable alternative. "In America, my children didn't thrive. They were for ever bending over books: here [in Palestine] they live in the open air and run about in the sunshine," explained an American at Merchavia.[68]

Moreover, if the parents had failed in America, Palestine was the place where a new generation could be raised with greater chance of success. Palestine had already begun to produce a "new type of man," a rejuvenation of the individual. Aaron David Gordon vividly expressed this process of reviving both the Jewish nation and the individuals involved in the process. In a prophetic tone he wrote:

CHAPTER 3

> Your sons and daughters will come to seek the interpretation of their dream in the land of their fathers. They will seek it with all the powers of their hands, with all the strength of their hearts. They will dig it out of hidden places; they will carry on every kind of work in the field and in the vineyard in seeking for it. They will renew the earth and their lives in their search. It will happen that as they search and work, they will grow and wax strong until in the end they will become great, greater than the mountain peaks on the face of the earth; they will see what no man saw before them, and they will become mighty on the earth.[69]

In addition, the image of the "sabra" (native-born Palestinian Jew) had already started to permeate the American Jewish consciousness. It was hoped that American youth would be invigorated with the spirit of the sabra.

THE SPATIAL DISTRIBUTION OF POTENTIAL IMMIGRANTS

An additional tack for understanding motivation for immigration may be taken by looking at the spatial distribution of potential immigrants. Such factors as distance from urban centers, the quality of the local society, and the availability of services are closely correlated to the different locations where potential American Jewish immigrants resided. Obviously, the largest number of immigrants—actual and potential—came from the American northeast. The largest concentration of Jews in the country lived in this region. However, other areas had higher per capita rates of actual and potential immigrants. And those who considered emigrating from America were not equally distributed throughout the country. Although sources of information are limited, and while no exact data is available regarding the place of residence before immigration of all individuals throughout the period of this study, certain trends can be determined. For example, the statistical report of applicants for immigration to Palestine from America for 1919 and the first five months of 1920 has been summarized and translated graphically.

Another means of ascertaining the spatial distribution of those who intended to emigrate to Palestine is examining the records of land companies—specifically, the American Zion Commonwealth and Migdal. These were not the only companies engaged in the sale of land, but they were the largest. Furthermore, their sales, unlike those of small *ahuza* companies, were not limited to a certain locale, city, or region, but were found throughout the United States. Certain limitations exist in the use of this data, however. The marketing of the product—land in Palestine—was not conducted with equal efficiently in all regions. The charisma and credibility of the sales representatives often influenced purchasers' decisions, and this is reflected in actual sales. In addition, the companies decided to focus their attention on certain regions, possibly those with the greatest potential. But both these companies advertised widely—the American Zion Commonwealth in the

Map 1a. U.S. and Canadian applicants for immigration to Palestine, 1919–20

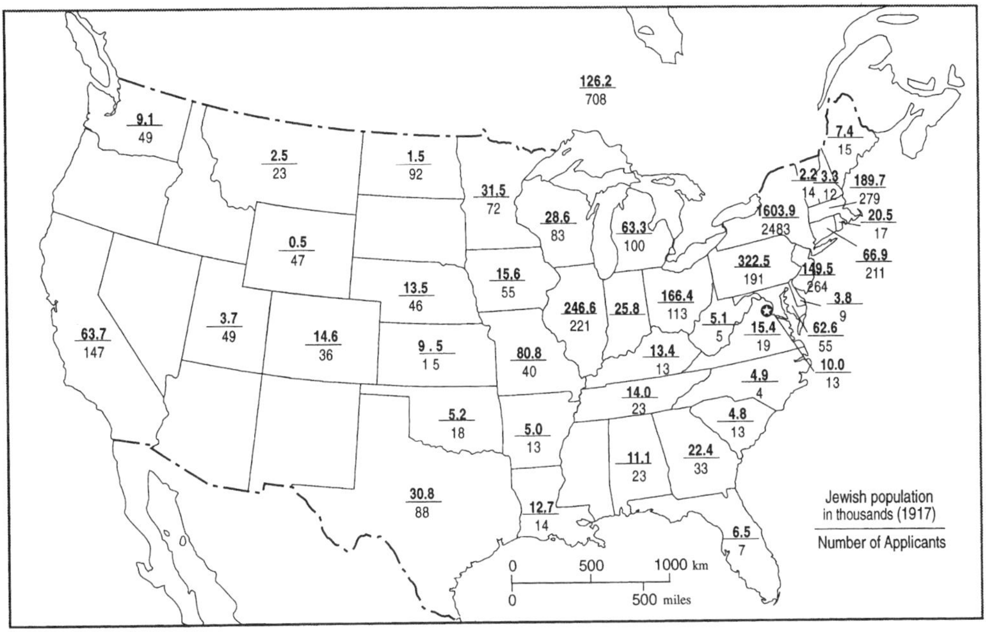

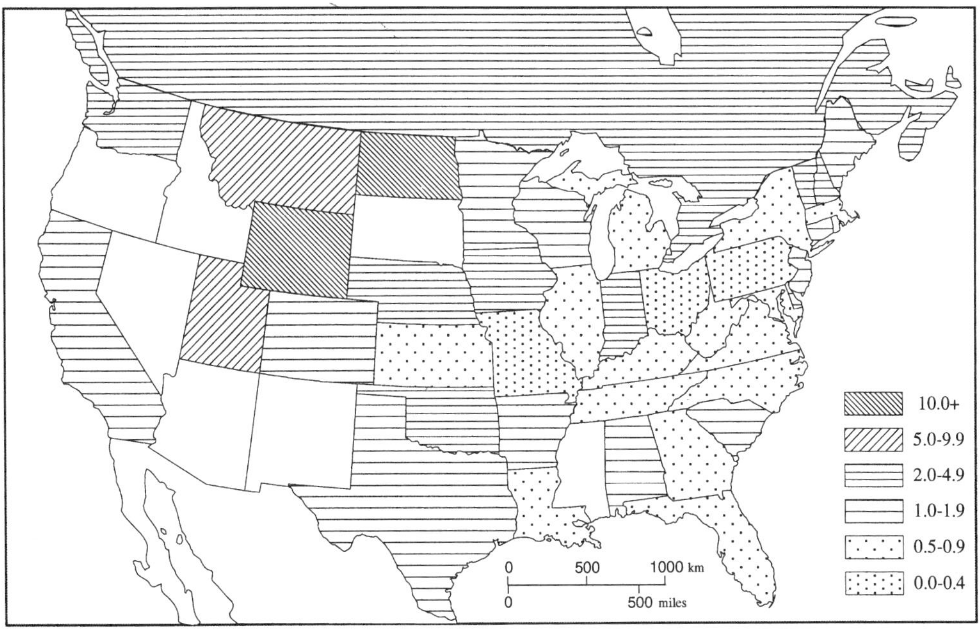

Map 1b. Ratio of U.S. and Canadian applicants relative to the total Jewish population, 1919–20

organs of the Zionist Organization of America, and Migdal in many local and national Jewish newspapers.[70] Together these companies had the largest number of purchasers, and thus their records provide some insight into the spatial distribution of those who acted in a practical manner, purchasing land that they hoped to eventually settle. A summary of this data has likewise been rendered graphically.

Among the 1919 applicants, a disproportionate per capita distribution of applicants *outside* the larger centers of Jewish population is noticeable. In states where the absolute numbers were the greatest—New York, Pennsylvania, Illinois, Massachusetts, Ohio, and Missouri—the ratio of applicants to the Jewish population was low. The southeastern states had not only a low ratio of applicants but a paltry absolute number. On the other hand, almost all the states to the west of the Mississippi River had a high ratio of applicants—with Wyoming, North Dakota, Utah, and Montana in the lead—though in absolute terms their numbers were quite low.

With regard to actual land purchasers there is a certain parallel with the figures for applicants. In states like Illinois, New Jersey, Massachusetts, New York, and Pennsylvania, the ratio of purchasers was lower than that of their proportion of the country's Jewish population. Similarly, in the periphery—the southern states of Alabama, Florida, Louisiana, and South Carolina—the ratio was very low.

There are certain discrepancies in the two sets of figures, and explanations can be found for some of these. Georgia, for example, with a low number of land purchasers, had a separate land purchasing group, known as Nahalat Atlanta; although this company had been founded under the auspices of the American Zion Commonwealth, their sales were not listed among those of the American Zion Commonwealth. In other states, *ahuza* companies continued to exist or were still being created during the period of this study. In New York, a large number of potential purchasers had joined the New York Achooza Aleph; this effectively lowered the proportion of New York land purchases from the American Zion Commonwealth and Migdal. However, the failure of pre–World War I *ahuza* companies tended to deter the purchase of land by people living in the states where they had been founded. This phenomenon is most notable in Missouri and Illinois, where, after the war, many reports reached local communities that described the negligence and eventual collapse of the Hoachoozo of St. Louis undertaking at Poria and the Chicago colony of Sarona.

In a further attempt to explain the distribution, we can note that in sparsely settled areas, particularly west of the Mississippi, it was difficult to sustain a Jewish lifestyle in the small towns and rural environment characteristic of these areas. Moreover, a significant proportion of the Jewish population residing in these regions was employed in agriculture and living in isolated settings.

Map 2a. Land purchases from the American Zion Commonwealth and the Migdal Company, 1927–31

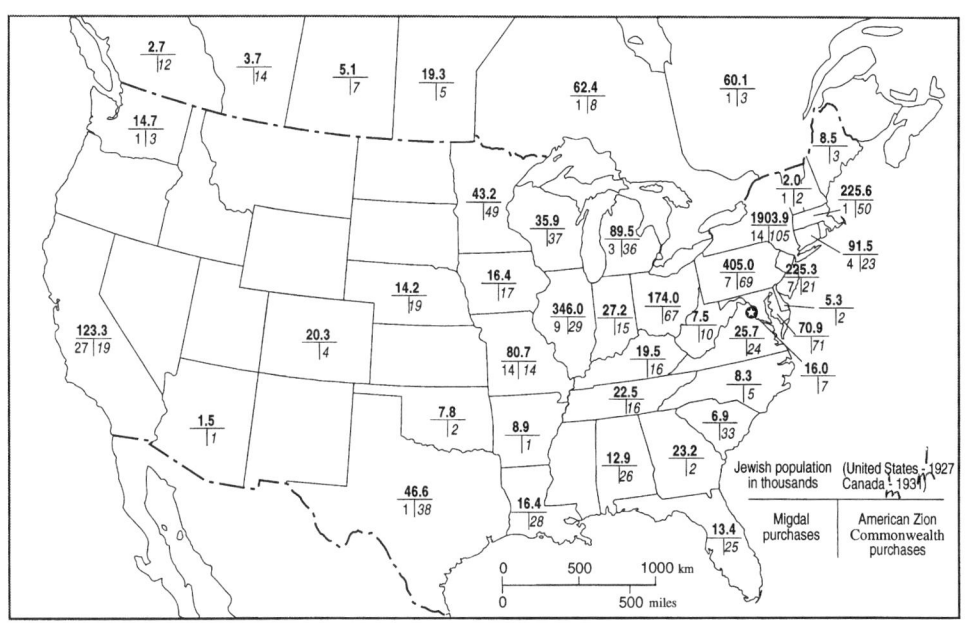

Map 2b. Ratio of land purchasers to the Jewish population, 1927–31

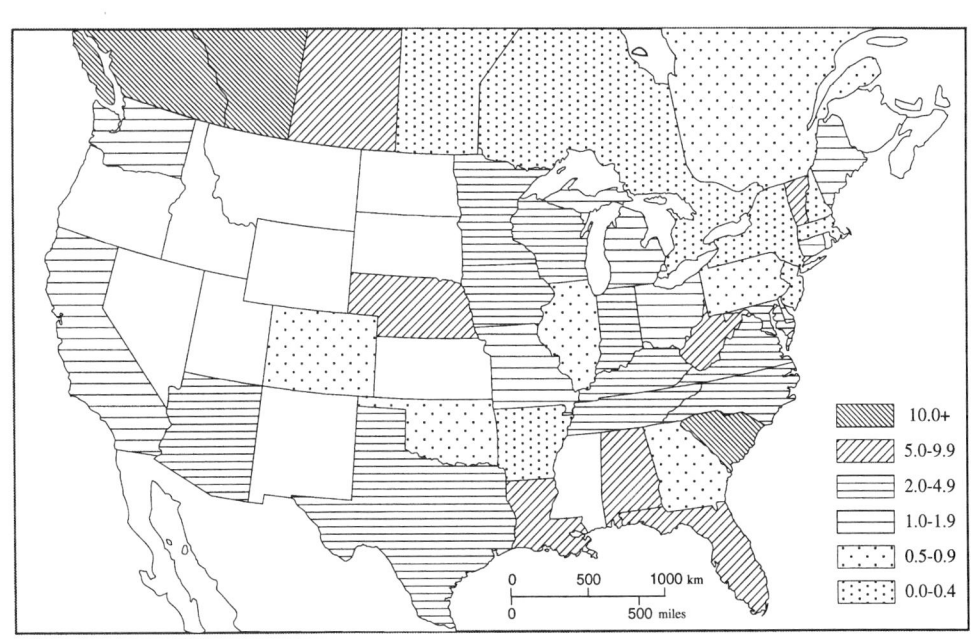

As explained by Gabriel Davidson in his survey of American Jewish farmers, the natural tendency of Jews was to settle in or near places that already had Jewish farmers because it was easier to maintain ties with relatives and friends and to have a social life.[71] Furthermore, a relatively large community was needed in order to establish and sustain essential community services—a synagogue, *mikveh* (ritual bath), school, and *shochet* (ritual slaughterer).[72] Without these services, the Jewish population was in danger of assimilation. Therefore the three choices open to Jewish farmers and their families were: (1) remain in the rural environment and possibly undergo a process of assimilation; (2) abandon agricultural endeavors and relocate to a larger community that could support the necessary services; or (3) move to Palestine, where there was an agrarian milieu that would sustain basic Jewish services.

In summarizing the Jewish Agricultural Society's 1934 study, Davidson explained that the "driving force" for American Jewish farmers "was the longing to exchange the restraints and inhibitions of the city for the peace and freedom of the country."[73] If this was indeed true, most Jewish farmers would elect the first or third choices listed here. Thus it can be concluded that American Jews residing on the periphery, outside the urban centers of the northeastern United States, had a greater tendency to immigrate, or that at least they considered this option more seriously than did their counterparts in the American industrial heartland.

In summary, American Jews found various reasons for immigrating to Palestine. These can be categorized into four basic kinds of motivation: *economic, social, geographic,* and *ideological.* It should be emphasized that in most cases, a single factor by itself was insufficient to generate immigration, but a combination of ideological motivation with one or more of the other three reasons was. *Ideological* reasons—Zionism, a "Zionist calling," Judaism, return to the soil, and the pioneer spirit—were motivations that facilitated the selection of Palestine as the destination for migration. The strength of this motivation alone could not move people to migrate, although certain individuals professed this as the key factor in their migration. Other factors considered when making a change in permanent residence included: *geographic*—peripheral location and alienation due to distance from concentrations of Jewish life; *social*—antisemitism, fear of assimilation, personal dissatisfaction, and unhappiness with American society in general; and *economic*—the Great Depression and the lack of available jobs in certain professions. Solutions to some of these problems might be found in America. For example, alienation could be alleviated through migration to areas of higher Jewish concentration. Antisemitism could be faced and combated within the framework of American society. In other instances, however, the entire American population was affected, as in the Great Depression, thus mitigating the weight of this pull factor on individual American Jews.

In order to quantify the strength of these motivations, it would be necessary to establish the scale of each factor or the parameters of the affected population. For example, how many American Jews were actually imbued with ideological motivation that would lead to emigration? If membership in Zionist organizations and groups is used as a criterion, this would expand the pool of potential immigrants to approximately 170,000 families in the United States.[74] However, not all the members of Zionist groups and organizations were affected by other forms of migrational motivation; they didn't feel alienated, or experience antisemitism or economic hardship, for example. Furthermore, not all of them regarded Zionism as a reason to migrate; many viewed it either as a commitment to the up-building of Palestine or as a social movement with which they could identify. With the other three factors any attempt to estimate the extent of the phenomena or its effect numerically is virtually impossible.

Moreover, taking into account the lack of support for migration to Palestine that existed within American Jewish society in general, it is not surprising that American immigration to Palestine was limited in its volume. The actual American Jewish immigration to Palestine, as such, expresses the determination of a select few, imbued with a certain ideology, their situation aggravated by one or more motivating migrational factors, and a willingness to resist the pressures of greater Jewish society. And once the decision was made to immigrate, the realities of immigration ordinances, the amount of capital on hand, and other restrictions might very well prevent an actual migration to Palestine.

4

The Screening Process: Immigration Policies and Regulations

> A delegation of about a hundred spirited young Zionists had bid Miriam a lusty farewell in New York. Miriam was only twenty-three years old but she went forth with the honest conviction that life must be lived in Palestine. Her baggage was slight, her pocketbook thin. Somewhere in her belongings was a labour certificate entitling her to live permanently in Palestine. She had waited long for this certificate. It was the envy of many of her friends who had come to bid her good-bye.
>
> Dorothy Ruth Kahn, *Spring Up, O Well*

Miriam was one of the lucky ones. During the 1930s, American Jewish immigration to Palestine was shaped not only by an individual's desire to immigrate but also by policies developed by the administration of Palestine and the translation of these policies into immigration ordinances. Not everyone who wanted to relocate to Palestine could do so legally. Playing an important role in determining who would be successful were various Zionist boards: the Zionist Executive in London; the Zionist administration in Palestine (Zionist Commission for Palestine 1918–21, Palestine Zionist Executive 1921–29, the Jewish Agency for Palestine 1929 onward); and the national Zionist organization in the United States. These administrative bodies significantly influenced the number and selection of immigrants. This chapter describes the regulations that controlled immigration, incidents and events that affected it, the role of the Zionist organization in America in determining immigration policies and practices, and various facilitators in the process.

The first group of American Jews to immigrate to Palestine after World War I were soldiers of the Jewish Legion, some of whom were demobilized in Palestine. Although not officially registered as immigrants, they constituted the initial influx of American Jews to Palestine under British rule.[1] Under the General Routine Order of 16 January 1919, American Jewish Legionnaires who wanted to remain in Palestine were required to demonstrate sound financial standing or possess a written guarantee of employment. The British military government requisitioned a small number of specialists from the ranks of the Jewish Legion for needed services, and it also permitted the Zionist Commission for Palestine to commandeer a number of soldiers. The Labor Bureau of the Poale Zion also issued certificates guaranteeing that employment in Palestine would be found for these soldiers.[2]

Demobilization in Palestine presented many technical difficulties. American Jewish Legionnaire Samuel Levine's letter to the Zionist Commission outlined his problems in obtaining the needed guarantees to remain in Palestine and provides insight into the general situation:

> That I may be forced to leave this country is hardly what I ever expected. . . . I have sacrificed everything for the sake of remaining in Palestine and be[ing] settled here. I have also lately arranged to have my money brought over here and I presume that the checks must be on the way. I did not know until last week that I will have to show the Government a written guarantee for employment. I might have been able to procure such guarantee had I known it for some time. At present we can not leave the camp and I can not go out to see anybody of the friends I have made while being here. Thus I am compelled to apply to you and beg you to see what you can do for me. I should be able to stop here if local demobilization will be allowed.[3]

Some of the former Legionnaires, unable to find employment in Palestine, had no choice but to return to America.

Nonetheless, with the end of the war, a rush of applicants for immigration to Palestine reached the Zionist Organization of America: 5,803 up to 9 December 1919, with an additional 198 through 31 May 1920. However, the Zionist Organization of America had no clear understanding of how to process these applications.[4] With Palestine still under British military administration, it was unclear what procedure American Jews should follow in order to receive permission to immigrate there. Despite the fact that no formal permission had been granted for immigration to Palestine, a number of Americans had already gone there, anyway.

Beginning in September 1919, immigrants from other countries began to enter Palestine. During the last quarter of that year, 806 Jews of Russian citizenship entered Palestine. From January through May 1920, 1,213 Jewish immigrants were reported to have been admitted.[5] Not until the last month of the British military administration of Palestine was immigration controlled by a military permits system. The system was enacted as a response to Arab protests against Jewish immigration and the Arab riots in Jerusalem in April 1920. Under the Military Regulations Governing Admission of Civilians into Palestine of 31 May 1920, a total of 434 individuals entered Palestine in June that year.[6] Official records do not list any Americans.

Following the establishment of the Civil administration in Palestine on 1 July 1920, immigration continued. The administration worked toward developing an immigration policy and drafting the necessary regulations, and consulted the Zionist Commission about how the policy might be formulated. On 26 August 1920, the first Immigration Ordinance was enacted, and a quota of 16,500 immigrant Jews was fixed for the first year. This ordinance became effective on the first of September.

The granting of visas to Palestine was carried out by British consulates worldwide. Instructions in this matter distinguished two categories—A (Zionists) and B (persons other than Zionists). Regarding the former, the consuls were to be informed, either by the Foreign Office or through His Majesty's local representative, as to the total number and class of Zionists to whom visas for Palestine might be granted during the period in question. Visas were to be given to those recommended by local Zionist offices, unless the individual was deemed definitely undesirable. A single visa included family members—wife, children, and persons wholly dependent upon the immigrant. The second group, persons other than Zionists, included anyone who could satisfy the consul that he or she was self-supporting or could produce evidence that he could obtain employment in Palestine. It also comprised persons of religious occupation, including Jews who came to Palestine for religious reasons and could satisfy the consul as to their means of maintenance.[7] The administrative instructions also specified that the Zionist Organization of America would be the body that recommended Zionists in the United States for immigration to Palestine.

The expected large influx of immigrants was weakened by external events. In late 1920 the Zionist Commission found itself hard-pressed financially and thus unable either to provide employment for new immigrants or secure financial support for them. Leonard Stein of the Zionist Executive met with the Passport Control Department to request that the immigration schedule be reduced. The November circular of the Zionist Executive revealed that it had reached an accord with the Foreign Office to cut back the number of certificates from 16,500 to 1,000 and to agree that only bachelors would be accepted as immigrants.[8]

The Zionist Executive in London encouraged the immigration of English-speaking laborers, although no guarantee was given that those individuals would receive employment upon their arrival in Palestine. It emphasized that they "could be utilized as foremen in the organized cooperative groups and thus facilitate the relations with the Government engineers and other authorities. . . . Furthermore, the skilled labourers . . . could much easier find employment with various Government Departments, such as the Railways, Public Works Department, Public Health Department and Military Authorities, if they could receive their instructions in English."[9]

The United States was omitted from the list of countries to which the Zionist Executive had allocated the first 1,000 certificates for immigrants without means. It explained that until the commencement of large-scale works in Palestine that would facilitate the economic absorption of new immigrants, only a few individuals without means—if any at all—should be admitted. Of course, those who possessed sufficient capital to be self-supporting could continue to apply for immigration to Palestine. From July 1920 until April 1921, 10,652 Jews immigrated to Palestine, the majority of whom—9,191 in number—were under Zionist Commission guarantee.[10]

On 1 May 1921, five days of rioting broke out in Palestine. The Jewish settlements of Jaffa, Petah Tikvah, Hadera, Rehovot, and Gadera were attacked by local Arabs. Forty-seven Jews were killed and 116 were wounded in the riots. Jewish immigration came to a standstill. Arab boatmen at Jaffa, who enjoyed a monopoly on this vocation, refused to transport new arrivals from anchored ships to the port. On 6 May the district governor of Ramle announced the administration's intention of halting Jewish immigration altogether in the near future; an official government announcement to this effect was issued on 14 May.

As a result of the riots, the Palestinian administration deemed it necessary to formulate a new policy. On 1 August 1921, new regulations governing the admission of immigrants into Palestine were implemented. The regulations stipulated that:

> Immigrants into Palestine are divided into five under-mentioned categories:
> "B" (1) Persons of independent means who intend to take up permanent residence in Palestine.
> "C" (2) Members of professions who intend to follow their calling.
> "D" (3) Wives, children and other persons wholly dependent on residents of Palestine.
> "E" (4) Persons who have a definite prospect of employment with specific employers or enterprises.
> "F" (5) Persons of religious occupations, including the class of Jews who have come to Palestine in recent years from religious motives and who can show that they have means of maintenance here.[11]

One effect of these changes was to curtail the power of the Zionist organization. It was required to certify immigrants in category E, and all decisions regarding persons in categories C, D, and E had to be referred to the Department of Immigration and Travel in Jerusalem.[12]

In 1922 the Palestine Zionist Executive reached an agreement with the Department of Immigration and Travel to allow 450 persons with skilled workmen permits to be admitted to Palestine. Twenty were allocated to the United States, with ten for bricklayers, masons, and stone dressers; five for locksmiths, blacksmiths, and mechanics; and five for plumbers. However, it appears that skilled American workmen did not arrive. In January 1923, Frederick Kisch reported to the Controller of Labor in Jerusalem that twenty permits for skilled workmen from the United States had not been utilized.[13]

Under the terms of the Churchill White Paper, a statement of British policy in Palestine issued on 3 June 1922, immigration could not exceed the current economic capacity of the country to absorb new arrivals. Further, a committee of the elected members of the Legislative Council would confer with the Administration of Palestine on matters relating to the regulation of immigration. Any difference of opinion between the two bodies would be referred to His Majesty's government in London.[14]

Over the following three years, the Colonial Office, the high commissioner, and the Palestine Zionist Executive ironed out the terms of the Immigration Ordinance of 1925. This ordinance redefined the previously established categories, basically dividing prospective immigrants into capitalists (persons of independent means), laborers, and dependents.

> A.—(i) Persons in possession of £E1,000 and upwards, and their families.
> A.—(ii) Professional men in possession of £E500 and upwards.
> A.—(iii) Skilled artisans in possession of £E250 and upwards.
> A.—(iv) Persons enjoying an assured income of £E4 per month.
> B.—(i) Orphans destined for institutions in Palestine.
> B.—(ii) Men and women of religious occupation, whose maintenance is assured, and their families.
> B.—(iii) Students whose maintenance is assured.
> C.—Working men and women and their families.
> D.—Dependant relatives of residents in Palestine, who are in a position to maintain them.[15]

The ordinance excluded individuals considered undesirable: the mentally ill, persons with mental retardation, prostitutes, anyone likely to become a pauper or a public charge, or anyone who had been convicted in any country of murder or an offense for which a sentence of imprisonment had been passed. It further left the high commissioner with the prerogative to exclude those of whom he had received official information as to their unsuitability—those likely to be dangerous to peace and good order. Certain medical conditions were also justification for non-admittance, including epilepsy, leprosy, syphilis, active tuberculosis, or other diseases deemed by the government medical officer to be a threat to public health. Furthermore, those granted visas to Palestine could be turned back at the discretion of the immigration officer at the point of entry into Palestine or by the chief immigration officer.[16]

The most important change brought about by the new ordinance was the establishment of the semiannual labor schedule. These schedules were prepared by the chief immigration officer, after considering any proposals made by the Palestine Zionist Executive, and with the final approval of the high commissioner. Following publication of the labor schedule, certificates were distributed to those with assured employment in Palestine and to the Palestine Zionist Executive for distribution among Zionist organizations outside Palestine. The number of certificates fluctuated according to the real or perceived economic situation in Palestine—from a high of 9,200 for April to September 1925, to a low of none at all for the period of October 1927 to September 1928. Moreover, the distribution of certificates varied among countries according to the perceived needs of the Zionist organization, which channeled labor certificates at its discretion to its countries of choice. The greatest number of certificates was allotted to Jews in Poland. For the period of May 1925 to December 1942, the United States had one of the lowest percentage of immigrants from any country receiving labor certificates—13 percent.[17]

During this period, correspondence was carried out between the Immigration Department of the Palestine Zionist Executive and the Zionist organizations of the United States. Once a certain number of labor schedule (*halutz*) certificates had been allocated, the local Zionist organizations selected their candidates from larger lists of applicants. Each and every applicant was scrutinized as to his/her fitness, from every point of view, for settling in Palestine. Almost every candidate was highly recommended by leaders of various Zionist parties as people of fine character and high morals. However, in some instances the candidates were not approved by Jerusalem.[18]

After another series of riots, in 1929, the Shaw Commission recommended that temporary restrictions be placed on immigration into Palestine, and such restrictions were issued. In 1932 a new Immigration Ordinance was enacted. While it was similar to previous ones, it widened the arbitrary powers of the director of immigration by placing further conditions on certain categories. The changes included: A.—(ii) members of liberal professions who possessed £P500 would be allowed entry if the director was satisfied that additional members of that profession were necessary in Palestine; A.—(iii) skilled tradesmen or craftsmen possessing £P250 were permitted entry if the director of immigration was satisfied that the economic capacity of the country allowed it. This new ordinance also introduced a fifth subsection: A.—(v) any person possessing £P500 was allowed entry if the director was satisfied that his settlement would not lead to undue competition. It also included as qualified persons in category C those who had a definite prospect of employment in Palestine.[19]

This ordinance remained in force until 1939, when, as a result of Arab pressure and other considerations, the British government redefined its immigration policy once again. The government promulgated the 1939 White Paper, which fixed Jewish immigration at 10,000 per annum for the

TABLE 12
Distribution of immigration according to categories for selected countries of origin, May 1925–December 1942

Country	Capitalists Percent	Students Percent	Labor Percent	Dependents Percent	Total
England	42	10	30	18	1,402
Germany and Austria	35	12	37	16	49,592
Lithuania	19	8	53	20	8,275
Poland	16	5	52	27	101,962
U.S.S.R.	25	0	45	30	9,917
Rumania	12	6	62	20	15,032
United States	77	0	13	10	5,861
Greece	9	0	81	10	5,785
Yemen	2	0	91	7	8,437

Source: David Gurevich, Aaron Gertz, and Roberto Bachi, *The Jewish Population of Palestine: Immigration, Demographic Structure and Natural Growth* (in Hebrew) (Jerusalem: Jewish Agency for Palestine, 1944), 64.

following five years, with an additional 25,000 refugees to be admitted at the high commissioner's discretion. This new policy, together with the outbreak of World War II, brought American Jewish immigration to a virtual halt.

In the period leading up to 1939, potential immigrants found ways to circumvent official immigration policies. Tourist visas frequently served as an important mechanism for individuals who had been unable to obtain immigration visas under the existing ordinances. British authorities attempted to prevent the permanent settlement in Palestine of individuals who entered the country under the guise of being tourists. However, these attempts were hindered by a number of official and unofficial policies. Under Article 13 of the Mandate, the British were to guarantee freedom of access to the holy sites; as such, they could not deny entry to a foreigner who claimed that he intended to tour the country for religious reasons. Indeed, British authorities were interested in developing the Palestinian economy through an increased flow of tourists. Moreover, the government wanted to expand its revenues through various taxes levied directly on tourists and through indirect taxes derived from tourists' expenditures in Palestine.[20]

The normal flow of tourists to Palestine had been halted due to World War I. In November 1919 the military government declared that it had no objection to a renewed flow, so long as the numbers were small enough to be properly supervised, and in January 1920, British authorities once again allowed tourists to enter Palestine. They issued tourist visas for periods of up to three months and required tourists to provide proof that they had obtained return passage. But tourists who were intent on remaining in Palestine often found work and housing during their visit, and then applied to change their status to immigrant, claiming that they had the means to support themselves. Between 1923–39 the government of Palestine authorized 1,661 American citizens who had originally entered the country as tourists to permanently settle in Palestine.[21]

During the 1930s, British authorities attempted to prevent tourists from remaining in Palestine. Their strategy was three-pronged. At the points of entry into Palestine, immigration officers carefully screened tourists, warned them that they would be expelled if they remained longer than permitted, and even turned away individuals with visas whom the authorities suspected of wanting to remain indefinitely in Palestine. They also required tourists not traveling first-class to leave a £P60 deposit and show a return ticket. The high commissioner also threatened to subtract the number of tourists authorized to settle in Palestine from the semiannual immigration schedule, in the hope that Jewish institutions would cease their assistance to these tourists. The authorities' third measure was to expel tourists who had overstayed their three-month visas. To this end, the Palestine police conducted wide-scale searches, demanding that passengers on trains and buses present documentation. The police often followed individuals suspected of remaining in Palestine on an expired visa, hoping to collect sufficient evidence to warrant their expulsion. In mid-1934 the Jewish Agency Executive called for a stop to this form of illegal immigration because, they said, it threatened their activities. After this, there was a distinct fall in the rate of American Jewish tourists authorized to settle in Palestine. For 1923–34 the number of illegal tourists averaged 112.8 per annum, but that number dropped to 37.4 for 1935–39.[22]

The Palestine Zionist Executive, and later the Jewish Agency, had significant discretionary powers with respect to immigration practices. Under relevant sections of various immigration ordinances, they were allowed to determine which Jews without means would be permitted entry into Palestine. The number of certificates allotted to each country was determined by the Palestine Zionist Executive. Each country was then left with the decision of how to distribute the certificates to the various organizations that were vying for them. In the United States, the Palestine Service and Information Bureau had this responsibility. The demand for certificates often exceeded the supply, and requests for additional certificates generally fell on deaf ears. The Palestine Zionist Executive was principally concerned with Eastern and Central European Jewry and their plight. The Palestine Information and Service Bureau attempted to find some alternative procedure to assist applicants to Palestine, for the number of applicants usually exceeded official opportunities. For example, during the last four months of 1930, 120 young American men and women applied for *halutz* certificates, of which only sixty were available. The bureau reclassified the remaining applicants, either as tourists who could eventually change their status and settle permanently, or as professional men—under section A.—(iii) of the 1925 Immigration Ordinances—with sufficient capital as required by law. The following year the gap between supply and demand for certificates increased greatly: fifty candidates were selected from a "big list of several hundred applicants."[23]

The actual distribution of the *halutz* certificates received by various local groups depended on the influence of each organization. In the United States a committee consisting of representatives of Poale Zion-Zeire Zion, Hechalutz-Hashomer Hatzair, Zionist Organization of America, and the Mizrachi-Hapoel Hamizrachi voted on the allocation. For example, the thirteen certificates granted for the period of March to October 1932 were distributed as follows: seven to Hashomer Hatzair, four to Hechalutz, one to Mizrachi, and one to the Cleveland Zionist district.[24]

As the situation deteriorated for German Jewry in the 1930s, fewer American Zionists received certificates. This was a blow to the prestige of the Zionist Organization of America and hindered the expansion of the Zionist youth movement in the United States.

> [O]n the strength of the large number of applications submitted by all parties, the Praesidium recently dispatched a cable to the Jewish Agency, signed by all parties, urging the allotment of at least 150 Certificates, including 50 for Miktzoim [skilled trades and craftsmen]. It is to be profoundly regretted that the Agency disregarded this request, granting such a small number unprecedented in the annals of American Aliyah. This not only is a severe blow to the hopes of American Chalutzim but also a humiliation, especially at a time when all parties in America are making every effort to develop the Chalutz movement, and at a time when Dr. [Enzo] Sereni, one of the foremost leaders of Hechalutz, is himself taking a leading part in this country on behalf of the movement.[25]

Although, as outlined above, the process of obtaining permission to immigrate and settle permanently in Palestine was conducted through the Immigration Office, the Palestine Zionist Executive, and later the Jewish Agency for Palestine, in certain instances the American consulate interceded on behalf of its citizens. On other occasions, companies or organizations carried out much of the paper work for the immigrant and helped him circumvent the bureaucracy. Sometimes organizations exercised their clout in an attempt to expedite the process of immigration. For example, the American Mizrachi turned to the Inter Allied Mizrachi Bureau in London, which in turn approached the Zionist Bureau in London, in an attempt to obtain permits for fifteen American Mizrachi members. The organization's leader, Rabbi Meir Berlin [Bar-Ilan], made it clear that this action would "greatly increase the prestige of Mizrachi." However, these permits, despite their importance to the American Mizrachi, were not granted.[26]

The Palestine Immigration Bureau was established in New York in order to expedite the process of travel and immigration to Palestine. The bureau served as a facilitator between the applicants and the British consulate at all stages of the process—completing application forms, developing strategies for the simplest way to acquire visas, advising how to arrange for bonds, intervening in more difficult cases, and receiving and distributing permits. Often the bureau would provide letters of introduction for American immigrants to potential connections in Palestine. Their final task was to see off the immigrants bound for Palestine and publicize a notice of their immigration in the American Jewish press.[27]

Although the American Zion Commonwealth never believed that all its land certificate holders would eventually settle in Palestine, it was inclined to provide assistance in obtaining visas for immigration to American members of their organization and their European relatives. American Zion Commonwealth involvement in this process began in late 1924, the year in which the United States tightened immigration regulations and in which the quota system was introduced. The commonwealth believed that providing assistance to immigrants would increase the company's sales. One possible solution to immigration restrictions was to have Americans settle their Eastern European relatives on American Zion Commonwealth land in Palestine, thus guaranteeing the entry of their relatives into Palestine at some later date. Since the American Zion Commonwealth was already entangled in the business of obtaining visas for relatives, there was no reason why it should not do the same for its American members.

The commonwealth reached an informal accord with immigration authorities. Charles Passman, director of the American Zion Commonwealth's Jerusalem office, explained that he had been "successful in making arrangements with the government officials here [in Jerusalem] that an AMZIC certificate should be considered the same as cash in connection with gaining admission into Palestine."[28] This meant that the American Zion Commonwealth Jerusalem office could issue letters certifying that money had been paid on account for land purchased in Palestine. These letters would be taken into consideration by the immigration authorities in calculating the £E500 (Egyptian pounds) needed in order to receive a capitalist visa. No definite agreement was made regarding the proportion of the needed £E500 the American Zion Commonwealth letter could be used for. Passman believed that an additional £E100 to £E150 in cash should be in the immigrant's possession when he arrived in Palestine. This would probably expedite the process of Americans receiving visas. Rather than applying through

STRICTLY PRIVATE AND CONFIDENTIAL

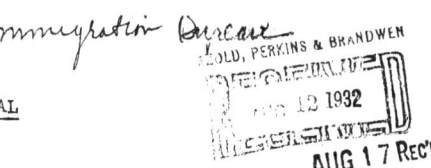

REGISTER OF THE PALESTINE IMMIGRATION BUREAU

FOR TWO MONTHS: JUNE 1 UNTIL AUGUST 1, 1932.

During the past two months, from June 1st until August 1st, 1932, the Palestine Bureau has acted upon the following applications for permits to settle in Palestine:

JUNE

	Name	Address	Capital
1.	N. L.	Roxbury, Mass.	$ 15,000.00
2.	Rabbi A. L.	New Bedford, Mass.	13,000.00
3.	Mrs. F. S.	Newark, N. J.	7,500.00
4.	S. B.	New York City	6,000.00
5.	S. S., wife & 2 Children	Brooklyn, N. Y.	6,500.00
6.	I. J. B.	New York City	5,500.00
7.	B. C.	New York City	5,000.00
8.	J. B.	Lakewood, N. J.	5,000.00
9.	B. W. & wife	Brooklyn, N. Y.	4,600.00
10.	D. N., wife & child	Elizabeth, N. J.	5,000.00
11.	L. W. & wife	Brooklyn, N. Y.	4,700.00
12.	I. G. & wife	Brooklyn, N. Y.	4,600.00
13.	A. N., wife & 6 Children	Bronx, N. Y.	4,000.00
14.	A. G.	Brooklyn, N. Y.	4,100.00
15.	Mrs. L. R.	Cleveland, Ohio	4,000.00
16.	M. K.	Detroit, Mich.	4,000.00
17.	G. P., wife & child	Milwaukee, Wisc.	4,000.00
18.	R. B. & child	Bronx, N. Y.	4,000.00
19.	R. A. & wife	New York City	4,105.00
20.	M. F.	New York City	4,300.00
21.	D. S. & wife	Detroit, Mich.	3,800.00
22.	M. N.	New York City	4,700.00
23.	B. R.	Rockaway, N. Y.	3,500.00
24.	M. L. & wife	New York City	4,300.00
25.	B. M.	Jersey City, N. J.	4,000.00
26.	F. W.	Brooklyn, N. Y.	4,100.00
27.	J. L.	New York City	4,000.00
28.	Miss G. F.	Long Beach, L. I.	4,000.00
29.	S. K.	New York City	4,000.00
30.	Mrs. S. D. & 2 Children	Trenton, N. J.	4,000.00

Fig. 15. Page 1 of the Register of the Palestine Immigration Bureau (New York) 1 June to 1 August 1932. (CZA S17/162)

the Palestine Bureau in New York, which forwarded the application to the British consulate in that city which relayed it to the immigration officer in Jerusalem, a faster and more direct way was found. The American Zion Commonwealth's Jerusalem office negotiated directly with the immigration officer, thus reducing expenses and decreasing the anxiety experienced by the immigrants, who frequently had to endure extended periods of waiting for answers to visa applications made through normal channels. Approximately fifty American families received such assistance from the American Zion Commonwealth.[29]

But by early 1926, the American Zion Commonwealth was no longer able to continue its role as a facilitator in procuring visas—either for its members in the United States or for their Eastern European relatives—since the Mandatory government now wanted to curtail immigration altogether. This clampdown first found expression in the more stringent 1925 Immigration Ordinance, and later with the cancellation of the unwritten accord the American Zion Commonwealth had reached with British authorities. The Immigration Department ruled that a visa could only be issued if land was actually registered in the name of the immigrant; a letter from the American Zion Commonwealth attesting to this was no longer regarded as sufficient. This decreased the role of the organization in the process of acquiring visas and made it quite difficult for certain of its members. Because of the company's financial crisis, and the complex and lengthy legal procedures governing the transfer of land, very few certificate holders were in actual possession of *kushans* (title) to their lands. Thus the capital invested in land could not be put toward the sum needed under immigration regulations. Nevertheless, the organization continued, whenever and wherever possible, to lend a hand to its American shareholders who were attempting to immigrate.[30]

In some instances, requests by the Zionist organization and its departments in Palestine to allow specific Americans to settle in Palestine received the support of British authorities. In 1919 the Zionist Commission for Palestine received permits for four Jewish Legionnaires from the United States to remain in Palestine. Their skills—physician, mechanic, bookkeeper, and journalist—were considered invaluable. In other cases, departments of the Palestine Zionist Executive, and later the Jewish Agency for Palestine, determined there was a need for individuals with specific skills generally unavailable in Palestine. Indeed, certain American enterprises established there had special labor needs. For example, I. Sacks and Sons, owners of the Meshi silk factory in Ramat Gan, applied to bring Morris Aaronovitch, an expert in silk manufacturing, to Palestine from the United States. Their request was forwarded to the Jewish Agency's Department of Commerce and Industry, which in turn approached the government of Palestine's Department of Immigration to obtain the required visas for this worker. Such forms of assistance were limited in scope, but they represent some of the alternative measures that could be taken to facilitate the entry of Americans into Palestine.[31]

Educational institutions also played an important role in facilitating immigration. Under the Immigration Ordinances, beginning in 1925 students accepted to the Hebrew University of Jerusalem could receive entrance visas to Palestine. The academic institution was obliged to guarantee that each potential student would have £P4 per month over a period of three years and had to attest that the student possessed an amount adequate for his or her maintenance. In addition, the university itself guaranteed a sum of £P15 that it would hold during the period in which the student was registered at the university. This was to assure the return of the student to his home should circumstances arise in which he or she would be deemed indigent or in need of charity. Thus the university bore a financial responsibility for the students whom it facilitated in receiving visas. For the academic year 1932–33, twenty-two of the thirty-one foreign students studying at the institution received student visas. Of the five American students in attendance, two received such Hebrew University–sponsored visas.[32]

The American consulate in Jerusalem also played a role in facilitating the immigration process. Until the signing of the Treaty of Versailles, the capitulation agreements with Turkey were technically still in force. Capitulations were commercial treaties concluded by Western powers, including the United States, with the Ottoman Empire. Under the terms of such agreements, the nationals of a foreign power were granted extraterritorial privileges. As such, Americans in the Ottoman Empire (which had included Palestine) were subject to the laws of the United States and were immune from Ottoman law.[33] Article 22 of the Covenant of the League of Nations in the Treaty of Versailles entrusted the Mandate for Palestine to His Britannic Majesty's government and thus allowed for the cancellation of the capitulation agreements under Article 8 of the Mandate. However, since the United States was not a member state of the League of Nations, it did not feel bound by the Mandate. So the American consulate continued to convene its consular court, claiming the right to the same conditions enjoyed previously under the Turkish regime. This practice continued even after publication of the 1922 Palestine Order-in-Council, in which Article 38 declared that, "The Civil Courts hereinafter described shall, subject to the provisions of this part of the Order, exercise jurisdiction in all matters and over all persons in Palestine."[34] On 3 December 1924, a convention was concluded between the United States and the British government with respect to the rights of the two governments and their nationals in Palestine; this agreement was based on the terms of the Mandate granted to Great Britain. The articles listed below related directly to American citizens.

Article 2, The United States and its nationals have and shall enjoy all the rights and benefits secured under the terms of the mandate to members of the League of Nations and their nationals, notwithstanding the fact that the United States is not a member of the League of Nations.

Article 3, Vested American property rights in the mandated territory shall be respected and in no way impaired. . . .

Article 5, Subject to the provisions of any local laws for the maintenance of public order and public morals, the nationals of the United States will be permitted freely to establish and maintain educational, philanthropic and religious institutions in the mandated territory, to receive voluntary applicants and to teach in the English language.[35]

With the exchange of ratification one year later—on 3 December 1925—the American consulate ceased to convene its consular court. The three articles cited above became the basis for any possible intervention of the consulate on behalf of its Jewish citizens. Henceforth there were only a few instances in which the consulate intervened on behalf of American citizens in order to help them obtain permission to reside or settle in Palestine. Unless there was some form of active discrimination against an American, there was no longer any legal or moral basis for the consulate to intervene.

One example of American consular intervention can be seen in the 1927 application for permanent residency by Dr. Olga Pickman Feinberg. She entered Palestine on a three-month visitor's visa but decided to stay on for a few years. Under the 1925 Immigration Ordinances it was necessary for her to have applied for residence status before she had arrived in Palestine. She had £P500 on deposit at the Anglo-Palestine Bank—the amount required for a capitalist visa. She was interested in doing charity work for the Hadassah organization and Ezrat Holim as well as assisting her uncle, Professor Boris Shatz, at the Bezalel School of Art and Crafts. The American consul at Jerusalem, Oscar Heizer, forwarded his recommendation to the chief immigration officer, stating, "It would appear to this Consulate that granting of a permanent permit of residence to Dr. Feinberg would be a benefit to Palestine, and in no way detrimental to the country, and this Consulate would be glad to see a permit granted to her, if an exception can be made in her case." The response was that Pickman would be authorized to settle in Palestine once she gave satisfactory guarantees regarding her employment for a year. Intervention by the consulate, however, was the exception, not the rule. And in the case of Olga Pickman, the consulate interceded merely with a recommendation.[36]

In other cases, the consulate did no more than report irregularities connected to the entry of American citizens into Palestine. For example, Consul Heizer wrote the U.S. State Department in 1927: "If the customs house official has doubts about the bona fide of the traveler he requires that a

CHAPTER 4

deposit of twenty pounds be made which will be forfeited to the Government in case the traveler does not leave the country. A case of this kind has just been brought to the notice of this Consulate by Mrs. Leah Visler who came on a traveler's visa instead of a visa for permanent residence."[37]

In another incident, Consul Heizer reported that the immigration authorities refused Mr. S. Gordon and his wife admittance into Palestine. They had arrived at Jaffa from New York on the SS *Sinaia* as first-class passengers with tourist visas. The *Palestine Bulletin* pointed out that they proved that they had a deposit of £P1,848 ($9,240) in Barclays Bank and £P200 ($1,000) in their possession—much more than the amount necessary to obtain a capitalist visa. According to the *Bulletin:* "The reason given for their non-admittance was that when Mr. Gordon was asked whether he intended to remain permanently in Palestine, he answered in the affirmative adding that he would apply for permanent residence in due course. The Immigration officer considered that he was guilty of giving wrong information and refused to allow him to land."[38] The American consulate did nothing in this matter.

In summary, American migration to Palestine was inhibited by a number of legal restrictions and bureaucratic decisions. The potential immigrant's moral character, health, and financial situation were all taken into account by the Mandatory government. Occasionally procedural irregularities that occurred in the application process would prevent the person from obtaining permission to settle in Palestine. Zionist organizations, worldwide and in the United States, were also involved in the screening process. Their role included issuing labor certificates, deciding the number to be issued to a certain country from the total allotted, and then selecting the appropriate candidates. Facilitators could speed the process, saving prospective immigrants time, money, and anxiety. Occasionally the recommendation of a facilitator would tilt the scale to benefit an immigrant. The legal and bureaucratic screening process significantly limited the number of American immigrants. Many were turned away, and others were delayed for such extended periods of time that they gave up their attempts to immigrate.

5

The Spatial Distribution of American *Olim*

> We landed at Jaffa Nov. 8 and as it was our plan to learn agriculture work we went to the workers union [Histadrut] and registered as workers, and asked them to send us to a [kibbutz]; they told us to call in a few days as it would take a number of days before they could give us an answer.
>
> In the meanwhile we looked up Mr. Bloominfeld mayor of Tel Aviv to whom we had a letter, who introduced us to Mr. Gauloop secretary of the Achdut HaAvoda. He promised to settle us in a kibbutz so he gave us a letter to the secretary of the Kibbutz Ain Harod. [W]e went there and they asked us to wait a few days till they would have a meeting to decide if we would be allowed to remain, after the meeting they told us that it would be impossible for us to remain as they had too many [comrades] at that particular time. They told us to go back to Tel Aviv and they would write a letter to [Merchavia] asking them if we would be taken in, and that they would write us a letter either yes, or no, as soon as they received word from [Merchavia]. We came back to Tel Aviv and started going day and night to Mr. Gauloop's home in the hope of getting a letter but, no letter came. One day we asked him why they did not send a letter, so he said, I'll tell you the truth boys, you're from America, and have plenty of money, so it dosent [*sic*] hurt if you go around a half year without work. [S]o you can see that the whole story about trying to put us in Ain Harod or [Merchavia] was a fake, it was just a good excuse to get rid of us.[1]
>
> Lewis Jack Kamenetzky and Morris Rosenstein, Tel Aviv, to American Zion Commonwealth, New York, 10 March 1926

Few contemporary sources detail the place of residence of American Jews in Palestine, thus hindering a detailed and accurate description of their spatial distribution. Subsequent interpretation is somewhat limited, and is drawn from the scanty data at hand. The 1918 *Census of the Jews of Eretz Israel* lists the location of American nationals and those born in the United States who were resident in Palestine during World War I. The information in the census is somewhat incomplete and includes some inconsistencies, yet certain patterns can be gleaned from it. First, during this period the majority of American nationals resided in an urban environment: 546 in Jerusalem, some 70 in Jaffa, with 9 individuals born in America residing in Haifa, Safed, and Tiberias. A minority of American nationals resided in a rural environment: 76 in Judaea (Petah Tikvah 58, Rishon Lezion 8, Rehovot 4, Ekron 1, Ein Ganim 2, and Gadera 3); 5 in Samaria (Zichron Yaakov 2, Hadera 2, and Meir Shefaya 1); and 32 in the Lower Galilee (Yavniel 5, Kfar Tavor 1, Merchavia 1, Menahemia 4, Beit Gan 3, and the American-initiated settlements of Poria 17, and Rama [Sarona] 1). The proportion of American nationals in these locales varied. In Jerusalem they represented 2 percent of the population, while in almost every other settlement where they were found their proportion was below 2 percent; an exception was Poria, where American nationals comprised 25 percent of the total population of 68.[2]

After World War I, the only reliable information on the spatial distribution of American nationals is the *Census of Palestine 1931*. It recorded 672 Jews born in the United States and resident in Palestine at that time, and 2,222 Jews who had American citizenship but were born outside the United States. These numbers include those who immigrated before World War I. Certain inconsistencies have been identified that affect these basic figures. First, since some Americans relinquished their former citizenship to embrace Palestinian citizenship, they were not designated as Americans. Secondly, these figures do not take into account individuals who were born outside the United States, resided in America for an extended period of time (more than five years), but never attained U.S. citizenship. Such individuals were listed under other countries of birth and citizenship.

Despite the shortcomings of the census information, certain trends can be observed with regard to the spatial distribution of American Jews in Palestine. The figures for citizenship show that this population group had a higher concentration in the Jerusalem and Southern districts than the rest of the Jewish population. This group was highly urban, with 77.3 percent living in the urban centers; this is slightly higher than the figure of 73.6 percent urban dwellers of the total Jewish population. These figures represent a low estimate, since they do not include Tiberias and Safed or other urban settlements, and thus they should be adjusted upward. In 1931 American Jews were concentrated in Jerusalem (38.3 percent) and in Tel Aviv (31.6 percent).[3]

Another source of data is a 1924 list of American citizens who had obtained provisional certificates of Palestinian citizenship. This provides details regarding the residence of 180 individuals. Although the list represents only a small portion of the American Jewish population in Palestine, it does indicate their spatial distribution as 80 percent urban and 20 percent rural.[4] This serves to strengthen the accuracy of the figures for rural-urban distribution as seen in the 1931 census.

Based on the 1941–42 Jewish Agency survey of the rural Jewish population, those originating in America—848 in number—made up only 0.6

TABLE 13
Distribution of American Jewish citizens in Palestine according to district, 1931

District/country of origin	United States		All Jews	
	Number	Percent	Number	Percent
Northern	267	12.02	40,928	23.44
Jerusalem	862	38.79	54,959	31.48
Southern	1,073	48.29	78,723	45.09
Total	2,222	100.0	174,610	100.0

Source: Eric Mills, *Census of Palestine 1931* (Alexandria: Whitehead Morris, 1933), 2:266–68.

TABLE 14
Distribution for rural settlements and selected urban centers of American Jewish citizens compared to the general Jewish population, 1931

Region or city	United States		All Jews	
	Number	Percent	Number	Percent
Urban	1,718	77.3	128,467	73.6
Rural	504	22.7	46,143	26.4
Total	2,222	100.0	174,610	100.0
Jaffa	7	0.3	7,209	4.2
Tel Aviv	702	31.6	45,564	26.1
Haifa	94	4.2	15,923	9.1
Jerusalem	851	38.3	51,222	29.3

Source: Eric Mills, *Census of Palestine 1931* (Alexandria: Whitehead Morris, 1933), 2:266–68.

percent of the Jewish rural sector. There appears to be a marked increase over the number of Americans in the rural environment from the 1931 census, although the comparison is between country of origin in 1941–42 and between citizenship in 1931.[5]

Possible explanations for these concentrations of American citizens can be deduced from the "pull" that a certain place or way of life may have had when immigrants chose their new place of residence. As the Holy City and center of the Mandate administration, as well as the home of Jewish national institutions and the fledgling Hebrew University, Jerusalem attracted certain Americans. Most members of Kollel America chose to reside in Jerusalem for religious reasons. Americans like Robert Kesselman found employment with the Mandatory government; others, like Gershon Agronsky, worked for various Jewish and Zionist organizations located there; and of course there were Americans who worked and studied at the Hebrew University of Jerusalem.

In September 1939 a census was taken of the Jewish population of Jerusalem, which listed 824 American citizens there. The census recorded the United States as the last place of residence of 730 of the city's inhabitants. These figures are lower than those cited in the 1931 census, but this does not necessarily indicate a decline in the city's American Jewish population, since presumably some American Jews had relinquished their United States citizenship. In addition, we know that in 1931 the American Jewish population was elderly, so the associated higher mortality rate could also explain the difference between the 1931 and the 1939 figures, despite the expected increase resulting from eight years of immigration.[6]

Tel Aviv appealed to American immigrants because of its position as the new "Jewish city"—the economic and cultural center of Jewish Palestine. The low proportion of Americans in Jaffa (0.3 percent as compared to 4.2 for the general Jewish population) probably reflects the fact that Americans could afford to live elsewhere—beyond the proximity of Jaffa's Arab population, which had attacked its Jewish neighbors, including some Americans, in 1921 and 1929.

The low ratio of American Jews (4.2 percent compared to 9.1 percent for the Jewish population) in Haifa appears somewhat incongruous, for Haifa was generally attractive to Americans. Indeed, the largest number of urban purchases made through the American Zion Commonwealth were in Haifa.[7]

Certain segments of the American immigrant population were specifically urban in nature. Members of Kollel America Tiffereth Yerushalaim, for example, were found mainly in Jerusalem, but also in Safed, Tiberias, Jaffa, Tel Aviv, and Petah Tikvah.[8]

While the percentage of American Jews in the rural environment in general was slightly lower than that of the larger Jewish population, there were high concentrations of American Jews in certain rural locations. In the settlements of Balfouria and Herzlia, for example, which had been established by the American Zion Commonwealth, Americans comprised 11.6 and 12.8 percent of the population in 1926. Significantly, this is much higher than the proportion of Americans to the entire Jewish population, which was 1.3 percent. In kibbutzim with American groups there was also a higher proportion of Americans than their national average. Ein Hashofet had 52 Americans (approximately 17 percent), and 32 Americans resided at Kfar Menachem (approximately 13 percent—with another 14 joining after

World War II).[9] The disproportionately higher distribution of Americans in settlements organized and founded by their compatriots would appear to be an obvious correlation, but this does not hold in all cases. In Afula—sponsored by Americans—they comprised 0.9 percent of the population in 1926.[10] Furthermore, the share of the population held by Americans in growing settlements like Herzlia and Raanana decreased over time as an influx of immigrants from other countries augmented and eventually eclipsed the American population.

In an attempt to create a complete picture of the spatial distribution of American Jewry in Palestine, an inventory was initiated by the author during the preparation of this study. Information about each individual was recorded, including place and duration of residence. Although the inventory is incomplete, it provides details of the various settlements in which Americans resided. In the Northern District, higher concentrations of Americans were found in Haifa and twenty-five other settlements, including Avihail, Balfouria, Merchavia, Tiberias, Safed, and Zichron Yaakov. In the Jerusalem District, concentrations of Americans were found in Jerusalem, Ben Shemen, and Hebron until 1929. In the Southern District, similar densities were found in Tel Aviv and Jaffa as well as in eleven other settlements, with higher concentrations in Herzlia, Petah Tikvah, and Raanana.

In some instances, American Jews decided on the location of their new residence as well as their occupation before they immigrated to Palestine, while other immigrants only made their decision after reaching Palestine. Detailed accounts of individual selection processes, coupled with the categorization of factors that shaped these processes, assist in formulating an explanation for the American spatial distribution in Palestine.

Locational decisions are a dynamic process. In the case of American Jews migrating to Palestine, the encounter with a new environment and its population often led to a modification of an earlier decision. It was frequently recommended that an individual visit Palestine first in order to make a clear choice. The prominent American rabbi and Zionist David de Sola Pool, while serving on the Zionist Commission, articulately explained this to an American who wanted to obtain a farm in Palestine. Pool suggested,

> the only way for you to come to any satisfactory grasp of the situation and for you to know exactly what would be before you, would be for you [to] come over to Palestine for a short while. You should count on a minimum of two or three weeks in Palestine, because, although the country is small, communication is still somewhat difficult and you could hardly come to a decision without having had occasion of making a judgment, based on an examination of the various possibilities which would be open to you.[11]

Some American immigrants, however, chose their future place of residence before departing for Palestine. They purchased a tract of land and even commissioned the construction of a home, or else made arrangements to rent a house, apartment, or room. Land purchasing agents and organizations, American and Palestinian, offered tracts of land in both urban and rural settings, and the immigrant's decision would be shaped by information presented by these agents.

In the following sections of this chapter, the activities of certain land purchasing and development companies are discussed, including details of their policies and some actual transactions. It is important to understand the options that were available to the potential immigrant as well as various changes in these companies' policies. In the case of the early activities of the American Zion Commonwealth, New York Achooza Aleph, and other such organizations, American Jews invested in lands without any inkling of the location, acreage, or quality of the land. In other instances, these factors were fully laid out by the land purchasing agent. Provided with maps, the purchasers knew, or at least thought they knew, the exact details of the land they were buying. It is also important to emphasize that most Americans had little understanding of the geography or settlement patterns of Palestine, and often enough the information they were given was inaccurate or misleading.

The first investors in the American Zion Commonwealth (AMZIC) and the *ahuza* societies, like New York Achooza Aleph, simply bought land in Palestine. These organizations needed to amass capital before they launched into activities in Palestine. Until 1919, the American Zion Commonwealth investor purchased "land certificates" for unspecified acreage. AMZIC and other advertisements merely advocated "buy a farming estate in Palestine," without mentioning where that estate might be located.[12] And the New York Achooza Aleph members at first made payments toward a share in some future colony whose site was not yet determined. Only after the representatives of these organizations actually purchased land did their constituents know the location of their possessions.

Similarly, members of *halutz* organizations had no notion of where they would be settled. They departed America simply knowing that through the offices of their organization, and after negotiations with the Palestine Zionist Executive (later the Jewish Agency), Jewish National Fund, and the Keren Hayesod, a site would be selected for them.

Later, once the American Zion Commonwealth and the New York Achooza Aleph began full-scale operations, purchasers knew which settlement or area they were investing in. The AMZIC offered land at Herzlia or Afula, and the New York Achooza first at Raanana then later at Gan Yavne. Other companies—for example, the Migdal Corporation and Menorah Palestine Building Corporation—offered its investors land in specific locales.

The next improvement in the land acquisition process was the sale of particular plots chosen from detailed maps made available by the land purchasing companies. Not only was the selection precise but the buyer had the possibility of knowing or determining who his neighbors would be as well as the plot's relative location to institutions, services, and transportation arteries. The American Zion Commonwealth listed available plots when it sold land in Haifa and Jerusalem neighborhoods, and in its planned Nordia settlement. In its 1932 brochure, the New York Achooza Aleph provided a plan of Gan Yavne.[13] The purchaser secured a definite tract and knew his future address before departing for Palestine.

Some Americans were disappointed by the arrangements made for them by their land purchasing agents. Some unscrupulous agents sold nonexistent tracts; other companies marketed plots that were not appropriate for settlement. The Rom Hacarmel project in the Haifa area, for example, was unsuitable for development. Sometimes the degree of infrastructure development in a project was not up to the standard advertised or promised (see chapter 10), as in the American Zion Commonwealth's new town of Afula. Thus in retrospect it appears that Americans would have fared much better if they had waited until they reached Palestine, retained a responsible representative, or, as David de Sola Pool suggested, visited first.

Immigrants who had not made previous arrangements began the process of selecting a dwelling place upon their arrival. Sometimes the prospective immigrant arrived in Palestine in advance of his family in order to select a location for their settlement. In other instances, a person who could afford an investigatory trip proceeded to Palestine, chose what appeared to be an appropriate abode, and then returned to America to collect his family.

In some instances, immigrants arrived in Palestine with a preference for a certain region, settlement, or type of settlement in which they wanted to reside. In other instances, they kept their options open. Often they postponed decisions until they could evaluate job opportunities and the possibilities for social integration, and had been able to gain an understanding of the real estate market. Most of these decision making processes were unique, reflecting individual needs. Nonetheless, a few detailed examples can highlight certain facets of the determining mechanisms and procedures, and these shed light on more general themes.

Realities of the local situation, particularly the availability of career opportunities, often affected the decision to settle in a particular spot. Dorothy Ruth Kahn related the trials of a man named Bill and his extended family from Brooklyn in their search for the right place to live. Among his various endeavors in America, Bill had been a cattle dealer. He thought his group of twenty should remain in Jerusalem for a month while he searched for land appropriate for raising cattle. In the interim, Bill's nephew received a job offer for an engineering position in Tel Aviv. Bill's mother-in-law wanted to remain in Jerusalem's Mea Shearim neighborhood with other elderly women whose companionship she found enjoyable. Bill's sister felt obligated to attend to her rheumatic mother in Jerusalem. The group thus began to fall apart. Bill learned that a tract of land large enough for a cattle ranch was expensive and beyond their means. In the end, Bill remained in Jerusalem and opened a restaurant.[14]

IDEAS AND AGENTS IN LAND TRANSACTIONS

There were three general ways for American Jews to invest in land in Palestine and settle on it. First, there was the possibility of semiprivate investment with the American Zion Commonwealth, which functioned as an agent or intermediary. The AMZIC provided for individual ownership and assisted in settling Americans if they so desired. The second direction was through private initiative; this involved using both American and Palestinian companies as intermediaries, since the procedures for land purchase in Palestine were quite complicated and usually drawn out over an extended period of time. Moreover, in most instances there were no regulatory controls on such real estate ventures. The third possibility was through the Jewish National Fund (JNF), which provided land for the founding of kibbutzim, moshavim *shitufiim,* and worker's neighborhoods in urban environments. This land was not necessarily settled by donors to the JNF, nor did American contributions necessarily serve to purchase lands for the benefit of American settlement groups. On occasion, however, pressure was brought to bear on the directors and representatives of the Jewish National Fund to establish Americans on these tracts.

As a rule, purchase of agricultural lands and urban tracts was not carried out by American settlement groups or individuals but instead by established companies in Palestine. Most of the settlement organizations discussed below had representatives in Palestine; the organizations were not in a position to, or indeed capable of, carrying out the transactions themselves. Land acquisition usually entailed extensive negotiations; this was frequently followed by difficulties in the transfer of title and the final registration. This process necessitated expertise in the field, achieved through long experience and with the aid of a support staff of lawyers, surveyors, and administrators. These limitations complicated the decision making process by American companies regarding the location of their tracts. In most cases, land agents in Palestine recommended tracts to be purchased by American organizations. In these instances, local intermediaries were often unable to find a single purchaser and thus needed the American organization's capital to complete the transaction.

The Palestine Land Development Company (PLDC) was founded in 1908 through the initiative of botanist and Zionist leader Professor Otto Warburg. This was one of many of his contributions toward advancing practical settlement work. Dr. Arthur Ruppin of the Palestine Office was appointed head manager of the company. Warburg hoped the PLDC would serve primarily as a land purchasing agent of the Jewish National Fund and as a semiprivate agent for groups interested in purchasing land for settlement. Companies or organizations that bought land through the PLDC paid the cost of the land and out-of-pocket expenses connected with the purchase—fees for title registration, the surveying and marking of boundaries, and gratuities paid to former cultivators—plus a 2 percent commission. Between 1910 and 1929 the PLDC purchased 443,187 dunams; more than half of this land was resold to the JNF, and 210,467 dunams were purchased by private clients. Between 1930 and 1939, the PLDC purchased approximately 180,000 dunams and sold most of this land to the JNF.[15]

The Zionist Organization of America (ZOA) was critical of the Palestine Land Development Company's activities, and particularly skeptical about Dr. Ruppin's involvement in the World Zionist Organization and the Jewish National Fund. The report of the ZOA Palestine Department dated 14 January 1921, contends that this constituted a conflict of interest, and the department recommended: "There should be only one Jewish land purchasing agency in Palestine and not a multiform purchasing agency as there seems to exist at present. According to correspondence Dr. Ruppin has been acting either for the [World] Zionist Organization or for the Palestine Land Development Company or for the Jewish National Fund or for all three at one and the same time."[16]

The Zionist Organization of America accused the Palestine Land Development Company of overcharging prospective buyers, promising tracts of land at one price and then delivering them at an inflated one. (However, it appears that these claims were the product of certain misunderstandings. Later on it became clear that the exclusivity of the PLDC's activities was, in fact, beneficial, for it prevented the inflation of land prices through speculation.) Abraham Goldberg of the ZOA expressed the consideration that it was his organization's duty, in full accordance with the Zionist Congress resolutions, to support the PLDC and facilitate its activities in the United States in every possible way, but if land prices were not reasonable, the ZOA could not sanction its activities.[17]

The Palestine Land Development Company sold lands not only to the Jewish National Fund and organizations or societies like the American Zion Commonwealth and the New York Achooza Aleph, but also to individuals. The question of the company's representation in America arose in 1922, when Pinhas Friedman was sent to the U.S. by the Geula Company and the PLDC to serve in this capacity. The Geula Company was founded in 1904 and cooperated with the PLDC in various transactions. Before the outbreak of World War I, the Geula Company had acquired 25,855 dunams of agricultural land and 83,000 square *amot* (47,476 square meters) of urban real estate in the Tel Aviv area and in Haifa. In 1921 the company was incorporated under the Mandatory Company Ordinances for the purpose of buying, renting, and exchanging land, buildings, gardens, orchards, and all types of real estate or rights to real estate in Palestine and adjacent countries. The Geula Company's incorporation papers further described various measures that should be taken for the improvement of these possessions.[18]

At the same time, the American Zion Commonwealth had been negotiating with the Palestine Land Development Company to become its sole representative in America.[19] Peter Schweizer and Abraham Goldberg, American Zionist delegates at the Zionist Congress of 1922, invited Ruppin to go to America to sell bonds, and they encouraged him to believe that he could sell tracts of land and PLDC shares.[20] In 1923 Ruppin wrote of the benefits of the agreement:

> Until now the Palestine Land Development Company has limited its activities to Palestine and Europe. Its propaganda did not reach American Jews. Now, however[,] the Palestine Land Development Company has entered into an agreement with the [American] Zion Commonwealth in New York, whereby the [American] Zion Commonwealth will be sole representative of the Palestine Land Development Company of the United States. The [American] Zion Commonwealth will be in a position to sell on behalf of the Palestine Land Development Company to any individual and to any group such a tract of land as is desired and is suitable, at very reasonable terms, and will assume full responsibility that land sold is suitable for the purpose for which it is sold. There are many Jews in the United States who have long desired to possess a parcel of land in Palestine, but did not know how to acquire it safely, with the knowledge that they are getting full value for their money.[21]

The American Zion Commonwealth continued to serve as the Palestine Land Development Company's agent in the United States until the AMZIC's collapse in 1926.

As can be seen from the preceding discussion, some companies were chiefly interested in the greatest possible return on their investment in land in Palestine. In other cases, the intercession of American companies in the Palestinian land market led to speculation by local agents. The American Zion Commonwealth questioned its own role in the speculative market. Charles Passman opened this question for discussion in a letter to the AMZIC board of directors. He was particularly concerned about the Sheinkin neighborhood on the periphery of the growing city of Tel Aviv. He was hesitant to market this tract, and he explained why.

> To speak, at present of Shunat [sic; should be *schunat;* Hebrew: neighborhood] Borochov as a part of Tel Aviv, where land can be sold in small plots of less than one dunam, is entirely out of the question, unless these plots are sold in America for speculation purposes only, the purchasers holding

their plots until such a time when Tel Aviv will extend in that direction, so that they will be able to make a profit on their purchase. This profit will also be limited, for, as a matter of fact, they will pay to the American Zion Commonwealth, at present, a much higher price than what the land is actually worth.[22]

Passman preferred that the company continue its policy of deterring speculation. To American investors, the American Zion Commonwealth clearly explained that it had no land for sale in Balfouria for speculation or investment purposes: "Our only object is to bring in as many Jewish families into Palestine and our contracts are accepted with the distinct understanding that in no event must the land remain idle for a longer period than one year from the date of signing of this contract, and we must have from you an expression, in writing, agreeing to the fact that within one year from date you will [have] on this land a Jewish family."[23]

Despite all its concern over real estate speculation, the issue of the American Zion Commonwealth's own profit taking arose. Harry Kotler of the New York office was shocked when profits from the Afula project showed a 100 percent return on the entire land cost instead of the 10 percent minimum needed for administrative and other expenses. Kotler contended that different prices had been charged to customers in Palestine and abroad.[24] No response to these accusations has been found.

With the growth in prominence of the American Zion Commonwealth, many local real estate agents in Palestine took notice of their activities. According to Yehoshua Hankin, "land speculators were following [Charles] Passman to find out what kind of land he was buying," with the hope of perhaps preempting the purchase, buying part of the tract, or purchasing another in close proximity. Once the AMZIC became involved in a certain area this inevitably created a stir in that market. Speculators believed that if they could sell nearby land—to buyers either in Palestine or the United States—they would turn a large profit.[25]

Many private real estate companies were established for the sole purpose of reaping profit. One such company was the Menorah Palestine Building Corporation, which was organized by Isaac Berman, an employee of the Mizrachi Organization. Two Jaffa merchants, [?] Turkenitz and Yaakov Perlstein, owned a tract between Jaffa and Rishon LeZion. Unable to dispose of it, they engaged Berman to sell it in America. The American Zion Commonwealth general manager explained that "the purchasers will, therefore, have to pay not only the expenses involved in the selling but also a fair profit to the Menorah Corporation as well as to the original owners of the land."[26]

Various attempts were made to curb speculation. The Tel Aviv Development Company—with £P40,000 capital equally invested by the Palestine

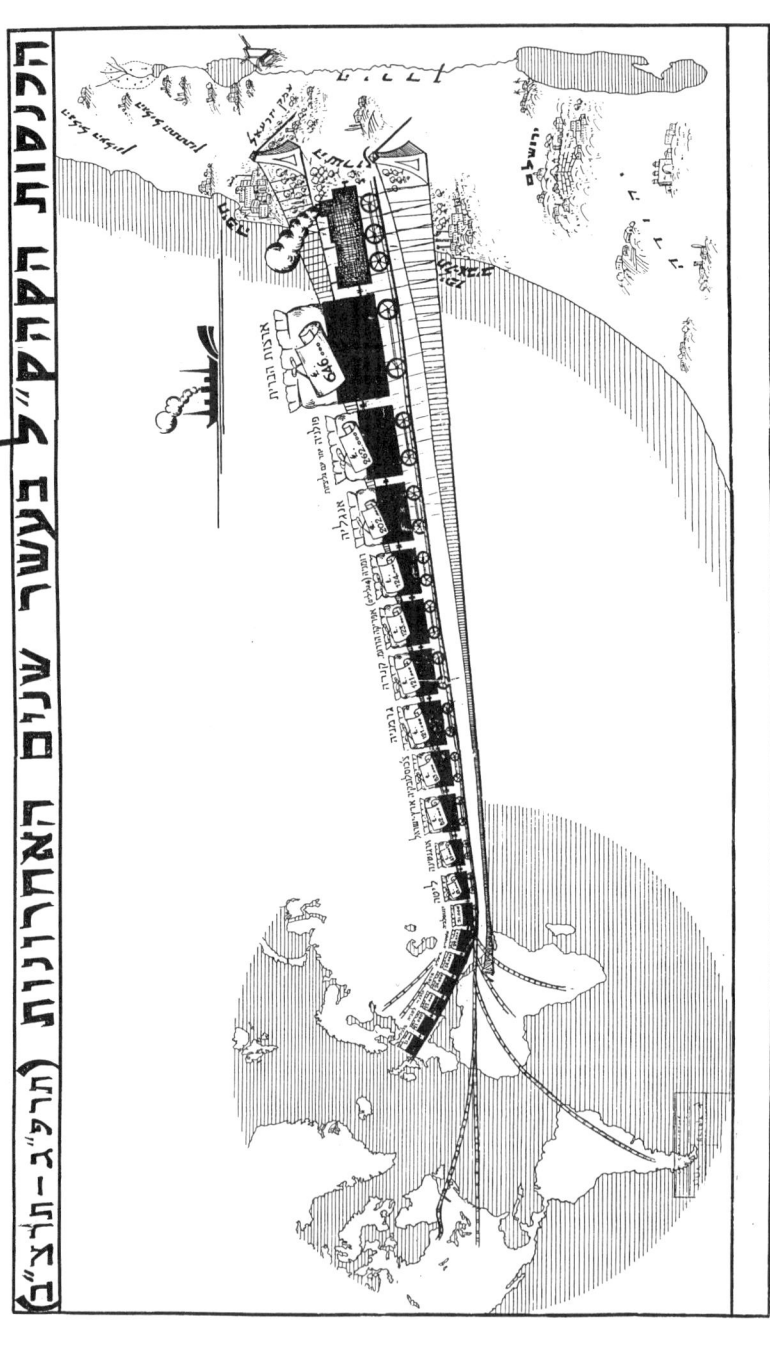

Fig. 16. Income of the Jewish National Fund according to country, 1923–32. *Right to left*: the United States, Poland including Galicia, England, Rumania, South Africa, Canada, Germany, Czechoslovakia, Palestine, Argentina, Lithuania, Yugoslavia, Austria, Italy, France, Holland, Latvia, and Belgium. (Jewish National Fund Map Archives, Hebrew University of Jerusalem, file 35, map 2,953)

Land Development Company, the American Zion Commonwealth, Geula, and the Anglo-Palestine Company—sought to buy large quantities of land in the Tel Aviv area. A large aggregate of land, it was believed, would create a kind of reserve and check speculation.[27]

There were two distinct types of investors in the Palestine land market in the period between the wars. One included *ahuza* companies and the American Zion Commonwealth; these can be defined as "national capitalists." Their motive was a Zionist ideological one—the expansion and promotion of Jewish settlement in Palestine. As Yossi Katz explained with regard to pre–World War I companies:

> Private enterprise was never motivated solely by commercial considerations and did not regard profit-making as an end in itself. Financial gain was primarily a means for attaining the ideological Zionist goal and not a goal in its own right. However, in order to guarantee the success and continuation of settlement activity, private enterprise operated according to economic and commercial criteria. Generally, it did not seek to maximize gains and was satisfied with a modicum of profit.[28]

The second type of investor, it appears, had little or no sense of mission in his activities. Profit was the key. These kinds of investors perceived Palestine as a lucrative and vibrant market with increased opportunity due to growing Jewish immigration. This profit motivated perspective often led investors into precarious and even dishonest practices, including misrepresenting the land they wanted to sell.

In addition to private and quasi-private investment, American Jews could play a role in the redemption of the Land of Israel through the Jewish National Fund. Prior to the first Zionist Congress of 1897, Professor Zvi Hermann Schapira developed a plan for a national land purchasing fund. He presented his plan to the first Zionist Congress, but only at the Fifth Congress in 1901 was a formal resolution passed approving the establishment of the JNF. In 1907 this "association limited by guarantee" was incorporated. Its purpose was to purchase lands in Palestine as the eternal possession of the Jewish people.[29]

Between 1902 and 1921, American Jewry contributed £159,000 ($795,000) to the Jewish National Fund; this represented 19 percent of the association's gross receipts of £835,400 ($4,177,000).[30] These sums, both the American contribution and the total amount, were relatively small in light of the investment needed to expand Jewish settlement activities following World War I. Up to 1920, the Jewish National Fund had purchased only 16,400 dunams. Could additional funds be collected in the United States, either through the JNF or the Keren Hayesod (the Palestine Restoration Fund), founded in 1920? European Jewry would be unable to help in this effort. Central and Eastern Europe had been ravaged by war, and Eastern

Europe was in turmoil as a result of the Bolshevik Revolution and the ensuing civil war in Russia. Through various relief agencies, American Jewry attempted to alleviate the suffering of their Eastern European brethren, but European Jews on the whole were not in a position to continue their role as primary supporters of Jewish national land purchasing. American Jewry, together with communities in South Africa, Canada, and Australia, were therefore asked to contribute more.

American Jewry began to express its concern about the manner in which its investments were being used, demanding greater accountability by the JNF. Thus, after the conclusion of World War I, the need for private and national capital in the development of Palestine became more apparent, and one cardinal element of the ensuing debate about Palestine was that of land ownership.[31] The second and third points of the Zionist Organization of America's 1918 Pittsburgh Program relate to this:

> Second, To insure in the Jewish national home in Palestine equality of opportunity we favor a policy which with due regard to existing rights, shall tend to establish the ownership and control by the whole people of the land, of all natural resources and of all public utilities.
>
> Third, All land, owned or controlled by the whole people should be leased on such conditions as will insure the fullest opportunity for development and continuity of possession.[32]

This attitude toward land reflects the concept of social justice that had developed in Palestine along the lines of "Social Zionism." This ideology drew upon ideas currently popular in America: Progressivism and Henry George's single tax movement. Bernard Rosenblatt, for example, was interested in changing the system of land taxation in Palestine to one that was based on the principle of land value taxation. This change would necessitate an enumeration of Palestinian landholding and improvements before World War I. These land values would be taken as basic values, and any increase would be taxed annually by the Jewish Commonwealth in Palestine on the basis of the normal increase in value or increased rental value. These ideas, adapted from the single tax movement, received support from various personalities in American Zionist circles, including Rabbi Stephen S. Wise and Mary Fels.[33]

The Zionist Organization of America's Pittsburgh Program did not address the question of private ownership. The organization's 1919 Chicago convention, although still supporting the primacy of the Jewish National Fund, also endorsed the land development activities of the American Zion Commonwealth.[34] At the 1920 London Conference, Justice Louis D. Brandeis and Chaim Weizmann differed over the means for up-building Palestine. On his return to America, Brandeis outlined his ideas in the Zeeland Memorandum:

To buy the land, and to provide the utilities for making it productive directly or indirectly (including in time afforestation of land acquired and perhaps even harbor facilities) such large contributions from Jews of the Diaspora will, for the immediate future and for many years indeed, be indispensable. These contributions may properly take the form of *investment in stock,* like in the Jewish Colonial Trust or the *Zion Commonwealth,* as in that form no obligation of paying a *return* would be incurred. But the contributions must not take the form of investment or bonds bearing interest—because interest cannot be earned for a long time to come and could be paid only from new contributions. We must not make any representations, expressed or implied, that any return by way of dividends may be expected soon on the stock to be issued. The obligation assumed must be limited to the assumption of the duty to expend the money wisely and efficiently, i.e., in a proper capital outlay in the best possible manner and with the greatest possible economy. If such an expenditure of the funds is made, the outlay will be a good investment. That is, one from which the Jewish people, and eventually individual owners of the shares of stock also, may hope to received a proper return.[35]

This policy guided his immediate followers. However, once the Brandeis group lost control of the Zionist Organization of America leadership in 1921, Zionists took two different directions. The first was in accord with Weizmann's policy and was supported by the new ZOA president, Louis Lipsky, and his followers. As a result, the Jewish National Fund and the Keren Hayesod became the official conduits for investment in land. Private ownership was not proposed, but it was accepted as a form of initiative. The Brandeis group continued to support the American Zion Commonwealth and looked for other sound, businesslike directions for developing Palestine. The Palestine Economic Corporation (PEC) appeared to be one such avenue. Although most of its activities were directed toward industry, it also invested in infrastructure and real estate development. From 1921 until 1938, the net contribution of American Jews to the JNF was £P1,065,000 or 25.44 percent of the total contribution to the JNF. Since American Jewry represented 25 percent of the world's Jewish population, American contributions accounted for one-fourth of the 396,906 dunams redeemed by the JNF between 1921–38.

Computation of private American Jewish purchasers is difficult because of incomplete and inconsistent listings. And determining an accurate sum is aggravated by the question of purchase versus ownership until 1939. Once the Jewish National Fund purchased a tract it remained in its possession in perpetuity. Private purchases were sold and often resold, not necessarily to other Americans, and sometimes they were donated to the JNF. Information collected for this study indicates that American Jews purchased at least 184,958 dunams in Palestine between 1920–39; this represents 19.8 percent of the total.

TABLE 15
Net income of the Jewish National Fund by region and selected countries, 1919–38

Region and countries	£P	Percent	Estimated Jewish population in 1933 (000's)	Percent
Continental Europe	1,524,000	36.40	9,355	59.04
United States	1,065,000	25.44	4,500	28.40
Great Britain and Ireland	428,000	10.22	335	2.11
South Africa	286,000	6.83	80	0.50
Palestine	240,000	5.73	200	1.26
Other countries	417,000	9.96	1,358	8.57
Total	4,187,000[a]	100.00	15,846	100.00

Sources: Net income of the Jewish National Fund is based on Adolf Boehm and Adolf Pollak, *The Jewish National Fund (Keren Kayemeth Leisrael): Its History, Function and Activity* (Jerusalem: Jewish National Fund, 1939), 110. Population figures are based on estimates by Arthur Ruppin, *The Jews in the Modern World* (London: Macmillan, 1934), 26–27.
[a]Does not include £227,000 in special income

QUANTITY AND QUALITY OF LAND PURCHASES

The extent of purchases made by various land purchasing agencies depended on both their familiarity with the Palestine real estate market and on the availability of land. A third factor that influenced their planning was the perception of the amount of land that was needed by an individual or family and how much was required to create a viable settlement.

The quantity varied according to land quality—which was generally synonymous with geographic location. The intensity of cultivation and the use of technology determined the necessary quantity of land. There were also political ramifications in the dispute over the Jewish up-building of Palestine and the connected issue of Jewish immigration; the greater question was what size population Palestine could support. Representatives of Zionist groups produced a number of internal memorandums on this issue and presented reports on the question to various British commissions. Mandatory functionaries likewise prepared estimates of the amount of land required to sustain an average Jewish farmer and his family.

TABLE 16
Summary of American land purchases up to 1939

Purchasers	Area in dunams	Percent of American purchases	Percent of Jewish purchases 1920–39	Percent of Jewish purchases up to 1939
American Zion Commonwealth	150,909	81.59	16.16	11.16
Ahuza companies (Poria, 3,545[a]; Sarona, 5,525[a]; New York Achooza Aleph, 12,753)	20,853	11.27	2.23	1.54
Medium-scale (Nahalat Shivim, 1,000; Pardes Hagdud, 680; Netanya, 140[b]; Gan Rashel, 700; Ramot Meir, 4,000; Agudat Netaim, 144)	6,664	3.60	0.71	0.49
Garden suburbs (Nachalat Zion, 1,650; Nahalat Itzhak, 1,050; Migdal, 343[b])	3,043	1.65	0.33	0.23
Individual purchasers (Sacks, 450; Silverman, 180; Warburg, 323; Lamport, 145; Shapira, 248[b] Bloom[c]; Kaplan, 400; Binenfeld, 1,762)	3,489	1.89		0.26
Total American purchases	184,958	100.00	19.80	13.68
Jewish purchases 1920–39	933,900	—	100.00	69.08
Total Jewish purchases up to 1939	1,352,000	—	237.10	100.00

[a]purchased before 1920
[b]minimum figure
[c]amount unknown

Arthur Ruppin, in his 1922 published letter "How Cheaply Can We Colonize," looked to developments in California and the writings of Professor Elwood Mead—a leading agricultural authority—for direction. California was often used as a model for comparison because it manifested similar climatic conditions to those in Palestine. California was also a land of new beginnings, where technology was employed to accelerate agricultural development. It was hoped that advances there could be applied to work in Palestine. Mead established that a single California farmer needed 30–40 acres (120–60 dunams) of irrigated land. Ruppin reckoned that much smaller areas would be sufficient in Palestine, assuming that more intensive cultivation methods were utilized.[36]

Another opinion was expressed by Yehoshua Hankin, who had a great amount of hands-on experience in the field. In 1890 he had purchased the lands on which the moshavah Rehovot was established; the following year he acquired the lands for Hadera. In addition, the Jewish Colonization Association used Hankin's services to acquire various tracts of land. Hankin was in the employ of the Palestine Land Development Company, and in 1932 he became the company's director. He is credited with the purchase of the Jezreel Valley and was known as "The Redeemer of the Valley." In a 1923 memorandum to Dr. Jacob Thon of the PLDC, Hankin outlined the amount of land required per farming family in different regions, based on his extensive experience: the Jezreel Valley, 100 dunams; Ir Jezreel (Afula), 20 dunams; the Judaean foothills, 100 dunams; along the Jaffa-Jerusalem road, 10 dunams; the foothills of Acre and Haifa, 20 dunams; and around the moshavot, 50 dunams. In a later report from 1927, Hankin reiterated most of the figures cited above, and he added to the list Beer Sheva and its environs, 300 dunams; the Galilee and Acre, 50–100 dunams; Samaria, 20–50 dunams; parts of Judaea which lack water, 100 dunams; and Trans-Jordan, 100 dunams.[37]

In late 1926 Chaim Weizmann approached Elwood Mead, then the commissioner of reclamation of the United States Department of the Interior, to chair the Joint Palestine Survey Commission and report on colonization prospects in Palestine to the World Zionist Organization. Mead and the commission members surveyed Palestine in 1927. The commission subsequently recommended that 160 to 320 dunams—with 240 dunams as a safer minimum—for dry cereal farming, with no distinction between geographical locations, could support an average Jewish family. Smaller units of irrigated land, 40 to 80 dunams, could support a similar family unit. To the dismay of the initiators of the survey, these figures greatly exceeded those accepted by Jewish experts in Palestine. If Mead's conclusions were indeed correct, the implication was that Palestine, agriculturally at least, could not support the size population than authorities had anticipated.[38]

In 1930 three of Palestine's agricultural experts, Joseph Weitz, David Stern, and Nahum Paper, prepared a report on land quality and the potential for settlement along the coastal plain. Unlike the more intuitive estimates made by Hankin, these three experts included a physiographic approach, which took into account the physical characteristics of soil, rainfall, and ground and surface water as determining factors of farm size. Their report divided coastal areas into seven sections. In the Acre region—Sulame Dezor (on the Lebanese border) to Acre—they suggested 60 dunams per family: 5 dunams in irrigated plantations, 10 dunams in plantations on the mountain slopes, and 45 dunams in partially irrigated plantations for extensive farming. In the Carmel region—Haifa to Atlit—they suggested 100-dunam parcels for extensive farming. In the Wadi Hawareth (Emek Hefer) region, they suggested 30 dunams: 7.5 dunams in plantations and 22.5 dunams in other crops. In the Sharon—extending southward to the Yarkon River—they recommended three types of farms, depending upon their location on an east-west axis: intensively cultivated farms consisting of 15 dunams; farms in transitional zones of 70 dunams; and extensively cultivated farms of 100 dunams. In the Petah Tikvah to Rehovot region they subdivided potential farms into three groups, starting their cross section on the coast and extending inland: intensive ones consisting of 15 dunams, 10 dunams for citrus plantations, and 5 dunams for other crops; those in transitional zones should consist of 30 dunams, including 7.5-dunam plantations and 22.5-dunam plots for other crops; and extensive ones consisting of 100 dunams. The next region, the Shephela (Judaean Foothills)—from Rehovot to Nahal Shariya—contained three types of farm: intensive, consisting of 25 dunams, of which 15 dunams were to be citrus plantations and 10 dunams other crops; transitional, consisting of 125 dunams, of which 15 dunams were to be plantations, 10 dunams irrigated, and 100 dunams dry farming; and extensive, consisting of 250 dunams, of which 5-dunam plots would be irrigated and 245-dunam plots used for dry farming.[39]

The Hankin memorandum and the Weitz, Stern, and Paper report emphasized the relationship between location and quantity. However, this information was not widely disseminated, and it did not become a factor in many of the decisions made in the United States. A large number of diverse opinions and ideas floated in American Zionist circles, adding to the confusion as to the amount of land that was needed for a colony and the type of agriculture that should be promoted.

A founder of the New York Achooza Aleph, Judah Leib Kazan, explained that the *ahuza* membership clearly lacked any accurate understanding of the situation in Palestine. They had no notion of the type of farms they were going to establish nor of the amount of land needed for settlement. Menachem Sheinkin tried to help them clarify their planning. Sheinkin, a Zionist leader first in Russia and then in Palestine, moved to Palestine in 1906 and had directed Hovevei Zion's information and immigration office in Jaffa. Sheinkin was also among the founders of the American Zion Commonwealth and organized groups for settlement in Palestine, but during World War I he had become stranded in America. In a 1916 lecture before the New York Achooza Aleph, he put forward a suggestion for a mixed farming economy. Drawing on his own experience in Palestine, he proposed a 20-dunam tract for each family, consisting of 4 dunams for cereal, 2 dunams for vegetables, 2 dunams for fruit trees and tobacco, 2 dunams for hay and flowers, 1 dunam for mulberry trees, 4 dunams for citrus groves, 1 dunam for the yard, 2 dunams for forest, 2 dunams for roads and paths, beehives, olive trees, and a barn. He estimated that the cost of land, house, tools, and preparation would be $1,700, and that a 20-dunam tract would provide an annual income of 1,200 francs ($240). His proposal was congruent with contemporary views in Palestine, which were in themselves a reaction to the monoculture colonies instituted under the tutelage of Baron Edmond de Rothschild at the turn of the century. Sheinkin did not specify the geographic location for such a settlement.[40]

Other organizations also consulted experts in Palestine. For example, the American Zion Commonwealth purchased land through the agency of the PLDC, as the company was well aware of the quantity of land available for purchase and settlement. The AMZIC wanted to purchase relatively large-scale tracts and thus turned to various experts to recommend what to purchase and how much to pay. The AMZIC board of directors resolved to consult with agronomist Aaron Aaronsohn, whose discovery of Emmer wheat in the Galilee in 1906 had earned him a strong reputation in scientific circles. In 1909 Aronsohn visited the United States at the invitation of the Department of Agriculture, and during his stay he successfully solicited the financial support of prominent American Jews for the founding of the Jewish Agricultural Experiment Station at Atlit. He returned to America twice, in late 1917 and again in the summer of 1918 at Chaim Weizmann's request for a political propaganda campaign to gain American support for the Zionist cause. Despite the directors' official resolution, neither Aaronsohn's diary entries nor the records of the AMZIC yield information about any such consultation with the AMZIC.[41]

The organization's representatives did suggest certain sizes for land holdings that would support prospective settlers. At first, the appropriate holding was defined according to the number of certificates. Menachem Sheinkin, then employed by the American Zion Commonwealth, explained that six certificates would provide a modest living, eight a good one, and ten a very good one. The price of each certificate was $250, and, according to Sheinkin, each certificate was redeemable for no less than 10 dunams but no more than 20 dunams.[42] Prior to the first land purchase by the AMZIC there was no actual translation of certificates into a defined area.

After gaining some experience in Palestine, the American Zion Commonwealth suggested that 75 dunams extensively cultivated in Balfouria would be sufficient for a family. This was translated into approximately eight land certificates.[43] This figure of 75 dunams is lower than any of the numbers suggested for this geographical region by the above mentioned experts. With hindsight, we can see that they were indeed correct in their assessment; the

AMZIC's reliance on the lower figure had definite repercussions for the success of their settlement. The colonists at Balfouria later told members of the Joint Palestine Survey Commission that they "believe they should have a farm unit of 75 acres," i.e., four times the amount allotted to them.[44] Later the American Zion Commonwealth sold plots according to size and quality, becoming much more specific as to the quantity necessary to support the intended settlers. For example, at Herzlia agricultural plots were 25 dunams, in line with estimates given by experts for irrigated tracts in this area.

Less well-informed planners drew their concepts of land use from their experience in America. The enormous difference between the physical size of Palestine and that of the United States was often not taken into account by American Jews, who overestimated the size of the estates they would purchase or be settled upon. Furthermore, specific information regarding Palestine, its soil, and its climate was usually not available to American Jews. As early as the 1870s, the Palestine Exploration Fund had surveyed and mapped the area, but this information did not include details about soil quality or the availability of water for agricultural use. During the late nineteenth and early twentieth centuries, various researchers had detailed the characteristics of the land and published their findings; the better known of these works was George Adam Smith's *Historical Geography of the Holy Land,* first issued in 1894.

Often American Jews who toured Palestine and inspected the landscape were unable to discern which land best suited their needs. They transferred their perceptions of soil productivity from their experience in the northern temperate climatic zone of the United States or from earlier experiences in Eastern Europe, where some had resided before immigrating to the United States. Frequently they had little understanding of soil and its relation to agriculture. They sometimes reached unfounded conclusions based on a short visit, having had only one season in which to formulate an image of the land.

Judah Leib Kazan and Isaiah Jarcho, representatives of the New York Achooza Aleph, toured Palestine in 1920 and were shocked by the PLDC's proposal that they purchase land with sandy soil. The two thought that nothing could be grown on it, whereas in fact this soil was appropriate for citrus culture, tobacco, vegetables, and a variety of other crops. On the other hand, they were impressed by the black soil in the Galilee; for them it was reminiscent of the very fertile chernozem soil found in sub-humid plains such as the Ukrainian steppes where they were born. Chernozem soil, however, is not found in the Galilee, nor in the rest of Palestine. The black earth Kazan and Jarcho encountered was actually grumosol or basaltic alluvium, much different in quality from chernozem soil.[45]

Quite often relative location or the availability of land was deemed as important or more so than soil quality. Indeed, in most documentation found with regard to prospective land purchases, no mention is made of soil quality. As a rule, only after the completion of a land transaction was any pedological survey conducted to determine which crops could be raised effectively. The Rosoff groups, however, which developed Gan Rashel and Ramot Meir, understood the importance of soil characteristics to the success of their ventures. To fulfill their goal—the development of citrus plantations—"a land of special quality has to be purchased, and a proper investigation of the conditions of the soil has to be conducted prior to planting."[46]

Quality signified not only the soil type but also the amount of water available. Yet even the best informed of the American immigrants had difficulty in estimating soil quality and the availability of water. Thus they sometimes purchased inappropriate lands at unsuitable prices, foregoing more potentially productive tracts.

Two American Zion Commonwealth tracts illuminate the difficulties of failing to investigate water supply—Herzlia with its drainage problems, and Afula with too little water. At Herzlia, winter rains accumulated behind the first kurkar ridge to the west of the Mediterranean Sea. Lacking proper drainage, the area was transformed annually into a swamp, rendering the area inappropriate for agricultural exploitation. These malarial swamps also posed a danger to the health of inhabitants in adjacent areas. Thus, in preparing these lands for settlement, the AMZIC bore an additional financial outlay for drainage of this swampy tract. The Afula land seemed to promise large quantities of water for agricultural, industrial, and domestic consumption. It was thought that wells could be bored to a depth where an underground river, originating at Mount Hermon, could be tapped. No such subterranean flow existed, however. Without the expected quantity of water, plans had to be adjusted for different types of settlement activities, in particular, extensive rather than intensive agriculture.

Not all land transactions were underlined by financial considerations. The importance of ownership, the sense of pride, self-esteem, honor, and self-worth partially motivated some purchasers. M. Talitman, the first secretary of Ramat Gan colony, noted an event in his journal which at first glance appears curious. An American visiting Palestine purchased land in Ramat Gan. Before his return, he asked the moshavah secretary to show it to him. The American then staged a photo opportunity—a calf in the background, with the secretary delivering the *kushan*—a good picture for the American newspapers.[47] The emotional aspect of land ownership should not be disparaged. According to Norman Bentwich, biographer of Judah Leib Magnes, Magnes's acquisition of land in Netanya was an expression of his desire "to be physically rooted in Palestine."[48]

The actual purchase of land in Palestine had important significance for the purchaser. Jewish National Fund contributions, expended for land purchase or amelioration through afforestation, gave donors the satisfaction of redeeming land from non-Jews and the sense that their contributions would help increase the possession of the Jewish people as a whole in Palestine. Both rich and poor could share in the joy of land redemption, through large contributions or through the donation of pennies in Jewish National Fund "Blue Boxes," slowly accumulating, just like the Jewish holding, dunam after dunam.

6

American Ahuza Colonies

> The Achoozah does not regard itself as a private society. True, it is private in its methods of work, but not in its aims and purposes. The leaders of the Achoozah are Zionists in the best sense of the word. They know that their work is of public value and they feel that they have the right to expect the cooperation and encouragement of every friend of the Jewish upbuilding of Palestine.[1]
> Avraham Revutsky [Abraham Revusky], "Raanana, the American Colony," *Jubilee Volume of the Jewish National Fund*

Prior to World War I, the *ahuza* agricultural settlement plan was proposed for the purpose of transferring capital to Palestine to establish agricultural colonies, to settle groups of Jews from the Diaspora in Palestine, and to provide employment for Jewish laborers in Palestine. To this effect, groups of approximately fifty families were formed. They pooled their resources, collecting regular installments until a sufficient sum had accumulated toward the purchase of a tract of land in Palestine. An American group would employ Jewish workers to prepare the land, plant fruit-bearing trees, and maintain them. After six or seven years, when the plantations bore sufficient fruit to provide an income for its owners, the land would be parceled and transferred to the individual owners waiting to immigrate, settle on their own land, and assume its maintenance.

Ahuza societies were set up in the United States, Canada, England, and Russia. Between 1908 and the outbreak of World War I, the following were established in American cities: Hoachoozo of St. Louis (1908); New York Ahuza Bet (1909); Brooklyn Ahuza Gimmel (1909); Chicago Ahuza Aleph (1911); St. Louis Ahuza Bet (1912); New York Achooza Aleph (1912); [Los Angeles] California Palestine Land and Development Company (1913); Cleveland Achuza No. 1 (1913); Worcester, Massachusetts, Ahuza (1913); Cincinnati, Ohio, Ahuza (1913); Chicago Ahuza Bet (1914); Pittsburgh Ahuza (1914); Philadelphia Ahuza (1914); Springfield, Massachusetts, Ahuza (1914); and Bnai Zion Achuza of Hartford.[2]

The activities of four American *ahuza* societies are discussed below. Two of them purchased land in Palestine and established colonies before World War I, while the other two acquired land after the war.

HOACHOOZO OF ST. LOUIS'S SETTLEMENT—PORIA

Simon Goldman organized the first American *ahuza* company in St. Louis in 1908. Goldman was born in Russia in 1859; in his youth he migrated to London, where he joined the local Hovevei Zion organization and gained experience in dealing with settlement in Palestine. From 1898 until 1902, he oversaw the administration of Hovevei Zion of England funds for the moshavah Bnai Yehuda on the Golan Heights. Following disagreements with Hovevei Zion, he returned to England and immigrated to the United States shortly afterward.

While living in St. Louis in 1908, Goldman adopted and promoted the *ahuza* plan. Two years later, through Arthur Ruppin's intervention, the St. Louis group bought 3,545 dunams, located 8.5 kilometers southwest of Tiberias, from the Jewish Colonization Association. The property extended along a north-south ridge approximately 250 to 350 meters above the Sea of Galilee. The colony was named Poria (Heb. fertile) as a symbol of their desire to make the abandoned and desolate land fruitful. In June of the following year, local Jewish and Arab workmen began development under the management of Eliyahu Israelite, the son of a farmer at the colony of Kastina (Beer Tuvia). The first American settler, Simon Goldman, established himself and his family at Poria in 1912.[3]

The development of the colony progressed well during its first years. A report in the newspaper *Hatzfira* in late 1912 praised Israelite for having transformed the tract into a Garden of Eden over a period of two years. By 1915, 2,000 dunams were planted with olive and almond trees.[4] The *Census of the Jews of Eretz Israel* for 1917 listed a population of 68 at Poria, of which 25 percent or 17 persons (4 adults and 13 children) had come from America.[5]

By 1918 the catastrophic events connected to the war in Palestine, aggravated by strained communications with America, had brought funding of the settlement to a virtual halt. The Turkish army appropriated wheat crops; cut down trees; carried away horses, cattle, sheep, machinery, and building material; and injured crops—though army officials promised to reimburse the colonists for the foodstuffs and livestock they had appropriated. Only after the situation was stabilized and the British military government established could interaction between the American *ahuza* society and its colony begin to return to normal. Efforts were then made to evaluate the situation and decide how to proceed.[6]

Unknown to Hoachoozo of St. Louis, other arrangements were being developed for its possessions in Palestine. Indeed, similar plans were also

CHAPTER 6

Fig. 17. The "Aliya" to Poria, 1912.
(CZA photograph collection 15,348)

being made for the Chicago *ahuza*'s colony of Sarona. Among the recommendations in a January 1919 report written by Akiva Ettinger and Yitzhak Vulcanski for the Agricultural Settlement Department was the placement of new settlers on existing private estates. The report recommended:

> On the lands belonging to private societies and to individuals, at least four hundred families engaged in agriculture could be settled. Should sufficient means be available from private sources for first technical improvements and sufficient funds for granting adequate advances on easy terms by an agricultural bank, even more intensive types of cultivation could be introduced than here anticipated, on private estates. In that case the free land in Jewish possession would be sufficient for perhaps double the number of settlers than here estimated.[7]

The two American *ahuzas* of Poria and Sarona (Rama) were among the thirteen private holdings under discussion by the department. The disbandment and eventual loss of ownership of the two colonies seemed predestined.

After the war, three American families—the Goldmans, Lewinsons, and Finkelsteins—remained at Poria. Eliyahu Israelite, the manager of Poria, attempted to reestablish contact with *ahuza* members in St. Louis in order to resume the flow of capital from the United States and continue development of the estate. The March 1919 report on the situation at Poria indicated that 2,500 of the colony's 3,500 dunams were covered with plantations.[8] Twenty-six Jewish and forty-two Arab laborers carried out the work in 1919. In the report's estimation, "thanks to the great energy and ability of Mr. Israelite, Poria suffered little during the war."[9] Because of capital flow problems, a loan was constructed to meet the expenses. The amount dispensed for land, building expenses, and the cost of planting 2,500 dunams was 626,000 francs ($125,200); a 200,000-franc ($40,000) loan was contracted to cover part of the expenses. The report predicted a profit for that year: a gross yield of the almond crop of about £4,000 ($20,000) and approximately £3,200 ($16,000) in expenses, leaving a net income of about £800 ($4,000). Until the sale of the year's crop, £1,000 ($5,000) was required to cover operating expenses. The report noted that this sum had to be transferred from St. Louis or borrowed in Palestine. It also predicted that the net yearly income would increase annually as the younger trees grew and their yield increased.[10]

Poria's future prospects depended upon its physical expansion. In 1914 the Jewish Colonization Association promised to sell 800 dunams on the colony's frontier. This, with the 3,500 dunams already in hand, would support forty-three families. The acquisition of 2,000 additional dunams on the colony's borders from a local effendi would allow its development into a larger colony.

Apart from a 30-dunam plantation, each colonist needed acreage for grain, vegetables, beekeeping, poultry, and dairy farming for personal consumption. For colonization to commence, approximately twenty members from St. Louis were needed to start working the land, with or without hired labor. In addition to the outlay for land and its improvement, each family had to contribute between £E800 and £E1000 ($4,000–5,000) to finance construction of communal buildings. It was hoped that wealthy members in St. Louis would advance a certain sum of money to poorer members willing to come immediately. In exchange, the land of those remaining in America would be cultivated by those with limited means. Thus, those at Poria would be provided with employment and a steady source of income until their own plantations reached the stage at which they could support the owners.[11]

In 1919 fifteen families affiliated with the American Mizrachi organization and members of the *ahuza* expressed their intention to migrate and settle in Poria, but they were not granted immigration permits. A later report stated that twelve settlers would arrive from the United States by March 1921. One settler intended to bring a tractor to use in the colony. The Mirsky family from Minnesota planned to settle at Poria in 1922, but because of the discouraging accounts they heard about the colony, they chose to reside in Herzlia instead.[12]

New York Achooza Aleph representatives Judah Leib Kazan and Isaiah Jarcho visited Poria in the summer of 1920. Their general impression was "it was but born and started to die." They found the almond trees yellow and wilting. The leader of the settlement, Simon Goldman, had died two years before their arrival. They reported that all but one of the American settlers had abandoned the colony.[13]

In 1921 the colonists expressed dissatisfaction with the method of working the plantations as a single unit. The manager and the eight families who by then were residing at Poria wanted to divide the land among the shareholders immediately. Newly arrived settlers hoped to use their private funds to develop their respective estates and did not wish to be burdened with collective problems. The response of the society in St. Louis was negative—it owed about £E8,000 ($40,000) to creditors, and most of this had to be paid back before anyone could obtain any part of the property, for they were mutually responsible for the debt. The society hoped that the present year's crop would pay off the greater part of the debt.[14]

In early 1922 more American stockholders abandoned Poria. The situation had worsened; the market for local almonds suffered due to competition from Italian almond growers. The colonists could not subsist on the almond plantations because the revenues failed to cover expenditures. One member, [?] Kaminis, lost his son in the 1921 riots and returned to America. Tzipora Finkelstein married in 1920, leaving Poria to settle at Degania Bet. The remainder of the Finkelstein family returned to the United States in 1922, settling in Boston until their return to Palestine and settlement in Herzlia in 1933. Six members of the Poria colony remained, with four working their own land. The situation was so grave that the tractor owner lacked funds for gasoline and oil. Requests for financial assistance from America were unrequited.[15]

In a letter to Harry Goldman, Arthur Ruppin explained that it was impossible to settle colonists on a piece of land if they could not be assured an income during the first year. He saw little hope for the colony if it followed the present direction of development. Other branches of agriculture, he thought—dairy and poultry farming, and some growing of wheat, barley, and fodder—should replace the almond plantations, for these crops would guarantee a secure revenue. To develop these other forms of agriculture, adjoining Jewish Colonization Association land was needed and a sufficient water supply pumped from the Sea of Galilee had to be assured. These changes would necessitate an expenditure of between £E20,000 and £E25,000 ($100,000 to $125,000).[16]

The bottom line was that in its present state, Poria could not support its owners. Ruppin made it clear that prospective settlers must have a thorough knowledge of agriculture, be able to conduct every kind of work, and be accustomed to the climate and conditions in Palestine. *Ahuza* members in America did not generally fit this description. Ruppin believed that the reorganization of Poria would be possible only when the owners relinquished all the colony's property to a group of local Jewish farmers. Ruppin suggested that the new farmers purchase the land and repay the original owners a sum equal to the fair market value of the property; his scheme provided for repayment, at a low interest rate, in twenty-five annual installments, beginning five years after the new families had been established in Poria. The property value would be estimated by a committee of experts, with owners and workmen equally represented.[17]

The American owners hoped that the Palestine Zionist Executive would provide the needed funds for the reorganization of Poria. However, the financial situation of the Palestine Zionist Executive and its various branches was itself critical, and the organization could barely maintain the settlements it had founded. Ruppin instead suggested that the *ahuza* society approach the American Zion Commonwealth with a proposal that the latter take over the colony. In July 1922, the AMZIC's response was negative: it was interested in redeeming land, not transferring money from its treasury to individual *ahuza* members in St. Louis. Nor was the AMZIC inclined to manage the colony, believing that this would only result in financial losses.[18]

In the summer of 1922, the Anglo-Palestine Company ordered the seizure of the entire almond crop, in repayment of part of the £E3,000 ($15,000) due from the colony. The colonists were left virtually penniless and, in certain cases, without the most elemental necessities of life. Israelite's report of October 1922 painted a bleak picture. Only four families, two of which were society members, remained at Poria, trying to eke out a livelihood from field crops. The 1922 census listed nineteen males and six females at the colony, less than half the population during the war. Colonists entreated Israelite's assistance in obtaining a loan of £E150 ($750) for seeds for the following year.[19]

In 1923 Poria's total debt reached £E9,000 ($45,000). Its members anticipated recouping some of their losses by filing two identical claims for $75,000 against the Turkish government for damages inflicted during the war—one claim with the British government through its manager in Palestine, and the second with the American government through its stockholders in St. Louis. Documented, itemized lists of all property that had appropriated and damaged were forwarded with the claims.[20]

Attempts to induce the Palestine Zionist Executive or the Keren Hayesod to take over Poria and settle *halutzim* there while providing the owners with some remuneration were without success. The *ahuza* society approached Zionist Organization of America president Louis Lipsky with the following request for assistance:

CHAPTER 6

> It is our hope that some solution should be found which will at least salvage something for our members who staked everything they had on the Colony. We feel that Dr. Weizmann might be able to arrange with the PLDC, or the Jewish National Fund or some other agency to take over the Colony, to pay its debts and to settle a few score families of Jewish colonists on the land. If it is impossible to induce any of the Zionist agencies to pay us money for the Colony either now or at some future time, possibly an arrangement can be made whereby we will be given in exchange for Poriah a parcel of land near Petah Tikvah or Tel Aviv, where land is in demand for building purposes.[21]

The *ahuza* could no longer bear the financial burdens of the colony. When the society was incorporated, it had assets of $120,000, but the outlay for Poria was about $160,000. It owed various creditors $25,000 to $40,000, much of this debt incurred because of the exorbitant rates of interest that had been charged. Sixteen years had passed since the founding of the *ahuza*. Some members had died, leaving widows and children in financial difficulties because of their investment in the colony. Other members were too old to work and support themselves. Of all of the stockholders, only three members were financially stable. During a visit to Palestine, member E. Davis spoke with Arthur Ruppin, of the PLDC, and Dr. Melech Zagrodsky, an agronomist and advisor on agricultural settlement. Davis asked why they had not been told the truth about conditions in Poria. It became clear that if the truth were told, the society would never have sent any money.[22]

The Jewish National Fund took the matter of Poria under consideration. It conditionally agreed to accept the lands if the *ahuza* society paid all connected debts. JNF fund-raisers in St. Louis would then collect money for the colony's expansion, and the JNF would match the amount, dollar for dollar. However, no formal accord was reached on this provisional agreement.[23]

Finally M. J. Slonim of Hoachoozo of St. Louis appealed directly to Chaim Weizmann—in his capacity as president of the World Zionist Organization—to intervene, explaining:

> I would not take up your valuable time with these sentiments, were it not for the fact that I have been called upon by the *Committee* representing the *Colony of Poriah* to inquire whether you are taking any steps toward the solution of their problem. They are particularly concerned at this time because they have received news from Palestine to the effect that Poriah has been placed on sale in order to satisfy certain obligations supposed to have been incurred by the Colony. I need not reiterate what is quite clear to you, namely that if the colony is wrested from these people without proper compensation being made, two scores of families will have lost all that they possess. Obviously, such a situation would do us great injury locally, and

would certainly do us no good nationally. The failure of Poriah would be bound to react unfavorably on our work in Palestine.[24]

In 1925 the American Zion Commonwealth was again contacted to take over Poria, its improvement, parceling and sale. The value of Poria was assessed at £E8,800 ($44,000). The price of the land was £E2.5 per dunam, totaling £E7,600; the infrastructure was assessed at £E1,200. The £E300 debt to the government of Palestine and the £E6,000 debt to creditors were to be paid from the sale of the colony. Money left over after outstanding debts were paid would be divided among the members of Hoachoozo of St. Louis. With the land in its possession, the AMZIC would transfer 1,000 dunams to the Jewish National Fund for Kvutzah Har-Kinneret and 500 dunams to the five families that remained at Poria. The AMZIC would have more than 2,000 dunams remaining for other colonization activities.[25]

This proposal appears to have been unsatisfactory to the *ahuza* because the society would recoup only £E1,500 ($7,500), a small fraction of the $160,000 it had invested. The St. Louis group had no recourse but to turn to Chaim Weizmann a second time, imploring him "to cause [the] Zionist Organization to settle [the] indebtedness of [the] Poria Colony and to have [the] land of this colony appraised by [an] impartial committee appointed by yourself so as to enable us to save investments through [a] new agreement."[26]

In 1926, with no end in sight, the Anglo-Palestine Company, a major debt-holder, warned the Palestine Zionist Executive that after three years of waiting, it had no option but to put the land up for public auction. To emphasize the seriousness of this action, the company called attention to a very sensitive issue in the Zionist approach to land redemption—that these lands might not remain in Jewish hands. The bank reported that an Egyptian land speculator, Selim Shadid, had taken an interest in Poria. Subsequently the High Court of Justice rendered a decision that the property was to be sold in a public auction. The Anglo-Palestine Company was the highest bidder, offering £E4,200. The president of the Haifa District Court, at the request of various parties, extended the sale period, since the highest bid was roughly half the assessed property value.[27]

In 1929 only two of the *ahuza* members—Hanoch Halperin and Shmaya Schwartz—remained at Poria. The property had fallen into decay and the land was being farmed by neighboring Arabs. The remains of structures were scavenged by Arabs and the villagers of Yavniel. Standing trees were foraged for firewood. Following the 1929 riots, the remaining settlers left Poria, and it was further looted and destroyed.[28]

In 1941 the land was resettled by a group affiliated with Hever Hakvutzot. In 1949 the *kfar avoda* Poria and the urban settlement Poria (Nave Oved) were founded. In 1955, another urban settlement, Poria Elit (Upper Poria), was established in this area. Poria is now a suburb of the city of Tiberias.

CHAPTER 6

CHICAGO AHUZA'S SETTLEMENT—SARONA

The *ahuza* plan was adopted by a group in Chicago in 1911. The following year, representatives of the Chicago Ahuza Society turned to Arthur Ruppin of the Palestine Land Development Company with the request that he acquire land in Palestine for the *ahuza*. Their specifications were for an area of 5,000 dunams, with the possibility of paying for it in installments. As various proposals were presented to the *ahuza,* specifications vis-à-vis the location of the tract were added. A proposal for land at Rafiah on the northern coast of the Sinai Peninsula was rejected since the location was distant from other settlements and conditions would not provide the standard of living expected by the prospective group of settlers from Chicago. Following this proposal, the *ahuza* specified a preference for land between Jaffa and Jerusalem. Karkur, a 6,000-dunam Jewish Colonization Association tract in the northern Sharon plain, was another possibility; however, it could not be purchased in installments.[29]

In 1913 the Jewish Colonization Association agreed to an installment purchase of a tract in the Lower Galilee. The 5,525-dunam Sarona tract was sold at 15 francs ($3) a dunam, with a down payment of 75,000 francs ($25,000). The total cost of the tract, including 17 percent interest over a period of repayment of ten years, was 262,000 francs ($52,400). The tract, which lay along a relatively flat ridge with an elevation of 250 meters above sea level, was ten kilometers southwest of Tiberias along the Yavniel-Kfar Tavor road, near the Muslim Arab village of Sarona.[30]

The new colony was named Rama, but was also known as Sarona.[31] Work began in 1913; the land was prepared for the planting of almond and olive trees. As of 1918, eleven persons resided in Sarona, only one of whom was American. It appears that he had arrived at the time of the founding of the colony and served as its administrator. Four workers and a family of six also dwelled there.[32]

Sarona, like Poria, suffered as a result of World War I. The 2,000-dunam almond plantation waned during the war. In addition, the burden of repaying the loan from the Jewish Colonization Association and the colony's upkeep strained the finances of its members. Some members in Chicago had passed away; others were left with limited resources. Those who did attempt to settle in Sarona found it in ruins, without any defense, no school or other necessities. None of them remained there. In 1919 the Chicago Ahuza sent Lee Berman and his family to administer Sarona. He arrived the following year, and was later joined by three other Americans, Pinhas Shamir, Abraham Kaplan, [?] Yakir, and some of their family members. As of 1922, there were fifteen Jews living in Sarona.[33]

In May 1922, Chicago Ahuza president M. Benamy sent a proposal to the Palestine Zionist Executive Agriculture and Settlement Department offering part of the colony to the Jewish National Fund. The *ahuza* was willing to forego 1,500 dunams if the JNF would pay the colony's £E1.35-per-dunam debt to the Jewish Colonization Association. Another stipulation was that the Palestine Zionist Executive would arrange for at least fifteen temporary workers until *ahuza* members could settle there. The agreement was worked out with the JNF, which requested that the permanent settlers be willing to live harmoniously with "bourgeois" Americans. The *ahuza* members hoped to develop an agricultural colony with more experienced pioneers, since almost all the Americans were from an urban background.[34]

At the end of 1922, a formal proposal was sent to the Jewish National Fund to transfer to it 2,000 dunams with the following conditions:

> 1. The Jewish National Fund would accept the debt to the Jewish Colonization Association for its part of the land, approximately $7.00 per dunam, and the Ahuza would no longer be responsible to the Jewish Colonization Association for it.
>
> 2. The Jewish National Fund would settle no less than twenty families in the summer of 5683 (1923).
>
> 3. The Jewish National Fund would send experts to measure and divide the land in the best way practiced in Eretz Israel.
>
> 4. The moshavah would be built on one site together with members of the Ahuza.
>
> 5. The Jewish National Fund would share proportionately in the uprooting of trees and the vineyard and all needs of the moshavah.
>
> 6. The Jewish National Fund would receive only 2,000 dunams of land but the Jewish National Fund would have no part of [our] live inventory [livestock] and inanimate inventory, not the houses, buildings or plantations in Sarona.[35]

At the same time, the former settlers at Rama wrote to Menachem Ussishkin with a similar proposal for the Jewish National Fund to take over 2,000 dunams. This proposal was for a moshav *ovdim,* not a moshavah.[36]

The matter of Sarona reached Chaim Weizmann's attention during his visit to Chicago in May 1923. Max Shulman discussed the problem with Weizmann, who agreed to have the Keren Hayesod use $10,000 raised in Chicago for the settlement of pioneers. That summer, a collective of pioneers known as the Brisk *kvutzah* left Kfar Yehezkel and settled in Sarona. They began plowing and sowing the fields, but the harvest was meager, and there was barely enough to feed them. They were unable to raise vegetables since the colony's supply of water was limited. The *kvutzah*'s debts multiplied. Because of the distance from potential places of employment, settlers were unable to find additional work to supplement their income. After two years the *kvutzah* concluded that it could not take root and develop at this particular site, and so it left Sarona. One American, Pinhas Shamir, remained in Sarona until 1928. In the end, the holdings of the Chicago Ahuza were returned to the Palestine Jewish Colonization Association (the heir of the Jewish Colonization Association).[37] The land lay idle for almost a decade. Only in 1938 was a moshav founded at the site by members of the Gordonia organization.

NEW YORK ACHOOZA ALEPH

On 17 July 1912, a group of Jews in the New York area founded the New York Achooza Aleph, which later established the colonies of Raanana and Gan Yavne. In December 1914, the *ahuza* was incorporated under the Business Corporation Law of the State of New York with capital of $10,000. Its stated purposes were:

> 1. To use all legal efforts in encouraging the emigration of Jews from the various countries into Palestine.
> 2. To aid in the settlement of immigrants and the establishment of Jewish Colonies in Palestine.
> 3. To purchase, own, mortgage, sell and lease ground and real estate. . . .
> 4. To conduct scientific or other investigations in agricultural, mining or other industries.[38]

Over two decades, the New York Achooza Aleph succeeded in attracting a large number of purchasers. They were "mostly of the middle class people—that is, professionals, teachers, small business men, laborers, that have only one idea in mind, and that is [to] establish themselves and their families in Palestine," as they explained to American Zionist leader Rabbi Stephen S. Wise. As of June 1931, 234 individuals had purchased 207.5 units (the minimum purchase was one-half unit). The value of the sales plus interest and taxes was $388,279, of which $315,224 was paid on account. This sum did not include the outlay on the improvement of the properties through plantings, the construction of houses, barns, and other buildings, and infrastructure.[39]

Before its incorporation, the company had collected $10,000 and decided to purchase a suitable tract. The *ahuza* approached Ruppin to intercede on their behalf; they specified that they required 6,000 to 7,000 dunams, which could be improved with olive and almond plantations, located in the vicinity of Jerusalem. The PLDC suggested various tracts—Karkur, Wadi Hawareth (Emek Hefer), Ein Hai, and Jemmama (Ruchama)—all of which were rejected by the *ahuza,* since the tracts were not close to Jerusalem.[40]

Simon Goldmann of the Hoachoozo of St. Louis, already in Palestine, was asked to assist in this endeavor. He was a familiar figure due to his activities promoting the *ahuza* plan in the United States and his bid to create an umbrella organization for American *ahuzot*. The New York *ahuza* was offered the Abu Shusha (Gezer) tract located 45 kilometers west of Jerusalem on the road to Jaffa. It had been purchased a year earlier by the Jewish Colonization Association from the estate of Peter Melville Bergheim and was not settled. Negotiations began but were not concluded, partially because this tract was reported to have poor water resources.[41]

New York Achooza Aleph president Michael Salit went to Palestine to complete arrangements, but the outbreak of hostilities prevented him from achieving his mission. He initiated unconcluded negotiations over the lands of the villages of Kuskus and Tivon, located on the fringes of Haifa Bay. In 1926 Meshek and the American Zion Commonwealth purchased 10,000 dunams from these villages (see chapter 7). This tract fell outside the society's locational specifications, and it is unclear from the correspondence of the New York Achooza Aleph whether it seriously considered making this purchase.

In 1916 the *ahuza* was "handed a rude jolt" when the Yiddish press reported that all the funds of the Anglo-Palestine Company in Jaffa had been confiscated by the Turks. The *ahuza* had $40,000 on deposit. As news of the seizure spread, certain members became disheartened and suggested abandoning the entire project. President Michael Salit, the *ahuza* treasurer Leopold Kehlman, and secretary Samuel Judenfreund persuaded members to persevere and continue their payments, which were deposited in the State Bank of New York. The following year word was received from David Zalman Levontin, the Anglo-Palestine Company's manager, that he had transferred all the company's funds safely to Egypt.[42]

After the war, the *ahuza* recommenced its quest for a suitable stretch of land. Two of its representatives, Isaiah Jarcho and Judah Leib Kazan, sailed to Palestine in 1920. The membership's declared preference was still for land in Judaea—not for economic reasons but because they were drawn to the region for its symbolic nature. Biblical and Talmudic sources alluded to Judaea as the heartland of the Holy Land and Jerusalem, its navel. To this end, one member proposed that the *ahuza* buy Sarona, the Templer colony, whose founders—German nationals—had been deported by the British during the war. The colony was in close proximity to Tel Aviv. Sarona, however, was not for sale.[43]

In 1920 the Palestine Land Development Company offered the *ahuza*'s representatives four possible tracts for purchase—33,000 dunams at Nuris, 22,000 at Tel Adas, 27,000 at Kfar Malul, and 800 dunams near Haifa. The first three proposed tracts were in the Jezreel Valley, and varied in quality and price. The Tel Adas tract was adjacent to the Balfouria tract. From Kazan's account, the Palestine Land Development Company was not enthusiastic about the *ahuza* settling in the Jezreel Valley, for this area demanded special preparation and improvement. Instead, the Palestine Land Development Company suggested tracts in the Galilee. Jarcho and Kazan toured Palestine, trying to gain an impression of available tracts. That year, the PLDC futilely attempted to purchase the Sidney Ali lands (also known as Jelil lands) for the *ahuza*. Other agents also attempted to find land for the New York society. Kazan met with one Jerusalem real estate agent who suggested a tract half an hour's travel east of Jerusalem in the Judaean desert. The proximity to the Holy City was deemed attractive but its aridity made it inappropriate for agriculture.[44]

Finally, the Palestine Land Development Company presented the two representatives an option for the tract of Khirbet Azun, an area of approximately 7,000 dunams. After hesitation and much uncertainty they reached an agreement. This property at least answered their desire for land in the vicinity of Judaea, but Jarcho demanded the PLDC satisfy certain conditions before the agreement was finalized. One was that the tract extend one kilometer to the north and another kilometer to the south of the planned main street leading to the railroad station at Kfar Saba. Furthermore, lands beyond these lines were to be taken off the *ahuza*'s hands immediately and the *ahuza* credited. These conditions were a result of a preconceived settlement plan. Already in New York, the organizers of the *ahuza* wanted a colony extending along one main axis. Symmetrical tracts would extend perpendicularly outward from the main thoroughfare.[45]

The Khirbet Azun tract totaled 8,527.24 dunams, of which two sections, the first 4,634.44 dunams and the second 870.19 dunams, were purchased by the New York Achooza Aleph. The deal was concluded at the end of 1921, and the purchase price was £E13,387 (£E2.432 per dunam). This area was known locally as "Old Raanana."[46]

In addition, the Sidney Ali tract was again suggested to the New York Achooza Aleph. This 6,000-dunam tract, 500 meters to the west of the *ahuza*'s lands and extending to the coast, was available at a price of £E5 per dunam plus transfer fees and other expenses. The terms of payment were £E2 per dunam at the time of transfer and the remainder in quarterly installments over three to four years. The Palestine Land Development Company expected to purchase the connecting section in the future. Instructions were forwarded from New York to halt the negotiations over the Sidney Ali tract until the land between it and Raanana could be secured.[47]

Two further transactions were negotiated through the Palestine Land Development Company. In 1928 the *ahuza* hoped to buy 2,000 dunams of the El Haram tract north of Herzlia. It also expected to purchase the tract of Tel Raanan—6,000 dunams adjoining the plantations of Lord Melchett at Tel Mond—to be named "Marshallia" in honor of Justice Louis Marshall. There was a good prospect of an early conclusion to negotiations. In 1929 the PLDC bought 6,600 dunams at El Haram; it then transferred 1,600 dunams to the New York Achooza Aleph and 5,000 dunams to the American Zion Commonwealth. Altogether, the PLDC purchased 10,322 dunams in Raanana and its environs, of which 9,898 were sold to private clients.[48]

In November 1930, the purchase of 1,300 dunams, also in the area of El Haram, from the El Omri family was considered, but because of the society's worsening financial situation, the New York Achooza Aleph did not obtain it. Instead, the Jewish Agency executive instructed the Jewish National Fund to finance the purchase. In 1931 Joseph Weitz investigated the Arsuf tract, a northern section of El Haram. He reported that the land was appropriate for intensive cultivation but not for settlement of workers under the "Thousand Settlement Plan." He suggested that it would be more suitable for the expansion of Raanana, allowing for its planned continuation to the coast.[49]

Prior to the formulation of the New York Achooza Aleph's constitution in 1914, the society's management and membership had no preconceived notions of the spatial organization and economy of the settlement they wanted to develop. Thus the society's constitution included a quite general definition of intentions, as shown in two relevant articles:

> 3. To purchase, own, mortgage, sell and lease ground and real estate; to engage in mining, or the sub-soil industries; to purchase and raise all kinds of poultry and livestock; to build and operate dairies & creameries for the production and manufacture of butter, cheese, and other products, purchase and dispose of them; to construct buildings of all kinds and to lease same or otherwise to dispose of the same; to develop dams and conserve water and to lay pipes; to construct ditches and flumes for irrigation purposes; to have electric and hydraulic power for the purpose of necessary machinery and to purchase oil and operate all kinds of machinery and appliances necessary or useful in directing general farming, stock raising, dairy operations, house building, mining or other sub-soil industries; to construct, equip, maintain and build public works of all kinds, including railways, railroads, docks, harbours, piers, wharfs, canals, reservoirs, sewers, water, gas, warehouses and buildings public and private and all other works of public or private use; and also to build, own, purchase or otherwise acquire for its own use and operation railways and railroads. . . .
>
> 4. To conduct scientific or other investigations in agricultural, mining or other industries.[50]

Following the war, the *ahuza* representatives Judah Leib Kazan and Isaiah Jarcho who were sent to purchase the land slowly became more familiar with the situation in Palestine, particularly with regard to land quality, prices, and agricultural opportunities. The two differed in opinion as to how to develop Palestine. Both supported the growth of industry, holding that it was more appropriate for their American constituents, most of whom

Map 3a. Raanana and its vicinity, 1938

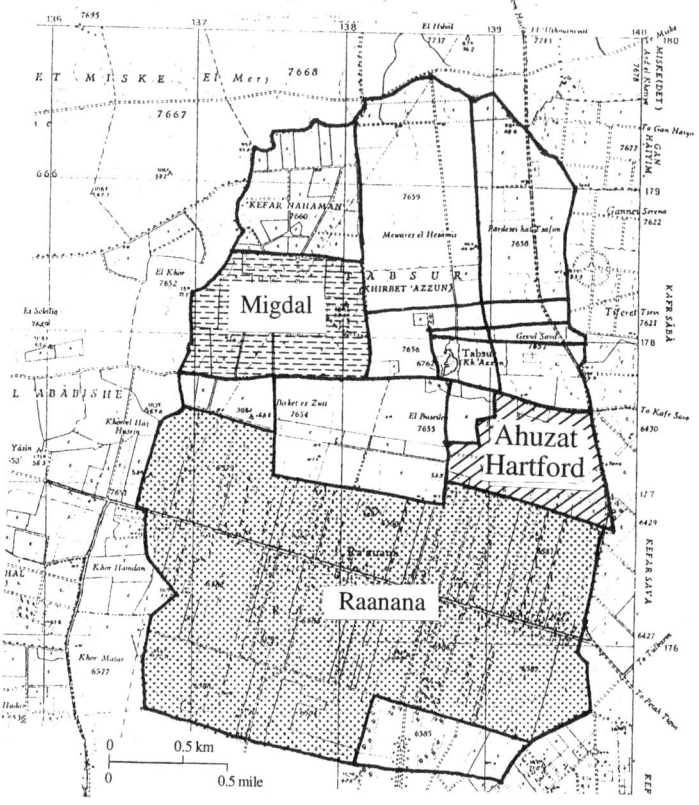

Map 3b. Plan of Raanana

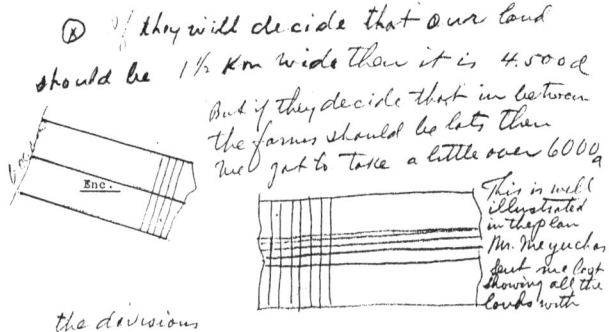

If they will decide that our land should be 1 2/2 km wide then it is 4.500 d[unams]. But if they decide that in between the farms should be lots then you got to take a little over 6.000 d[unams]. This is well illustrated in the plan Mr. Meyuchas sent me last showing all the lands with the divisions. (CZA L18/94/1)

were middle-aged or elderly and had no agricultural experience. Kazan did not want to determine the exact shape of the future settlement, preferring to await the arrival of the members. Jarcho, an engineer, insisted that an exact plan be drawn up. With their orientation to industry, they envisioned that plots would be ten dunams and not fifty as needed for agriculture; this effectively changed the general concept of the settlement from a moshavah to a garden city.[51]

The New York management of the *ahuza* chose to follow the agricultural route and decided on large plots of approximately fifty dunams. The *ahuza* disapproved of selling smaller parcels, asserting that an American family could not make a comfortable living from ten or fifteen dunams and would need a secure income from other sources. The society divided the tract following the conceptualization developed in New York. American Zionist leader and *ahuza* member Julius Haber reminisced over its planning and provided his impressions of the colony.

> Looking down the colony's main avenue some five and a half kilometers long, and the only one of its kind in all of Israel, I was reminded of the many evenings we had spent together in the early 20's as members of the Achuza's executive in the home of the president Nathan Chazan, discussing the layout of the colony. Though everyone in Palestine had advised us against planning such a vast length of thoroughfare, with the colony laid out alongside it (most favored was the usual radial layout developed by other colonies for reason of defense) the engineer on our executive Board, Joshua Jarcho had an entirely different idea. He saw in the plans for Raanana a pleasant suburban type of development created to allow for flexibility in growth and [a] more leisurely, less formal layout than that imposed by the radial plan. We supported him in his contention and today we can see the wisdom of his viewpoint for the main thoroughfare of Raanana is the pride of the colony's 12,000 residents.[52]

In keeping with this concept, one principal east-west street was laid out with perpendicular, elongated plots, 62 meters along the main street by 750 meters deep. The exact size of each plot was 46.5 dunams. In addition, certain sections were allocated for public space, institutions, and structures, including a water tower. The site for the water tower was carefully selected atop the kurkar ridge that traversed the colony.[53]

Even before settlement began, ten American families arrived in Palestine and waited for the day when details of the transaction would be finalized and they could claim their tracts. On 18 May 1922, a group planted the Stars and Stripes, the Union Jack, and the Zionist flag on the hill of Raanana. Landowners hurried to build their own homes, mainly wooden shacks and tents. Most had insufficient funds to afford the proper building materials that were brought from Tel Aviv.[54] At that time, no road connected this new

CHAPTER 6

Fig. 18. View of the main street of Raanana, 1927.
(Raanana Municipal Archives photograph collection 437)

settlement directly to Tel Aviv, thus hindering communication and increasing transportation costs.

The first settlers in Raanana commenced by plowing and planting vegetables and barley. Having had little or no agricultural experience, they nonetheless "were filled with the joy of seeing the products of their labors." These efforts may have pleased the farmers, but they were insufficient for their maintenance. The first years saw attempts to plan the colony's economy and develop various agricultural branches that could supply Tel Aviv with fresh produce; this was, of course, conditional upon improved transportation. Vegetables, poultry, and dairy farming seemed logical types of agriculture, but the dairy branch failed due to low milk prices, and the others were hindered by transportation problems.[55]

Another crop that looked promising was tobacco. Fields were planted and a drying shack was constructed, but tobacco was cultivated for only one year. The farmers' inexperience, their inability to compete with the extremely low labor costs of the Balkan countries producing Turkish tobacco, the depressed American demand for Turkish tobacco, and government taxation all led to great losses, which were absorbed by the farmers.[56]

Finally, an appropriate and profitable kind of farming—citriculture—was introduced to Raanana, with the thrust beginning in 1928. The previous year 112 dunams were put to citrus cultivation; this acreage would begin producing a crop in 1932. In 1928, 566 dunams were planted with trees that would start to bear marketable fruit in 1933. Ownership of this citrus plantation was divided: twenty growers resident in Raanana farmed 317 dunams,

172

Fig. 19. American-style house in Raanana, 1927.
(Raanana Municipal Archives photograph collection 436)

an average of 15.85 dunams per holding; thirteen absentee American owners held 361 dunams, an average of 27.78 dunams per holding. The total area under citriculture increased to 1,657 dunams in 1935.

One drawback of this kind of farming was the five-year period between planting and the first yield. Many Americans chose to remain in the United States during this maturation process in order to continue working at jobs that would finance their investment; they put off their departure for Palestine until their groves could provide them with an income that would sustain them. Tending the orchards of the absentee owners during their first years provided employment to farmers in Raanana and other Jewish laborers. Some of the work was contracted to Yakhin, the agricultural cooperative association of the Histadrut. American techniques as practiced in California were introduced in some orchards. To allow the tractors proper access between the rows, farmers planted thirty-six saplings per dunam instead of sixty as locally practiced. This spacing and the use of tractors did not, in the end, yield any particular advantage; indeed, it resulted in lower productivity per dunam.[57]

Though Raanana specialized in orange cultivation, other crops such

CHAPTER 6

Fig. 20. Tobacco drying at Raanana, 1927.
(Raanana Municipal Archives photograph collection 762)

as grapefruit, bananas, table grapes, and vegetables were also developed. In 1935 bananas were planted on 52 dunams and cereals sown on 3,672 dunams. Other means of economic development were also attempted. In 1929 there were two factories, six workshops, and three stores. Throughout the 1930s there was a continuous decrease in the number of persons gaining their livelihood from agriculture: in 1936, for example, 58.8 percent of Raanana's inhabitants subsisted from agriculture, whereas almost all of the original residents were farmers.

As for services and infrastructure, in 1929 Raanana had seventy dunams of forest and public gardens. By 1932 there were a number of community and public buildings—a local council hall, synagogue, post office, school, two kindergartens, clinic, workers' center, and two sport clubs (Maccabi and Hapoel). The colony also possessed a modern water system. "To one who does not know Palestine," Abraham Revusky wrote, "this may not mean very much. Suffice it to say it is one of the most characteristic earmarks of a progressive community in the whole of the Near East." Raanana's wells, equipped with seven electric pumps, had a capacity of over 35,000 gallons (132.5 cubic meters) an hour.[58]

With regard to the population's changing composition, Raanana began with the settlement of ten American families in 1922 (five of whom still resided in Raanana in 1949). The hardships of life in the settlement led some to leave—either for Tel Aviv or Jerusalem, or to return to the United States. Others flourished in the new colony. Baruch Ostrowsky, an *ahuza* member who had left the United States in 1930 to manage the settlement, later became mayor of Raanana. Non-Americans also populated Raanana, for the colony needed additional workmen. The New York Achooza Aleph had a specific policy that only Jewish labor be employed even if this meant increased costs; the policy was in line with the concept of "conquest of labor." The *ahuza* went one step further, however: only organized Jewish labor was employed. Thus Yakhin, the agricultural cooperative association of the Histadrut, worked with the Palestine management of the *ahuza*. The 1927 population of Raanana was 156. Two years later it had increased to 550, with many Jewish workers absorbed into the colony. The moshavah grew further with the influx of German immigrants during the 1930s. As of September 1936, the population of Raanana was 2,299.[59]

Raanana's achievements were numerous. Its economic success, derived from the citrus groves, created a flourishing settlement that attracted a large Jewish population. In 1931 its population ranked fourteenth among Jewish rural settlements, rising to tenth in 1936. Foundations were laid during this period which transformed the colony into one of the more prosperous cities in Israel.

Was there a relationship between Raanana's design and its long-term success? In a 1932 article focusing on Raanana, Abraham Revusky wrote about the advantages and disadvantages of the moshavah's design.

> The "American plan" adopted in Raanana has many advantages. It brings the colonist into more intimate contact with his plantation, it facilitates his work and observation, it makes the growing generation more soil-conscious and more expert in agricultural work. . . .
>
> On the other hand, the experience of Raanana has revealed some of the defects of this plan. It affects adversely the social life of the individual and the community and necessitates various additional expenditures, such as result from the installation of a regular bus service for school children and so forth.

In conclusion, Revusky compared the American conception to its European counterpart:

> On the force of this experience the present membership of Ahuza seems to be more in sympathy with the European plan of settlement adopted in most of the other colonies in Palestine. That plan provides for a village, centrally located, where the settlers dwell, and for the fields and plantations

thrown out in a circle around the village. The settlers go to work daily in their plantations, sometimes at a considerable distance from their homes.[60]

Revusky's observations were appropriate for Raanana as an agricultural settlement. But as noted above, by 1936 the percentage of those engaged in agriculture had declined to 58.8 percent. This dropped even further with the growth of the service sector and the beginnings of industry.

As it turned out, the original plan was well-suited to the needs of a less agriculturally-oriented settlement. The organization of the lots and thoroughfares was particularly appropriate for later development—the rapid urbanization of the region and the transformation of the colony into a suburb of Tel Aviv. The boundaries of the perpendicular plots served as the roads. Today the main thoroughfare, Ahuza Street, is the commercial center of the city, with strip retailing. Indeed, an important factor in the colony's success was its readiness to repeat the main street scheme. The society's second colony, Gan Yavne, followed another American plan: the garden city design.

From the perspective of American Jewish settlement, Raanana was a magnet for North American *olim.* Mayor Baruch Ostrowsky pointed out that there were some 100 American and Canadian families in Raanana in 1949, and "Today they are the leaders and policy-makers in all social and community activities."[61] The colony's population reached 5,300 in 1948, and in the late 1990s it is a city within the Tel Aviv metropolitan area with 57,500 inhabitants.

GAN YAVNE, THE SECOND COLONY

Unable to purchase additional land in the vicinity of Raanana, the New York Achooza Aleph continued to try to develop an agricultural colony in a second location, at Gan Yavne. In 1930 it began negotiations to acquire lands from the village of Kfar Barka, near the historical Jewish settlement of Yavne in Judaea. Located in the southern coastal plain, Yavne had the appropriate climatic conditions for the development of citrus plantations. This form of economic exploitation had rapidly gained popularity among both foreign and local investors. Land in the southern Sharon was at a premium, and prices in the southern coastal plain were lower. The New York Achooza Aleph bought a 4,600-dunam tract at £P4 per dunam. (In 1921 the average price per dunam at Raanana was £E2.72, but by 1929 it had risen to £P6.67.) The transfer was completed in 1931, and the total cost—including expenses, taxes, and commissions—was £P19,569.[62]

The new colony began in 1932, with the preparation of 400 dunams for planting orange groves. The early development of Gan Yavne reflected the success of Raanana. American investors continued to be attracted by this form of venture. Moreover, the experience already acquired in citriculture

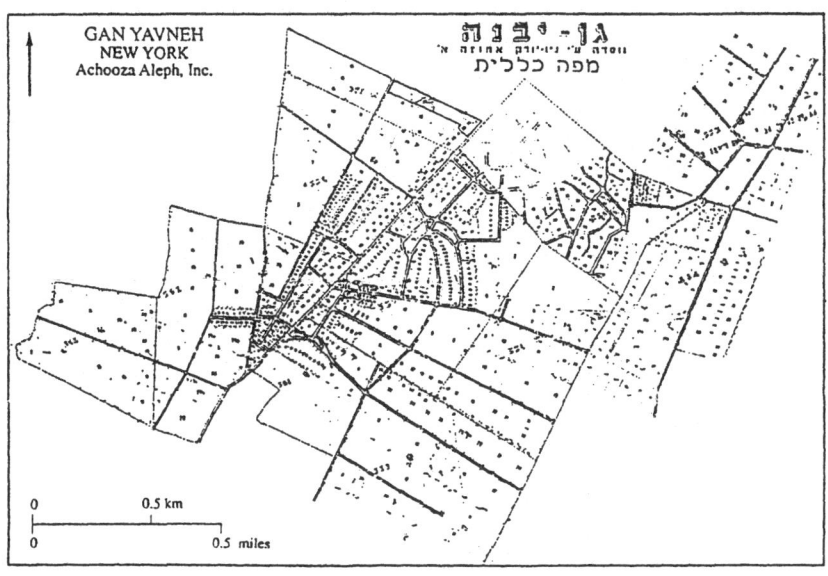

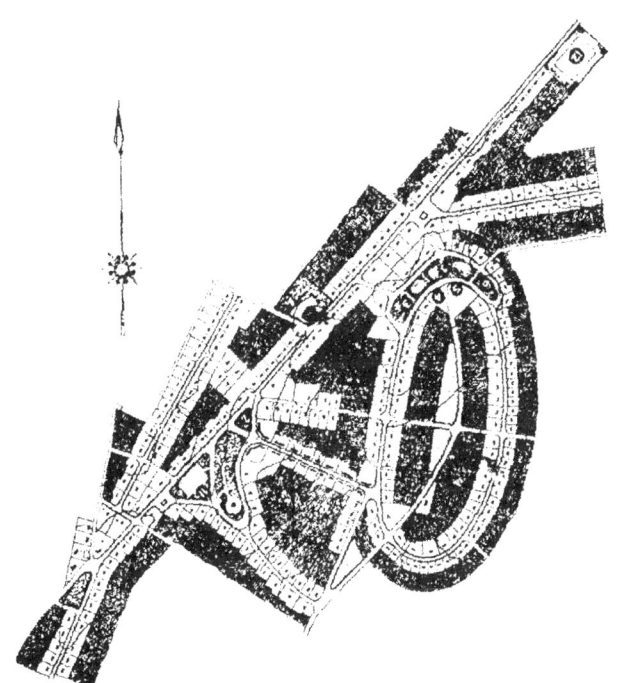

Map 4. Gan Yavne, general map and settlement plan, 1933. (*Top*) Gan Yavne and surrounding agricultural lands. (*Bottom*) Detailed plan of the settlement.

could be applied to the southern colony. Adjacent to the colony, an agricultural workers' settlement was established on thirty-two dunams of Jewish National Fund land. Under the auspices of Yakhin, the workers planted, tended, and later harvested the orchards. As of 1936, 1,631 dunams were under citrus plantations and 263 under irrigated crops. The land was divided into 14 plots of less than 20 dunams, and 78 over 20 dunams. Of the 92 farms, 77 were based primarily on citriculture.[63]

The workers' colony and the *ahuza* colony were united under municipal jurisdiction. By 1936, the colony's population reached 272 or approximately 140 families, of which only eight or nine were members of the *ahuza*. This created conflict within the local committee because the interests of the workers differed from those of the landowners, particularly with respect to taxation and education.[64]

With regard to the size of the American population, research indicates that the highest figure at any one time was ten families. One event that contributed to this low number occurred in 1936, when the plantations were attacked by Arab rioters and partially destroyed. The effect of this attack can be illustrated by the example of Abraham Singer, a former Legionnaire who had bought land in Gan Yavne. When the Arab revolt broke out in 1936, he was already en route to Palestine, but he abandoned his plans to settle at Gan Yavne and returned to his native Tulsa, Oklahoma. The ensuing unrest, which continued intermittently until 1939, probably also dissuaded other *ahuza* members from settling on their tracts.[65]

One of the colony's problems was its isolation: it was surrounded by six Arab villages. A road that would connect Gan Yavne with other Jewish communities was needed for its continued development. As a resident explained in a letter to Rabbi Stephen S. Wise in 1937: "It is more than certain that without a highway, Gan Yavneh will go under, and the fortune of hundreds of members of the Achooza will be lost. Six hundred workers employed in Gan Yavneh will go idle." It is unclear whether the *ahuza* was updating Wise or appealing to the president of the Zionist Organization of America. But the letter pointed out the problems of personal safety and of transporting produce to market. Between 1936 and 1938, negotiations began with the Mandatory government, and later a paved road was constructed.[66]

In 1948 the settlement had a population of 302. Today it is an urban settlement of 5,660 within the Tel Aviv metropolitan area.

BNAI ZION ACHUZA, HARTFORD, CONNECTICUT

A second *ahuza* society active in Palestine following World War I was Bnai Zion Achuza of Hartford, Connecticut. An attempt to merge with New York Achooza Aleph for a joint purchasing and colonization project was made, but the Hartford group's funds were insufficient.[67] Another possible explanation for the New York *ahuza*'s disinterest in a merger was its desire to retain its independence. Indeed, New York Achooza Aleph had earlier withstood pressure from the Zionist Organization of America to join the American Zion Commonwealth.

In 1923 Bnai Zion of Hartford gave American *oleh* Emanuel N. Mohl, manager of the Palestine Building Loan and Savings Association, the authority and power of attorney to approve the selection of appropriate lands proposed by the Palestine Land Development Company. The tracts that were offered bordered on Raanana. The first tract was on the northeast border of Raanana, in Khirbet Azun; it consisted of 686 dunams. Approximately 300 more dunams nearby were under negotiation, bringing the potential size of the tract to 1,000 dunams. A second tract of 176 dunams was located to the west of Raanana and bounded by the lands of another American association. The third tract, 736 dunams in area, was located in the northeastern corner of Khirbet Azun. In all, the PLDC offered 1,598 dunams for sale, with another 300 dunams still under negotiation. The 686-dunam tract in Khirbet Azun was purchased in April that year for £P1,606, the *ahuza* placing a £P800 down payment. By 1924 some members of the society anticipated moving to Palestine and settling on their tract. However, Bnai Zion of Hartford had received no detailed information about the land they had purchased. They appealed to Jacob DeHaas, requesting details and asking his assistance in clearing up the matter.[68]

Although the New York Achooza Aleph turned down plans for a merger with the Hartford group, the latter's purchase created the possibility of mutual financial savings if the two groups would share certain outlays. Finally in 1928 an agreement was reached incorporating the Hartford *ahuza*'s possessions under the auspices of Raanana. The two *ahuza* societies shared expenses for water and irrigation. The Hartford settlement was thus irrevocably tied to Raanana.[69]

The Ahuza Plan and Its Effectiveness for American Settlement

The *ahuza* plan created a great amount of excitement when it was first promoted in America. *Ahuza* members hoped that they would be able to purchase and develop their own plots in Palestine, allowing each individual to live on the produce of the land.

The American *ahuza* colonies established before World War I had failed because of the effects of war and the indebtedness incurred at that time. The drawbacks of the *ahuza* plan were appropriately summarized by Akiva Ettinger. His comments also reflect a certain ideological slant: it will be recalled that he was the one who had recommended the transfer of American *ahuza* tracts to more experienced or at least more ideologically imbued *halutzim.* The first three points he made regarding detrimental aspects of the *ahuza* plan focused on planning, and the fourth on human resources:

1. formation of too small bodies (generally of only 40–50 members) intending to settle in Palestine as soon as their plantations become productive.
2. inadequacy of the estimates worked out for the establishment of the individual families.
3. overlooking of the communal requirements of the prospective settlement (schools, medical aid, etc.)
4. lack of preparedness, on the part of the members for their intended profession.[70]

Ettinger did not refer specifically to American *ahuzot.*

Bernard Sandler was another observer who proposed certain explanations for the deficiencies of the *ahuza* program, paying particular attention to Poria and Sarona. He concluded that failure of settlements was due to "absenteeism," the lack of "farming experience," and an extended "waiting period." On the other hand, he viewed the success of the New York Achooza Aleph and its colonies as a result of "obstinacy" and "resoluteness."[71]

In their evaluations of the accomplishments of the New York group, neither Ettinger nor Sandler took into account the period of activity, the location of the settlements, or their economy. The earlier settlements of Poria and Sarona most certainly failed because of the difficulties caused by World War I. Chances were that if the New York *ahuza* had been engaged in developing land during the war, it too would have become disheartened and failed. Under British rule, New York Achooza Aleph enjoyed better conditions, including relative economic and political stability. Moreover, Poria and Sarona were in peripheral locations at a distance from large commercial and service centers. They found it difficult to market their produce and obtain services, and their problems were compounded by a sense of isolation. By contrast, Raanana, in particular, and, to a slightly lesser extent, Gan Yavne were located in the heartland near Tel Aviv-Jaffa. They were only a short distance from markets, services, and cultural activities, and strong links were formed between Raanana and Tel Aviv. Furthermore, the citrus industry, viable in the coastal plains and expanding from the late 1920s onward, provided added opportunity to Raanana and Gan Yavne. Poria and Sarona, however, gambled their economies on almond and olive plantations. The almond market collapsed after World War I, and the olive crops—in the quantities produced by these Galilee *ahuzot*—never produced a high income. Period and place were the determining factors in the success of an *ahuza* colony; planning, organization, and the human element were of lesser importance.

7

The American Zion Commonwealth (1914–1928)

> When the American Zion Commonwealth office was informed by the Palestine Zionist Executive, through Col. Kisch, who arranged the entire itinerary of Earl Balfour in Palestine, that the Earl would visit and have luncheon in the colony bearing his name—Balfouria—we immediately started making arrangements and preparations for that momentous day. The colonists of Balfouria were immediately informed; the hotelkeeper, Mr. Saletzky, formerly of Chester, Pa., was given instructions to prepare a suitable luncheon for the distinguished guest and his friends; reporters were communicated with; flags from Tel Aviv and Jerusalem were collected—while hundreds of others were made up in Balfouria itself—British flags, Zionist flags, and, of course, American flags, for is not Balfouria a colony created thru the efforts and fund of American Jews?—so that the hustle and bustle was great indeed. In fact, we all felt that Balfour's visit to Balfouria must be an impressive and memorable one not only to the many participants, who would greet him, but to Balfour himself.
>
> Keren Tannenbaum, letter from Jerusalem, to American Zion Commonwealth, New York, 17 April 1925

Established in New York in 1914, the American Zion Commonwealth (AMZIC) outlined its purpose in its constitution as "aiding in the settlement of Jews in Palestine, and of securing for our members and their descendants rights, interests and privileges in lands occupied by the Zion Commonwealth Inc., to the end that social justice, in harmony with the ideals of the prophets of Israel, may be the cornerstone of the Jewish Commonwealth in Zion."[1]

Members would receive the rights to the agricultural exploitation of the surface of the land while the American Zion Commonwealth retained the rights over commercial, industrial, and mineral interests. At least 10 percent of all AMZIC land was to be set aside as communal lands—utilized for commercial, industrial, and mineral purposes, and for the development of settlements. Members could sell or transfer their lands, but the AMZIC reserved the right to veto such transactions and to repurchase lands at an assessed value. The constitution further granted exclusive rights to the

Zionist Congress through the Jewish National Fund or any Zionist Congress–appointed agency to purchase at any time all or any AMZIC lands.[2] These conditions guaranteed that its lands would remain in Jewish hands, even if they belonged to private investors. Moreover, they provided for the possibility of these lands becoming part of nationally owned land. As a land purchasing and development company that operated along parallel lines with the JNF and cooperated in the nationalist endeavor of promoting ownership of the Land of Israel by the Jewish people, the AMZIC adopted a policy that explicitly prohibited the sale of land to non-Jews.[3]

The American Zion Commonwealth differed from the Jewish National Fund in that it provided investors or contributors a voice in decisions related to the land redeemed through their financing. It created a bond between individuals or a community and a specific geographic area. This method was later adopted by the Jewish National Fund in its pairing of a Diaspora community with the redemption of a certain tract—for example, Canadian Jewry and the Emek Hefer purchase. The AMZIC created a conduit for American Jewish involvement that went beyond investment for building Palestine. However, the ideas developed in its constitution were criticized by the World Zionist Organization. Furthermore, some of the company's objectives could not be realized because of conditions in Palestine.

The policies set by the Executive of the World Zionist Organization at the London Conference of July 1920 included the assertion that "the fundamental principle of Zionist land policy is that all land on which Jewish colonization takes place should eventually become the common property of the Jewish people. . . . The organ for carrying out Jewish land policy in town and country is the Jewish National Fund."[4] This directly challenged the American Zionist program, which supported the Jewish National Fund but simultaneously advocated land development along capitalist lines, albeit without excessive profit.

The final paragraph of the 1920 policy statement relating to land expresses the pragmatism of the period and openly acknowledges that the large-scale funding needed to insure the success of the Jewish National Fund could not be readily obtained. Certain channels of funding had dried up due to the political changes brought about by World War I and the ensuing economic devastation in Eastern Europe. The World Zionist Organization expected that American Jewry and Jews in the British Empire (South Africa and Canada) would possibly back the JNF, but their support proved to be insufficient. It became apparent that private capital investment in land would have to be tapped—at least in the short term. Another possibility that was explored but not realized was to reach an accord with the British Mandatory government to purchase government lands on a long-term basis with easy payments. A compromise was reached between the World Zionist and American leadership as expressed in the decisions of the London Conference[5]: "In order to bring large portions of the land of Palestine into Jewish possession as rapidly as possible, the Jewish National Fund shall devise means by which alongside of the capital of the Jewish National Fund itself, private capital can also be utilized for the purchase of land under conditions which will assure the eventual transference of land so brought into the national capital."[6]

Louis D. Brandeis spearheaded the American position, which held that private investment had a pivotal role to play in the development of Palestine, alongside gifts from Jews throughout the world. Gifts directed toward the regeneration of Palestine's infrastructure (e.g., afforestation and the eradication of malaria) and the development of its human capital would ensure more conducive conditions for investment. While en route to the United States following the London Conference, Brandeis incorporated his ideas of landownership into the Zeeland Memorandum in which he elaborated on the idea of transforming Palestine into a self-governing commonwealth. One of the specific difficulties he foresaw was the acquisition of land—the cornerstone of development. Another was the raising of necessary funds. Brandeis contemplated three kinds of land purchasing funds: investments, quasi-investments, and gifts. Investment would be ventured through the purchase of stock in the Jewish Colonial Trust, the Anglo-Palestine Company, and mortgage banks and would provide the investor with a return. Quasi-investments would be directed through the American Zion Commonwealth and provide the investor with title to land and future returns. Gifts would go to the Jewish National Fund. The donors would have the satisfaction of expanding landownership in Palestine and of improving it for the Jewish people.[7]

Later that year Brandeis's sentiments were endorsed by the Buffalo Convention of the Zionist Organization of America (ZOA). Donations for land acquisition were to be solicited through the Jewish National Fund, and investment funds would be sought through the sale of American Zion Commonwealth land certificates.[8]

Over the following decade or so, American contributions to the Jewish National Fund increased greatly compared to the period before the war. Between 1921 and 1928, American contributions totaled £436,318. As of February 1928, the American Zion Commonwealth had $2,314,825 (£462,965) in assets and $1,768,117 (£353,623) in liabilities, leaving a surplus of $421,708 (£84,342).[9] Reports during this period show that the AMZIC investment was slightly higher than the total of American contributions to the JNF, an indication of the AMZIC's popularity in American Jewish circles. Fears among World Zionist leadership that they would lose control of resources were not unfounded. The AMZIC, although it usually cooperated

Fig. 21. American Zion Commonwealth landownership certificate. (CZA L65/190)

with World Zionist leadership, channeled a substantial sum according to its own policies.

The AMZIC's popularity was generated by the support given the American Zion Commonwealth by prominent American and World Zionist leaders—including, to his own dismay, Chaim Weizmann—who showed public support for the AMZIC, but would have preferred that the funds be channeled to the Jewish National Fund or the Keren Hayesod, two funds controlled by the World Zionist Organization.[10] Further, it was accredited by the Zionist Organization of America as "the only recognized Palestine land selling agency of the Zionist Organization of America." In turn, the AMZIC became the agent for certain Palestinian land purchasing and development companies, including the Palestine Land Development Company (PLDC), Geula, and Agudat Netaim, which had been founded in 1905 by agronomist Aharon Eisenberg of Rehovot to serve individuals and groups. In May 1921, the AMZIC resolved to use the services of Agudat Netaim temporarily to assist individuals who wanted to proceed to Palestine immediately. Once the AMZIC was able to provide ameliorated land, it would no longer require the offices of agents such as Agudat Netaim.[11] Additionally, the American Zion Commonwealth reached an accord with the Mizrachi Organization of America to serve as the Palestine Land Development Company's representative for land sales to Orthodox congregations and organizations in the United States.[12] This expanded the opportunity for sales in communities to which the AMZIC and its representatives had limited access.

In trying to attract investment, the American Zion Commonwealth emphasized to potential backers that Jews had a natural urge to possess their own property—"land hunger"—which could be satisfied through the offices of the AMZIC. This marketing approach is evident in an excerpt from its brochure describing lands at Afula.

> The Jews have been a landless people and in consequence the hunger for land is powerfully developed in them. "Every man under his vine and every man under his fig tree, and none to make them afraid," is an ideal which Jews have always cherished but not often realized. Since men construct their ideals in terms of what they miss most in their actual lives, it is natural that the Jewish land ideal should occupy a prominent place in their dreams and striving. "Let all who are hungry come and eat." Buy a portion of the land of Israel and satisfy your own land hunger of your people.[13]

The company also iterated the idea put forward by Brandeis that in addition to the contributions made to the Jewish National Fund and the Keren Hayesod, millions of dollars of private capital were needed—and the best means of investing was through the American Zion Commonwealth. It assured prospective buyers that this would be a secure and productive investment. It further emphasized the connected goals of improving the land and providing profitability to the purchaser. The AMZIC denied that this opened the door to land speculation in Palestine; rather it should be seen as an opportunity to make a sound investment that would be to the advantage of both investors and Palestine.

The vicissitudes of the economic situation in Palestine during the 1920s affected the ability of the American Zion Commonwealth to sell land there. In 1926 reports reached America that Palestine "is going through a severe financial panic[,] that land values are dropping daily and that it is only a question of time when most of the money invested by American Jews will be wiped out owing to the drop in land value." In 1924 and 1925 large amounts of capital had been infused into the land market and the construction sector, thus inflating prices. By the spring of 1926, with the beginning of the economic depression that continued through 1929, land prices dropped drastically. Harry Kotler of the AMZIC New York office explained that although there were "unfavorable and self-evidently untrue, rumors," they were hurting the AMZIC's cause and retarding its work. Kotler questioned the feasibility of developing its most recent project at Haifa Bay, expending millions of dollars during a period of uncertainty among potential investors in America.[14]

Despite the strong tendencies of the Zionist Organization of America to funnel funds for land through the Jewish National Fund and the American Zion Commonwealth, to the ZOA's dismay other land purchasing companies also attempted to sell land to American Jews. The private companies included *ahuza* societies (such as the New York Achooza Aleph and the Hartford Achouza); private real estate agencies like Hanoteah, the Migdal Corporation, the Menorah Company, the Jerusalem-America Land Company, and the American-Palestine Real Estate Agency, to name a few. In addition, private investors were also selling land: Max Shoolman and Isaac Harris, both of Boston, were particularly successful in this endeavor.[15] Some companies and individuals were approved by the American Zionist establishment, while others were condemned outright.

In December 1919 the New York Achooza Aleph petitioned the Zionist Organization of America for recognition and for the kind of special relationship it had established with the American Zion Commonwealth. After the ZOA National Executive Committee had discussed this question, Bernard Rosenblatt, a member of the committee and founder of the AMZIC, pointed out that the *ahuza* societies were in fact stockholding companies. *Ahuza* companies had previously been denied endorsement on the grounds that their activities were not practical and that their operations were not in accordance with the ZOA's Pittsburgh Platform. Rosenblatt noted that many *ahuza* companies had already joined the AMZIC. Ahuza Erez of New York and the Cleveland Ahuza No. 1, for example, became AMZIC members in 1915 and 1918 respectively. Further discussion resulted in the adoption of a motion forwarded by executive committee member Henrietta Szold, "to invite the [New York] Achouza Aleph in conference and endeavor as best it can to secure the adherence of the Achouza Aleph to the Zion Commonwealth."[16] The New York Achooza Aleph did not join the AMZIC, however, and operated without the endorsement of the ZOA. Only in 1932, several years after the collapse of the American Zion Commonwealth, did the Zionist Organization of America convention declare that it "extends appreciation to the New York Achooza Aleph for its efforts to stimulate the settlement of American Jews in Palestine."[17]

In the late 1920s a number of companies attempted to fill the void that resulted from the demise of the American Zion Commonwealth. Hanoteah, the Bnai Binyamin plantations and colonization department, called public attention to the fact it had been officially recognized by the Zionist Organization of America, the AMZIC, and the Palestine Jewish Colonization Association. Indeed, these organizations had all extended aid and credit to Bnai Binyamin and its members. With this backing, Hanoteah had set aside 1,200 dunams for orange groves and 300 dunams for houses for American clients at its settlement Netanya. Eliezer Babli, chief of the Palestine Zionist Executive Colonization Department, Moshe Smilansky, president of the Jewish Farmer's Federation of Palestine, and a host of local planters lent their approval to the Netanya settlement scheme.[18]

Yakhin, the cooperative contracting association of the General Jewish Federation of Labor in Palestine (Histadrut), also filled part of the void left by dissolution of the American Zion Commonwealth. Its modus operandi included every phase of cultivation, from the planting of seedlings to the picking, packing, and export of the fruit for landowners in Palestine. Yakhin also assisted in organizing groups of Jews outside Palestine willing to invest in Palestine, and helped Americans purchase suitable areas of land.[19]

By contrast, the Migdal Corporation, which operated coextensively with the American Zion Commonwealth, was charged by the AMZIC with engaging in land transactions for the sake of excessive profit. The commonwealth asserted that Migdal's activities contradicted the concept of the ownership of land in Palestine by the Jewish people. According to AMZIC president Solomon J. Weinstein.

> The Migdal Corporation is not a public organization, is not recognized by the Zionist Organization, and does not even propose to engage in the land business for the public welfare; but they are frankly admitting that they entered into the sale of land in Palestine for private gain. The Migdal

Enterprise . . . is netting them a considerable profit, as they are selling land in Migdal from which they have paid to Mr. Glickin, ten (10) pounds [$50] per dunam (which, in itself, is an exorbitant price), and at the rate of 40–50 pounds [$200–$250] per dunam. In their prospectus, they are pledging certain improvements on the land, such as streets, boulevards, planted trees, etc.[20]

These charges, although slightly exaggerated, were not unfounded. The price per dunam advertised in the Migdal Garden Villa brochure started at $125—relatively expensive when compared to garden city prices in Herzlia or Afula.[21] A partial explanation for the excessive price was the precarious financial situation of Migdal enterprises following the Bolshevik Revolution. Most of the company's investors were Russian Jews, some of whom had died and others of whom went bankrupt. Migdal's manager attempted to salvage the situation by taking out exceedingly large loans to support its development. By the end of 1920, lenders were demanding repayment. Even after selling 200 dunams of prime real estate to Lord Melchett (Sir Alfred Mond), Migdal was still unable to repay the loan or continue running the estate. A plan was developed to transform the property into a "garden city" whose lands could be sold at a high price, allowing for the losses to be recouped.[22]

Migdal was not the only real estate company criticized by Zionists. For instance, claims of false representation were lobbed against the American Palestine Real Estate Agency. In 1924, its representative [?] Goldberg was offering 20,000 dunams in Afula at £E3 ($15) per dunam, including all the expenses of parceling, transfer, and registration. This was an impossibly low figure. The agreement concluded between the owners—the Sursocks and the PLDC—stipulated that the Sursocks would have to pay a £E10,000 ($50,000) penalty if they did not sell the tract to the PLDC. Furthermore, the advertised price was lower than that offered to the Sursocks by the PLDC. Charles Passman, the representative of the American Zion Commonwealth in Palestine, explained that whenever the American Palestine Real Estate Agency found that the PLDC was negotiating for the purchase of some land, they approached the owners and offered a higher price. Passman summarized their activities thus:

> In general, the methods of the American Palestine Real Estate Corporation [*sic*] are such that no decent person or organization, who is familiar with their methods, would care to associate with them. . . . In my cable, I stated that Goldberg's connections with the American Palestine Real Estate Corporation are scandalous, and this may sound a very strong term, but I can assure you that if I had found in the Code Book a stronger word, I would have used it, for I believe that if a Zionist official comes to Palestine and

attempts to undermine the existing Zionist Organization, there is no excuse for it, particularly so when the object is for mere personal profit.[23]

Another real estate company, the Menorah Palestine Building Corporation, was successful in attracting wealthy American investors, some of whom were willing to lay out $150,000 or more for land in Palestine. This company was founded by Isaac Berman in the early 1920s, apparently in order to assist two Jaffa merchants, [?] Turkenitz and Yaakov Perlstein, to sell in America a tract between Jaffa and Rishon Lezion. According to the American Zion Commonwealth's Bernard Rosenblatt, they could "offer the investor much more than what the AMZIC can. Therefore, if it came to a battle with those companies, on purely business grounds, we would surely lose out." Rosenblatt suggested that the AMZIC establish another land purchasing company that could interest wealthy Jews in investing large sums of money. At the same time, he was unwilling to have the AMZIC itself be transformed into such a company, for it was principally involved in work of a pioneering nature.[24]

Competition among land companies over American investors took many forms. For example, Oved Ben-Ami, secretary of the Bnai Binyamin organization between 1924–28 and founder of Netanya, was asked for advice regarding investing in citrus plantations in Herzlia. He expressed the opinion that the land was not suitable for orange groves. Instead, he explained, "Nathanyah is much more desirable for this specific purpose."[25] This was a direct attempt to persuade the potential investor to buy land from the Bnai Binyamin organization rather than from the American Zion Commonwealth.

The AMZIC perceived a significant aspect of its role as preventing both speculation and the purchase of inappropriate lands by investors—as in the case of individuals like Max Shoolman and Isaac Harris, who purchased large tracts of land simply as an investment. Such investment activities were occasionally supported by Zionist figures, including Chaim Weizmann. In some situations, however, the AMZIC attempted to intervene. When [?] Harris of New Jersey attempted to purchase land in the vicinity of Herzlia, Passman wrote, "if this Mr. Harris should enter into any negotiations for the purchase of that tract, I will try to stop it." In a similar situation, when Mr. [?] Schuldinger of New York was considering the purchase of a 650-dunam tract near Schunat Borochov, Passman explained the AMZIC's policies—and his own point of view—regarding land speculation: "While the American Zion Commonwealth is in no way interested in the purchase of that tract, nevertheless, in order not to give Schuldinger a chance to acquire it, I deem it advisable to take a hand in it . . . but in all events I will not let Schuldinger acquire that tract."[26]

CHAPTER 7

The American Zion Commonwealth held a special position within American Zionist circles. Its founding followed the pre–World War I *ahuza* experiences. Initially, the company was meant to serve as an umbrella organization for these *ahuzot*. Later, ideological elements were incorporated into its constitution, specifically "Social Zionism" as espoused by the company's founder, Bernard Rosenblatt. In addition, AMZIC policies reflected Louis D. Brandeis's sentiments regarding the up-building of Palestine, particularly up-building through investment and not by donations. Furthermore, with a single large and centralized land purchasing and development organization that did not operate solely for the sake of profit, Americans could channel their funds more efficiently for the purpose of developing Jewish settlement in Palestine. Integrity, competence, and a sense of purpose were the underlying ideals of the AMZIC. The company sought to monopolize the American market for land purchase in Palestine. Its motivation was not to increase profits but rather to limit undue competition in a fixed and restricted land market. It was apparent to Brandeis, Rosenblatt, and others involved in the AMZIC that an increased number of competitors would hinder general progress in Palestine.

AMERICAN ZIONIST COMMONWEALTH PURCHASES AND SETTLEMENTS

Bernard Rosenblatt published a pamphlet in 1919 announcing the purchase of the first tract—Balfouria—and plans for its future development. There was great excitement among the American Zion Commonwealth membership, and a number of individuals set out for Palestine ready to take possession of their land. However, when four members arrived in 1921 they found no land awaiting them. The situation was brought to the attention of the American consulate in Jerusalem:

> We may mention 4 American Jews who bought land upon the apparently glowing promises and the representations of the [American] Zion Commonwealth Society of New York City and came recently to Palestine to take possession and enjoy the fruits thereof. They found that the Society had not yet acquired land in Palestine and was therefore unable to make delivery of that which it had sold. Upon complaint of one of these land purchasers in question (Hyman Raflowitz) this Consulate informally approached the local representative of the Zion Commonwealth Society and learned that he had been making frantic efforts to secure land to meet the demands of these and other arriving stockholders from the U.S. He thinks that he has been successful but even so the average American stockholder is unlikely to secure living returns upon investment at the exceedingly high land prices prevailing in Palestine even if he were willing to spend several years at the severest and most exacting forms of agricultural labor, which he is generally

neither trained nor willing to do. These back-to-the-land Zionists have taken somewhat too literally and applied to Palestine the poetic description of land that is "tickled" with a hoe and laughs with a crop. Just about twice as much "tickling" is required to get a profitable crop from the average Palestine land available to these builders of the new Zion as is required for real agricultural land in the U.S.[27]

The needs of some constituents were met, at least by narrow definition, through the provision of tracts procured through the offices of Agudat Netaim. One example has been found in which Hirsh (Harris) Skakolsky of New York received land at Hefzibah near Hadera in 1921. It consisted of a four-dunam plot for his house and forty dunams for agriculture: cereals and plantations. Despite the original hardship of settling the land, Skakolsky was proud of his perseverance. In an open letter to the members of the Third Zionist district of New York, he reported on his activities and his feelings.

> I did not write up till now because my first few months were very hard and I did not want to follow the example of the ancient spies who spied the land in forty days and brought out an evil report. I have done all kinds of hard work and I worked as a laborer in the field, and this in the hottest time of the year, and as I feel, thanks to God, better in health than I ever did before, I might say that the climate is not bad at all. I thank God that I came at last to find rest and bread in our own land.[28]

Despite the enthusiasm he expressed in this letter, after three years of hard work Skakolsky was unable to make a success of his farm, and he returned to America.

Eventually the American Zion Commonwealth succeeded in acquiring land, and began the process of establishing colonies and settling them with American Jews. While planning the settlements, the AMZIC discussed various possibilities. Initially their inclination was to establish agricultural settlements, but by 1921 their direction had turned to developing "garden villages," conceived as "a communal center, placed in a larger area of farming land, which will bring together the high thinking of the city with the plain living of the farm."[29] This change in policy came about because of lessons learned at their agricultural colony, Balfouria, and it was endorsed by Jacob G. Lipman as more appropriate for American constituents.[30] The "garden village" plan was realized in the later settlements of Herzlia and Afula. A new phase in AMZIC propaganda—"American Zion Commonwealth by the Various Communities"—commenced. By 1921 arrangements had already begun in Boston, Pittsburgh, and New York to create specific sections within the garden villages for emigrants from those cities. As in Herzlia, the AMZIC promoted the settlement of groups from designated areas of the United States within a concentrated area in each new colony. This encouraged a population that was bound by social or even familial ties to reside together in a single area.³¹

Following World War I, the American Zion Commonwealth began the actual process of land purchase in Palestine. The company bought large tracts in the Jezreel Valley, the southern Sharon plain, and in the Zebulon Valley (Haifa Bay). At a later period it also entered the urban real estate markets of Tel Aviv, Haifa, and Jerusalem.

Lacking the necessary representation, manpower, and practical understanding of the land market, the American Zion Commonwealth, like many other Jewish companies and individuals, depended on the Palestine Land Development Company for advice and services. In a 1921 report to the U.S. secretary of state, the American consul in Jerusalem outlined the relationship between these two companies: "The Palestine Land Development Company resells this land to Zionist enterprises and to individual Jewish immigrants interested in the building of the new Zion in Palestine. An American organization known as the New York Zion Commonwealth [*sic*] has just concluded a purchase of nearly two thousand acres of the land from the development company."³²

To fully understand the land purchases made by the American Zion Commonwealth it is important not only to grasp the relationship between this company and the Palestine Land Development Company but the greater framework of the PLDC as an informal extension of the World Zionist Organization and the Jewish National Fund. According to researcher Irit Amit, it appears that between 1919 and 1924 the AMZIC "did not adopt any clear-cut policy with regard to land acquisition and settlement. Tracts were purchased as opportunity arose, while clarifications were made as to which areas were slated for development."³³ Amit is correct in her analysis that the AMZIC purchased tracts when the opportunity arose. Furthermore, the company often served as the proxy of the World Zionist Organization and the JNF. In 1925, for example, in the case of the Jidro purchase (Haifa Bay), the JNF contemplated buying these lands but lacked the necessary funds. It chose to forego this tract, preferring one in the Jezreel Valley that lay between existing settlements on JNF land. The JNF contacted the PLDC and the AMZIC and received assurance of an option for half the area. According to its constitution, the AMZIC was obliged to concede for the benefit of the JNF all land that it purchased or would purchase, if it were so decided by the World Zionist Congress.³⁴

In 1921 Chaim Weizmann of the World Zionist Organization praised the American Zion Commonwealth for its efforts in land acquisition and encouraged its contemplated purchase of Tel Adas (part of the colony of Balfouria), since it was a district with little Jewish settlement. Weizmann urged the AMZIC to consider purchasing land in the Gaza district, which he viewed as very good land that might prove profitable, but no evidence has been found of American Zion Commonwealth interest in Gaza at that time. However, in 1925 Gaza was reconsidered; Yehoshua Hankin drew up a plan to construct two Jewish towns, one in the north near Ashkelon and the other ten kilometers to the south. Together with Beer Sheva as a third point, a triangle of Jewish settlement would thus be created.[35]

The American Zion Commonwealth particularly aspired to purchase and develop contiguous territory. In the case of Balfouria, it was "resolved that insofar as practicable, the President of the Commonwealth shall endeavor to buy land in Amak [sic] Israel, so as to have a large continuous territory for development."[36]

After the registration of the company as a nonprofit organization in August 1924—enabling it to operate under Mandatory laws—company agents in Palestine were asked to present a plan of activity. Three individuals instrumental in forming this policy were Charles Passman, Bernard Rosenblatt, and Solomon J. Weinstein.[37]

Because the AMZIC focused on purchasing lands that were marketable in America, it turned down a request from the Vaad (local council) of Rehovot to assist with a loan to purchase a few thousand dunams to expand the colony. The company feared that the Vaad of Rehovot would not agree to turn over any of the land for sale in America and would insist on selling the entire tract for immediate settlement by those already in Palestine. Since no Americans would settle this land, such a transaction would not benefit the AMZIC. Its only gain would be a minimal profit on the transaction. It did agree, however, to attempt to facilitate the Vaad of Rehovot in receiving a loan from other sources. Another reason for the company's disinterest was that small-scale purchases could not be developed into colonies. The Rehovot transaction involved an area of only 2,000 dunams, and the AMZIC felt that small-scale purchases were acceptable only if they were adjacent to existing AMZIC colonies and would thus augment them.[38]

Another company policy was to purchase land from non-Jews in the spirit of the redemption of Palestine and the expansion of Jewish holdings. Although this policy was extended to land worked by Jews, the American Zion Commonwealth decided not to enter into negotiations for Arab-owned lands that Jews had previously entered.[39] Furthermore, the AMZIC did not see the rescue of other Jewish colonization undertakings in dire financial straits as one of its functions; this attitude was illustrated in its response to the needs of Poria (see chapter 6).

By March 1926 the American Zion Commonwealth had ceased its purchasing activities; by this time the cash flow had dried up, even though assets both in Palestine and the United States exceeded liabilities by $60,000 and $125,000 respectively. Outstanding debts by American purchasers had reached $800,000, half of which was long overdue. Quite often individuals made an initial payment toward a land purchase but did not follow through with subsequent installments as they came due.[40] Although the AMZIC appeared solid on paper, it failed because it was unable to amass the funds needed to purchase lands. But this was not the only reason. Rosenblatt concluded that: "Sad experience has taught us that it is impossible to manage an active institution at a distance of five thousand miles. No matter how independent our Directorate may be, they will not be able to direct, not only colonization activities, but even the problem of judicious purchase of land in Palestine, from the New York headquarters."[41]

Unable to fulfill its financial commitments and make payments on lands purchased, the American Zion Commonwealth turned to banks in the United States as well as to the Zionist Organization of America, the United Palestine Appeal, and the Palestine Zionist Executive for loans or guarantees. This action caused great distress to the Zionist leadership in America and elsewhere. Weizmann, for example, wrote that the "American Zion Commonwealth has received £60,000 from us through the American Keren Hayesod (to which my blood sticks) and owes the banks £40,000; it will lose its best asset [Haifa Bay], and then we can whistle for our money."[42] To prevent default on mortgage payments, some parcels were sold to pay off loans received from various Zionist organizations; other tracts were transferred to the Jewish National Fund. The individual purchases and the sale or transfer of the tracts involved in this process are detailed in the following sections.

BALFOURIA, THE FIRST AMERICAN ZION COMMONWEALTH COLONY

As mentioned above, in 1912 the Palestine Land Development Company contracted to purchase a large tract in the Jezreel Valley from the Sursock family of Beirut and Alexandria in 1912 but was unable to complete the transaction due to the World War. From at least the seventeenth century, the Sursocks were tax farmers for the Ottoman government, a position that facilitated their acquisition of land in various parts of the Ottoman Empire. By the mid-nineteenth century, family members were engaged in international shipping, silk manufacture, banking, real estate, and investment in the stock market and in public works projects (the Suez Canal, the Beirut-Damascus carriage road, the port of Beirut). The family owned urban properties (residences, warehouses, shops, and vacant land) in and around Beirut, Mersine, Tarsus, and elsewhere in southern Turkey, and in Alexandria as well. They also owned rural property in Mount Lebanon, and whole villages in Palestine and Egypt. Their property in Palestine included some 181 square kilometers in the Jezreel Valley.[43]

In 1915 Shmuel Pevsner, a businessman from Palestine stranded in the United States during the war, proposed that the Zion Commonwealth purchase a 3,000-tract in the Jezreel Valley known as Tel Adas at $12 per

Map 5. Land purchases by Americans in Palestine up to 1939

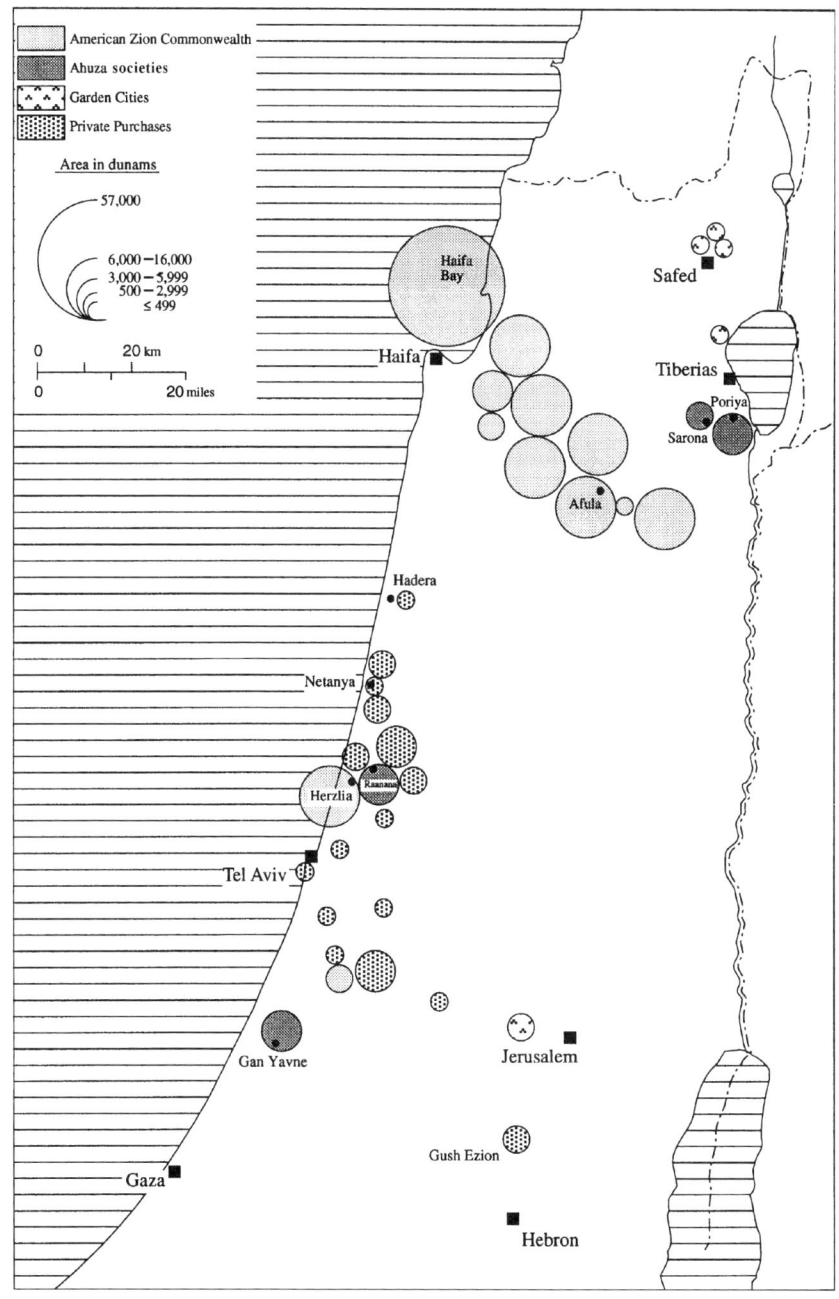

TABLE 17
Agricultural land purchased by the American Zion Commonwealth 1919–26

	Years of purchase			
Location	1919–23	1924	1925	1926
Balfouria	12,992	—	—	—
Herzlia	—	14,000	—	—
Afula	—	16,000	—	—
Kafrata	—	—	10,000	—
Majdal	—	—	4,000	—
Jiddah	—	—	9,700	—
Zarnuqa	—	—	2,575	—
Haifa Bay	—	—	57,000	—
Shunam	—	—	—	10,000
Kuskus-Tivon	—	—	—	10,000
Merchavia	—	—	—	497
Khirbaj-Khartia	—	—	—	3,000
Total	12,992	30,000	73,275	23,497

Source: American Zion Commonwealth, Jerusalem, to Jewish National Fund, Jerusalem, 14 March 1927, CZA KKL5/2002.

dunam, with an option for an additional 10,000 dunams. The directors of the Zion Commonwealth discussed the proposal with Sylvan Robison. He argued that the company should not, at that time, bind itself "for the purchase of such a large quantity of land and on the motion of Mr. S. J. Weinstein, it was resolved that the contract be entered into for only 1,500 dunams, with an option for 12,000 dunams more until January 1916."[44] Because of war-related communication problems, information flowed slowly to the Zion Commonwealth. In early 1917, Jacob Thon, manager of the PLDC, communicated that full title to Tel Adas could probably be procured after the war. A motion was carried by the shareholders recommending that the board of directors purchase Tel Adas.[45]

After the cessation of hostilities, there was some uncertainty as to whether the owners would still sell the land to the PLDC. Nevertheless, Yehoshua Hankin strongly believed the PLDC would eventually obtain the tract, although probably at a higher price. On 18 December 1918, the PDLC concluded an agreement with Nagib and Albert Sursock for the purchase

The American Zion Commonwealth

of 71,356 dunams in the Jezreel Valley, including Tel Adas. The Jewish National Fund agreed to purchase a major portion of the tract. However, the transaction could not be completed because the government had not yet opened the Land Registry Books.[46]

By the end of 1918, the American Zion Commonwealth had a subscribed capital of $339,750, of which $26,077 had been paid up. During the first six months of 1919, it considerably increased its financial base: $783,875 was added to its subscribed capital, and cash receipts were augmented by $105,363. With this accumulated capital, and promised capital of over $1.1 million, the AMZIC could begin its actual undertakings in Palestine. Its president, Bernard Rosenblatt, toured Palestine during July and August 1919 searching for a tract where they could establish their first colony. In his memoirs he stated that "Mr. Chankin said that there was a small area, near the colony of Merhavia in Lower Galilee, which might be secured. He offered to travel with us 'to spy out the land.' "[47] Hankin showed Rosenblatt a 7,000-dunam tract at Tel Adas, and pointed out that the AMZIC could take over the PLDC's two-year lease of these lands until the agreement was finalized.

Rosenblatt was concerned about what would happen to the buildings, wells, plantations, and other infrastructure developed over the two-year lease period in the event the Tel Adas tract could not be purchased. Hankin suggested that the American Zion Commonwealth lease an adjoining 1,000 dunams of Jewish National Fund land in Merchavia and develop the capital investment there. At worst, the JNF would benefit from this section of Merchavia's development. Rosenblatt agreed to lease the Tel Adas lands on the condition that the JNF would lease 1,000 dunams at Merchavia. The JNF agreed, and the accord was finalized on 6 August 1919. The purchase price was £3.600 per dunam, and the AMZIC leased 8,000 dunams in all. The purchase from the Sursocks was eventually completed, and in late 1920, these 7,000 dunams were registered in the *tabu* (land registry).[48]

Some organizers felt this quantity of land was insufficient for American Zion Commonwealth expansion plans. Louis D. Brandeis advised Rosenblatt that "As a colony [Balfouria], I should think success more nearly attainable with a larger area than you now have."[49] The board of directors therefore resolved in May 1921 to purchase, in large or small quantities, land contiguous to Balfouria, and in December 1921 an agreement was concluded with the Palestine Land Development Company for the purchase of 8,000 dunams at Rub-El-Nazra from Henri and Marie Sursock of Beirut. By order of the government of Palestine, an option was given to Arab cultivators of the land to purchase it at any time during the following six years. In the end, 5,000 dunams at £E4.000 per dunam were added to the AMZIC's land reserve at Balfouria through the Rub-El-Nazra purchase (a tract bordering Balfouria on the east). Thus the Balfouria purchase totaled 12,992 dunams, with an additional 1,000 dunams leased from the Jewish National Fund.[50] In 1926 a

Map 6a. Balfouria, plan of the settlement and various structures, 1923

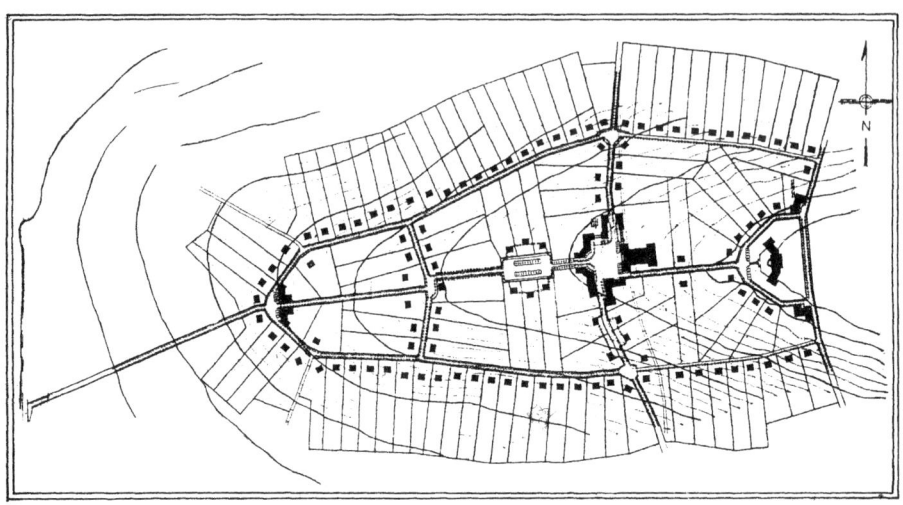

Typical barn

Front view

Floor plan

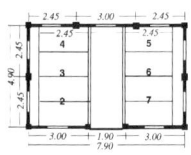

Typical house

View from the street

View from the garden

Floor plan

Side view

Map 6b. Balfouria and Rub-El-Nazra purchases, 1926

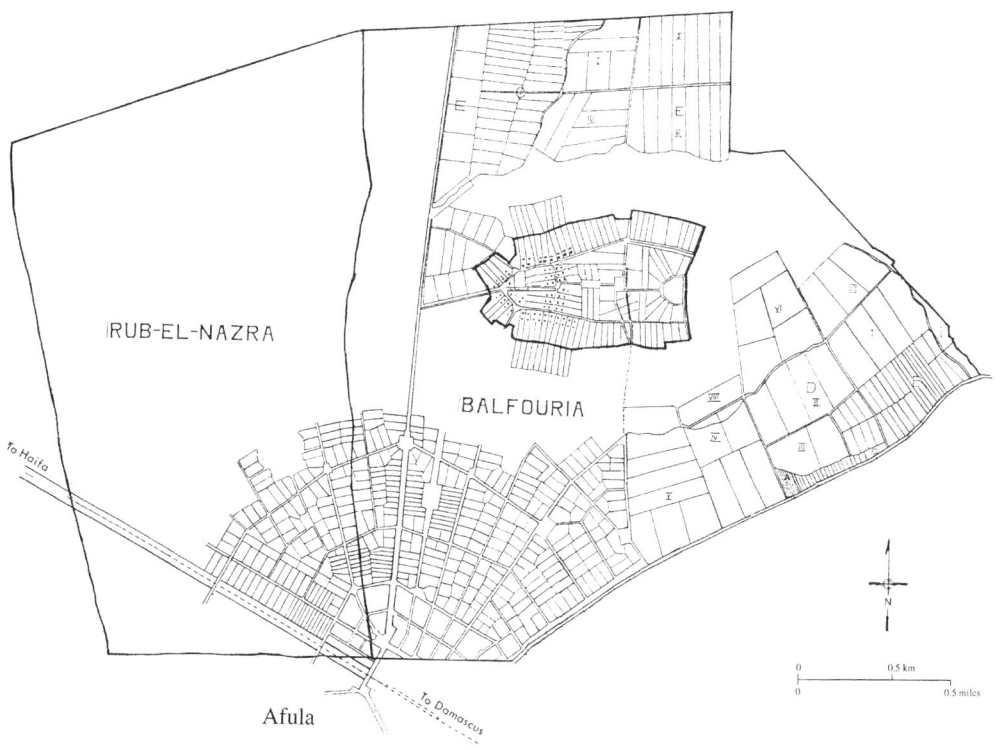

third tract of 497 dunams was acquired at Merchavia, but since the AMZIC was unable to pay for it, the tract was sold instead to the JNF.

After the land for the new agricultural colony had been acquired, Lord Arthur J. Balfour was asked if he would approve the naming of the colony in his honor. It was Balfour who, in a letter to Lord Lionel Walter Rothschild dated 2 November 1917, had outlined British support for the establishment of a Jewish homeland in Palestine. Chaim Weizmann wrote to Balfour in August 1919 asking him to lend his name to the settlement, and Balfour gave his consent.[51]

Balfouria was of great importance to the Zionists in America, particularly those who were at the forefront of the conflict with the World

CHAPTER 7

Zionist leadership over the methods and means for up-building Palestine and over their potential intervention there. In this regard, Brandeis wrote to Rosenblatt, "as you know, I feel we must make a success of Balfouria whatever the cost."[52] It was to be a model settlement for future American activity in Palestine.

> This dream embodied a vision, but an essentially practical one; a dream of a modern colony planted in the ancient Homeland, possessing qualities which will attract the man and woman accustomed to a European or an American standard of living. The methods and system of working, the performance of the various tasks connected with building of the colony were also to be as modern as possible, so that this colony may serve as the *model* for all future similar enterprises in Palestine [emphasis in the original].[53]

Hopes for the colony, however, exceeded the AMZIC's capacity to bring them to fruition. As noted above, Brandeis believed the colony needed to be established with a larger area if it was to succeed. Yet he warned Rosenblatt that "a large colony will require an even bigger man as colony manager—than would a small colony. No doubt you have this in mind and have or expect to get a man of sufficient caliber to lead the undertaking." Until then, the American Nellie Straus had served as manager of the project, but her performance did not live up to the company's expectations. She had trouble mediating between the company and the construction workers for the colony. Brandeis also understood that this project required additional resources. In a letter to Rosenblatt, he commented: "I assume you have figured on the cost of the larger enterprise and have assured yourself that you will have ample cash. We are entering upon a period during which it will be particularly undesirable to be a borrower."[54]

The extent and scale of the original plans for Balfouria are unclear. According to the *Judaean Magazine:*

> The village of Balfouria which will consist of about 150 farm houses, excluding the public buildings, is situated on an oblong-shaped hill, in the center of a stretch of 13,000 dunams of flat land. Each colonist has a 5-dunam plot in the village, in the center of which is situated his house and barn, the surrounding area comprising of his farm-land. The land surrounding the houses will be utilized by each farmer for raising vegetables and planting fruit trees. Balfouria will be the first colony which from its inception, will be provided with a modern water system. Each farmer will have water brought into his house and will have the necessary outlets to irrigate his surrounding garden as well.[55]

Architect and town planner Richard Kaufmann drew up the plan for Balfouria. Similar to Kfar Yehezkel and other moshavim, it was designed with communal structures in the center encircled by houses. Contrary to the report in the *Judaean Magazine,* the settlement was divided into 111 residential plots and 11 others designated for public buildings.[56] Irving Fineman, in his description of Henrietta Szold's visit to the colony in June 1920, pointed out one fault in the planning: "Although the new colony of Balfouryah had been designed in America it repeated the fundamental mistake of others: the stables were too near the dwellings."[57]

The foundations of the colony were laid by former Jewish Legionnaires. After full consultation with the head of the Zionist Agricultural Department in Palestine, Rosenblatt offered to employ a maximum of 100 Jewish Legionnaires for a two-year period at a fair wage. During this time the land would be surveyed and divided, infrastructure laid out, and houses and barns built. It was further hoped that some of the Legionnaires would become permanent settlers, either leasing or mortgaging land.

In 1919 Rosenblatt appointed Nellie Straus as the American Zion Commonwealth representative in Palestine and gave her the job of finding agricultural experts to prepare Balfouria for settlement. However, as Alice L. Seligsberg explained, it was "a task too great for her inexperience and too heavy for her frail health. For from the day of her birth Nellie Straus suffered from a heart ailment that often incapacitated her and that made the knowledge of the imminence of death her ghost companion throughout her life." Straus was assisted by Emanuel Mohl, former secretary of the Zionist Society of Engineers and Agriculturists, who had taken up residence in Palestine. Rosenblatt believed that Mohl's efforts would spell the difference between success and failure.[58]

Almost immediately, conflicts arose between Straus and the Zionist Commission vis-à-vis the commission's lack of support and attempts to claim credit for the project. Misunderstandings developed between the American Zion Commonwealth and the ex-Jewish Legionnaires as well. The former soldiers thought that all decisions connected to Balfouria would be left in their hands, and they acted under the misconception that the land would eventually be turned over to them for their settlement. The AMZIC, however, only intended to use them as laborers. This would at least provide them with employment, facilitate their demobilization in Palestine, and allow them to gain experience in a variety of vocations connected to agriculture and construction. From the AMZIC's perspective, former Legionnaires who possessed sufficient funds would be welcome to purchase a tract at Balfouria and settle there.[59]

Henrietta Szold, together with Dr. Isaac Max Rubinow and Julia Aronson, visited Balfouria in 1920. Szold's biographer described the health and security conditions at Balfouria.

> Dr. Rubinow proposed to remove the colony's doctor to Kinneret where he was very much needed, while the men at Balfouryah, a new colony, were so healthy they hardly needed a resident physician. Whereupon one of the

CHAPTER 7

Fig. 22. Road in the Moshav Balfouria, ca. 1930. (CZA Keren Hayesod L65/190)

colonists, who was indeed a robust specimen of young manhood, protested that they were expecting to be attacked any day and that there were bound to be casualties and, from what he had seen at other colonies which had been attacked, they would certainly need a doctor on hand.[60]

In 1921 thirty workmen, some of whom had served in the Jewish Legion, were employed at Balfouria. They were organized in a cooperative society and, according to Arthur Ruppin, their work was done in a satisfactory manner. However, a dispute over the Jewish Legionnaires' claim to be entitled to settle in Balfouria led to their ostracism from participation in construction activity. Instead, a number of *kvutzot* (collectives, sing. *kvutzah*)—Kvuzat Brenner, Kvuzat Tzerifin, Kvuzat Collective, Kvuzat Tetelbaum, and the Valley Company—supplied workers to Balfouria. Nearly 200 people were engaged in building the first structures.[61] Some workmen involved in the construction were derisive; they thought that the American Zion Commonwealth was a colonization society, "an organization upheld by rich American millionaires who are wasting their money in this way."[62]

The most up-to-date American machinery—tractors, pumps, stone-crushers, cement mixers, and cement block presses—was used in the construction of Balfouria. A provisional narrow-gauge railway was extended from the Afula station along the Valley railroad (the 1905 extension of the Hijaz railroad to Haifa) to Balfouria. This greatly facilitated the transportation of large quantities of building material arriving daily from Haifa.[63]

Within the territory of Balfouria there were a number of small springs. Improper drainage over the years had led to the growth of swamps that expanded and contracted seasonally. The swampy areas were breeding grounds for the mosquitoes that transmit malaria; this chronic parasitic disease often retarded progress in the development of Palestine by disabling workers. To solve this problem and better utilize the water from the springs, canals were dug in 1923 to collect spring water, and pipes were laid to convey the water to storage reservoirs. This system improved the quality of life in the settlement, but lack of maintenance resulted in the eventual blockage of the canals and, by the early 1940s, the slow regrowth of the swampy areas.[64]

Balfouria was officially founded on 2 November 1922, the fifth anniversary of the Balfour Declaration. By March 1923, the physical inventory of the colony included fourteen barns under construction, three of which already had roofs; eight houses under construction; and the foundations for twenty-two more houses to be completed over that summer. In 1926 the cornerstone was laid for the school, and in 1930 a synagogue was built at a cost of £P419. Zvi Blumenfeld of Memphis, Tennessee, a landowner, contributed $1,500 toward the construction of the synagogue.[65]

With regard to the population of the colony, the *Judaean* reported: "Beginning in June [1922], forty American Jews will leave the United States monthly for Palestine. All are artisans pursuing various crafts and are bringing with them from $2,000 to $10,000 each. They will settle in Balfouria."[66] This number of people, however, was not actually en route to settle the colony, so an accord was reached with the Palestine Zionist Executive Agriculture and Settlement Department to populate the colony with farming families. The American Zion Commonwealth provided 100 dunams each, a house and barn, and a start-up loan to approximately thirty-two families. Each of these families had eight to ten years of agricultural experience. They were drawn from the workers' groups (*kvutzot*) and included some American veterans.[67] These people were not required to invest their own money in the colony; their contribution was a willingness to settle in Balfouria and farm the land. This action by the AMZIC became a sore point for the company's American members who had paid in full for their land. In the following years, there were constant conflicts between the two groups of settlers. In 1926 the population of Balfouria was 275, consisting of 61 families. Only seventeen families holding certificates of ownership settled in Balfouria, and the majority of them were European relatives of AMZIC stock owners. Altogether there were seven American families living in Balfouria in 1926.[68]

TABLE 18
Country of origin of family heads in Balfouria, 1926

Country of origin	Number	Percent	Country of origin	Number	Percent
Russia	19	31.1	Austria	6	9.8
Poland	9	14.7	Bessarabia	5	8.2
Palestine	7	11.6	Danzig	1	1.6
United States	7	11.6	Hungary	1	1.6
Lithuania	6	9.8	Total	61	100.0

Source: Moshe De Shalit, "Balfouria, Herzlia and Afula" (in Yiddish), New York, ca. 1926, CZA L65/292.

The 1927 census of agriculture listed 342 individuals in Balfouria, but this figure appears too high, for it suggests an increase of 67 individuals over the space of one year. Indeed, the number of families in Balfouria between 1926 and 1928 decreased from 61 to 60. By 1936 Balfouria's population was 300, having remained stable over the decade from 1926.[69]

Actual farming at Balfouria commenced in the autumn of 1919, when Asher Cucuy and his sons, immigrants from Western Canada, plowed the land and planted it with wheat, barley, and vegetables. In 1921 the American Zion Commonwealth consulted with agricultural expert Jacob G. Lipman, who suggested that during the first two or three years all the land should be worked as a single unit, with regular crop rotation—including alfalfa and clover, which would enrich the depleted land. Lipman stressed the importance of parceling the land so that each settler would know which land and which crop was his, although the parcels would be cultivated communally. He also expressed apprehension about the adjustment of the mainly urban American Jews to rural life. He supported the proposal to use lands not settled by certificate holders as a model training farm to allow American Jews inexperienced in agriculture to acquire the necessary knowledge and skills. Lipman's model farm was, however, never created.[70]

In late 1923 the lands were surveyed, mapped, and divided, marking the beginning of the permanent population of the colony. The first settlers were individuals with agricultural experience already resident in the country, though American landowners were making their way to Balfouria at that time.[71]

Regarding the first settlers, Akiva Ettinger (acting within the framework of the Palestine Zionist Executive Department of Agriculture and Settlement policy and in accord with the American Zion Commonwealth) agreed to lend £E200 ($1,000) to a maximum of twenty-five families of settlers, at the department's usual interest rates. The principal condition was that the AMZIC would provide the necessary land and be responsible for providing water, laying down roads, clearing malarial swamps, and lending money to build stone houses and barns. Only £E100 ($500) would be provided within any single year because of the Palestine Zionist Executive's poor financial position and numerous requests for assistance from settlers in other places. Ettinger petitioned the AMZIC to provide the £E100 for the purchase of tools and animals, to be returned within a year in cash or in the form of building supplies. Thirty-three families were settled in this manner. They were organized as a small-shareholders cooperative, a moshav.[72]

The situation of American landowners and their relatives was different from that of the first settlers of Balfouria. For one thing, the size of their holdings depended upon the number of land certificates in their possession: Each certificate was translated into eleven dunams. The number of certificates held by Americans ranged from one—enough land for a house—to thirteen or more. Thus the economic situation of American colonists or their relatives varied greatly. Some of the tracts were too small to support their owners. Furthermore, most American settlers or their relatives were not members of the settlement cooperative. This was typical of the organization of a private holding colony, a moshavah. Because of its two distinct population groups, Balfouria developed organizationally into two distinct settlements at the same site. The settlement comprised a moshav alongside a moshavah in a single colony, although the form of the colony as a whole was that of a moshav.

Those who had been assisted by the Zionist Organization sowed their land with winter and spring grains immediately upon their settlement. The primary economic basis was to be dairy cattle and sheep, since the plots were only 100 dunams. Settlers would be unable to exist from grain cultivation on such small plots, so they planned to raise fodder for livestock. Despite the experience gained in 1923, Charles Passman, the company's local representative, still contended in 1924 that 75 dunams extensively cultivated in Balfouria was sufficient for a family.[73]

Americans were responsible for certain agricultural innovations at Balfouria. Zvi Blumenfeld of Memphis, who owned land in Balfouria, experimented with the cultivation of broom corn on his plot with seeds sent from the United States. At the suggestion of Eli Solomon, another American farmer at Balfouria, Blumenfeld also promoted the development of a modern poultry farm To this end, he sent equipment—incubators and brooders—and the best American breeds of poultry—Rhode Island Reds, Plymouth Rocks, and South Carolina White Leghorns—from the United States.[74]

In addition to income from agriculture, Balfouria also had a hotel. American settler Mordechai Saletsky commissioned the construction of

CHAPTER 7

Hotel Jezreel in 1924 through the American Zion Commonwealth at a price of £E650, partially financed through a £E150 loan from the Palestine Zionist Executive. In 1950 Saletsky explained that the idea for the hotel came from Yehoshua Hankin. As a frequent visitor to the Saletsky home, Hankin often asked Saletsky's wife, Hannah, to prepare meals for him and his guests. In his opinion, Balfouria was ideally located—on the Jerusalem-Jenin-Haifa road—for a hotel, and he promised to recommend it to friends and acquaintances. The Saletskys hosted the luncheon for Lord James Balfour and distinguished guests during their 1925 visit to the colony. Hotel Jezreel eventually closed; it could not compete with nearby hotels that were established in Afula after its founding in 1925.[75]

By 1928 there were 60 families residing in Balfouria: the population included the 33 agricultural laborers mentioned above; 17 others engaged in agriculture; 10 occupied in crafts; outside labor possessing plots of land; and a number of professionals.[76] During the 1920s, Balfouria had not expanded. One major deterrent to growth was the limited amount of water available. While it was hoped that large underground sources could be tapped and utilized for irrigation, thereby transforming the agricultural economy from extensive to intensive, no such resources were found.[77]

In 1929, following the failure of the American Zion Commonwealth, the members of the Balfouria worker's moshav requested assistance from the Zionist Organization in Palestine. They wanted first to receive immediate aid through interest-free or low rate loans for no less than five years; in addition, they asked for a committee of experts to help the moshav members work out a development plan to be presented to the next Zionist Congress. Economic decline had begun in 1927, when milk prices dropped by 40 percent. During the following two years the herds were decreased by 50 percent and milk production fell from 13,000–14,000 liters a month to 4,000. The moshav cooperative took out various loans and incurred debts that by 1929 stood at £P3,400. The moshav hoped that a Palestine Zionist Executive loan of £P2,500, in addition to one covering the deficit, would allow them to continue their activities. Later that year another request came from the moshav for aid, stating that thirty-five to forty families had no funds with which to start the coming season. Ten families with no prospects of income registered with the employment bureau in Afula. The cooperative estimated that altogether, £P1,000 was needed for seed and essential household needs.[78]

The 1927 census of Jewish agriculture enumerated five farms of less than 10 dunams at Balfouria and fifty-three over 10 dunams. Of the 9,657 dunams of land worked by farmers, 246 had plantations; 8,768 were crop land and fallow; 519 were idle but fit for cultivation; and 2,360 dunams were available for settlers. The total area of the settlement was 12,017 dunams. There were 246 cows and 80 work animals. The number of buildings (including houses, barns, storage sheds, and public buildings) totaled 233. In 1935 the lands of

Balfouria were catalogued as 118 dunams of plantations, 11,263 of taxable cereal land, 256 of uncultivable land, 227 of roads, and 235 of built-up area—for a total of 12,099 dunams. The change in the farming economy over the previous eight years was negligible. Although the 1927 figures detail actual utilization and the 1935 figures outline the evaluation of the land for taxation by the government of Palestine, a decrease in land under plantation and an increase in crop land can be noted. This would not, however, have resulted in any substantial increase in farming income for the colony.[79]

The colony persevered throughout the period of the British Mandate. In 1948 there were 289 residents, and today Balfouria remains a small settlement, with 266 inhabitants.

HERZLIA, THE SECOND COLONY

The American Zion Commonwealth altered its strategy in developing its second colony. It recognized that the Balfouria purchase was not well-suited to the needs of its American constituents. This was due both to the agricultural economy—extensive cultivation—and to its location at a significant distance from urban centers. Thus for its second colony, the AMZIC searched for tracts that could be intensively exploited and were situated nearer to Jewish population centers.

The foundations for the establishment of a second colony, Herzlia, began in 1921, when Balfouria was in its infancy. In September of that year, Yehoshua Hankin concluded an agreement for the purchase of 16,072 dunams from the villages of Jelil and El Haram in the southern Sharon plain. Lacking the necessary funds to pay for this purchase, the Palestine Land Development Company directorate met with members of the Zionist Commission and the Jewish National Fund to discuss how to proceed. Hankin, the intermediary for this purchase, emphasized the importance of the purchase at that specific time. Negotiations had been initiated before the war, and if the purchase fell through now it was uncertain whether they could buy it later. But even if they could, the price would surely rise. Menachem Ussishkin, head of the Zionist Commission, stated that according to the dictates of settlement considerations, the agreement should not be canceled. The principal problem was how to raise the funds. Ussishkin was sure that Arthur Ruppin, then in America, could find buyers there and that every effort should be made to get additional time from the owners. The unanimous decision was therefore to draw out the negotiations as long as possible until definitive information could be obtained from Ruppin. It was decided to offer an additional £E3,000 if the owners would accept the first payment a year later.[80]

Ruppin, during his visit to America in the winter of 1922–23, succeeded in convincing Bernard Rosenblatt and, in turn, the American Zion

CHAPTER 7

Fig. 23. Cover of *Palestine Pictorial* 1 (April 1927).

Commonwealth of the importance of this purchase. On his speaking tour of America, Ruppin attempted to find subscribers for the Tel Aviv Bond Issue and Palestine Land Development Company shares, but he encountered several difficulties. In a letter to his wife, Ruppin related "It is not possible to extract money from hard-boiled American Jews by letter or through

Fig. 24. Middle-class settlement at Herzlia, 1928. (CZA Keren Hayesod photograph collection)

third person, but I personally may yet be able to achieve something. I now sometimes 'shout to the skies with delight, sometimes am grieved to death,' depending on whatever my prospects appear to be."[81]

Ruppin apparently had little difficulty selling the Jelil and El Haram properties to the American Zion Commonwealth, who saw this as an opportunity to obtain prime real estate just north of Tel Aviv. The directors of the AMZIC agreed to risk the initial funds to complete the purchase, which was immediately marketed to the American Jewish public. The AMZIC agreed to purchase 8,000 dunams, and the Polish Mizrachi Organization, which established a society named "Menucha ve Nahalah," also agreed to purchase land. By June 1924, the Palestine Land Development Company concluded the Jelil purchase and was involved in administering the land transfer and registration. One sticking point was how to divide the land between the prospective Jewish owners and the Arabs who retained part of the land. The original agreement made no provision for the delineation of the different holdings; legal action could be taken, but this would lengthen the process and create ill will with the Arab owners. In the midst of efforts to resolve the problems, the AMZIC increased its stake to 13,000 dunams, and the Polish Mizrachi was to receive 3,000 dunams. The PLDC presented Mizrachi with four alternative proposals, but in the end the Polish Mizrachi did not purchase any land because its financial status was severely weakened by economic problems in Poland during 1923–24. The AMZIC, understanding the potentially lucrative nature of the tract, agreed to purchase the entire 8,760 dunams of the Jelil lands, which were sold to the AMZIC at £E4.500 per dunam. This purchase did not include the El Haram lands.[82]

The American Zion Commonwealth made every effort to expand its land holdings in the vicinity. The preferred direction of expansion was south toward Tel Aviv. Concurrently, many other Jewish real estate speculators attempted to purchase lands between Herzlia and Tel Aviv. Bordering the Jelil tract to the south was *wakf* (Muslim religious endowment) land that was not for sale. Further south there was the Sheikh Munis tract of 11,000 dunams continuing to the Audja (Yarkon) River. This tract had piqued the interest of many local and foreign prospective purchasers, including the Winnipeg Ahuza Society. In 1925 the AMZIC, intent on purchasing this land, solicited Yehoshua Hankin's services. At the insistence of the Palestine Zionist Executive, the AMZIC reached an accord with the Palestine Land Development Company that if the tract was purchased, 5,000 dunams would be sold to the Jewish National Fund for the establishment of Zelig Soskin's workers' settlement.[83] However, in the end, the Sheikh Munis tract was not sold to the AMZIC.

The Palestine Zionist Executive had for many years considered establishing an agricultural experimental station at Herzlia. Yitzhak Vulcanski, agronomist and researcher, explained the advantages of its location on the coastal plain that extended from the sea to the second kurkar ridge, the heart of the citrus belt. In 1924 the Palestine Zionist Executive urged the Jewish National Fund to purchase 1,500 dunams of the Herzlia tract from the American Zion Commonwealth, but the latter was not in a position to sell any of the Jelil lands. The company had received less land than it expected and had committed 13,000 dunams to purchasers in America. One suggestion was that the JNF appeal directly to American purchasers to contribute a certain percentage of their land for the station. The JNF could then receive approximately 1,000 dunams gratis. Eventually, however, the agricultural experimental station was established near Rehovot.[84]

Unlike Balfouria, Herzlia was both agricultural and suburban in nature. Richard Kaufmann was again commissioned to design this new colony. The plan designated four separate zones, each distinct in nature and each taking into account the topographical and geographical conditions. The coastal area from the Mediterranean Sea to the first kurkar ridge included zones 1 and 2. The narrow strip adjacent to the beach would have a boardwalk serving as the focus for the resort town, an "Atlantic City" on the Levantine coast. In addition to single family dwellings, zone 1 would include bathing facilities, parkland, a boardwalk, and various commercial facilities. This zone was 915 dunams in area, including 88.7 (6.7 percent) for streets, 136 (14.6 percent) for parks, and 75.3 (9.0 percent) for plazas. Inland a residential area, including the principal public buildings, was planned. Zone 2, the seashore land, comprised 964.4 dunams consisting of single-family dwellings. It would also have synagogues, public halls, kindergartens, schools, hospitals, convalescent homes, the town hall, shops, markets, parks, playgrounds, sports grounds, hotels, restaurants, water towers, and a railway station. The plan reserved 65.4 dunams (8.9 percent) of this zone for streets, 12.8 (1.3 percent) for parks, and 112.4 (11.9 percent) for plazas. Zone 3, the 2,024.3-dunam garden city, was planned for the western kurkar ridge, with an additional 3,033 dunams reserved for agriculture. The built-up area would support single-family dwellings, and would include various public and commercial buildings. Within this zone, 115.1 dunams (8.1 percent) were set aside for streets, 240.6 (11.8 percent) for parks, and 180.8 (8.8 percent) for plazas. Zone 4 was located on the second, eastern kurkar ridge. This area, an agricultural settlement, was distanced from the first three zones by the swampy depression between the two kurkar ridges. Because of its relative isolation, this zone would have its own public buildings and commercial facilities as well as agricultural infrastructure. An industrial area was also planned for zone 4, which in total consisted of 6,925 dunams. The basis for agricultural development would be plantations; some of these would be planted and maintained by local workers until their American owners arrived.[85]

A few years later, negotiations for the El Haram tract were completed. In May 1929, 5,000 dunams of El Haram were sold to the American Zion Commonwealth for £P6.400 per dunam. The Palestine Land Development Company bought 6,600 dunams. The remaining 1,600 dunams were sold to the New York Achooza Aleph to augment their colony of Raanana. With this addition to Herzlia, zone 1 was supplemented by 733 dunams, zone 2 by 554.5 dunams, zone 3 by 3,024.63 dunams, and zone 4 by 686.06 dunams.[86] The price to American purchasers was $100 per dunam in zone 1, $75 in zone 2, $65 in zone 3, and $40 in zone 4. The payment schedule was 20 percent due on signing of the contract, followed by five equal payments every three months. In addition, the purchaser agreed to pay the government Land Tax—approximately 1 percent of the land value. Upon completion of payment, the *kushan* (title deed) would be received. Each purchaser agreed to contribute a share of his land, as outlined in the plan, for roads, parks, and other public spaces.[87]

David Ben-Gurion, secretary-general of the Histadrut, envisioned a workers' settlement with both agriculture and industry on a section of

Map 7a. Plan and location of Herzlia, 1924, zones 1, 2, and 3.

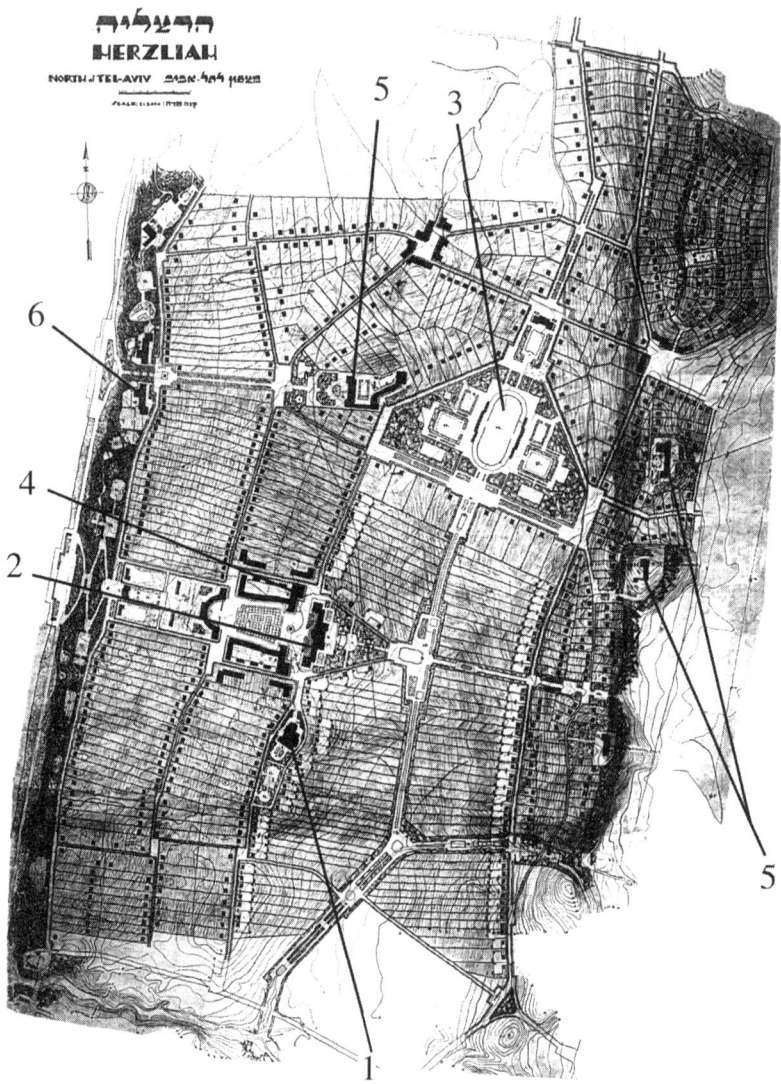

Map 7b. Plan and location of Herzlia, 1924, zone 4.

Key for Herzlia, zones 1, 2, 3, and 4
(1) town hall
(2) public hall
(3) sports ground
(4) market
(5) schools
(6) hotels

the Herzlia lands. He thought such a settlement would be instrumental in the development of Herzlia. Three types of settlers were suggested: farmers engaged in intensive cultivation, workers engaged in construction and industry with small farms to supplement their income, and cooperative industrial workers residing in workers' neighborhoods. Between 8,000–10,000 dunams in the southern section were suggested for this cooperative. The terms called for repayment of the original purchase price plus payment of a prime interest rate over forty-nine years. Ben-Gurion's proposal, which involved the majority of the American Zion Commonwealth holding, was rejected by the company.[88]

The American Zion Commonwealth was quite successful in selling its Herzlia land in the United States. Groups of purchasers were formed on a local or regional basis in line with the AMZIC policy for creating community garden villages. The Cleveland Herzlia Group bought 800 dunams—100 dunams in zone 1, 100 in zone 2, 350 in zone 3, and 250 in zone 4. The Nahalat Atlanta group purchased 200 dunams. The New England American Zion Commonwealth purchased 60 dunams in zone 1, 50 in zone 2, 485 in zone 3, and 225 in zone 4, totaling 820 dunams.[89] The intention was to create east-west strips of American settlers from different regions in the United States. But, as described below, few Americans settled in Herzlia, and these strips were never created.

Zone 4 was the first area to be actually developed. The initiative was taken by individuals from a group of twenty Herzlia landowners already in Palestine. On 23 November 1924, seven members—including Shimon Zeev Levine of Chattanooga, Tennessee—ventured to the site and erected the first structure. Within a short time, [?] Fein and his sons from New York completed a second building. By themselves, these few settlers were insufficient for the creation of the kind of colony envisioned by the American Zion Commonwealth. One hundred settlers were needed to create a nucleus, but since they were not hurrying from America, settlers were sought in Palestine. Additionally, Charles Passman tried—unsuccessfully, as it turned out—to enlist new immigrants from Transylvania and Poland. The AMZIC then concluded successful negotiations with the Bnai Binyamin organization for settling its members. The company realized that an assembly of sons of local farmers would inject life into Herzlia and serve as a stable foundation. Nonetheless, the AMZIC wanted to retain control over Herzlia, and thus it limited the Bnai Binyamin settlers to twenty-five. The company sold this group twenty-five dunam plots at £E8 ($40) per dunam and required a down payment of £E50. It also extended £E250 loans to the Bnai Binyamin farmers for the construction of houses, barns, and chicken coops. Bnai Binyamin members would put £E150 down as a first payment, and the remainder would be repaid over eighteen years.[90]

The American Zion Commonwealth then proceeded to develop the infrastructure. It organized and funded a drainage system at a cost of £E5,000. As noted above, the area between the two kurkar ridges had deteriorated over the centuries into a swamp. Unless the source of malaria could be eradicated, the population of this fledgling colony would most probably have fallen prey to disease, as had many other colonies. The man-made tunnel dating back to the Roman period that cut the western ridge was cleared, thus opening the flow of winter rain from behind the ridge to the sea. Included in this project was the laying of sewers, which were later incorporated into a larger drainage system. In addition, two wells were bored, one twenty-one meters deep and the second twenty-four. The cost, including motors for pumping, was £E5,000. Moreover, the road connecting Herzlia to Tel Aviv was repaired and improved. Within a year, several hundred families had settled in zone 4. The water system branched out and was extended to homes and barns. A school was built, medical facilities were developed, and an hourly bus service to Tel Aviv was organized.[91]

In June 1925 a group of Americans who owned land in zone 3 were intent on developing their holdings in this area. The American Zion Commonwealth was hesitant because of this area's distance from zone 4, because of the swampy depression that separated the two areas, and because the ownership of certain parts was still under dispute. Beyond these considerations, the number of settlers who were prepared to build immediately was limited. One American owner, Herman Harris, suggested building houses as an investment, hoping to sell or rent them to local Jews; he expected a return of 7 percent. Passman attempted to dissuade Harris, explaining that it would be difficult to attract individuals when zone 3 was in its infancy. Another approach Harris pursued was the development of plantations in zone 3. Passman viewed this tack favorably. By autumn 1926, work had already commenced on the six-meter-wide improved dirt road from Tel Aviv that passed through the entire length of zone 3, and bids were submitted for the construction of houses in this area.[92]

In 1927 one source enumerated 353 buildings in Herzlia. Two years later, a more detailed account listed a physical inventory of 120 houses, 60 shacks, 9 public buildings, 1 factory, 12 workshops, 10 stores, 5 other businesses, 2 public wells, and 11 irrigation wells; altogether there were 230 structures and 2,000 meters of roads.[93] Up to 1939, only zones 3 and 4 were developed. The coastal area, zones 1 and 2, were developed at a later phase; today these zones are known as Herzlia Pituah.

The chief economic foundation of Herzlia was the citrus industry. In the 1920s this was the most important and lucrative branch of horticulture in Palestine. The area of Herzlia under citrus plantations increased from 140 dunams in 1927 to 2,882 dunams in 1935. Both farmers in Herzlia and American absentee owners invested in this area.[94] In 1932 Hanoteah attempted to fill the role of maintaining and developing plantations that had earlier been filled by the American Zion Commonwealth. Hanoteah began offering American owners of Herzlia lands its services in planting these lands.[95]

In 1925 and 1926, the Vaad of Herzlia, having observed previous settlement activities, decided to try to develop an intensive and mixed agricultural economy. The committee showed an interest in crops such as bananas, potatoes, and tobacco, as well as the development of a dairy industry. In 1927 their discussions were widened to include structuring the farm economy in accordance with the demands of the export market. They were particularly interested in poultry and vegetables. Bananas were first grown that year, with 110 dunams being planted and the produce marketed in Tel Aviv and Jerusalem. In 1935 this crop became more important, with 85 dunams in Herzlia and 112 in El Haram planted with bananas. To provide ample fodder for the dairy cows, experiments were conducted for a better and cheaper type of grass, using seeds imported from the United States. By 1927 there were 3,450 dunams of crop land and fallow, of which 340 were idle but fit for cultivation. There were also 222 head of dairy cattle, some imported from Holland. The dairy products were marketed in Tel Aviv. The land was divided into ten farms of less than ten dunams and eighty farms over ten dunams. The economy of Herzlia also included commerce and industry. In 1929 there were twelve workshops, one factory, ten stores, and five other businesses. No apparent explanation has been found for the smaller number of buildings in 1929 than in 1927. It is important to emphasize that on the basis of a decision in principle by the settlement committee and the American Zion Commonwealth, the labor for Herzlia was exclusively Jewish.[96]

The population at Herzlia originally consisted of three groups: Americans, relatives of Americans, and residents of Palestine (including members of the Bnai Binyamin organization). Information available for 1926 details the country of origin of the 108 family heads in Herzlia.

In 1929 Israel Fine of Baltimore, owner of 50 dunams in zone 4, wished to provide assistance to Yemenite Jews and settle them on his land. Beginning in 1881 and continuing throughout the late Ottoman period, Jews from Yemen settled in groups in Palestine, usually without any capital. Many lived on the fringe of existing settlements and provided a source of inexpensive labor. Underlying Fine's decision may have been an element of American— both Jewish and Christian—romanticism toward Yemenite Jews. As early as the 1880s the Yemenites were referred to as the Gadites, one of the ten lost Tribes of Israel. Henrietta Szold commented once about the Yemenites: "Constituted as they are, tenaciously and loyally Jewish, intellectually alert, Arabic in speech and habit, accustomed to work in field and shop, they are destined, unless all signs fail, to be a cement between Arab and Jew, between the industrially-minded Jew of the city and agriculturally-minded Jew of the country, between Sefardi and Ashkenazi." Despite their noble

TABLE 19
Country of origin of family heads in Herzlia, 1926

Country of origin	Family heads	Percent	Country of origin	Family heads	Percent
Russia	25	23.1	Latvia	3	2.7
Palestine	22	20.3	Germany	2	1.8
Poland	21	19.9	Rumania	2	1.8
United States	14	12.8	Bulgaria	1	0.9
Lithuania	9	8.3	England	1	0.9
Hungary	8	7.5	Total	108	100.0

Source: Moshe De Shalit, "Balfouria, Herzlia and Afula" (in Yiddish), New York, ca. 1926, CZA L65/292.

position, the Yemenites were, in Benjamin Gordon's judgment, "poverty-stricken and spiritually crushed." "[F]rom a national and economic point of view," he continued, "they form a valuable asset to Jewish colonization, constituting the best labor material for Jewish settlements whose honesty and intelligence can be depended upon."[97] It seemed clear to everyone that Yemenites deserved material assistance. However, despite the American Zion Commonwealth's intention to cooperate with Israel Fine, no Yemenite colony was established in Herzlia at that time.

The colony's population grew rapidly. In 1926 there were 306 persons; in 1927, 575; and in 1929 approximately 1,000. By 1929 the labor force was divided between 170 farmers and 350 workers, though it should be noted that some of the workers were temporary or seasonal. The settlement grew rapidly in the 1930s, and its 1936 Jewish population was 4,917, with an additional 308 persons in El Haram.

Using calculations and research conducted by Herzlia resident Shoshana Migdal, it can be determined that 64 of the 1,088 settlers in the first decade were Americans.[98] There was a decline in the proportion of Americans in Herzlia over the years, from some 13 percent in 1926 to about 6 percent in 1934. By comparison, in 1934 Americans comprised approximately 3 percent of the Jewish population of Palestine.

Herzlia attracted the interest of American Jewry and became a symbol of the American contribution to the up-building of Palestine. Bernard Rosenblatt brought Max Shoolman to Herzlia in December 1924. Earlier Shoolman, a highly successful builder from Boston who was considering investing in Palestine, had been disappointed by the inferior construction of buildings in Tel Aviv and wanted to leave Palestine, losing interest in the whole endeavor. Rosenblatt persuaded Shoolman to stay on and inspect Herzlia, an example of effective investment. Shoolman was impressed by the view of the Mediterranean Sea and the winter climate. During that visit Rosenblatt pointed out the first American settler, Shimon Zeev Levine, riding by on horseback. This image, which likened the new Jew to a pioneer in the American West, so impressed Shoolman that he extended his visit in Palestine. Later, Shoolman advanced the American Zion Commonwealth £P6,000 to make the mortgage payment for Herzlia, and he also invested substantially in Haifa.[99]

In 1926 Colonel Frederick Herman Kisch of the Palestine Zionist Executive praised the activities of the American Zion Commonwealth and the progress made at Herzlia.

> The progress made in the short time since the settlement was established is really astonishing, and [demonstrates] what can be accomplished in this form of colonization when arranged and executed under the auspices of an efficient organization. Not only has there been most remarkable material progress, but I found the [spirit] among the settlers all that could be desired. I was particularly pleased to find a spirit of cooperation and the best possible neighborly relations existing between such varying elements as on the one hand the young Palestinian-born members of Bnai Benjamin, and on the other hand, new arrivals from America and other countries.[100]

The settlement may have appeared impressive, but in 1930 the situation in Herzlia was considered grave by owners in America who had received communiqués from the colony.

> Herzlia is in danger because the Arabs are occupying the land and are threatening murder. The land was sold to us individually for over $650,000 but [we] received no deeds. The American Zion Commonwealth mismanaged our funds. We have no more confidence in the American Zionists organization to rebuild our homeland[.] [W]e cannot dispossess the Arabs and cannot get any loan. We are losing over one-thousand purchasers willing to work with [us.] [Y]ou are instead threatening to take this matter to the federal courts and create a Jewish scandal which will affect your work as well as the reputation of all Jews[.] I cannot hold the purchasers back any longer[.] [I]mmediate action is necessary[.] [W]e want to place our hope and trust in your leadership and want to work with you. Please save the two hundred and fifty families which are on the land[.] [M]ake the place safe for the future American settlers and help us to get deeds[.] [H]elp Herzlia to help our homeland.[101]

Over the following years Herzlia continued to expand. In 1948 it had a population of 5,300. Its proximity to Tel Aviv accelerated its growth, and today it is one of the Tel Aviv metropolitan area's larger suburbs, a city with 83,800 inhabitants.

The Agricultural Zone of Afula

Once again, in an attempt to defray the heavy financial burden of the Afula purchase, the World Zionist Organization sought Jewish investors abroad. Having successfully attracted the AMZIC in the Balfouria purchase, the organization approached the company again. In addition, the World Zionist Organization persuaded the Polish Meshek Company to invest in the Afula purchase. An important selling point of the Afula area was that it would likely develop into a prosperous city, a central place for the growing rural hinterland that included Balfouria and Merchavia (indeed, the area eventually included dozens of settlements within a ten-kilometer radius). Moreover, American purchasers, mainly members of the urban middle class, would probably prefer an urban setting. If buyers still wanted to engage in agriculture, they could take it up in the garden neighborhood or agricultural zone of the new town. It was believed that "as the Plain [of Esdrelon] becomes peopled with Jews, it will need an industrial center, nearer to it than Haifa—and Afulah will be that industrial center. The Emek will need a commercial center, and Afulah should become the shopping district of the Emek."[102] Furthermore, Afula's development was guaranteed to accelerate due to its prime location on transportation routes, both rail and highway, within Palestine and internationally.

On 27 August 1920, Yehoshua Hankin reconfirmed a preliminary agreement with the Sursocks, and the process of purchase and transfer began. The financial institutions of the World Zionist Organization lacked the funds required for another large project in the Jezreel Valley. In the end, the Twelfth Zionist Congress approved the Jewish National Fund's purchase of only 41,300 dunams in the valley. It was obvious to Zionist leadership in the autumn of 1920 that other Jewish purchasers were needed. Chaim Weizmann would have preferred that all these lands be redeemed through national capital but, having little choice in the matter, he turned to the American Zion Commonwealth. On 26 November 1920, he cabled Bernard Rosenblatt a confidential request that the AMZIC participate in the purchase. Weizmann offered 16,000 dunams of the "best land in Palestine," immediately irrigable, at a price of £5 per dunam, but £100,000 would have to be transferred within a month. The World Zionist Organization's requirement that the AMZIC remit payment in such a short period of time underscores the fact that this was one of its last alternatives. The AMZIC agreed to the purchase, but at the same time there were rumors that the Sursocks had sold the land to the American-Palestine Real Estate Corporation; these rumors proved to be false.[103]

Under the terms of the final agreement, Arab tenants in Afula were given four years to purchase the land or part of it. In the interim, they could continue cultivating it. Hankin negotiated with the sharecroppers, and, for

Map 8a. Plan of Afula, 1925

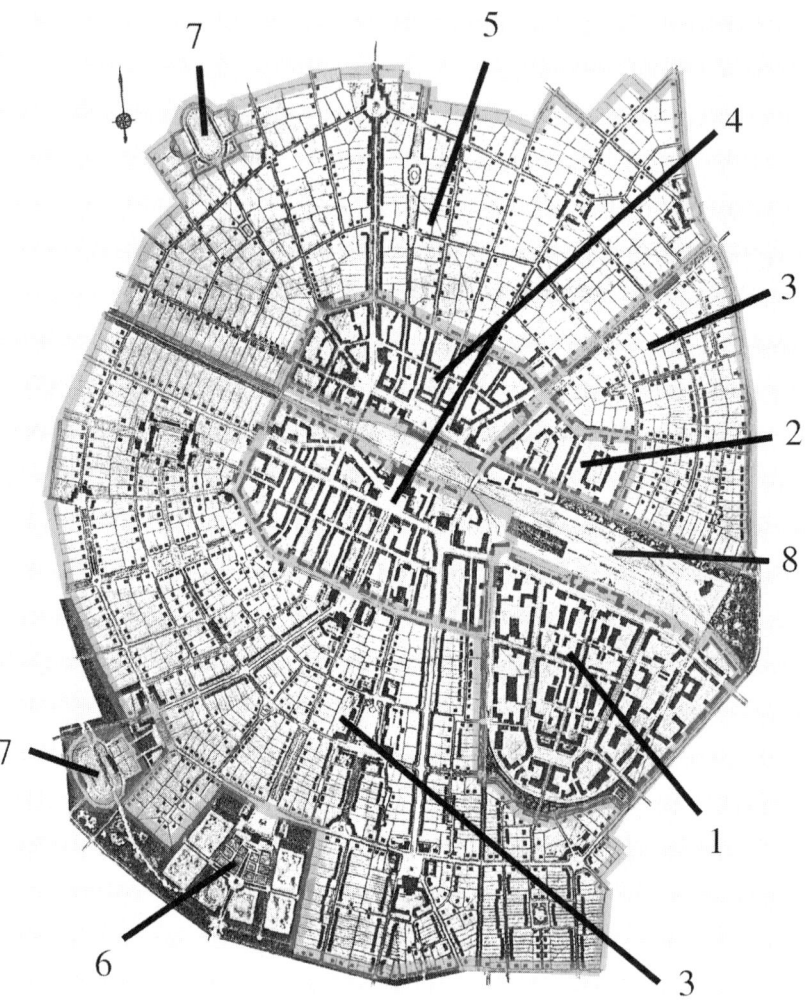

(1) heavy industry
(2) light industry
(3) residential area
(4) commercial center
(5) garden city
(6) cemetery
(7) stadiums
(8) railroad station and facilities

Map 8b. Afula, 1939

a price, they agreed to quit the lands they were farming before 25 January 1925. If they failed to leave, they would pay an indemnity to the purchasers. The Afula purchase totaled 15,964 dunams at £E4.250 per dunam.[104]

The purchase was divided into two sections: an area that was to be developed into an urban center of 5,000 dunams (see chapter 10), and an agricultural area of 11,000 dunams. To facilitate the immediate growth of Afula, Charles Passman contracted the sale of 1,000 dunams of agricultural land to a group of sixteen Jews from Mechov, Poland; eventually, however, the company sold 500 dunams to the Polish group and 300 dunams to five German Jews.

From the AMZIC's perspective, it was both more efficient and more profitable to sell these first parcels to Poles rather than to Americans. The Polish settlers would arrive within a few months and immediately begin cultivating the land. It would have taken much longer for American purchasers to reach Palestine. Moreover, the Polish purchasers agreed to make a first payment of 50 percent of the purchase price and pay the remainder over three years; by contrast, American purchasers usually paid only 20 percent as the first installment. By selling to Polish Jews, the American Zion Commonwealth would realize a larger proportion of its investment and receive an infusion of capital that could be reinvested in the development of the colony's infrastructure. The New York office of the AMZIC opposed this transaction since it would reduce the amount of land available for sale in America and diminish the extent of activity there.[105] Nevertheless, tracts were sold to Polish Jews through the Meshek Company, to Jews in Palestine by the local AMZIC office, and in America by the AMZIC.

Development of Afula began in 1927, when the American Zion Commonwealth facilitated the establishment there of a women's training farm. Six such farms existed in Palestine in 1930, providing young immigrant women with equality of opportunity and the possibility of gaining experience in various branches of agriculture instead of entering service-related occupations when they settled permanently on a kibbutz. Through the offices of the Agricultural Center of the Labor Federation and the Working Women's Council, the AMZIC set aside 100 dunams for the training farm at Afula, and this was supplemented by 25 dunams provided by the Bank Hapoalim in Afula.[106] Once a group of women had established the Afula farm, the land would be turned over to the Jewish National Fund. The AMZIC promised to supply this farm with 60 cubic meters of water per day.

The 1927 census of Jewish agriculture listed 940 inhabitants of Afula: 337 men, 335 women, and 278 children under age 15; the census did not distinguish between persons in the agricultural zone and those in the urban zone. The total area of the settlement was 13,665 dunams. The agricultural units consisted of 12 farms of less than 10 dunams and 30 over 10 dunams. Of the 4,081 dunams of land worked by farmers, 19 had plantations, 3,327 were crop land or fallow, and 510 were idle but fit for cultivation. Still available for settlers were 9,584 dunams. The census also enumerated 117 cows and 60 work animals, and determined that the number of both urban and rural buildings was 425.[107]

Afula's agricultural economy suffered during the late 1920s. Wheat prices dropped with the lifting of duties on imported grain; many farmers who had cultivated wheat left their fields fallow. John Hope-Simpson, who was sent to Palestine on behalf of His Majesty's government to survey and evaluate the situation in Palestine following the 1929 riots, noted in his 1930 report that the fields of Afula were the source of a regional rodent infestation.[108]

As with neighboring Balfouria, grain cultivation in this region was not a lucrative form of agriculture, despite government of Palestine attempts from 1930 onward to protect local wheat producers by imposing duties on imported wheat. Local farmers sought alternative ways to earn a livelihood through agriculture. At a 1932 meeting called by the Council of Afula, it was decided that grapefruit cultivation was the most promising alternative. The Jewish National Fund agreed to assign 500 dunams of its lands in the settlement to the inhabitants of Afula for this purpose, subject to sufficient irrigation water being made available. A second well was bored by the American Zion Commonwealth. This augmented the colony's water supply and facilitated the expansion of irrigated agriculture; 130 dunams were planted with apple, plum, and pear trees. By 1936 there were 520 dunams with plantations, of which 220 had citrus groves. In addition, 4,020 dunams were planted with field crops. Livestock was also raised in Afula; there were 121 head of cattle and 1,500 poultry. Altogether, agriculture provided a livelihood for 152 of Afula's 1,354 residents.[109] However, agriculture never played a substantial role in the economy of this settlement, at least in part because the agricultural sections were not fully brought under cultivation. (The discussion of the town of Afula is continued in chapter 10 on urban development.)

The Haifa Bay Lands

In 1924 Chaim Weizmann approached Bernard Rosenblatt with a national mission: redemption of the Haifa Bay lands, between Haifa and Acre and along the Kishon and Naaman rivers. Weizmann asked Rosenblatt to convince the American Zion Commonwealth's board of directors to undertake this project. Though he understood the significance of the project, Rosenblatt questioned why the Jewish National Fund did not undertake this acquisition. Weizmann explained that the JNF had overextended itself in the vast financial undertaking of the Jezreel Valley purchases. Rosenblatt saw two principal obstacles to the success of his efforts: the vast scope of the purchase—the tract comprised 57,000 dunams—and the limited funds the AMZIC had on hand. However, he was resolved to realize this project, and thus he approached the directors in New York. He explained to them that the articles of the constitution had made appropriate provisions for this type of purchase. Moreover, the AMZIC would be performing a national duty in redeeming the Haifa Bay lands. Rosenblatt also pointed out that they would retain the land until the time, if ever, that the JNF exercised its option and purchased it from the AMZIC.[110] The directors were persuaded.

In order to defray the large costs, the American Zion Commonwealth entered into negotiations with Joseph Loewy, representing the Sommerfeld Group, and the representatives of the Meshek Company for the formation of a new company to develop these lands—the Haifa Bay Development Company. The three partners each invested £E10,000. A tentative agreement was drawn up on 7 December 1924, with 25 February 1925, set as the date for making a final agreement.[111] Apparently Loewy stood behind the initiative for this project. Indeed, a year or so before the formation of this company, he had forwarded "far-sighted and ambitious plans for the development of the Bay lands."[112] But despite his intentions, he could not draw together the necessary capital for the venture. In the end it was the Palestine Land Development Company that was responsible for the actual purchase, since, as mentioned above, the Jewish National Fund lacked the capital for this project. In addition, there were ideological considerations—the JNF preferred agricultural lands, not industrial lands such as were offered in Haifa Bay. The PLDC, through Arthur Ruppin's initiative and with Weizmann's assistance, brought all the players together.

The Haifa Bay property belonged to the Sursock family, who had purchased it from the Ottoman government in 1872. The tract was known as the Jidro lands, and included the villages of Jidro, Kafrata, Darbeide, Kurdani, Majdal, and Khirbaj-Khartia. The area, exclusive of Kafrata, Majdal, and Khirbaj-Khartia, comprised approximately 45,000 dunams. In addition, the government of Palestine granted a 99-year concession for 12,000 dunams of dunes adjoining the tract. This brought the total area to 57,000 dunams. (The Kafrata, Majdal, and Khirbaj-Khartia tracts are discussed in the next section.)

With the completion of the Haifa Bay purchase, plans were forged for the development of settlements in this area. Solomon J. Weinstein believed that "there is no doubt that the establishment of the colony by America[n settlers] in Haifa Bay would become very popular among the America[n] Jewish public, and, therefore, I have good reason to believe that our sales campaign would prove even more successful than the Herzlia campaign."[113] The Haifa Bay area was slated for accelerated development. Until this time, the coast of Palestine lacked a modern harbor, and government resources were budgeted for the construction of modern port facilities at Haifa. The surrounding areas would enjoy speedy development as Haifa became the industrial hub of Palestine. The population would increase rapidly in order to service the new port and facilities, the associated industries, and the required service sectors. New neighborhoods and settlements would sprout up quickly to house the sizable population increase. In turn, this would most likely lead to the development of nearby agricultural settlements to satisfy the urban area's need for dairy and poultry products, fruits, and vegetables.

Two plans were drafted for Haifa Bay, the first by Richard Kaufmann and the second by Patrick Abercrombie. Kaufmann's plan, drawn up in 1926, called for the area to be divided into seven zones. The 1,500-dunam zone 1 in the south was reserved for the continued urban development of Haifa. Zone 2, a 10,000-dunam area, was set aside for the new port and large-scale industry. Zones 3 and 4 were targeted for agricultural colonization. Zone 3's 3,500 dunams were to be subdivided into 5-dunam plots on which new immigrants would be housed. These new settlers could supplement their incomes by growing vegetables and raising dairy cows and poultry. Zone 4's 9,500 dunams were planned for intensive cultivation of orange and banana plantations in 20-dunam plots. On the 8,000-dunam zone 5, a garden town, to be named Kordani, was planned. The town was compared to Heliopolis, Ostend, and Atlantic City. It would be parceled into lots of 1.5–3 dunams, with low density housing. Zone 6, 11,000 dunams in area, was designated for intensive agriculture in plots of 5–10 dunams. Zone 7—5,000 dunams in area—would be taken up by villas on 3-dunam lots that would line both sides of the planned 50-meter-wide road from Haifa to Acre. These villas were intended to attract wealthy American Jews who would retire to this site for the winter months instead of Florida or California. The area around the villas would be adorned with exotic gardens, cypress trees, and fountains; it would also include recreational amenities, such as tennis courts and golf courses. The principal road running through zone 7 was compared to Paris's Champs-Élysées.[114]

One variation of Kaufmann's plan combined zones 6 and 7 into an area that would be offered for sale in America. To honor Judge Louis D. Brandeis—and increase sales by giving the new settlement a popular name—the American Zion Commonwealth suggested naming this area Brandeisia. Henrietta Szold supported this proposal and was willing to meet with Brandeis to gain his approval. Should Brandeis decline permission—which indeed he did—the new settlement would be called Nordia, in honor of Max Nordau, noted Zionist leader and Herzl's right-hand man.[115]

By August 1926 planning had reached the stage at which the American Zion Commonwealth could announce: "preparations are under way for a new agricultural settlement, 12 km. from Haifa, to be named Nordia in memory of Dr. Max Nordau. This settlement will be the third of the American Zion

Commonwealth holdings immortalizing men who have rendered historic services to Zionism, the first having been Balfouria, the second Herzlia. The Commonwealth anticipates that colonization in this settlement will commence shortly after Passover."[116]

After hearing of the plans for Nordia, Akiva Ettinger commented that in his estimation, the lands in the possession of the American Zion Commonwealth were appropriate for an "orchard settlement." This term, as Ettinger explained, related to a modern irrigated settlement planted with European fruit trees (apples, pears, apricots, plums, and so forth), table grapes, and field crops with potential for export (cauliflower, eggplant, artichokes, and strawberries). Ettinger referred to this kind of modern, specialized agriculture as "horticultural industry"; he indicated that in order to carry out this type of agricultural activity, the settlement would need a nursery, a canning factory, and cold storage. Ettinger tried to dissuade the American Zion Commonwealth from its plan to sell the land in the United States. The human resources needed to develop Nordia would not, he thought, be found in America but in Palestine. The role of Americans, Ettinger argued, was to finance the project, either by assisting their relatives or by providing funds through a colonization bank.[117]

Nonetheless, the American Zion Commonwealth proceeded to sell Nordia lands in the United States. Its circular to the company's sales representatives explained the special nature of the new colony: "we offer in this case such improvements as were never known to be given in Palestine, not even by the American Zion Commonwealth." The villas and the agricultural lands would be supplied with piped-in water. Each plot would be located on a street. The Haifa-Acre highway would be 50 meters wide. At its own expense, the AMZIC would provide public buildings—synagogues, schools, kindergartens, a hospital, bathhouses, ice and creamery plants. The company also emphasized the development of the port, the oil pipeline from Mosul, Iraq, and the already existing local industries: the "Nesher" cement factory, the "Shemen" oil factory, the "Grands Moulins de Palestine" flour mills and matzo bakery, and the Rutenburg Power Station.[118]

Through the American Zion Commonwealth and Meshek, lands were sold to the Jewish National Fund and to individuals around the world, including the United States, Palestine, Europe (Austria, Bulgaria, England, Germany, Latvia, Lithuania, Poland, Romania, the Soviet Union, and Sweden), and Egypt. Americans were offered various plots, but in the end only a small amount of land was purchased by clients in the United States. Altogether, Americans bought only 70 dunams, although plans were drawn up for a 4,700-dunam garden town in zone 6 specifically for American investors.[119]

The principal reason for this shortfall in American sales was that by 1925 potential purchasers in the United States had lost confidence in the American Zion Commonwealth. Meshek had also experienced financial difficulties due to the worsening economic conditions in Poland. These and other factors resulted in the AMZIC's inability to fulfill its financial responsibilities with respect to mortgage payments for the land—although Bernard Rosenblatt attempted to obtain loans through the Jewish Colonial Trust and various American banks. The Haifa Bay Development Company owed £P250,000, and there was fear that foreclosure would result in the restoration of the land to its former Arab owners. The magnitude and severity of the situation caused great distress among the Zionist leadership both in America and internationally.

Other investors, like the Palestine Economic Corporation and some non-Jewish entrepreneurs, saw the land around Haifa as an area with great potential. Plans for the new harbor, the Baghdad-Haifa railroad, and the Iraqi Petroleum Company's pipeline from Mosul to Haifa made the property even more attractive. But the Zionist leadership, particularly Weizmann, opposed the involvement of the PEC. Although the PEC was founded in 1925 as an American Jewish venture for the development of Palestine, it was an instrument of the Brandeis group's policy, supported by American non-Zionists and not a self-proclaimed Zionist organization.

The Jewish National Fund, Keren Hayesod, and the Palestine Zionist Executive all became involved in the purchase discussions, attempting to keep these lands out of the hands of private investors. (Leah Doukhan-Landau's article carefully and adeptly outlines the process of trying to retain possession of the Haifa Bay territory.) The end result of these discussions was the transfer of 5,000 dunams to the PEC and the remainder to the JNF. The Bayside Land Corporation, a joint venture of the PEC and the JNF, was specifically established for the development of the Haifa Bay lands. In addition, through pressure applied by the Mandatory government, 3,200 dunams were sold to the Iraqi Petroleum Company.[120] In the end, the AMZIC did not retain any land for its constituents.

The American Zion Commonwealth did, however, remain extensively involved in the purchase and sale of nearby lands. For example, it bought several tracts to the east of the Haifa Bay purchase, extending the territory by 14,000 dunams. In 1925 the company also purchased 10,000 dunams at Kafrata at a price of £E4.500 per dunam; acting on behalf of a group of Polish Hasidim, Avodath Israel, it set aside 6,400 dunams of this tract for them. The AMZIC sold 1,000 dunams of this parcel to private investors and 2,600 dunams adjacent to the Haifa Bay tract to the Haifa Bay Development Company. The Avodath Israel group was unable to finance its full commitment, and in the end it received only 3,600 dunams. To help settle its debts to the AMZIC, it sold 2,924 dunams to the Jewish National Fund.[121]

The American Zion Commonwealth also served the interests of two other groups of Hasidim, one from Yablonov and the other from Kozienice. The company purchased 4,000 dunams at Majdal (also to the east of Haifa

Map 9. American Zion Commonwealth purchases in Haifa Bay and the Jezreel Valley, 1926

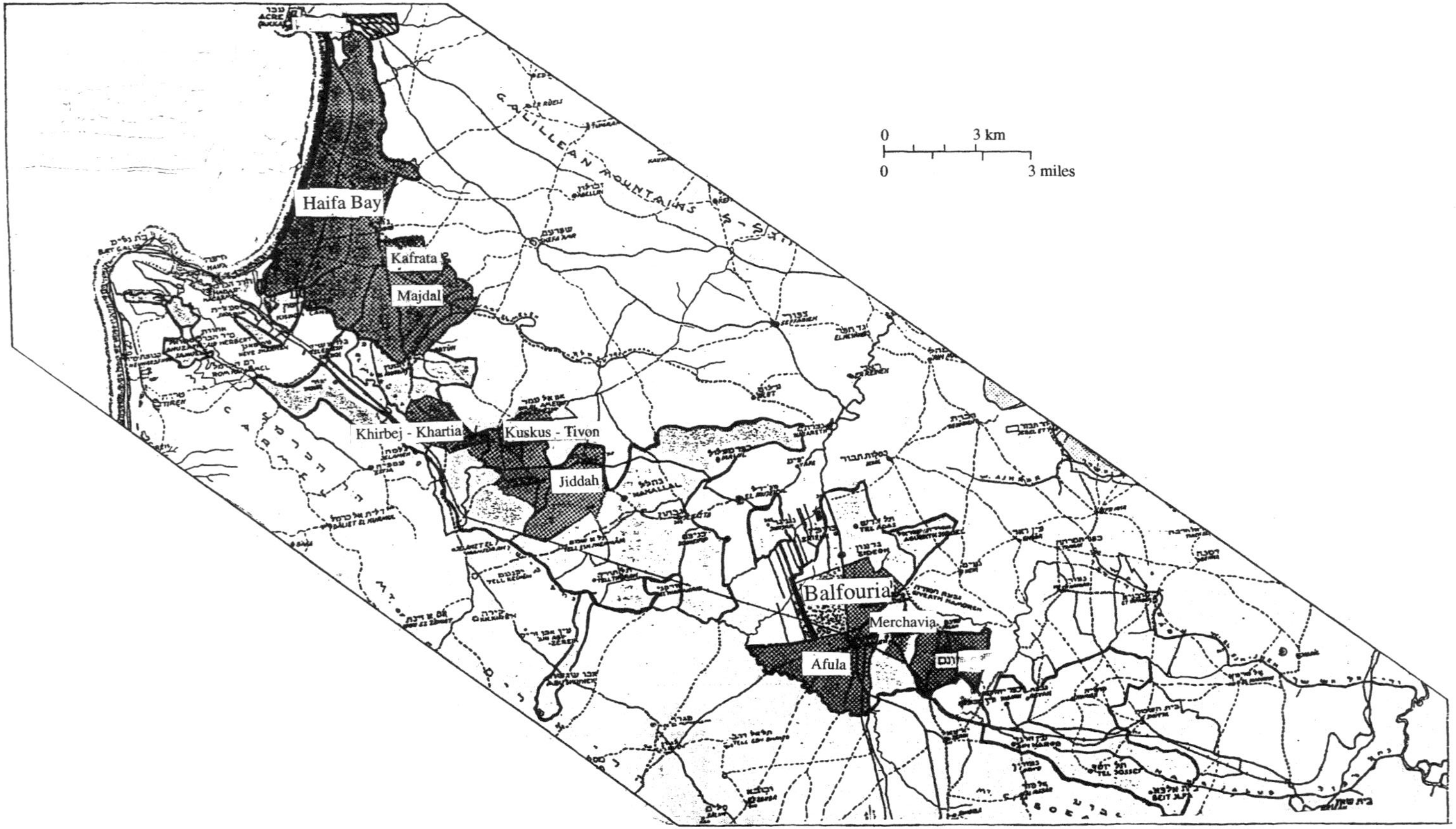

Bay) at £E4.500 per dunam. In 1925 the group from Yablonov founded Nahalat Yaakov and the Hasidim from Kozienice founded Avodat Yisrael. Shortly after settling, however, members of these groups were obliged to abandon the site because of the economic crisis in Poland. Upon the cancellation of their purchase, the AMZIC sold the entire tract to the Jewish National Fund. In 1926 a third group affiliated with Hapoel Hamizrachi settled on the land. The three settlements were amalgamated that same year and named Kfar Hasidim. Two years later, an organization was established in the United States to assist the Hasidim at Nahalat Yaakov. A $40,000 loan, administered by the Palestine Zionist Executive, was organized for the construction of buildings. (In 1939 the moshav consisted of 85 units and a population of approximately 600.) In addition, the AMZIC purchased 3,000 dunams in the adjacent village of Khirbaj-Khartia in 1926. It is unclear what happened to this tract; although it is listed among the company's purchases, no further mention of it can be found in the company's records.[122]

In 1929 Professor Patrick Abercrombie of Liverpool University, one of Britain's most prominent town and regional planners, was asked to advise on the development of Haifa Bay. Abercrombie and Clifford Holliday together produced an initial draft of the Emek Zebulun scheme in January 1934. Two years later, Abercrombie completed the scheme, and this plan was eventually approved by the high commissioner in January 1938. The scheme retained "something of the essence of Kaufmann's vision."[123] As with Kaufmann's plan, the area would be developed with different settlements and neighborhoods. Zones 3 and 4 would include the middle-class settlement Kiryat Motzkin (1934), moshav Kfar Bialik (1934), the German immigrant neighborhood Kiryat Bialik (1934), the residential quarters of Kiryat Haim (1932), the Kiryat Shmuel quarter for religious Jews (1936), and Kiryat Yam (1946). Zones 4, 6, and 7 would include Zur Shalom, Kibbutz Ein Hamifratz (1938), Mishmar Hayam (1939, later moved to Afek), Kibbutz Kfar Masaryk (1938), and the private estate Karei Naaman (1955).[124] (Developments that occurred on lands sold to the PEC are discussed in the following chapter.)

OTHER RURAL ACTIVITIES

During the 1920s, the American Zion Commonwealth purchased several tracts of agricultural land on which it never established settlements. Some parcels were contiguous with other AMZIC tracts. After the financial collapse of the company, the Jewish National Fund purchased some of these lands and either attached them to existing settlements or used them to found others.

In 1925, for example, the American Zion Commonwealth purchased 10,000 dunams of the village of Jiddah in the Jezreel Valley at a price of £E5 per dunam. The Jewish National Fund acquired 1,000 dunams of this tract to settle a group of Yugoslavian Jews. The AMZIC had entered this transaction on behalf of two Polish companies, the Manor Textile Company Limited and the Jezreel-Jaffa Company. They purchased 5,000 and 4,000 dunams respectively for the two companies. The Manor Textile Company erected a textile factory, whose employees were to engage both in industry and agriculture. Twenty-seven families settled on this tract, but because of the economic difficulties in Poland, neither company was able to fulfill the terms of its commitment. After negotiations, the Manor Textile Company received 1,500 dunams against the sum it had already paid, and the Jezreel-Jaffa Company 1,328 dunams. The AMZIC sold a large segment of the tract—5,895 dunams—to the JNF. Of this total, 500 dunams of hilly lands and forest remained under the supervision of the JNF. The remainder was leased to three moshavim to augment their holdings: 2,850 dunams to Kfar Yehoshua, 1,950 dunams to Nahalal, and 165 dunams to Beit Shaarim.[125]

Additional purchases in the area included the Meshek Company purchase of 10,000 dunams in the vicinity of the villages of Kuskus and Tivon (east of Haifa Bay) on behalf of private purchasers. After the failure of this company, the American Zion Commonwealth, which had taken over 80 percent of it, transferred 30 percent of these lands to private owners, and the remaining 7,025 dunams were transferred to the Jewish National Fund. Of these lands, 2,800 dunams were forest retained by the JNF, and 4,225 dunams were divided between moshav Kfar Yehoshua and Kibbutz Geva for their expansion.[126]

In 1925 the American Zion Commonwealth purchased 2,225 dunams in the village of Zarnuqa, located to the west of Rehovot. This transaction was not facilitated by the Palestine Land Development Company, but achieved through direct negotiations with the three owners, formerly of Ramleh and at that time resident in Jerusalem. However, after the disbursement of the first installments the tract was not transferred by the date agreed upon. The AMZIC claimed the return of its outlay, interest, damages, and legal fees. Later a portion of this land was sold to private individuals and the rest to the Jewish National Fund for the development of an agricultural experimental station.[127]

With the land boom of 1925, Trans-Jordan was seen by the American Zion Commonwealth as a possible area for development. Since the Jewish National Fund had already shown an interest in the Hula Valley, the Beit Shaan Valley, and the Negev, the AMZIC was excluded from these areas. Trans-Jordan was perceived as the only region large enough for the continuation of the AMZIC development. One million dunams could be purchased at a cost of £E1.000 to £E1.500 per dunam. This acquisition would relieve the pressure for land in Palestine and afford the AMZIC an area for future expansion. Alternatively, it could be sold to landless Arabs who had been displaced when the land they had worked as sharecroppers was sold from under them. Since the AMZIC's finances prevented the purchase of any land in Trans-Jordan at that time, its officers endeavored to interest private capital in the project.[128]

The American Zion Commonwealth also investigated other tracts in Palestine and entered negotiations for their purchase. In 1925 Rosenblatt and the Vaad of Rishon Lezion discussed the possibility of developing the sand dunes of Rishon Lezion into a garden city. These dunes represented an area of over 20,000 dunams, and they were located just one kilometer to the south of the Jubeliah area (Bat Yam). Under Ahmed Jamal Pasha, commander of the Turkish Fourth Army in Palestine and Syria during World War I, Rishon Lezion received permission to plant the dunes with trees. This was in essence a gift, for eventually this land, if revitalized, could become a permanent holding with *kushans* issued to Rishon Lezion. When the settlers started their plantings, they believed that this investment would ensure their inalienable right to ownership, but later their right to the land was contested. The AMZIC believed that the question of ownership would eventually be resolved in favor of Rishon Lezion, so the company drew up an agreement in which the Vaad of Rishon Lezion gave it the right to exploit half the area. The issue of ownership was not settled until 1942.[129]

In 1925 Eliyahu Zeev Lewin-Epstein of New York, on behalf of his brother Levi of Warsaw, approached the American Zion Commonwealth with an offer for the sale of two estates. The first was in the colony of Sedjera. Over 20,000 dunams had been colonized by Baron Rothschild's administration in 1899 and later by the Jewish Colonization Association. Thirty-five families were settled on 10,000 dunams, and 10,200 dunams were purchased by Levi Lewin-Epstein. His lands included plantations, forests (3,000 dunams of eucalyptus trees), and a number of houses and public buildings. Lewin-Epstein proposed that the land be subdivided and sold in 100-dunam plots. The sale price to the AMZIC would be £E6.500 per dunam, with 50 percent due immediately and the remainder paid over ten years at 5 percent interest. The suggested resale price was £E10 to £E12 per dunam. One problem with this proposal was that the AMZIC was not interested in acting merely as a land selling organization for a private owner.

Levi Lewin-Epstein's second tract comprised 4,000 dunams in Nimrin, a village eleven kilometers west of Tiberias. The Polish Mizrachi organization was to sell 1,000 to 1,500 dunams of this tract at £E3.250 per dunam. Lewin-Epstein was eager to sell the balance at £E2.750 per dunam plus the expenses of the *mafruz* to the AMZIC.[130] However, adhering to its policy not to purchase land from Jews, the AMZIC passed up this opportunity as well as Lewin-Epstein's previous proposal.

CHAPTER 7

Summary

The American Zion Commonwealth succeeded in establishing three settlements—Balfouria, Herzlia, and Afula—that continued to develop even after the company's demise. Realizing that American owners would not arrive in Palestine en masse, it took the practical approach of first settling local and European Jews on the land. This measure differed markedly from the operations of the failed *ahuza* companies and guaranteed the success of the projects. If Americans did not want to take the initiative during the founding stage of one of the AMZIC settlements, vibrant and developing colonies would be established which they could join at a latter phase. Another factor in the success of these three projects was the sensible approach taken to the economic development of the settlements. Unhindered by rigid ideological perceptions about economic development, the AMZIC could adapt—usually quite quickly—to new agricultural ideas, and it was willing to foster industrial development as well. This flexible attitude fostered a dynamic process in the growth of the colonies. Further, the AMZIC often learned from its own mistakes. From experience with the Balfouria colony, the company discerned the disadvantages of being located at a great distance from an urban center. Thus a prominent factor in the AMZIC's decision to develop Herzlia was that colony's proximity to Tel Aviv-Jaffa. Similarly, the Haifa Bay project was chosen not only because of its national importance but because of its propinquity to the growing port city of Haifa. With regard to Afula, however, the AMZIC erred in assuming that the community's location in the heart of the Jezreel Valley at a crossroad would foster its growth. The AMZIC did not fully comprehend the ideological factors prevailing in the surrounding socialist settlements. (This is discussed at greater length in chapter 10.)

Financial overextension led to the failure of the American Zion Commonwealth and a loss of confidence by the American public. Believing in the great mission of redeeming the land, the AMZIC too often gave affirmative answers to World Zionist Organization requests to enter into transactions of national importance. As Kenneth Stein pointed out, "the quantity of Arab land offered for sale was in excess of the Jewish ability to purchase."[131] The American Zion Commonwealth was placed in an extremely awkward position: there was always more land available than it could afford to purchase. The Haifa Bay purchase simply did not make good business sense. Including the tracts of Kafrata and Majdal, it represented twice the total amount of land the company had purchased up to this point in time.

Nevertheless, the greatest achievement of the company was the purchase of over 150,000 dunams in the short span of seven years. As of 1927, Jewish land holdings in Palestine totaled 864,700 dunams. The company's land was used to establish colonies, furnish Jewish settlers with acreage, and, when transferred to the Jewish National Fund, add significantly to the national land reserve.

Following the transfer of Haifa Bay lands to the Jewish National Fund, Bernard Rosenblatt summarized his perception of the American Zion Commonwealth's contribution in a letter to Menachem Ussishkin:

> Please accept my sincere congratulations on the conclusion of the successful negotiations of the Keren Kajemeth for securing the Haifa Bay lands. When it became evident that the Commonwealth could not carry through this project, Passman and myself were working along a consistent program to make it possible for the Jewish National Fund to become the heir. I am glad that it finally resulted in saving the land, not only for the Jewish people, but particularly because it becomes the *inalienable* property of the Jewish people, through the ownership of the organization, which you head [emphasis in the original].[132]

Rosenblatt continued,

> It now appears that instead of criticism, I deserve praise—in which I am not really interested, as long as Haifa Bay lands are safe under your jurisdiction. Incidently [*sic*], the original constitution of the American Zion Commonwealth, contains a provision that at any time the Zionist Congress may insist in transferring its lands to the Jewish National Fund, a provision which was written by me and approved by Justice Brandeis. In a roundabout way, the dream of those who organized the Commonwealth and worked so hard for it—particularly Passman and myself—has found fruition, for the benefit of Eretz Israel.[133]

8

Private Development in the Rural Sector

> I beheld my grove at last in full-grown state. All through the depression I had managed to send money for its upkeep, and last season there had been a first crop, but Arab vandals had destroyed it, and they had also burned my packing shed. This year as I arrived I was greeted with news of a local hailstorm which had ruined half my crop. Alas, my dreams of sometime living here in modest ease and writing epics on the proceeds from my grove were like the dreams of all genteel buyers of chicken farms in New Jersey and little ranches in California. There was just then a glut of oranges on the market because of too-rapid expansion of the citrus industry, and many groves were being abandoned. So I crammed myself with oranges during my week in Nathanyah, as the sole return of my seven-year investment.
>
> Meyer Levin, *In Search: An Autobiography*

In the 1920s and 1930s, several American groups and a number of individuals whose motivations were pragmatic rather than ideological were involved in rural development in Palestine. However, some of their projects and initiatives were influenced by social and Zionist considerations—including Jewish redemption of land and its amelioration through agricultural development; the expansion of the Jewish economy through growth in production and employment of Jewish labor; and the establishment of workers' settlements, often adjacent to plantations that provided an income for the inhabitants. These private projects differed to some degree from those of the *ahuza* companies and the American Zion Commonwealth. These companies had established constitutions that laid out well-defined directions for their activities; their mode was a kind of quasi-investment—upbuilding the land, but with no desire for excessive profits. By comparison, planting as a private investment was based on the premise of reaping high returns.

The Gan Haim Corporation, with a capital of £P100,000, was founded in 1927 to create large citrus plantations in Palestine. Its founders included Canadians, British, Australians, Americans, and local inhabitants. Among the more prominent backers were Asher Pierce of Montreal, David Dunkelman of Toronto, Max Shoolman of Boston, and Sir Alfred Mond (later Lord Melchett). Other Americans included Nathan Goldberg, a construction engineer from the Bronx who served as chairman of Gan Haim in 1933, and Israel Matz, a New York Zionist and Hebraist who settled in Palestine in 1926. The corporation's ultimate objective was to divide the groves, once they were fully developed, into various sized plots to be sold to settlers on easy payment terms.

In 1927 negotiations began for the purchase of 2,500 dunams in the area of Miske (today the area of Ramat Hakovesh). By 1928, 975 dunams had been transferred and registered in the company's name. On this site the large estate of Gan Haim was founded, honoring Zionist leader Chaim Weizmann, a personal friend of some of the investors. (The corporation also initiated negotiations for the purchase of 8,000 dunams extending southward from Birket Ramadan [the swampy depression of the Poleg River] toward Herzlia, but this transaction was not realized.) By spring 1928 about 220 of the 975 dunams were planted with orange groves; by 1936, 892 dunams had been planted. In addition, large nurseries were created for the future development of the company's land.[1]

Abraham Revusky, commenting on the success of Gan Haim, noted: "The largest and most important of these groups, the Gan Haim, owns extensive orange plantations in the Sharon to the north of Kfar Saba. It has proven to be highly successful from the investment point of view. It has pursued a liberal labor policy, encouraging the permanent settlement of their workers on small holdings adjoining the large plantations. Owing to this policy it forms the base for rapidly growing settlements in the vicinity."[2]

Asher Pierce, one of the more active investors in this group, applied his experience in Western Canada and his business acumen to this and other endeavors in Palestine. In late 1929, without consulting the corporate directors, he decided to expand Gan Haim, believing this would be beneficial to the development of the estate as well as to the workers. But coming as it did after the stock market crash, such an investment was regarded by the shareholders as a breach of confidence, and Pierce's initiative created an unbridgeable rift between company owners who supported the expansion and those who opposed it.[3]

As of 1929 Gan Haim consisted of 3,500 dunams, of which 1,000 were planted with orchards, 5 dunams had forests and public gardens, and 500 dunams were ready for planting orchards. The estate structures were spread over 25 dunams. The infrastructure and machinery consisted of eleven houses, five shacks, two public buildings, a workshop, four irrigation wells, and two tractors. There were sixty-five inhabitants, of whom fifty were Jewish workers. By 1933, 1,700 dunams of citrus groves had been developed. Part of the plantation had reached the fruit-bearing stage, and that year 12,000 cases of oranges were harvested. The number of workers increased to between sixty and sixty-five. At that time, two packing houses were under construction, and during the following years production would increase greatly.[4]

In 1935 the Jewish National Fund had leased land adjacent to Gan Haim to a group of twenty-five workers there. Each member of the group received 10 dunams for his home and a small farm. This new settlement was originally named Gan Haim Bet, but eventually it gave up its independent status and became part of Gan Haim.[5]

Among the employees at Gan Haim were a number of Americans. Pierce had solicited Americans with experience in citrus culture, particularly those employed in educational institutions in California, to manage the enterprise. Among these recruits was Mendes Sacks, who had completed his studies at the University of Maryland and Harvard University and then specialized in citriculture at the University of California. His wife Celia was also an agronomist. In 1932 they arrived in Palestine, where he began as technical manager of the estate and within a few years rose to become full manager of the Gan Haim holdings. Sacks and his wife built their home amid the orchards.[6]

Private investment also boosted development near Haifa. When the American Zion Commonwealth encountered financial difficulties, the PEC began to invest in land in Haifa Bay. For this purpose, the PEC established a subsidiary, the Bayside Land Company, in partnership with the Jewish National Fund. In 1928, following the final transfer of the Haifa Bay lands to their new owners, the company commissioned Patrick Abercrombie to create an outline plan for the area. As noted above in chapter 7, Abercrombie's scheme differed from Richard Kaufmann's. The new plan divided the parcel into three sections: an industrial area of 15,441 dunams located in the southern section of the tract adjacent to the harbor; a residential area of 21,015 dunams to the north of the industrial zone; and an agricultural zone to the north of the residential area.

At that time an oil pipeline was planned from Iraq to Haifa. The Iraqi Petroleum Company purchased 4,685 dunams in the industrial zone for the pipeline and a refinery, as well as 73 dunams in the residential zone. In addition, a deal was struck with the government of Palestine, which acquired 1,285 dunams for an airport and railroad warehouses. According to the original agreement, the Bayside Land Corporation was to receive 5,000 dunams in the industrial zone, but instead it received only half this amount. To further the industrial development of this area, the Bayside Land Corporation constructed and offered for lease eight industrial buildings with a total area of 3,205 square meters.[7] In exchange for relinquishing its share in the industrial zone, the Bayside Land Corporation received 2,400 dunams in the residential zone. The settlement of Kiryat Yam was established on this section in 1940.

Fig. 25. Water tower at Gan Haim, ca. 1935.
(CZA Keren Hayesod photograph collection)

In addition, the Bayside Land Corporation held (in partnership with the Jewish National Fund) 8,000 dunams of agricultural land.[8]

Adjacent to the Haifa Bay lands were the State Domains. In 1932 the Department of Lands undertook the division of this land into parcels that would be leased to small landholders. In a letter to the U.S. secretary of state (with a copy to Emanuel Neumann), the American consul in Jerusalem, Alexander K. Sloan, pointed out that "this might be an excellent opportunity to American citizens wishing to lease land for industrial or agricultural purposes."[9] But American investors did not take up the challenge.

The settlement of Haifa Bay was, however, facilitated by the PEC, which held 78 percent of the Palestine Mortgage and Credit Bank. This bank provided 200 mortgages of £P100 for new home owners in the workers' neighborhood of Kiryat Haim, founded in 1933. The PEC's interest was clear—as the area became developed, additional settlers and investors would be drawn to it and would, in turn, purchase land from the PEC.[10] In all, the Palestine Economic Corporation contributed to the development of the Haifa Bay region through two types of initiative: participation in land redemption, and encouraging settlement of the area by providing lands for housing as well as mortgages.

Another investment project was initiated by a single individual—Meyer L. Rosoff. A report of the activities of the Rosoff Group Plantations described how "Already in 1926, after his first trip to Palestine, Dr. M. L. Rosoff started to think about possibilities of making investments in some constructive enterprises undertaken along agricultural lines in that land."[11] Dr. Rosoff (1886–1948), an oral surgeon from New York City, investigated several possible means of achieving "a successive realization of smaller individual investments." With the advice of social workers and the assistance of Mr. M. Cohen, Rosoff envisioned creating agricultural colonies in Palestine that would unite individual investors into groups "which would have to be constructed in such ways as to have possibilities of controlling all the work, no matter how small, and every cent which is to be invested in such an enterprise."[12] This plan for oversight was drawn up in reaction to the sometimes unaccountable and dubious business practices of various companies engaged in work in Palestine.

Beginning in 1927 and continuing until 1935, six corporations were organized under the umbrella of the Rosoff Group: Gan Rashal, Gan Hadar Corporation; Gan Hadar Beth, Inc.; Tel Hadar, Inc.; Pri Hadar, Inc.; and Reyem, Inc. These corporations engaged the Yakhin company to plant and tend their orange groves. Gan Rashal was developed on a 700-dunam tract bordering on Herzlia. The other five corporations purchased and developed the land of Naane in the vicinity of Rehovot. The majority of corporate members in each of these groups resided in the United States, but there were also some European owners. Under Rosoff's direction, these investors sought land of special quality; they understood the importance of thoroughly investigating soil quality and water availability before the land was purchased and planted. The corporations ventured to select "healthy trees of a desirable variety and uniform fruit"; to engage "a reliable contractor for development work"; to select "a supervision management, consisting of experts"; and to construct a well. At the same time, Rosoff deemed it cardinal to carefully select the investors. He realized that investors needed to be able to bear the financial burden for at least five years before seeing any return. This apparently was a reaction to problems encountered by *ahuza* companies and the American Zion Commonwealth. Investors, excited by the prospect of owning land in Palestine, often made an initial down payment but did not follow through on the following payments, nor did they uphold their commitments to pay taxes and subsidize improvements. To remedy this situation, Rosoff stressed that it was "very important to study the financial possibilities of every prospective investor before he undertakes such an obligation."[13]

As noted above, the first project was Gan Rashal in the Sharon. This name was an acronym, constructed from the initials of the biblical matriarchs: Rachel, Sarah, and Leah. Five American investors purchased 700 dunams in 1927, of which 200 were planted in the spring of 1928. As of 1 January 1933, the total investment had reached $109,000. The settlement included a "first class" well connected to a "California system of water irrigation." The inventory also comprised "a special iron tank for additional water supply, a house built on the well, a packing house and a large nursery and other subtropical plants." As of 1929, twenty Jewish workers and a guard were employed at Gan Rashal. The estate was later included under the jurisdiction of Herzlia.[14]

The Gan Hadar Corporation was organized in 1928, and the following year it purchased 600 dunams near Rehovot. Though the climatic conditions of the location were considered quite suitable for plantations, there was apprehension about the availability of water. Development work was postponed until the spring of 1931, when the boring of an appropriate well was completed. Initially, 350 dunams were planted and irrigated by utilizing the California system. Here, too, the project was supervised by Yakhin and employed members of the 125-strong Kvutzah of Hanoar Haoved that was settled nearby.[15]

Plans for additional settlements were made in 1931, but these were hindered by the difficulty of acquiring a large enough tract in the possession of one owner. One tract that seemed feasible comprised approximately 2,000 dunams of undeveloped land lying between Gan Hadar and the railroad station at Naane. The Land Settlement Department of the Mandatory government had completed its survey and division of lands in the area. Local villagers owned small parcels, few of which exceeded 10 dunams (this was in contrast to other areas, where large tracts of land were owned by urban Arab effendis). Thus, if these American groups wanted to continue purchasing land, it would be necessary to proceed cautiously, buying tract after tract from villager after villager. Negotiations had to be discreetly conducted with each owner so as not to inflate land prices. Local landholders had been unsuccessful in their attempts to drill for water, but if they believed water was available, they would raise the price of their acreage. The Rosoff companies purchased a 150-dunam tract from an Arab owner who had bored a 215-meter well that came up dry. After completing the transaction, the American owners continued drilling until they struck water at a depth of 237 meters. The Rosoff group kept the discovery a secret so they could continue securing land in the vicinity. By February 1932, 200 dunams had been purchased for Gan Hadar Beth, bordering Gan Hadar.[16]

In March 1933, a 150-dunam tract at the Naane railroad station became available for purchase. This section would be strategically important for the development of plantations, for it could be the site of transportation services to all the investment groups in the area and allow the transit of produce by rail to the port of Haifa or to Egypt—the second largest market for Palestinian citrus fruit. After the tract was acquired, it was decided to utilize it for the benefit of all the companies in the area. Pri Hadar obtained 497.5 dunams by October 1933, of which 334 were planted. Tel Hadar acquired 300 dunams, which were planted with 10,000 trees.[17]

At first no thought was given to establishing a settlement for the American owners. Indeed, these plantation groups did not expect to create any continuous zone of ownership. It was assumed the company would only obtain noncontiguous and dispersed tracts of land. If owners did consider immigrating to Palestine, they could settle nearby in some existing Jewish colony. With the accumulation of some 1,500 dunams near Naane, however, foundations were laid for a 200-dunam settlement for American landowners, located near a workers' settlement that had been established on Jewish National Fund land. The tract would be parceled into 2.5-dunam plots. Half a dunam of each parcel would be set aside for roads and public buildings. The settlement was called Ramot Meir, in honor of Meyer Rossoff, but it was also known as Ganei Hadar.[18]

The company reported in January 1933 that during the coming year many of its American owners were expected to settle permanently in Palestine. If they did, it appears they did not settle at Ramot Meir, for the *1936 Census of Jewish Agriculture* reported that 1,825 of the 4,000 dunams had been planted with citrus trees; the colony was divided into 95 plots of 20 or more dunams, but no one lived there. The plantations of the Rosoff Group did provide employment and thus financial support for the workers' colony at Naane. In 1931, 69 Jewish workers resided there, and by 1936 their number had increased to 472. They were settled on 1,079 dunams belonging to the

Map 10. Rosoff group settlements between Rehovot and Naana, ca. 1935

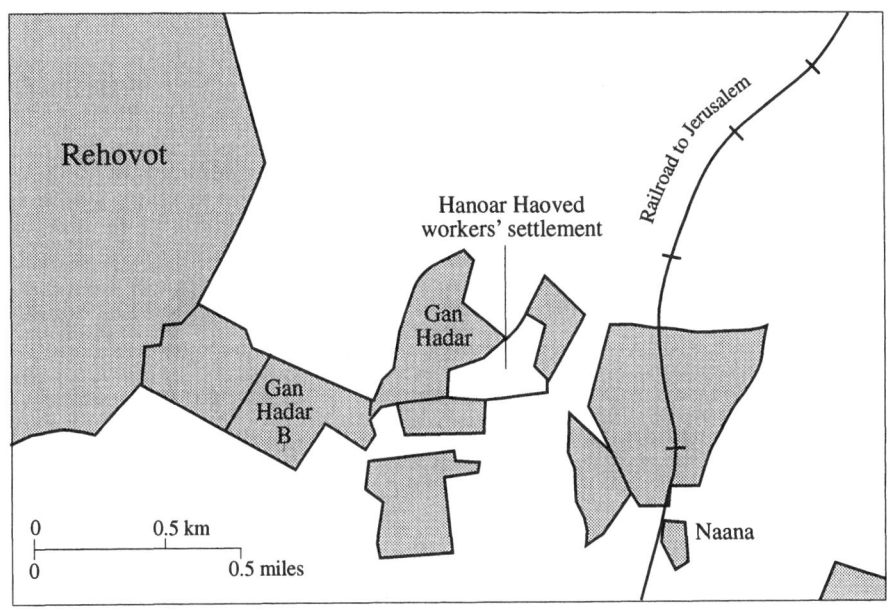

Fig. 26. Orchards at Ramot Meir, 1940.
(CZA photograph collection 6,895)

Jewish National Fund. Agricultural use was divided: plantations comprised 100 dunams, of which 70 had citrus orchards; 795 dunams were farmed with field crops, of which 49 were irrigated. These workers also had 35 head of cattle as well as poultry.[19]

All in all, the Rosoff Group succeeded in redeeming a substantial amount of land. The amelioration of the land increased Jewish agricultural production. It also provided employment for Jewish workers and income for adjacent workers' settlements.

During this period, Americans also channeled investments through Jewish land development companies in Palestine. In 1905 Aharon Eisenberg, an agronomist and founding member of Rehovot, organized a stock company—Agudat Netaim (Heb., planting association)—to purchase and plant lands. On the eve of World War I the company had purchased five tracts totaling over 18,000 dunams at Sedjera, Rehovot, Atta, Zeita, and Hefzibah—the latter three in the vicinity of Hadera. Of Agudat Netaim's 102 listed investors, four were Americans, including Dr. Harry Friedenwald of Baltimore.[20]

Dr. Friedenwald (1864–1950), a professor of ophthalmology, was also an ardent Zionist who had visited Palestine in 1911. He purchased 100 dunams of the 1,800-dunam Hefzibah tract near Hadera and planted his land with almond trees. With the decline of this branch of agriculture, the trees were replaced with more lucrative orange groves. In 1947 Friedenwald transferred his land to the Jewish National Fund, and the village Yaar Shalom was established there. The scheme was to provide land and housing for Yemenites in the vicinity of the small town of Hadera; today it is known as Hefzibah. Friedenwald also purchased a second tract at Atta, near Hadera, which was improved with orange groves.[21]

In addition to providing a means of direct investment by American Jews, Agudat Netaim served as an agent for the American Zion Commonwealth before it purchased land in Palestine. An example has been found in which Hirsh (Harris) Skakolsky of New York received land at Hefzibah in 1921, consisting of a 4-dunam plot for his house and 40 dunams for agriculture, cereal, and plantations. (This purchase is discussed in greater detail in chapter 7.) No other American purchasers from Agudat Netaim have been identified, however. During the years prior to World War I, the company marketed lands mainly to Eastern European Jews and Jews in Palestine. There appear to have been only limited attempts by Agudat Netaim to draw on the potential market in the United States.

American investment was also directed through the Bnai Binyamin organization, founded in 1921 by sons of established Jewish farmers in Palestine to further "cultural and agricultural aid for its members; the successful building of the land by establishing new colonies; the making possible a self-supporting livelihood on the land." These men had been raised on moshavot founded prior to World War I, most of which lacked a reserve of land for settlement by the second generation. The Jewish Colonization Association was able to establish only a few second-generation settlers in its colonies of Binyamina and Pardes Hannah. Thus a grassroots movement was created to find a solution for the landless farmers. To further this purpose, Bnei Binyamin established two institutions, a bank and an agricultural contracting company. The bank allowed for the accumulation of capital for land purchasing, and loans for housing and infrastructure development. The contracting company provided employment for some farmers, particularly in developing tracts for absentee owners. As of 1928, the organization and its affiliated institutions had financed the settlement of twenty-eight families at the American Zion Commonwealth colony of Herzlia and twenty families at Kfar Aaron. Assistance was also provided to allow 228 families to settle in various established settlements, including Petah Tikvah, Rishon Lezion, Binyamina, Yesod Hamaalah, Kfar Tavor, Nes Ziona, Ekron, Kfar Saba, Zichron Yaakov, and Rosh Pinnah.[22]

The Co-operative Bank Bnai Binyamin was established in 1923 with initial capital of $100,000. Among the shareholders were Americans Mary Fels and Nathan Straus, and Baron Felix de Menashe of Alexandria. Hanoteah, the Development of Plantations and Colonization of the Bnai Binyamin organization, was a private contracting firm organized on strictly capitalistic lines. The first project developed, not exclusively for the settlement of Bnai Binyamin members, was Netanya. Land was offered abroad, and the planting would be conducted by Hanoteah.[23]

The Bnai Binyamin organization also distributed brochures in the United States promoting various avenues for American participation and investment. In 1928, Hanoteah attempted to promote "orange groves for private investors." This idea was conceived during a trip to Greece by Oved Ben-Ami and Ittamar Ben-Avi. There, these two key figures in Bnai Binyamin observed the employment of peasants in maintaining lands owned by wealthy Greek expatriates. They hoped that a similar arrangement could be reached between Diaspora Jews and Jewish laborers in Palestine. Hanoteah advertised the possibility that people of moderate means could profitably rebuild Palestine and some day settle there. It emphasized that it was the only profitable business in Palestine that gave workers permanent employment. An additional selling point was that it would offer employment to many of the Eastern European relatives of American Jews who could not enter the United States because of new immigration restrictions. Netanya, a 10,000-dunam colony on the coast of the central Sharon, was named in honor of the American Jewish philanthropist Nathan Straus. The plan allotted 1,200 dunams for orange groves and 300 dunams for homes of foreign investors. Each unit comprised ten dunams of groves and two-and-a-half for building, at a cost of $4,400 payable over five years.[24]

Among the investors were Dr. Isaac Berkson, Alexander M. Dushkin, and Dr. Israel Kligler—Americans resident in Jerusalem who spent some of the summer months at the coast. Owners in America included Israel Chipkin; Miss Eudice Elkin of New York; Al P. Schoolman, director of the Central Jewish Institute in New York; and Rabbi Morris M. Schusheim of New York. Indeed, Schoolman had organized this particular group of Jewish educators. No information has been found regarding their total holdings, but details have been located specifying the planting of 120 dunams with citrus trees by Hanoteah. In addition, some of the owners leased from the Jewish National Fund two-dunam plots on the shoreline cliffs for their homes. American owners specified that "only a certain and definite percentage of Arab labor is to be used on our groves."[25] The entire project was named Gan Berakhah (Garden of Blessing), a reference to Berakhah, the Hebrew name of Bertha Schoolman.

In 1932 a pamphlet in English and Yiddish, *An Orange Grove on the Mediterranean: Nathanyah, An Ideal Plan for American Settlers,* did not stress the profitability of the investment, but rather emphasized the idea of the actual settlement of middle-class Americans at Netanya. It pointed to the geographic advantages of Netanya that would make it a new regional center.

Instead of splitting their energies in "mushroom" plantation-settlements of a few hundred dunams each, scattered over Palestine, whenever a land bargain offered, far from centers of Jewish population and roads and transportation services, the experienced members of Hanotaiah, with an eye to the future, regarded Nathanyah as a nucleus and proceeded to expand in accordance with a preconceived plan for bringing their work in line with a scientific regional plan for the ultimate development of the whole Jewish orange belt. Nathanyah is already developing into the natural center of the entire Plain of Sharon. All other settlements in the Plain will eventually resort to Nathanyah for their social life and avail themselves of its beach facilities, making it the Tel Aviv of the Sharon.[26]

The promoters of Netanya promised sound prospects of a safe income and pleasant living conditions for middle-class Americans. Possible investors were assured that the plan was highly approved by Palestine's outstanding agricultural experts, including Moshe Smilansky, Mordechai Chefetz, P. Pascal, and T. Z. Miller. The size of a holding was 10 dunams; fully planted, this represented an investment of £P800 (about $3,000) spread over a five-year payment period. Net annual income was estimated at £P150 per annum, approximately 19 percent of the investment cost. Hanoteah promised to deliver a complete orange grove in fruit-bearing condition after five years. An added stimulus was that payments were to be made in Palestine currency—and the Palestine pound had recently been devalued. Compared to the previous year's price, in 1932 the cost of an orange grove in American currency was between 25 to 30 percent less. In 1933 Hanoteah began to develop the shoreline land designated for residential use, selling parcels at a rate of £P300 per dunam (£P200 to American grove owners). Few Americans were able to procure land at this time, however, since the United States was in the midst of the Great Depression.[27]

In 1929 Netanya consisted of 10,000 dunams, of which 500 dunams were set aside for building plots. Twenty houses, one shack, and two public buildings had been constructed. It had been planted with 500 dunams of orchards, 30 dunams of vineyards, 100 dunams of forests, and public gardens. An additional 1,000 dunams were ready for planting orchards. By 1936 the 4,734 dunams of the 11,414-dunam total were covered with citrus plantations, and 800 dunams were under field crops. The land was subdivided into 227 units—133 of less than 20 dunams, and 94 of 20 or more dunams.[28]

In 1947 the Jewish National Fund asked the American owners of these plots to sell their land so that a workers' settlement could be constructed for the growing town of Netanya. The owners agreed: It was for the good of Palestine. Moreover, while the owners had gained personal pleasure from their property over some fifteen years of investment, they had received no profit.[29]

CHAPTER 8

Fig. 27. Aerial view of Netanya from the Mediterranean Sea, 1938.
(CZA Keren Hayesod photograph collection)

At one point Hanoteah attempted to expand its activities into the area of Judaea. It advertised an additional tract for development near Naane. In the end, however, its sole achievements consisted of the colony of Netanya and providing contracting services to American orange grove owners.[30]

To the north of Netanya, Pardes Hagdud (the Legionnaires' Plantation) was launched for the settlement of a number of former members of the Jewish Legion. Instrumental in this process were American Sam Friedlander and local resident Avraham Freidman, who had met at the military training base at Windsor, Nova Scotia. These men shared the belief that a land worth fighting for was worth settling. They conceived the idea that after the war the Legionnaires should remain together, and no better way could be found to achieve this than through a special project of their own postwar Jewish Reconstruction of Palestine.[31] (See chapter 9 for a detailed discussion of the settlement of Jewish Legionnaires.)

Friedlander returned to America in 1920. A builder with experience in finance, he attempted to raise capital for the project. Freidman, an agronomist by training, remained in Palestine and searched for suitable land. He obtained an option for land in the Jezreel Valley, but by the time the funds reached Palestine, the tract had already been sold. In 1926 efforts began for the purchase of a 600-dunam stretch of land in the vicinity of the village Um-Haled in the Sharon plain. Friedlander urged former Legionnaires in the United States to buy sections of this land, and Friedman did likewise among the Legionnaires in Palestine. Together they formed a company and registered it in the United States as "Pardes Hagdud Inc."[32]

It appears they had no clear preference for either geographical location or any particular type of agricultural activity. However, it is certain that with Freidman's professional experience and knowledge, whichever tract was chosen would be appropriate for cultivation and would probably provide an income sufficient to maintain its owners. The initially considered Jezreel Valley land was appropriate for cereal or mixed farming. By comparison, the Sharon tract was in the citrus belt; this form of agricultural activity was more profitable and becoming more popular. Furthermore, citrus farming demanded a smaller commitment on the part of the investors. They need not settle, but if they did, they did not have to have experience in agriculture. The next year Friedlander arrived in Palestine to finalize the deal. The company acquired 680 dunams, of which 114 were government-owned, at a price of £P4 per dunam. The corporation issued six shares. Avraham Freidman and Noah Lipman each held half shares, and the remaining investors—Pesach Kaplan and the Americans Sam Friedlander, J. Jonas Jacobs, Aaron Herr, and Jacob Trachtenberg—each had a full share. Serving as the first manager, Freidman arranged for the immediate preparation and planting of groves in 1929.[33]

On the southern edge of Pardes Hagdud, a two-storied building was erected that included a water pump. This structure was used as both a watchman's lookout and a residence for the workmen. In the northern section, a large, four-room residence with many American conveniences—including a bathtub—was built for the Friedlander family. In 1931 Sam Friedlander returned to Palestine with his wife and three daughters and took over the post of manager. Until the lands were divided among the owners in 1935, Pardes Hagdud was operated cooperatively.[34]

In addition to various partnership arrangements, Americans invested in private estates throughout Palestine. The concept of isolated or individual farms and homesteads was somewhat alien to Palestine. Rural settlement was generally concentrated in clustered villages, mainly for security reasons. This concentration also made it easier for settlers to contract social and economic services. An American member of the Zionist Commission, David de Sola Pool, after consulting with Akiva Ettinger of the Settlement Department, explained to an American intent on purchasing a farm in Palestine that "Farms, such as are obtainable in America, do not come [o]n the market in Palestine. The usual procedure, for anyone who wishes to take up country life, is to buy a piece of ground and start from the beginning, building the house and preparing the ground, according to his own plans."[35]

In the early 1920s in Palestine there were only a handful of private estates. These were found in the coastal zone, particularly in the vicinity of Jaffa in the form of *bayyarat* (sing. *bayyara*—Arabic for watered orchard). No American private estates have been identified, though limited information and obscure references are available regarding the ownership of citrus plantations and other tracts in existing settlements by individual Americans. Ownership of private property is usually poorly documented in institutional repositories, and thus the descriptions are scanty and quite incomplete. Nonetheless, there are allusions to the private ownership and development of tracts consisting of a few thousand dunams of land.

For example, according to a 1932 article in the *Palestine and Near East Economic Magazine,* "The noted American Zionist worker, Mrs. Archibald Silverman, is reported to have decided to settle in Palestine and has acquired 180 dunams of orange-grove near Rishon LeZion, which will be planted next spring." Ida M. Silverman was vice-president of Hadassah, the Zionist Organization of America, and Young Judaea. Despite this report, Mrs. Silverman did not settle in Palestine.[36]

Another non-settler was Zionist activist Samuel C. Lamport of New York, who owned 145 dunams in Kfar Saba. In 1929 he entered into negotiations with the Yakhin company for planting and maintenance. Eventually the lands were sold and developed into a neighborhood bearing Lamport's name.[37]

Private American investors also included Isaac Sacks, the owner of the Meshi textile and Argeman dyeing factories in Ramat Gan. Sacks (see chapter 10) purchased 450 dunams of orchards in the vicinity of Nes Ziona and Petah Tikvah. His expenses comprised £P46,200 for orange groves purchased from the Palestine Jewish Colonization Association, £P1,300 for transfer fees, £P5,000 for improvements, and £P20,000 in agricultural land. The purchase of these lands represented Sacks's attempt at diversification: during the 1930s, the groves provided an income that subsidized his industrial endeavors. During World War II, with the interruption of marine transportation between Palestine and its European markets, the citrus industry collapsed.[38]

Similarly, Samuel S. Bloom of Philadelphia, the owner of the American Porcelain Tooth Manufacturing Company (see chapter 10), invested in agriculture as well as industry. He purchased land for orange groves near Karkur, Bnai Brak, and in the Sharon near the site of a later settlement, Even Yehuda.[39]

Another diversified investor was Meir Shapira, who was born in Lithuania in 1884 and immigrated to America in 1898. In the early 1920s, he settled in Tel Aviv, bringing with him a large amount of capital—approximately $950,000. Initially his investing activity focused on the urban real estate market in Tel Aviv, but in 1930 he extended his interest to rural areas. Shapira entered into an agreement to purchase 800 dunams at Latrun from the Trappist monastery. Envisioning this as an opportunity to develop a settlement between Jerusalem and Tel Aviv, he intended to name it the Shapira Brothers Village. However, only 148 dunams were transferred to Shapira. He began legal proceedings over the transfer of additional land, and eventually the Supreme Court in London ordered the monastery to relinquish another 100 dunams to Shapira.[40]

Zvi Arieh Binenfeld, also an American, was involved in negotiations for the purchase of land in the Judean Mountains between Bethlehem and Hebron. In 1934 he signed a contract for 3,300 dunams of *musha* land in the village of Nahalin with the promise of an additional 6,000 dunams. The price was £P7 per dunam—£P23,000 altogether. Binenfeld paid out £P12,000 and received a *kushan* for 441 dunams of *musha* land. The actual area was 1,762 dunams, however, because the *kushan* was issued during the Ottoman period when the villagers attempted to avoid taxes by registering a much smaller area. It is not clear what motivated Binenfeld—whether he wished to assist in the founding of an agricultural settlement for a group of Gur Hasidim or purchased the land solely for the sake of investment. Binenfeld passed away in the late 1930s without completing the transaction or settling ownership claims.[41]

Binenfeld's heirs offered this land to the Jewish National Fund in 1940. They were willing to absorb a substantial loss and receive payment over five years. Funding for this purchase came from the Nahalat Herzog Project, which the American Mizrachi organization had organized months earlier. This $100,000 campaign, launched in Baltimore in May 1940, honored Palestine's Chief Rabbi Isaac Halevi Herzog. In the end, the money was used to secure another tract in the area, the site of the settlement Mesuat Itzhak. The Binenfeld lands and others tracts at Nahalin were transferred to the Jewish National Fund in 1947.[42]

Information on other purchases by Americans is even more scanty and less reliable. Far more numerous than the actual purchases by American Jews were the proposals and plans for such. Before the opening of the *tabu* (land registry) in 1920 there was a race to organize the purchase of lands, particularly in the vicinity of Tel Aviv-Jaffa. Marcus Eastman, the American Zion Commonwealth representative, listed seven organizations active in 1920. Of the seven, one had a distinct American connection, at least in name. According to Eastman's report, the Society of English and American Jews in Palestine—a registered organization—had thirty-five members. Their number, according to Eastman's communiqué, increased at every meeting. The society wanted to purchase 100 parcels of land for a total of 1,000 dunams.[43] Additional information about this organization has not been located.

Private American initiatives represented between 5 to 10 percent of American land purchases in Palestine in the period between the two World Wars. These purchases varied from small sections of larger settlement initiatives to tracts in the thousands of dunams. They also represented various points on a broad spectrum between fantasy and reality. Some purchasers were wholly unrealistic, while others regarded Palestine as a serious investment and took every measure to insure their success. Lack of available information has restricted the study of these private projects. Nonetheless, it is evident that they represent the diversity of American Jewry. These projects reflect attitudes based on a variety of ideological approaches, diverse regional origin, and different levels of business acumen.

9

American Jewish Settlement on Jewish National Fund Lands

> I was reminded of having sat on the floor in discussion with the youth of Hashomer Hatzair in such places as Brooklyn, The Bronx, Boston, Detroit, Montreal, and Toronto, when we talked with American young newcomers on the floor of a tent in Mishmar Ha'emek, and I had an opportunity to learn the traditional experiences of these young people from the Western world. They had now been here about a year. Young city dwellers had been changed by the training they had received into pioneer workers on the land; I recognized the transformation worked in their lives by the clear-cut purpose which they had made their own.
>
> No longer pale city dwellers, their bronzed young faces glowed in the light of the single oil lamp hanging from the tent pole; their eyes shone with the inner light seemingly characteristic of all the halutzim of Palestine. They had fully accepted their rigorous discipline and training needed to reach their chosen goal, and were [as] intent on meeting the tests as any young Americans trying out for college baseball teams or Olympic trials.
>
> Irma Lindheim, *Parallel Quest: A Search of a Person and a People*

American Jewish settlement was not limited to privately owned lands. Certain groups received financial support through the Jewish National Fund (JNF, or Keren Kayemet L'Yisrael) in the form of land, and assistance for development of settlements through the Keren Hayesod (Palestine Foundation Fund). Under the Herut Plan, the JNF cultivated a program for the settlement of middle-class American Jews on JNF land with amelioration underwritten by the settlers themselves. In other cases, American Jews were settled on JNF land and received financial support for the settlement from such bodies as the Keren Hayesod. American groups involved in this development process included the Jewish Legionnaires and *halutzim* of Hashomer Hatzair, Habonim, and other pioneer organizations.

CHAPTER 9

Middle-Class Settlement on Jewish National Fund Lands

Unlike the *ahuza* societies and their offshoots, which were forms of private investment, the Jewish National Fund attempted to combine private and national capital. JNF land would be leased for forty-nine years to middle-class settlers; the agricultural company Yakhin would prepare the plots, planting orange groves for the settlers who would eventually immigrate to Palestine.

Akiva Ettinger, as head of the Land Acquisition Department of the Jewish National Fund, proposed in September 1931 a scheme for settling American families in Emek Hefer. At this time, a growing number of Americans were interested in settling in Palestine, for the Great Depression induced the fear that whatever capital they possessed would be lost if it wasn't invested carefully. Palestine was enjoying an economic boom, and the American dollar had greater buying power there than in the U.S. Ettinger apparently wanted to cash in on the available capital by directing it to the development of JNF lands and providing employment for Jewish workers. By 1931 the fund's land reserve had expanded considerably through the Haifa Bay, Emek Hefer, and Tel Mond purchases. American capital should thus be used to replace some of the Keren Hayesod funding for the development of these lands. Ettinger's proposal was forwarded to the Zionist Organization of America with a request that the scheme be adopted without investigation or delay. Nevertheless, there were doubts about the feasibility of Ettinger's plan. Criticism was leveled on two planes, economic and social. The expert opinion of the president of the Farmers Union (Hitachdut Haikarim), Moshe Smilansky, was solicited, and he concluded that the plan was "far from being suitable." He declared that fifteen, not eight dunams, were needed to support a family; the settlers' inexperience would raise the planting costs; the production of export-quality citrus fruit was overestimated; and other expenses were underestimated. All in all, Smilansky estimated that £P2,000—not £P860 as Ettinger had proposed—would be required to settle an American family.[1] Emanuel Mohl, an American engineer who had been involved in various development projects in Palestine for a decade, emphasized the very serious problem of malaria, for which there was no means of eradication. He also stressed the need for Americans to be fully prepared. Mohl recommended Pardes Hannah on the Palestine Jewish Colonization Association's land as a preferable location for the settlement of middle-class American Jewish families. Similarly, when Yehoshua Hankin, Victor Cohen, and I. Rosenfeld of the Palestine Jewish Colonization Association, Harry Vitales, Robert D. Kesselman, Israel Shochat, Dr. A. I. Kastelianski, and Joseph Nahmani were asked for their opinions, not one of these experts lent his approval to the scheme.[2]

At the time Ettinger was advancing his proposal, the future of the citriculture was also being questioned. According to Revusky, some local experts had expressed grave concern regarding the ability of European markets to absorb a greatly increased citrus export, and they warned against further expansion of citrus plantations in Palestine. The most pessimistic among them even envisioned serious difficulty in marketing oranges and grapefruit once the already existing plantations reached full productivity. This view was explicitly communicated to the American Economic Committee for Palestine. In a memorandum to Rehabiah Lewin-Epstein, A. Barroway wrote: "We have had a number of conferences with Mr. Vitales about encouraging Americans to continue to plant new orange groves. . . . I need only tell you that Mr. Vitales and his associates are not optimistic about the prompt solution of the marketing difficulty and in view of this difficulty, they are hesitant about encouraging further cultivation of new orchards, especially where the investor will be dependent upon his income at an early date for a livelihood."[3]

Beyond the question of the profitability of orchards was the great amount of misleading information that traversed the Atlantic. Avraham Moshe Koller, the Yakhin representative in America, complained about the "disparity" between the expectations of the various cultivating organizations. The New York Achooza Aleph quoted a cultivation cost of £P40 per dunam, excluding initial land purchase and boring wells but including irrigation installation. This low figure made it impossible for Yakhin to compete effectively, for the public had been led to expect they could contract for labor at a much lower price than Yakhin set. Other confusing quotations existed in advertisements. Rabbi Yehuda Leib Zlotnick's organization Boaz advertised in a Yiddish newspaper, the *Montreal Adler,* that for a mere Can$3,600 a family could settle happily on an orange grove in Palestine. Furthermore, a controversy was raging in the Yiddish newspapers as a result of Revusky's article calling for regulation of activities. Koller had asked the American Economic Committee for Palestine to intervene in the controversy. The committee planned to make a public statement, based on a consensus of opinion, regarding costs, returns, and minimum requirements for an average American family.[4] On this issue, Louis Brandeis had already explained to Ettinger:

> I think you are wise in calling the attention of possible settlers to the low standard of living which they must expect if they conclude to settle on the land. But I think it would be wise to send with the statement some one of the published descriptions of life on the small plantations with its worthy social joys, so that those middle-class Jews may realize that they are not being relegated to dreary, barren life common on isolated, small American farms. I have some doubt whether a man of 45 will be too old for the adventure. I have also a doubt of whether you should not make clearer that the $4,300

CHAPTER 9

do not include travelling expenses or the necessary expenses incident to landing etc. in Palestine.[5]

Brandeis concluded, "It is good to know also from you of the favorable economic conditions of Palestine, relative to the rest of the world. I trust this may continue, and draw from America many middle-class Jews who would be happier and useful in Palestine."[6]

Yakhin subsequently developed its own scheme, known as the Herut Plan, for middle class settlement.

> "Yakhin," the Agricultural Concentrating Cooperative Association of the Histadruth and the directorate of the Jewish National Fund recently reached an agreement whereby the settling of 200 families on a large new tract of land in Vadi Havarith [Emek Hefer] was entrusted to Yakhin. Yakhin has taken upon itself the task of organizing in different countries two hundred working and middle class families who can in a period of from five to six years set aside the sums necessary for the cultivation of the orange groves. According to the plan, by the time [the] orange groves mature, the families will be in a position to settle in Palestine and be assured of a living.[7]

Three settlements were organized under this scheme: in 1931, Herut Aleph (later Tzofit), consisting of twenty families; in 1932, Herut Bet (later Bet Herut), for sixty-five families; and in 1933, Herut Gimmel, which was to consist of fifty families. Herut Aleph and Bet provided ten dunams for each of the settlers; both communities had non-American as well as American members. Herut Gimmel, located adjacent to Herut Bet, was designed specifically for North Americans, with twenty dunams to be supplied for each holding.

Despite the anticipated numbers, only fifty-nine North American Jewish families actually signed contracts for these three settlements. No Americans ever settled at Herut Gimmel. Only five or six American families settled in Herut Aleph (Tzofit).[8] Molly Lyons Bar-David, resident in neighboring Gan Hasharon, developed strong social ties with the Americans in this colony and described their settlement: "Zofit planted a mile-long boulevard of magnolia, leading from the gate to the end of their holding where one day the graveyard would be. Right now the clinic at the front of the land was the busy place. The settlers were young and all the wives were pregnant, and they were receiving prenatal care from their co-operative medical service."[9] By contrast, however, an American who had settled at Bet Herut asserted that this venture was unsuccessful "primarily because the *chaverim* who joined the group did not come to settle in Israel."[10]

In 1933, Herut Bet members in the United States held a meeting in Chelsea, Michigan, to discuss the future of their settlement. The groves had not yielded sufficiently to provide for their minimum needs. A majority of members were in favor of transforming the settlement into a moshav *shitufi*, but a minority prevented this change. It was decided instead that the members should deal directly with Yakhin. For this purpose, an office was opened in New York and a second in Minneapolis to serve the Midwest. A year later, a second conference at Cleveland approved the plan to change the settlement into a moshav *shitufi*, with two variations: families could construct houses according to their own specifications and finances, and two dunams adjacent to each house could be worked privately. This agreement represents a very early appearance of this type of settlement organization; the first moshav *shitufi* was founded at Kfar Hittim in the Lower Galilee in 1936.[11]

A number of the children of Herut Bet members were sent to Palestine to train in agriculture. In 1939, along with some older members, they took on the responsibility of developing and administering the settlement for others in America. Before World War II, only six American families had settled in the colony. Following the war, however, the number increased to seventeen families.[12] More Americans joined after Israel's War of Independence, and in 1960 there were sixty members—half of whom were members of the American Habonim movement. Nibby Penn, an American settler, summarized the group's achievement up to 1960: "Its story follows the pattern of a settlement that made its way in Israel to become one of the 'showplaces.' It has grown to a community with one thousand dunam of orange groves, two hundred and fifty of fishponds, one hundred of tropical fruits, four hundred dunam of field crops, vegetables, and grain, some thousands of turkeys and six thousand chickens, etc., with a large silk-screen printing plant and a woodworking factory."[13] The settlement was renamed Bet Herut, and today it has a population of 396.

Various groups in America hoped to receive some assistance for their settlement through Palestine national institutions. One such group from Chicago, calling itself the Chalutzim Organization, requested information from the Jewish National Fund in 1932. From the questions they asked, it appears that the group attempted to obtain JNF land and planned to use their own capital for its development. The basic concepts forwarded by this group for settlement appear similar to the Herut plan for middle-class American settlement, but with certain variations. The members of this group were interested in growing wheat, barley, and other field crops, and raising poultry and dairy cattle. They did not specify any interest in plantations. The questions show they were preoccupied with the quantity of land, its readiness for utilization, and its geographic location. Another deviation from the Herut plan was the fact that the membership of the Chalutzim Organization came from a single geographic area. Although this is similar to the *ahuza* plan, under the Herut plan members would come from throughout the North American continent. Not specified in the Chalutzim Organization's proposals were details about using labor in Palestine for the amelioration of the land, and the period of time that would be needed to prepare the tracts.[14]

The Jewish National Fund responses to the Chalutzim group were favorable. Land for settlers with capital was available: "Such land is to be found in the region of the Haifa Bay which it is considered will be most suitable for your purposes. It is soil very favourable for growing cereals and vegetables and being in the vicinity of good communications, both by rail and road to the growing town of Haifa adds to its advantages." The lands referred to were probably those the American Zion Commonwealth had sold to the JNF. As of 1932, the Haifa Bay area had been partially developed with only one settlement, Kiryat Haim. Land was thus available for additional colonies. However, members of the organization would have to fulfill certain conditions before they could be seriously considered: namely, they should have adequate financial resources and be qualified as agriculturalists.[15] No further information has been found regarding the activities of this organization, nor indeed about any American group in the Haifa Bay area.

JEWISH LEGIONNAIRE SETTLEMENT ON JEWISH NATIONAL FUND LAND

The story of the Jewish Legionnaire settlement is a decade-long saga about the establishment of these World War I veterans on the land. At the end of the war, various proposals were forwarded to facilitate the demobilization of American soldiers in Palestine. One avenue was through agricultural settlement, training those who possessed no previous experience and employing them as manual laborers in agricultural colonies, or directly settling Jewish Legionnaires who had farming experience. The Palestine Office negotiated with various *kvutzot* to accept demobilized Legionnaires into their ranks and give them agricultural training.[16]

Among the small-scale plans was one mentioned by American Legionnaire Samuel Levine. He explained to the Zionist Commission for Palestine his proposal for a small dairy near Jerusalem: "I have a small capital of $1,500 and 12 years of practical experience in dairy farming. I had some time ago a talk with Mr. Hershfield of Jerusalem about establishing a small dairy near Jerusalem by ex-soldiers of practical experience in dairying. He seemed to be interested himself in it and if conditions would be more favorable at present we might have had a chance right now."[17] However, current conditions were not appropriate for their scheme, and no information has been found as to whether Levine remained in Palestine and became engaged in dairy farming. Another failed attempt (described in chapter 6) was to find employment for one hundred Jewish Legionnaires, and possibly permanent settlement for them at Balfouria.

In February 1920, the Zionist Commission allocated £E4,800 for the maintenance of sixty ex-Legionnaires in the Upper Galilee for a period of eight months. Twenty veterans would go to Tel Hai, twenty to Kfar Giladi, and twenty to Hamara. The decision to send them to these particular settlements reflected a need to fill the political and military vacuum that had developed in that area. Britain and France had not agreed upon the demarcation line between their respective mandated territories. These three settlements were situated in no-man's-land, and they were particularly vulnerable to attacks by local Arabs. Demobilized soldiers were deemed necessary for the defense of this area. Detailed information has not been found as to the national origin of the forces detached to these settlements, but among the defenders of Tel Hai were two American Legionnaires, Wolf (Zeev) Sharf and Jacob Toker, both of whom fell in battle on 1 March 1920.[18]

Several large-scale plans for the agricultural settlement of Legionnaires were forwarded to the British authorities. Although these schemes were not specifically designed for Americans, it is likely that some would be part of any group of former soldiers. In 1919 and 1920 detachments of the Jewish Legion were camped at Rafiah and El Arish, and some dreamed of settling there. Shmuel Yavnieli designed a plan for settlement: "the founding of a new city on the coast at Rafiah, a large harbour beside it, road and rail connections to other cities." When a request was made to settle there, the proponents were referred to other locations, as Rafiah and El Arish were not within the boundaries of the Palestine Mandate.[19]

More realistic proposals were forwarded as well. In June 1919 Akiva Ettinger penned a memorandum on the provision of land in Palestine for the settlement of Jewish ex-soldiers. He called on the British authorities to provide about 300,000 dunams to settle 1,000 ex-soldiers; the Zionist Organization would provide the capital for buildings and equipment. Ettinger justified this claim by pointing out that the provision of land for ex-servicemen had become policy in Great Britain and the Dominions—Canada, Australia, and New Zealand. Without entering into great detail, he emphasized certain aspects of his plan. Colonies should have approximately 100 families each to allow for an economy of scale. He preferred that the colonies be established in close proximity to each other, and he particularly recommended southern Judaea as an area of settlement.[20] Ettinger may have been concerned both to avoid isolated settlements that would be vulnerable to Arab attack and to create a contiguous zone of Jewish settlement.

In 1921 High Commissioner Sir Herbert Samuel promised to grant the demobilized soldiers government land in Palestine. Discussions were opened with the land commissioner in October. The inventory of government lands included 60,000 dunams in the Hula Valley, 600,000 in the Beit Shaan Valley, 60,000 in the vicinity of Jericho, 25,000 near Tel Arad, 36,000 around Beer Sheva, and 1,500,000 in other parts of the Negev. The Discharged and Demobilized Soldiers Association entered into negotiations for its membership of 2,000—although the actual number of would-be settlers was estimated to be between 200 and 300, a few of whom were Americans. (In the ranks of the 39th Battalion, for example, there were at least ten Americans with agricultural experience.[21])

Legionnaires and Jewish authorities preferred lands in either the north or the east, which were considered to have greater agricultural potential. Strategically, these areas would augment the defense of existing Jewish settlements in the vicinity against threats of attack from Syria and Trans-Jordan. The Land Commission clearly stated that it was prepared to lease certain government lands for settlement and intensive cultivation purposes, but only after a corporation would register and submit articles of association to the Legal Department for approval. It immediately ruled out the area of Beit Shaan because of the tenuous situation there: The government of Palestine was undergoing negotiations with sharecroppers over their rights to the land. In the end, discussions regarding the Jewish soldiers never led to any actual settlement. Among the problems were the choice of lands, financial backing for the project, and the procrastination of the British authorities. Ettinger's plan, like many others, faded into oblivion.[22]

Among the Jewish Legionnaires were a number of graduates of the Baron de Hirsch Agricultural and Industrial School at Woodbine, New Jersey. Eight of them organized themselves, together with Eliezer Joffe and Melech Levine (already settled in Palestine), to form a colony.[23] At a meeting held at the Mikveh Israel agricultural school in February 1919, discussion focused on the direction of the colony, including whether it should be a cooperative society. Eliezer Joffe, regarded as the initiator of the moshav *ovdim* concept, advocated his own viewpoint: "From my experience I can say that if each member will be compelled to be a partner, we will not succeed. Everyone must be independent, and when the need comes, if he wants to become a partner in the work, he can do so, but no compulsory partnership."[24] Melech Levine vehemently stated his opposition to the cooperative system based on his own previous experience: "Each and everyone individually will make a better success. It will be well to imitate the system of the American farmer." He argued that cooperation or partnership bred jealousy and meanness and often led to the loss of initiative.[25] Nonetheless, the four-point program that outlines the basic tenets of the group shows the influence of Joffe's preference for a moshav *ovdim:*

1. A modern diversified farm colony.
2. The land should be bought by the Baron De Hirsch fund together with the [Jewish] National [F]und.
3. The Colonies should operate the farms individually, but wherever co-operation is possible to do it on co-operative basis.
4. The money for the purchase of the land should come from the Baron

De Hirsch Fund and should be given on long term credit to be repaid with interest.[26]

The colonists hoped to attract fifty or more members.

Their appeals for financial assistance from the Baron de Hirsch Fund were not realized, however. They were told that since the deed of trust specifically earmarked monies for immigrants to America, trustees could not disperse funds for use outside American territory. Furthermore, it did not appear practical for the trustees to finance a project that was too far away to supervise.[27] This decision brought an end to plans for the colony.

No agricultural settlement for the Jewish Legionnaires materialized during the first years following the war. Some of the demobilized soldiers found their way to existing settlements, while others were among the founders of new settlements. The ambition of some ex-Legionnaires was specifically to establish settlements similar to Pardes Hagdud (described in chapter 8). Various promises were made both in Palestine and the United States to assist in their colonization.

In America, two organizations were founded for this purpose: the Hagdud Haivri League and the American Palestine Settlers Association. The Hagdud Haivri League was incorporated under New York State law in November 1929, in reaction to the riots in Palestine a few months earlier. The League's declared intention was:

> To create and establish in Palestine colonies or settlements of and for Jewish men, who during the world war served in Palestine. . . . [T]o establish legionaries in Palestine in every conceivable place, capacity and occupation; to voluntarily aid and assist its members in the U.S.A., or legionnaires in countries other than the U.S.A., to emigrate to Palestine for colonizing or settling there; to safeguard and foster Zionist aims as defined by the second Zionist Congress.[28]

The League further proposed the establishment of a Jewish self-defense system in Palestine. Their plans extended to a network of colonies in Palestine, possibly along the Jordan and Syrian frontiers. This would serve as a bulwark against Arab invasion across these frontiers and provide Palestine with a number of Jewish American pioneers engaged in constructive work.[29] Apparently the organization did not receive the support to which it aspired. A Zionist leader in Wilmington, Delaware, Louis Topkis, shared his evaluation of the organization with Avraham Harzfeld: "I regret exceedingly to advise you that the American Ex Legionnaires Organization have no leadership and besides they cannot go out and raise $25,000, such as you state in your letter. In fact when I left America on July 15 I made arrangements with one of their men to go out to raise funds and up until the time that I came back they did not raise $1.00."[30]

CHAPTER 9

The American Palestine Settlers Association was established with a more specific purpose than the Hagdud Haivri League: the settlement of American Jews in Palestine. Turning to the Jewish Agency and the Jewish National Fund as well as to the Palestine Jewish Colonization Association, it looked for help in establishing two colonies. Each would consist of 100 members and be devoted to citrus growing. Furthermore, each member would receive 25 dunams, of which 10 were to be planted. The association anticipated that the JNF would provide the land, and it attempted to raise $1,000,000 through bonds or stocks, possibly under the rubric of the "Louis Marshall Colonization Fund," to assist in financing the settlement. The colonists themselves would invest no less than 10 percent of the $1,000 cost of settling. To the dismay of the American Palestine Settlers Association, pledges collected in various American cities amounted to only $86,750. A questionnaire distributed among ex-Legionnaires revealed that 109 individuals desired to settle in Palestine: 72 in 1930, 22 in 1931, and 15 in 1932.

After various delays, the first Jewish Legionnaire settlement was founded in 1933 (its name, Avihail [avi, "father"; and hail, "soldier"] reflected its population). In May 1930, the JNF had agreed in principle to grant a 2,000 dunam stretch of land in Emek Hefer to the association.[31] However, it was not until August 1932 that the Jewish National Fund's regional plan for Emek Hefer was completed. During the following months the land was surveyed and the exact boundaries of each settlement delineated. The plan allocated land for 100 settlers. However, problems in financing required gradual development of the colony: twenty families had settled by November 1933, another thirty were expected within a year-and-a-half, and the rest four years later.[32] Although the land had been acquired from the Jewish National Fund, capital for the development of the tracts came from the settlers themselves. Those whose personal funds were insufficient were not eligible for assistance from the Keren Hayesod or the Jewish Agency. However, the Zionist Organization of America placed at the disposal of the Legionnaires $40,000 that had been bequeathed by Mrs. Rebecca Zundelowitz of Texas.[33]

In 1936 the population of Avihail reached 280. The 1,884 dunams received was divided into seventy-six farms. Since the tract was spread over areas with different soils, each farmer received land adjacent to his home, in the plantation zone, and in the field crop area. The colony was planted with 673 dunams of orchards, mainly citrus, and 350 dunams were cultivated with field crops. Not all the members resided in the colony. According to a list dated April 1936, there were at that time fifty-three families (fourteen of them North Americans) on the land at Avihail, and twenty-six families (seven of them North Americans) residing outside the settlement.[34]

The American Palestine Settlers Association had eighty-one members in 1938. Forty-four of them resided in Avihail, where they worked in agriculture and received loans from various national institutions. Thirty-seven

Map 11. Settlement of American *Halutzim*, 1918–39

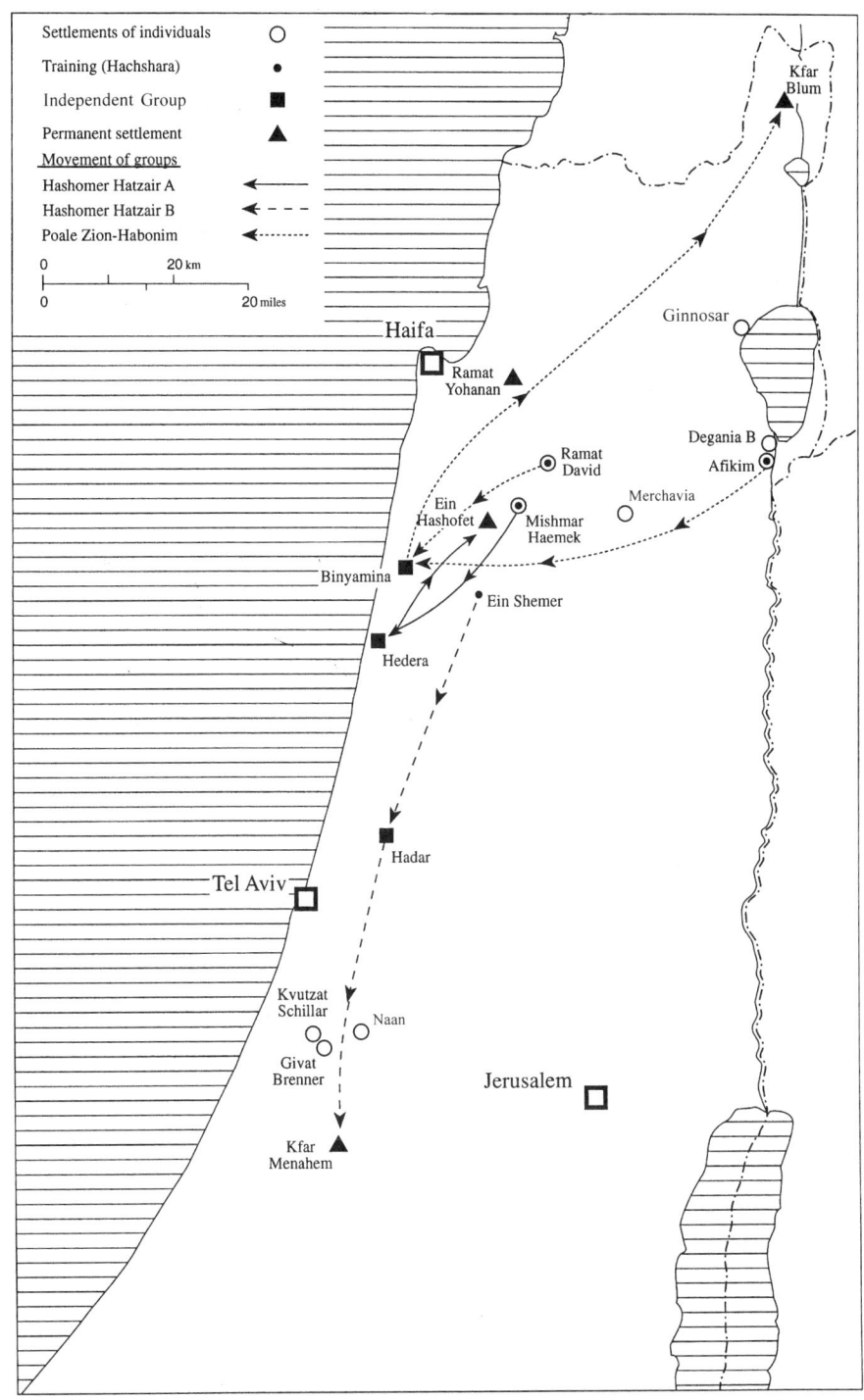

lived outside Avihail in the city and earned their livelihoods from other enterprises; their land at Avihail was worked by others, and their property financed through private efforts. Eventually a dispute broke out between residents and nonresidents. In his description of the background to the dispute, Asher Sapir pointed out that the organization had not been founded on the basis of mutual interests. The only common denominator was service in the 38th, 39th, and 40th battalions of the Royal Fusilliers. As volunteers they had common moral and spiritual ideals. But there were significant discrepancies in economic, personal, and social standing among those who organized the cooperative agricultural endeavor and founded Avihail. While the organization's members were attempting to obtain land and money for the development of the village, they worked together, more or less. Once their initial purpose was achieved and began to bear fruit, however, individuals became more interested in their private affairs, and thus disputes arose. These were resolved when the moshav's institutions were reorganized, with one cooperative society for water and another for services—including security, education, health, and representation before the authorities. This agreement allowed those who had actually settled in Avihail to have greater control over its destiny.[35]

The Legionnaires' struggles to develop an agricultural settlement in Palestine resulted not only in the establishment of Avihail, but also a private orchard colony, Pardes Hagdud, and a workers' colony, Ein Haoved, which had also been established on JNF land. Eighteen workmen earned their livelihood in Pardes Hagdud, and in their spare time they tilled their own plots on the 350-dunam settlement of Ein Haoved.[36] Avihail, Pardes Hagdud, and Ein Haoved were eventually integrated, and services available at Avihail were extended to the other two. Laborers from Ein Haoved were employed in the other two settlements. Two of the owners of Pardes Hagdud, Aaron Herr and Sam Friedlander, settled in Avihail. In 1946 the settlements of Avihail and Ein Haoved were united. Today, this moshav with 892 inhabitants is on the edge of the growing city of Netanya.

SETTLEMENT OF *HALUTZIM*

Halutzim represent a small proportion of the total American aliya, but they are a relatively well-documented group thanks to various histories and recorded recollections.[37] In 1931 the Jewish Agency published statistical data for agricultural settlements to which it had given financial support in 1929. It listed the countries of origin of settlers and the types of settlement. Out of a total of 7,556 persons only fifteen (0.2 percent) were from America. (The term "America" probably included all of the Western Hemisphere, but mainly those from the United States.) The detailed information placed four Americans in cooperative groups (*kvutzot*) with a total population of 2,143;

two in moshavim with a total population of 3,036; seven in supported settlements that comprised 849 people; none on girls' farms, which housed 167 persons; none on Yemenite settlements, which had 1,255 inhabitants; two Americans among the ninety-three persons in various cooperative groups; and none among the thirteen at experimental stations.[38] Both Americans' absolute number and their proportion to the total population increased during the 1930s with the rise of the *halutz* movement in America.

In a 1944 article, Ben Halpern explained some of the background behind the concentration and spatial distribution of American *halutzim:*

> Unlike Hashomer Hatzair whose members were grouped together and made important partners in founding new settlements, the others [unaffiliated pioneer youth and Young Poale Zion members] scattered in small numbers, and frequently became associated with long established settlements, where they were an insignificant part of the membership. Slowly, insensibly, their identity as Americans was sunk, and they merged in the general body of the collective. This, in fact, was almost the deliberate policy of many of them.[39]

The American *halutzim* came both individually and in groups. Those who arrived alone found various means of obtaining places in cooperative groups, although none of them was easy or simple. As is evident in the example of Lewis Jack Kamentzky and Morris Rosenstein, even the most ardent American settlers sometimes found it impossible to join a kibbutz: These two Americans reached Palestine in November 1925, and after four months, all their efforts ended in frustration.[40] According to Saadia Gelb, an American *halutz* who later settled at Kfar Blum, 1929–39 was the decade of assimilation. The policy of the Young Poale Zion Alliance was "to go to Palestine and assimilate into the Yishuv. Going in groups was permissible but perpetuating a special American identity was not." Some Americans were integrated into various kibbutzim, including Naan, Degania B, Ginnosar, Afikim, Ramat David, and Givat Brenner[41] (see map 11).

Most of the pioneers arrived in Palestine in groups. They had usually made arrangements beforehand, through affiliated organizations, to train or settle on a specific kibbutz. During World War I, American members of pioneer organizations reached Palestine as part of the Jewish Legion. Poale Zion members hoped to remain in Palestine after the war and play a part in developing Palestine, as members of either a collective or a kibbutz. As outlined earlier in this chapter, there was little support for the organized settlement of former Legionnaires, but some demobilized soldiers did join kibbutzim and moshavim.

Following the war, entire groups of *halutzim* began to arrive. In July 1921, a group of twenty-two American Poale Zion members reached Palestine, among them Golda Meyersohn (Meir). She had hoped to join Kibbutz Merchavia because a friend from Milwaukee had gone there. Morris and

Golda Meyersohn's application was met with a curt response and deferred until September. The kibbutz twice voted against accepting them: "Not only because we were Americans, but because we were a married couple. The thirty-two men were all bachelors and they wanted single girls."[42] Other members of the Meyersohns's group chose not to go to a collective settlement; they felt they were not prepared mentally or physically for such a change in lifestyle.

The first group of *halutzim* to undergo preparatory training in America was Kvutzat Gordonia from Philadelphia, founded in 1925. At the suggestion of Yosef Baratz of Degania A, nine members studied poultry farming for two years at Petaluma, California, in 1927. Five members migrated to Palestine in 1929 and remained together for two years as a *kvutza*. No information has been found as to where they eventually settled.[43]

Subsequently other independent groups of *halutzim* left America for Palestine. One of these was the Detroit Kvutza, organized in 1927. During the first stage of preparation, the twelve members worked in their own trades; together they studied Hebrew as well as Zionist and Jewish history. In January 1930 they enrolled in a course at the Michigan State College of Agriculture at East Lansing. Their curriculum included general agriculture, poultry, dairy production and butter and cheese making, and farm engineering. From March until November 1930, the group trained at the Hightstown, New Jersey, farm operated by Hashomer Hatzair. Ten individuals departed for Palestine in December, and when they arrived, the Histadruth arranged for their entry into Kvutzat Hatzafon. A year later, upon receiving Jewish National Fund land in Emek Zevulun, the group from Detroit founded Kibbutz Ramat Yohanan.[44] In 1932 another group, consisting of twenty-eight pioneers, set sail for Palestine; their destination was Degania B. Another group, seven members of Hechalutz Hatzair (the youth movement of Kibbutz Hameuchad), departed the following year, going first to Kinneret and then permanently settling at Afikim.[45]

The largest group of *halutzim* from America to settle in Palestine were from the ranks of the Hashomer Hatzair (see chapter 2). Its ideology stressed the necessity for members to establish themselves in collective settlements. The settlement process of American members of Hashomer Hatzair in Palestine was divided into three phases. First came absorption, training, and acclimatization in an established kibbutz. The second stage involved a period of waiting and consolidation on a small tract of land near an existing settlement—usually near colonies in the coastal plain that could provide employment for the *kvutza* members in orchards or in other jobs. The final phase was permanent settlement on Jewish National Fund land.

In 1931 a group of six American Hashomer Hatzair members reached Palestine and joined Kibbutz Aleph. The success of this group was considered extremely important for the future of the movement in America. Since they were small in number and too inexperienced to establish a kibbutz of their own, the group's viability worried the Hashomer Hatzair Executive in Warsaw; it was suggested that they seek help from affiliated kibbutzim in absorption, training, and acclimatization. The group initially considered Mishmar Haemek, Karkur, and Merchavia, but as the first two were already engaged in the absorption of other groups, they were ruled out. Because Merchavia had considerable experience in absorbing new pioneers, it was deemed the most appropriate choice. The American group was divided, with four going to Mishmar Haemek and two proceeding with a *kvutza* from Mishmar Haemek to the Palestine Electric Corporation's hydroelectric power plant at Naharaim.[46]

The following year the number of Americans at Mishmar Haemek increased to seventeen. Proposals were forwarded to allow this group to remain in the vicinity. Dr. Maurice Hexter, an American member of the Jewish Agency Executive, explored various avenues of increasing funding from the Colonization Department. At a 1932 meeting of the executive committee, he noted that "Each of the colonies receiving maintenance was more or less composed of homogeneous groups, most of whom had friends abroad who might be induced to grant them loans for the purpose of consolidation." He continued, using the group of American *halutzim* at Mishmar Haemek as an example: "If they get a loan of say £6,000 we would be relieved of maintenance." Chaim Arlosoroff, head of the Jewish Agency's political department, opposed this "principle of Landsmanschaftliche assistance," fearing that Diaspora communities would attempt to exercise too much control. Despite the opposition of Arlosoroff and Dr. Werner David Senator, "a decision was adopted by the Executive to accept Dr. Hexter's suggestion and that he should be empowered to try and see what he could do in the way of getting such loans."[47] However, it appears that this system of financing colonization was not explored any further.

By 1933 there were thirty Americans at Mishmar Haemek, and the Hashomer Hatzair attempted to force the hand of various settlement bodies for the permanent establishment of its *halutzim*. It proposed that an amount raised above the yearly income of the JNF in the United States be used for that purpose. They suggested promoting increased donations to the JNF by using the slogan "Land for American Chalutzim" in fund-raising efforts. These extra funds would be used to purchase a 10,000-dunam strip of land between Mishmar Haemek and the archaeological site of Megiddo. (This tract appears to have been Khirbet El Mansi, later the site of the moshav Midrach Oz.) The site was attractive because of its potential for general and diversified farming, which suited the training that American *halutzim* had received. Furthermore, it was appropriate for the application of American methods and machinery.[48] Irma Lindheim, a former president of American Hadassah and closely associated with the Hashomer

CHAPTER 9

Fig. 28. American Banir group leaving Kibbutz Mishmar Haemek to occupy the land of Juara (Ein Hashofet), 5 July 1937.
(CZA Keren Hayesod photograph collection)

Hatzair movement, was contacted to go to America to collect $100,000 for that purpose, but objections were raised to this fund-raising mission: "The principal objection is the fact that it represents an effort in behalf of one group in Zionist life. . . . Another objection . . . was that at the present time, when the situation of German Jewry is so urgent, every effort should be made for their settlement in Palestine."[49] Indeed, the fund-raising campaign was never conducted. Lindheim settled on kibbutz Mishmar Haemek and later became a member.

In 1934 the American *halutzim* left Mishmar Haemek for a 15-dunam tract of Jewish National Fund land near Hadera. This represented the second phase of the group's settlement process. Together with a group from Poland, they worked as hired labor in the moshava of Hadera while they awaited their turn for land to be allocated to them for settlement. This period also served the additional purpose of consolidating the group. Over the years the number of Americans increased to fifty-three. They remained at Hadera until July 1937, when the first members established themselves at the settlement site of Juara in the Samaritan mountains, later known as Ein Hashofet.[50] Its name (Heb. spring of the judge) was in honor of the American Zionist leader Judge Louis D. Brandeis. He had retained strong

Fig. 29. An American couple at Kibbutz Ein Hashofet.
(CZA Keren Hayesod photograph collection)

connections with the American settlers and personally provided them with financial assistance.

While this group remained in Hadera, American Yiddish journalist Abraham Revusky held intimate talks with them. Revusky was "strongly impressed by the idealistic spirit of these young men and women, nearly all high school graduates or college students, who came to participate personally in the building of a new country under the still-trying conditions of Palestine."[51] In 1943 the population of Juara reached 299, with 4,500 dunams of land. By 1947, the kibbutz's economy was based on mixed farming (cereals, fodder, vegetables, fruits, dairy, poultry, sheep, and bees) and contract trucking (six trucks for transportation between Haifa, Tel Aviv, and Jerusalem); it also had shares in Hever—the Haifa urban and suburban bus cooperative.[52] Today Ein Hashofet has 799 inhabitants.

In 1935 the second group of American Hashomer Hatzair members, fourteen in number, began their settlement process in Kibbutz Ein Shemer. Known as Kibbutz Bet, this group continued on to Hadar in the southern

CHAPTER 9

Fig. 30. Aerial view of Ein Hashofet, 1939.
(CZA Keren Hayesod photograph collection)

Sharon at the end of 1936 to join the Polish group Krit for a three-month trial period. The original intent of the American group was to achieve independent existence through reinforcements from America. However, in light of the difficulties in obtaining immigration certificates, it was deemed best by the group already in Palestine and the Vaad Hapoel of the Hashomer Hatzair movement that the American and Polish groups unite. Their temporary kibbutz in Hadar was founded on 8 dunams belonging to the Jewish National Fund, and an additional 30 dunams were leased. The period at Hadar consisted of work in the citrus plantations of adjacent colonies as well as in the carpentry workshop, in construction, transportation, on a small dairy farm, and other outside labor.[53]

The process of choosing a site for America-Krit began in 1938. Information regarding all the options considered and the decisions that led to the choice of the final location is incomplete. However, it appears that one possibility was at Hanita in the western Galilee. An expeditionary force of five members was sent to the place. They vied with other settlement organizations also interested in colonizing the land but did not succeed in receiving permission to remain. A second possibility was Um-es-Suf,

Fig. 31. Kibbutz America-Krit celebrating settlement of the land of Kfar Menachem, 6 December 1939. (CZA Keren Hayesod photograph collection)

a tract close to Kibbutz Ein Hashofet. Fifteen members were sent to secure the site, founding an outpost. Eight months were spent guarding the spot, while problems connected to ownership of the land obstructed settlement. The Palestine secretariat of Hashomer Hatzair hoped that the new kibbutz (which included the second American contingent) would be established near Ein Hashofet. They also hoped to influence Avraham Harzfeld to intervene in this direction, but to no avail.[54]

Authorities were eager to move the America-Krit group, if not near Ein Hashofet, then to the Beit Shaan Valley or near the Hula Basin. In 1939 American Jewish National Fund President Dr. Israel Goldstein explained, in a personal letter to Menachem Ussishkin, that the move "could give encouragement to this group of pioneers, who have proven their worth and who have a special significance as an American Kibbutz." The lands of Khiam Walid, north of the Hula concession, and Rahania, northwest of Ein

CHAPTER 9

Hashofet, were also offered to the America-Krit group. But at the kibbutz meeting of 29 July 1939, a decision was made not to settle at either location.[55]

Finally, with the failure of the Menachem Organization—a moshav in the southern Judaean foothills—lands were made available for the America-Krit kibbutz. This 3,650-dunam tract had been purchased in 1935. Two years later, a moshav was founded but was unable to sustain itself. On 6 December 1939, Kibbutz Kfar Menachem (named in honor of Menachem Ussishkin) was established as a tower and stockade colony with thirty-two Americans.[56] In 1943 it had 245 inhabitants. Its economy was based on mixed farming (grains, vegetables, cattle, sheep, and poultry) and industry (carpentry shop and garage). Today Kfar Menachem has a population of 605.

A third American Hashomer Hatzair group was organized in 1937, but its arrival in Palestine was delayed until after World War II. In the autumn of 1945, 62 North American members of this group arrived in Palestine, joining a group of Palestinian and Bulgarian Jews to found Kibbutz Hatzor.[57]

American *halutzim* affiliated with Hechalutz, Habonim, and the Young Poale Zion Alliance arrived in Palestine in 1938 and 1939, and began their own venture toward settlement. The process included several months of training in existing kibbutzim—Ramat David and Afikim. These Americans joined together with an Anglo-Baltic group situated at Binyamina and waited to be assigned a site for permanent settlement. They worked at the farms at Binyamina, the quarry there, and the saltworks at Atlit. They also entered the timber industry, cutting planks and preparing firewood. In addition, they purchased machinery to produce clothes-pegs. In 1943, with money raised by the Jewish labor movement in America, the Jewish National Fund purchased the lands of Naame on behalf of this group. On 13 November 1943, the cornerstone was laid for the first building of the new kibbutz for the American and Anglo-Baltic groups. Named Kfar Blum, in honor of French Jewish Zionist Léon Blum, its initial population was 157, with 800 dunams of land. During its first year, the kibbutz raised cereals, vegetables, fodder, cattle, and sheep, later adding bees and poultry. The clothespin factory was transferred to the kibbutz, and its location on the banks of the Jordan north of the Hula swamp allowed for the development of fish ponds.[58] Kfar Blum has grown to a settlement of 615 residents.

Haluztiut, the pioneer spirit—an idea that motivated thousands from Eastern Europe to immigrate and build Palestine—likewise inspired a few hundred Americans. Immediately after World War I, the movement represented only a small volume, but it greatly increased in number during the 1930s. The magnitude of the population mass and their ideologies, coupled with the policies of various settlement organizations and movements, determined the spatial distribution of American pioneers. The involvement of American Zionist organizations in trying to facilitate the process for local constituents was unique in the settlement of Palestine. Beyond having an interest in the settlement of their *halutzim,* these organizations believed that their actions would be to their own benefit by encouraging fund-raising and local involvement. The founding of the first collective settlement to include an American group represented a turning point in the American pioneering effort. The ensuing publicity generated prestige and inspired greater activity. It is also important to note with regard to spatial distribution of American pioneers that while efforts were made to create a regional concentration of these settlers in the Carmel and Menashe hills, circumstances connected to the availability of Jewish National Fund land led to the dispersion of kibbutzim with American members throughout Palestine.

Molly Lyons Bar-David has pointed to one significant contribution to the kibbutz movement by Americans:

> There was something masochistic in the spirit of kibbutzim. They cultivated a pleasure in unnecessary privation and discomfort. . . . It took the peppering of the kibbutz movement with a few Americans to bring changes into something of this attitude. An American was not satisfied with a handmade killin rug for his bed, a Van Gogh print on the wall and a shelf of books only. The Yanks brought radios, electric kettles, upholstered chairs from back home to fix up their rooms. Pretty soon they introduced private showers and toilet and a kitchenette nook in their housing. Comfort had ceased to be a sin. Other settlements began to follow suit. Before long even a bachelor could have a room of his own. Maybe it meant a contented cow less in the dairy. But it also meant a contented kibbutznik.[59]

These *halutzim,* middle-class settlers of the Herut plan and the ex-Legionnaires at Avihail, are representative of the efforts to settle Americans on Jewish National Fund lands. Circumstances in Palestine, particularly the limited amount of territory held by the JNF, checked the number of Americans who could settle on national lands. Many more Americans would have been willing to settle in Palestine if they had been provided with assistance: namely, land to settle on. Moreover, immigration restrictions and the long, drawn out process of receiving such land hindered and slowed the migration of Americans.

10

Americans in the Urban Environment

> If Nazareth took us back into the past, Tel-Aviv held us within the present, save when it swept us fast and far into the future. Twenty years ago there were miles of sand dunes on the shores outside the ancient city of Jaffa. Now, on these same dunes, there stands a municipality of thirty-eight thousand souls, as thriving and busy as any typical American town. Tel-Aviv is nearer one hundred per cent Jewish than a much-advertised soap is one hundred per cent pure. It is accurately described as the only one-hundred-per-cent Jewish city in the world. Its inhabitants, with a few scattered exceptions, are all Jews; its mayor, judges, police force, merchants, teachers, artisans, street cleaners, garbage collectors, all are Jews. Here is no segregation of Jews into a ghetto, into a few traditional trades, into circumscribed and traditional types of life. Jews in Tel-Aviv are occupying all the positions of society, and therewith proving their fitness for every type of leadership and labor. It is an amazing spectacle—this modern city of emancipated Jews.
>
> John Haynes Holmes, *Palestine To-day and To-morrow: A Gentile's Survey of Zionism*

The development of the Jewish urban landscape of Palestine during the British Mandate was influenced by the ideological schism between pioneering Zionism and other schools of thought along the Zionist spectrum. Researcher Erik Cohen showed that the pragmatism of the pioneering ideology emphasized the rejuvenation and restructuring of Jewish society in Palestine rather than in the Diaspora. *Halutzim* advocated returning to the soil and developing the rural sector. They perceived the city as the embodiment of social evils and the deterioration of society.[1] Among American Jewish immigrants to Palestine, this anti-urban view was held by only a small minority, and they were usually affiliated with the pioneering movements. Most American Jewish immigrants had resided in urban centers in the United States, and, on the whole, they did not see the city as a threat. Indeed, the Orthodox population—most of whom were associated with Kollel America Tiffereth Yerushalaim—not only accepted the city but were ideologically opposed to the concept of pioneering rural settlement. In 1927, 84 percent of American Jews lived in cities of 100,000 or more, and 9 percent in cities between 25,000 and 100,000.[2] Before leaving America, most of them searched for a city in Palestine in which to settle. They perceived the city as the focus of industrial and commercial development—essential sectors for the growth of a healthy economy. And American Jews were also attracted to the variety of cultural activities that were available in cities.

These immigrants from the United States brought with them to Palestine untainted views of investment in urban real estate, speculation, and development. They considered these kinds of investment as legitimate means of furthering the healthy economic growth of the *Yishuv*. They organized the purchase of urban tracts in much the same way that their compatriots organized the purchase of agricultural lands: individually or through associations. As with rural tracts, urban land purchases ranged from whole neighborhoods to sections of them and individual plots. During the period covered by this study, the most prominent American purchasing organization was the American Zion Commonwealth (AMZIC), which sometimes promoted its own projects and sometimes represented those of the Palestine Land Development Company (PLDC). The AMZIC and the PLDC were active in the three largest cities—Jerusalem, Tel Aviv, and Haifa—as well as in the new town of Afula.

When transactions were concluded in America, the agents in Palestine were usually local real estate agents or companies like the Palestine Land Development Company and Geula. These companies prepared elaborate brochures describing plans for the new neighborhoods, the advantages of site and relative location, and future amelioration. The prospectus generally included maps that depicted physical layout and available plots for purchase. Several American groups developed plans for "garden villages"—Migdal, north of Tiberias; Nahalat Itzhak, west of Jerusalem; and a section of Har Canaan near Safed. On a smaller scale, a number of real estate agencies were founded in Palestine with American capital or by American representatives for the purchase and resale of land and its development. Among these agencies were the American-Palestine Real Estate Agency, the Jerusalem-America Land Company, and the Menorah Palestine Building Corporation.

American investment in urban real estate was complicated by the distance between the United States and Palestine as well as by a poor communication apparatus. Americans' lack of familiarity with the landscape and situation in Palestine often led to misconceptions about the actual transaction. The real estate market was riddled with irregularities and false promises, and so Americans, like other immigrants, often fell prey to shady dealers, as exemplified in this American consular report.

> A widow lady Mrs. Rebecca Schneider came recently from San Francisco to Palestine, imbued with Zionist ideas, and purchased a building lot in the

vicinity of Jerusalem upon which to construct a residence, paying therefor the usual inflated price. She complains that the organization (not American) which sold her the land is unable to locate it for her excepting on paper. She wishes now to return to the comforts of her San Francisco home, having changed her mind about residence in Palestine, and is trying to get her money back. The promoting organization offers a refund of 75% but requires 25% for expenses in encouraging her to assist in building up the new Zion.[3]

This chapter focuses on American Jewish activity in the three urban centers—Jerusalem, Tel Aviv-Jaffa, and Haifa—and the new town of Afula. It examines the size and growth of the American Jewish immigrant population, spatial distribution, land purchase and development processes, and economic and other forms of activity. The American presence in Safed, Tiberias, and Hebron is also described, as are various attempts to develop garden villages.

JERUSALEM AND ITS ENVIRONS

From the mid-nineteenth century up to 1914, both spontaneous and planned development transformed Jerusalem from a densely populated, traditional Middle Eastern city confined within a walled area of less than one square kilometer to a vibrant, westernized city with a built-up area of over five square kilometers. By the outbreak of World War I, the population of Jerusalem had reached 70,000, but the war led to a decline in the city's population. In 1922 Jerusalem had 62,700 residents, of whom 34,100 were Jews—a substantial decline from the estimated 45,000 Jews in 1914. By 1931, however, Jerusalem's population had grown to 93,100 and the number of its Jewish inhabitants to 53,800. Eight years later, the Jewish population of the city was an estimated 80,850.[4]

A number of American companies and organizations were active in the development of Jerusalem. Groups in Palestine also turned to America for investment and the sale of property. In addition, there was noncommercial development through Kollel America Tiffereth Yerushalaim.

Foremost in Jerusalem land sales to Americans was the Palestine Land Development Company. Its 1923 pamphlet, *Building Plots at Jerusalem,* advertised land in six different sections of the city—Talpiot, Givat Eliyahu, Amos Land, Zanzariah (Rehavia), the Garden of Antimos, and the business center. Sometimes the PLDC sold land directly to individuals and sometimes it sold tracts through the American Zion Commonwealth.

During his 1922–23 visit to North America, Arthur Ruppin met with Zionist leaders and convinced the American Zion Commonwealth to purchase urban tracts in Jerusalem. In March 1924, the AMZIC purchased 93,223 square meters for £E8,500 ($42,500) in the Givat Eliyahu neighborhood, and 18,750 square meters in the Talpiot neighborhood for £E3,600

TABLE 20
Lands purchased in Jerusalem by the American Zion Commonwealth and the Palestine Land Development Company up to 1929, in square meters

Area	Palestine Land Development Company	American Zion Commonwealth	Percent
Mount Scopus	124,186	—	—
Talpiot	180,407	18,750	10.39
Mekor Haim	57,127	—	—
Rehavia	125,501	—	—
Givat Eliyahu	113,627	93,223	82.04
Ramat Rachel	90,348	—	—
Business center	17,449	—	—
Antimos, Ben Yehuda	50,199	—	—
Total	758,844	101,973	13.44

($18,000). The AMZIC sold plots to individuals across the United States; *kushans* (title deeds) were issued for 36 plots—among them, fifteen to buyers in Los Angeles and fourteen to members of the Rabalsky Group of Boston.[5]

In 1926, to accelerate the growth of Talpiot, the Palestine Land Development Company decided to sell additional land in America. It wanted the American Zion Commonwealth to conduct this campaign, but if they were unwilling, the PLDC would do so itself. Moshe Ben Zeev Cohen, a member of Vaad Schunat (neighborhood committee) Talpiot, went to the United States to induce American owners to invest capital for building and to sell lands belonging to other (non-AMZIC) owners. The conditions of Cohen's activities were subject to the AMZIC's approval, since it was the sole agent in America for the PLDC. The agreement concluded with Cohen allowed him to add 25 percent to the list price. The terms of the sale were one-third upon signing the contract with the remainder due within a year-and-a-half.[6]

Land owned by foreigners who did not immigrate to Palestine often represented a deterrent to growth. Plots that were underdeveloped yet unavailable for purchase impeded the expansion of neighborhoods such as Talpiot. The merchant and philanthropist Nathan Straus was one of the Americans who had purchased land in Talpiot. In 1923 he was asked by the Vaad to donate his property for the construction of the Jewish National Fund headquarters and other projects that the Vaad believed would accelerate the growth of Talpiot. Straus denied their request. Three years later he was again

CHAPTER 10

Map 12. Development of Jerusalem up to 1937

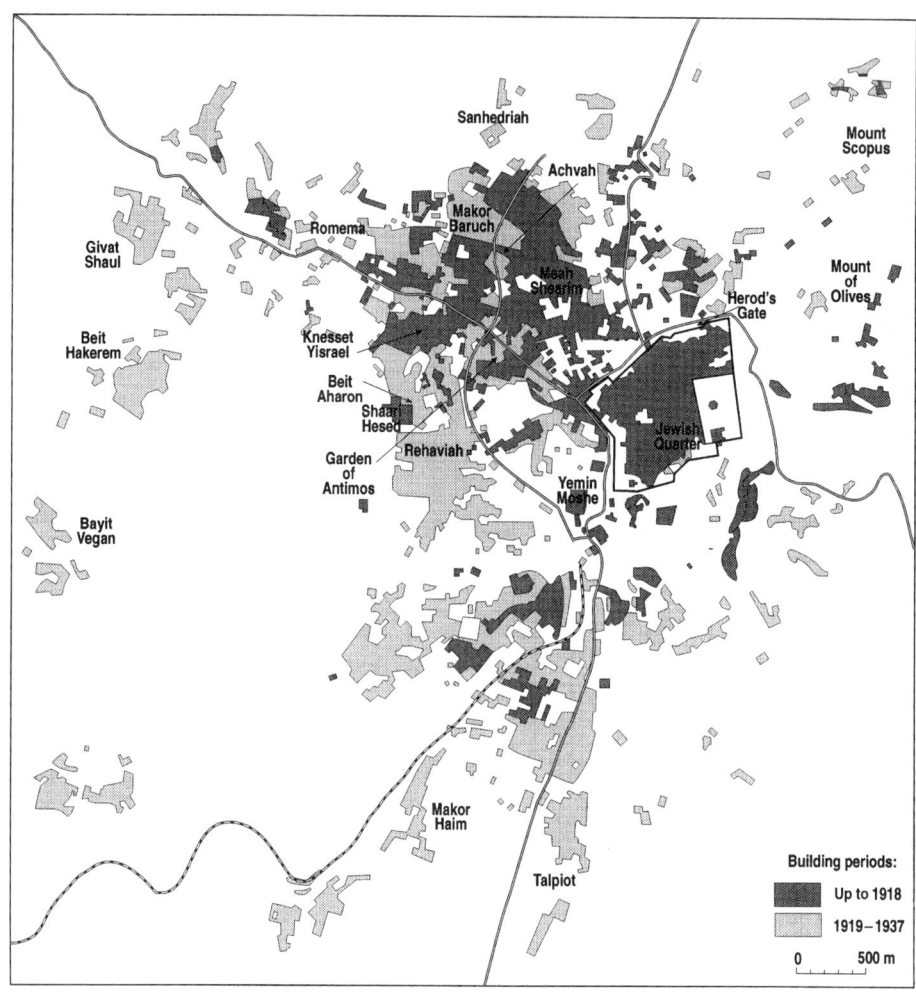

approached by the Vaad and asked to set aside 28 percent of his land for public use; he objected to this proposal as well.[7] Another example of the problems caused by foreign ownership is the Kesselman family—Americans who in 1924 had purchased a plot in the Beit Hakerem neighborhood. As Robert Kesselman explained to his wife, "The people of Beit Hakerem demand of me to build, and if I don't they want to take away from me the plot and give me instead of it another not so suitable." About the same time he became interested in another garden suburb, Talpiot. He acquired a plot there too, on which he eventually built his family house.[8] Altogether, only a score or so Americans resided in Talpiot.

In 1920 American capital was used to form the American-Palestine Real Estate Agency for the purchase, parceling, and resale of lands in Palestine. Two years later, Mary Fels, a Zionist and widow of a millionaire industrialist, became interested "in promoting a building scheme—whether through the medium of a partnership, a limited company of otherwise." She entered an agreement with Israel Tannenbaum, Israel Blumenfeld, and Moritz Grunhut of the American-Palestine Real Estate Agency to act as intermediaries for land purchases in Jerusalem. Fels was particularly interested in lands on Mount Scopus, an area of 160 dunams. It is unclear if the company was able to purchase the sites she wanted, but in 1922 and 1923 a series of contracts was drawn up with various landowners on Mount Scopus. Mary Fels later donated some of this land to the Hadassah organization to augment its holdings there, and in 1934 the cornerstone was laid for Hadassah's Mount Scopus Medical Center.[9]

In 1923 the American-Palestine Real Estate Agency agreed that Ittamar Ben-Avi would act for it by selling land on a commission basis during his business tour of Europe and the United States. Ben-Avi was probably chosen because he was well-known as the first Hebrew-speaking child in modern Palestine. No information has been found regarding the outcome of this venture.[10] The agency also offered building plots in Jerusalem, Haifa, and Jaffa. Lots were advertised in Jerusalem on Mount Scopus and near the neighborhoods of Talpiot, Romema, and Beit Hakerem. The agency boasted of prominent American clients like Mary Fels, Nathan Straus, Solomon Rosenbloom of Pittsburgh, H. Simons of Detroit, and Samuel C. Lamport of New York. In addition, the company claimed to have agricultural land available in the Jordan Valley, in the vicinity of Hadera and other locations.[11]

A number of Jerusalemites joined together with a group of Americans to establish the Jerusalem-America Land Company for the purchase of lands in Jerusalem, Tel Aviv, and Haifa. This company had over half-a-million dollars in capital, and in 1925 American stockholders included Aaron and Samuel Bernstein, Boris Hershenov, Michael Salit, Aaron Jacobs, and Joseph Kaplowitz, all of New York. The extent of the company's activities is unclear, but following the economic crisis of 1927–30, it was unable to honor its debts. It had purchased most of its lands on credit. Three of its eight unsold parcels were located in Jerusalem: the company owned 12,836 square meters at Mekor Baruch, 16,737 square meters at Kreisha,[12] and 14,938 square meters at Beit Aharon near Rehavia. The Beit Aharon neighborhood, named in honor of the company's founder Aaron Bernstein, was located between the neighborhoods of Rehavia and Shaare Hessed (the houses along Haran Street). Because the Vaad Schunat Rehavia had fenced off the road passing through Rehavia to Beit Aharon, the Jerusalem-

American Land Company had difficulty selling plots in this area. It turned to the town planning commission to find some solution to the problem of accessibility, but the neighborhood's construction did not begin until the 1930s.[13] The neighborhood of Mekor Baruch, founded in 1926 and located near the Syrian (Schneller) Orphanage, was named in honor of an American, Boris (Baruch) Hershenov, with reference to Proverbs 5:18. The company developed plans for 207 plots, but once again construction of houses did not begin until the 1930s.[14]

Upon the liquidation of the Jerusalem-American Land Company in 1929, irregularities were found in its records. Some of its managers were arrested and put on trial. An attempt was made to reach an arrangement with the debt holders—Barclays Bank and others—for the continued operation of the company. It was proposed that if lands could be parceled and developed, a large profit could still be achieved. The company's American stockholders appealed to the court in Jerusalem to have liquidator Eliyahu Eliachar be sent to the United States to help clear up the matter. Under advisement from the attorney general, Judge J. M. de Freitas agreed to allow Eliachar to serve as the court-appointed representative, empowered to take statements and meet with the stockholders. In the end, the company's lands were sold and developed by others.[15]

Throughout the 1920s and 1930s, Americans purchased plots in various Jerusalem neighborhoods. References to American purchases are sporadic, but they do show an American presence in several parts of the city. For example, in 1926 *Mischar Ve-Taasiah* (Trade and Industry) reported that through the auspices of the Nahalat Bayit company of the Mizrachi Hatzair, the neighborhood of Sanhedriah would be expanded from 70 to 110 lots; an unspecified number of these were sold in America. As of 1928 only five structures existed in Sanhedriah. Its principal development followed the 1929 riots. The majority of Nahalat Bayit's membership came from the Ashkenazi and Kurdish communities. No information has been found to verify American purchases or settlement, though one American, Shimon Lifshitz, contributed to the construction of the neighborhood synagogue.[16]

Another example is the Binyan Hayishuv Company of Jerusalem. With Rabbi Yosef Rivlin acting as its agent, the company sold lots in that city to Americans. Binyan Hayishuv received the blessings of Chief Rabbis Avraham Isaac HaCohen Kook and Yaakov Meir, as well as the endorsement of the Mizrachi leader Rabbi Meir Berlin (Bar-Ilan). One American, H. Rubenstein of Kansas City, who bought land through this company, turned to the Zionist Organization of America to receive further information. As he explained, "I did not have the time to investigate this matter thoroughly but several of my friends in this City bought lots, including Rabbi Braver so I also bought a lot." Although the project was said to be located "a few miles out of the City of Jerusalem,"[17] it was actually adjacent to Mekor Haim in southern Jerusalem, a residential area later named Mizpeh Yerushalaim. The 625-square-meter plots in this tract were mainly purchased by Americans. By the time of the outbreak of the 1929 riots, only one building had been completed, and the area was subsequently abandoned.[18]

Several Americans, including Mary Fels, were among the investors of Agudat Betar. This company was registered in May 1929 for the purpose of establishing a Jewish neighborhood and all that was necessary for its development on the lands of the Arab village of Battir. As the site of the ancient town of Betar, the center of the Bar Kochba revolt, it was especially attractive to investors. The company purchased 5/6 of a 139.6-dunam tract for £E414. Each investor was to receive 5 dunams. Although located at some distance from the city, the tract had the advantage of being near a station on the Jerusalem-Jaffa railroad line. The tract was not developed, however, and the company halted its activities. In 1936 the registrar of companies ordered an investigation into the company's affairs, and this led to a decision to disband it. The company's chairman intended to divide the land among the investors, but the troubles of the period and the riots prevented this; in 1945 the company sold the tract to the Jewish National Fund.[19]

A number of individual American purchases are of interest. Moses Rabalsky, brother of Boston Zionist leader Benjamin Rabalsky, purchased plots in Rehavia. In the same neighborhood, Dr. I. J. Biskind constructed his home in the distinct architectural style developed during this period.[20] In 1921 Mrs. S. I. Hyman and Alfred Kornfeld each subscribed for 2 dunams in the Bayit Vagan garden suburb, a 400-dunam project that was the initiative of the Mizrachi organization. After thirteen years the subscribers had still not received the *kushan* for this property—a not uncommon occurrence that was obviously a source of great anxiety to the purchasers. Another American, Aharon Mordechai Ashinski, was among the owners of land in Bayit Vagan.[21] Also, David Klein of San Francisco owned a 635-square-meter plot in the Givat Shaul garden suburb.[22]

In addition to these projects and purchases, American capital in the form of loans and mortgages was used to support the construction of houses in Jerusalem. The Brandeis-Mack group, through the Palestine Cooperative Company, extended financial backing to help found the Palestine Building Loan and Savings Association, which was registered in 1922 with an authorized capital of £E25,000. Located in Jerusalem, the association was managed by American engineer Emanuel Mohl. During its first year it provided loans for the construction of 300 houses, mainly in Jerusalem (in the Talpiot and Beit Hakerem neighborhoods) and Haifa (the Bat Galim neighborhood), as well as in Jaffa. Using the $36,000 capital extended by Judge Louis D. Brandeis, the company also provided loans for the 40-unit workers' suburb of Kfar Brandeis near Hadera.[23]

Among American immigrants to urban areas of Palestine, the American ultra-Orthodox population was distinctive by virtue of its ideology, social organization, and economic activity. These immigrants were affiliated with the "Old *Yishuv*" and segregated themselves from most other Americans. The majority of this group was affiliated with a form of *landsmanschaft*, the Kollel America Tiffereth Yerushalaim. Others reestablished contacts with their Eastern European communities of origin and affiliated organizations in the Holy Land. The ultra-Orthodox contribution to the development of the landscape was limited, as their religious beliefs included opposition to the concepts of land redemption and up-building. Nonetheless, they supported a number of projects for urban and rural development. Some members of this group were involved in various economic activities. Perhaps the most important contribution of the ultra-Orthodox Jews was the import of capital; though this money was not necessarily invested in the development of settlement or other enterprises, it generated an economic ripple effect. Funds from abroad were used to purchase goods and services, and this provided employment for various sectors of the local population—Old *Yishuv*, New *Yishuv*, and Arab.

Kollel America Tiffereth Yerushalaim was founded in 1896 by American Jews in Jerusalem to support not only American Jews in the Holy Land, but needy Jews coming from other countries as well. American Consul Edwin Sherman Wallace reported that prior to 1896, the *kollel* collected $45,000 annually in America, but only $6,000 ever reached Jerusalem. Despite the opposition of Jerusalem rabbis, the fledgling *kollel* received the support of American Jewry and the American consul. An accord was reached with the Vaad Haklali (General Committee of the Kollelim) in Jerusalem stipulating that two-thirds of the money collected in America would go to the Vaad Haklali and the remaining one-third to Kollel America.[24]

Membership in Kollel America increased in the early twentieth century. A report from 1912 listed 216 heads of families connected to the *kollel*—altogether about 550 souls. Of these 216 heads of families, 92 were non-Americans, and this led to claims that the *kollel*'s funds were not being used as intended. The organization's basic principle was "that only American registered citizens who are without any means of support should receive the Hallukah, and other such necessary aid as a free house to reside [in] in his declining years."[25] An attempt was made to exclude non-Americans, as well as those with independent means (45 family heads), from receiving financial support. By 1913 the *kollel*'s membership in Jerusalem was reported at 485. It was one of three *kollelim* that granted members an income "halfway adequate for decent living, though it is not the richest." Although it also intended to provide housing, the *kollel* did not do so before World War I. In 1912 each individual received 6 francs ($1.14) per month support, but it was hoped that after reforms this sum would rise to 15 francs ($2.85).[26]

The Chicago Kollel was another independent organization. In 1912 it reportedly had 150 individuals connected to it.[27] No additional information has been found about this group, nor has an explanation been found as to why a separate American *kollel* was established. It appears that the Chicago Kollel was disbanded after World War I, and that its members then joined Kollel America.

In the early years of the war, *kollel* members still resident in Palestine were supported by funds sent from America, but when the United States entered the war in 1917, funds could no longer be sent directly from America to Palestine. Instead they were sent via Sweden on behalf of the Joint Distribution Committee of New York. Some of the persons who received payment were *kollel* members.[28]

As British forces approached Jerusalem, Americans in the city were ordered to report to the Turkish authorities, who would send them into exile in the interior. The Turks threatened them with charges of espionage if they failed to report within twenty-four hours. A few Americans reported at the fixed time, but many hid, hoping to be liberated by the advancing British troops. Approximately 200 Americans were rounded up and sent into exile. Not all returned to Jerusalem when the war ended.[29]

Kollel America continued its activities under the British Mandate. Its new constitution opened with the following preamble:

> The KOLLEL AMERICA is the only Organization of American and Canadian Jews residing in Palestine, and the home for every American Jew making his residence in the Holy Land.
>
> The KOLLEL AMERICA takes care of the needful American Jews in Palestine supporting them in the form of decent monthly subsidies, free loans, to facilitate industry, to assist workers, etc., free dwellings, free medicines, etc.
>
> There is no other institution nor an organization where the American or Canadian Jews can find help in his distress, except KOLLEL AMERICA . . . .
>
> The KOLLEL AMERICA has in [its] possession own houses which are given FREE by casting lots for three successiv [sic] years to poor American and Canadian Jews residents of Palestine.
>
> A part of their income is being set aside to buy houses and settle them and thus, in addition employment will be given to workers, etc.
>
> The Kollel has also in [its] possession a Synagogue, kept open day and night for prayer and study.[30]

The three years following the war were prosperous ones for the *kollel*. Funds that had been collected during the war and held in the U.S. began to flow to Jerusalem after 1919. The more favorable dollar-to-pound exchange rate also increased the value of the *kollel*'s funds. But with prosperity, the moral integrity of the *kollel* and the fair distribution of its funds became important concerns of Jewish communities in the United States and Canada. In 1923 the United States Consular Court ordered an investigation into the *kollel*'s accounts and operations because of accusations of mismanagement and misappropriation of funds. The president of the Consular Court in Jerusalem appointed Israel Klaiman receiver and manager of Kollel America.

Klaiman opened his report with this statement: "It appears from the records and careful investigation that this organization, which pretends to have come into existence with a view of establishing better management and fairer distribution, has wasted all the funds, intended for the American poor, that have come into their hands."[31] A series of charges and countercharges were made by Kollel America members, who pointed to various persons as those responsible for abuse of funds. *Palestine Weekly* reporter Zalman White furnished Klaiman with a secret report on the *kollel*'s financial improprieties. He listed seven individuals who, according to his sources, had abused the process of distributing funds. In response, individual members attempted to explain why they deserved these funds although others had claimed that they did not.[32]

Klaiman's report alleged that there had been gross abuse of the money collected for the *kollel:* "It appears from the records of the Kollel that for each dollar paid out by the organization to the needy beneficiaries a sum of seven dollars is collected from donors in the United States." As Klaiman described it, a significant amount of money had been diverted to pay commissions (of between 33 and 50 percent) to fund-raisers. The expenses of the New York offices (25 percent of the funds) were subtracted from the amount that remained after commissions were paid. Salary and office expenses in Jerusalem further reduced the sum by 44 percent. According to Klaiman, distribution of money to undeserving and well-to-do people accounted for 50 percent of the balance. This left only fourteen cents of every dollar for the truly deserving cases.[33]

These specific claims of misuse of funds led to a general debate in the American Jewish community about the methods of supporting charitable institutions in Palestine. Judah Magnes served as the chairman of a committee investigating the problem. Its purpose was "to institute a thorough statistical investigation of all the charitable and educational institutions in Palestine not supported by the Keren Hayesod, with a view of safeguarding the Jews in America and elsewhere from any possible imposition and in order to bring about a general economy in both the method of collection and in the administration of the institutions." As part of this investigation, the Klaiman report was presented to influential Jewish and Zionist leaders in the United States—Julian Mack, David de Sola Pool, Solomon Sorrenstein, Samuel Lamport, and Samuel A. Goldsmith.[34]

According to a report issued in 1932, 249 families (about 500 persons) were receiving financial assistance from Kollel America. This consisted of monthly subsidies (500 mils for adults and 250 for children under the age of six), assistance in times of need, medical services, rent for two to three years in *kollel*-owned apartments, and provisions for certain holidays (e.g., matzo and other necessities for Passover). Seven or eight years earlier, the number of *kollel* families receiving assistance had been 600; the sharp decrease reported in 1932 reflected the smaller number of remissions arriving from Depression-struck North America. The *kollel*'s worsening financial situation led to stricter controls on its distribution of funds in Palestine. For example, when beneficiaries died or left Palestine, Kollel America did not accept new beneficiaries in their place.[35]

In 1933, at a meeting of American and Canadian Jews residing in Palestine, four resolutions were unanimously passed that marked a turning point in Kollel America's assumption of financial responsibility for its members in Palestine who depended solely on contributions from abroad. The first resolution called for the registration of Canadian and American Jewish members of Kollel America who would make a commitment to contribute at least $50 annually. The other resolutions called for additional forms of support for the American and Canadian poor in Palestine. It was hoped that these reforms would impress potential and actual contributors in North America to continue to support this worthy cause. For the years 1920 through 1932, total income for Kollel America reached over $250,000.[36] This provided a significant flow of funds into the Palestinian economy. In addition, members' personal assets and other sources of income helped boost the local economy.

The available quantitative information describing Kollel America is limited. Various sources provide numbers of family heads supported by the institution; they do not, however, indicate the number of people who were affiliated with the *kollel* but were not supported by it. Following World War I there was a steady increase in the number of heads of families supported by Kollel America. No clear reasons have been found for this trend, although suppositions can be advanced, including greater longevity due to better sanitation and medical services in Palestine, and increased economic mobility of the American population, for example.

From the responses to questionnaires distributed to Kollel America members in 1932, some characteristics of this population can be discerned. This data has limited application, since it represents the responses of only 148 family heads (60 percent), comprising 371 persons (74 percent). Nonetheless, it appears to be an accurate reflection of certain attributes of the *kollel* society: members were elderly, with 56.8 percent over the age of 61. The vast majority were not born in American (only 1.4 percent were). Of this group, 4.1 percent had lived in North America for less than five years, 33.8 percent between five and ten years, 32.4 percent between eleven and twenty years, and 27.0 percent more than twenty-one years. This points to the temporary nature of *kollel* members' residence in North America; as previously argued,

TABLE 21
Number of persons supported by Kollel America Tiffereth Yerushalaim for various years

Year	Family heads	Individuals	Location
1912	216	500	—
1913	—	485	—
1921–22	155	[321][a]	—
1922–23	164	[339]	—
1928	Over 200	[414]	—
1932	249	Approximately 500	Jerusalem, Safed, Tiberias, Jaffa, Tel Aviv, Petah Tikvah
1937	270	Approximately 525	Mainly Jerusalem, but also Jaffa, Tel Aviv Haifa, Tiberias, and the moshavot

[a]Estimates of the population are based on an average family size of 2.07.

America was for them just a place to stay while they accumulated some wealth to insure their final resting place in the Holy Land. This supposition is strengthened when viewed in conjunction with the occupations of Kollel America's members in Palestine: 52.7 percent had no occupation, 23.0 percent were involved in Jewish ritual occupations (scribes, kosher butchers, and so on), and 11.5 percent were merchants. A small group of wealthy members of the *kollel* probably were not included in these statistics; members of this type had been mentioned in the 1925 report as undeservedly receiving funds. Included in the list of undeserving was a landlord worth $100,000; the owner of two clothing stores, one in Jerusalem and the other in Haifa; the Palestinian representative of the American Manischewitz Matzo Factory; and an accountant employed by Solel Boneh, to name a few.[37]

In the possession of Kollel America was property for public use. A synagogue, called Tifferet Yerushalaim, was located in the Mea Shearim quarter, which also served as a yeshiva for its members. There was also property for the use of a select part of the membership. After World War I, Kollel America purchased houses in the Achvah neighborhood that had been founded in 1908. The first phase of that neighborhood's development was the purchase of land by twenty-two members of Achvah, the secret religious organization, in 1906. Two years later, twenty-five houses were completed by this group. After the war, construction continued in this neighborhood,

TABLE 22
Age of family heads of Kollel America, 1932

	<16	16–20	21–30	31–40	41–50	51–60	61–70	71–80	80>	Total
Number	1	1	5	16	17	24	35	40	9	148
Percent	0.7	0.7	3.4	10.9	11.5	16.2	23.7	27.0	6.1	100

but it was carried out by individuals, not by the original Achvah organization. In the southern section of the neighborhood, construction was sponsored by Kollel America, which transferred its offices to this sector.[38]

The *kollel* owned houses in Jerusalem which it allocated to needy members (selected by lot every two or three years), rent-free or for a small payment to cover taxes. The property included fourteen apartments: six units on Meah Shearim Street, one in the Kerem Quarter, three in the Knesset Yisrael neighborhood, two in the Milner Quarter, and two in the Wittenburg Quarter.[39] Most Kollel America members resided in privately owned homes in Jerusalem. In some cases they received interest-free loans from the *kollel* for the construction or purchase of their homes. In the mid-1920s, 126 *kollel* family heads indicated that their place of residence was in Jerusalem. Of these, 32 reported that they resided in the Meah Shearim Quarter and another 12 in the Beit Yisrael Quarter. A population cluster is evident: 54 percent resided in the Meah Shearim Quarter and adjacent neighborhoods, and 20 percent in neighborhoods along Jaffa Road. In addition, smaller clusters of 5–6 percent each were located in the Old City and in the Yemin Moshe and Shaarei Hesed quarters. Almost no Kollel America family heads were listed as residing in the newer and garden suburbs.[40]

In 1928 a group of local Orthodox Americans organized the Agudath Achim, Anshei America, a mutual aid society. These American Jews, rooted in Jerusalem, had found needy individuals among their ranks and decided to take responsibility for their plight. This *landsmanshaft*-like society planned to develop an American neighborhood in Jerusalem. The society invested £P1,700 of amassed funds in a four-dunam cemetery on the ridge of the Mount of Olives. It advertised the plots in the United States and went so far as to state that the cemetery was "like paradise." The society recouped £P1,000 after having sold 12 percent of the plots, and intended to use the profits to build houses for the American poor and Torah scholars. The society also promoted visits to the American sick and elderly. Members of Agudath Achim, Anshei America met regularly in the home of a Newark immigrant, Zvi Arie Loewe, in the Jerusalem Achvah Quarter and studied Torah together.[41]

Although the members of Kollel America Tiffereth Yerushalaim and like-minded Americans in the city represented a substantial segment of the American Jewish population in Jerusalem, their involvement in the development of the city was limited. Most lived out their lives studying Torah. They had little desire to transform the economy or the landscape.

Yet some American businessmen were actively involved in a variety of ventures for the commercial and industrial development of Jerusalem. For instance, the Palestine Securities Company entered into negotiations over the construction of a hotel in Jerusalem, with George Barsky as their first partner. Steps were taken to proceed with the organization of a corporation, under State of New York laws, to erect this hotel. The required capital was $1,000,000, and the proposed location was on a rise between the Allenby Hotel (near today's Kikar Davidka) and the train station. Leading local citizens promised $100,000 in subscriptions. Barsky found other investors and left the association, but he did not build the hotel. Instead, Palestine Securities entered into an agreement with [?] Amdursky, who operated the second-best hotel in Jerusalem. Together with Louis J. Rosenblatt, he purchased a lot on King George V Boulevard (today's Kikar Hachserat Hayishuv). Other investors were approached, including Sir Elly Kadoorie of Shanghai and the Anglo-Palestine Company. Arrangements were made with Solel Boneh (the building and contracting organization of the Histadrut) to construct the hotel, but this was not realized.[42]

Americans helped develop the King David Hotel through the PEC, which invested in Palestine Hotels, Ltd.—a company founded in 1921 by the wealthy and influential Mosseri family of Cairo and Alexandria. In 1929 the company purchased 18 dunams half-a-kilometer from the Old City; two years later the six-story, 200-room hotel was completed. It had the most up-to-date facilities, including hot and cold running water. In 1934 the Palestine Economic Corporation's investment in the King David Hotel stood at $117,000.[43]

Americans were also involved in smaller-scale enterprises. Prior to World War I, a handful of American Jews in Jerusalem were engaged in small retail businesses (groceries, dry goods, books, crockery, glassware, and clothing stores); in manufacturing (flour mills and bakeries); finances (money exchange); and in services (bath houses).[44] Following the war, many prospective immigrants to Palestine expressed their intention to engage in business there. Some meant to transfer their special backgrounds to their new surroundings, while others planned to take up a new vocation. Projects proposed by applicants for immigration included importing and exporting, retailing, hotel operation, automobile maintenance, and manufacturing of hats, lace, shoes, soap, and preserves. Some prospective immigrants indicated they wanted to engage in such activities in Jerusalem.[45]

Records reveal that during the period of this study, American businessmen established a wide variety of manufacturing operations in urban areas of Palestine. In 1921, for example, Menachem Mendel Freidman of Norfolk, Virginia, after investigating local cigarette manufacturing, decided to enter a partnership with a local producer. Freidman relocated their £E200 business, with six workers in one room, to five rooms in Jerusalem's Succat Shalom neighborhood. This new plant was in full compliance with government health department standards. The tobacco, packaging, and other production material were imported from Egypt. Because of the owners' lack of personal experience in the field and an inept manager, the company could not compete with the cheaper, inferior foreign cigarettes. Additional competition came from the Ketura factory in Safed, which, unlike Freidman's enterprise, received full backing from the Zionist Organization's Department of Commerce and Industry. (The Safed factory was deemed important in that it was one of the few industries employing Jews and it used tobacco produced by Jewish settlers in northern Palestine.) Freidman's options were either to modernize—switch from a hand-made to a machine-made product—or to close the workshop, and in 1923, having absorbed substantial losses, he shut down the factory. In a critique of Palestine industries, Moshe Novomeysky—a chemist, industrialist, engineer, and later the founder of the Dead Sea Works Company—suggested that Freidman failed because of "the lack of funds required for a rational organization of the work." It also appears that Freidman's efforts were premature; only two years after the failure of his venture, there was a boom in the cigarette manufacturing industry. From 1925 to 1926, exports of locally produced cigarettes increased seven-fold with the introduction of new factories and the expansion of existing ones.[46]

Throughout the 1920s, other manufacturing companies began operations in Jerusalem. The Palestine Knitting Works was the first and only power-driven plant of its kind in the Near East when it was established in 1921. It had first-rate machinery and an expert in charge. The factory produced scarves, shawls, jumpers, blankets, underclothing, dress materials, ties, and other clothing from wool, artificial silk, and a mixture of the two. The business was founded by Robert Kesselman's friend and Zionist coworker Alexander Landsberg. Originally from Brooklyn, Landsberg returned to America to settle his affairs after being demobilized from the Jewish Legion. He sold his long-established business in New York and returned to Palestine via Poland, where he purchased a fully equipped knitting factory. He also arranged for the immigration of a staff of mechanics to install and operate his plant. Kesselman helped his friend establish the factory in the Kerem neighborhood by negotiating with customs authorities and with national groups who were promoting support for "home industries." One of Landsberg's difficulties was a lack of working capital; another was his decision to use artificial silk, for he soon discovered that local demand for woolen goods was heavier. Yet his business expanded to an annual production of £E10,000 and employed twenty-five workers. Demand for the factory's products was so great that it could have operated three shifts, but lack of skilled labor allowed only one full and one partial one. The Arab boycott after the 1929 disturbances brought this flourishing enterprise to a ruinous end, when an order from Damascus worth over £P4,000 was withdrawn because the material was a Zionist product. Despite all the skill and energy that had been invested, this factory was forced to shut its doors.[47]

American investment often tapped the skills of the local population. Eight months after the liquidation of the Marbadia Carpet Company, the New Marbadia Carpet Company was established in Jerusalem to produce handwoven carpets and rugs. New capital was infused, and the company was incorporated in New York State with capital of $300,000. According to American Zionist Julius Haber, the men involved in this project were Philadelphia manufacturer Israel Greenblatt, Pittsburgh builder B. Pearlman, and I. Z. Josephson of New York. Another source from 1927 lists an investment of £P2,550 in New Marbadia by two Americans—Pearlman of Pittsburgh with £P700 and Felix Warburg of New York with £P200. New Marbadia took advantage of skilled labor among the Persian, Bukharian, Algerian, and Tunisian immigrants living in Jerusalem. The plant was located in the city's Bukharian quarter. In 1926 it had over 100 employees, mainly women, at its factory, and others working in their own homes. In the first half of that year, New Marbadia exports reached £E2,000.[48]

One American entrepreneur—and his European partner—attempted to gain a foothold in Palestine's furniture industry. Judah Leib Kazan, a representative of the New York Achooza Aleph, lived in Jerusalem from 1921 to 1927, during which time he managed the Danish-American furniture company. His memoirs describe the factory as employing some 150 persons directly and many indirectly. He emphasized that the business trained many workers who themselves became experts and instructors. In a second reference, Kazan mentioned that there were more than 100 Jewish workers at this facility; he noted the contribution made by this factory in providing employment for new immigrants. In his words, it was "an Aliyah Bureau."

Theoretically, the woodworking industry in Palestine had certain advantages: freight costs on wood were cheaper than those on furniture; moreover, import duty on wood was 3 percent, while for furniture it was 12 percent. In addition, wood need not be packed, whereas furniture demanded elaborate and comparatively expensive packing. Unfortunately, with the depreciation of the currencies of Germany, Austria, and Czechoslovakia—the major suppliers of furniture to Palestine—prices for these goods dropped sharply, and local producers were unable to compete. It was hoped that once these currencies were stabilized, the cost of imported furniture would rise and Palestinian enterprises would succeed. Moshe Novomeysky explained that the failure of the Danish-American Company was a combination of competition with the aforementioned European producers and irrational working methods. Although the owners suffered a financial loss with the factory's failure, Kazan noted that his former workers opened a smaller, cooperative operation, with private factories and workshops. Some of these workers were able to purchase the tools and machinery of the liquidated business.[49]

In the food service sector, a number of American establishments attempted to capture a specific niche—the American tourist and resident trade. Near Zion Circus (now Zion Square), an American named Bill owned a small shop where he served American chocolate sodas, hamburgers, and percolated coffee. His establishment became a rendezvous for Americans and eventually was popular among Jerusalemites as well, who took a liking to these American delicacies.[50] Libby Berkson, in partnership with Lillian Friedlander, opened an American-style tearoom, "Al Cos Te" (Over a Cup of Tea). It provided the clientele—locals and American tourists—with apple pie and American coffee in a pleasant setting. At the time, "there was no shortage of rather ugly, but otherwise adequate, eating places," explained Sylva Gelber. "We welcomed the proposal for a congenial establishment, where we could obtain wholesome American-style meals in friendly surroundings."[51]

In addition to fostering business enterprises, American philanthropic activity had a dramatic effect upon Jerusalem's landscape. The Hadassah organization founded and maintained hospitals, day care centers, health stations, infant welfare stations, school luncheon programs, and playgrounds. The Hadassah Medical Center on Mount Scopus was inaugurated in 1939. Between 1917–45, Hadassah was responsible for 9.1 percent (£P3,915,000) of the £P42,758,000 in income of Jewish funds and institutions in Palestine. During this period, 17.3 percent of the organization's expenditure was for education and culture, and 82.7 percent for health care and social work. Nathan and Lina Straus funded the establishment of the health center that bears their name and which opened its doors to all races and creeds in 1929. The Strauses contributed over $2,000,000 to various Palestinian causes, mainly in Jerusalem.[52]

A survey of American activities in Jerusalem leads to the question of whether some parts of the city had higher concentrations of Americans. Clearly one group of Americans, members of Kollel America, organized themselves in one section of Jerusalem, in and around the Mea Shearim Quarter. Other groups of Americans were not as highly concentrated. Edwin Samuel mentioned a number of Americans (including Dr. Israel Kligler, Dr. Judah Magnes, and archaeologist Dr. Nelson Gluck) who lived among British and Jewish families outside Herod's Gate as tenants of Muslim Arab landlords. The Americans were part of the local elite. However, Jewish families left the area after the riots at the Wailing Wall in August 1929. Correspondence of the American consulate in Jerusalem during the period of the 1929 riots indicates that there was one group of American Jews in the Rehavia neighborhood and another in Talpiot. Available statistical information does

CHAPTER 10

Fig. 32. Straus Medical Center, Jerusalem, ca. 1935.
(CZA Keren Hayesod photograph collection)

not provide details, but various descriptive sources suggest that while there were pockets of Americans, there were no exclusively or mainly American projects or neighborhoods. These pockets were not the result of the activities of real estate ventures or of settlement organizations such as the American Zion Commonwealth. Rather they were formed because Americans were drawn to neighborhoods that had amenities which appealed to persons with their socioeconomic backgrounds. Thus, for example, pockets of Americans existed in Jerusalem's Talpiot, Rehavia, and Romema neighborhoods.[53]

TEL AVIV-JAFFA AND VICINITY

Jaffa underwent rapid growth as a commercial center in the late nineteenth century. Its population increased from roughly 8,000 in the 1870s to approximately 50,000 at the outbreak of World War I. The 1922 census placed the population of Jaffa-Tel Aviv at 47,709, of whom 20,699 were Jews. Over the following nine years the population more than doubled. The 1931 census enumerated 97,967, of whom 52,773 were Jews. The built-up area of Jaffa expanded from 108 dunams in 1841–42 to 1,550 dunams in 1917–18.[54] Tel Aviv underwent two development booms, the first in 1924–25 and the second between 1932–37. By 1939 the Jewish population of Tel Aviv-Jaffa had grown to 177,000, more than triple its size at the beginning of the decade.

Beyond Jaffa's numerical and spatial growth, the city developed as the social and cultural center of the new Jewish settlement in Palestine. In the late nineteenth century, it rose to become the chief town of the New *Yishuv*, with a cosmopolitan atmosphere. Concepts of productive labor and Hebrew culture found a nurturing surrounding for their development. Jaffa embodied the range of institutions involved in the transformation of Jewish society from conservative Orthodoxy to its national revival.[55] This was extended and then transferred to Tel Aviv. In 1909 the Jewish garden neighborhood of Achuzat Bayit, originally a suburb of Jaffa, became the focal point for Tel Aviv, the first new Jewish city. Tel Aviv became an independent entity under the Township of Tel Aviv Order issued on 11 May 1921, symbolic of a new beginning. In contrast to its sister city Jaffa, Tel Aviv was the city of the future, a site in which new concepts of planning and urban life could be initiated.[56]

Pioneer Zionist circles viewed the growth of Tel Aviv with considerable apprehension since the city drew a large proportion of Jewish immigrants away from rural surroundings and agricultural pursuits. Tel Aviv was criticized as being "built on sand" with no solid economic foundations.[57] Zionists in America, on the other hand, were proud of this new city. Author and reporter Ludwig Lewisohn viewed Tel Aviv as "A City Unlike New York." His 1924 description actually compared Tel Aviv to the summer resort town of Far Rockaway, New York; he likened their seaside locations and their strongly Jewish environments. Lewisohn also remarked: "The houses in Tel-Aviv are not beautiful. Some of them are cheap and pretentious and seem to have been built in imitation of the worst period of American domestic architecture." Despite the unattractiveness, Lewisohn found beauty in the gardens, the light, and the sea. Certain streets reminded him of Charleston, Savannah, and New Orleans. He took pride in the fact that the street names honored famous Jews. Lewisohn was well aware of the city's problems—its shaky economic foundations and land speculation. But he noted that "The city glows with life, with a spontaneous and powerful will to be. . . . The people are building the city with joy." He differed from his radical Zionist friends in that he saw the need for both rural and urban development in Palestine; he opposed the "romantic myth that the country is pure and the city foul, that a merchant is essentially and necessarily more ignoble than he

TABLE 23
Floor area of new buildings, selected years from 1923–40, in square meters

Year	Area m^2	Year	Area m^2	Year	Area m^2
1923	33,507	1928	23,612	1933	353,322
1924	91,134	1929	28,710	1934	424,504
1925	236,669	1930	43,690	1936	261,224
1926	53,983	1931	65,795	1938	150,994
1927	12,720	1932	128,079	1940	42,045

Source: Palestine and Middle East Economic Magazine 8 (January 1933): 39; David Gurevich and Aaron Gertz, *Statistical Handbook of Jewish Palestine*, 1947 (Jerusalem: Jewish Agency for Palestine, 1947), 266.

who cultivates the soil, that the work of the hand has a moral value which the work of the mind lacks."[58] Many of his sentiments were shared by other Americans, who were pleased by the development of this exclusively Jewish, growing urban center.

American Zionists assisted in the development of Tel Aviv in various ways. For example, they provided financial assistance for the improvement of the municipal infrastructure through the Tel Aviv Bond Issue. In the spring of 1922, Bernard Rosenblatt, while serving on the Palestine Zionist Executive, proposed to Mayor Meir Dizengoff that a loan could be procured in America for public works—the development of a water supply as well as a sewage system and road improvements. The loan was approved by the local council of the Township of Tel Aviv and sanctioned by the High Commissioner Sir Herbert Samuel. Rosenblatt was empowered to negotiate with well-established banking institutions for floating the Tel Aviv Bond Issue.[59] The terms of this £75,000 bond issue were 6½ percent per annum for twenty years, with repayment on a semiannual basis. The interest rate was lower than bonds issued at that time by other municipalities—e.g., Copenhagen at 8 percent and Paris at 7 percent. According to Rosenblatt, the low rate was possible because "only when we have a sentimental appeal, with the business aspects emphasized, can we succeed in a substantial way."[60]

American investment in Tel Aviv was poured into the construction of homes, commercial buildings, and neighborhoods, both during the booms and in slower periods. The American Zion Commonwealth developed land on the fringe of Tel Aviv. In 1921, a workers' neighborhood, Schunat Borochov, was founded east of the Yarkon River on Jewish National Fund land. An additional 600 to 700 dunams to the south of this neighborhood came on the market, and a host of investors—including Mr. Schuldinger of New York, the AMZIC, and the JNF—took an interest in the tract. In 1922 Charles Passman expressed a preference for this site over the Jelil tract (Herzlia) as the spot for an AMZIC garden city. Two years later, the JNF wanted to purchase the tract but did not possess the necessary capital. Passman suggested that the AMZIC purchase it in order to prevent Schuldinger or other investors who did not have the well-being of the Zionist enterprise in mind from acquiring it. He pointed out that the land could either be sold to the JNF or to investors in Palestine at a considerable profit.[61]

In October 1924, the AMZIC purchased 679 dunams at a price of £E15 ($75) per dunam, plus approximately 10 percent for expenses, to be paid in installments over two years. An accord reached with the Jewish National Fund gave it a five-month option on one-half of the tract, which it subsequently exercised. This tract was named Schunat Sheinkin after Menachem Sheinkin, a Zionist figure popular among Americans for his cooperation with the American Zion Commonwealth. The AMZIC considered purchasing an adjacent 600-dunam tract for future expansion, but this proposal was not concluded.[62]

After deducting space for wadis, parks, streets, public spaces, and buildings, plans were drawn up for 470 one-dunam building plots. Setting aside land for the Jewish National Fund, 240 dunams remained in the possession of the American Zion Commonwealth, which grappled with such issues as price and market strategy. The New York office proposed selling the land in America at $400 per dunam, but Passman suggested that marketing be oriented toward the local population and the price set at $175 per dunam. At the lower price, the AMZIC would have realized a profit of $34,000 on the transaction. At the higher price, company profits would have been increased by $135,000—to $169,000.[63]

One potential purchaser for part of Schunat Sheinkin was the Tel Aviv Town Council, which was seeking 40 to 45 dunams for slaughterhouses, quarantines, and a cattle market. The mayor hoped that the abattoir would provide job opportunities for several dozen families as well as lower the price of kosher meat. The American Zion Commonwealth agreed with the council's proposal, on the condition that the AMZIC would receive half the purchase price immediately. The accord fell through, however, since the Tel Aviv Town Council did not have the necessary funds. The AMZIC then objected to having an abattoir near its development: not only would it be a nuisance, it would surely lead to a decrease in property values.

As mentioned above, the AMZIC believed it would reap higher profits by selling the land in America.[64] Yet by 1926 American sales had proved extremely disappointing. American Zion Commonwealth correspondence does not explain prevailing consumer attitudes. The shortfall in sales may simply be a reflection of the loss of public confidence in the company due to its well-publicized financial difficulties. The AMZIC received requests for cancellation and the return of money. Although forty-one Americans entered into contracts for land purchases in Schunat Sheinkin, in the end only twenty-seven *kushans* were issued. In 1929 the adjacent neighborhood, Schunat Borochov, attempted to expand and wanted to purchase 100 to 150 dunams from the AMZIC, but because of disagreement over the price, no accord was reached. Nonetheless, the AMZIC cooperated with Schunat Borochov by developing infrastructure for both communities. By 1936 the 367-dunam neighborhood had a population of 400, of whom 70 earned their livelihood from agriculture; citrus groves had been planted on 18 dunams. No Americans have been identified as having settled in this neighborhood.[65]

In an effort to thwart speculation in an uncontrolled market, four equal partners—the Anglo-Palestine Company, Geula, the Palestine Land Development Company, and the American Zion Commonwealth—founded the Tel Aviv Development Company in 1925 with a combined capital of £P10,000 ($50,000). The Township of Tel Aviv also entered into this arrangement; though it put up no capital, it received a share of the profits. The principal purpose of the partnership was to purchase large tracts of land in order to curb speculation. The consortium sought land near the mouth of the Yarkon River, an area where it believed a port would eventually be built.[66]

The expansion of the Tel Aviv real estate market served as an avenue of activity and investment for individual Americans. Some of this coincided with the boom of the mid-1920s, although in general the tone of reports on these investments does not allude to maximization of profit. While some Americans sought sound investments, others wished to participate in the Zionist enterprise and utilize experience they had gained in the United States. Researcher Natan Harpaz emphasized that many American immigrants to Tel Aviv were experienced businessmen with capital and a knowledge of American commercial construction methods, which served as a thrust for economic development. The American projects that have been identified are outlined below; however, since more than 700 American Jews lived in Tel Aviv-Jaffa in 1931, it is likely that there were more projects of varying scale.

After his first visit to Palestine in 1924, Louis Rosenblatt (Bernard's father) decided to return and spend his last years there. After attempting to develop various business activities, Rosenblatt formed a partnership to purchase land from Arabs in the area of Tel Aviv and resell it in small plots to prospective Jewish homeowners. As few settlers had ready cash, he furnished them with long-term mortgages, conditional upon the building of houses on the premises. He was responsible for opening up the area near the Geula land company's Lev Tel Aviv project; his development work occurred along Rothschild Boulevard, west of Allenby Street up to the area of Habimah Theatre. Rosenblatt presented the land for Habimah Theatre to the Tel Aviv

Map 13. American activities in Tel Aviv up to 1939

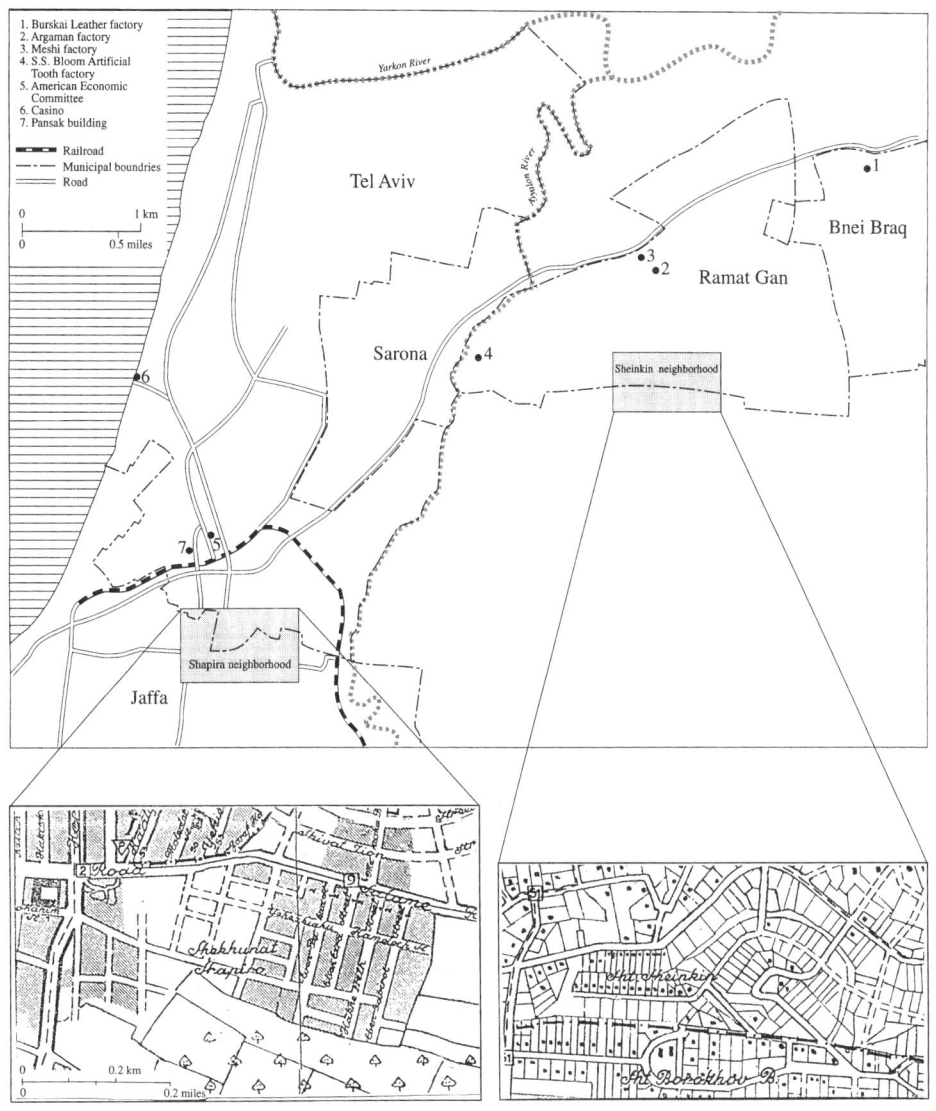

Town Council as compensation for the construction of roads through his lands. According to his son, Rosenblatt reaped only a modest profit on the resale of these lands, but the interest and amortization of mortgages allowed him to live comfortably. Bernard claimed that "in this pioneer work he was employing methods learned in America."[67]

Although Rosenblatt's marketing orientation was not necessarily toward Americans, one example of a purchase by an American in this area is that of Dr. Jacob P. Norman, originally of Boston, who decided to purchase a plot for £E550 ($2,750) in cash in 1924. He built a two-story house with ten rooms for £E1,500 ($7,500). Norman wanted construction to begin immediately, for, in his opinion, renting a house at £E12–15 ($60–75) a month was too expensive.[68]

In the early 1920s, the Menorah Palestine Building Corporation also undertook the development of land adjoining Bayit Vegan, an area south of Jaffa. It sold plots to "a large number of Jews from America." Two areas—Menorah Aleph and Menorah Bet—were offered, but they were not developed at the time. In 1926 the urban settlement of Bat Yam was founded on the Bayit Vagan lands. The economic crisis in the late 1920s slowed development, but by the 1930s, growth in this section took off, new homes were built, and land prices increased.[69]

Another American initiative was that of immigrant Meir Shapira, who purchased 15 dunams between Tel Aviv and Jaffa that was later known as Schunat Shapira. One fifth of the land was set aside for roads and public space, and the remainder was divided into 36 plots of 333 square meters each. Shapira attempted to have this area incorporated in the Jaffa municipal jurisdiction instead of that of Tel Aviv, since taxes in Jaffa were lower. This caused a rift between Shapira and Tel Aviv mayor Meir Dizengoff, who lobbed the insult that Shapira was not a Zionist.[70]

The Jerusalem-American Land Company owned a 9,724-square-meter tract in Jaffa near the railway station; its exact location has not been identified.[71] The company, it appears, sought to develop the area, but the collapse of the real estate market in Tel Aviv in 1926 probably arrested any such attempt.

Two other American-initiated projects were the Casino and the Pansak Passage. In 1921, to allow direct access to the casino, Allenby Street was redesigned so that it would curve toward the beachfront. The casino building was destroyed in 1939 because it blocked the view of the sea. The second structure, a commercial center on Herzl Street, was initiated by Mordy Pansak in 1921. This three-story building, to which a fourth floor was later added, included stores and workshops. Within its courtyard was the first freight elevator in Tel Aviv. This was a typically American enterprise, creating rentable floor space and the necessary amenities for small industry and commerce.[72]

The Fish Family of Brooklyn found a special niche in providing hospitality services for visitors to Palestine, particularly American Jews. Sarah Fish originally went to Palestine in order to provide her three young children the opportunity to live and learn in a Hebrew-speaking environment. She intended to remain for a year, but instead she extended their sojourn, and the family's father Avraham eventually joined Sarah and the children. With worsening economic conditions in the United States, the couple decided to seek a life in Tel Aviv and earn their livelihood there. Sarah truly enjoyed entertaining. On one occasion, she opened her home to members of the American team participating in the 1932 Maccabiah Games, and when she ran out of rooms she made beds for them on the floor. According to Sarah's youngest son, it was at her initiative that they opened their first family business in Palestine: Pension Fish on Ben Yehuda Street in 1933. Two years later they moved their business to Yarkon Street and renamed it Hotel Fish. In 1941 the Fish family procured the "American House" on Yehuda Halevi Street, a modern hotel that had been established in the late 1930s with American capital. Occupying the upper two floors of a three-story building, this twenty-five-room hotel had all the modern conveniences: an elevator, central heating, and showers in every room. The Fish family kept the hotel's original name, since it reflected the owners' country of origin and the type of hospitality one could expect at this hotel.[73]

Americans were also engaged in the industrial development of Tel Aviv-Jaffa, but there were numerous barriers to the success of these ventures. In March 1927, the Urban Settlement Department of the Palestine Zionist Executive organized a meeting of American capitalists who were visiting Tel Aviv. Mr. Stone, the secretary, and Mr. Rodovsky expressed their trepidation regarding investment in Palestinian industries. Stone complained of high salaries, wasted money, and unfair administration. Rodovsky expressed a need for change. The Mandatory government, he charged, did nothing to assist the development of industry; indeed, in certain instances it actually hindered growth—for example, by placing heavy duties on raw materials. Second, he saw a need for public participation through the purchase of locally manufactured goods. Third, Rodovsky called for the Histadrut to cooperate in the endeavor and not obstruct it.[74]

Another example of private American initiative is Shimon Zeev Levine of Chattanooga, Tennessee, who immigrated to Palestine in 1922. Until he relocated to Herzlia in 1924, he operated a cigarette factory called Ashna on Ahad Haam Street in Tel Aviv. He also marketed his products in a retail store in Tel Aviv.[75]

The Jewish leather processing industry in Palestine began on a small scale under primitive conditions but expanded during the 1920s. The 1921–22 census of Jewish industry listed only one tannery with three workers; this was located at Motza, on the outskirts of Jerusalem. The industry increasingly specialized in cattle hides and became geographically focused in the Tel Aviv-Jaffa area. By 1926 there were six Jewish tanneries: three in Tel Aviv, and one factory each in Motza, Haifa, and Acre. Three years later, however, only four of them remained in operation—three in Tel Aviv-Jaffa and the one in Motza.[76] American entrepreneurs were involved in the expansion of this sector. In January 1923 it was reported that "[The Shapiro Tannery in Tel Aviv] is a new concern, with paid-up capital of $10,000, that is manufacturing cheveau, chrom and other kinds of leather. The Near East are heavy importers of leather articles. This fact is of vital importance to those interested and experienced in the leather business, for they can see that the 'Tannery Co.,' properly financed, will, after enlarging its plant and providing better machinery, be in a position to gain possession of the leather markets in the whole of the Near East." A year later, however, the tannery had closed; the chief reason for its failure was the lack of funds required for rational organization of the work.[77]

David Naphtali Diamant and Ch. Kvashnievsky developed the Bourskai, Palestine Leather Factory in a building in Jaffa rented from Arabs; its offices were in the Wilson House on Ramban Street in Tel Aviv. As of 1923, £E1,900 was invested: £E1,100 in immovable property and cisterns, and £E800 in liquid capital, tools, implements, chemicals, skins, and leather. The factory received loans from the Zionist Organization, Kupat Milveh, and Louis Topkis. Topkis's interest provided the factory with certain advantages. As Zeev Jabotinsky explained to the Palestine Zionist Executive, Topkis was an important supporter of the Keren Hayesod and other Zionist projects. Jabotinsky suggested that the executive help the operation by obtaining an appropriate site for the factory in Tel Aviv and assist in the process of rescheduling its loans.[78]

Various reports describe attempts by Americans to invest in the leather industry. According to one active American Zionist, Julius Haber, "A Chicagoan named Leopold Lowenstein sought the authorization from the Zionist Organization of America to raise funds for establishing a saddle-making shop in Jaffa, to employ fifty Jews." Haber also mentioned that "a group in Syracuse organized a $50,000 corporation to open a tannery in Jaffa for the processing of native hides."[79] Another report describes the Association of American and Palestinian Leather Workers established in New York to develop the leather industry in Palestine. The organization's members each invested $20 for a total of $20,000, and then entered into negotiations over the development of the industry in Palestine.[80]

Americans attempted to transfer textile industries to Palestine, but only one took root in the Tel Aviv area. In 1932 the building of the "Meshi" artificial silk factory commenced at Ramat Gan. The owner of the factory, Isaac Sacks of Paterson, New Jersey, operated a similar concern in the United States. To insure a sufficient supply of energy for the factory and other new developments nearby, the Palestine Electric Corporation set up a transformer nearby. It is noteworthy that Sacks purchased £P4,000 in shares in the utility. To assist the new factory, which was to provide employment for 100 workers, the Ramat Gan Council provided certain tax exemptions and reduced water rates. Sacks invested over £P150,000 in Palestine, including £P77,320 in the factory. It must be emphasized that from the outset, the factory operated at a disadvantage, particularly vis-à-vis international competitors. The cost of Japanese labor, for example, was one-fifth that of Palestinian labor. High duty on raw material and low tariffs on manufactured goods would further hinder the growth of this industry. Nonetheless, the factory held out the promise not only of employing Jewish workers but also of encouraging the growth of cocoon production by the agricultural sector. In 1933 there were sixty-six mechanical looms in Sacks's factory, with another twenty en route from the United States.[81]

One of the most successful American enterprises established in Palestine was the American Porcelain Tooth Manufacturing Company, Ltd.—although it was initially expected to fail because of the limited market for its products in Palestine. Lithuanian-born Samuel Simon Bloom immigrated to the United States in 1882 at the age of twenty-two and slowly built up a successful artificial tooth factory. He developed strong Zionist sympathies, visiting Palestine and taking an active role in fund-raising. As early as the 1909 American Zionist convention in New York, he expressed his intention to open a branch factory in Palestine. Bloom later became affiliated with the Brandeis group.[82]

In 1926 Bloom settled in Palestine, founding a factory on Maged Street, Nahalat Itzhak, Tel Aviv. At that time, international demand for artificial teeth exceeded the supply. The factory required no specialists, and Palestine afforded relatively cheap labor. Eighty percent of the employees would be girls aged fourteen to twenty, whose work would be clean and easy. By February 1927, it employed 42 workers and was operating at 50 percent capacity, producing 15,000 teeth a day. It was hoped that the factory would eventually employ between 200 and 250—possibly even 500 workers. However, conditions in Palestine were not conducive to this industry, for the raw materials it needed—feldspar, gold, and platinum—had to be imported with a 12–15 percent ad valorem duty. Since completed artificial teeth were admitted into Palestine custom-free, Bloom thought that it was illogical to tax the raw materials.[83]

On 26 February 1927, Bloom, "very bitter," announced that he would soon close the factory, in which he had already invested £P10,000. He believed that his efforts to succeed had been hindered by many factors. He protested to the Executive Council of the Zionist Organization in London, writing, "I am compelled to seriously consider giving up my task and closing the factory. And why? Because the mismanagement of the Zionist Office

Fig. 33. Advertisements for American Tooth Manufacturing Company and Judea Insurance Company, American firms in Palestine. (*Palestine and Near East Economic Magazine,* 20–22, 540, 544).

holders here is unbearable for any truthful Zionist." He went on to explain that he had been promised assistance regarding exemption from duty on raw materials. Furthermore, he had gotten caught up in the rivalry between different national bodies—for example, the mayor of Tel Aviv had prevented High Commissioner Lord Plumer from visiting the factory. Bloom was warned that to avoid trouble he should join the Histadrut and hire only Histadrut workers.[84]

Despite Bloom's threat to shut down the factory, his product gained a good reputation among dentists in Britain and was much in demand. In 1929 the factory had fifty-eight employees receiving £P3,250 in wages annually. The capital invested in the factory was £P7,003. Expenditures on raw material and energy were £P3,536 and £P459 respectively, with principal expenditures totaling £P7,245. That year production reached £P10,776. At the end of 1932, seventy-two workers were employed and were considered highly skilled in their trade; in fact, the high quality of their products led to

Fig. 34. Interior of the American Porcelain Tooth Manufacturing Company, 1931. (CZA photograph collection 696)

attempts to imitate the company's trademark. By 1934 approximately 180 workers were employed, and artificial teeth held an important place in the Palestinian export economy.[85] Louis Brandeis took particular pride in this enterprise: "The sale of £P10,000 [in 1930] of artificial teeth to England is an indication of what Jewish ingenuity, courage and determination can achieve for Palestine."[86]

The local construction industry attracted Samuel Wilson, who had been a mason and contractor in Hartford, specializing in bakers' ovens. Wilson began to build private homes in Palestine in 1909, and after World War I, his early initiative provided the foundation for a successful building career in Tel Aviv. He emphasized the professionalism and integrity of his enterprise by including the words "American Contractor" in his logo. Wilson may well be the entrepreneur mentioned in this excerpt from an American consular report: "A Palestine-American factory in Jaffa which has supplied building materials for 40 houses intends to increase its production and improve its equipment."[87]

TABLE 24
Palestinian exports of artificial teeth and industrial products

Year	Exports of artificial teeth (£P)	Industrial exports (£P)	Artificial teeth as percent of industrial exports
1930	10,325	365,350	2.82
1932	13,429	312,392	4.30
1934	28,585	294,243	9.71
1936	34,431	417,078	7.72
1938	30,732	639,604	4.80

Source: Statistical Abstract of Palestine, 1937–38, 74–75.

Tel Aviv attracted numerous American professionals. In 1922 there were twelve American professionals out of 383 enumerated. In the field of education, New York-born Isaac Meir Kanowitz studied at Columbia University and the Teacher's Seminary, New York. Arriving in Palestine in 1924, he taught in Tel Aviv and eventually became headmaster of one of the city's high schools.

Americans were elected to the municipal council as well. Nathan D. Kaplan, a Chicago attorney and leading Zionist in the American Midwest, immigrated to Palestine in 1927. He was a member of the Tel Aviv municipal council from 1936 to 1941. He was chosen to be mayor but refused the post, saying that it should go to a native-born citizen. Zvi Lavon also served on the Tel Aviv municipal council. Samuel Wilson served as the chair of the Tel Aviv building committee, as a member of the town's executive, and as the head of the volunteer firefighters.

From the activities detailed above, it is clear that Americans played a variety of roles in the development of Tel Aviv and its vicinity. They helped expand the housing supply through the redemption of lands as well as the construction of houses and neighborhoods. Moreover, they also expanded the industrial and commercial sectors. Two factories were especially significant in the period between the two World Wars. Between them, Meshi and the American Porcelain Tooth Manufacturing Company employed hundreds of Jewish workers and helped facilitate the absorption of new immigrants.

HAIFA AND MOUNT CARMEL

Haifa developed rapidly during the late Ottoman period, eventually overtaking its neighboring rival Acre in population and the amount of built-up area. In 1880 it had 6,500 inhabitants; this number increased to 24,000 in 1922. Linking the Hijaz railroad to Haifa in 1905 gave further impetus to its progress. From 1895 to 1922, the city's Jewish population multiplied at an even faster pace—from 810 to 6,230, close to an eightfold increase.

British intentions to transform Haifa into the principal port of Palestine augmented the city's status, inducing interest and drawing investment in land and industrial projects. Discussions in the 1930s concerning an oil pipeline from Iraqi deposits to Haifa enhanced the city's importance. New industries and the Palestine Electric Corporation benefited the city and attracted new residents. Government and Jewish institutional administrations for the Northern District of Palestine were located in Haifa. In 1931 the city had 50,500 residents, of whom 31.7 percent were Jews. Over the following eight years, the Jewish population grew to 69,000, chiefly because Haifa attracted a large portion of the Central European and Polish Jewish migration. Advertisements placed Haifa in the center of the world, with the Levant and Iraq as its hinterland. American Jews invested in the development of new residential neighborhoods and in commercial structures such as the business center. However, only a small percentage of Jewish American immigrants settled in Haifa.

The Palestine Land Development Company played a pivotal role in the city's development. It purchased over 10 million square meters in the first decade of British rule and, in turn, commissioned the planning of neighborhoods, their parceling, and initial development. Plots were sold directly to purchasers or buyers abroad through agents, such as the American Zion Commonwealth. Additional companies, some of questionable repute, offered other tracts for foreign investors.

The American Zion Commonwealth purchased various tracts in the Haifa area with the intention of reselling them in America. Although it took no active role in the development of these tracts, the company assumed a moral responsibility toward the American Jewish consumer. It realized that if it did not fully serve the requirements of the American public, potential purchasers would turn to other real estate agents, some of whom had rather questionable business practices. By contrast, the AMZIC demanded that honest business practices be followed in this mission of national importance. Through the efforts of the Palestine Land Development Company, plans were drawn up and the new neighborhoods subdivided into plots, with areas set aside for roads, parks, public space, and buildings. The AMZIC was provided with maps and detailed lists of the lots it could sell in America.

The Palestine Land Development Company and the Palestine Real Estate Company purchased the land of Hadar Hacarmel before World War I, and conducted parceling and development. A provisional committee was organized to steer the area's development and expansion. Acknowledging the sizable number of owners who lived abroad, the PLDC arranged that two of the nine committee members represent the interests of foreign owners. In 1924 the American Zion Commonwealth purchased 15,625 square meters,

CHAPTER 10

Map. 14. American activities in Haifa to 1927

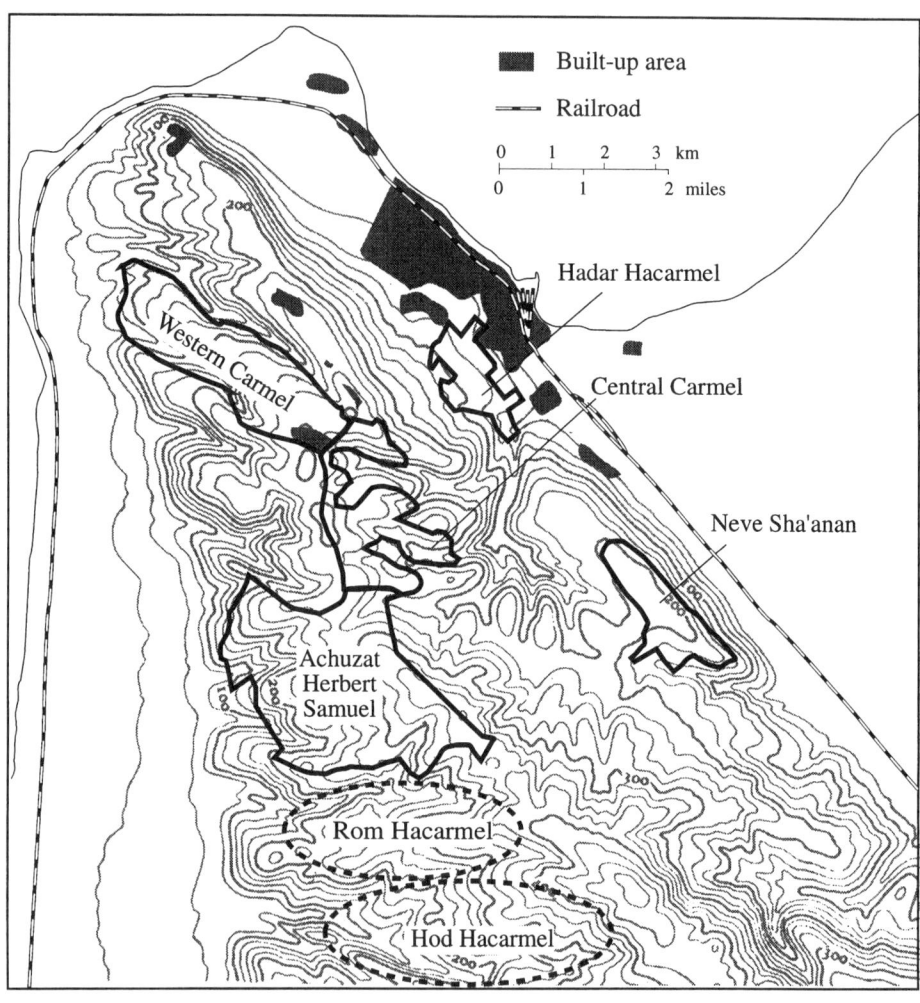

the equivalent of 25 lots, for £E3,300 ($16,500) for sale in America. The price per lot ranged from £E100 ($500) to £E180 ($900). Due to the heavy demand, seven additional plots were offered and sold in the American market. This led to problems, however, as these seven plots were occupied by local inhabitants who had built wooden barracks there. Although they were squatters, they intended to eventually pay for the land, and their tenancy had received the approval of the Vaad of Hadar Hacarmel. The PLDC had full knowledge of the sale of these seven plots, but since it had not received immediate payment from the American purchasers, decided to sell the land right from under them.

The Vaad viewed with trepidation the purchase of lands under its jurisdiction by Jews residing in the Diaspora. The committee was wary of purchasers abroad who did not intend to take up permanent residence but rather were involved in speculative activities. This would likely escalate land prices and retard development by creating a market out of reach of potential buyers who did intend to take up residence there. Moreover, foreign owners generally did not pay taxes to the Vaad, and these were necessary for the development of the area's infrastructure. Further complications had arisen because the PLDC sent incomplete information to the AMZIC in New York. The AMZIC then sold lots at incorrect prices, in some instances with the wrong area being quoted or the wrong zone, and this led to confusion among the purchasers.[88]

By the 1930s, Hadar Hacarmel had become an affluent neighborhood. Bernard Rosenblatt, the founder of the American Zion Commonwealth, settled there with his family in 1930. At first he rented a house while building his own at the corner of Balfour and Melchett streets. Rosenblatt's memoirs outline some of the difficulties he experienced in building his house and link these to his being an American: "We wanted to build a modest home," he explained, "but our architect would have none of it. He was building for an American family, he said, and he was no more to be overruled than the typical American Jewish waiter in a restaurant in New York. The result was that three years later we sold the house because my wife objected to rented quarters."[89]

A larger transaction, lands in the Central and Western Carmel, was negotiated between the Palestine Land Development Company and the American Zion Commonwealth. Architect and planner Richard Kaufmann designed the schemes for these areas. In 1924 the AMZIC bought 140,000 square meters, the equivalent of 140 lots, for £E6,600 ($33,000). Although this area was deemed attractive by foreign investors, local settlers disagreed with this judgment. They thought it was too isolated, too far from the city center, and suffered from antiquated and inefficient road connections. In addition, they pointed out, the topography would make it more difficult to develop. Only in the 1930s, with the large wave of German Jewish immigration, did development take place in these areas.[90]

Another portion of Mount Carmel in which the American Zion Commonwealth sold lands was the "Red Carmel," better known as Neve Shaanan. Founded in 1921, this area had the advantage of a subtle topography and protection from maritime winds, yet its disadvantages included proximity to the swampland of the bay and the lack of a road connecting it to Haifa (this was not constructed until 1926). Although there were 230 members of the organizing group, its first settlers numbered approximately 100. By 1926

Neve Shaanan's population had increased to 600. The AMZIC offered 85 one-dunam plots in this settlement, located in four zones. The prices were $400, $500, $550 and $600 for each area. By 1926 only 22 plots had been sold, the majority in the most expensive zone.[91]

Another campaign for Haifa land sales, Carmelia, began in July 1926. This area lay west of the Central Carmel area. As it became increasingly evident that the American Zion Commonwealth was undergoing financial difficulties, the company looked to serve as an intermediary rather than as a developer. It justified this transaction because it recognized the considerable interest in the American market for lands on Mount Carmel. In addition, the AMZIC could combat so-called real estate agencies selling so-called "Carmel land" at very high prices. Moreover, sales could be conducted simultaneously with the Afula and Haifa Bay campaigns without hindering them. Finally, it was argued, this transaction would not entail additional expenditures; on the contrary, it would yield extra profits that would cover the company's budget and increase its capital reserve.

The owner of the Carmelia land, Yehuda Itin, was intent on selling it in the United States. So as to block or eliminate competition, the AMZIC was willing to purchase the entire holding, which consisted of 439,425 square meters divided into 303 plots. The transaction involved $270,000 worth of land, 49 percent of which was already sold by November 1926. Solomon J. Weinstein considered this sale "somewhat satisfactory," but a downward trend in the land market was apparent. Over the following year, only an additional 5 percent of the land was sold in the United States. With the financial failure of the AMZIC, a syndicate was created to take over the Carmelia project. This group assumed the $92,057 debt for the balance of payments of plots previously sold and the sale of 140 unsold plots valued at $123,500. The entire tract of land was transferred and registered in the name of the group's treasurer in May 1928. Two years later, the administration of sales was transferred to the New York Achooza Aleph.[92]

The America-Palestine Agency for Land Transactions was also involved in Mount Carmel land sales. In a detailed brochure, the agency described its aim as the redemption of building plots and agricultural lands at inexpensive prices and on easy terms. It announced the redemption of more than 4,000 dunams on Mount Carmel from non-Jews. Noting that one of the agency's principles was "carefulness and exactness," it emphasized that this area included lands for which they actually had *kushans*—not land in the process of being purchased. The agency claimed 2,000 plots atop the Carmel in an area it called Rom Hacarmel. The three-dunam plots would assure light, air, a view, and no crowding. In addition, lands were set aside for public gardens and forests, as well as roads wide enough to accommodate electric trams. The brochure claimed that the majority of the plots were sold to American Jews, who would be pioneers in building the city, investing their energies in its improvement. This advertising campaign was in fact chiefly directed toward the Jewish population of Palestine. Tracts were also marketed in Europe.[93]

In 1924 the Palestine Land Development Company had this tract investigated. Richard Kaufmann was convinced that because of the large number of gullies, it would be impossible to carry out the original plans. Engineer Nahum Paper claimed that the company had misrepresented the extent of its holdings. The map of Rom Hacarmel included parts of Achuzat Herbert Samuel and Abu Dib, neither of which belonged to the company. Precisely because of its difficult topography, Rom Hacarmel had been rejected by the PLDC. All in all, the land was inappropriate for the proposed development. A 30 percent building allowance was deemed more fitting; the agency's plans— designed as if for a flat terrain—were grossly unsuited to the topographic reality.[94] Moreover, the America-Palestine Agency was entangled in a legal dispute over the tract's northern boundary. In the end, this area was not developed during British rule.

The Menorah Palestine Building Corporation offered Americans the opportunity to purchase building plots in its development of Hod Hacarmel A, adjacent to Rom Hacarmel. Its circular suggested to purchasers: "Take a direct part in the upbuilding of Palestine. Become an owner in one of the most beautiful parts of the Carmel in Haifa. Every Jew should possess a home in the Jewish Homeland. It is a praiseworthy step towards its upbuilding. A safe and profitable investment for you." The company conducted its affairs through a New York office. Two-dunam plots were offered in an area that also included space set aside for public buildings and parks. Roads, water, and sewage were to be provided at the company's expense. No information has been found regarding prices, although the period of payment was specified as one year. The Menorah Corporation's advertising campaign succeeded in attracting some American purchasers, including Louis Abrahamson of St. Paul, Minnesota, for example, but details have not been uncovered as to the extent of sales in America. This area was also undeveloped during the British Mandate.[95]

The Jerusalem-American Land Company also focused its activities in Haifa. Abraham Aaron Spector, a prominent Haifa resident, was involved in the process. In miscellaneous documents, references to a few tracts have been found. As of the end of 1928, the company had three unsold tracts in Haifa: the 13,409-square-meter Keller parcel and the 13,256-square-meter Rehald tract, both near the government building; and the 1,588-square-meter Suliman-Bey Nassif parcel on the Carmel. With the liquidation of this company, two other tracts near Kiryat Eliyahu (Ard El Hayeh) were sold. The first was subdivided into thirty-three parcels varying in size from 19 to 1,500 square meters, totaling 15,222. The second tract measured 12,772 square meters.[96]

Real estate investment was not limited to residential neighborhoods. A local consortium of Jewish businessmen, with Shmuel Pevsner as its president, acquired land from the Palestine Land Development Company to build a commercial center, which the consortium felt would be instrumental in furthering the development of downtown Haifa. This three-story structure was to include shops, flats (later to be converted to offices), banks, a cinema, a hotel, and two restaurants. Arthur Ruppin and Max Shoolman of Boston negotiated the funding for this commercial center, and in 1925 Shoolman's son arrived in Haifa to supervise the project.[97] An article in *Palestine Correspondence* explained Shoolman's involvement.

> Max Shoolman of Boston did not stage a full-dress debate on the question of investments versus money provided for Jewish Reconstruction in Palestine, a fond perdu. A hard-headed business man, accustomed to doing things on a large scale, Mr. Shoolman was attracted to Palestine via his work as Chairman of the Keren Hayesod in Boston. He had come, he said, to look things over and concluded his visit by advancing to the Jewish businessmen of Haifa, the town that is beginning to throb with new life and hope, about $200,000 for a period of about 15 years. The one to interest Mr. Shoolman in Haifa and its possibilities was Mr. Isaac Harris, a prominent Boston Zionist, who has come to Palestine for a year and Mr. Harris became interested in Haifa because his three children are going to school there. Both Mr. Harris and Mr. Shoolman, having become interested in Haifa are now Haifa boosters. They are contemplating the building of a school-house and theater [and] have purchased some land on Mt. Carmel and are proud of everything in Haifa.[98]

In 1933 a syndicate was organized to buy the properties of the Count Selim Jedid of Alexandria. In 1925 the count had purchased large tracts in northern Palestine. He died in 1927, and his estate remained unsettled until September 1933, when, through a decision by the Privy Council in London, it became possible for his heirs to dispose of the larger part of these lands. The syndicate was headed by Bernard Rosenblatt and Joseph Loewy, and relied on information from Dr. Abraham Weinshall, the lawyer handling the estate. Loewy was a Rumanian-born Jew, educated and trained in Germany. He pioneered the development of Haifa Bay lands and was among the founders of Nahariya and Yaarot Hacarmel. The count's lands included a tract stretching from Hadar Hacarmel to the Central Carmel, a large stretch of land near the port of Haifa, and large areas in and around the old town of Tiberias.[99]

All in all, Haifa was a most attractive place for American investment in urban properties in Palestine. However, as noted above, the city was home to only a small number of Americans—272 in 1938. Among their ranks were a number of professionals who found homes and employment opportunities in this rapidly developing port city. In 1922, five American professionals (two doctors, two engineers, and one nurse) resided in Haifa. A few examples will illustrate the achievements of American professionals in Haifa. Aaron Joseph Agranat, an American dental surgeon, practiced in Haifa and was elected president of the Palestine Association of Dentists. Perz Willard Etkes was a prominent engineer who arrived in Palestine in 1920. His previous experience included work at General Electric Company workshops at Harrison, New Jersey, and the Public Service Commission of the State of New York. In Palestine he started as clerk of works in the Public Works Department and was promoted to senior execution engineer in 1929. During his career, his achievements included the building of 500 kilometers of main roads and most of the important bridges in Palestine. He was also involved in the maintenance of Haifa harbor from 1933 to 1943. Eliyahu Einzelbauch, a leader of the American Mizrachi, immigrated in 1931 and served as a rabbi at Eliyahu Hanavi synagogue in Haifa.[100]

American Jewish settlement and investment were underrepresented in Haifa. The city had a positive image as an aesthetically attractive city offering economic opportunity. Further, Haifa symbolized the modernization of Palestine. Yet it appears that these factors were not sufficient to rival the attractiveness of Tel Aviv or Jerusalem, the two cities where American Jews were overrepresented.

Hebron

Toward the end of World War I, the Jewish community of Hebron numbered some 700, declining to 430 in 1922. American Jews attempted to reinforce the Jewish presence in this holy city, and in 1924, with the financial assistance of a group of New York Jews, Knesset Israel Yeshiva of Slobodka was relocated in Hebron. This signified the return of one of the centers of religious study to Palestine and the revitalization of the holy city of Hebron. Students from Lithuania, Poland, and even the United States attended the yeshiva there, and some of them settled permanently in Hebron. In 1929, thirty-six of 194 yeshiva students were Americans.[101] Rabbi Leo Gottesman, an American himself, explained the attraction to Hebron.

> It would have been unnatural, therefore, if our practical efforts to reclaim Palestine as [a] national homeland had not included an earnest endeavor by the contemporary leaders of Jewish Torah-culture to rehabilitate the land in its deeper sense as Palestine. . . . One of the noteworthy undertakings of this character has been the transfer of part of the Yeshivah of Slobodka to Hebron. Long famous as a seat of the highest Torah-culture, this Yeshivah had been a center to which many of the most promising young scholars of Eastern Europe flocked to imbibe Torah at the feet of revered teachers. One perceives, however, the importance of Palestine to modern Jewry from the

fact that no sooner did the Slabodka Yeshivah become the Hebron Yeshivah than it took on a broad national character and began to attract young men even from America—devoted students of Torah even from the land which, it had once seemed, could produce only pessimists and skeptics on the subject of traditional Judaism.[102]

The transition to Hebron was trying for Americans; the standard of living there was low, for the infrastructure had not developed as in other cities and the local Arab population was hostile. Gottesman continued,

> I had found a good deal of difficulty in locating permanent quarters in Hebron that would suit my tastes and standards. Many of the young men who came to study in the yeshivah were easily accommodated in the not very comfortable homes of some of the Hebron Baale Batim [homeowners]. Where they came from they had not been accustomed to better living conditions. In my case, as with a number of other American boys, I was not easily suited; and most of those who owned modern homes were disinclined to take in roomers.[103]

The Brooklyn-based kosher food manufacturer Israel Rokeach attempted to establish a colony for Orthodox Jews (not necessarily Americans) in the vicinity of Hebron. Originally he "intended to give $20,000 to a fund which should give to twenty Jewish artisans $1,000 on a first mortgage" for houses that would be established near a large Jewish colony. Wives and children could assist in supporting the family by cultivating a small plot of land. After a conversation with Rabbi Moses Mordechai Epstein, the head of the Knesset Yisrael Yeshiva in Hebron, Rokeach agreed to the idea of establishing such a settlement near Hebron. These plans coincided with the 1924 relocation of the yeshiva from Slobodka, which had been made possible through contributions from American Jews. Thus the new settlement Rokeach agreed to sponsor would be "in the same form as Tel-Aviv near Jaffa"—a new Jewish town near a predominantly Arab city—and he considered buying a tract and donating some of the land to the yeshiva.[104]

To this purpose Dr. Isaac Levy, manager of the Anglo-Palestine Company, was engaged to buy 100 dunams near Hebron. Levy, an agronomist by training, served as an inspector of agriculture for the Ottoman government and then as the manager of the Jewish Colonization Association colonies in Judaea from 1901 until 1904. He was later employed by the Geula Company to locate lands for purchase, survey them, and negotiate with the Ottoman authorities. In 1904 he began his many years in the employ of the Anglo-Palestine Company. In 1926 he obtained 500 dunams approximately six or seven kilometers from Hebron, but this tract proved unsuitable for Rokeach's purpose, and Levy hoped to recover at least part of the deposit.[105]

It appears that further attempts to establish a settlement near Hebron were aborted in 1929, when the Jewish community in that city suffered a catastrophe during the riots. As conveyed in a telegram from the American consulate in Jerusalem, Americans in Hebron were among the victims: "Moslem attacks on Jews at Hebron Friday and Saturday resulting in 45 Jews killed, 51 seriously wounded, 20 slightly wounded of which Mr. Simon, of the Consulate General recognized a number of wounded and 12 dead all American students Slovodka-Talmudic school."[106] Following these attacks, the entire Jewish population abandoned the city, bringing an end to the American Jewish presence in Hebron during the British Mandate.

SAFED AND TIBERIAS

Because of their status as holy cities, Safed and Tiberias attracted American Jewish residents. The Jewish populations of these cities were mostly affiliated with the Old *Yishuv,* and numbered 2,700 and 3,100 respectively in 1918. During the British Mandate, Safed's Jewish population declined, to 2,000 in 1939, while Tiberias's Jewish population steadily increased, reaching 7,000 in 1939. Information is scanty regarding American residents of these two cities, although it is known that their settlement predated the British Mandate. They too suffered from events connected to the war, and some were exiled. The majority of American inhabitants were members of the Orthodox community; for example, the *mohel* (ritual circumciser), Rabbi Wolf Lauterbach, was originally from New York. As of 1923, twenty-five individuals from America were receiving support from Kollel America in the two cities. By the mid-1920s at least thirty-two families were registered by Kollel America. The American consulate registered three Americans in Safed and two in Tiberias who obtained provisional certificates of Palestinian citizenship. As with Jerusalem, these cities generally attracted an elderly American population who desired to live out their last days in a holy place. Not all the American population was connected to the Old *Yishuv,* however. The Hadassah medical organization operated a hospital in Safed, and among its personnel were some American doctors and nurses.[107]

Americans invested in land on the outskirts of Tiberias. Beginning in 1927, Bernard Rosenblatt organized the purchase of the Tiberias Hot Springs concession. He was the largest stockholder in the company that was formed to develop the spa, which tapped into subterranean thermal springs. Rosenblatt organized a holding company with an authorized share capital of £P55,000 in 1929. He found investors in Palestine and South Africa but not in America, because of the economic crisis there. In the mid-1930s, Africa Palestine Investments assumed a large financial stake in the company. Unfortunately, the enterprise did not produce the profits anticipated in the company's prospectus, for the spa failed to attract a large number of visitors.[108]

CHAPTER 10

Fig. 35. Panorama of Afula, 1926.
(CZA Keren Hayesod photograph collection)

AFULA AND THE AMERICAN ZION COMMONWEALTH

As previously discussed, the Afula purchase consisted of two sections, 5,000 dunams to be developed into an urban center and an agricultural area of 11,000 dunams. Afula was to become an industrial and shopping center for the Plain of Esdrelon.[109] It was assumed that Afula's development was guaranteed to accelerate due to its prime location on transportation routes, both rail and highway, within Palestine and internationally.

The Valley City (Afula) was designed by Richard Kaufmann as a focal point for the Jezreel Valley. Situated at the crossroads of the north-south axis from Jenin to Nazareth and the east-west axis from Haifa to Damascus, it possessed the advantage of superior location. It was also in the heart of a growing hinterland of Jewish agricultural settlements. Kaufmann envisioned the development of the city through the introduction of industry: canning factories would process fruits and vegetables from the surrounding agricultural settlements, and there would be tobacco, sugar, and textile industries as well. Furthermore, Afula was intended to serve as a center for the repair and improvement of farm machinery and implements, and possibly their manufacture. Afula could also function as the site of hospitals, asylums, and other medical and veterinary services. Kaufmann wanted to create a city that would develop organically.

A city organism must be compared to a human or to an animal organism, an organism whose life center is fed by means of a certain system, which divides into certain sections of the organism which streams out and together which concern [*sic*] in the building of the system and upon this foundation, the whole mass becomes a living organism. So is the system of this place to be compared which from the heart of the organism streaming from larger canals leads into the finest arteries [and] carries the living elements of the district into the structure of the organism of this place. Also to be compared is the inhalation system of the city with the lung and respiratory system in order that the organism of the city may be completely supplied with fresh air.[110]

With the railroad station at its heart, Afula was divided into distinct sections—commercial, heavy industry, light industry, workmen's neighborhoods, and garden neighborhoods—spreading out in a radial pattern. This design would segregate different land uses in different areas and insure sufficient space for future expansion.

Raising funds for this project was a drawn-out affair. In 1925 the American Zion Commonwealth had entered into negotiations with Sir Elly (Eliezer Silas) Kadoorie, a millionaire philanthropist who was the president of the Keren Hayesod in Shanghai. Kadoorie was asked to organize a group of Far Eastern Jews who would provide financial support for a new garden and industrial city, which would be named "Kadooria" in his honor. At the outset, the intent was to develop 3,000 dunams in the radial section on the road to Haifa, which could later be enlarged and grow toward the port city. The AMZIC agreed to provide the land without receiving any compensation; money for settlement would be collected through a special fund of the Keren Hayesod. Dr. Ariel Bension, a local Sephardi leader and Keren Hayesod emissary to the eastern Jewish communities, was to serve as the managing director of the project in Palestine. But less than half-a-year after the agreement was signed, the AMZIC appeared to have doubts whether Kadoorie would fulfill his commitment to raise a minimum of £E15,000 per annum over five years. The AMZIC later offered him an opportunity to select an alternate location for the project either in the vicinity of Tel Aviv or Haifa Bay. However, nothing came of this project.[111]

The first stage of Afula's development was the razing of the Arab village to allow for the development of the modern Jewish city. The land was transferred in October 1924, then it was surveyed and the town plan laid out. In November of that year, when sixty Jews went out in a wagon convoy to plough the land, hostilities erupted. Some fifty Arabs attacked the convoy, and a skirmish ensued, leaving one Arab dead and a number of persons wounded on both sides.

Despite this setback, the American Zion Commonwealth began to develop Afula's infrastructure. A well was bored, and when water was found at 90 meters, the boring continued to 110 meters. Engineers erroneously presumed that they had tapped an underground river originating at Mount Hermon, and thus early reports claimed sufficient water for 15,000 inhabitants. Streets and roads were laid out. The position of Afula was augmented when it became a township on 1 May 1925, under section 2 of the Town Planning Ordinance of 1921. The township comprised land in a radius of 1.5 kilometers from the railroad station, together with all lands within a 2.5 kilometer radius to the south and southwest of the same point. On 1 July 1925, the founding of Afula was celebrated, and several notables of the *Yishuv* were in attendance.[112]

To enhance the new city's status and accelerate its expansion, the American Zion Commonwealth negotiated with Pinhas Rutenberg to erect an electrical substation at Afula. The AMZIC offered the government of Palestine four dunams near the railway station for a police station with stables. The government agreed and constructed the station, which served the entire Jezreel Valley. In addition, a postal, telegraphic, and telephone office was built. In 1926 government authorities decided to establish a regional hospital for the Jezreel Valley. The AMZIC lobbied various organizations in Palestine and the United States in an attempt to have Afula chosen as the site. Kupat Holim, the main financier behind the project, preferred other sites in the vicinity, near Kfar Hayeladim or at Kfar Yehezkel, and the latter location was chosen. This decision dealt a serious blow to the new urban center by removing a potentially major employer and an important service from the city. However, another event proved more auspicious. On 16 April 1926, Rabbi Dov Kook, brother of the chief rabbi of Palestine, was inducted into office as the rabbi of the town's new synagogue. This eminent scholar's presence enhanced the settlement's status, particularly for the religious population.[113]

By June 1926 a number of stores and small industries were established in Afula that engaged in transactions with farmers in some of the surrounding villages. Yet Afula did not develop at the rate expected nor to the dimensions envisioned. In 1931 its population reached 874, and grew to only 1,354 by 1936. In 1941 the population stood at 1,650.[114]

There were a number of reasons for the city's stagnation. Some contemporary observers saw its lack of growth as an expression of the general economic crisis of the period. Zionist settlement policy was also blamed for showing preferential treatment to rural settlement over urban.[115] Later observers pointed out that the American campaign had begun to falter: "Due to the fact that Afula is at present entirely discredited and therefore, unpopular with the public, the sales in the colony are extremely disappointing." Sales were poor, and requests were received for the cancellation of contracts and return of money paid in. Shimon Levine of Herzlia learned from Afula's experience. "I saw to it that we'd (in Herzlia) have none of the sort of goings-on that I saw in Afula," he asserted, "where they sold corner plots opposite the site designated for the opera house for $995."[116]

It appears that Afula's development was hindered by the attitudes of the socialist organizations in Palestine as well. Afula represented a capitalist venture in contrast to the kibbutzim and moshavim in the surrounding areas. The city offered religious services, adding to the ideological contrast between urban and rural settlement.[117] Furthermore, many of the outlying settlements had developed closed economies, and thus they were less in need of the services offered by the new town. When outside services were needed, rural settlers often turned to Haifa instead.

AMERICAN GARDEN VILLAGES

During the British Mandate, a series of garden suburbs or garden villages was planned in areas around cities throughout Palestine. The idea was clearly drawn from the work of British town planner Ebenezer Howard. In *Garden Cities of To-Morrow,* Howard reintroduced a concept of city planning drawn from the ancient Greek tradition that recognized a natural limit to the growth of an organism or organization. His scheme represented a reaction to the uncontrolled organic expansion of cities, with attendant congestion, slums,

CHAPTER 10

Fig. 36. Aerial view of Afula, 1937.
(CZA Keren Hayesod photograph collection)

and pollution. Howard was of the opinion that from the beginning a city must be limited in size, density, and number of inhabitants. It should have all the essential urban functions—namely, business, industry, administration, and education as well as parks and private gardens—to insure a pleasant and healthy environment. An important aspect of this planning was that the new urban unit would be encompassed by a permanent agricultural greenbelt. This would guarantee close proximity of the rural surroundings and inhibit urban sprawl. Howard figured that a garden city would ideally have a population of 32,000, with 2,000 in the neighboring agricultural zone.[118]

In the Palestinian setting the garden city took on the form of a garden suburb. The Ahuzat Beit project, the area of Jaffa that developed into the city of Tel Aviv, has been referred to as the first garden city in Palestine. In essence, this 1909 pioneer project created a relatively spacious residential area, with formal by-laws that controlled density and land use and promoted a green setting. Building was permitted on only 30 percent of the land. Furthermore, a building setback of at least three meters from the road was required, and this was reserved for gardens. However, the by-laws did

316

not integrate the wide range of urban activities that Ebenezer Howard had foreseen in his conceptualization. For example, no provision was made for commercial activities.[119]

Following World War I, the garden city concept found greater acceptance and expression in Palestine as new neighborhoods were developed with the intention of providing a pleasant environment for residents. The principal stipulations of the garden suburb plan were low densities and large green areas in the form of public parks, boulevards, private gardens, and even green gardens for raising fruits and vegetables that would supplement the income of the inhabitants. Richard Kaufmann, who was well-acquainted with Ebenezer Howard's ideas and those of the garden city movement in England, integrated many of these ideas into the garden suburbs that he designed for Jerusalem.[120] Although Americans were not actively engaged in developing these garden suburbs, many of them chose to live in such neighborhoods because of their attractiveness.

Another form of the garden city, the garden village, was also developed in Palestine. It differed from the garden suburb in that it was located at a greater distance from the city and had a higher level of agricultural activity. This hybrid between the village and the garden suburb found a welcome market among American buyers and immigrants. It allowed residents to live in a rural setting yet have many urban amenities and services. Furthermore, the garden suburb offered inhabitants the opportunity to engage in agriculture to varying degrees, from full-time farming to working in the city and living in a house with a large garden.

The principles behind the development of the garden village are outlined in a document found in the American Zion Commonwealth archives; this document lists ten points important in the proper development of garden villages. Although it is unclear who drew up this proposal, the ideas provide a framework for studying three American-initiated garden villages. The suggested location was 9 to 10.6 kilometers from a large town with a strong economy. Travel time to the town by bus should not exceed twenty to thirty minutes. The site should have an ample supply of water and not suffer from malarial infection. Before settlement, a proper infrastructure of roads, water supply, and sewage system must be completed. The document distinguishes four categories of settlers: (1) those who are exclusively dependent on agriculture; (2) those mainly dependent on agriculture but possessing other sources of income; (3) those mainly dependent on nonagricultural income but supplementing that through agricultural work; and (4) those who earn their income in urban occupations but who seek better and healthier living conditions. The land to be allocated to each type of settler was: (1) 25 dunams, of which five to ten must be irrigated; (2) 10 dunams, of which two to three must be irrigated; (3) 5 dunams, of which one to two should be irrigated; and (4) 1.5 to 2 dunams. In cases where all the land had inferior agricultural potential, provisions should be made for larger allotments. The proposal included total capital expenditure for each type of settler, taking into account the amount and type of land ($50 per dunam for agricultural and $125 for building plots), first improvements (roads, water supply, drainage, and so on), building, and inventory. Estimates for these capital expenses and improvements were $5,000, $3,500, $2,675, and $1,950 respectively.[121]

The settlement of Migdal, originally established as an estate in 1910, was developed into a garden village in the 1920s. It had been founded through the investment of Moscow Jews, including Professor Otto Warburg, and covered about 5,000 dunams. During its first years, this strip along the shores of the Sea of Galilee, six kilometers north of Tiberias, was transformed from a barren and distant estate to one planted with fruit trees and irrigated for vegetable cultivation. From the beginning, Moshe Glikin managed the estate, training and employing Jewish men and women. Even though Migdal marketed some of its produce, it was burdened with heavy debts, like the *ahuzot* of Poria and Sarona. Moreover, regular infusions of capital from Russia ceased with the outbreak of World War I.[122]

By 1922 Migdal's liabilities totaled £E100,000 ($500,000); 90 percent of this was owed to the Anglo-Palestine Company and the remainder to the Palestine government. Many of the original Moscow investors had either died or were financially ruined, so Warburg and the shareholders put forward a proposal to develop the estate. Glikin approached Robert Szold, president of the Palestine Cooperative Company, with the request for a loan of $60,000 to help underwrite the proposal. Under the shareholders' scheme, Migdal would be transformed into a settlement for over 100 families. It would consist of two parts. The first, along the coastline, would be divided into thirty-five to forty residential lots of 10-dunams each that would be sold to private individuals for villas and orchards. The second section was planned for intensive farming; 100 lots of varying size, from 10 to 12 dunams, would be developed there. These plots would be sold in installments. The plan also called for the construction of houses and other buildings, the purchase of equipment, the improvement of irrigation and sewage systems, and provision of communal services.[123]

Unable to persuade the Palestine Cooperative Company to invest in the scheme, Glikin sold 500–1,000 dunams to the newly established Migdal Corporation, which purchased the land from Glikin at £E10 ($50) per dunam for resale at £E40–50 ($200–250) per dunam in America. In its prospectus, the Migdal Corporation pledged certain improvements, such as streets, boulevards, and planted trees. Salesmen were engaged and received, to Glikin's dismay, an unheard of 15 percent commission. The American Zion Commonwealth bitterly criticized the Migdal Corporation, emphasizing that it was not a public organization, it was not recognized by the Zionist Organization of America, and made no pretense that it was in the land business for the public welfare. However, the Migdal Corporation frankly admitted that it had entered into real estate in Palestine for private gain. Indeed, the Migdal enterprise was netting its investors a considerable profit.[124]

In 1924 Glikin entered negotiations with a number of New York investors to develop a garden village on another section of the estate. Migdal Garden Villa, Inc., was established for this purpose. Small plots and a more densely developed area were planned, to yield higher profits. During Glikin's 1925 visit to the United States, the American Migdal Hotel Co., Inc., a New York corporation, was established for the purpose of erecting a hotel at Migdal. The sale of shares to Americans would infuse further capital into the area.[125]

In 1925 Bernard Rosenblatt reported that there were only "12 houses being built, with one or two American families there."[126] This illustrates the failure of the various Migdal companies to develop the area as promised. By 1932 eight Americans, including Rabbi Abba Hillel Silver, had purchased plots varying in size from 5–20 dunams in the agricultural area (altogether 80 dunams). In the garden village, 205 Americans had purchased 1–3-dunam plots (altogether 281 dunams). In addition, Americans invested thousands of dollars in the hotel scheme. Since nothing had come of any of these projects, the Jewish National Fund organized an appeal to the owners in 1932 to donate their idle land so that the JNF could amass a sufficient tract for a viable settlement there.[127]

Another group of American investors formed the Nachalat Zion Company to promote the sale of small plots in garden cities in the Galilee. This Boston company's president, Mr. [?] Shankman, met with American Zion Commonwealth representatives and detailed his company's activities. It owned three tracts in Har Canaan, Ein Zeitim, and Kfar Ivri, which the company was in the process of selling to Americans. The first, Har Canaan, was located near Safed. (The history of this area includes many attempts to establish garden cities. For example, the Jewish Colonization Association had purchased 14,500 dunams in the area before World War I, then in turn sold sections of this tract to various organizations.) The Nachalat Zion Company came into possession of 1,000 dunams, for which it paid £E1 ($4.50) per dunam. The land was subdivided into 2,000 lots of 225 square meters, and lots were sold for $20 each. The remaining land, half the area, was set aside for streets. Nachalat Zion gave no details regarding other land use or public buildings. By 1922 the company had sold 250 lots, and its profit per dunam was $40.50.[128]

This company also owned 500 dunams at Ein Zeitim near Safed. This had been the site of Jewish agricultural settlement from as early as the eleventh century through to the mid-nineteenth century, and in 1891 an association of Russian Jews attempted to revive the village. The lands were entrusted to the Jewish Colonization Association, which brought in

CHAPTER 10

Map 15. Migdal garden city and estate plans, ca. 1925

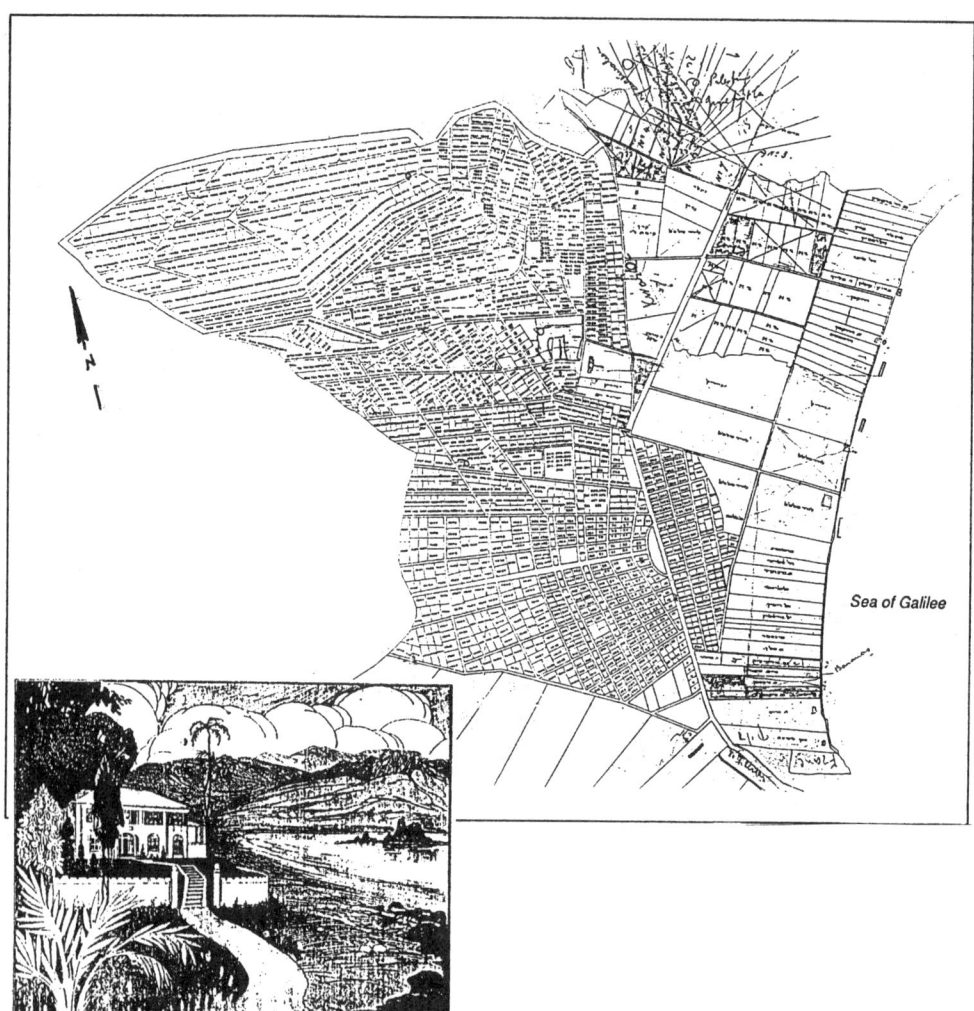

additional colonists. The few who remained at Ein Zeitim in 1914 were forced to leave the colony during the war. It appears that the Nachalat Zion Company purchased a section of the colony from the JCA after the war. It planned to sell 450 dunams in 10-dunam plots at $60 per dunam, though there is no indication of whether the land would be used for agriculture. Fifty dunams were set aside for an orphanage and farm, funded through profits from lots sold at Har Canaan at $12.50 per lot. Ein Zeitim was not redeveloped until 1925, when former settlers and young settlers from Safed reestablished a community. Their attempt was short-lived; it came to an end following attacks during the 1929 Arab riots.[129]

The third section offered by the Nachalat Zion Company was 150 dunams at Kfar Ivri. The company advertised 5-dunam lots for $160 each—a price that appears to be incorrect, since it is only half the price of most 5-dunam lots offered in Palestine around that time. The campaign seems to have been quite successful. Twenty-five lots were bought by Americans, though it is unclear whether Nachalat Zion was the intermediary in this process.

The American Zion Commonwealth continued to be skeptical of Nachalat Zion's real intentions. Solomon J. Weinstein asserted that "the company really had no right to sell the land . . . it is not worth the price that the purchaser pays for it." The AMZIC was asked "Whether the Nachalat Zion was a meritorious enterprise for the upbuilding of Palestine" and whether the company was fair in dealing with its purchasers. Was Nachalat Zion harming Zionist endeavors in America? In response, the company president, Mr. Shankman, stated, "they do not sell to Zionists, but to any Jews who are interested in buying land in Palestine." He added, "he is entitled to make profits from Zionism as well as from any other source," claiming that "Zionism owes him a living as well as America, because he has always been a strong Zionist and he is entitled to benefit therefrom."[130] Nevertheless, Nachalat Zion did not develop its projects at either Har Canaan or Ein Zeitim.

Other Americans made plans to establish another garden city west of Jerusalem. Isaac Feller—an Eastern European immigrant to the United States, an ardent Zionist, and honorary secretary of the Mizrachi of Greater New York—twice visited Palestine before his eventual settlement in 1931. During his first stay in 1925, he bought 131 dunams, and during his second journey, in 1928, he purchased two more tracts of 405 and 374 dunams.[131] Feller wanted to establish a residential area for Orthodox American Jews, though subsequently members of the local Orthodox population were also regarded as potential clients. This private enterprise received the support of the Mizrachi organization and the chief rabbinate of Jerusalem.

Feller published a brochure offering purchasers a dunam of land in the Holy Land. The pamphlet emphasized its location just "15 minutes ride from Jerusalem." The climate was described as "dry, and the air is sweet and healthy," and the water coming from "sweet, good water wells." The land was depicted as "good for planting grapes, almonds and olives"—although the tracts offered consisted of only one dunam. Feller's advertisement played on almost every emotion.

> If you want the Holy Land to be in the hands of the Jewish people. . . . If you want to invest your money in secure investment and reap a profitable

business. . . . If you want the Holy Land redeemed. . . . If you want a spot where you can make a comfortable livelihood. . . . If you want your name inscribed in Jewish History, as one who helped build the Holy Land. . . . If you want to inspire your children with true Jewish existence. . . . If you want to increase Jewish strength, Jewish might, and the existence of Judaism. . . . If you want to strengthen the spirit of Judaism—Buy a dunam land in Nachlas Itzchak, near Jerusalem.[132]

The tract, south of the Jerusalem-Jaffa road, was parceled into approximately 360 one-dunam plots, with land allocated for roads and a public garden. A dunam plot was insufficient to support a family who intended to make their living from agriculture. Moreover, unlike the property described in the brochure, the land was either rocky and uncultivable or rocky with 20 percent patch cultivation. Information has not been found regarding sales of Nahalat Itzhak in America, although there is evidence that some plots were sold to residents of Jerusalem. Development of the project came to a halt after Isaac Feller's sudden death in 1934. Two years later, Nahalat Itzhak had a population of 30, and the area included 1,050 dunams, with 115 planted with fruit trees and 415 under field crop cultivation.[133] Feller's garden city was never established, although some of the land was exploited for agriculture.

Another project of note was the Mizrach Hatzair of Palestine's settlement Kfar Ivri (Neve Yaakov). In 1918 a group of Orthodox Jerusalemites, imbued with the idea of "the Land of Israel for the Jewish people according to the Torah of Israel," initiated the development of agricultural settlements in order to improve the spiritual and material condition of the religious youth of Eretz Israel. Local rabbi Itzhak Avigdor Orenstein served as the organization's secretary. In 1921 the organization established the "Kfar Ivri" (Hebrew Village) cooperative society, whose stated purpose was "to establish garden villages in the vicinity of the city for the benefit of its members."[134]

Following its registration in February 1922, the society contracted the purchase of 650 dunams to the north of Jerusalem. With the receipt of the *kushans* in 1924 its members commenced settlement activity. The settlement was named Neve Yaakov in memory of Rabbi Itzhak Yaakov Reines, the founder of the Mizrachi movement. According to the original plans, each settler was to purchase a five-dunam plot; this would allow a settler to construct a house, plant various fruit trees, grow vegetables, and build a chicken coop and barn for dairy cows. Income from agriculture would supplement his other earnings. The society viewed the garden city as a transitional phase from an unhealthy urban life to a healthy one entirely devoted to agricultural activity. Society by-laws required all members and their families to farm their land; it was hoped that what began as an obligation would in the end become a labor of love. There was also a nationalist undertone to the society's plan: to provide Jewish produce to the Jewish inhabitants of Jerusalem. Members recalled the shortages that followed the 1921 Arab riots, when Arab women from villages around Jerusalem would not sell their agricultural produce in Jewish neighborhoods.[135]

Two considerations were factored into Kfar Ivri's locational decisions. The society favored a tract that would be within an hour's walk of Jerusalem and preferably along an established road, and, if possible, near a spring. The second prerequisite reflected the need for a secure source of water. With these considerations in mind, two society representatives, Rabbi Orenstein and Dov Natan Brickner, investigated tracts within a ten-kilometer radius of Jerusalem. In the end they selected a tract eight kilometers to the north of Jerusalem in the village of Beit Hanina, even though it did not have a source of fresh water. The society decided that since there was a limited number of springs around Jerusalem, the ideal solution would be to repair existing cisterns and construct large covered pools to store rainwater.[136]

Richard Kaufmann designed the Kfar Ivri settlement, parceling the land into 200 lots of two-and-a-half dunams—half the area originally envisioned by the society. The houses were to be erected close to the road, with barns, coops, and storage buildings behind the houses. The remaining area would be planted with vegetables and fruit trees. The price paid for each plot was £E30 ($150).[137] Land at Kfar Ivri was marketed in the United States by the American Mizrachi organization. Purchasers included 140 individuals and five societies, among them twenty-five Americans and three American groups. None of the American purchasers settled on the land.[138] However, one American family—the Zeligs from Philadelphia—resided in Kfar Ivri from 1934 to 1939. The Zeligs immigrated to Palestine at the insistence of the mother, Haya Sarah, a devout Orthodox woman who feared that if her children remained in America, they would stray from Orthodox practice and assimilate. Kfar Ivri provided a suitable religious environment for the Zeligs.[139]

During the early stages of the settlement's development, organizers were unable to draw financial support from the World Mizrachi organization and Zionist institutions. The latter opposed agricultural settlement in the Judaean mountains, viewing this region as impractical for viable Jewish colonization. Financial assistance was obtained instead through two loans. The first was from Baruch H. Snor, the treasurer of the American Mizrachi Organization from 1915 to 1918; he provided £E200 ($1,000) for each of the first ten houses. The Brandeis group loaned the society £P250 ($1,250) for up to thirteen more houses.[140]

After reviewing American attempts to build garden villages, it seems clear that their prospects for success were dubious. Migdal and Nachalat

Map 16. Nahalat Itzhak, 1933

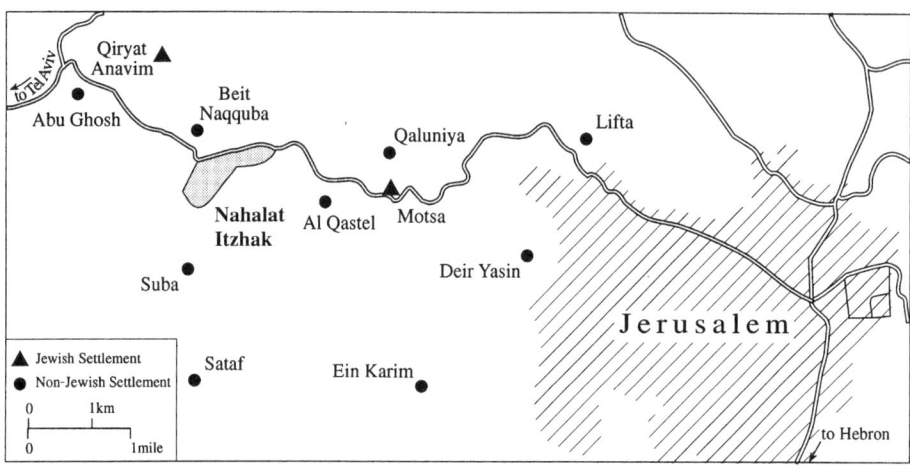

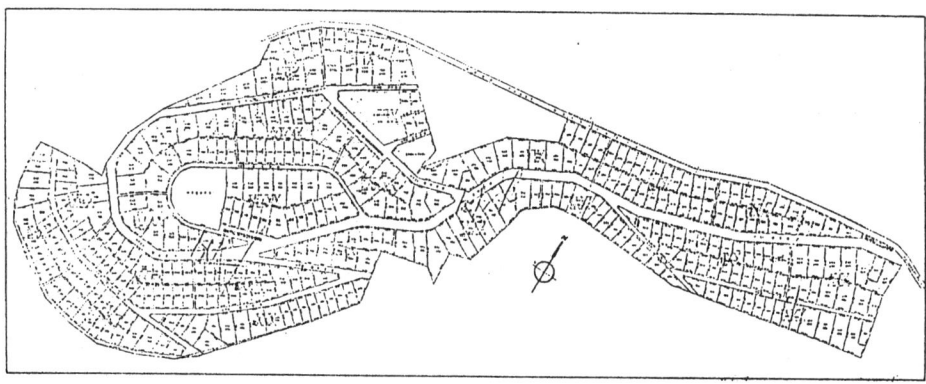

Zion, for example, were near cities that were too small to provide a strong economic basis for the employment of village residents. Nahalat Itzhak, although close enough to a prosperous urban center, competed with the proliferation of garden suburbs in Jerusalem. In addition, lands were sold in each of these three villages before their infrastructure was developed. Almost no account was taken in the plans for different types of settlers in garden villages. Finally, these projects were usually directed toward Americans, the majority of whom had no intention of settling in Palestine. With no critical mass of population to launch these garden cities, they remained mired in the planning stages.

Summary of Urban Development

Most American immigrants to Palestine were attracted to urban areas because these were familiar and suitable to their lifestyle. The majority of American immigrants chose to live in Jerusalem and Tel Aviv-Jaffa. Each of these cities had its special attractions. Jerusalem was for some the Holy City, while for others it was the capital city, with a variety of institutions. Tel Aviv was viewed as the new city of the Zionist enterprise, a cultural center and a city of commerce and industry.

Fewer immigrants settled in Haifa and Afula. Nonetheless, these two urban centers attracted American investors who considered the possibility of moving to Palestine in the future. Indeed, the largest number of urban tracts sold through land agents abroad were in Haifa and Afula. Haifa was seen as the city of the future: nestled on beautiful Mount Carmel overlooking the new harbor yet also a center of industry. It was thought that Afula, a new city, would play an important role in the development of the Jezreel Valley. Moreover, it had been carefully designed, following the most modern theories of urban planning. It was considered ripe for investment but not for immediate settlement.

It is important to distinguish between urban sites where immigrants thought they could live comfortably and earn a livelihood, and those in which purchasers thought the best investment was to be made. In general, Jerusalem and Tel Aviv-Jaffa were considered places for residence; by contrast, Haifa and Afula were places for investment.

Conclusion

The migrational movement of American Jews to Palestine between the two World Wars was unique. Most Americans who re-emigrated during this period returned to their country of origin.[1] From 1915 to 1937, total Jewish emigration from the United States was negligible—an estimated 8,949—resulting in a re-emigration rate of 2.2 per hundred.[2] Yet during this same period, American Jewish immigration to Palestine was 6,353, according to Jewish Agency figures, or 8,231, according to government of Palestine figures.[3] It appears that the majority of Jews who left the United States were destined for Palestine, rather than—as was the case with other American émigrés—for their country of origin.

American Jewish immigration to Palestine was "free migration" not "forced migration." During the period covered by this study, the vast majority of Jewish immigrants to Palestine came from Eastern Europe and Central Europe; war, economic hardship, persecution, and other adversities led to their departure. By contrast, those who freely migrated to Palestine came from various regions: the Americas (Canada, Argentina, Brazil, and Mexico), Western Europe (Great Britain, Denmark, Belgium, Finland, France, Sweden, Switzerland, Finland, the Netherlands), South Africa, and Australia—as well as Middle Eastern and Mediterranean basin countries.

The phenomenon of free migration can be explained in terms of the five basic questions connected to any migrational movement. Why did migration occur? Who migrated? What was the rate of migration and its direction? What was its effect on the country of origin? What was its effect on the country of destination? To further understand American Jewish migration, it

TABLE 25
American Jewish emigration versus American Jewish immigration to Palestine, 1915–37

	Emigration rates from the U.S.		Jewish immigration to the U.S.	Jewish emigration from the U.S.	Immigration to Palestine	
Year	General	Jewish			Jewish Agency	Government of Palestine
1915–20	56.6	4.3	78,966	3,396	163	—
1921–24	25.8	0.7	222,831	1,560	600	617
1925–37	40.0	3.8	105,000	3,993	5,590	7,614
1915–37		2.20	406,797	8,949	6,353	8,231

Source: C. Bezalel Sherman, "Immigration and Emigration: The Jewish Case," in *The Jew in American Society*, ed. Marshall Sklare (New your: Behrman House, 1974), 55.

will be compared to migration movements in other Diaspora communities, particularly in Canada and South Africa.

WHY DID MIGRATION OCCUR?

American Jewish migration to Palestine was numerically insignificant within the contexts of American society in general and American Jewry in particular. The low number of émigrés reflects both the national and Jewish social and economic frameworks. Furthermore, it illuminates the nature of "free ideological migration."

In the late nineteenth and early twentieth centuries, America was the destination for most immigrants. It was the "Golden Land" or the "Land of Promise," offering countless opportunities for prosperity. Particularly for Europeans, America was a magnet. Yet some discovered that America was not the right place for them, and not all who took their chances there succeeded. Some émigrés returned to their homelands no better off than when they had left. Even among those who became prosperous or accustomed to American life, there were some who returned to their homelands. Most Jews who thought about returning to Eastern Europe realized this was not a viable option due to the hardship and oppression there. Palestine, the new Jewish homeland undergoing development, offered a more hospitable, more Jewish environment. And in the 1930s, an economic boom made Palestine particularly attractive to many prospective immigrants.

CONCLUSION

For most American Jews who moved to Palestine, migration was an illogical act, not explicable in rational terms. Yet while Zionist ideology in its various forms motivated almost all these immigrants, it was not the only determinant. Immigration to Palestine was often ideological, but it was usually influenced as well by geographic, economic, and sociological factors. Moreover, the importance of political or religious ideology in migration decisions is not unique to the Jewish experience in America. Ideological motifs were significant factors underlying the migrational movements of other groups, too, including African Americans, American communists, and Armenian-Americans.

The Back-to-Africa movement, for example, was an expression of black Zionism—"the ideal held by millions of blacks in America and the Caribbean of returning to the land from which their forefathers were wrenched."[4] As researcher David Jenkins explained:

> Africa . . . was a land of growth and freedom and ancestry and redemption and purity and deliverance, a land of giants, of the darkest and lightest shades of soul, the signal for the end of Diaspora and all suffering. In short, an antithesis of the plantations of the Southern United States and the Caribbean, a place where the spirit could roam free. The imagined Africa became a fountainhead of inspiration and pride of the downtrodden blacks in the Southern cotton areas, and in the exploitative industrial North of America.[5]

Marcus Garvey, a Jamaican journalist, roused African Americans to mass political action and created the Universal Negro Improvement Association. In 1920 he exhorted a gathering of 25,000 in Madison Square Garden: "We shall now organize that 400,000,000 Negroes of the world into a vast organization to plant the banner of freedom on the great continent of Africa." "We do not desire what has belonged to others, Garvey noted, "though others have always sought to deprive us of that which belonged to us. . . . If Europe is for the Europeans, then Africa shall be for the Black peoples of the world."[6] The Garvey movement did not, however, lead to any mass migration to Africa. Millions may have been needed, but only hundreds were ready to go. In fact, the Liberian government refused to allow anyone connected to the Garvey movement to land in its territory; indeed, it voiced irrevocable opposition in principle and in fact to Marcus Garvey's Universal Negro Improvement Association. The Liberian government would have been willing to accept a small number of useful immigrants but not thousands or millions.[7]

Another example of ideologically motivated migration is that of American communists. Although this phenomenon is poorly documented, a number of American communists migrated to the Soviet Union during the 1920s and 1930s for ideological and personal reasons. While American communists wanted to join the ongoing endeavor to build up the Soviet Union, they were also fleeing persecution in the United States. Some individuals had been blacklisted and were unable to find employment because of their involvement in Communist Party or union activities. The Soviet government, in an attempt to further the process of industrialization, recruited American workers who had communist leanings. Socialist Sam Herman of Detroit, for example, agreed to go to Russia: "to work at the Ford's auto plant. To make the machines run and to build a great future for all men." He planned to give three years "to build a great Socialist world," but in the end the Herman family remained in Nizhni-Novgorod (Gorky). American workers were also found in tractor factories at Stalingrad and Kharkov, a coal mine at Kemerova, as well as at hydroelectric stations and airplane factories.[8]

Another ideologically inspired migration movement was that of Armenians. The Armenian dispersion was the direct result of a Turkish policy of genocide and deportation, and displaced Armenians were charged with a longing for their homeland. Albert H. Hourani claimed that "the great majority of Armenians . . . desire ultimately to return to the Caucasus and rebuild their national life there," though he failed to point out that Armenians who had accumulated property or large interests in their new locations were often content to stay there. Personal safety was as important as ideology in this migration movement. Hourani pointed out that Armenians were "not popular" with Lebanese and Syrian Christians "for having [come] into the country destitute and being now prosperous."[9] Repatriation would end the insecure, minority existence of these people and allow them "to live in the shadow of Mount Ararat." The spokesman for the Armenian Repatriation Committee in Jerusalem asserted that "their reason for leaving is not necessarily economic, or that they are unhappy in the countries where the families of some have lived for hundreds of years, but their desire to live as a national group in their own country after centuries of persecution and massacres."[10]

On 12 November 1945, the government of Soviet Armenia resolved to allow the repatriation of Armenians from abroad, and when the policy statement was approved by Moscow, it heralded a new era. This resolution was reminiscent of the biblical declaration of Cyrus, or the Balfour Declaration.[11] Approximately 110,000 Armenians dispersed in ten countries—Iran, Lebanon, Syria, Palestine, Iraq, Egypt, Greece, Bulgaria, France, and the United States—settled in Soviet Armenia in the late 1940s. About 1,000 of the 180,000 Armenian-American population registered for repatriation, but only 153 actually departed for Soviet Armenia. A statement to the press on behalf of the returnees explained why some chose to re-emigrate:

> America gave us refuge when the Armenian people were on the brink of total extermination. . . . The democratic institutions of America afforded us

an opportunity to build life anew. We did our utmost to serve America well. [Their return to Armenia] was impelled by one of the deepest emotions of the human heart—the desire to live and work in the land where for countless generations before us our ancestors have lived, struggled, and brought forth a matchless civilization.[12]

Seen in the context of other re-emigration movements, Zionism—with its notion of personal fulfillment through aliya—was not unique. Behind all these migrations there was not necessarily dissatisfaction with America or American life, nor any strong attraction to another place for its actual qualities. The motivation was rather an ideal—an ideal that without regard for past place or future destination transcended temporal reality. And a common theme prevailed in all these re-emigration movements: appreciation and gratitude for all that America had offered them. American Jews had a variety of reasons for migrating to Palestine. Some did not find religious fulfillment in the new Jewish society that had developed in the United States. Many wanted a more traditional Jewish milieu, such as the ones that existed in their old homelands in Europe or in Palestine.

Who Migrated?

Unlike other Diaspora communities, the United States did not experience the kind of political and economic upheaval that necessitated emigration. The turmoil in Eastern Europe following World War I led to mass Jewish migration there. Between 1918–20, hardship and persecution caused the outflow of hundreds of thousands from Eastern Europe. Although the sense of imminent danger subsided during the 1920s, economic restrictions on Jews and antisemitism were dominant factors in Jewish emigration from Poland, Rumania, Latvia, and Lithuania. With the rise of Hitler to power in Germany in 1933, another Diaspora community was added to the list of countries with an outflow of Jews.

By contrast, American Jews could freely choose to leave the United States. So, who decided to leave? Four distinct groups of American Jewish immigrants to Palestine have been identified in this study: 1) Orthodox Jews, 2) middle-class agriculturalists, 3) *halutzim,* and 4) urban professionals.

Orthodox Jews often failed to find religious fulfillment in the United States. The elderly hoped to live out their last years in the Holy Land, studying Torah until they were interred in its sacred soil. For the younger members of this group, Palestine offered a milieu where they could study Torah in a more traditional environment.

The migration of middle-class agriculturalists resulted from a hybrid of motivations. On the one hand there were religious motifs, including a wish to return to the soil in the Land of Israel. References to earning a living from the land were also not uncommon, nor were various expressions of disappointment with American society and urban life.

American *halutzim* combined two ideologies—Zionism and socialism. Many were young, American-born, and the children of working-class parents. They were mainly secular but in search of a Jewish national identity. They were dissatisfied with capitalist society and criticized its treatment of society's weaker constituents. They were a radical element in a period when society in general was pressing its members to integrate and become part of its "melting pot." For this group, the Great Depression marked a turning point. After 1929, an increasing number of young Jews joined various *halutz* organizations to express their disappointment in capitalism and their sense of hopelessness in the American future. Becoming part of the new socialist society developing in Palestine seemed a viable alternative for these young American Jews.

The urban professionals came from an environment that was similar to the *halutzim*'s. A major difference between the groups is that the urban professionals embraced the ideology of Zionism but rejected socialism. They were also somewhat older, having completed their vocational training; some were married and had young children.

In all, the American Jewish immigrant population was not homogeneous. It consisted of an almost equal number of men and women. There was a wide spectrum of ages, from infants to the elderly. There was also great variation in economic status. Some arrived almost penniless while others brought with them hundreds of thousands of dollars. Levels of education ranged from rudimentary schooling to bachelor's degrees and doctorates. But in almost all cases, the principal motivation for immigrating was adherence to Zionist tenets or the sense of Jewishness.

THE MIGRATION RATE AND ITS DIRECTION

The population movement of Jews between the United States and Palestine was not only in one direction. There was a two-way flow, with a certain percentage of immigrants eventually returning to America. During the period covered by this study, there were approximately 9,000 American Jewish immigrants to Palestine. From 1919 to 1939, the annual average was 450, but the flow varied widely, with no immigrants in 1919 to a maximum of 1,862 in 1935.[13] Above average years for migration include 1925 and the period 1932–35.

The immigration rate of American Jews was similar to that of other Jewish nationals. For example, during this period Jewish immigration from Greece was almost equal to the American total, and it reached a peak in 1933–36. Similarly, above average migration was recorded for German Jews in

TABLE 26
Relative rates of Jewish immigration to Palestine for selected countries, 1919–39

	U.S.	Germany	Poland	U.S.S.R.	Greece	Yemen	Total
Total 1919–39	6,380	37,109	130,392	30,472	6,134	7,523	327,691
Annual Average	304	1,767	6,209	1,451	292	358	15,604
Index of migration (annual average = 100)							
1919	0	0	0	56	0	0	0
1920	54	10	41	152	19	0	64
1921	49	10	29	261	3	0	63
1922	66	2	42	250	6	0	50
1923	29	4	35	203	26	51	48
1924	53	10	91	205	99	113	82
1925	109	15	276	536	88	147	217
1926	61	4	121	132	23	60	84
1927	9	1	13	35	3	17	17
1928	23	0	5	19	2	0	14
1929	26	2	32	27	4	157	34
1930	43	3	38	29	10	104	32
1931	56	2	26	25	10	47	26
1932	162	9	48	8	39	122	61
1933	350	325	207	28	382	335	194
1934	338	396	271	40	515	532	271
1935	527	309	474	31	721	374	396
1936	81	326	208	40	117	198	191
1937	34	151	58	18	24	90	68
1938	20	191	54	4	5	90	82
1939	9	330	30	1	5	51	105

Source: Report by His Majesty's Government in the United Kingdom of Great Britain and Northern Ireland to the Council of the League of Nations on the Administration of Palestine and Trans-Jordan for the Years 1922–1939.

1933–39, for Polish Jewry in 1925–26 and 1933–36, and for Yemenite Jews in 1924–25, 1929–30, and 1932–36. With respect to total Jewish migration to Palestine, above average years were 1925, 1933–36, and 1939. These figures demonstrate the unusual "pull" of Palestine in the years 1924–26 and 1933–36—periods of economic prosperity there. "Push" factors were also important, such as economic difficulties in Poland in the early 1920s, the Great Depression in the early 1930s, and the persecution of Jews in Germany and later Austria in the 1930s. One nation did not follow the pattern of the others: Immigration from the Soviet Union was above average for the years 1920–26, but after that the numbers dropped sharply, due to Soviet restrictions on the exodus of its Jewish population.

Some immigrants were disappointed by life in Palestine or failed to become acclimatized to the new society. This led them to emigrate from Palestine and return to the United States. Insufficient statistical information exists to determine the rate of this return. A figure not substantiated by concrete evidence but repeated in various sources indicates that one in three American *olim* (immigrants) returned to America. But emigration from Palestine was not unique to the American Jew. For the years 1920–30, British sources listed 27,852 Jews emigrating from Palestine as compared to 109,987 new arrivals—or approximately one Jew leaving for every four entering the country.

MIGRATION'S EFFECT ON THE COUNTRY OF ORIGIN

The migration of some 9,000 American Jews from 1918 to 1939 had little effect on the United States or on its Jewish community. From the American perspective, these émigrés were a drop in the bucket compared to the total population of the United States—an estimated 103 million in 1918 and 131 million in 1939. At the beginning of this period, the American Jewish population stood at approximately 3.6 million, and it increased to 4.5 million at the close. Thus one American Jew in five hundred left for Palestine. Neither the actual nor relative loss had any great effect on the Jewish community at large.

The flow of capital out of the United States was insignificant as well. Using a figure of $5,000 as a multiplier (the minimum required for a capitalist and his family to receive a capitalist's visa), the total amount of departing capital would have been $45 million. However, the actual capital transfer by immigrants is next to impossible to calculate. Figures exist for only part of the immigrant population. For example, for the months July to September 1932, 128 family heads declared they had brought $904,205 to Palestine. However, some individuals would declare only the required amount, though in reality they had more in their possession.

With regard to human capital, many American Jewish immigrants to

Palestine had received a high school education and some were university graduates. There was also the loss of a few American industries to Palestine, which may have had a negative effect on local economies. Such industries included Samuel Bloom's artificial tooth enterprise in Philadelphia, and Isaac Sacks's silk dying and cloth weaving factories in Paterson, New Jersey. In addition, there were attempts to transfer other industries that had suffered during the Great Depression.

With respect to the American Jewish community, the principal loss was qualitative. Some of the immigrants were community and Zionist leaders. Prominent émigrés included Judah L. Magnes, Henrietta Szold, Rabbi Meir Berlin, Irma Lindheim, and Bernard Rosenblatt. The immigration of a local community leader would have had a significant impact on smaller Jewish communities. In all, however, the effect of immigration on America and its Jewish community was negligible.

THE EFFECT OF MIGRATION ON PALESTINE

Immigration played a significant role in the development of Palestine. This study has detailed the contribution of actual *olim* and potential ones, including those who purchased land in Palestine. The underlying assumption of most land purchasing organizations was that eventually their members would migrate. Many Americans who used the services of real estate companies harbored thoughts of ultimately living on their own land in Palestine. There was a direct influence on the landscape, economy, and society of Palestine through five American Jewish activities: land purchase; amelioration through agricultural development; the development of new settlements and expansion of existing ones; the populating of new and existing settlements; and the introduction of new industrial, economic, and professional policies. Indirectly, American Jewish activity resulted in the employment of Jewish workers; the development of settlements dependent upon American Jewish agricultural investment; improvement in the quality of life in Palestine; the attraction of capital to Palestine; and the introduction of new ideas and social norms.

Clearly the contribution of American Jews—immigrants, potential immigrants, and those who wanted to develop Palestine but did not intend to settle there—to the redemption of the land far exceeded their actual numbers. Between 1920 and 1939, American Jews purchased over 180,000 dunams in Palestine—in effect, 19.35 percent of the total Jewish land purchases during that period. Moreover, their contributions to the Jewish National Fund for the years 1921–38 accounted for 25 percent of the organization's receipts.

The concept of acquiring land and then developing and settling it was attractive to many Americans, and prior to World War I, American *ahuza*

Conclusion

companies were pioneers in land purchase. *Ahuza* groups sprouted up across the country, and two *ahuza* settlements were established. During the war there were attempts to reorganize and unify the *ahuza* companies. This brought about the establishment of the American Zion Commonwealth, which aspired to create more centralized and efficient activities and a low unit cost for land and its development. Following the war, the AMZIC succeeded in purchasing large tracts of land. Two *ahuza* companies, New York Achooza Aleph and the Hartford *ahuza,* also purchased land. But both the AMZIC and the *ahuza* companies were unable to convince investors to settle in Palestine or even maintain continued financial support for the land they had purchased. Some American Jews made initial payments but sent no more money after that.

Weakened cash flows led to the disbanding of most *ahuza* companies and the collapse of the American Zion Commonwealth. It was feared that if mortgage payments to the original owners were not made, the land would revert to non-Jewish ownership and be sold at public auction to whoever offered the best price. In the end, however, lands that the *ahuza* companies or the AMZIC could not maintain were sold to the Jewish National Fund, and thus they remained in Jewish hands.

Lands purchased by American immigrants and investors were developed through their own initiatives. Agriculture was the most significant kind of development undertaken by the first wave of settlers and investors, and the most popular form of agriculture was the planting of orange groves. American-sponsored settlements accounted for 8.7 percent of the Jewish agricultural land in 1936, with 16,694 dunams of citrus groves or 11.2 percent of the Jewish total. These settlements were generally less oriented toward field crops, with only 6.5 percent (21,348 dunams) of the Jewish total. In all, 1,563 dunams were under irrigation. It's important to note that these figures do not include American-owned land in other settlements, such as Netanya or Kfar Saba, for example.

American efforts also led to the establishment of agricultural settlements. In none of these colonies were American Jews the majority, but they provided the financial backbone for the settlements, which attracted local farmers and new immigrants from other countries. And their critical mass drew others to American-initiated settlements. The list of colonies established by American investors includes Balfouria, 1922; Raanana, 1922; Herzlia, 1924; Afula, 1925; Gan Haim, 1928; Pardes Hagdud, 1929; Avihail, 1933; Tzofit, 1933; and Bet Herut, 1933. Settlements with an American component include Migdal, 1910, and Netanya, 1929. Americans were also found in various kibbutzim—Merchavia, Ramat David, Afikim, Degania B., Mishmar Haemek, Ginnosar, Naan, Givat Brenner, and Kvutzat Schiller. Moreover, Americans were partners in the founding of Ein Hashofet in 1937, Kfar Menachem in 1939, and Kfar Blum in 1943.

CONCLUSION

In the urban centers, American activity found expression in the purchase of land, the development of neighborhoods, and in building various structures. Although approximately three-quarters of American immigrants resided in cities, their influence was less distinctive in urban settings than rural ones. One reason for this is the fact that despite concentrated purchases in neighborhoods made through the American Zion Commonwealth or various real estate agencies—as with Talpiot in Jerusalem or Hadar and the Western Carmel in Haifa—there were few well-defined clusters of Americans in Palestinian cities. American influence on neighborhood design was negligible, but it sometimes found expression in the construction of individual houses.

An important American contribution to urban development in Palestine was the introduction of new industries and professional activities. Industrial development was sponsored and supported by the Brandeis-Mack group of American Zionists. Successful American enterprises employed dozens and even hundreds of Jewish workers, expanding the industrial output of the *Yishuv* and its exports. This had a trickle-down effect on the Jewish economy and allowed the absorption of more Jewish immigrants.

American agricultural endeavors also provided employment for local Jews. When the colonies of Poria and Sarona were established before World War I, Jews were employed in preparation of the land and its upkeep. This policy of preference for Jewish labor over Arab labor continued after the war and was incorporated into the policies of various land development companies, including the American Zion Commonwealth and New York Achooza Aleph. In certain instances, work in American-owned fields represented an opportunity to train inexperienced workers, increasing their skills so that eventually they could operate their own farms. In some cases, workers' colonies were established adjacent to American sponsored colonies: Naan beside Ramot Meir, Gan Haim B beside Gan Haim, and Ein Haoved beside Pardes Hagdud and Avihail. The inhabitants of these colonies earned their livelihood by working in the American settlements as well as on their own land.

American activities also supported Jewish workers in construction—for example, in the colony of Balfouria. American-financed projects in the urban and rural sectors needed Jewish workers to build and pave roads and to construct houses, apartment, and public facilities. American immigrants were also found among construction workers.

The presence of Americans in Palestine attracted further U.S. investment there. The endorsement of personalities like Robert Kesselman, Judah Magnes, Emmanuel Mohl, and Bernard Rosenblatt encouraged others to buy and develop land, and to pursue other avenues of investment.

American activities in the fields of health, education, and social services

Conclusion

led to substantial improvements in the quality of life in Palestine. The Hadassah organization played a central role in this process. Some of its employees were Americans, and a number of them had arrived earlier with the American Zionist Medical Unit. Hadassah financed hospitals, educational programs, infant and mother health care programs (*Tipat Halav*), and other activities. As a result of cooperative efforts, the Jewish infant mortality rate dropped substantially. In 1937–39, it was 56 per thousand, substantially lower than the Northern European rate of 64 per thousand. By 1940–43, it was almost on a par with that of the white population of the United States—44 per thousand in Palestine as compared to 43 per thousand in the United States. Statistics for Muslims and Christians in Palestine also improved during this time, for the American policy was to extend medical assistance to all races and creeds. Death rates became lower in the adult population as well. The American contribution to the public health system was eclipsed, however, when the wave of German-Jewish immigration—with its large number of medical practitioners—occurred in the 1930s.

American activity also introduced new ideas and norms to the local society. Although these cannot be quantitatively measured, their impact was significant. In the field of education, Deborah Kallen introduced John Dewey's ideas, which were eventually adopted by the Israeli educational system. Alexander Dushkin was another prominent figure in education in the late 1930s, lecturing in pedagogy at the Hebrew University of Jerusalem and working as principal of the Beit Hakerem secondary school. Robert Kesselman trained a generation of bookkeepers with a value system and work ethic from America. In the area of recreation, Americans lent a hand to the growth of Scouting in Palestine and the development of playgrounds. American ideas were also pervasive in the political arena. Judah Magnes helped found Brit Shalom, a Jewish organization devoted to the promotion of a peaceful modus vivendi between Zionism and Arab nationalism, and the establishment of a binational state.

Other Americans took on administrative duties, and their activities were undoubtedly affected by their American background. Serving on the Palestine Zionist Executive and later the Jewish Agency Executive were Bernard Rosenblatt (1921–23), Henrietta Szold (1927–30), and Emanuel Neumann (1931–34). Henrietta Szold was elected to the Vaad Leumi (National Council) in 1930. Golda Meir held various positions in the labor movement in Palestine. Eliezer Joffe, an American who immigrated prior to World War I, was instrumental in defining the organization and structure of the moshav *ovdim*—a compromise between the kibbutz (communal settlement) and the moshavah (private colony). The moshav *ovdim* became a widespread form of settlement during the British Mandate and after the founding of the State of Israel.

CONCLUSION

AMERICAN ALIYA AND OTHER DIASPORA COMMUNITIES

How do these American Jewish immigrants compare with those from other Diaspora communities? Research conducted simultaneously on Canadian Jewish immigration patterns reveals many similarities as well as some differences. Zionism was more popular in Canada than in the United States, and that country had higher rates of membership in Zionist organizations. Canadian Zionist groups were less fragmented, and there was much less opposition to ideology. Furthermore, the controversy over dual loyalty was a moot question in Canada.[14] Potential immigrants to Palestine resided in a more supportive environment; Canadian Jews did not face hostility if they chose to immigrate.

Canadian motives to immigrate were quite similar to American motives, with one significant variation: The Jewish population in the Canadian prairies suffered from a sense of isolation and alienation due to the dispersed nature of settlement in this region. Over time, most of this population migrated away from farmsteads and small settlements. Some hoped to continue their agricultural endeavors; when they looked for a more hospitable place for Jewish life, they found it in Palestine. The "pull" of rural settlements resulted in higher rates of migration from Western Canada (Manitoba, Saskatchewan, and Alberta) than from the rest of the country. Similarly, though to a lesser degree, the rate of American Jewish immigration from the sparsely settled Great Plains states was higher than from urban areas.[15]

In other respects, the actual migration from Canada was not different from American immigration; both countries had low rates of migration— approximately one per thousand for the period 1919–34. Countries with comparable rates were England, France, Holland, Hungary, Argentina, and Morocco.[16]

Once Canadian Jews arrived in Palestine, their activities were similar to those of the Americans described in this study. Canadian Jewish immigrants can be divided into the same four groups as Americans: Orthodox, middle-class agriculturalists, *halutzim,* and urban professionals. Moreover, there was often cooperation between the nationals of these two countries. Certain organizations, including Kollel America Tiffereth Yerushalaim, Hashomer Hatzair, the American Zion Commonwealth, and the Herut settlement program traversed the international border. One difference, however, lay in the scale of activity: Canadian aliya was a fraction of American aliya, and Canadians' contribution to Palestine was proportionate to the size of their migration.

American Jewish immigrants can also be compared with those from South Africa. Gideon Shimoni's study illustrated a significant difference between the two groups: Zionism was widespread in South Africa, probably because most South African Jews had originated in Lithuania, an environment more supportive of Zionism. Furthermore, anti-Zionism was almost nonexistent in South Africa, and "dual loyalty" was a non-issue. As Shimoni noted, "South Africa's peculiar inter-colour pluralism and intra-white dualism was conducive to the cultivation of a national mode of identification for Jews."[17] Shimoni also described South African Jewry's attitude toward aliya.

> For Jews in South Africa, no less than in America, confidence in the continued viability of Jewish life in their new-world home imparted a vicarious quality which enabled them to identify with the notion of a return to Zion without regarding it as directly applicable to themselves. However the Zion which they vicariously sensed as absolutely vital as a haven for distressed European Jewry, was, they also sensed, a vital complement for their own future as Jews in the Diaspora. The recreation of a Jewish national home in *Eretz Israel* would normalize the position of the Jews, solve or at least ameliorate the problem of anti-Semitism, enhance the status and self-esteem of the Jews and provide a spiritual-cultural centre for the entire Jewish people. Zion was thus a complement rather than a substitute for their South African Diaspora, and the idea of *aliyah* as a personal obligation for the adherent of Zionism was scarcely incorporated within their universe of discourse prior to the late 1940s. At best, *aliyah* was perceived as an act of altruistic service to the cause, or as an ultimate act of personal fulfillment.[18]

Between 1919 and 1934, some 100 immigrants from South Africa settled in Palestine. Shimoni estimated that there were approximately three hundred former South Africans residing in Palestine in 1937.[19] These immigrants may be divided into two groups: urban professionals and *halutzim*. South Africans did not attempt to organize or establish agricultural colonies. Instead, they were involved in investment companies and industry. The list of their enterprises includes South Africa-Palestine Enterprises, the Tiberias Development Company, the Palestine Cold Storage and Supply Company, Dubek Cigarettes, and Electra Appliances.[20]

The examples of both Canada and South Africa serve to strengthen our understanding of ideological free migration and its particular expression in the ideological context of Zionism and the country of destination, Palestine. The United States, Canada, and South Africa have certain common denominators that account for the similarity in their migrational patterns to Palestine. The host countries all drew on British political traditions. Religious freedom and sectarian equality were considered the norm. And, in each of these countries, Jewish communities were essentially immigrant societies.

Given these common denominators, the similarities in migrational motivation and patterns—as well as activities in Palestine—are reasonable. But variations among them can be traced to different relations between the host countries and their Jewish communities. In the United States, American Jews were in the troublesome position of having to address the issue of dual loyalty; this was not an issue for either Canadian or South African Jews. Moreover, the Jewish populations in these nations had developed different ideological perspectives because of their original countries of origin. There were two distinct waves of Jewish immigration to the United States: the German-Jewish immigration of the 1850s to the 1880s was followed by a large-scale Russian migration. By contrast, South African Jews were almost exclusively from Lithuania. Canadian Jews, on the other hand, were mainly from Russia and Poland. In all these cases, immigrants brought with them the attitudes toward Judaism and Zionism that were traditional in their former European homelands.

AMERICAN JEWRY AND THE *YISHUV:*
THE DYNAMICS OF THE RELATIONSHIP

American Jewry fostered and shaped the development of the *Yishuv* both from within and from a distance. The approximately 9,000 immigrants infused Palestine with their American "cultural baggage," shaping its landscape, institutions, and society. They transported American values, ideas, and technologies—including democracy, separation of church and state, religious freedom and pluralism, as well as the precepts of capitalism and other economic systems. American Jewry, both Zionists and non-Zionists, attempted to graft American values and ideas onto the developing structure of Palestine. Sometimes the immigrants' initiatives fell on fertile ground. The *Yishuv* accepted certain American ideas, and integrated them into policy and practice. American contributions were most noteworthy in the fields of social welfare and education. In other areas, however, American approaches were deemed ill-suited to the new environment; attempts to integrate these perspectives inevitably failed.

The long-distance relationship between American Jewry and the *Yishuv* became a confrontation. America, the greatest potential source of funding for the development of the *Yishuv,* was led to believe that it was a partner in the great endeavor because it held the purse strings. Yet when Americans attempted to influence the *Yishuv* with American values and ideas from afar, they often found they had no voice, and their ideas were rarely accepted. This led to rivalry, conflict, and a lack of cooperation between Zionist leaders in the *Yishuv* on the one hand, and the World Zionist Organization and American Jewry on the other. Searching for alternative avenues to shape the development of Palestine, American Jewish leadership created its own institutions. In this atmosphere of conflict and despite it, American activity was highly effective, particularly in light of the relative size of its immigrant population to Palestine. Indeed, from 1917 to 1939, American Jewry in the "New Zion" made a significant contribution to the development of the new Jewish homeland, its landscape, and society in the "Old Zion."

NOTES

INTRODUCTION

1. An attempt was made to create a database of all North American immigrants to Palestine. Unfortunately the information collected is incomplete, and no conclusions can be drawn regarding the North American Jewish immigrant population as a whole.

2. Calvin Goldscheider, "American Aliya, Social and Demographic Perspectives," in *The Jew in American Society,* ed. Marshall Sklare (New York: Behrman House, 1974), 347–51, devotes these pages to the Mandatory period and a critical discussion of the following three studies: (1) Moshe Sircon, "Immigration to Israel, 1948–1953, Statistical Supplement" (Jerusalem: Falk Project for Economic Research in Israel and Central Bureau of Statistics, Special Series No. 60, December 1957), 6, Table A8; (2) Jacob Lestschinsky, "Jewish Migration, 1840–1956," in *The Jews,* ed. Louis Finkelstein (Philadelphia: Jewish Publication Society, 1960), 2:572, Table 8, and 2:1584, Table 14, provides a total of 8,043 Jewish immigrants originating from the United States for 1919–43, or 2.4 percent of the total, but the source of this information in unclear; (3) Pinhas E. Lapide, *A Century of U.S. Aliya* (Jerusalem: Association of Americans and Canadians in Israel, 1961), 132. Chaim I. Waxman, *American Aliyah: Portrait of an Innovative Migration Movement* (Detroit: Wayne State University Press, 1989), 78, skirts the question of the number of immigrants, and mentions Goldscheider's and Lapide's findings.

3. Ruth Kark, *American Consuls in the Holy Land, 1832–1914* (Jerusalem: Magnes Press; Detroit: Wayne State University Press, 1994), 199–204.

4. William Coffin, United States Consul, Jerusalem, to Jacob Hardegg, American Consular Agent, Jaffa, 16 March 1911, USNA RG 84 Jaffa 5964.

5. Palestine Office of the Zionist Organization, *Census of the Jews of Eretz Israel* (in Hebrew) (Jaffa: 1918), 1:20, 23, 31, 43, 47, 110.

6. Kark, *American Consuls,* 199–204; Palestine Office of the Zionist Organization, *Census of the Jews of Eretz Israel,* 2:5, 14, 22, 36, 71, 110–11.

7. Eric Mills, *Census of Palestine 1931* (Alexandria: Whitehead Morris, 1933), 1:61.

8. Histadrut of Jewish Labor in Palestine, Department of Statistics and Information, *Labor Immigration, 1919–1947* (Tel Aviv: Histadrut of Jewish Labor in Palestine, March 1949), 1–8. This study is critical of the different sources of information.

9. Mills, *Census of Palestine,* 1:61; David Gurevich, "Fifteen Years of Aliya to Eretz Israel," *Aliya: Collection on Aliya Matters* (in Hebrew) (Jerusalem: Jewish Agency for Palestine, 1935), 2:58.

10. Album of the Jewish Legion, BHMA, a collection of questionnaires sent to former Legionnaires and their families at the time of the founding of the museum in 1959. Not all responded and often the information is incomplete.

11. Resolution for the Settlement of 100 Jewish Legionnaires in Palestine, circa 1929, CZA F25/118.

12. Qtd. by Dr. S. Bernstein, Director, Palestine Bureau, New York, to Immigration Department, Jewish Agency for Palestine, Jerusalem, 4 August 1938, CZA S6/3216.

13. Report on Kolel America Tiferet Jerusalem, Jewish Community of Palestine General Council (Vaad Leumi), Department for Social Service, Information Bureau, August 1932, CZA A110/32.

14. Mills, *Census of Palestine,* 1:64–65. The calculation used was (1922–31 x 1.23) + (1932–39 x 1.1).

15. Report Number 3 of the Palestine Zionist Executive, Immigration Department, 16 November 1923, CZA S6/388.

16. Lapide, *Century of U.S. Aliya,* 127, arrived at 31–32 per hundred by piecing together various unspecified sources. Ralph G. Martin, *Golda: A Biography* (New York: Ivy Books, 1988), 118, mentions one in three.

17. Mills, *Census of Palestine,* 2:166–67, 210–11.

18. *Palestine Bulletin,* 29 August 1926; Mills, *Census of Palestine,* 1:70–71.

19. Oscar S. Heizer, United States Consul, Jerusalem, to the Secretary of State, Washington, D.C., 15 May 1924, USNA RG 84 353/82 0040–0052.

20. Joseph C. Grew, Department of State, Washington, D.C., to Oscar S. Heizer, United States Consul, Jerusalem, 27 November 1925, USNA RG 84 353/82 0082.

21. O. Eisenberg, *Census of the Jewish Population in Haifa, 1938* (in Hebrew) (Haifa: 1940), Table 9, pp. 20–21.

22. Mills, *Census of Palestine,* 2:184–85, 229.

23. David Gurevich, *The Jewish Population of Jerusalem: A Demographic and Sociological Study of the Jewish Population and Its Component Communities, Based on the Jerusalem Jewish Census, September, 1939* (Jerusalem: Department of Statistics of the Jewish Agency for Palestine, 1940), 27–31.

24. Report on Kolel America Tiferet Jerusalem, Jewish Community of Palestine General Council (Vaad Leumi), Department for Social Service, Information Bureau, August 1932, CZA A110/32.

25. David Gurevich and Aaron Gertz, *Statistical Handbook of Jewish Palestine, 1947* (Jerusalem: Jewish Agency for Palestine, 1947), 58–59.

26. David Gurevich, Aaron Gertz, and Roberto Bachi, *The Jewish Population of Palestine: Immigration, Demographic Structure and Natural Growth* (in Hebrew) (Jerusalem: Jewish Agency for Palestine, 1944), 155.

27. The total number of liberal professionals enumerated was 1,223. In the tables, their countries of origin are divided into six geographic regions: Eastern Europe, Central Europe, Western Europe, North and South America, other countries, and Palestine. For North and South America, footnotes list the actual countries—usually the United States and Canada.

28. Zionist Organization of America, Palestine Service and Information Bureau, "Statistical Report on Applicants and Registrants for Immigration to Palestine from America," 31 May 1920, CZA F25/33.

29. List of recipients of labor schedule certificates for the period of January–March 1933, CZA S6/2630. The professionals included: 1 accountant, 1 teacher, 1 engineer, 1 rabbi, and 1 lawyer. The craftsmen included: 5 mechanics, 2 carpenters, 3 painters, 1 leather worker, 1 printer, 1 photographer, 3 plumbers, 1 electrician, and 1 locksmith.

CHAPTER 1

1. Gershon Greenberg, *The Holy Land in American Religious Thought, 1620–1948* (Lanham, Md.: University Press of America, 1994), 269–70, 335–36.

2. Dovid Ben Nachum, "100 Years of Dreaming" (Ein Dor: unpubl. ms., 1991), 12.

3. Greenberg, *The Holy Land,* 335–36.

4. Cyrus Adler and Aaron M. Margalith, *With Firmness in the Right: American Diplomatic Action Affecting Jews, 1840–1945* (New York: 1946; reprint, New York: Arno Press, 1977), 44; Consul Joseph G. Wilson, Jerusalem, to Secretary of State, Washington, D.C., 28 March 1879, USNA RG 59 T471/4; Simcha Fishbane, "The Founding of Kollel America Tifereth Yerushelayim," *American Jewish Historical Quarterly* 64 (December–June 1974): 129–35.

5. Yossef Fund, "The Attitude of Agudat Israel Leaders to Aliyah" (in Hebrew), in *Ingathering of Exiles: Aliyah to the Land of Israel, Myth and Reality,* ed. Dvora Hacohen (Jerusalem: Zalman Shazar Center for Jewish History, 1998), 69–80; Samuel Halperin, *The Political World of American Zionism* (Detroit: Wayne State University Press, 1961), 67–69.

6. Meyer Waxman, "The Mizrachi," *Jewish Communal Register of New York City, 1917–1918* (New York: n.p., 1918), 1350–53.

7. Charles B. Chavel, "The Fostering of the Settlement and Cultivation of Palestine in the Halaka," in *Mizrachi Jubilee Collection in Honor of Twenty-Five Years of the Mizrachi Organization in America,* ed. Pinhas Horgin and Arieh Leib Goelman (New York: n.p., 1936), 59. This volume contains sections in Hebrew, Yiddish, and English. See also Marnin Feinstein, *American Zionism, 1884–1904* (New York: Herzl Press, 1965), 267–69; Hyman B. Grinstein, "Orthodox Judaism and Early Zionism in America," in *Early History of Zionism in America,* ed. Isidor S. Meyer (New York: 1958; reprint, New York: Arno Press, 1977), 220–22; Ze'ev Safrai, "The Influence of the Babylonian Talmud on the Attitude to Aliya" (in Hebrew), in *Ingathering of Exiles,* ed. Hacohen, 27–50.

8. Eliezer Don-Yehiya, "Religious Zionism and Issues of Immigration and Immigrants' Absorption in the Yishuv Period" (in Hebrew), in *Ingathering of Exiles,* ed. Hacohen, 81–87.

9. Solomon Schechter, "Zionism—A Statement," in *Tradition and Change: The Development of Conservative Judaism,* ed. Mordecai Waxman (New York: Burning Bush Press, 1958), 458–60.

10. Herbert Parzen, "Conservative Judaism and Zionism (1896–1922)," *Jewish Social Studies* 18 (October 1964), 235–64. See also Moshe Davis, *The Emergence of Conservative Judaism: The Historical School in 19th Century America* (New York: Burning Bush Press, 1963), 268–74.

11. Mordecai M. Kaplan, "A Program for the Reconstruction of Judaism," *Menorah Journal* 6 (4 August 1920), 181–93; Jack J. Cohen, "Reflections on Kaplan's Zionism," in *The American Judaism of Mordecai M. Kaplan,* ed. Emanuel S. Goldsmith, Mel Scult, and Robert M. Seltzer (New York: New York University Press, 1990), 401–14.

12. Mordecai M. Kaplan, *Judaism as a Civilization: Toward a Reconstruction of American-Jewish Life* (New York: Reconstructionist Press, 1957), 215; see also 65–67, 174, 273–76.

13. Conference of Reform Rabbis, "The Pittsburgh Platform (1885)," in *The Jew in the Modern World: A Documentary History,* ed. Paul R. Mendes-Flohr and Jehuda Reinharz (New York: Oxford University Press, 1980), 370–71.

14. Greenberg, *The Holy Land,* 261–65.

15. Ibid., 265–66.

16. *Central Conference of American Rabbis, Year Book* 27 (1917): 132. See Gary L. Zola, "Reform Judaism's Pioneer Zionist: Maximilian Heller," *American Jewish History* 73 (June 1984): 375–97.

17. *Central Conference of American Rabbis, Year Book* 28 (1918): 133–34. See also Greenberg, *The Holy Land,* 326–29.

18. Irving Levitas, "Reform Jews and Zionism, 1919–1921," *American Jewish Archives* 14 (April 1962): 3–19.

19. Michael Alper, "Reform Judaism and Zionism," in *The Brandeis Avukah Annual of 1932,* ed. Joseph Shalom Shubow (Boston: n.p., 1932), 585–91.

20. *American Israelite,* 19 September 1930, qtd. in Alper, "Reform Judaism and Zionism," 591.

21. Armond E. Cohen, "Palestine and Our Rabbinical Schools," in *Brandeis Avukah Annual of 1932,* ed. Shubow, 593.

22. Michael A. Meyer, *Response to Modernity: A History of the Reform Movement in Judaism* (New York and Oxford: Oxford University Press, 1988), 326–33.

23. Aron Horowitz, *Striking Roots: Reflections on Five Decades of Jewish Life* (Oakville, Ontario: Mosaic Press, 1979), 30: "Davka organized Reform Judaism was the first to send some [of] its Rabbinic students to spend a year at the Hebrew University, the very first one having been Theodore Cook, who was 'drafted' by Dr. Judah Magnes, president of the Hebrew University, when he visited Hebrew Union College in 1932." Others listed by Horowitz were Alan Green and William Chomsky. "List of American Students Who Have Studied at the Hebrew University," HUJA, file 620, names several Hebrew Union College students: Walter Rothman, 1929; Joshua Liebman, 1931; Arthur Zuckerman, 1931; Joseph Cooper Levine, 1933; and Samuel W. Chomsky, 1936; this list does not include Cook or Green.

24. "The Columbus Platform (1937)," in *Jew in the Modern World,* ed. Mendes-Flohr and Reinharz, 410–12, 323–26.

25. Halperin, *Political World of American Zionism,* 99.

26. Neil Larry Shumsky, " 'Let No Man Stop to Plunder': American Hostility to

Notes to Chapter 1

Return Migration, 1890–1924," *Journal of American Ethnic History* 11, no. 2 (1992): 56–75; Jonathan D. Sarna, "The Myth of No Return: Jewish Return Migration to Eastern Europe, 1881–1914," *American Jewish History* 71 (December 1981): 267–68; Arthur Hertzberg, *The Jews in America: Four Centuries of an Uneasy Encounter—A History* (New York: Simon and Schuster, 1989), 182–95.

27. Nachman Syrkin, "Collective Settlement and Achva," *HaAchdut* 31 (1914), 1–5, qtd. in Bernard I. Sandler, "The Jews of America and the Resettlement of Palestine 1908–1934—Efforts and Achievements" (Ph.D. diss., Bar Ilan University, 1978), 115.

28. Shumsky, " 'Let No Man,' " 70–75.

29. A. Zeiger, "Emma Lazarus and Pre-Herzlian Zionism," in *Early History of Zionism,* ed. Meyer, 90–92.

30. Menachem Kaufman, *An Ambiguous Partnership: Non-Zionists and Zionists in America, 1939–1948* (Jerusalem: Magnes Press; Detroit: Wayne State University Press, 1991), 11–22.

31. Louis Marshall (chairman), Proceedings of the Non-Partisan Conference to Consider Palestinian Problems, Astor Hotel (New York, 17 February 1924), 9, AJA.

32. Edward Warburg, interview by Moshe Davis and Menahem Kaufman, New York, 14 April 1975, Oral Documentation, Institute of Contemporary Jewry, Hebrew University of Jerusalem (128), 45.

33. Richard J. H. Gottheil, "The Aims of Zionism," in *The Zionist Idea: A Historical Analysis and Reader,* ed. Arthur Hertzberg (New York: Atheneum, 1982), 500.

34. *New York Times,* 20 December 1902.

35. Richard Gottheil to Theodor Herzl, CZA HV III/289, qtd. in Moshe Davis, "Jewish Distinctiveness within the American Tradition: The Eretz Yisrael Dimension," in *America and the Holy Land: With Eyes Toward Zion—IV* (Westport, Conn.: Praeger, 1995), 56.

36. Theodor Herzl, "Zionism and Patriotism," *Maccabean* 9 (November 1905), 243, qtd. in Davis, "Jewish Distinctiveness," 56–57.

37. *American Hebrew,* 10 June 1898, 172.

38. Israel Freidlander, "The Present Crisis of American Jewry," in *Past and Present: Collected Essays* (Cincinnati: Ark Publishing, 1919), 341–42.

39. Allon Gal, *Brandeis of Boston* (Cambridge, Mass.: Harvard University Press, 1980), 137–207.

40. Louis D. Brandeis, Boston, to Alex Cantor, n.p., 14 November 1914, in *Letters of Louis D. Brandeis,* ed. Melvin I. Urofsky and David W. Levy (Albany: State University of New York Press, 1971–78), 3:357.

41. Louis D. Brandeis, "The Jewish Problem and How to Solve It," in *Brandeis on Zionism: A Collection of Addresses and Statements by Louis D. Brandeis* (Washington, D.C.: Zionist Organization of America, 1942), 24, 28.

42. *Menorah Journal* 4 (February 1918): 2–10; 4 (August 1918): 195–203.

43. Theodor Herzl to Joseph Zeff, 14 October 1899, qtd. in Feinstein, *American Zionism,* 164; Yonathan Shapiro, *Leadership of the American Zionist Organization 1897–1930* (Urbana: University of Illinois Press, 1971), 35.

44. Joseph Zeff (in Hebrew), *HaTehiya* 2 (29 June 1900), 4.

45. Allon Gal, "Independence and Universal Mission in Modern Jewish Nationalism:

A Comparative Analysis of European and American Zionism (1897–1948)," in *Israel: State and Society, 1948–1988—Studies in Contemporary Jewry,* ed. Peter Y. Medding (New York: Oxford University Press for the Institute of Contemporary Jewry, Hebrew University of Jerusalem, 1989), 5:242–55, 269–74. See responses to Gal by Arnold Eisen, ibid., 256–58; Arthur A. Goren, 259–62; Yosef Gorny, 263–65; and Ezra Mendelsohn, 266–68. See also Ben Halpern, "The Americanization of Zionism, 1880–1930," in *Solidarity and Kinship: Essays on American Zionism,* ed. Nathan M. Kaganoff (Waltham, Mass.: American Jewish Historical Society, 1980), 56–87; Judd L. Teller, "America's Two Zionist Traditions," *Commentary* 20 (October 1955): 343–52.

46. Henry L. Feingold, "Assessing an Assessment: The Case of American Zionism," *American Jewish History* 75 (December 1985): 168. See also Evyatar Friesel, "The Influence of American Zionism on the American Jewish Community, 1900–1950," *American Jewish History* 75 (December 1985): 144–46.

47. Melvin I. Urofsky, "Response [to Evyatar Friesel]," *American Jewish History* 75 (December 1985): 163.

48. Rabbi Samuel Mohilever, "Proclamation to the Learned Rabbis" (in Hebrew), *HaIvri* 6 (19 June 1896): 3.

49. "The Pittsburgh Program," *Maccabean* 31 (August 1918): 237.

50. Melvin I. Urofsky, *American Zionism from Herzl to the Holocaust* (Garden City, N.Y.: Doubleday Anchor Press, 1975), 234–41.

51. Horgin and Goelman, ed., *Mizrachi Jubilee Collection,* English section, 6–13, 26–9, 47–51.

52. Michael Brown, *The Israeli-American Connection: Its Roots in the Yishuv, 1914–1945* (Detroit: Wayne State University Press, 1996), 48; Esther Stein-Ashkenazy, "The Dispute within Revisionist Circles: The *Aliyah* of Beitar Members, Option or Obligation (1925–1935)" (in Hebrew), in *Ingathering of Exiles,* ed. Hacohen, 145–64.

53. Margalit Shilo, "On the Way to the Moshav: Ha-Ikar Hatzair, the 'American Group' in the Second Aliyah" (in Hebrew), *Cathedra* 25 (September 1982), 79–98; Joseph Brandes, *Immigrants to Freedom: Jewish Communities in Rural New Jersey Since 1882* (Philadelphia: Jewish Publication Society of America, 1971), 243–46.

54. For a history of these American organizations, see Samuel Grand, "A History of Zionist Youth Organizations in the United States from their Inception to 1940" (Ph.D. diss., Columbia University, 1958). See also Mark A. Raider, *The Emergence of American Zionism* (New York: New York University Press, 1998), 140–42.

55. Chaim Arlosoroff, *Surveying American Zionism* (New York: Zionist Party "Hitachduth" of America, 1929), 31–32; Grand, "History of Zionist Youth Organizations," 37, 53. Among the Young Judaean *olim* were Mrs. Israel Friedlander, Jessie Sampter, Lotte Levensohn, Mrs. Bernard Rosenblatt, Jaques Shapiro, Gershon Agronsky, Emanuel Neuman, Louis Ehrlich, Esther Davis, Leon Hoffman, and Rechavia Lewin-Epstein.

56. *Young Judaean* (September 1933): 9.

57. Jonas S. Friedenwald, "The Intercollegiate: A Retrospect," *Kadimah* (New York: 1918; reprint, New York: Arno Press, 1977), 193–211; *Menorah Journal* 4 (February 1918): 2–10; *Menorah Journal* 4 (August 1918): 195–203.

58. *New Palestine,* 10 July 1925, 45.

59. Arlosoroff, *Surveying American Zionism,* 30–31; Grand, "History of Zionist Youth Organizations," 93–96, 105, 117–19, 123.

60. Grand, "History of Zionist Youth Organizations," 165, 177–78; Sophie A. Edin, ed., *The Palestine Year Book,* 2 (New York: Zionist Organization of America, 1946): 559.

61. Grand, "History of Zionist Youth Organizations," 165, 177–78.

62. Aharon Antonofsky [Aaron Antonovsky], "American Roots [of Hashomer Hatzair]," *Youth and Nation* 16 (August 1948): 14.

63. Stuart E. Knee, *The Concept of Zionist Dissent in the American Mind, 1917–1941* (New York: Robert Speller & Sons, 1979), 154–79; Halperin, *Political World of American Zionism,* 157–75; Chaim Zhitlovsky, "Our Future in America" in *Jew in the Modern World,* ed. Mendes-Flohr and Reinharz, 388–89.

64. *New Masses,* 19 February 1935, 11, qtd. in Halperin, *Political World of American Zionism,* 171.

65. Louis D. Brandeis, "The Jewish Problem and How to Solve It," in *Brandeis on Zionism,* 28; see also Benjamin L. Gordon, *New Judea: Jewish Life in Modern Palestine and Egypt* (Philadelphia: 1918; reprint, New York: Arno Press, 1977), 214–34. Gordon concluded that Palestine could accommodate four million inhabitants.

66. Fromenson, "Some Zionist Conventions of the Past," *Maccabean* 30 (June–July 1917): 278, qtd. in Shapiro, *Leadership of the American Zionist Organization,* 52, n. 83.

67. *Bulletin of the Zionist Society of Engineers and Agriculturalists* 1 (November 1919): 3–8, CZA F25/298; Louis D. Brandeis, Washington, D.C., to Jack Mosseri, n.p., 24 September 1919, in *Letters of Louis D. Brandeis,* ed. Urofsky and Levy, 4:426–27; Shapiro, *Leadership of the American Zionist Organization,* 130, 139–40.

68. Shapiro, *Leadership of the American Zionist Organization,* 139, 150.

69. Louis D. Brandeis, Washington, D.C., to Israel Benjamin Brodie, n.p., 16 February 1930, in *Letters of Louis D. Brandeis,* Urofsky and Levy, 5:419; Brandeis wrote Kesselman, who was considering leaving Palestine in 1927 because of the difficult economic situation: "It would be a misfortune to Palestine ... for you to leave after these many years of service on the firing line. You are among the few significant human contributions which America has made to the force for upbuilding; and there will be great need of your aid in the trying time immediately before us." Brandeis to Robert Kesselman, n.p., 27 November 1927, in ibid., 5:314.

70. Gershon Agronsky, "American Zionists and Their Palestinian Luggage," *New Palestine,* January 1925, CZA A209/86.

71. "What's the Matter with the Jews? Asks Famous Palestine Surgeon," *Judaean* 3 (January 1923): 173.

72. Irma L. Lindheim, Jerusalem, to Stephen S. Wise, New York, 19 November 1929, AJHSA P-134, file 113/13.

73. Samuel M. Melamed, "The Basis of Civilization," *Reflex,* 1 (January 1928): 1–10.

74. "Program of the Poale Zion Party," 1918, 33–34, CAHJP, P3/771.

75. Ibid., 35–36.

76. Bernard Rosenblatt, interview by Moshe Davis, Jerusalem, 20 November 1963, Oral History Collection, Institute of Contemporary Jewry, Hebrew University of Jerusa-

lem, Jerusalem; Synopsis of discussion at the conference between the representatives of the American Zion Commonwealth and Professor J. G. Lipman, n.p., 28 June 1921, CZA A405/37a.

77. Shapiro, *Leadership of the American Zionist Organization,* 252–53.

78. Y. Greenbaum, "Problems of Aliyah" (in Hebrew), in *Aliyah: A Collection Regarding Aliyah* (Jerusalem: Immigration Department of the Jewish Agency for Palestine, 1935), 2:9–13.

79. Table 21, Countries of Immigrants' Last Residence by Categories, in David Gurevich, "Fifteen Years of Immigration," 2:xxx–xxxi. To obtain a capitalist visa, the applicant needed £P1,000 ($5,000); Gurevich, Gertz, and Bachi, *Jewish Population of Palestine,* Table 12, Countries of Last Residence by Immigration Categories during May 1925–December 1942.

80. Alex Bein, ed., *Arthur Ruppin: Memoirs, Diaries, Letters* (Jerusalem: Weidenfeld and Nicolson, 1971), entry for 1 March 1923, p. 203.

81. Chaim Weizmann, n.p., to Eric Forbes-Adam, n.p., 23 July 1919, qtd. in Elias Gilner, *War and Hope: A History of the Jewish Legion* (New York: Herzl Press, 1969), 327; Sandler, "Jews of America," 147–48.

82. Gilner, *War and Hope,* 320–33. Gilner postulates that it was either because the Americans were undisciplined or because of their democratic background.

83. David Ben-Gurion, Jaffa, to the Central Committee of Poale Zion in America, n.p., 10 October 1919, qtd. in *Ben-Gurion Letters* (in Hebrew), ed. Yehuda Erez (Tel Aviv: Am Oved and Tel Aviv University, 1971–74), 2:8–9.

84. Zeev Tzahor, "David Ben Gurion's Attitude toward the Diaspora," *Judaism* (1983): 10–11, 13.

85. David Ben-Gurion, Jaffa, to Central Committee of Poale Zion in America, n.p., 10 October 1919, in *Ben-Gurion Letters,* ed. Erez, 2:11.

86. Telegram from Chaim Weizmann and [?] Cohen, London, to Zionist Organization of America, New York, 18 November 1920, in *The Letters and Papers of Chaim Weizmann,* ed. Leonard Stein (Oxford: Oxford University Press, 1968), 10:88.

87. Chaim Weizmann, London, to Sir Wyndham Deedes, Jerusalem, 13 December 1921, in *Letters and Papers of Chaim Weizmann,* ed. Stein, 10:331.

88. Chaim Weizmann, Boston, to Sir Alfred Mond, London, 18 May 1921, in *Letters and Papers of Chaim Weizmann,* ed. Stein, 10:193.

89. Chaim Weizmann, aboard *S.S. Paris,* to Vera Weizmann, London, 1 March 1923, in *Letters and Papers of Chaim Weizmann,* ed. Stein, 11:267.

90. Chaim Weizmann, "Why Palestine?—An Address Delivered at Boston, May 16, 1923," *Judaean Magazine* 3 (May–June 1923), 276.

91. Bogrei Hechalutz America, *Pioneers from America: 75 Years of Hechalutz 1905–1980* (Tel Aviv: Bogrei Hechalutz America, 1981), 55.

92. Chaim Arlosoroff, *To the Jewish Youth: Address of Dr. Chaim Arlosoroff before the Washington Chapter of 'Avukah'* (New York: Zionist Party "Hitachduth" of America, 1928); Arlosoroff, *Surveying American Zionism.*

93. David Ben-Gurion, n.p., to A. Tomshov, New York, 9 April 1924, in *Ben-Gurion Letters,* ed. Erez, 2:202–3. Tzahor notes Ben Gurion's disillusionment "at having failed to create a constructive immigration movement," Tzahor, "David Ben Gurion's Attitude Toward the Diaspora," 14. See also Brown, *Israeli-American Connection,* 216–17.

Notes to Chapter 1

94. David Ben-Gurion, Cleveland, Detroit, to comrades, n.p., 7–31 December 1930, in *Ben-Gurion Letters,* ed. Erez, 3:178–85.

95. "Astounding Progress in Palestine: Sir Alfred Mond Finds All Money Usefully Employed," *Palestine Correspondence* 18 (25 February 1925), 2–3, CZA A209/1.

96. J. J. Goldberg and Elliot King, eds., *Builders and Dreamers: Habonim Labor Zionist Youth in North America* (New York: Herzl Press, 1993), 72–75, 81–82, 90–92; Shmuel Ben Zvi, "25th Anniversary of American Kibbutz Aliya," *Israel Horizons* 4 (May 1956): 28; David Breslau, ed., *Arise and Build: The Story of American Habonim* (New York: Ichud Habonim Labor Zionist Youth, 1961), 29.

97. Abraham Revusky, *Jews in Palestine* (London: P. S. King & Son, 1935), 259–60; the reference to Degania relates to members of Haikar Hatzair.

98. Martin, *Golda: A Biography,* 118.

99. Leo Gottesman, *The Martyrs of Hebron* (New York: 1930; reprint, New York: Arno Press, 1977), 55. For another example, see Meyer Levin, *In Search: An Autobiography* (New York: Horizon Press, 1950), 41.

100. Revusky, *Jews in Palestine,* 272.

101. Arthur Ruppin, *Three Decades of Palestine: Speeches and Papers on the Upbuilding of the Jewish National Home* (Jerusalem: Schocken, 1936), 66–80.

102. Arthur Ruppin, n.p., to Harry Goldman, Chicago, 3 January 1922, CZA S15/156b. Ruppin viewed American Zionists mainly as the source of financial support. See entries for 17 December 1919 and 3 January 1922, in *Arthur Ruppin,* ed. Bein, 180, 195.

103. Goldie Hoffman, Jerusalem, to Leon Goldman, Executive Secretary, Zionist Organization of Canada, Montreal, 30 March 1921, NAC MG 28, V81, vol. 7.

104. *A Survey of Palestine Prepared in December 1945 and January 1946 for the Information of the Anglo-American Committee of Inquiry* (Jerusalem: Government Printer, 1946), 1:17. The report was not published at the time.

105. Ibid., 18–19; American Consul in Charge, Jerusalem, to the Secretary of State, Washington, D.C., 4 May 1921, USNA RG 84 353/79.

106. English summary of Arab comment on Zionism, 7 November 1926, USNA RG 84 353/88 0628.

107. See Naomi W. Cohen, *The Years After the Riots: American Responses to the Palestinian Crisis of 1929–1930* (Detroit: Wayne State University Press, 1988), for examples of American responses.

108. Saadia Gelb, "The Founding of Habonim (1930–1935)," in *Arise and Build,* ed. Breslau, 9.

109. *Survey of Palestine,* 1: 31. Memorandum to the High Commissioner, 25 November 1935; Supreme Arab Committee resolution, 25 April 1936; referred to in *Survey of Palestine,* 1:33, 35.

110. Molly Lyons Bar-David, *My Promised Land* (New York: G. P. Putnam's Sons, 1953), 74–75.

111. Addison Southard, American Consul in Charge, Jerusalem, to the Secretary of State, Washington, D.C., 14 March 1922, USNA RG 84 353/88 748–9.

112. See Naomi W. Cohen, *American Jews and the Zionist Idea* (n.p.: Ktav Publishing House, 1975), 114–24, for a similar discussion of the period 1945–1967.

Chapter 2

1. This applies to "free migration," not primitive, forced, impelled, or mass migration. W. Petersen, "A General Typology of Migration," in *Readings in the Sociology of Migration,* ed. Clifford J. Jansen (Oxford: Pergamon Press, 1970), 49–68.

2. Paul E. White and Robert I. Woods, eds., *The Geographical Impact of Migration* (New York and London: Longman, 1980), 7–9.

3. There are another nineteen occurrences in the Bible.

4. American Zion Commonwealth brochure, circa 1925, CZA F38/560.

5. Louis D. Brandeis, Washington, D.C., to Akiva Jacob Ettinger, n.p., 1 November 1931, in *Letters of Louis D. Brandeis,* ed. Urofsky and Levy, 5:486–87.

6. Dorothy Ruth Kahn, *Spring Up, O Well* (London: Jonathan Cape, 1936), 197.

7. Hertzel Fishman, "A Zionist Childhood in St. Albans, Vt.," *Kfari* (February 1989): 5.

8. Hertzel Fishman, interview by author, Jerusalem, 13 February 1994.

9. Jacob Katzman, *Commitment: The Labor Zionist Life-Style in America—A Personal Memoir* (New York: Labor Zionist Letters, 1975), 176–78.

10. Louis D. Brandeis, Chatham, Mass., to Robert Szold, n.p., 19 August 1930, in *Letters of Louis D. Brandeis,* ed. Urofsky and Levy, 5:446–47. Brandeis further explained: "Meetings of 15 to 25 persons would probably be most productive, at least at first, and the speaker must realize that every occasion secured is one worth while—no matter what the character of the audience. No one can tell what a person really interested by the discussion may [do] thereafter to help the cause" (448).

11. Brown, *Israeli-American Connection.*

12. Meyer Weisgal, *Meyer Weisgal . . . So Far: An Autobiography* (London and Jerusalem: Weidenfeld and Nicolson, 1971), 37–42, 57–58, 64–74. Weisgal, a supporter of Chaim Weizmann, described the conflicts within American Zionism between the Brandeis and Lipsky camps and the ramifications upon these Zionist publications. He was editor of *New Palestine* between 1921–29.

13. "Palestine Immigration," *New Palestine,* 1 May 1925, 549–50.

14. Agronsky, "American Zionists and Their Palestinian Luggage."

15. Arlosoroff, *Surveying American Zionism,* 18–21.

16. These periodicals included: *Bitzaron,* a Hebrew monthly published from 1933; *Bnai Zion Voice,* an English monthly published from 1931; *Farband Stimme* (Alliance Voice), a Yiddish and English bimonthly published by the Jewish National Workers' Alliance (*Farband*) from 1935; *Hadassah Newsletter,* issued every six weeks by Hadassah and Junior Hadassah from 1921; *Hadoar,* a Hebrew weekly published by Histadruth Ivrith from 1921; *Harofe Haivri* (Hebrew Medical Journal), an English and Hebrew semiannual published from 1926; *Jewish Frontier,* an English monthly published from 1934; *Jewish Horizon,* an English monthly published by Hapoel Hamizrachi of America from 1938; *Land and Life,* an English monthly published by the Jewish National Fund in New York City from 1938; *Mizrachi Weg and Jewish Outlook,* an English and Yiddish monthly published from 1937; *News Bulletin of the Hebrew University in Jerusalem,* issued three times a year in English by the American Friends of the Hebrew University from 1938; *Niv,* a Hebrew bi-monthly published by Hanoar Haivri from 1939; *Pioneer Woman* (*Die pionern froy*), a Yiddish and English monthly, published by the Pioneer Women for Palestine from 1928; *Yiddisher Kemfer,* a Yiddish weekly, published by Poale Zion from 1919; *Young*

Judaean, an English monthly of Young Judaea of America, published from 1913; and *Youth and Nation,* in English and Hebrew, published by Hashomer Hatzair from 1933. "Zionist Periodicals," in *Palestine Year Book,* ed. Edin, 2:578–83.

17. Minutes of the meeting of the Acting Executive Committee of the American Economic Committee for Palestine, 20 February 1933, CZA S17/161.

18. Louis Lipsky, *Thirty Years of American Zionism* (New York: Nesher, 1927), 214.

19. Ibid., 215–16.

20. Isaac Metzker and Harry Golden, eds., *A Bintel Brief: Sixty Years of Letters from the Lower East Side to the Jewish Daily Forward* (New York: Schocken Books, 1971), 157–58; Albert Waldinger, "Abraham Cahan and Palestine," *Jewish Social Studies* 39 (Winter–Spring 1977): 75–92.

21. *Palestine and Near East Economic Magazine* 1 (25 November 1926): 315.

22. Ibid. See also Raider, *The Emergence of American Zionism,* 106, for a description of Louis D. Brandeis's interest in *Palestine and Near East Economic Magazine.*

23. Jessie Sampter, ed., *A Guide to Zionism* (New York: Zionist Organization of America, 1920), 3; Bertha Badt-Strauss, *White Fire, The Life and Works of Jessie Sampter* (New York: Reconstructionist Press, 1956), 44.

24. Gordon, *New Judea,* 7.

25. Ibid., 73.

26. Katzman, *Commitment,* 89.

27. Shabtai Teveth, *Ben-Gurion: The Burning Ground, 1886–1948* (Boston: Houghton Mifflin, 1987), 109–18.

28. Hillel Tryster, "'The Land of Promise' (1935): A Case Study in Zionist Film Propaganda," *Historical Journal of Film, Radio and Television* 15, no. 2 (1995): 188.

29. CZA L65/236, L65/295, J88/25.

30. Barbara V. DePorte, Acting Director, Palestine Service and Information Department, New York, to Dr. Jacob Thon, Palestine Office, Jaffa, 6 March 1919, CZA S15/20076.

31. Daily Register of the Palestine Immigration Bureau, 8–16 January 1931, CZA F38/624.

32. *American Economic Committee for Palestine Report,* 1933, 2, New York Public Library.

33. Ibid.

34. Ibid.; "The American Economic Committee for Palestine, Information Service," *Palestine and Near East Economic Magazine* 7 (December 1932): 542.

35. Maurice Boukstein, New York, to Horace Kallen, New York, 20 April 1938, Horace M. Kallen Papers, YIVO, box 2, folder 22; Minutes of the Meeting of the Acting Executive Committee of the American Economic Committee for Palestine, New York, 20 February 1933, CZA S17/161.

36. Brandes, *Immigrants to Freedom,* 71–72, 126–42.

37. Martin, *Golda: A Biography,* 100. See also Raider, *The Emergence of American Zionism,* 128–30, for a description of activities of the Junior Poale Zion Club of Hartford for the years 1919–21.

38. Bogrei Hechalutz America, *Pioneers from America,* 49, 89.

39. Bulletin No. 2, Hashomer Hatzair Organization of North America, New York, November 1931, CZA KKL5/4931.

40. "Resolutions Adopted by the Convention of American Hechalutz," 31 December 1931, in Bogrei Hechalutz America, *Pioneers from America,* 40–41.

41. Yaacov Levin, "Kvutzat Gordonia in Philadelphia," in Bogrei Hechalutz America, *Pioneers from America,* 46–47; Kenneth L. Kann, *Comrades and Chicken Ranchers: The Story of a California Jewish Community* (Ithaca and London: Cornell University Press, 1993), 22–27.

42. Grand, "History of Zionist Youth Organizations," 79, 87.

43. Ibid., 253.

44. Ibid., 255.

45. Yona Goldberg, "California Farm," Report of Hechalutz Organization of America, 1947, CZA S6/2030.

46. Grand, "History of Zionist Youth Organizations," 262, 274. See also CZA S6/2170; GHA RG T-1, box 19, file 4, 13–14; and Nahum Guttman, "The Anoka Farm, Minnesota, 1933: 'Together We Switched to Agriculture,' " in *Builders and Dreamers,* ed. Goldberg and King, 46–49.

47. L. Wilson, President of the Dr. Leon Pinsker Camp No. 41, Order Sons of Zion, New York, to Dr. Pick(heltz), Petah Tikvah, 8 November 1918; Yaacov Ettinger, n.p., to L. Wilson, Bronx District No. 13, Zionist Organization of America, Bronx, 20 February 1919 (in Hebrew), CZA S15/20076.

48. Gershon Agronsky, Philadelphia, to Arthur Ruppin, Jaffa, 17 May 1914; Ruppin to Agronsky, 4 June 1914, CZA A209/12; Ruppin, *Three Decades,* 88–149.

49. A. H. Friedland, Cleveland, to Louis Lipsky, Zionist Organization of America Chairman, New York, 26 April 1926; Lipsky to Schmaryahu Levin, New York, 29 April 1926, CZA A20/63. In another instance, M. M. Freidman of Norfolk asked Menachem Ussishkin and Ben-Zion Mossinsohn if he should immigrate to Palestine: Menachem Mendel Freidman, "Memoirs" (in Hebrew), 117, TAUA T-11/263.

50. Jessie E. Sampter, Rehovot, to Edgar Wachenheim, Jr., n.p., 11 March 1930, CZA A219/2/2.

51. Ruhama and Mordecai Morahg, *Towards Joy Profound* (Holon: M. and R. Project, 1990), 84–92. The story is based on actual events and on individuals who participated in them.

CHAPTER 3

1. Mark Wischnitzer, *To Dwell in Safety: The Story of Jewish Migration Since 1800* (Philadelphia: Jewish Publication Society of America, 1948), 141–223.

2. A number of studies deal with the motivation for immigration of North American Jews to Israel and these immigrants' adaptation to their new environment. See Aaron Antonovsky and David Katz, *Americans and Canadians in Israel* (Jerusalem: Israel Institute of Applied Social Research, 1969); Gerald S. Berman, *The Experience of Aliyah Among Recently Arrived North American Olim: The Role of the Shaliach* (Jerusalem: Work and Welfare Research Institute, Hebrew University of Jerusalem, 1977); Gerald S. Berman, *The Work Adjustment of North American Immigrants in Israel* (Jerusalem: Work and Welfare Research Institute, Hebrew University of Jerusalem, 1978); Gerald Engel, "Comparison between Americans Living in Israel and Those Who Returned to

America," *Journal of Psychology* 74 (January 1970): 195–204, and 75 (July 1970): 243–51; Goldscheider, "American Aliya"; Simon N. Herman, *American Students in Israel* (Ithaca: Cornell University Press, New York 1970); Harry Leib Jubas, "The Adjustment Process of Americans and Canadians in Israel and Their Integration into Israeli Society" (Ph.D. diss., Michigan State University, 1974); Waxman, *American Aliyah.*

3. Aaron Antonovsky, "Social and Cultural Factors in Coronary Heart Disease: An Israel-North American Sibling Study," *Israel Journal of Medical Sciences* 7 (December 1971): 1578–83.

4. Aaron Antonovsky and Abraham David Katz, *From the Golden Land to the Promised Land* (Darby, Penn., and Jerusalem: Norwood Editions, 1979), 13–20; discussion between Aaron Antonovsky and the author, Jerusalem, 10 June 1993.

5. Antonovsky and Katz, *From the Golden Land,* 13–32.

6. Goldscheider, "American Aliya," 347–51.

7. Waxman, *American Aliyah,* 77–82.

8. Ibid., 79.

9. Yohai Goell, "Aliyah in the Zionism of an American Oleh: Judah L. Magnes," *American Jewish Historical Quarterly* 65 (1975–76): 114–15; Arthur A. Goren, ed., *Dissenter in Zion: From the Writings of Judah L. Magnes* (Cambridge, Mass.: Harvard University Press, 1982), 28–29, 203–7; Daniel P. Kotzin, "An Attempt to Americanize the Yishuv: Judah L. Magnes in Mandatory Palestine," *Israel Studies* 5, no. 1 (2000): 1–23.

10. Antonovsky and Katz, *From the Golden Land,* 50–53.

11. Fishman, "A Zionist Childhood," 5; Hertzel Fishman, interview by author, Jerusalem, 13 February 1994.

12. Samuel Rodman, "Ha-Gedud Ha-Ibri," in *Kadimah* (New York: 1918; reprint, New York: Arno Press, 1977), 22.

13. Zionist Organization of America, Palestine Service and Information Bureau, "Statistical Report on Applicants and Registrants for Immigration to Palestine from America," 31 May 1920, CZA F25/33.

14. Menachem Mendel Freidman, "Memoirs, 1878–1963" (in Hebrew), 116, TAUA T-11/263.

15. Louis Ginsberg, "The Assimilator," *Judaean* 3 (November 1922): 136, 138.

16. Confidential Report of the American Consulate in Jerusalem, Concession Policy in Palestine, to the Secretary of State, Washington, D.C., 18 October 1921, USNA RG 59 353/86, 64.

17. Open letter from Jacob Goell, n.p., circa 1929, CZA A404/576.

18. Open letter from Elias Ginsburg, Chairman of the America Palestine Jewish Legion, n.p., circa 1930, CZA F25/118; Cohen, *Years After the Riots,* 35–36.

19. Tenets of the American Palestine Settlers Association, circa 1930; Jacob De Haas, Report to the National Committee of the American Palestine Settlers Association, CZA A404/576.

20. The word *halutz* has three meanings: part of the army that goes before the rest; first to conquer, for a project that paves the way for others; and young person who made aliyah to realize Zionist ambitions and participate in the building of pre-1948 Palestine through manual labor (*Even Shoshan New Dictionary,* 1969 [in Hebrew]). Aryeh Tartakover, "The Essence of Labor Zionism," in *Struggle for Tomorrow, Modern Political Ideologies of the*

Jewish People, ed. Basil J. Vlavianos and Feliks Gross (New York: Arts, 1954), 53–70; David Yaroslavsky, "Links in the Chain," in Bogrei Hechalutz America, *Pioneers from America,* 35–39; S. Ilan Troen, "Frontier Myths and Their Applications in America and Israel: A Transnational Perspective," *Israel Studies* 5, no. 1 (2000): 303–5.

21. Moshe Furmansky, "What is Halutziut?" in Bogrei Hechalutz America, *Pioneers from America,* 33.

22. Kahn, *Spring Up,* 60.

23. Bernard A. Rosenblatt, *Social Zionism (Selected Essays)* (New York: Public Publishing, 1919), 13.

24. Bertha Schoolman, "3 American Pioneers in Israel," *Hadassah Newsletter* 36 (January 1956): 15.

25. Kahn, *Spring Up,* 79–80.

26. Unsigned letter from Alabama City to Meir Dizengoff, Tel Aviv, 4 July 1925, TAJMA RG 3, file 150.

27. Jewish Community of Palestine General Council, Department of Social Service, Information Bureau, "Kollel America Tiffereth Yerushalaim," August 1932, CZA A100/32. Of these 148 family heads, 24 were aged 51–60, 35 were aged 61–70, 40 were aged 71–80, and 9 were over 80 years old.

28. Dr. S. Bernstein, Director of the Palestine Bureau, New York, to Palestine Zionist Executive, Jerusalem, 14 September 1925, CZA S6/382. Similar letters can also be found in this file.

29. Gottesman, *Martyrs of Hebron,* 53.

30. Julius Haber, *The Odyssey of an American Zionist: Fifty Years of Zionist History* (New York: Twayne, 1956), 239.

31. Arieh Goren, "A Two Way Street: Visitors, Sojourners and Settlers from America to the Land of Israel," lecture presented at the Field Study Course in Israel, "America and the Holy Land, 1620–1948," Institute of Contemporary Jewry and Rothberg School for Overseas Students, Hebrew University of Jerusalem, Jerusalem, 6 July 1988; Joseph B. Glass, "American Jewish Women and Palestine, Their Immigration," in *Women in the Yishuv and the Early Years of the State of Israel,* ed. Margalit Shilo et al. (Jerusalem: Yad Izhak Ben-Zvi, (in press).

32. Marlin Levin, *Balm in Gilead: The Story of Hadassah* (New York: Schocken Books, 1971), 81–84; Sylvia M. Gelber, *No Balm in Gilead: A Personal Retrospective of Mandate Days in Palestine* (Ottawa: Carleton University Press, 1989), 104–5.

33. Jessie Sampter, Jerusalem, to Lotta Levinsohn, New York, 28 December 1920, CAHJP, P3/851.

34. Schoolman, "3 American Pioneers in Israel," 15.

35. Revusky, *Jews in Palestine,* 268.

36. Ibid., 269.

37. Robert Kesselman, Jerusalem, to Frank Katz, New York, 13 October 1922, CZA A168/3.

38. Revusky, *Jews in Palestine,* 56.

39. David Horovitz, "Why Palestine's Present Immunity from the Crisis?" *Palestine and Near East Economic Magazine* 7 (September 1932): 356. Horovitz was head of the Jewish Agency for Palestine Economic Department from 1935 to 1948.

40. Revusky, *Jews in Palestine,* 268. For a general discussion of capitalist immigration, see Aviva Halamish, "Immigration of Jewish 'Capitalists' to Palestine between the Two World Wars" (in Hebrew), in *Ingathering of Exiles,* ed. Hacohen, 193–232.

41. "Daily Register of the Palestine Immigration Bureau," 8–15 January 1931, CZA F38/624.

42. A. M. Hillman, San Francisco, to Rabbi Meir Berlin, San Francisco, 1 March 1932; A. M. Hillman to I. H. Farbstein, Jewish Agency, Jerusalem, 18 May 1932, CZA S8/2290a.

43. C. Bezalel Sherman, "Immigration and Emigration: The Jewish Case," in *Jew in American Society,* ed. Sklare, 53–55; Sarna, "Myth of No Return." See also table 25 in the conclusion.

44. Antonovsky and Katz, *From the Golden Land,* 51; William A. Scott and Ruth Scott, *Adaptation of Immigrants: Individual Differences and Determinants* (Oxford: Pergamon Press, 1989), 3–4.

45. TAJMA, RG 8, files 445–47.

46. Kahn, *Spring Up,* 81–82.

47. Ibid., 83–84.

48. Olga Rubinow Lurie, "Living Here in Palestine from 1920 to 1922: A Young Girl's Diary," *Moment* 11 (December 1986): 48.

49. Antonovsky and Katz, *From the Golden Land,* 51.

50. *Shabbosdige Post* (St. Paul, Minn.), 1 (21 October 1921), 242 (in Yiddish); Mordechai Naor, ed., *The Pioneers of Herzliya: The Story of the First Settlers, 1924–1934* (in Hebrew) (Herzlia: n.p., 1990), vol. 2.

51. Samuel N. Eisenstadt, *The Absorption of Immigrants: A Comparative Study Based Mainly on the Jewish Community in Palestine and the State of Israel* (London: Routledge & Kegan Paul,1954), 29.

52. Myriam Harry, *A Springtide in Palestine* (London: E. Benn, 1924), 51.

53. Ben Halpern, *The American Jew: A Zionist Analysis* (New York: Schocken Books, 1983), 16.

54. Naomi Patai and Raphael Patai, "A Builder of Zion: The Life and Letters of Robert D. (Reuven David) Kesselman," (unpubl. ms.), 67 in CZA A168/13; see also Ginsberg, "Assimilator," 135–36, 138, 141, for an account of the connection between antisemitism in America and aliya.

55. Metzker and Golden, eds., *A Bintel Brief,* 153–55. Editor Abraham Cahan's response was: "Your son is a very sensitive and thinking person. Since he is an adult you must let him go his way and do what he wants to do."

56. Jessie Sampter, Jerusalem, to her sister, n.p., 1 June 1920, CZA A219/2/1.

57. Lyons Bar-David, *My Promised Land,* 40.

58. Irving Fineman, *Woman of Valor: The Story of Henrietta Szold* (New York: Simon and Schuster, 1961), 350–52.

59. Herman, *American Students in Israel,* 96–102, 205–7.

60. Isidore B. Hoffman, "In the Beginning: From a Student's Notebook," *New Palestine* 8 (27 March 1925): 365. Isidore Hoffman and Simon Greenberg are listed as attending the university in 1925. See George M. Hyman, Jerusalem, to Dr. Ben Selekman, New York, 7 June 1929, HUJA 620 1929 Publicity file. On 22 December 1924, the Institute

of Jewish Studies was opened, offering noncredit courses in Talmud, the Septuagint, and Palestinology. The university was formally opened on 1 April 1925.

61. Moshe Davis, *The Formative Year: A Journey to Europe and Eretz Israel, on the Eve of the Holocaust—A Decade before the Founding of the State of Israel* (in Hebrew) (Jerusalem: Department for Jewish Education and Culture in the Diaspora, 1993); "Moshe Davis," *Encyclopedia Judaica* (Jerusalem: Keter, 1975), 5: col. 1369.

62. List of American Students Who Have Studied at the Hebrew University, HUJA 620/1938IV.

63. Cohen, "Palestine and Our Rabbinical Schools," 593.

64. Meyer Greenberg, New York, to Dr. David Werner Senator, Jerusalem, 15 February 1939; Senator to Dr. Bernard Levy, New York, 15 February 1939, HUJA file 120/1939.

65. Lyons Bar-David, *My Promised Land,* 76. See also "The New York Times' Correspondent Describes the School in Jerusalem," *Bulletin of the American Schools of Oriental Research* 35 (October 1929): 18–21, qtd. in *The Holy Land in American Protestant Life, 1800–1948,* ed. Robert T. Handy (New York: Arno Press, 1981), 48–51. The article mentions that "the many American students, a large majority of whom are young ministers and rabbis, have practically all departed for home," p. 48.

66. Irma L. Lindheim, n.p., to Stephan S. Wise, n.p., 21 May 1929, AJHSA P-134 Wise Papers, 113:3; Irma L. Lindheim, *Parallel Quest: A Search of a Person and a People* (New York: Thomas Yoseloff, 1962), ix–x, 356–72, 381–84.

67. Antonovsky and Katz, *From the Golden Land,* 51.

68. Harry, *Springtide in Palestine,* 51.

69. Aaron David Gordon, *Selected Essays* (New York: League for Labor Palestine, 1938), 138–39. By 1930 some of Gordon's writings had appeared in English in the United States. See *Aharon David Gordon: A Bibliography, 1904–1972, on the Fiftieth Anniversary of his Death* (Degania A: Yachdav and Beth Gordon, 1979).

70. Advertisements for Migdal were placed in the *San Francisco Lodge Bulletin,* I.O.B.B., 4 (September 1927): 24; the *Jewish Monitor* (Fort Worth-Dallas), 15 (20 January 1928): 10; *Texas Jewish Herald* 45 (16 February 1928): 5; *International Jewish News* (Denver), 51 (22 December 1927): 1; NLA, Migdal Collection, V264a.

71. Gabriel Davidson, "The Jew in Agriculture in the United States," *American Jewish Yearbook* 37 (1935–1936): 104.

72. Marshall Sklare, *America's Jews* (New York: Random House, 1971), 46. For a detailed discussion of this thesis from the perspective of the Canadian prairies, see Joseph B. Glass, "Isolation and Alienation: Factors in the Growth of Zionism in the Canadian Prairies, 1918–1939" (in preparation).

73. Davidson, "The Jew in Agriculture," 130.

74. In 1918 there were 149,235 Zionist Organization of America members and 18,000 Mizrachi members. In 1927, 141,221 shekels were purchased in the United States. This reflects the majority of dues-paying Zionists; see Halperin, *Political World of American Zionism,* 327–28.

Chapter 4

1. Izhak Ben-Zvi, Rafiah, to Rachel Ben-Zvi, n.p., 5 August 1919, in Izhak Ben-Zvi,

Notes to Chapter 4

The Jewish Legion: Letters (in Hebrew) (Jerusalem: Yad Izhak Ben-Zvi, 1967), 100–101. Ben-Zvi specified 800, but in other accounts the numbers vary from 400 to 1,500.

2. Gershon Agronsky, "A Survey of the Jewish Battalions Prepared at the Request of the Zionist Commission," June 1919, CZA A209/1.

3. Samuel Levine, Bir Salem, to Zionist Commission, Jerusalem, 28 July 1919, CZA L3/25VIII.

4. Zionist Organization of America, "Statistical Report on Applicants and Registrants for Immigration to Palestine from America," 31 May 1920, CZA F25/33.

5. M. Mossek, *Palestine Immigration Policy under Sir Herbert Samuel: British, Zionist and Arab Attitudes* (London: F. Cass, 1978), 6; David Gurevich, *Statistical Abstract of Palestine 1929* (Jerusalem: Keren Hayesod, 1930), 46–47.

6. Mossek, *Palestine Immigration Policy,* 6, 17.

7. Ibid., 157–64, which includes "Immigration Ordinance, August 26, 1920" and "Instructions to Consuls Regarding Granting of Visas for Palestine, August 20, 1920."

8. Ibid., 8–14.

9. Executive Secretary, Zionist Executive, London, to the Zionist Organization of Canada, Montreal, 8 and 10 December 1920, CZA Z4/360. Similar letters were sent to the Zionist Organization of America, see Executive Secretary, Zionist Executive, London, to the Zionist Organization of America, New York, 23 November 1920, CZA Z4/731.

10. Mossek, *Palestine Immigration Policy,* 169.

11. "Public Notice—Admission of Immigrants into Palestine, August 1, 1921," in Mossek, *Palestine Immigration Policy,* 165–66; Addison Southard, American Consul in Charge, Jerusalem, to the Secretary of State, Washington, D.C., 8 August 1921, USNA RG 59 353/82, p. 476.

12. Mossek, *Palestine Immigration Policy,* 35–40.

13. Palestine Zionist Executive, Jerusalem, to Department of Immigration and Travel, Jerusalem, 5 July 1922; F. H. Kisch, Jerusalem, to Controller of Labour, Jerusalem, 29 January 1923, CZA S6/274.

14. Mossek, *Palestine Immigration Policy,* 58–60.

15. John Hope-Simpson, *Report on Immigration, Land, Settlement and Development* (London: H.M. Stationary Office, 1930), 120.

16. Government of Palestine, *Immigration Ordinances 1925–1926 and Regulations, Orders, etc., Made Thereunder* (Jerusalem: April 1926).

17. Ibid.

18. Dr. S. Bernstein, Director, Palestine Bureau, New York, to Immigration Department, Jewish Agency Executive, Jerusalem, 15 June 1931, CZA S6/2630.

19. "Immigration," *Palestine and Near East Economic Magazine* 7 (October 1932): 421.

20. David H. Shpiro, *Aliya by Any Means: The History of Jewish "Illegal" Immigration into Eretz Israel under British Rule until the Thirties (1918–1937)* (in Hebrew) (Tel Aviv: Am Oved, 1994), 65–72, 154–64.

21. Ibid.; Gurevich, Gertz, and Bachi, *Jewish Population of Palestine,* Table 17.

22. Shpiro, *Aliya by Any Means,* 154–64; Gurevich, Gertz, and Bachi, *Jewish Population of Palestine,* Table 17.

23. Dr. S. Bernstein, New York, to Robert Szold, New York, 11 December 1930, CZA F38/624; Dr. S. Bernstein, New York, to Jewish Agency Executive, Immigration Department, Jerusalem, 15 June 1931, CZA S6/2630.

24. Minutes of the Meeting of the Palestine Office, 19 August 1936, CZA S6/3818; List and Details of Applicants to Whom Certificates, including 10 Middle-class Certificates, Have Been Granted for the Period of March–October 1932, CZA S6/2630.

25. Minutes of the Meeting of the Palestine Office, 19 August 1936, CZA S6/3818.

26. Meir Berlin, New York, to the Inter Allied Mizrachi Bureau, London, 1919; Lazarus Cohen, Secretary, Inter Allied Mizrachi Bureau, London, to S. Landman, Secretary, Zionist Bureau, London, 7 July 1919, CZA Z4/252.

27. "Daily Register of the Palestine Immigration Bureau," 8–16 January 1931, CZA F38/624.

28. Charles Passman, Jerusalem, to American Zion Commonwealth, New York, 11 September 1924, CZA L65/386.

29. Ibid.; "Herzlia Settlers through assignments from American relatives (visas obtained through Amzic) as of July 20, 1925," CZA L65/348; "List of people for whom visas were procured or applied for," n.d., CZA L65/385.

30. Solomon J. Weinstein, Jerusalem, to American Zion Commonwealth, New York, 12 March 1926, CZA L65/365.

31. Gershon Agronsky, "A Survey of the Jewish Battalions prepared at the Request of the Zionist Commission," June 1919, CZA A209/1; Arieh Shenkar, Chairman of the Manufacturers' Association of Palestine, Tel Aviv, to Department of Commerce and Industry, Jewish Agency, Jerusalem, 20 November 1932, CZA S8/2290a.

32. *The Hebrew University of Jerusalem: Yearbook 5690* (in Hebrew) (Jerusalem, n.p., 1931), 122–23. Details about the organization of entry visas for students to Palestine, 11 January 1933, HUJA, file 210/1935.

33. Kark, *American Consuls,* 55–67.

34. Norman Bentwich, ed., *Legislation of Palestine, 1918–1925: Including Orders-in-Council, Ordinances, Public Notices, Proclamations, Regulations, etc.* (Alexandria: Whitehead Morris, 1926), 1:11.

35. Convention between the United Kingdom and the United States of America Respecting the Rights of the Two Countries and Their Respective Nationals in Palestine, signed at London, 3 December 1924, USNA RG 84 353/81, p. 195.

36. Oscar S. Heizer, American Consul, Jerusalem, to Albert M. Hyamson, Chief Immigration Officer, Jerusalem, 22 September 1927; Hyamson to Dr. Olga Pickman Feinberg, Jerusalem, 30 August 1927; Heizer to Secretary of State, Washington, D.C., 5 October 1927, USNA RG 84 353/82, p. 568–69, 572–73.

37. Oscar S. Heizer, American Consul, Jerusalem, to Secretary of State, Washington, D.C., 28 December 1927, USNA RG 59 353/82, pp. 574–75.

38. Ibid.; *Palestine Bulletin,* 18 December 1927.

Chapter 5

1. The letter continues with a description of the two men attempting to be accepted to the Mikveh Israel agricultural school in order to receive the necessary training for settlement. Unsuccessful, they worked as day laborers in construction in Tel Aviv. Summarizing their trials, they wrote: "In the whole time that we are in Palestine we

can truthfully say that we have goen [sic] every other day to register in the workers union. [W]hen you go to register they ask you where you come from, naturally you must tell them the truth, so you tell them America. [W]hen they hear America, they give you a look and let out a laugh that makes the shivers run up and down your spine: then they give you a cross examination, what insane asylum broke loose? because they figure anyone who comes to Palestine from America must be crazy with out doubt. Who chased you out of America? Why did you pick Palestine? Oh, I guess you have a few thousand dollars, you didn't come here to work, you better go back to America and make money so you can send it here to us. [W]e need your money more than we need you, and a thousand more such foolish questions. [T]he result is, that you stop and wonder if it really was worth while to come to Palestine, maybe it would be better if we did go back[.] [I]nstead of giving you courage, they break down your spirit to such a low standard that you feel like running away, no matter where, just so it shouldn't be Palestine." Lewis Jack Kamenetzky and Morris Rosenstein, Tel Aviv, to President, American Zion Commonwealth, New York, 10 March 1926, CZA L65/400.

2. Palestine Office of the Zionist Organization, *Census of the Jews of Eretz Israel* (1918), 1:20, 23, 31, 43, 47; (1919), 2:5, 14, 22, 36, 53.

3. Mills, *Census of Palestine.*

4. Oscar S. Heizer, United States Consul, Jerusalem, to the Secretary of State, Washington, D.C., 15 May 1924, USNA RG 84 353/82 0046–0052. Urban distribution was as follows: Jerusalem 51 percent, Tel Aviv-Jaffa 19 percent, Haifa 7 percent, Safed 2 percent, and Tiberias 1 percent. Rural settlements included Petah Tikvah, Zichron Yaakov, Nes Ziona, Ben Shemen, Merchavia, Yavniel, Rishon LeZion, and Nahalal.

5. Gurevich and Gertz, *Statistical Handbook of Jewish Palestine,* 58–59.

6. Gurevich, *Jewish Population of Jerusalem,* 27, 31.

7. List of purchasers of American Zion Commonwealth tracts in Palestine, n.d., CZA L65/436.

8. Report on Kollel America Tiferet Jerusalem, Jewish Community of Palestine General Council (Vaad Leumi), Department for Social Service, Information Bureau, Jerusalem, August 1932, CZA A110/32.

9. List of American *halutzim* at Ein Hashofet and Kfar Menachem, circa 1947, GHA RG T-1, box 26, file 3; Edwin Samuel, *Handbook of the Jewish Communal Villages in Palestine* (Jerusalem: Zionist Organization Youth Department, 1945), 73–75. The 1943 populations were: Ein Hashofet, 299; Kfar Menachem, 245; and Kfar Blum, 157.

10. Moshe De Shalit, "Balfouria, Herzlia and Afula" (in Yiddish), New York, circa 1926, CZA L65/292, pp. 14, 39, 55.

11. David De Sola Pool, n.p., to H. Saletan, New York, 22 August 1920; Akiva Ettinger, Jerusalem, to De Sola Pool, Jerusalem, 19 August 1920, CZA L3/66II.

12. Advertisement of the Zion Commonwealth, CZA Z4/762.

13. Circular #2 Colony Nordau, 23 February 1927, CZA L65/35; New York Achooza Aleph, "Present Opportunities for American Jews in Palestine," New York, 1932, CZA F25/253.

14. Kahn, *Spring Up,* 207–12. See also Joseph B. Glass, "An American Jewish Woman's Place in the Promised Land, Their Spatial Distribution and Locational Decisions in Palestine, 1917–39," in *Untold Stories: American Jewish Women in the Yishuv and Early State of Israel* (forthcoming).

15. Dr. Arthur Ruppin, n.p., to Zionist Organization of America, New York, 28 February 1921, CZA L18/44/11; Leah Doukhan-Landau, *The Zionist Companies for Land Purchase in Palestine, 1897–1914* (in Hebrew) (Jerusalem: Yad Izhak Ben-Zvi, 1979), 98–121; "Agricultural Land Acquired by the P.L.D.C. in the Years 1910–1929," *Palestine and Near East Economic Magazine* 5 (22 July 1930): 255; Adolf Boehm and Adolf Pollak, *The Jewish National Fund (Keren Kayemeth LeIsrael): Its History, Function and Activity* (Jerusalem: Jewish National Fund, 1935), 59; Aminadav Ashbel, *60 Years of Hachshevet HaYishuv: The Israel Land Development Company* (in Hebrew) (Jerusalem: Israel Land Development Company, 1969), 93–157.

16. Dr. Arthur Ruppin, n.p., to Zionist Organization of America, New York, 28 February 1921, CZA L18/44/11.

17. Ibid.; minutes of meeting held at the Zionist Office, New York, 6 October 1922, CZA L18/115/2.

18. For the history of Geula, see Yossi Katz, *The "Business" of Settlement: Private Entrepreneurship in the Jewish Settlement of Palestine, 1900–1914* (Jerusalem: Magnes Press and Bar-Ilan University Press, 1994), 29–142.

19. Solomon J. Weinstein, New York, to Dr. Jacob Thon, Jerusalem, 25 October 1922, CZA L18/115/3.

20. *Arthur Ruppin,* ed. Bein, 200.

21. Arthur Ruppin, "Geulath Haaretz," *Judaean* 3 (January 1923): 171.

22. Charles Passman, Jerusalem, to American Zion Commonwealth, New York, 28 November 1924, CZA L65/317.

23. Harry Kotler, New York, to Th. L. Miller, Chicago, 1 July 1925, CZA L65/412.

24. Harry Kotler, New York, to Solomon J. Weinstein, 8 April 1926, CZA L65/365.

25. Minutes of the American Zion Commonwealth Board of Directors' Meeting, New York, 24 February 1925, CZA L65/263.

26. General Manager, American Zion Commonwealth, New York, to Jacob Marcus, New York, 29 October 1923, CZA L65/127.

27. Minutes of the American Zion Commonwealth Board of Directors' Meeting, New York, 24 February 1925, CZA L65/263.

28. Katz, *"Business" of Settlement,* 310.

29. Doukhan-Landau, *Zionist Companies for Land Purchase,* 53–97; Zvi Shilony, *Jewish National Fund and Settlement in Eretz-Israel, 1903–1914* (in Hebrew) (Jerusalem: Yad Izhak Ben-Zvi, 1990), 5–37.

30. Gurevich, *Statistical Abstract of Palestine,* 226–27.

31. Jacob Metzer, *National Capital for a National Home, 1919–1921* (in Hebrew) (Jerusalem: Yad Izhak Ben-Zvi, 1979), 50–53; Yigal Drori, "The Attitudes of Jabotinsky, Gluecksohn and Levontin on Land and Settlement in the Early 1920s," in *Redemption of the Land of Eretz-Israel: Ideology and Practice* (in Hebrew), ed. Ruth Kark (Jerusalem: Yad Izhak Ben-Zvi, 1990), 199–208.

32. "The Pittsburgh Program," *Maccabean* 31 (August 1918): 237.

33. Bernard Rosenblatt, n.p., to Jacob DeHaas, n.p., 7 January 1919, CAHJP P3/803. A copy was sent by Julius Simon, London, to N. de Lieme, The Hague, 18 April 1919. See also Rosenblatt, *Social Zionism;* Stephen S. Wise, *Challenging Years: The Autobiography of Stephen Wise* (New York: G. P. Putnam's Sons, 1949), 7.

34. Allon Gal, "Brandeis's Views on the Upbuilding of Palestine, 1914–1923," *Studies in Zionism* 6 (Autumn 1982): 211–40.

35. "Zeeland Memorandum," in Metzer, *National Capital for a National Home,* 157.

36. Ruppin, *Three Decades,* 96.

37. Qtd. in Shalom Reichman, *From Foothold to Settled Territory: The Jewish Settlement, 1918–1948* (in Hebrew) (Jerusalem: Yad Izhak Ben-Zvi, 1979), 165, 168.

38. *Report of the Joint Palestine Survey Commission* (London: Press Printers, 1928), 66–67; Frank Adams, "Palestine Agriculture," *Annals of the American Academy of Political and Social Science* 164 (November 1932): 79–80.

39. Joseph Weitz, David Stern, and Nahum Paper, "The Coastal Plain: Survey of the Conditions of the Land and Possibilities for Settlement," 13 March 1930, in Reichman, *From Foothold to Settled Territory,* 190–202.

40. Judah Leib Kazan, *From New York to Raanana* (in Hebrew) (Tel Aviv: M. Neuman, 1954), 10–11.

41. Minutes of the Special Meeting of the Board of Directors of the Zion Commonwealth Inc., 24 February 1918, CZA L18/447; Yoram Efrati, ed., *Yoman Aaron Aaronsohn, 1916–1919* (Aaron Aaronsohn's Diary, 1916–1919) (Zichron Yaakov, 1978) 358–63, 422–24.

42. Morris Cherpowitz, New York, to the Directors of the American Zion Commonwealth, New York, CZA L65/172. Cherpowitz complained that the amount of land he received was less than Shenkin had promised.

43. Charles Passman, Jerusalem, to American Zion Commonwealth, New York, 11 September 1924, CZA L65/386.

44. *Report of the Experts Submitted to the Joint Survey of Palestine* (Boston: n.p., 1928), 2:54.

45. Kazan, *From New York to Raanana,* 35, 88; Yoel Dan, "Soils of the Galilee," in *The Lands of the Galilee* (in Hebrew), ed. Avshalom Shmueli, Arnon Sofer, and Nurit Kliot (Haifa: Haifa University and Israel Ministry of Defence), 1:95, 101–7.

46. "The Activities of the Committee of Rosoff Group Plantations," AMJLM IV-104-102-37.

47. *Ramat Gan Jubilee Book, 1921–1946* (in Hebrew) (Ramat Gan: Local Council, 1946), 103.

48. Norman Bentwich, *For Zion's Sake: A Biography of Judah L. Magnes, First Chancellor and First President of the Hebrew University of Jerusalem* (Philadelphia: Jewish Publication Society of America, 1954), 141.

CHAPTER 6

1. The spelling of *ahuza* (pl. *ahuzot*) varies according to the method of transliteration employed in different sources, e.g., *achouza, achooza, ahusa, achuza.* I have adopted the transliteration used by the *Encyclopedia of Israel and Zionism*—except in references—in order to preserve the integrity of the sources.

2. Bernard I. Sandler, "Hoachoozo—Zionism in America and the Colonization of Palestine," *American Jewish Historical Quarterly* 65 (December 1974): 142–45. An *ahuza* company was in existence in Baltimore in 1921; see Simon A. Neuhausen, Baltimore, to Zionist Organization, London, 8 Shvat 5681/17 January 1921, CZA 24/5361. An *ahuza* company also existed in Hartford, but it is unclear when it was founded.

3. Yossi Katz, "Achouzat Poria—The First Achouza in Eretz Israel" (in Hebrew), *Ofakim Be-Geographia* (Horizons, Studies in Geography) 4 (1979): 59.

4. Ibid.

5. Palestine Office of the Zionist Organization, *Census of the Jews of Eretz Israel* (1919), 2:65.

6. M. J. Slonim, "Statement on Poriah—A Colony in Palestine," 6 August 1923, CZA S15/199a.

7. Report by Akiva Ettinger and Yitzhak Wilkansky on the "Enlargement of the Existing Settlements," Jaffa, January 1919, CAHJP P3/803.

8. Sandler, "Jews of America," 88–89; report on Poria, March 1919, CZA S15/75.

9. Report on Poria, March 1919, CZA S15/75. The use of Arab labor rebuts Sandler's conclusion regarding the contribution of the St. Louis *ahuza* in employing Jewish labor; see Sandler, "Jews of America," 93. On the "Conquest of Labor," see Yakir Plessner, *The Political Economy of Israel: From Ideology to Stagnation* (Albany: State University of New York Press, 1994), 154–57.

10. Report on Poria, March 1919, CZA S15/75.

11. Ibid.; Melech Zagorodsky, Poria, to Arthur Ruppin, Jerusalem, 19 March 1921, CZA S15/75.

12. Melech Zagorodsky to Arthur Ruppin, 19 March 1921, CZA S15/75; Meir Berlin, New York, to Inter Allied Mizrachi Bureau, London, 1919, CZA Z4/252; Naor, ed., *Pioneers of Herzliya,* 2: entry for Avraham and Batzion Mirsky.

13. Kazan, *From New York to Raanana.* 48–52.

14. Hoachoozo Palestine Land & Development Co., St. Louis, to Arthur Ruppin, Jerusalem, 20 January 1921; Melech Zagorodsky to Ruppin, 19 March 1921, CZA S15/75.

15. Melech Zagorodsky to Arthur Ruppin, 19 March 1921; Report of the meeting of the Poria Committee, M. Israelite, S. Schwartz, M. Sower, H. Halperin, M. Goldstein, Z. Goldman in attendance, Poria, 24 April 1924 (in Hebrew), CZA S15/75; Katz, "Achouzat Poria," 59–60; Ever HaDani [Aaron Feldman], *Settlement in the Lower Galilee: Fifty Years of History* (in Hebrew) (Ramat Gan: Masada, 1956), 459; Naor, ed., *Pioneers of Herzliya,* 3: entries for the Finklestein children—Tzipora Pat, Zvi, and Isaachar Shoham.

16. Arthur Ruppin, n.p., to Harry Goldman, Chicago, 3 January 1922, CZA S15/156b.

17. Ibid.

18. Ibid.; Solomon J. Weinstein, New York, to Harry Goldman, Chicago, 18 July 1922, CZA L65/93.

19. Report of A. Israeli's visit to Poria on October 18–20, 1922 (in Hebrew), Jerusalem, 25 October 1922, CZA S15/156b; Slonim, "Statement on Poriah"; J. B. Barron, *Palestine: Report and General Abstracts of the Census of 1922* (Jerusalem: Greek Convent Press, 1922), 39.

20. Slonim, "Statement on Poriah."

21. M. Cohen, E. Davis, and N. H. Massie, Haachoozo Palestine Land & Development Co., St. Louis, to Louis Lipsky, Chicago, 27 December 1923; Lipsky, New York, to Arthur Ruppin, New York, 15 January 1924, CZA S15/199a.

22. N. Massie, St. Louis, to Emanuel N. Mohl, n.p., 22 February 1924, CZA S15/199a.

23. Jewish National Fund, Jerusalem, to Emanuel N. Mohl, Jerusalem (in Hebrew), 13 March 1924, CZA S15/199a.

24. M. J. Slonim, St. Louis, to Chaim Weizmann, New York, 8 April 1924, CZA S15/199a.

25. Summary of Conference held on November 17, 1925 concerning Poria, present: Louis Lipsky, Bernard Rosenblatt, Charles Passman, Arthur Ruppin, S. Kaplansky, and [?] Stern, CZA Z4/1175.

26. Telegram, M. Kaufmamn, St. Louis, to Chaim Weizmann, London, 26 September 1926, CZA S9/1840c.

27. Anglo-Palestine Company, Tiberias, to Palestine Zionist Executive, Jerusalem, 10 January 1926, CZA S9/1840c; Protocols of the meeting of Palestine Zionist Executive, 29, Jerusalem, 24 December 1926, CZA S100/7B; Copy of the decision by Chief Justice Thos. Haycourt, High Court of Justice, 30 July 1926, CZA L51/882; General Manager, Anglo-Palestine Bank, n.p., to H. Sterling, London, 28 January 1929, CZA L51/882.

28. Summary of the sharecropping of Poria, Tiberias, 22 May 1929, CZA L51/883; HaDani, *Settlement in the Lower Galilee,* 459.

29. Yossi Katz, "Mifalei Ha-achuzot Be-eretz Yisrael Bein Ha-shanim 1908–1917 (The achouza project in Eretz Israel, 1908–1917)" (Master's thesis, Hebrew University of Jerusalem, 1979), 34–35.

30. Ibid.

31. There were at least four different biblical settlements named Ramah: one in the territory of the tribe of Benjamin (Joshua 18:25), the residence of Samuel the prophet (1 Sam 7:17); and three in the tracts of the tribes of Simon, Asher, and Naphtali (Joshua 19:8, 19:29, 19:36). The last is closest to the Chicago Ahuza colony. However, *Ramah* (pl. *Ramot;* poss., *Ramat*), Hebrew for plateau, is a common name for settlements on flat high ground. Sarona was named for a settlement in the vicinity. The new Jewish colony was situated one kilometer to the north of the Arab village. The Palestine Exploration Fund survey from the 1870s listed 250 inhabitants. Gottlieb Schumacher's population list for 1887 enumerated 60 adult males. The census of 1922 listed 77 Muslims and 15 Jews. See Yehoshua Ben-Arieh and Amiram Oran, "Settlements in the Galilee on the Eve of Zionist Settlement," in *The Lands of the Galilee,* ed. Shmueli, Sofer, and Kliot, 1:343.

32. Palestine Office of the Zionist Organization, *Census of the Jews of Eretz Israel* (1919), 2:70.

33. Pinhas Shamir, Ramah, to Menachem Ussishkin, Jerusalem, 16 December 1922, CZA S15/160a; Sandler, "Jews of America and the Resettlement of Palestine," 87–88; Acting Chairman of the Zionist Commission, Jerusalem, to Major Reed Kerr, Assistant Administrator, Jerusalem, 18 July 1919, CZA L3/66II; HaDani, *Settlement in the Lower Galilee,* 459. In 1921 Abraham and Dina Kaplan arrived at Sarona with their four children, only to move to Herzlia in 1925. See Naor, ed., *Pioneers of Herzliya,* 3.

34. M. Benamy, Chicago, to Agriculture and Settlement Department, Palestine Zionist Executive, Jerusalem (in Hebrew), 3 May 1922, CZA S15/76.

35. Formal proposal from Samuel Matshis, Chicago, to Jewish National Fund, n.p. (in Hebrew), 10 December 1922, CZA S15/160a.

36. Pinhas Shamir, Ramah, to Menachem Ussishkin, Jerusalem, 16 December 1922, CZA S15/160a.

37. Max Shulman, Chicago, to Leon Zolotkoff, Jaffa, 1 June 1923; Akiva Ettinger,

Jerusalem, to Executive of the Keren Hayesod, London, 8 July 1923, CZA S15/160a. David Ofir, "Wanderings—The History of the Settlement of the Brisk Kevutza at Ramat David," in *Sefer Ha-aliya Ha-shilishit (Third Aliyah Book)* (in Hebrew), ed. Yehuda Erez (Tel Aviv: Am Oved, 1964), 491–92.

38. Kazan, *From New York to Raanana,* 5–10; Certificate of Incorporation of the New York Achooza Aleph, Inc., December 1914, CZA L18/94/4.

39. New York Achooza Aleph, New York, to Rabbi Stephen Wise, New York, 15 July 1937, CZA F25/253; "New York Achooza Aleph Ltd., Annual Statement," 30 June 1931, CZA J86/47.

40. Katz, "Achouzot," 35–36; Sandler, "Jews of America," 165.

41. Simon Goldmann, Sarona, to Dr. Jacob Thon, n.p., 8 January 1914, CZA L18/255; Ruth Kark and Tzvi Shiloni, "Renewal of the Settlement at Gezer" (in Hebrew), in *Sefer Zev Vilnay: Essays on the History, Archaeology, and Love of the Holy Land, Presented to Zev Vilnay,* ed. Eli Schiller (Jerusalem: Ariel 1984), 336–37.

42. Kazan, *From New York to Raanana,* 5–10; Haber, *Odyssey,* 164, cites a lower figure of $25,000.

43. Kazan, *From New York to Raanana,* 20.

44. Ibid., 37, 93–101; Palestine Land Development Company, Jerusalem, to I. Jarcho, Jaffa, 5 November 1920, CZA L18/94/4. The description is not sufficiently detailed to identify the agent or the tract near Jerusalem.

45. Kazan, *From New York to Raanana,* 106–7; I. Jarcho, Tel Aviv, to Dr. Jacob Thon, Jerusalem, 10 February 1922, CZA L18/94/1.

46. Palestine Land Development Company, "Situation of the Purchases in Kirbet Azun," Jerusalem, 4 March 1923, CZA L18/228/2; Avraham Revutsky [Abraham Revusky], "Raanana, the American Colony," in *Jubilee Volume of the Jewish National Fund* (New York: Jewish National Fund, 1932), 88; "New York Achooza Aleph Annual Statement," 30 June 1931, CZA J86/47.

47. Dr. Jacob Thon, Jerusalem, to Secretary of New York Achooza Aleph, Brooklyn, 9 October 1922; Isaiah Jarcho, Tel Aviv, to Thon, 15 August 1922, CZA L18/94/1.

48. Board of Directors of New York Achooza Aleph, New York, to Louis Marshall, 28 May 1929, CZA F25/253; "Agricultural Land Acquired by the P.L.D.C. in the Years 1910–1929," *Palestine and Near East Economic Magazine* 5 (22 July 1930): 255.

49. Protocol of Palestine Executive of the Jewish Agency, 17 (19 November 1930), CZA S100/12B; Yosef Weitz, Memorandum on the lands of El Haram, 15 January 1931, CZA KKL5/507.

50. Certificate of Incorporation of the New York Achooza Aleph, Inc., December 1914, CZA L18/94/4.

51. Kazan, *From New York to Raanana,* 114–18.

52. Haber, *Odyssey,* 394–95.

53. Revutsky, "Raanana," 92; Kazan, *From New York to Raanana,* 146–47.

54. Kazan, *From New York to Raanana,* 133.

55. Ibid., 143, 159–60; Haber, *Odyssey,* 207.

56. Kazan, *From New York to Raanana,* 159–60; Haber, *Odyssey,* 207.

57. "Report about Raanana," 11 November 1946, CZA S9/1187; "Expansion of the Orange Industry in Palestine," *Palestine and Near East Economic Magazine* 3 (15 August

1928), 361; Kazan, *From New York to Raanana,* 160–63; Government of Palestine, *Village Statistics* (Jerusalem, 1938), 55.

58. Kazan, *From New York to Raanana,* 162; Government of Palestine, *Village Statistics,* 55; Revutsky, "Raanana," 89. Sixty dunams of vineyards were listed in "Statistics of Citrus Moshavot on the Coastal Plain," 1929; see Vulcanski Archives, in Reichman, *From Foothold to Settled Territory,* 184–89; New York Achooza Aleph, "Present Opportunities for American Jews in Palestine," New York, 1932, CZA F25/253.

59. Haber, *Odyssey,* 394; Sandler, "Jews of America," 169, provides a figure of 60 Americans in 1929 out of 200 registered members. Depending on family size, sixty persons would likely have represented 10 to 15 families or members. See also Revutsky, "Raanana," 90; Gurevich, *Statistical Abstract of Palestine,* 92–93 Statistics of Citrus Moshavot on the Coastal Plain, 1929, Vulcanski Archives, in Reichman, *From Foothold to Settled Territory,* 184–89; Government of Palestine, *Village Statistics,* 55.

60. Revutsky, "Raanana," 90.

61. Baruch Ostrowsky, "Raanana—A Little American Town in Israel," *Land and Life* 12 (Fall 1949): 30.

62. "New York Achooza Aleph Annual Statement," 30 June 1931, CZA J86/47; Revutsky, "Raanana," 92.

63. *Palestine and Near East Economic Magazine* 7 (August 1932): 328; Jewish National Fund, Jerusalem, to Nir Company, Tel Aviv, 5 June 1935; Nir Company, Tel Aviv, to Jewish National Fund, Jerusalem, 13 December 1935, CZA KKL5/998; "Gan Yavne, Municipal Interests," 18 May 1937, AMJLM IV-208-1-1603.

64. David Gurevich and Aaron Gertz, *Jewish Agricultural Settlement in Palestine (General Survey and Statistical Abstracts)* (Jerusalem: Department of Statistics of the Jewish Agency for Palestine, 1938), 2.

65. "Gan Yavne, Municipal Interests," 18 May 1937, AMJLM IV-208-1-1603; Abraham Singer, Album of the Jewish Legion, Beit Hagdudim Museum, Avihail.

66. New York Achouza Aleph, New York, to Rabbi Stephen Wise, 15 July 1937, CZA F25/253; Barcochba Meirovitch, Jerusalem to M. Shertock, 9 August 1938, CZA S9/1001.

67. Sandler, "Jews of America," 167.

68. Dr. Jacob Thon and M. Elazari-Vulcani, Jerusalem, to Emanuel Mohl, Jerusalem, 21 February 1923; Mohl to Palestine Land Development Company, Jerusalem, 21 March 1923; Bill from the Palestine Land Development Company, Jerusalem, to Bnai Zion Association, Hartford, 21 August 1923, CZA L18/138/10; Louis Glazer, Hartford, to Jacob DeHaas, n.p., 15 April 1925, CZA A404/209.

69. Sandler, "Jews of America," 169.

70. Jacob Ettinger, "Planting 'On Shares'—A Solution for Would-Be Planters With Limited Means," *Palestine and Near East Economic Magazine* 2 (28 February 1927): 83.

71. Sandler, "Jews of America," 93, 176.

CHAPTER 7

1. Constitution of the Zion Commonwealth, Inc., CZA Z4/762. Sandler, "Jews of America," 187–204, partially describes American Zion Commonwealth activities. Sandler's research drew only on the minute books and pamphlets of the AMZIC, leading to some errors and misconceptions about the institution's policies and activities. He did

not make use of the AMZIC New York office archives (originally in the Zionist Library and Archives, New York, but now in the Central Zionist Archives, Jerusalem), which provide a wealth of material.

2. Ibid.; Irit Amit, "American Jewry and the Settlement of Palestine: Zion Commonwealth, Inc.," in *The Land that Became Israel: Studies in Historical Geography,* ed. Ruth Kark (Jerusalem: Magnes Press; New Haven: Yale University Press, 1990), 253. Amit did not, however, emphasize the restrictions that safeguarded Jewish ownership.

3. American Zion Commonwealth, New York, to George Chorover, Swampscott, Mass., 7 April 1926, CZA L65/4.

4. Reports of the Executive of the Zionist Organization to the 12th Zionist Congress, Part III: Organization Report (in English), London 1921, in Metzer, *National Capital,* 141.

5. Metzer, *National Capital,* 50–53.

6. Reports of the Executive of the Zionist Organization to the 12th Zionist Congress, Part III: Organization Report, London 1921, in Metzer, *National Capital,* 142.

7. Louis D. Brandeis "The Zeeland Memorandum," 24 August 1920, cited in Metzer, *National Capital,* 157.

8. Resolutions Adopted by the Zionist Organization of America at the Buffalo Convention, 28 November 1920, cited in Metzer, *National Capital,* 165–67.

9. Gurevich, *Statistical Abstract of Palestine,* 226–27. Report of Committee on the American Zion Commonwealth appointed by the United Palestine Appeal, 1928, CZA KKL5/2296.

10. Weizmann perceived the American Zion Commonwealth as a competitor to the Keren Hayesod. See Chaim Weizmann, Paris, to Julius Simon, London, 17 October 1920, in *Letters and Papers of Chaim Weizmann,* ed. Stein, 10:64–65. During the following years, Weizmann lent guarded support to the AMZIC, assisting it in receiving credit from the Jewish Colonial Trust. See Chaim Weizmann, New York, to the Jewish Colonial Trust, Walbrook, England, 27 December 1923, CZA L65/177.

11. Minutes of Special Meeting of the American Zion Commonwealth Board of Directors, New York, 20 May 1921, CZA A405/37a; Minutes of meeting held at the Zionist Office, 6 October 1922, CZA L18/115/2.

12. Agreement between the Palestine Land Development Company, Jerusalem, and the Mizrachi Organization of America, New York, 29 June 1923, CZA L65/440.

13. Brochure of the American Zion Commonwealth, circa 1926, CZA F38/560; the reference resembles Micah 4:4.

14. Harry Kotler, American Zion Commonwealth, New York, to Charles Passman and Solomon J. Weinstein, Jerusalem, 26 February 1926, CZA L65/364.

15. Shoolman and Harris, together with [?] Cohen-Kaplan, were in Palestine representing the "Habonim Organization," founded in New York in 1922 to build homes in Palestine for members of the organization. Its subscribed capital was $100,000, with $20,000 paid up. Shoolman and Harris were searching for an appropriate tract. *Mischar Ve-Taasiah* (Trade and industry) 3 (15 February 1922): 17. No other relevant information has been found.

16. Minutes of the Meeting of the Zionist Organization of America National Executive Committee, New York, 11 January 1920, CZA L3/38I; Minutes of the Special Meeting of the Zion Commonwealth Board of Directors, New York, 28 April 1915, p. 71, CZA

Notes to Chapter 7

L65/447; Statement of agreement between Cleveland Ahuza No. 1 and AMZIC, 18 July 1918, CZA L65/195. For a history of the *ahuza* in Cleveland, see Lloyd P. Gartner, *History of the Jews of Cleveland* (Cleveland: Western Reserve Historical Society in cooperation with the Jewish Community Federation of Cleveland, 1987), 252. Cleveland Ahuza No. 1's joining the American Zion Commonwealth answers Gartner's query—"The disaster of war put an end to brave plans, and what happened to their painfully gathered funds is not known."

17. New York Achooza Aleph, "Present Opportunities for American Jews in Palestine," New York 1932, CZA F25/253.

18. Anon., *The Story of Nathanyah: The Aim, Ambition, and Outlook of Eretz Yisroel's Youngest Colony,* 1928; Anon., *An Orange Grove on the Mediterranean: Nathanyah on the Mediterranean, A Model Orange Settlement for Americans* (New York: Palestine Settlers' Service, 1932).

19. "What is Yakhin?" AMJLM IV-104–102-37.

20. Solomon J. Weinstein, New York, to Dr. Jacob Thon, Jerusalem, 25 October 1922, CZA L18/115/3.

21. Migdal Garden Villa Incorporated Brochure, circa 1924, CZA L65/317.

22. Yosef Katz, "The Development of Ahuzat Migdal, 1910–1921" (in Hebrew), *Cathedra* 42 (January 1987): 149–51.

23. Charles Passman, Jerusalem, to American Zion Commonwealth, New York, 8 July 1924, L65/387.

24. Two references to the "Menorah" company were found: the Menorah Palestine Building Corporation, room 208, 111–13 Delancy Street, New York ("Building Plots on Mt. Carmel," CZA L65/295); and Menorah Palestine Land Selling Company, Markel Brothers Bank, 92 Canal Street, New York (*Mischar Ve-Taasiah* [Trade and Industry] 18 January 1925). Apparently these two companies are one and the same; Bernard Rosenblatt, Jerusalem, to Harry Kotler, New York, 15 December 1925, CZA L65/365.

25. O. Ben Ami, Tel Aviv, to S. J. Fox, c/o American Zion Commonwealth, New York, 30 October 1928, CZA L65/240.

26. Morris Cherpowitz, New York, to the Directors of the American Zion Commonwealth, New York, n.d., CZA L65/172; Charles Passman, Jerusalem, to AMZIC, New York, 25 July 1924, L65/388.

27. Addison E. Southard, American Consul in Charge, Jerusalem, to Secretary of State, Washington, D.C., 18 October 1921, USNA RG 84 353/86.

28. Hirsh Skakolsky, Hadera, to the members of the 3rd Zionist District in New York and to the President of the District, Mr. Miller, New York (22 September 1951); Solomon J. Weinstein, New York, to Sam Skal, New York, 30 March 1922; *Herald Tribune,* 12 June 1925, in CZA L65/25.

29. Bernard Rosenblatt, New York, to Julian Mack, New York, 30 January 1921, CZA A405/37b.

30. Jacob G. Lipman, born in Russia in 1874, emigrated to the United States in 1888. His family joined the agricultural colony at Woodbine, New Jersey, sponsored by Baron Maurice de Hirsch. Jacob studied at the colony's agricultural school and later graduated from Rutgers College, receiving an M.A. and a Ph.D. from Cornell University. He returned to Rutgers to establish a department of soil chemistry and bacteriology. His career included the post of director of the New Jersey Agricultural Experiment Station,

NOTES TO CHAPTER 7

and he was considered a world expert in soil science. Selman A. Waksman, *Jacob G. Lipman* (New Brunswick, N.J.: Rutgers University Press, 1966).

31. Emanuel Mohl, "Synopsis of discussion at the conference between the representatives of the American Zion Commonwealth and Prof. Jacob G. Lipman," 28 January 1921, CZA A405/37a; Bernard Rosenblatt, New York, to Julian Mack, New York, 30 January 1921, CZA A405/37b.

32. Addison G. Southard, American Consul in Charge, Jerusalem, to Secretary of State, Washington, D.C., 31 December 1921, USNA RG 59 353/85, p. 396.

33. Amit, "American Jewry," 258.

34. Summary of the Protocols of the Directorate of the Jewish National Fund, 6 February 1925, CZA KKL5/1204, cited in Reichman, *From Foothold to Settled Territory*, 175–77.

35. Minutes of the Meeting of the Advisory Council of the American Zion Commonwealth (with Chaim Weizmann in attendance), Cleveland, 7 June 1921, CZA L65/474; Bernard Rosenblatt, Jerusalem, to Solomon J. Weinstein, New York, 5 October 1925, CZA L65/397.

36. Minutes of the Regular Meeting of the American Zion Commonwealth Board of Directors, 2 March 1920, CZA L65/447.

37. Amit, "American Jewry," 259.

38. Charles Passman, Jerusalem, to Bernard A. Rosenblatt, New York, 16 February 1925, CZA L65/321; Passman, to American Zion Commonwealth, New York, 8 March 1925, CZA L65/390; Minutes of the Second Meeting of the AMZIC Palestine Committee, New York, 22 February 1921, CZA L65/474, p. 103.

39. Minutes of a Special Meeting of the American Zion Commonwealth Board of Directors, New York, 9 June 1920, CZA L65/447; Minutes of the Second Meeting of the AMZIC Palestine Committee, New York, 22 February 1921, p. 103, CZA L65/474.

40. Solomon J. Weinstein, Jerusalem, to Louis Lipsky, New York, 23 May 1926, CZA L65/177.

41. Bernard Rosenblatt, New York, to Louis Lipsky, President, Zionist Organization of America, New York, n.d., CZA F38/560.

42. Protocols of the Meeting of the Palestine Zionist Executive, 25 August 1926, CZA S100/6B; Chaim Weizmann, London to S. Salman Schocken, Zwickau, 25 February 1925, in *Letters and Papers of Chaim Weizmann*, ed. Stein, 13: 385–87.

43. Leila Tarazi Fawaz, *Merchants and Migrants in Nineteenth-Century Beirut* (Cambridge, Mass.: Harvard University Press, 1983), 91–94; Ruth Kark, "Changing Patterns of Land Ownership in Nineteenth Century Palestine: The European Influence," *Journal of Historical Geography* 10 (1984): 357–68; Kenneth W. Stein, *The Land Question in Palestine, 1917–1939* (Chapel Hill: University of North Carolina Press, 1984), 223–25.

44. Minutes of the Special Meeting of the Directors of the Zion Commonwealth, Inc., New York, 15 April 1915, CZA L65/447.

45. Minutes of the Adjourned Annual Meeting of the Shareholders of the Zion Commonwealth, Inc., New York, 4 February 1917, CZA L65/447.

46. Stein, *Land Question*, 54–60. See Ariel L. Avneri, *The Jewish Land Settlement and the Arab Claim of Dispossession* (in Hebrew) (n.p.: Hakibbutz Hameuchad, 1980), 97–103, for details of land purchases in the Jezreel Valley.

Notes to Chapter 7

47. "Subscribed Capital and Cash Receipts of the American Zion Commonwealth," January 1920, CZA L3/38II; Bernard A. Rosenblatt, *Balfouria* (New York: Zionist Organization of America, 1920), 3; idem, *Two Generations of Zionism: Historical Recollections of an American Zionist* (New York: Shengold Publishers, 1967), 76; Bernard Rosenblatt, New York, to Julian Mack, New York, 13 November 1919, CZA Z4/762.

48. Bernard Rosenblatt, New York, to Judge Julian Mack, New York, 13 November 1919; Akiva J. Ettinger, Jaffa, to Jewish National Fund Directorate, The Hague, 12 August 1919, CZA Z4/762; Agreement between Palestine Land Development Company and JNF, and American Zion Commonwealth, Jerusalem, 6 August 1919, CZA KKL5/2003; JNF, Jerusalem, to Zionist Commission, Jerusalem, 14 May 1920, CZA KKL2/134.

49. Louis D. Brandeis, Washington, D.C., to Bernard Rosenblatt, n.p., 10 November 1920, in *Letters of Louis D. Brandeis,* ed. Urofsky and Levy, 4: 499.

50. Minutes of the Special Meeting of the American Zion Commonwealth Board of Directors, New York, 20 May 1921, CZA A405/37a; Memorandum of Agreement between Palestine Land Development Company and AMZIC, 16 December 1921, CZA L18/79/3.

51. Chaim Weizmann, London, to Arthur J. Balfour, Paris, 14 August 1919, in *Letters and Papers of Chaim Weizmann,* ed. Stein, 9: 193.

52. Louis D. Brandeis, Washington, D.C., to Bernard A. Rosenblatt, n.p., 10 November 1920, in *Letters of Louis D. Brandeis,* ed. Urofsky and Levy, 4:499. Brandeis also stated: "The action we should take, in the first instance . . . [is] to put Balfouria on the road to success"; Brandeis to Julian William Mack, Stephen Samuel Wise, Bernard Flexner, Jacob de Hass, Felix Frankfurter, Robert Szold, and Alexander Sacks, n.p., 6 February 1921, in ibid., 4:530.

53. "Balfouria: A Bit of America in Palestine," *Judaean Magazine,* 3, no. 12 (May-June 1923), 284.

54. Louis D. Brandeis, Washington, D.C., to Bernard A. Rosenblatt, n.p., 10 November 1920 in *Letters of Louis D. Brandeis,* ed. Urofsky and Levy, 4:499.

55. "Balfouria: A Bit of America in Palestine," 284.

56. Richard Kaufmann Album, Map Library Collection, Department of Geography, Hebrew University of Jerusalem, Jerusalem.

57. Fineman, *Woman of Valor,* 303.

58. Alice B. Seligsberg, "Nellie Straus Mochenson," *Hadassah Newsletter* 18 (March 1938): 109; Minutes of joint meeting of the Zionist Commission for Palestine and American Zion Commonwealth representatives, 8 December 1919, CZA Z4/762; Bernard Rosenblatt, n.p., to Louis D. Brandeis, Washington, D.C., 23 January 1920, CZA A405/37b.

59. Nellie Straus, American Zion Commonwealth, n.p., to Jacob Ettinger, Palestine Office, Jaffa, 18 September 1919, CZA L3/25VIII; Minutes of joint meeting of Zionist Commission for Palestine and AMZIC representatives, 8 December 1919, CZA Z4/762; Rosenblatt, *Balfouria,* 4–5.

60. Fineman, *Woman of Valor,* 302.

61. Arthur Ruppin, n.p., to Director of the Department of Industry and Commerce, Jerusalem, 27 February 1921, CZA L18/79/3; Rosenblatt, *Balfouria,* 4–5; Report of Dr. Melech Zagorodski, 27 March 1923, CZA S15/156b; Yehuda Erez, ed., *Sefer Ha-aliya Ha-shlishit* (Third Aliya Book) (Tel Aviv: Am Oved, 1964), 306–7, 390, 396.

62. Report Rendered by Peter J. Schweitzer on His Visit to Balfouria, 25 May 1921, CZA L65/451.

63. "Balfouria: A Bit of America in Palestine," 284; Report of Dr. M. Zagorodski, 27 March 1923, CZA S15/156b.

64. Shragga Irmai, "Notes—The Drying of the Swamps in the Jezreel Valley Is Not a Legend" (in Hebrew), *Cathedra* 32 (July 1984): 194. Yoram Bar-Gal and Shmuel Shamai, "The Swamps of Emek Yizre'el (Jezreel Valley)—Myth or Reality" (in Hebrew), *Cathedra* 27 (March 1983): 163–74; and various reactions to this article in *Cathedra* 30 (December 1983): 161–95, and *Cathedra* 32 (July 1984): 182–201.

65. Report of Dr. Melech Zagorodski, 27 March 1923, CZA S15/156b; Invitation for the Laying of the Cornerstone of a school in Balfouria, 13 May 1926, CZA S15/319a; Rabbi Haim Michlin, Jerusalem, to Palestine Zionist Executive, Jerusalem, 9 February 1930, CZA S30/1915; plans for a synagogue at Balfouria, 1930, CZA S15/618b.

66. "Palestine Colonization," *Judaean* 3 (June 1922): 11.

67. Report of Dr. M. Zagorodski, 27 March 1923, CZA S15/156b; "Balfouria: A Bit of America in Palestine," 285.

68. American Zion Commonwealth, New York, to Jewish Agency for Palestine, Jerusalem, 8 January 1933, CZA S17/122.

69. Moshe De Shalit, "Balfouria, Herzlia and Afula" (in Yiddish), New York, circa 1926, CZA L65/292; Gurevich, *Statistical Abstract of Palestine,* 96–97. Both sources provide a breakdown of the population according to age and sex, but their divisions do not overlap. See also Memorandum of the Settlement of Balfouria to the Experts Commission, n.d., CZA S15/429a; Government of Palestine, *Village Statistics* (Jerusalem, 1938), 18.

70. Bernard Rosenblatt, n.p., to Louis D. Brandeis, Washington, D.C., 23 January 1920, CZA A405/37b; Emanuel Mohl, "Synopsis of discussion at the conference between American Zion Commonwealth representatives and Prof. Jacob G. Lipman," 28 January 1921, CZA A405/37a. See also Joseph B. Glass, "The Settlement of Prairie Jews in Palestine, 1917–39," *International Journal of Canadian Studies* 16 (Fall 1997): 215–44.

71. Solomon J. Weinstein, New York, to Jacob Thon, Jerusalem, 25 October 1922, CZA L18/115/3; a larger number—fifty houses and barns—is mentioned in "Balfouria: A Bit of America in Palestine," 285; Bill presented to American Zion Commonwealth, Jerusalem, by Palestine Land Development Company, Jerusalem, 12 December 1924, CZA L18/231/3.

72. Akiva Ettinger, Jerusalem, to Charles Passman, Jerusalem, 17 October 1922, CZA S15/156b. By 1923, 24 settlers had received loans of between £E75 to £E125 for farm animals and implements; Report of Dr. Melech Zagorodski, 27 March 1923, CZA S15/156b. This reached Chaim Weizmann's attention during his 1923 North American tour: Chaim Weizmann, New York, to the Keren Hayesod, London, 27 December 1923, in *Letters and Papers of Chaim Weizmann,* ed. Stein, 12: 83–84.

73. Report of Dr. Melech Zagorodski, 27 March 1923, CZA S15/156b; "Balfouria: A Bit of America in Palestine," 285; Charles Passman, Jerusalem, to American Zion Commonwealth, New York, 11 September 1924, CZA L65/386.

74. Minutes of the Annual Meeting of the American Zion Commonwealth, 28 October 1924, CZA L65/263; Eli Solomon, Balfouria, to H. Blumenfeld, Memphis, 12 July 1925, CZA L65/92.

75. Charles Passman, Jerusalem, to the American Zion Commonwealth, New York,

Notes to Chapter 7

7 October 1924, CZA L65/88; Passman to Treasury Department, Palestine Zionist Executive, Jerusalem, 24 February 1925, CZA S1/542; Letter to the editor of *Yediot Achronot* from the Saletskys, Balfouria, n.d., CZA J33/95; *Palestine Bulletin,* 24 February 1925, 3. For a detailed study of the Saletsky family, see Nili Fox, "Balfouriya: An American Zionist Failure or Secret Success?" *American Jewish History* 78 (June 1989): 497–512.

76. Memorandum of the settlement of Balfouria to the Experts Commission, n.d., CZA S15/429a.

77. "Balfouria: A Bit of America in Palestine," 285.

78. Members of Moshav Balfouria, Balfouria, to Zionist Organization, Jerusalem, 4 March 1929, CZA S15/542a; Shimon Mekler, Afula, to the Settlement Department of the Zionist Executive, Jerusalem, 15 November 1929, CZA S15/618d.

79. Gurevich, *Statistical Abstract of Palestine,* 96–97; Government of Palestine, *Village Statistics,* 18.

80. Contract for the purchase of the lands of Jelil and El Haram, 11 September 1921, CZA L18/48/11; "Agricultural Land Acquired by the P.L.D.C. in the Years 1910–1929," *Palestine and Near East Economic Magazine* 5 (22 July 1930): 255; Ashbel, *60 Years of Hachsharat HaYishuv,* 56–57.

81. Arthur Ruppin, New York, to his wife, 20 February 1923, in *Arthur Ruppin,* ed. Bein, 203; Rosenblatt, *Two Generations,* 121–22.

82. Rosenblatt, *Two Generations,* 121–22. Contracts between various individuals and American Zion Commonwealth, representative of Palestine Land Development Company in America, CZA L18/169/2; PLDC, Jerusalem, to Mizrachi, Warsaw, 18 June 1924, and attached four maps, CZA L18/228/3.

83. Protocols of the Palestine Zionist Executive, 101, 104, 107 (12 and 21 January and 1 February 1925), CZA S100/5b; Minutes of the American Zion Commonwealth Board of Directors Meeting, New York, 24 February 1925, CZA L65/263. Katz, *"Business" of Settlement,* 221–22.

84. Protocols of the Palestine Zionist Executive, 5 (6 July 1924), CZA S100/4b; Protocols of the Palestine Zionist Executive, 112 (16 July 1925), CZA S100/5b; Yitzhak Vulcanski, Palestine Zionist Executive, Tel Aviv, to Jewish National Fund, Jerusalem, 21 July 1924; Charles Passman, Jerusalem, to JNF, Jerusalem, 21 November 1924, CZA KKL5/1532.

85. Table of Survey of the Area (gross & net) in Zones 1, 2, 3 of Herzlia, September 1925, CZA L65/31.

86. Report on the Activities of the American Zion Commonwealth, 1930, CZA Z4/3445II; Summary of purchases at Herzlia and letter to Yehoshua Hankin, Tel Aviv, 18 August 1932, CZA L18/700.

87. American Zion Commonwealth contract for the purchase of a 10-dunam plot in Herzlia Zone 3, 3 October 1924, General Custodian's Office, HW/a, citation graciously provided by Irit Amit; Agreement between the Cleveland Herzlia Group and the AMZIC, 6 June 1924, CZA L65/47.

88. David Ben-Gurion, Jerusalem, to the American Zion Commonwealth, New York, 4 March 1924 (in Hebrew), in *David Ben-Gurion Letters,* ed. Erez, 2: 202–3.

89. Agreement between the Cleveland Herzlia Group and American Zion Commonwealth, 6 June 1924, CZA L65/47; Sol I. Golden, Atlanta, to AMZIC, New York, 28 February 1931, CZA L65/396.

NOTES TO CHAPTER 7

90. Photocopy of the protocols of the Herzlia Committee, 1 (11 November 1924), CZA J33/144; Bernard Rosenblatt, "Afternoon Tea in Herzliah," 17 December 1924, CZA L65/389; Charles Passman, Jerusalem, to Solomon J. Weinstein, New York, 9 March 1925, CZA L65/392; Mordechai Naor, Zeev Inbar, Zeev Segal et al., ed., *Herzlia: Ha-Yovel Ha-rishon* (Herzlia: The First Jubilee) (Herzlia and Tel Aviv: n.p., 1979), 26–27, 31–37; Vered Shatzman, "Histadrut Bnai Binyamin—Yessuda Ve-peiluta, 1919–1929" (The Bnei Binyamin Organization—Its Founding and Its Activities, 1919–29) (Master's thesis, Hebrew University of Jerusalem, 1989), 77–82.

91. Bernard Rosenblatt, Jerusalem, to Solomon J. Weinstein, New York, 5 October 1925, CZA L65/397; Naor et al., eds., *Herzlia: The First Jubilee,* 37–39; Annual Report of American Zion Commonwealth, June 1926, CZA L65/264.

92. Charles Passman, Jerusalem, to American Zion Commonwealth, New York, 25 June 1925, CZA L65/391. Passman to Herman Harris, New York, 14 September 1925; Memorandum on the Bids for the Construction of Houses in Herzlia, 1 July 1926; Memorandum on the Construction of Roads in Herzlia, 5 October 1926, CZA L65/363.

93. Gurevich, *Statistical Abstract of Palestine,* 92–93; Statistics of Citrus Moshavot on the Coastal Plain, 1929, Vulcanski Archives, in Reichman, *From Foothold to Settled Territory,* 184–89.

94. "Expansion of the Orange Industry in Palestine," *Palestine and Near East Economic Magazine* 3 (15 August 1928): 360, 375–82; Gurevich, *Statistical Abstract of Palestine,* 92–93; Government of Palestine, *Village Statistics,* 54.

95. Anon., *Orange Grove on the Mediterranean.*

96. Protocols of the Herzlia Committee, 10, 14 February 1925, CZA J33/144; Memorandum from the Committee of the Moshav Herzlia to Solomon J. Weinstein, Jerusalem, 26 March 1926, CZA L65/363; M. De Shalit, Jerusalem, to American Zion Commonwealth, New York, 21 February 1927, CZA L65/366; Naor et al., eds., *Herzlia: The First Jubilee,* 32, 71–72; Government of Palestine, *Village Statistics,* 54; Gurevich, *Statistical Abstract of Palestine,* 92–93.

97. American Zion Commonwealth, New York, to Moses De Shalit, Jerusalem, 19 November 1929, CZA L65/193; Henrietta Szold, *Recent Jewish Progress in Palestine* (reprint from *American Jewish Year Book 5676*; Arno Press: New York 1977), 96–97; Gordon, *New Judea,* 69–70.

98. Statistics of Citrus Moshavot on the Coastal Plain, 1929, Vulcanski Archives, in Reichman, *From Foothold to Settled Territory,* 184–89; Government of Palestine, *Village Statistics,* 54; Naor et al, eds., *Pioneers of Herzliya* 3 vols. Shoshana Migdal was a member of the committee that produced this work; her calculations are based on entries in the book and corrected lists of country of origin. For example, see S. W. Levine (vol. 2), whose country of origin is listed as Russia; he was born there but lived in the United States from 1903 until 1922.

99. Bernard A. Rosenblatt, *Two Generations,* 122–23.

100. Frederick H. Kisch, Jerusalem, to Solomon J. Weinstein, Jerusalem, 26 May 1926, CZA L65/406.

101. [?] Oberstein, chairman of Herzlia purchasers group, Brooklyn, to Zionist Organization, Central Office, London, 25 March 1930, CZA S30/1915.

102. Gershon Agronsky, "Afulah in the Great Plain of Esderelon," *New Palestine,* 12 June 1925, 691.

Notes to Chapter 7

103. Stein, *Land Question,* 54–60; Avneri, *Settlement,* 97–103; Charles Passman, Jerusalem, to American Zion Commonwealth, New York, 8 July 1924, CZA L65/387. Although Weizmann partially supported the AMZIC, he would have preferred that the Jewish National Fund and the proposed Keren Hayesod receive control of the Jezreel Valley lands. He explained to Julius Simon, on the eve of his visit to North America, "I can only go on that trip if I have an opportunity of starting a great movement, not to found joint stock companies or to promote the [American] Zion Commonwealth" (Chaim Weizmann, Paris, to Julius Simon, London, 17 October 1920, in *Letters and Papers of Chaim Weizmann,* ed. Stein, 10: 64–65); Telegram from Chaim Weizmann, London, to Bernard Rosenblatt, New York, 26 November 1920, in ibid., 10: 97.

104. Abdullah Muhammmad Jawish et al., Nazareth, to Yehoshua Hankin through the District Officer, Nazareth, 28 December 1924, CZA S25/3368 (English trans. from Arabic), in Stein, *Land Question,* 54–56; Report on the Activities of American Zion Commonwealth, 1930, CZA Z4/3445II.

105. Charles Passman, Jerusalem, to American Zion Commonwealth, New York, 28 April 1925; Harry Kotler, New York, to Passman, New York, 22 May 1925, CZA L65/323.

106. Ada Maimon, *Women Build a Land* (New York: Herzl Press, 1962), 108–9.

107. Gurevich, *Statistical Abstract of Palestine,* 96–97.

108. Quoted in *Ir Yizrael: Afula Bat Kaf-Hay, 5685–5710/1925–1950* (City of the Jezreel: Afula at Twenty-Five, 5685–5710/1925–1950) (Afula: n.p., 1950), 9.

109. Ibid., 10; *Palestine and Near East Economic Magazine* 7 (August 1932): 32; Gurevich and Gertz, *Jewish Agricultural Settlement in Palestine,* 7.

110. Rosenblatt, *Two Generations,* 126–27.

111. Charles Passman, Jerusalem, to American Zion Commonwealth, New York, 3 February 1925, CZA L65/390; Report on the Haifa Bay Development Co., Ltd., Haifa, 22 November 1927, CZA J15/5688; Doukhan-Landau, "The Haifa Bay Lands"; Iris Graicer, "Cooperation between Private and Public Capital in the Development of the Zebulun Valley (Emeq Zevulun)" (in Hebrew), in *Studies in the Geography of Israel* (Jerusalem: Israel Exploration Society, 1992), 13:159–78.

112. Gilbert Herbert and Silvina Sosnovsky, *Bauhaus on the Carmel and the Crossroads of Empire: Architecture and Planning in Haifa during the British Mandate* (Jerusalem: Yad Izhak Ben-Zvi, 1993) 158.

113. Memorandum from Solomon J. Weinstein, New York, to the Board of Directors, American Zion Commonwealth, New York, 29 November 1926, CZA F38/560.

114. Haifa Bay Development Co., Ltd., Haifa, 12 April 1926, CZA J15/5688.

115. Harry Kotler, n.p., to American Zion Commonwealth, Jerusalem, 26 February 1926, CZA L65/364; Memorandum from Solomon J. Weinstein, New York, to the AMZIC Board of Directors, New York, 29 November 1926, CZA F38/560.

116. *Palestine Bulletin,* 26 August 1926, in USNA RG 84 353/88, p. 489.

117. Akiva Ettinger, "Nordia: A Proposal for the Founding of an Orchard Colony near Haifa," 12 September 1926, CZA L65/294.

118. American Zion Commonwealth sales circular, 20 February 1927, CZA L65/35.

119. Charles Passman, Jerusalem, to American Zion Commonwealth, New York, 10 January 1927, CZA L65/394.

NOTES TO CHAPTER 8

120. Bernard Rosenblatt, New York to Menachem Ussishkin, Jerusalem, 8 January 1929, CZA KKL5/2296; Doukhan-Landau, "Haifa Bay Lands"; Julius Simon, *Certain Days: Zionist Memoirs and Selected Papers,* ed. and essay by Evyatar Friesel (Jerusalem: Israel Universities Press, 1971), 279–80; Chaim Weizmann, London, to S. Salman Schocken, Zwickau, 13 February 1928, in *Letters and Papers of Chaim Weizmann,* ed. Stein, 13: 365; Chaim Weizmann, New York, to Zionist Executive, London, 29 March 1928, in ibid., 13:421.

121. Situation of the Lands of AMZIC and Meshek, 16 March 1928, CZA KKL5/2296; Report on the Activities of the AMZIC, 1930, CZA Z4/3445II; Report on lands received from the American Zion Commonwealth by the Jewish National Fund, Jerusalem, 22 December 1931, CZA S15/566.

122. Ibid.; Protocols of the Palestine Zionist Executive, 39 (18 June 1928), CZA S100/8b.

123. Herbert and Sosnovsky, *Bauhaus on the Carmel,* 186–202.

124. Yehuda Hayut, "The Founding of the Krayot in Haifa Bay" (in Hebrew), in *Haifa and Its Development, 1918–1948,* ed. Mordechai Naor and Yossi Ben-Artzi (Jerusalem: Yad Izhak Ben-Zvi, 1989), 130–46.

125. Ibid.

126. Ibid.

127. Contract between Abd-el Rahman Beck Nafiz El Taji El Faruki et al. and American Zion Commonwealth, Jerusalem, 31 July 1925; Statement of claim by the AMZIC against Abd-el Rahman Beck Nafiz El Taji El Faruki et al., Jerusalem, 3 June 1926, CZA A417/6.

128. Charles Passman, Jerusalem, to American Zion Commonwealth, New York, 8 March 1925, CZA L65/390; Bernard Rosenblatt, Jerusalem, to Solomon Weinstein, New York, 5 October 1925, CZA L65/397.

129. Ibid.; Aminadav Ashbel, *The Palestine Land Development Company: Episodes and Activities in the Cities of Israel, Jerusalem, Tel Aviv and Haifa* (in Hebrew) (Jerusalem: Israel Land Development Company, 1976), 161–86.

130. Ran Aaronsohn, "Building the Land: Stages in First Aliya Colonization (1882–1904)," in *The Jerusalem Cathedra: Studies in the History, Archaeology, Geography and Ethnography of the Land of Israel,* ed. Lee Z. Levine (Jerusalem: Yad Izhak Ben-Zvi; Detroit: Wayne State University Press, 1983), 3:269–70; E. W. Lewin-Epstein, Brooklyn, to American Zion Commonwealth, New York, 11 November 1925, CZA L65/248; Solomon Weinstein, London, to AMZIC, New York, 9 February 1926, CZA L65/364.

131. Stein, *Land Question,* 69.

132. Bernard Rosenblatt, New York, to Menachem Ussishkin, Jerusalem, 8 January 1929, CZA KKL5/2296.

133. Ibid.

CHAPTER 8

1. "The Gan Chaim Corporation Ltd.," *Palestine and Near East Economic Magazine* 3 (30 April 1928): 239; Gurevich and Gertz, *Jewish Agricultural Settlement in Palestine,* 4; Asher Pierce, Tel Aviv, to High Commissioner, Jerusalem, 4 April 1928, CZA L18/1169; *Palestine Bulletin* (26 January 1928): 2; Memorandum from E. Lewin-Esptein to A.

Baroway, 24 May 1933, CZA A123/18; Irit Amit, "Private Jewish Investors in Palestine in the 1920s," in *The Mosaic of Israeli Geography,* ed. Yehuda Gradus and Gabriel Lipshitz (Beer Sheva: Ben-Gurion University of the Negev Press, 1996), 451–60.

2. Revusky, *Jews in Palestine,* 265–66.

3. Sydney Pierce, "Asher Pierce, 1867–1936" 1980, CJCNA RG 2B/Asher Pierce, pp. 4–5; Irit Amit, "Jewish Land and Settlement Policy in the Southern Sharon between the Years 1918 and 1929: The Role of National Capital and Private Enterprise in Shaping the Region" (in Hebrew) (Ph.D. diss., Hebrew University of Jerusalem, 1993), 298–312.

4. Statistics of Citrus Moshavot on the Coastal Plain, 1929, Vulcanski Archives, in Shalom Reichman, *From Foothold to Settled Territory,* 184–89; *Palestine and Middle East Economic Magazine* 8 (March 1933): 127.

5. List of Renters of the Gan Haim Organization, Jerusalem, 11 September 1935; Gan Haim Organization, Gan Haim, to Head Office, Jewish National Fund, Jerusalem (in Hebrew), 25 February 1934, CZA KKL5/6935.

6. Knowles Ryerson, Los Angeles, to Asher Pierce, Montreal, 23 July 1928, CZA L18/1169; Yaacov Morris, *On the Soil of Israel: Americans and Canadians in Agriculture* (Tel Aviv: Association of Americans and Canadians in Israel, 1965), 41–42.

7. Julius Simon, *An American Corporation at Work in Palestine* (Tel Aviv: Palestine Publishing, 1939), 3–8; Graicer, "Cooperation between Private Capital and National Capital"; Hayut, "Founding of the Krayot."

8. Graicer, "Cooperation between Private Capital and National Capital," 164–75; Hayut, "Founding of the Krayot," 136, 144.

9. Alexander K. Sloan, American Consul, Jerusalem, to the Secretary of State, Washington, D.C., 23 December 1932, CZA S17/161.

10. Simon, *An American Corporation,* 3–8.

11. "The Activities of the Committee of Rosoff Group Plantations," AMJLM IV-104-102-37.

12. Ibid.

13. Ibid.; "The Development of Ramoth Meyer," n.d., CZA J88/29.

14. Ibid. Statistics for the Citrus Moshavot on the Coastal Plain, 1929, in Reichman, *From Foothold to Settled Territory,* 184–89. *HaOlam* (in Hebrew) 6 (20 January 1928): 53; 6 (14 September 1928): 707. The five investors were: Dr. M. L. Rosoff, Dr. L. Shiffman, Mr. M. L. Schupak, Dr. S. L. Auerbach, and Mr. M. Kastoff. The first three had 200 dunams each, and the last two owned 50 dunams each.

15. "Activities of the Committee of Rosoff Group Plantations," AMJLM IV-104-102-37.

16. Ibid.

17. Ibid.

18. Ibid.

19. *Palestine and Middle East Economic Magazine* 8 (January 1933): 39; Eric Mills, *Census of Palestine,* 1:22; Gurevich and Gertz, *Jewish Agricultural Settlement,* 3.

20. List of members of Agudat Netaim (in Hebrew), CZA A182/53. The other three were A. Abramson from Chicago, A. Lubrosky from New York, and [?] Akram from Baltimore. It appears they subscribed to the company but did not purchase any land. For a history of Agudat Netaim up to 1914, see Yossi Katz, *"Business" of Settlement,* 143–202.

21. Robert Kesselman, Jerusalem, to Dr. H. Friedenwald, Baltimore, 23 May 1941; "Yaar Shalom," CZA A182/4. Correspondence dealing with the purchase before 1914 is found in CZA A182/53. See also Alexander Lee Levin, *Vision: A Biography of Harry Friedenwald* (Philadelphia: Jewish Publication Society of America, 1964), 211, 324.

22. Anon., *Story of Nathanyah.*

23. Ibid.; Revusky, *Jews in Palestine,* 266.

24. *Story of Nathanyah;* Rachel Kleinman, Yehoshua Ben-Arieh, and Dan Giladi, "The Beginnings of Netanya as an Agricultural Moshavah, 1928–1933," (in Hebrew) in *The Netanya Book,* ed. Avshalom Shmueli and Moshe Brawer (Tel Aviv: Am Oved, 1982), 115–16.

25. *Story of Nathanyah;* A. P. Schoolman, New York, to Dr. I. Berkson, Jerusalem, 5 September 1933; A. P. Schoolman, n.p., to Hanotaiah, Tel Aviv, 12 March 1934, CZA A348/126; Alexander M. Dushkin, *Living Bridges: Memoirs of an Educator* (Jerusalem: Keter, 1975), 190–91.

26. *Nathanyah on the Mediterranean.*

27. Ibid.; Bernard Joseph, Jerusalem, to Israel B. Brodie, New York, 6 July 1932, CZA S17/162. See also, Contract between Isaac B. Berkson, Jerusalem and Hanotaiah, 16 March 1932, CZA A348/126. On 6 April 1932, £P = $3.81, as compared to a relatively stable rate of £P = $5.00. Moshe Smilansky was an agronomist and president of the Jewish Farmers' Federation of Palestine; P. Pascal was an agronomist and planted in Petah Tikvah; [?] Chefetz of Petah Tikvah and T. Z. Miller of Rehovot were also planters. A. P. Schoolman, n.p., to Hanotaiah, Tel Aviv, 12 March 1934, CZA A348/126.

28. Statistics of Citrus Moshavot on the Coastal Plain, 1929, Vulcanski Archives, in Reichman, *From Foothold to Settled Territory,* 184–89; Gurevich and Gertz, *Jewish Agricultural Settlement,* 5.

29. Dushkin, *Living Bridges,* 190–91.

30. Map of Hanotaiah tracts in Amit, "Sharon," appendix 15, p. 384.

31. Morris, *On the Soil of Israel,* 30–31.

32. Ibid.; Sam Friedlander, Beit Hagdudim Museum Album, Avihail; Ruth Zamir, daughter of Sam Friedlander, interview by author Avihail, 3 May 1990.

33. Yitzhak Minster, interview by author, Avihail, 10 May 1990. J. Jonas Jacobs was president of Publicity Printing Corporation, New York City; Aaron Herr was president of Essex Metal Ceiling Co., Newark, N.J.; Jacob Trachtenberg was a wholesale grocer in Norfolk, Va.

34. Ibid.; Sam Friedlander, Beit Hagdudim Museum Album, Avihail; Ruth Zamir, interview by author, Avihail, 3 May 1990; Morris, *On the Soil of Israel,* 32–33.

35. Akiva Ettinger, Jerusalem, to David De Sola Pool, Jerusalem (in Hebrew), 19 August 1920; David De Sola Pool, n.p., to H. Saletan, New York, 22 August 1920, CZA L3/66II.

36. *Palestine and Near East Economic Magazine* 7 (August 1932): 329; Ben Rubinstein, New York to Ittamar Ben-Avi, n.p., 15 November 1932, YIBZA 5/2/6/8. Ida Silverman was the cofounder of the Herzlia Development Company in 1932.

37. [?] Horin, Tel Aviv, to A. M. Koller, New York, 31 October 1929, AMJLM, IV-204-102-11; Shlomo Angel, *Kfar Saba: 70 years to the Founding of Kfar Saba (1903), 80 Years to the Redemption of Its Land* (in Hebrew) (Kfar Saba: Kfar Saba Municipality, 1973).

38. David Tidhar, *Encyclopedia of the Pioneers of the Yishuv and Its Builders* (in Hebrew) (Tel Aviv: Sifriat Rishonim, 1947), 1:420; N. J. Thischby, Jerusalem, to the Chairman, Standing Committee for Commerce and Industry, Government of Palestine, Jerusalem, 22 November 1933, CZA S8/2093a; Shoshana Migdal, interview by author, Herzlia, 13 February 1995. Migdal identified Pardes Zacks as being located to the south of the road leading to Givat Brenner; this may be a different tract than the Nes Ziona tract referred to in the text.

39. Tidhar, *Encyclopedia,* 1:204.

40. Anat Tal-Shir, "Latrun Battle 93" (in Hebrew) in *Seven Days: Friday Supplement to Yediot Achronot,* 21 May 1993, 21, 23, 25; citation graciously provided by Prof. Ruth Kark.

41. Yossi Katz, *Jewish Settlement in the Hebron Mountains and the Etzion Bloc: From "Nahalat Herzog" to Gush Etzion* (in Hebrew) (Ramat Gan: Bar-Ilan University, 1992), 19–20.

42. Ibid., 25–35.

43. Marcus Esterman, Jaffa-Tel Aviv, to American Zion Commonwealth, New York, 8 November 1920, CZA A405/37b.

Chapter 9

1. Moshe Smilansky, Tel Aviv, to Israel B. Brodie, New York, 27 October 1931, CZA S17/162.

2. Emanuel Mohl, n.p., to Israel B. Brodie, New York, circa 1931; Memorandum on the Jewish Agency's Scheme for Middle-Class Settlement on Jewish National Fund Land in Wadi El-Hawareth, circa 1931; Yehoshua Hankin, Tel Aviv, to Brodie, 26 October 1931; Harry Vitales, Jerusalem to Brodie, 8 November 1931, CZA S17/162.

3. Memorandum from Aaron Baroway, n.p., to Rehabiah Lewin-Epstein, n.p., 16 November 1932, CZA S17/161.

4. Ibid., 9 December 1932, CZA S17/161.

5. Louis D. Brandeis, Washington, D.C., to Akiva Jacob Ettinger, n.p., 1 November 1931, in *Letters of Louis D. Brandeis,* ed. Urofsky and Levy, 5:486–87.

6. Louis D. Brandeis, Washington, D.C., to Robert D. Kesselman, n.p., 5 February 1932, in *Letters of Louis D. Brandeis,* ed. Urofsky and Levy, 5: 495.

7. "An Extensive Colonization Scheme in Palestine," New York, 27 February 1933, CZA S17/161.

8. Emanuel Liebes, *History of Moshav Beit Herut* (in Hebrew) (Beit Herut: private publication, 1994), 3.

9. Lyons Bar-David, *My Promised Land,* 51–52.

10. Nibby Penn, "Moshav Bet Cherut," in *Arise and Build: The Story of American Habonim,* ed. David Breslau (New York: Ichud Habonim Labor Zionist Youth, 1961), 211.

11. Ibid.; Efraim Orni and Elisha Efrat, *Geography of Israel* (Jerusalem: Israel Program for Scientific Translations, 1966), 230. A moshav *shitufi* is a type of cooperative smallholders' settlement representing an intermediate form between the kibbutz and the moshav. It is based on a collective economy and collective ownership, combining the mechanical and technological advantages of large-scale enterprises with individual living.

12. Emanuel Liebes, *History of Moshav Beit Herut,* 3, 36–38.

13. Nibby Penn, "Moshav Bet Cherut," 212.

14. David Gerstein, President of Chalutzim Organization, Chicago, to Jewish National Fund, Jerusalem, 5 April 1932, CZA S15/2488.

15. General Secretary of Jewish National Fund, Jerusalem, to Chalutzim Organization, Chicago, 12 May 1932, CZA S15/2488.

16. Izhak Ben-Zvi, Tel Aviv, to Rachel Ben-Zvi, n.p., 30 October 1919, in Ben-Zvi, *Jewish Legion,* 119–21.

17. Samuel Levine, Bir Salem, to Zionist Commission, Jerusalem, 28 July 1919, CZA L3/25VIII.

18. Nakdimon Rogel, "Who Defended Tel Hai" (in Hebrew), *Kivunim,* 38 (March 1990): 130–31, 139–40. These two Americans were forgotten in the historiography of the defense of Palestine's northern frontier. With the exception of Rogel, most sources do not refer to them at all. A press report, "Last Days in Upper Galilee," described the scene at Tel Hai following the attack: "One of the demobilized American Judeans, Tuker[,] lay dead together with those belonging to the village. On ascending above they were confronted with a terrifying spectacle[.] Sara Chisik, Munter and one of the demobilized Americans, Sharf, were cut in pieces by a bomb" (translated from *Ha'aretz* [8 March 1920] in CZA Z4/16083). In addition, a physician observing the incident was Dr. George Gershon Garry, a demobilized American Legionnaire. Garry was best known for attending to Joseph Trumpeldor's fatal wounds and testifying to Trumpeldor's famous last words, "It is good to die for our country."

19. Mordechai Eliav, "The Rafah Approaches (Pithat-Rafiah) in the History of Jewish Settlement" (in Hebrew), *Cathedra* 3 (February 1977): 161.

20. Jacob Ettinger, "Memorandum on the Provision of Land in Palestine for the Settlement of Jewish ex-Soldiers," Jaffa, June 1919, CZA L2/208II.

21. Circular to the Members of Discharged and Demobilized Soldiers Association describing its second conference on 20 Iyar 5681 (26 May 1921); Executive Committee of Discharged and Demobilized Soldiers Association, Jerusalem, to the Chairman of the Land Commission, Jerusalem, 7 January 1920 [*sic;* should be 1921] CZA A209/1; Louis Kaskin, n.p., to Jacob Ettinger, Jaffa, n.d., CZA L2/208II. The ten Americans with agricultural experience were: Louis Kaskin, Samuel Schwartz, Lazar Lipnar, I. Miller, Harry Stone, Isaac Landa, Samuel Gitlin, M. Itzikof, Samuel H. Garekol, and Nathan Goldstein.

22. Ibid.; Gershon Agronsky, Jerusalem, to the Land Commissioner, Jerusalem, 15 October 1920; [?] Abrahamson, Chairman of the Land Commission, Jerusalem, to Agronsky, 28 October 1920, CZA A209/1.

23. The eight graduates were: [?] Brondse (1918), Samuel H. Garekol (1913), Samuel Gitlin (1917), Nathan Goldstein (1913), Isaac Landa (1918), Lazer Lipner (1916), [?] Srebnick (1918), and Harry Stone (1918). Originally there were fifteen members. Eliezer Yoffe and Melech Levine also studied at the Baron de Hirsch Agricultural School at Woodbine, New Jersey. They were members of HaIkar HaTzair in the United States who settled at the Kinneret farm. See Shilo, "On the Way to the Moshav."

24. Minutes of the meeting held by the Graduates of the Baron de Hirsch Agricultural School of Woodbine, N.J., at Mikvah Israel, 16 Adar I, 5679 (19 February 1919), AJHSA I-43, box 3. On the development of the moshav *ovdim* idea, see: Michal Oren, "The Development of the *Moshav Ovdim* Idea," in *Land That Became Israel,* 215–32.

25. Ibid.

26. English translation of letter from Samuel Garekol, Tel Aviv to [?] Rapkin, n.p., circa 1919, AJHSA I-54, box 3.

27. Bernard A. Palitz, New York to Eugene S. Benjamin, White Sulphur Springs, W. Va., 17 March 1919; Palitz to Samuel Garkol and Melech Levine, Jaffa, 1 April 1919, AJHSA I-54, box 3.

28. Certificate of Incorporation of Hagdud Haivri League, Inc., 5 November 1929, CZA F25/186.

29. Ibid.; General letter from Elias Ginsburg, New York, n.d., CZA F25/118.

30. Louis Topkis, Wilmington, Del., to Avraham Harzfeld, Tel Aviv, 16 October 1929, AMJLM IV-235–3-321.

31. American Palestine Settlers Association, Report to the National Committee by Jacob De Haas, n.p., n.d.; Plan for Establishing Two Legion Colonies in Palestine within the Next 2 Years, n.p., n.d.; General letter of the American Palestine Settlers Association, 12 June 1930, CZA A404/576. Memorandum submitted by the American-Palestine Jewish Legion to the Conference for the United Palestine Campaign, CZA F25/118. Joseph Weitz, Jerusalem, to the Demobilized Soldiers Organization, Tel Aviv, 16 December 1931, CZA KKL5/6001. Memorandum to Palestine Jewish Colonization Association, n.p., from Association of American ex-Legionnaires, "Agricultural Settlers in Palestine," n.d., Yosef Binyamini Archives, YIBZA 5/6/1/13.

32. L. Bawly to Emanuel Neumann, 30 September 1932, CZA S17/150; Letter to Julius Simon, n.p., 26 November 1933, CZA KKL5/6876.

33. Declaration for the creation of the Zundelowitz Fund in America, CZA S15/1972; List of loans from the Zundelowitz Fund to Avihail Settlers, CZA S15/1979; Haber, *Odyssey,* 201.

34. List of Settlers on the Settlement (Avihail), 29 April 1936, CZA S15/1972; Gurevich and Gertz, *Jewish Agricultural Settlement,* 5.

35. Asher Sapir, Tel Aviv, to the Registrar of Cooperative Organizations of the Palestinian Government, Jerusalem, 22 July 1938, CZA S15/1978a.

36. Yitzhak Minster, interview by author, Avihail, 10 May 1990.

37. Bogrei Hechalutz America, *Pioneers from America;* Breslau, ed., *Arise and Build;* Goldberg and King, eds., *Builders and Dreamers;* Yona Goldberg and Natan Friedel, eds., *Hechalutz: Builders and Fighters* (New York: Hechalutz, 1947); Ariel Hurwitz, ed., *Against the Stream: Seven Decades of Hashomer Hatzair in North America* (Givat Haviva: Association of North American Shomrim in Israel and Yad Yaari, 1994); Lapide, *A Century of U.S. Aliya;* Morris, *On the Soil of Israel;* Morris, *Pioneers from the West.*

38. The supported settlements included Ramatayim, Gedera, Magdiel, Beit Shaarim, Kefar Aharon, Kefar Saba, Herzliya, Bnei Brak, and Balfouria. Among the population of these colonies, 203 farms with 849 persons received financial assistance. These cooperatives included the Karkur and Schiller groups. Together they had a population of 93: 55 men, 29 women, and 9 children. "Census of Agricultural Settlements," *Palestine and Near East Economic Magazine* 6, nos. 10–11 (1931), Tables 1, 5.

39. Ben Halpern, "Vanguard of an American Aliya," *Furrows* 3 (November 1944): 10.

40. Lewis Jack Kamenetzky and Morris Rosenstein, Tel Aviv, to the President of the American Zion Commonwealth, n.p., 10 March 1926, CZA L65/400 (see chapter 5, note 1 for part of the text).

41. Saadia Gelb, "Poale Zion and Habonim Settlements," in Bogrei Hechalutz America, *Pioneers from America*, 65–67.

42. Marie Syrkin, ed., *Golda Meir Speaks Out* (London: Weidenfeld and Nicolson, 1973), 38–42; Martin, *Golda: A Biography*, 100, 110, 117–18.

43. Levin, "Kvutzat Gordonia in Philadelphia," 46–47.

44. Their average age was 20.4 years, ranging from 18 to 23. Two were born in North America and the rest in Eastern Europe. Five had American citizenship, one had Canadian citizenship, and the rest had no passports. "Information about immigrants that came from America via Kantara," 30 December 1930; Description of the Detroit Kvutza, CZA S6/1592c. Grand, "History of Zionist Youth Organizations," 214–15; M. Ben Zvi and Moshe Zamir, "The Kvutza of Detroit," in Bogrei Hechalutz America, *Pioneers from America*, 48–50.

45. "A Call to All Hechalutz Branches . . . ," 19 December 1932; "To Our Departing Chalutzim," CZA F25/194; Breslau, ed., *Arise and Build*, 28–29.

46. Y. Hazan, Shomer Hatzair World Executive, Warsaw, to Shomer Hatzair Executive, Mishmar Haemek (in Hebrew), 8 April 1931, GHA RG H1.2, box 4, file 2; Hashomer Hatzair Bulletin, November 1931, 5, GHA RG T-1, box 1, file 5; Morris, *Pioneers from the West*, 26–27.

47. Minutes of the Palestine Executive of the Jewish Agency Meeting, 3 July 1932, CZA S100/13b.

48. "Memorandum on the project of supplying land for the settlement of the first American Kvutzah of Hashomer Hatzair Organization in Palestine," 2 March 1933, CZA KKL5/4931.

49. Elias M. Epstein, General Secretary, Jewish National Fund, Jerusalem, to Dr. Israel Goldstein, President, JNF of America, New York, 17 April 1934; Goldstein to Epstein, 10 May 1934; Irma Lindheim, Haifa, to Epstein, 5 July 1934, CZA KKL 5/6335. I. H. Rubin, JNF, New York, to JNF, Jerusalem, 30 March 1933, CZA KKL5/4931.

50. Morris, *Pioneers from the West*, 27–29. See the file Kibbutz America-Banir at Hadera, 1934–1938, CZA S9/465, for details of conditions at the Hadera camp.

51. Revusky, *Jews in Palestine*, 270.

52. Joshua Liebner, "Our First Kibbutz: Ein Hashofet," *Youth and Nation* 16 (August 1948): 17–20.

53. Bulletin Kibbutz B, 8 (October 1936), 9 (January 1937), GHA RG T-1, box 7 file 1. Kibbutz Hashomer Hatzair, America-Krit, Memorandum to the Agricultural center of the Histadrut, 16 June 1937, GHA RG H-3, box 18, file 1. Morris, *Pioneers from the West*, 36. Luba Greenbaum, interview by author, Kibbutz Kfar Menachem, 6 November 1993.

54. "And This is the History of Kfar Menachem" (in Hebrew), GHA RG 101, box 1.36, file 22; Protocols of Hashomer Hatzair Secretariat meeting, Tel Aviv, 29 June 1938, GHA RG 5, box 1B, file 2I; "We Await the Day: Second American Colony Prepares to Settle," circa 1939, GHA RG T-1, box 7, file 1; "The End of the Um-es-Suf Episode" (in Hebrew), in *In the Beginning: Kfar Menachem Bulletin* 171 (17 September 1965): 5, KKMA.

55. Dr. Israel Goldstein, New York, to Menachem Ussishkin, Jerusalem, 14 November 1939, GHA RG T-1, box 26, file 3; "And This is the History of Kfar Menachem" (in Hebrew), GHA RG 101, box 1.36, file 22.

56. Ibid.; Chaim Goldberg, "Kfar Menachem: An Epic of American Pioneering in Palestine," *J.N.F. News Bulletin* 8 (Spring 1945): 1–2, 8.

57. Morris, *Pioneers from the West,* 54–56; Lapide, *Century of U.S. Aliya,* 78–79.

58. Breslau, ed., *Arise and Build,* 203–5; " 'We Will Rebuild Galilee': A Year of Habonim Settlement of Kfar Blum," *Furrows* 3 (November 1944): 2–22.

59. Lyons Bar-David, *My Promised Land,* 53.

CHAPTER 10

1. Erik Cohen, "The City in the Zionist Ideology," *Jerusalem Urban Studies* 1 (1970): 2–9.

2. Harry S. Linfield, *The Jews in the United States, 1927: A Study of Their Number and Distribution* (New York: American Jewish Committee, 1929), 14.

3. Addison E. Southard, American Consul in Charge, Jerusalem, to Secretary of State, Washington, D.C., 18 October 1921, USNA RG 84 353/86, p. 64.

4. Yehoshua Ben-Arieh, *Jerusalem in the 19th century: The Old City* (Jerusalem: Yad Itzhak Ben Zvi Institute; New York: St. Martin's Press, 1984), 357–58; U. O. Schmelz, "Modern Jerusalem's Demographic Evolution," *Jewish Population Studies* 20 (Jerusalem: Institute of Contemporary Jewry, Hebrew University of Jerusalem and Jerusalem Institute for Israel Studies, 1987), 28; Government of Palestine Office of Statistics, *Statistical Abstract of Palestine, 1942* (Jerusalem: Government Printing Press, 1942), 11.

5. Aminadav Ashbel, *Palestine Land Development Company,* 58; Bill presented to the American Zion Commonwealth by the Palestine Land Development Company for land purchases, Jerusalem, 12 December 1924, CZA L18/231/3; List of American Zion Commonwealth purchasers, CZA L65/436; Correspondence between Benjamin Rabalsky, Boston, and American Zion Commonwealth, New York, 1925–30, AJHSA P-153, Benjamin Rabalsky papers.

6. Charles Passman, Jerusalem, to Solomon J. Weinstein, New York, 3 December 1926; Dr. Jacob Thon, "Instructions for the sale of Palestine Land Development Company to American Jews," Jerusalem, 3 December 1926, CZA L65/381.

7. Protocols of the meeting of the Vaad of Talpiot Garden City, 20 and 27 Tevet 5683 (8 and 15 January 1923), JMA RG Vaad Garden City Talpiot, box 194; Gideon Biger, " 'Garden Suburbs' in Jerusalem—Planning and Development under Early British Rule, 1917–1925" (in Hebrew), *Cathedra* 6 (December 1977): 110.

8. Patai and Patai, "Builder of Zion," 246, CZA A168/13.

9. Memorandum of Agreement between Emanuel N. Mohl, attorney of Mary Fels and Israel Tannenbaum, Israel Blumenfeld, and Moritz Grunhut, Jerusalem, 23 October 1922, CZA A417/116; various contracts for the purchase of land on Mount Scopus, 1922–23, CZA A417/14.

10. Agreement between Ittamar Ben-Avi and the American Palestine Real Estate Agency, Jerusalem, 1 October 1923, YIBZA 5/2/46/1. Ittamar Ben-Avi, *With the Dawn of Our Independence: Memoirs of the First Hebrew Child* (in Hebrew) (n.p.: Public Committee for the Publication of the Writings of Ittamar Ben-Avi, 1966); in his memoirs, Ben-Avi makes no mention of his activities.

NOTES TO CHAPTER 10

11. Advertisement in *Mischar Ve-Taasiah* (Trade and Industry) (in Hebrew) 5–6 (9 April 1924): 201–2. Rosenblum (1866–1925) donated $250,000 to the Palestine Development Fund in 1922, and later $250,000 to the Hebrew University of Jerusalem. His widow endowed the university with $500,000. See Jacob S. Feldman, *The Jewish Experience in Western Pennsylvania: A History, 1755–1945* (Pittsburgh: Historical Society of Western Pennsylvania, 1986), 227–28.

12. The location of the Kreisha tract has not been identified.

13. "Names, Addresses and Description of Subscriber [sic]," 2 June 1925; Joseph R. Raskas, Jerusalem American Land Company, Jerusalem, to Town Planning Commission, Jerusalem, 27 September 1926, CZA A430/4. "Jerusalem-American Land Co. Ltd., Unsold Land," 31 December 1928, CZA A417/63; map of Rehavia, 1930, JMA box 490.

14. Zeev Vilnay, *Jerusalem—Capital of Israel: The New City* (in Hebrew) (Jerusalem: Achiavar, 1963), 230; Biger, "Development of Jerusalem," 261; Boris (Baruch) Hershenov, a New York merchant, appears as Boris Aharonov in certain documents.

15. Elie Eliachar, *Living With Jews* (in Hebrew) (Jerusalem: Y. Marcus and Partners, 1981), 164–66.

16. *Mischar Ve-Taasiah* (Trade and Industry) (in Hebrew) 4 (21 March 1926): 126; Biger, "Development of Jerusalem," 258–59; N. Ben-Yehuda, "Around Jerusalem" (in Hebrew) *Hatzofeh* (14 Iyar 5698/1938).

17. H. Rubenstein, Kansas City, to Zionist Organization of America, New York, 24 August 1924, CZA L65/82.

18. Binyamin Kluger, *Jerusalem: Neighborhoods Surrounding Her* (in Hebrew) (Jerusalem: n.p., 1979), 263–64; Biger, "Development of Jerusalem," 273.

19. Yair Paz, "Jewish Land Purchases in the Vicinity of Jerusalem in the years 1920–1932" (in Hebrew) (Master's thesis, Department of Geography, Hebrew University of Jerusalem, 1992), 135–36.

20. Palestine Land Development Company, Jerusalem, to Benjamin Rabalsky, Boston, 2 February 1926, AJHSA P-153; David Kroyanker, *Jerusalem Architecture—Periods and Styles: The Period of the British Mandate 1918–1948* (in Hebrew) (Jerusalem: Keter, 1989), 298, 337.

21. "Memorandum concerning parcel of land in Bayith V'gan Belonging to Mrs. S. I. Hyman," n.d., CZA A348/100; George M. Hyman, Syracuse, to Libby Berkson, Jerusalem, 18 January 1934, CZA A348/97; Entry for Aharon Mordechai Ashinski in Account Book, JMA, Bayit Vegan Cooperative Society, 13/1, p. 12.

22. David Klein, San Francisco, to Zionist Organization of America, New York, 3 May 1934, CZA L65/154.

23. Hannaniah Caiserman, n.p., to Asher Pierce, Hirsh Volofsky, Lyon Cohen, and Abraham Levin, n.p., 3 January 1923, CJCNA RG DA.1, H. M. Caiserman files, box 9; Palestine Economic Corporation, Report of the Proceedings of the Meeting of Shareholders held on 31 October 1934, Temple Emanu-El, New York, p. 10, NYPL.

24. Fishbane, "The Founding of Kollel America Tifereth Yerushelayim," 120–28; Edwin Sherman Wallace, *Jerusalem the Holy* (New York: 1898; reprint, New York: Arno Press, 1977), 309–10.

25. Report on the Activities of Kollel America, 1912, CAHJP P3/517.

26. Ibid.; Nachum Dov Freiman, ed., *Jerusalem Memorial Book: A Detailed List of Our Spiritual and Material Possessions in Jerusalem* (in Hebrew) (Jerusalem: 1913;

reprint, Jerusalem: Ariel, 1980) 60; Szold, *Recent Jewish Progress*, 104. The rate of exchange used was 1 franc = $0.19; see *Encyclopedia Britannica* (11th edition, 1910–11), 17–18:706.

27. Report on the Activities of Kollel America, 1912, CAHJP P3/517.

28. Rear Admiral Mark Selmistol, United States Navy, Constantinople, to the Secretary of State, Washington, D.C., 6 December 1921, USNA RG 84 353/84, pp. 974–76, 982–83.

29. Sigfried Hoofien, *Report of Mr. S. Hoofien to the Joint Distribution Committee of the American Funds for Jewish War Sufferers* (New York: 1918; reprint, New York: Arno Press, 1977), 45, 89–91, 125–30.

30. Constitutios [*sic*] of the Kollel America Tiphereth Jerusalem, n.p., n.d., opposite p. 1, JMA RG Old Yishuv, file 78.

31. Israel Klaiman, Report on Kolel America Tiphereth Jerusalem, Jerusalem, August 1925, JMA, Shuchman Archives, 5/2581.

32. Zalman White, Jerusalem, to Israel Klaiman, Jerusalem, 19 November 1923; Samuel Bruner, Jerusalem, to United States Consul, Jerusalem, 3 December 1923; Rachel Weinberg, Jerusalem, to United States Consul, Jerusalem, 17 December 1923; Morris Sacks, Jaffa, to George Gregg Fuller, United States Vice Consul, Jerusalem, 17 December 1923, JMA, Shuchman Archives, 5/2581.

33. Recapitulations for the years 5682 (1921/1922) and 5683 (1922/1923); List of recipients of *haluka* 5682 and 5683; Israel Klaiman, Report on Kolel America Tiphereth Jerusalem, Jerusalem, Palestine, August 1925, JMA, Shuchman Archives, 5/2581.

34. Recommendations by Israel Klaiman, 6 April 1925; Julian W. Mack, David De Sola Pool, Solomon Sorrenstein, Samuel C. Lamport and Samuel A. Goldsmith to Israel Klaiman, 12 April 1926, JMA, Shuchman Archives, 5/2581.

35. Report on Kolel America Tiferet Jerusalem, Jewish Community of Palestine General Council (Vaad Leumi), Department for Social Service, Information Bureau, August 1932, CZA A110/32.

36. Report of the general meeting of American Jews, Tel Aviv, 1 Nissan 5693/3 March 1933 (in Hebrew), JMA RG Old Yishuv, file 78; this calculation is based on "Summary of Kollel America's activities until 1936," CZA A110/32.

37. Report on Kolel America Tiferet Jerusalem, Jewish Community of Palestine General Council (Vaad Leumi), Department for Social Service, Information Bureau, August 1932, CZA A110/32; Israel Klaiman, Report on Kolel America Tiphereth Jerusalem, August 1925, JMA, Shuchman Archives, 2581/5.

38. Pinchas Ben Zvi Grayevski, *From the Archives of Jerusalem* (in Hebrew) (Jerusalem 1930), 7:n.p.; Ben-Arieh, *Jerusalem*, 217–21.

39. Report on Kolel America Tiferet Jerusalem, Jewish Community of Palestine General Council (Vaad Leumi), Department for Social Service, Information Bureau, August 1932, CZA A110/32; The first phase of Knesset Israel was founded in 1891. American contributions paid for the construction of 31 of the 92 houses in the neighborhood (£E300 for a single house and £E400 for a double). See Knesset Israel brochure, circa 1925, JMA RG Old Yishuv, file 78.

40. Of the 228 registration forms filled out by Kollel America members, 178 indicated their place of residence; 68.9 percent indicated they resided in Jerusalem. See YIBZA RG 4/2.

41. *A Message from the President for the Fifth Anniversary of Agudath Achim Anshei America* (in Yiddish) (Jerusalem: P. Einav Printers, 1932), TAUA RG D-11/2295 Agudath Achim, Anshei America. For a general description of *landsmanshaft*, see Gerald Sorin, *A Time for Building: The Third Migration, 1880–1920* (Baltimore: John Hopkins University Press, 1992), 97–98, 258.

42. George Barsky, Jerusalem, to the American Consul, Jerusalem, 5 March 1924, USNA RG 84 353/85, pp. 26–28; Minutes of the Meeting of the Board of Directors of the American Zion Commonwealth, 24 February 1925, CZA L65/263.

43. *(Palestine Economic Corporation) Economic News* 3 (1 January 1934): 3.

44. List of Kollel America, their means and possessors of property, enabling them to exist without the Hallukah, 1912, CAHJP P3/517. Registrants include: Abraham Arkin—grocery shop; Moses I. Burkey—flouring mill and money exchange; Joel and Isaac White—large clothing store; Pesach Meltzer—bakery shop; Moses Silberstein—grocery shop; Moses Wein—grocery shop; Israel Morgenstern—crockery and glassware shop; Mordechai Fenster—proprietor of bathhouse; and Samuel Brunner—dry-goods shop.

45. Statistical report on applicants and registrants for Palestine from America, Palestine Service and Information Bureau, Zionist Organization of America, 31 May 1920, CZA F25/33.

46. Zionist Organization Department of Commerce and Industry, Jerusalem, to Menachem Freidman, Jerusalem, 28 March and 2 April 1922, CZA S8/1359. Menachem Mendel Freidman, "Memoirs, 1878–1963" (in Hebrew), TAUA T-11/263, pp. 128–299; Moshe Novomeysky, "The Industries of Palestine: Its Conditions and Prospects," *Bulletin of the Palestine Economic Society* 4–5 (May 1924): 16; "The Cigarette Industry," *Palestine and Near East Economic Magazine* 2 (28 February 1927): 91.

47. "Trade and Commerce in Our Land," *Judaean* 3 (January 1923): 177. *Rough Notes* 8 (9 December 1923): 2–3. Patai and Patai, "A Builder of Zion," 255. Palestine Knitting Works, "Statement of Income, Profit & Loss, for the period of four months, from September 1 to December 31, 1922," Jerusalem, CZA S8/2093.

48. Haber, *Odyssey*, 168; Nachum I. Thischby, Jerusalem, to Harry Sacher, Jerusalem, 1 December 1927, CZA S25/286; *Rough Notes* 11 (22 January 1924): 2. See also Itzhak Eilam, *Jerusalem Facets* (in Hebrew) (Tel Aviv: Am Oved—Tarbut Vechinuch, 1973), 113–14 for a description of the strike to shorten the work day from thirteen or fourteen hours down to eight hours at Marbadia. This was one cause of the failure of this enterprise. "The New Marbadia, Ltd.," *Palestine and Near East Economic Magazine* 1 (September 1926): 199.

49. Novemeysky, "Industries of Palestine," 16–17, 21–22; Kazan, *From New York to Raanana*, 112, 131, 148–50. According to Bernard Rosenblatt, one of the founders of the Danish-American Furniture Factory was [?] Goldstein of Terre Haute, Indiana. The name of the factory had a simple origin, as Goldstein explained to Kazan: "I and my friend were cheder boys in Russia. When the war broke out, I managed to go to America and he went to Copenhagen. We met in Jerusalem. So it is Danish-American furniture company." Bernard Rosenblatt, interview by Moshe Davis, Jerusalem, 20 November 1963, Oral History Division, Institute of Contemporary Jewry, Hebrew University of Jerusalem (22) 1.

50. Kahn, *Spring Up*, 207–8.

51. Gelber, *No Balm in Gilead*, 44–45; Sylva Gelber, interview by author, Ottawa, Canada, 2 October 1990.

52. Gurevich and Gertz, *Statistical Handbook of Jewish Palestine,* 366–67. See also Joseph B. Glass, "American Olim and the Transfer of Innovation to Palestine, 1917–1939," in *Moshe Davis Memorial Volume,* ed. Jonathan D. Sarna and Eli Lederhendler (forthcoming); Levin, *Balm in Gilead,* 35–163.

53. Edwin Samuel, *A Lifetime in Jerusalem: The Memoirs of the Second Viscount Samuel* (Jerusalem: Israel Universities Press, 1970), 92. Nelson Gluck was the director of the American School for Oriental Research during 1932–33, 1936–40, and 1942–47. "Talpioth, Jewish suburb Jerusalem where several American families resided was evacuated without casualties and homes afterward looted by Moslems," telegram from U.S. Consul General Paul Knabenshue, Jerusalem, to Secretary of State, Washington, D.C., 25 August 1929, USNA RG 84 353/83, p. 120. Cohen, *Years After the Riots,* 25, mentions a telegram to the State Department in which it was reported that "thirty-three Americans from Rehavia, mostly women and children, had sought refuge in the consulate." In addition, see *Address Book of the Residents of Rehaviah, Sivan 5695/June 1935* (in Hebrew) (Jerusalem: Rehavia Committee, 1935). Entries include American residents Rabbi Meir Berlin and Emanuel Neuman. Moshe Goodman spoke of an "American colony" in Jerusalem's Romema neighborhood in the late 1920s; Moshe Goodman, interview by author, Jerusalem, 16 June 1994. Neither the informant nor further research could determine if this was an opportunistic or a planned collection of Americans.

54. Ruth Kark, *Jaffa: A City in Evolution, 1799–1917* (Jerusalem: Yad Izhak Ben-Zvi, 1990), 125–37, 262–72.

55. Ruth Kark, "Jaffa—the Social and Cultural Center of the New Jewish Settlement in Palestine," in *Jerusalem Cathedra,* ed. Levine, 3:215–32.

56. Government of Palestine, *Official Gazette* (1 June 1921), no. 44.

57. Cohen, "The City," 10–13.

58. Ludwig Lewisohn, "A City Unlike New York," *Menorah Journal* 11 (April 1925): 167–72. In the early 1920s, Lewisohn was literary editor of the *Nation* and had published a number of books. He was sent to Palestine by Meyer Weisgal, editor of the *New Palestine,* to write a series of impressionistic articles; see Weisgal, *Meyer Weisgal . . . So Far,* 65–66.

59. Rosenblatt, *Two Generations,* 110–15; Power of Attorney from the Township of Tel Aviv to Bernard A. Rosenblatt, Tel Aviv, 31 May 1922; Meir Dizengoff, "Prospectus–Loan of £75,000 of the Township of Tel Aviv, Bearing Interest at the Rate of 6½% Per Annum," Tel Aviv, 31 May 1922, USNA RG 84 353/85, pp. 180–87.

60. Bernard Rosenblatt, New York, to Sigfried Hoofien, Jaffa, 5 October 1923, CZA L51/196.

61. Charles Passman, Jerusalem, to American Zion Commonwealth, New York, 25 September 1924, CZA L65/388.

62. Charles Passman, Jerusalem, to American Zion Commonwealth, New York, 17 March 1925, CZA L65/390; Passman, Jerusalem, to AMZIC, New York, 28 November 1924, CZA L65/317. The New York office wrote "Buy" on the letter beside the paragraph detailing the adjacent parcel of land.

63. Charles Passman, Jerusalem, to American Zion Commonwealth, New York, 17 March 1925, CZA L65/390; Bernard Rosenblatt, Jerusalem, to Solomon J. Weinstein, New York, 5 October 1925, CZA L65/397; Passman, Jerusalem, to AMZIC, New York, 1 December 1925, CZA L65/352.

64. Palestine Small Cooperative Society Ltd., Tel Aviv, to Meir Dizengoff, Tel Aviv, 18 November 1924, TAJMA RG 3, file 157; Meir Dizengoff, Jerusalem, to Bernard A. Rosenblatt, Jerusalem, 2 December 1925; Charles Passman, Jerusalem, to American Zion Commonwealth, New York, 1 December 1925, CZA L65/352.

65. Memorandum from S. J. Weinstein, New York, to the Board of Directors, American Zion Commonwealth, New York, 29 November 1926, CZA F38/560; List of AMZIC purchasers, CZA L65/436; Contract between the Borochov Neighborhood Committee and the AMZIC, 1926; Borochov Neighborhood Committee, Tel Aviv, to AMZIC, Jerusalem, 3 March 1929; AMZIC, Jerusalem, to Borochov Neighborhood Committee, Tel Aviv, 25 November 1929, AMJLM IV-235–20; Gurevich and Gertz, *Jewish Agricultural Settlement*, 3.

66. Minutes of the Meeting of the Board of Directors of the American Zion Commonwealth, New York, 24 February 1925, CZA L65/263.

67. Rosenblatt, *Two Generations*, 133–34.

68. Dr. Jacob P. Norman, Zichron Yaakov, to Benjamin Rabalsky, Boston, 15 November 1925, Zionist Association of Greater Boston Correspondence, 1915–1925, AJHSA P-153. Norman was born in Baki, Russia, in 1888. Upon his arrival in the United States in 1906 he studied at Boston University and received his medical degree in 1911. Then he immigrated to Palestine and practiced at Metulla until 1914, when he resumed his studies at the Bostonian Institute for Tropical Diseases. After the war he worked for six years at hospitals in Safed and Haifa. He pursued post-graduate studies in Berlin, and then returned to Palestine and opened a private practice in Tel Aviv. In 1929 he returned to Boston. David Margalith, *Physicians: Forerunners of Modern Israel* (Tel Aviv: Jerusalem Academy of Medicine, 1973), 78.

69. Advertisement in *Mischar Ve-Taasiah* (Trade and Industry) (18 January 1925); General Manager, American Zion Commonwealth, n.p., to Jacob Marcus, New York, 29 October 1923, CZA L65/127; Joseph Landman, Washington, D.C., to Zionist Organization of America, New York, 16 October 1933, CZA L65/153.

70. A. Y. Brawer, "Chapters in the Geography and Topography of Tel Aviv" (in Hebrew), in *Tel-Aviv Book*, ed. A. Drianov (Tel Aviv: Vaad Sefer Tel Aviv, 1926), 291; Tal-Shir, "Latrun Battle 93," 21, 23, 25.

71. "Jerusalem-American Land Co. Ltd., Unsold Land," 31 December 1928, CZA A417/63.

72. Natan Harpaz, "From Dream Houses to Box Houses: The Architectural Revolution of the 1930s in Tel Aviv" (in Hebrew), in *Eidan 3: Tel-Aviv in Its Beginning, 1909–1934*, ed. Mordechai Naor (Jerusalem: Yad Izhak Ben-Zvi, 1984), 94–95; Dov Gavish and Roi Raviv, "The Casino of Tel Aviv" (in Hebrew), *Ariel* 48–49 (1987): 134–39.

73. Ben-Ami Fish, Tel Aviv. Telephone interview by author. Jerusalem, 6 September 1998.

74. *Mischar Ve-Taasiah* (Trade and Industry) 5–6 (30 March 1927): 142–43.

75. Naor, ed., *Pioneers of Herzliya*, 2:n.p.

76. "Survey of Trades, Industries and Liberal Professions, 1921–1922," 3:58; "The Palestine Industry according to Location and Type of Production," *Mishchar Ve—Taasiah* (Trade and Industry) 11–12 (11 July 1929): 305, 310–11; David Gurevich, "Census of Hebrew Industry and Crafts," *Statistical Booklet (of the Jewish Agency for Palestine)* 19 (1931): 29.

Notes to Chapter 10

77. "Trade and Commerce in our Land," *Judaean* 3 (January 1923): 183; Novomeysky, "Industries of Palestine," 16.

78. Nahum Tishbi, "The Position of Diamant and Kvaskniewski," 7 June 1923; Zeev Jabotinski, New York, to Palestine Zionist Executive, Jerusalem, 9 June 1922; Louis Topkis, Wilmington, Del., to Palestine Zionist Executive, Jerusalem, 5 June 1922, CZA S8/1361I.

79. Haber, *Odyssey,* 167.

80. *Mischar Ve-Taasiah* (Trade and Industry) 16 (September 1925): 486.

81. *Palestine and Near East Economic Magazine* 7 (August 1932): 330 and 7 (September 1932): 374–75; N. J. Thischby, Jerusalem, to the Chairman, Standing Committee for Commerce and Industry, Government of Palestine, Jerusalem, 22 November 1933, CZA S8/2093a. Sacks paid an average of 250 mils for an eight-hour day. Labor costs per 100 yards of silk fabrics were £P4.000 in Palestine as compared to £P0.800 in Japan.

82. Haber, *Odyssey,* 167.

83. Frederick H. Kisch, n.p., to S. Patterson, Director of Customs, Excise and Trade, Jerusalem, 27 February 1927, CZA S25/525; Samuel S. Bloom, Tel Aviv, to S. Patterson, Director of Customs, Excise and Trade, Jerusalem, 20 February 1927, CZA S25/525; reference to this file graciously provided by Prof. Michael Brown. "Artificial Teeth," *Palestine and Near East Economic Magazine* 1 (15 July 1926): 84; "Artificial Teeth Factory," *Palestine and Near East Economic Magazine* 2 (28 February 1927): 91; Tidhar, ed., *Encyclopedia,* 1:204.

84. Samuel S. Bloom, Tel Aviv, to the Executive Council of [World] Zionist Organization, London, 3 April 1927, CZA S25/525.

85. *Palestine and Middle East Economic Magazine* 8 (January 1933): 42; Gurevich, "Census of Hebrew Industry and Crafts," 27.

86. Louis D. Brandeis, Chatham, Mass., to Maurice Beck Hexter, n.p., 7 September 1930, in *Letters of Louis D. Brandeis,* ed. Urofsky and Levy, 5:453.

87. American Vice Consul George Gregg Fuller, Jerusalem, to Department of State, Washington, D. C., Report on the Extent of Industrial Prosperity in Palestine, 17 December 1923, USNA RG 84 353/86, p. 12; Tidhar, *Encyclopedia,* 2:608–9; Haber, *Odyssey,* 167.

88. Bein, ed., *Arthur Ruppin,* 125; Description of Hadar HaCarmel, 1931, HMA RG 15, file 107; Arthur Ruppin, Haifa, from [?], Haifa, 10 November 1921, HMA RG 15, file 395; Agreement between the Palestine Land Development Company and American Zion Commonwealth, New York, 26 March 1924, CZA L18/231/3; List of lots sold to AMZIC, n.d, CZA L18/538; Charles Passman, Jerusalem, to AMZIC, New York, 21 and 29 April 1925; Vaad Hadar HaCarmel, Haifa, to AMZIC, Jerusalem, n.d., CZA L65/322.

89. Rosenblatt, *Two Generations,* 165.

90. Agreement between the Palestine Land Development Company and American Zion Commonwealth, New York, 26 March 1924, CZA L18/231/3; Shimon Stern, "The Development of Haifa's Urban Network, 1918–1947" (Ph.D. diss., Hebrew University of Jerusalem, 1974), 41–42.

91. "Red Carmel, purchases by the American Zion Commonwealth, 1926," CZA L65/376; Stern, "Haifa" 39–40.

92. The members of the syndicate were: Feibas Kobak, Louis Germain, Jacob Goell, Irving Rosenzweig, Isaac Meister, and David Freiberger of New York. Solomon J.

Weinstein, "Carmel Lots," n.p., 21 January 1926, CZA L65/190; Memorandum from Solomon J. Weinstein, New York, to the Board of Directors, American Zion Commonwealth, New York, 29 November 1926, CZA F38/560. David Freiberger, New York, to Adolph Held, Amalgamated Bank of New York, New York, 7 December 1927; Deed and Certificate of Registration for Carmelia Land, Haifa, 9 March 1928, CZA L65/100.

93. *The Carmel* (in Hebrew) (n.p.: America-Palestine Agency for Land Transactions, n.d.), 15. A discrepancy exists between the amount of land in the agency's possession (4,000 dunams) and land available for development (2,000 plots at 3 dunams each, plus the public space). The prospectus was published in Hebrew, and those interested in purchasing a plot were directed to local representatives. This reference was graciously provided by Prof. Yossi Ben-Artzi. Contract between the America-Palestine Real Estate Agency and A. Aubrin [?] of Warsaw, n.d., n.p., CZA A417/14.

94. Yitzhak Elazari-Volcani, Jerusalem, to Arthur Ruppin, New York, 20 February 1924; Nahum Paper, "Location of the Land, Rom HaCarmel," Jerusalem, 20 February 1924, CZA L65/253.

95. "Building Plots on Mt. Carmel in Haifa," CZA L65/295; Rabbi Herman M. Cohen, St. Paul, to Zionist Organization of America, New York, 5 February 1934, CZA L65/154.

96. "Jerusalem-American Land Co. Ltd., Unsold Land," 31 December 1928, CZA A417/63; Memorandum of agreement between Eliyahu Eliachar and Joseph Cohen Hemsi and Salomon Angel, 1943, CZA A417/12.

97. Herbert and Sosnovsky, *Bauhaus on the Carmel*, 110–21.

98. *Palestine Correspondence* 5 (23 January 1925): 1–2.

99. *Palestine Post* (23 February 1934); Rosenblatt, *Two Generations*, 157–59.

100. Alexander Aurel and Peretz Cornfeld, eds., *The Near and Middle East Who's Who 1945–1946*, vol. 1: *Palestine, Jerusalem* (Jerusalem, Tel Aviv, and Haifa: Near and Middle East Who's Who Publishing Co., 1946), 12, 55.

101. Oded Avisar, ed., *Hebron Book: City of the Fathers and Its Settlement in the Perspective of the Generations* (in Hebrew) (Jerusalem: Keter, 1978), 143.

102. Gottesman, *The Martyrs of Hebron*, 8–9.

103. Ibid., 15–16.

104. Eliyahu W. Lewin-Epstein, New York, to Siegfried F. Hoofien, Anglo-Palestine Bank, Jaffa, 17 December 1926 and 22 April 1927; Hoofien to Lewin-Epstein, 6 April 1927, CZA L51/281. Lewin-Epstein was Rokeach's nephew.

105. Ibid.

106. Telegram from Consul General Paul Knabenshue, Jerusalem, to Secretary of State, Washington, D.C., 25 August 1929, USNA RG 84 353/83, p. 0120.

107. Chaim Goldmann, Safed, to Israel Klaiman, Jerusalem, n.d., JMA Shuchman Archives, 2581/5; List of American Citizens who have obtained Provisional Certificates of Palestinian Citizenship, USNA RG 84, 353/82, pp. 46–52; *Bulletin of the Palestine Economic Society* 1 (May 1924): 116. Of the 228 registration forms filled in by Kollel America members, 178 indicate a place of residence; 17.5 percent of registrants indicated they resided in Safed; see YIBZA RG 4/2.

108. Rosenblatt, *Two Generations*, 139–42; *Palestine and Near East Economic Magazine* 7 (May 1932): 257–58.

Notes to Chapter 10

109. Agronsky, "Afulah," 691.

110. Richard Kaufmann, "Explanatory Report to Accompany the Plans of the Valley City," March 1925, CZA L65/227.

111. Agreement between the Kadoorie-Bension Group of Eastern Jews and the American Zion Commonwealth, New York, 23 September 1924; Elly S. Kadoorie, London, to Harry Kottler, n.p., 10 November 1924; Letter to Ezra Kadoorie, Paris, 3 February 1925, CZA L65/290.

112. Frederick Hermann Kisch, *Palestine Diary* (London: Victor Gollancz, 1938), 154–55; F. M. Plumer, "Order under the Town Planning Ordinance, 1921," 1 May 1925, CZA A175/15; Bernard Rosenblatt, Jerusalem, to Solomon Weinstein, New York, 5 October 1925, CZA L65/397; Annual Report of American Zion Commonwealth, June 1926, CZA L65/264.

113. *Palestine Bulletin* (16 August 1926): 3; Memorandum from Harry Kottler, New York, to Meyer Weisgal, New York, 24 October 1926, CZA F38/560; Memorandum on the condition of Ir Jezreel (Afula) (in Hebrew), 7 Elul 5687 (4 September 1927), TAJMA, Idelson RG, file 4. A. L. Perlman [?], Tel Aviv, to Gershon Agronsky, Jerusalem, 25 January 1927; Letter to Nathan Ratnoff, New York, 17 November 1926, CZA A209/15. Annual Report of American Zion Commonwealth, June 1926, CZA L65/264.

114. Gurevich, *Statistical Abstract of Palestine, 1929,* 51.

115. Israel Rosoff, "The City in Palestine" (in Hebrew), *Mischar Ve-Taasiah* (Trade and Industry) 13–14 (August 1927): 255–57.

116. Memorandum from Solomon J. Weinstein, New York, to the Board of Directors, American Zion Commonwealth, New York, 29 November 1926, CZA F38/560. Sarah Honig, "The Nevos: Herzliya Pioneers," *Jerusalem Post Magazine,* 15 November 1974.

117. Cohen, "The City," 13–14.

118. Ebenezer Howard, *Garden Cities of To-Morrow* (London: Faber and Faber, 1974); Lewis Mumford, *The City in History: Its Origins, Its Transformations, and Its Prospects* (New York: Harcourt, Brace & World, 1961), 514–24.

119. Kark, *Jaffa,* 118–24.

120. Ruth Kark and Michal Oren-Nordheim, "Colonial Cities in Palestine?: Jerusalem under the British Mandate," *Israel Affairs* 3 (Winter 1996): 71–73; Biger, " 'Garden Suburbs,' " 108–31.

121."Garden Cities," n.d., n.p., CZA L65/251.

122. Memoirs of Moshe Glikin (in Hebrew; transcribed by Ruth Bein), CZA A175/28; Yossi Katz, "The Development of Ahuzat Migdal" (in Hebrew) *Cathedra* 42 (January 1987): 129–52.

123. Moshe Glikin, New York, to Robert Szold, New York, 15 March 1922, CZA L51/95.

124. Solomon J. Weinstein, New York, to Dr. Jacob Thon, Jerusalem, 25 October 1922, CZA L18/115/3; Memoirs of Moshe Glikin, CZA A175/28, pp. 35–36.

125. Palestine Zionist Executive, Jerusalem, to the United States Consul General, Jerusalem, 2 September 1924, CZA S25/553; Gerald de Waltoff, Jr., Brooklyn, N.Y., to Secretary of State, Washington, D.C., 26 November 1929, USNA RG 84 353/82, p. 296.

126. Bernard A. Rosenblatt, Jerusalem, to American Zion Commonwealth, New York, 16 January 1925, CZA L65/344.

127. Vaad Moshavah Migdal, Migdal, to the Jewish National Fund, Jerusalem, 12 January 1932, 26 February 1932, and 16 August 1932, CZA KKL5/5761.

128. Memorandum of meeting of Solomon J. Weinstein, Mark Esterman, Mr. Shankman, and Dr. Waxman, New York, 17 August 1922, CZA L65/270. The calculations mentioned in the memorandum were not always correct. The exchange rate used was £E1 = $4.50.

129. Ibid. Yossi Ben Arzti, "The Tragic Story of En Zetim," *Israel—Land and Nature* 6 (Spring 1981): 122–23.

130. Memorandum of meeting of Solomon J. Weinstein, Mark Esterman, Mr. Shankman, Mr. Shultz, and Mr. Nichelson, New York, 11 September 1922, CZA L65/270.

131. I would like to thank Amos Ron for graciously placing documents relating to Nahalat Itzhak at my disposal. Contract between Angel and Jean Rahil and Isaac Feller, Jerusalem, 16 July 1925; Deed of Sale between Isaac Feller and Ismail Bey, Jerusalem, 19 September 1928; Tidhar, *Encyclopedia,* 15: 4766.

132. Brochure of Nachlas Itzhak, New York, circa 1931.

133. Beit Nekuba 1933, 1:10,000, Survey of Palestine, March 1934; Nachlat Ichak, partitioning plan of land situated between kilometers 10–12 on the Jaffa-Jerusalem Road, 1933, 1:1,000, Jewish National Fund map archive, file 32, map 2572. Land Contract between Isaac Feller and Shlomo Haim Aga Davidoff, Jerusalem, 3 July 1934; Gurevich and Gertz, *Jewish Agricultural Settlement,* 6.

134. Shmuel Even-Or (Orenstein), "Neve Yaakov from a Personal Perspective" (in Hebrew), in *Shomron and Binyamin,* ed. Zeev Erlich (n.p.: Yehuda and Shomron College, 1993), 3:125–28.

135. Ibid., 128.

136. Ibid., 129, 133–35.

137. Ibid., 130.

138. Shmuel Even-Or (Orenstein). Telephone interview by author. Jerusalem, 16 September 1998.

139. Even-Or, "Neve Yaakov from a Personal Perspective," 131, 135–36.

140. The mother and four (Yosef, Moshe, Avraham, and Eliezer) of her seven children arrived in Palestine in February 1934; they were later joined by the father, David Zeev. In the end, only the mother and Avraham remained permanently in Palestine. Avraham Zelig. Interview by author. Tel Aviv, 16 September 1998.

Conclusion

1. Bernard Axelrod, "Historical Studies of Emigration from the United States," *International Migration Review* 6 (1972): 32–49; Sarna, "Myth of No Return," 256–68.

2. See table 24. According to Wilcox's figures and calculations (based on the re-emigration rate multiplied by actual immigration), for the periods 1915–20 and 1921–24 both emigration and re-emigration exceeded immigration to Palestine. However, during 1925–37 American emigration was less than American immigration to Palestine. The difference is not significant enough to shake the integrity of the American emigration figures. The difference may be a result of errors in American or Palestinian records or a fault in the registration process. Some American immigrants may have left the United States registered as tourists rather than emigrants, though they eventually settled in Palestine. The difference for the aggregate shows that emigration exceeded immigration

to Palestine either by 718—according to British sources—or 2,596—according to Jewish Agency information. For Wilcox's statistics see his tables 2 and 3.

3. Sherman, "Immigration and Emigration," 53–55.

4. David Jenkins, *Black Zion: The Return of Afro-Americans and West Indians to Africa* (London: Wildwood House, 1975), 9.

5. Ibid.

6. Ibid., 115.

7. Ibid., 118; Richard West, *Back to Africa: A History of Sierra Leone and Liberia* (London: Jonathan Cape, 1970), 273.

8. Victor Herman, *Coming Out of the Ice: An Unexpected Life* (New York: Harcourt, Brace, Jovanovich, 1979), 6–41.

9. Albert Habib Hourani, *Minorities in the Arab World* (London: Oxford University Press, 1947), 37, 66–67, 84.

10. Armin Alighanian, Chairman of the Armenian National Committee, Letter to the Editor, *New York Times,* 22 November 1947; *Jewish Agency Digest of Press and Events* (Jerusalem), 26 October 1947; both qtd. in Schechtman, *Population Transfers,* 54.

11. Joseph B. Schechtman, *Population Transfers in Asia* (New York: Hallsby Press, 1949), 58.

12. Schechtman, *Population Transfers,* 64–65; *New York Herald Tribune,* 2 November 1947, quoted in Schechtman, 65.

13. The figure of 9,000 is based on estimates described in the introduction. Other figures are taken from government of Palestine sources.

14. Michael Brown, "The Americanization of Canadian Zionism, 1917–1982," in *Contemporary Jewry—Studies in Honor of Moshe Davis,* ed. Geoffrey Wigoder (Jerusalem: Institute of Contemporary Jewry, Hebrew University of Jerusalem, 1984), 129–58.

15. Glass, "Isolation and Alienation."

16. Gurevich, "Fifteen Years of Aliyah," 2: tables 1 and 10, pp. I and xv. The rates are based on the estimate of population in the early 1930s divided by the aggregate of the migration to Palestine for 1919–34. Countries with high rates included: Greece, 49.3; Lithuania, 37.3; Poland, 26.3; Germany, 25.4; and Turkey 23.90. Medium rates occurred for: Iraq, 16.4; Latvia, 16.2; Rumania. 10.2; Russia. 10.1; and Austria 8.0. Countries with low rates included: England, 2.1; Holland, 2.1; France, 1.7; Hungary, 1.7; United States, 1.1; Canada, 1.0; Morocco, 0.8; and Argentina 0.8.

17. Gideon Shimoni, *Jews and Zionism: The South African Experience (1910–1967)* (Cape Town: Oxford University Press, 1980), 27.

18. Ibid., 32–33.

19. Ibid., 33; Gurevich, "Fifteen Years of Aliyah," xlv–xlvi.

20. Shimoni, *Jews and Zionism,* 27–60; Philip Gillon, *Seventy Years of Southern African Aliyah: A Story of Achievement* (n.p.: Adar Publishing, 1992), 7–12, 69–83.

BIBLIOGRAPHY

MANUSCRIPT SOURCES

American Jewish Archives (AJA), Cincinnati, Ohio, U.S.A.
Record group
    Proceedings of the Non-Partisan Conference to Consider Palestinian Problems, Astor Hotel, New York, 17 February 1924

American Jewish Historical Society Archives (AJHSA), Waltham, Massachusetts, U.S.A.
Record groups
    I-54 Baron de Hirsch Agricultural and Industrial School, Woodbine, New Jersey
    P-28 Adolphus S. Solomons papers
    P-134 Stephen S. Wise papers
    P-153 Benjamin Rabalsky papers

Archives and Museum of the Jewish Labor Movement (AMJLM), Tel Aviv, Israel.
Record groups
    IV-104 Abraham M. Koller papers
    IV-124 Public Works department
    IV-208 Executive Committee of the Histadrut
    IV-235 Agricultural Center

Beit Hagdudim Museum Archives (BHMA), Avihail, Israel.
Record group
    Album of the Jewish Legion

Canadian Jewish Congress National Archives (CJCNA), Montreal, Quebec, Canada.
Record groups
    DA.1, H. M. Caiserman files
    2B/Asher Pierce
    Poale Zion Archives 1922–34 (temp. loc.)

BIBLIOGRAPHY

Central Archives for the History of the Jewish People (CAHJP), Jerusalem, Israel.
Record groups
    P3 Judah Leib Magnes
    Inv. 2077 Kollel America Tiffereth Yerushalaim
    IL/SA Archives of the Jewish community of Safed
Central Zionist Archives (CZA), Jerusalem, Israel.
Record groups
    A20 Shmaryahu Levin papers
    A24 Menachem Ussishkin papers
    A110 Ina Brichgi-Shamir papers
    A123 Emanuel Neuman papers
    A125 Henrietta Szold papers
    A168 Robert David Kesselman papers
    A175 Richard Kaufmann papers
    A182 Harry Friedenwald papers
    A209 Gershon Agron (Agronsky) papers
    A219 Jessie Sampter papers
    A251 Israel Brodie papers
    A348 Isaac B. Berkson papers
    A404 Jacob DeHaas papers
    A405 Julian Mack papers
    A417 Mordechai Eliash papers
    F25 History of Zionism in the United States collection
    F38 Zionist Organization of America
    F43 Palestine Economic Corporation
    J15 Palestine Jewish Colonization Association
    J33 History of the Yishuv, various documents
    J86 Gan Yavne, New York Achooza Aleph
    J88 Ramot Meir (Rosoff settlements)
    KKL2 Jewish National Fund, Cologne, The Hague
    KKL5 Jewish National Fund, Jerusalem
    L2 Palestine Office, Jaffa, Tel Aviv, Jerusalem
    L3 Zionist Commission, Jerusalem
    L18 Palestine Land Development Company
    L51 Anglo-Palestine Company (Anglo-Palestine Bank)
    L65 American Zion Commonwealth, New York
Palestine Zionist Executive and Jewish Agency for Palestine, various departments
    S1 Financial department
    S6 Immigration department
    S8 Trade and Commerce department
    S9 Labor department
    S15 Agricultural Settlement department
    S17 Economic department
    S25 Political department
    S30 Economic secretariat
    S48 Henrietta Szold's bureau
    S55 Arthur Ruppin's bureau
    S100 Protocols of the executive's meetings
    Z3 Central office of the World Zionist Organization, Berlin

Bibliography

Z4 Central office of the World Zionist Organization, London
Givat Haviva Archives (GHA), Givat Haviva, Israel.
Record groups
    Hashomer Hatzair archives
    H-1.2 Leadership in Palestine
    H-3 Correspondence of the Kibbutz Hartzi secretariat
    T-1 Hashomer Hatzair in the United States and Canada
    5 Secretariat of the Kibbutz Hartzi
    101 Histories of settlements
Haifa Municipal Archives (HMA), Haifa, Israel.
Record group
    15 Hadar Hacarmel committee
Hebrew University of Jerusalem Archives, The (HUJA), Jerusalem, Israel.
Record groups
    210 Student registrar
    620 Correspondence with the office of the American Friends, New York
Hebrew University of Jerusalem, The; Map Library Collection, Department of Geography, Jerusalem, Israel.
Record groups
    Jewish National Fund map archive
    Richard Kaufmann album
Jerusalem Municipal Archives (JMA), Jerusalem, Israel.
Record groups
    Bayit Vegan Cooperative Society
    Garden City of Talpiot committee
    Old Yishuv
    Rehavia neighborhood
    Shuchman archives
Kibbutz Kfar Menachem Archives (KKMA), Kfar Menachem, Israel.
National Archives of Canada (NAC), Ottawa, Ontario, Canada.
Manuscript group
    28, V81 Zionist Organization of Canada archives
National Library Archives (NLA), Jerusalem, Israel.
Record groups
    V264a Migdal collection
    4°1203/23 Kollel America Tifferet Yerushalaim
New York Public Library (NYPL), New York, New York, U.S.A.
Tel Aviv-Jaffa Municipal Archives (TAJMA), Tel Aviv, Israel.
Record groups
    2 Executive and secretariat of Tel Aviv, 1919–24
    3 Executive and secretariat of Tel Aviv, 1923–26
    4 Executive and secretariat of Tel Aviv, 1926–66
    8 Community committee and religious council
    102 Abraham Idelson papers
Tel Aviv University Archives (TAUA), Tel Aviv, Israel.
Record groups
    D-11/2295 Agudath Achim, Anshei America
    T-11/263 Menachem Mendel Freidman papers
United States National Archives, (USNA), Washington, D.C., U.S.A.

BIBLIOGRAPHY

Record groups
    59 T471 Dispatches from United States Consuls in Jerusalem, Palestine, 1856–1906
    84 Jaffa Records of the Foreign Service Posts of the Department of State, Jaffa
    84 M353 Records of the Department of State relating to the Internal Affairs of Turkey, 1910–29
Yad Itzhak Ben-Zvi Archives (YIBZA), Jerusalem, Israel.
Record groups
    4/2 Kollel America Tifferet Yerushalaim
    5/2 Ittamar Ben-Avi papers
    5/6 Yosef Binyamini papers
YIVO (Jewish Institute for Historical Research) Archive, New York, New York, U.S.A.
Record group
    Horace M. Kallen papers

ORAL HISTORIES

Even-Or (Orenstein), Shmuel. Telephone interview by author. Jerusalem, 16 September 1998.
Fish, Ben-Ami. Telephone interview by author. Tel Aviv, 6 September 1998.
Fishman, Hertzel. Interview by author. Jerusalem, 13 February 1994.
Gelber, Sylva. Interview by author. Ottawa, Canada, 2 October 1990.
Goodman, Moshe. Interview by author. Jerusalem, 16 June 1994.
Greenbaum, Luba. Interview by author. Kibbutz Kfar Menachem, 6 November 1993.
Migdal, Shoshana. Interview by author. Herzlia, 13 February 1995.
Minster, Yitzhak. Interview by author. Avihail, 10 May 1990.
Rosenblatt, Bernard. Interview by Moshe Davis. Jerusalem, 20 November 1963. Oral History Collection, Institute of Contemporary Jewry, Hebrew University of Jerusalem, Jerusalem.
Warburg, Edward. Interview by Moshe Davis and Menahem Kaufman. New York, 14 April 1975. Oral Documentation, Institute of Contemporary Jewry, Hebrew University of Jerusalem (128), 45.
Zamir, Ruth, daughter of Sam Friedlander. Interview by author. Avihail, 3 May 1990.
Zelig, Avraham. Interview by author. Tel Aviv, 16 September 1998.

PUBLISHED SOURCES

Newspapers, Magazines, Yearbooks, and Encyclopedias

American Economic Committee for Palestine Report
American Hebrew
Bulletin of the Palestine Economic Society
Central Conference of American Rabbis, Year Book
Encyclopedia Britannica
Encyclopedia Judaica
Furrows
Hadassah Newsletter
Haivri (Hebrew)
Haolam (Hebrew)
Hatehiya (Hebrew)

Hatzofeh (Hebrew)
International Jewish News, Denver
Jerusalem Post
Jewish Monitor, Fort Worth-Dallas
J.N.F. News Bulletin
Judaean
Judaean Magazine
Kfari
Maccabean
Menorah Journal
Mischar Ve-Taasiah (Hebrew)
New Palestine
New York Times
Official Gazette (Government of Palestine)
Palestine and Middle East Economic Magazine
Palestine and Near East Economic Magazine
Palestine Bulletin
Palestine Correspondence
Palestine Post
Rough Notes (of the Secretary for Trade and Industry of the Palestine Zionist Executive)
San Francisco Lodge Bulletin, I.O.B.B.
Shabbosdige Post, St. Paul (Yiddish)
Texas Jewish Herald
Yediot Achronot (Hebrew)
Young Judaean
Youth and Nation

Books, Articles, Dissertations, and Official Publications

Aaronsohn, Ran. "Building the Land: Stages in First Aliya Colonization (1882–1904)." In *The Jerusalem Cathedra, Studies in the History, Archaeology, Geography and Ethnography of the Land of Israel,* vol. 3, ed. Lee I. Levine, 236–79. Jerusalem: Yad Izhak Ben-Zvi; Detroit: Wayne State University Press, 1983.

Adams, Frank. "Palestine Agriculture." *Annals of the American Academy of Political and Social Science* 164 (November 1932): 72–83.

Address Book of the Residents of Rehaviah, Sivan 5695/June 1935 (in Hebrew). Jerusalem: Rehaviah Committee, 1935.

Adler, Cyrus, and Aaron M. Margalith. *With Firmness in the Right: American Diplomatic Action Affecting Jews, 1840–1945.* New York: 1946; reprint, New York: Arno Press, 1977.

Gershon Agronsky, "Afulah in the Great Plain of Esderelon," *New Palestine,* 12 June 1925.

Aharon David Gordon, A Bibliography, 1904–1972, on the Fiftieth Anniversary of His Death. Degania A: Yachdav and Beth Gordon, 1979.

Alper, Michael. "Reform Judaism and Zionism." In *The Brandeis Avukah Annual of 1932,* ed. Joseph Shalom Shubow, 585–91. Boston: n.p., 1932.

Amit, Irit. "American Jewry and the Settlement of Palestine: Zion Commonwealth, Inc." In *The Land that Became Israel,* ed. Kark, 250–71.

———. "Jewish Land and Settlement Policy in the Southern Sharon Between the Years

1918 and 1929: The Role of National Capital and Private Enterprise in Shaping the Region" (in Hebrew). Ph.D. diss., Hebrew University of Jerusalem, 1993.

———. "Private Jewish Investors in Palestine in the 1920s." In *The Mosaic of Israeli Geography,* ed. Yehuda Gradus and Gabriel Lipshitz, 451–60. Beer Sheva: Ben-Gurion University of the Negev Press, 1996.

Angel, Shlomo. *Kfar Saba: 70 Years to the Founding of Kfar Saba (1903), 80 Years to the Redemption of Its Land* (in Hebrew) Kfar Saba: Kfar Saba municipality, 1973.

Anon. *An Orange Grove on the Mediterranean: Nathanyah on the Mediterranean, A Model Orange Settlement for Americans.* New York: Palestine Settlers' Service, 1932.

Anon. *The Story of Nathanyah: The Aim, Ambition, and Outlook of Eretz Yisroel's Youngest Colony.* N.p., 1928.

Antonofsky, Aharon [Aaron Antonovsky]. "American Roots [of Hashomer Hatzair]." *Youth and Nation* 16 (August 1948): 14–16.

———. "Social and Cultural Factors in Coronary Heart Disease: An Israel-North American Sibling Study." *Israel Journal of Medical Sciences* 7 (December 1971): 1578–83.

Antonovsky, Aaron, and David Katz. *Americans and Canadians in Israel.* Jerusalem: Israel Institute of Applied Social Research, 1969.

———. *From the Golden Land to the Promised Land.* Darby, Pa. and Jerusalem: Norwood Editions, 1979.

Arlosoroff, Chaim. *To the Jewish Youth, Address of Dr. Chaim Arlosoroff before the Washington Chapter of 'Avukah.'* New York: Zionist Party "Hitachduth" of America, 1928.

———. *Surveying American Zionism.* New York: Zionist Party "Hitachduth" of America, 1929.

Ashbel, Aminadav. *60 Years of Hachshevet HaYishuv. The Israel Land Development Company* (in Hebrew). Jerusalem: Israel Land Development Company, 1969.

———. *The Palestine Land Development Company: Episodes and Activities in the Cities of Israel, Jerusalem, Tel Aviv and Haifa* (in Hebrew). Jerusalem: Israel Land Development Company, 1976.

Aurel, Alexander, and Peretz Cornfeld, eds. *The Near and Middle East Who's Who 1945–1946,* vol. 1: *Palestine, Jerusalem.* Jerusalem, Tel Aviv, and Haifa: Near and Middle East Who's Who, 1946.

Avisar, Oded, ed. *Hebron Book: City of the Fathers and Its Settlement in the Perspective of the Generations* (in Hebrew). Jerusalem: Keter, 1978.

Avneri, Ariel L. *The Jewish Land Settlement and the Arab Claim of Dispossession* (in Hebrew). N.p.: Hakibbutz Hameuchad, 1980.

Axelrod, Bernard. "Historical Studies of Emigration from the United States." *International Migration Review* 6, no. 1 (1972): 32–49.

Badt-Strauss, Bertha. *White Fire: The Life and Works of Jessie Sampter.* New York: Reconstructionist Press, 1956.

Bar-David, Molly Lyons. *My Promised Land.* New York: G. P. Putnam's Sons, 1953.

Bar-Gal, Yoram, and Shmuel Shamai. "The Swamps of Emek Yizre'el (Jezreel Valley)—Myth or Reality" (in Hebrew). *Cathedra* 27 (March 1983): 163–74.

Barron, J. B. *Palestine: Report and General Abstracts of the Census of 1922.* Jerusalem: Greek Convent Press, 1922.

Bein, Alex, ed. *Arthur Ruppin: Memoirs, Diaries, Letters.* Jerusalem: Weidenfeld and Nicolson, 1971.

Bibliography

Ben-Arieh, Jehoshua. *Jerusalem in the 19th Century: The Old City.* Jerusalem: Yad Izhak Ben-Zvi Institute; New York: St. Martin's Press, 1984.

———. *Jerusalem in the 19th Century: Emergence of the New City.* Jerusalem: Yad Izhak Ben-Zvi Institute; New York: St. Martin's Press, 1986.

Ben-Arieh, Yehoshua, and Amiram Oran. "Settlements in the Galilee on the Eve of Zionist Settlement" (in Hebrew). In *The Lands of the Galilee,* ed. Avshalom Shmueli, Arnon Sofer, and Nurit Kliot, vol. 1, 315–52. Haifa: Haifa University and Israel Ministry of Defense, 1983.

Ben-Avi, Ittamar. *With the Dawn of Our Independence: Memoirs of the First Hebrew Child* (in Hebrew). N.p.: Public Committee for the Publication of the Writings of Ittamar Ben-Avi, 1966.

Ben Arzti, Yossi."The Tragic Story of En Zetim." *Israel—Land and Nature* 6 (Spring 1981): 122–23.

Ben Nachum, Dovid. "100 Years of Dreaming." Ein Dor: unpubl. ms., 1991.

Bentwich, Norman. *For Zion's Sake: A Biography of Judah L. Magnes, First Chancellor and First President of the Hebrew University of Jerusalem.* Philadelphia: Jewish Publication Society of America, 1954.

———, ed. *Legislation of Palestine, 1918–1925, including Orders-in-Council, Ordinances, Public Notices, Proclamations, Regulations, etc.* 2 vols. Alexandria: Whitehead Morris, 1926.

Ben-Zvi, Itzhak. *The Jewish Legion, Letters* (in Hebrew). Jerusalem: Yad Izhak Ben-Zvi, 1967.

Ben Zvi, Shmuel. "25th Anniversary of American Kibbutz Aliya." *Israel Horizons* 4 (May 1956): 25–30.

Berman, Gerald S. *The Experience of Aliyah among Recently Arrived North American Olim: The Role of the Shaliach.* Jerusalem: Work and Welfare Research Institute, Hebrew University of Jerusalem, 1977.

———. *The Work Adjustment of North American Immigrants in Israel.* Jerusalem: Work and Welfare Research Institute, Hebrew University of Jerusalem, 1978.

Biger, Gideon. " 'Garden Suburbs' in Jerusalem—Planning and Development under Early British Rule, 1917–1925" (in Hebrew). *Cathedra* 6 (December 1977): 108–32.

———. "The Development of Jerusalem's Built-Up Area during the Final Decade of the British Mandate, 1920–1930" (in Hebrew). In *Jerusalem in the Modern Period,* ed. E. Shaltiel, 255–78. Jerusalem: Yad Izhak Ben-Zvi and Ministry of Defence, 1981.

Boehm, Adolf, and Adolf Pollak. *The Jewish National Fund (Keren Kayemeth LeIsrael): Its History, Function and Activity.* Jerusalem: Jewish National Fund, 1935.

Bogrei Hechalutz America. *Pioneers from America: 75 Years of Hechalutz 1905–1980.* Tel Aviv: Bogrei Hechalutz America, 1981.

Brandeis, Louis D. *Brandeis on Zionism: A Collection of Addresses and Statements by Louis D. Brandeis.* Washington, D.C.: Zionist Organization of America, 1942.

Brandes, Joseph. *Immigrants to Freedom: Jewish Communities in Rural New Jersey Since 1882.* Philadelphia: Jewish Publication Society of America, 1971.

Brawer, A. Y. "Chapters in the Geography and Topography of Tel Aviv" (in Hebrew). In *Tel-Aviv Book,* ed. A. Drianov, 266–320. Tel Aviv: Vaad Sefer Tel Aviv, 1926.

Breslau, David, ed. *Arise and Build: The Story of American Habonim.* New York: Ichud Habonim Labor Zionist Youth, 1961.

Brown, Michael. "The Americanization of Canadian Zionism, 1917–1982." In *Contemporary Jewry—Studies in Honor of Moshe Davis,* ed. Geoffrey Wigoder, 129–58. Jerusalem: Institute of Contemporary Jewry, Hebrew University of Jerusalem, 1984.

BIBLIOGRAPHY

———. *The Israeli-American Connection: Its Roots in the Yishuv, 1914–1945*. Detroit: Wayne State University Press, 1996.

Carmel, The (in Hebrew). N.p.: America-Palestine Agency for Land Transactions, n.d.

Chavel, Charles B. "The Fostering of the Settlement and Cultivation of Palestine in the Halaka." In *Mizrachi Jubilee: Publication of the Mizrachi Organization of America*, ed. Pinhas Horgin and Arieh Leib Goldman, 58–66. New York: n.p., 1936.

Cohen, Armond E. "Palestine and Our Rabbinical Schools." In *The Brandeis Avukah Annual of 1932*, ed. Joseph Shalom Shubow, 592–98. Boston: n.p., 1932.

Cohen, Erik. "The City in the Zionist Ideology." *Jerusalem Urban Studies* 1. Jerusalem: Hebrew University of Jerusalem, 1970.

Cohen, Jack J. "Reflections on Kaplan's Zionism." In *The American Judaism of Mordecai M. Kaplan*, ed. Emanuel S. Goldsmith, Mel Scult, and Robert M. Seltzer, 401–14. New York: New York University Press, 1990.

Cohen, Naomi W. *American Jews and the Zionist Idea*. N.p., Ktav Publishing House, 1975.

———. *The Years After the Riots: American Responses to the Palestinian Crisis of 1929–1930*. Detroit: Wayne State University Press, 1988.

Dan, Yoel. "Soils of the Galilee" (in Hebrew). In *The Lands of the Galilee*, ed. Avshalom Shmueli, Arnon Sofer, and Nurit Kliot, vol. 1, 91–110. Haifa: Haifa University and Ministry of Defence, 1983.

Davidson, Gabriel. "The Jew in Agriculture in the United States." *American Jewish Yearbook* 37 (1935–36): 99–134.

Davis, Moshe. *The Emergence of Conservative Judaism: The Historical School in 19th Century America*. New York: Burning Bush Press, 1963.

———. *The Formative Year: A Journey to Europe and Eretz Israel, on the Eve of the Holocaust, a Decade before the Founding of the State of Israel* (in Hebrew). Jerusalem: Department for Jewish Education and Culture in the Diaspora, 1993.

———. *America and the Holy Land: With Eyes toward Zion—IV*. Westport, Conn.: Praeger, 1995.

Don-Yehiya, Eliezer. "Religious Zionism and Issues of Immigration and Immigrants Absorption in the Yishuv Period" (in Hebrew). In Hacohen, ed., *Ingathering of Exiles*, 81–106.

Doukhan-Landau, Leah. *The Zionist Companies for Land Purchase in Palestine, 1897–1914* (in Hebrew). Jerusalem: Yad Izhak Ben-Zvi, 1979.

———. "The Haifa Bay Lands and the American Zion Commonwealth Crisis (1925–1930)" (in Hebrew). *Cathedra* 41 (October 1986): 173–99.

Drori, Yigal. "The Attitudes of Jabotinsky, Gluecksohn and Levontin on Land and Settlement in the Early 1920s" (in Hebrew). In *Redemption of the Land of Eretz-Israel: Ideology and Practice*, ed. Ruth Kark, 199–208. Jerusalem: Yad Izhak Ben-Zvi, 1990.

Dushkin, Alexander M. *Living Bridges: Memoirs of an Educator*. Jerusalem: Keter, 1975.

Edin, Sophie A., ed. *The Palestine Year Book*. 2 vols. New York: Zionist Organization of America, 1946.

Efrati, Yoram, ed. *Yoman Aaron Aaronsohn, 1916–1919* (Aaron Aaronsohn's Diary, 1916–1919) (in Hebrew). Zichron Yaakov: n.p., 1978.

Eilam, Itzhak. *Jerusalem Facets* (in Hebrew). Tel Aviv: Am Oved—Tarbut Vechinuch, 1973.

Eisenberg, O. *Census of the Jewish Population in Haifa, 1938* (in Hebrew). Haifa: n.p., 1940.

Bibliography

Eisenstadt, Samuel N. *The Absorption of Immigrants: A Comparative Study Based Mainly on the Jewish Community in Palestine and the State of Israel.* London: Routledge & Kegan Paul, 1954.

Eliachar, Elie. *Living With Jews* (in Hebrew). Jerusalem: Y. Marcus and Partners, 1981.

Eliav, Mordechai. "The Rafah Approaches (Pithat-Rafiah) in the History of Jewish Settlement" (in Hebrew). *Cathedra* 3 (February 1977): 117–208.

Engel, Gerald. "Comparison between Americans Living in Israel and Those Who Returned to America." *Journal of Psychology* 74 (January 1970): 195–204.

Erez, Yehuda, ed. *Sefer Ha-aliya Ha-shilishit* (Third Aliyah Book) (in Hebrew). Tel Aviv: Am Oved, 1964.

———, ed. *Ben-Gurion Letters* (in Hebrew). 2 vols. Tel Aviv: Am Oved and Tel Aviv University, 1971–74.

Even-Or (Orenstein), Shmuel. "Neve Yaakov from a Personal Perspective," (in Hebrew). In *Shomron and Binyamin,* vol. 3, ed. Zeev Erlich, 125–77. N.p.: Yehuda and Shomron College, 1993.

Ever HaDani [Aaron Feldman]. *Settlement in the Lower Galilee: Fifty Years of History* (in Hebrew). Ramat Gan: Masada, 1956.

Fawaz, Leila Tarazi. *Merchants and Migrants in Nineteenth-Century Beirut.* Cambridge, Mass.: Harvard University Press, 1983.

Feingold, Henry L. "Assessing an Assessment: The Case of American Zionism." *American Jewish History* 75 (December 1985): 165–74.

Feinstein, Marnin. *American Zionism, 1884–1904.* New York: Herzl Press, 1965.

Feldman, Jacob S. *The Jewish Experience in Western Pennsylvania: A History, 1755–1945.* Pittsburgh: Historical Society of Western Pennsylvania, 1986.

Fineman, Irving. *Woman of Valor: The Story of Henrietta Szold.* New York: Simon and Schuster, 1961.

Fishbane, Simcha. "The Founding of Kollel America Tifereth Yerushelayim." *American Jewish Historical Quarterly* 64 (December–June 1974): 120–36.

Fishman, Hertzel. "A Zionist Childhood in St. Albans, Vt." *Kfari* (February 1989).

Fox, Nili. "Balfouriya: An American Zionist Failure or Secret Success?" *American Jewish History* 78 (June 1989): 497–512.

Freidlander, Israel. *Past and Present: Collected Essays.* Cincinnati: Ark Publishing, 1919.

Freiman, Nachum Dov, ed. *Jerusalem Memorial Book: A Detailed List of Our Spiritual and Material Possessions in Jerusalem* (in Hebrew). Jerusalem, 1913; reprint, Jerusalem: Ariel, 1980.

Friedenwald, Jonas S. "The Intercollegiate: A Retrospect." In *Kadimah.* 193–211. New York: Federation of American Zionists, 1918; reprint New York: Arno Press, 1977.

Friesel, Evyatar. "The Influence of American Zionism on the American Jewish Community, 1900–1950." *American Jewish History* 75 (December 1985): 144–46.

Fund, Yossef. "The Attitude of Agudat Israel Leaders to Aliyah" (in Hebrew). In *Ingathering of Exiles,* ed. Hacohen, 69–80.

Gal, Allon. *Brandeis of Boston.* Cambridge, Mass.: Harvard University Press, 1980.

———. "Brandeis's Views on the Upbuilding of Palestine, 1914–1923." *Studies in Zionism* 6 (Autumn 1982): 211–40.

———. "Aspects of the Zionist Movement's Role in the Communal Life of American Jewry (1898–1948)," *American Jewish History* 75 (December 1985): 149–58.

———. "Independence and Universal Mission in Modern Jewish Nationalism: A Comparative Analysis of European and American Zionism (1897–1948)." In *Israel: State and Society, 1948–1988—Studies in Contemporary Jewry,* vol. 5, ed. Peter Y.

Medding, 242–55, 269–74. New York: Oxford University Press for the Institute of Contemporary Jewry and Hebrew University of Jerusalem, 1989.

Gartner, Lloyd P. *History of the Jews of Cleveland.* Cleveland: Western Reserve Historical Society in cooperation with the Jewish Community Federation of Cleveland, 1987.

Gavish, Dov, and Roi Raviv. "The Casino of Tel Aviv" (in Hebrew). *Ariel* 48–49 (1987): 134–39.

Gelber, Sylva M. *No Balm in Gilead: A Personal Retrospective of Mandate Days in Palestine.* Ottawa: Carleton University Press, 1989.

Gillon, Philip. *Seventy Years of Southern African Aliyah: A Story of Achievement.* N.p.: Adar, 1992.

Gilner, Elias. *War and Hope: A History of the Jewish Legion.* New York: Herzl Press, 1969.

Glass, Joseph B. "Balfouria: An American Zionist Colony." *Studies in Zionism* 14, no. 1 (1993): 53–72.

———. "American and Canadian Jews in Eretz Israel: Settlement and Initiatives for the Development of the Landscape during the Beginning of British Rule (1917–1932)" (in Hebrew). Ph.D. diss. Hebrew University of Jerusalem, 1995.

———. "American Olim and the Transfer of Innovation to Palestine, 1917–1939." In *Moshe Davis Memorial Volume,* ed. Jonathan D. Sarna and Eli Lederhendler. Forthcoming.

———. "Isolation and Alienation: Factors in the Growth of Zionism in the Canadian Prairies." In preparation.

———. "An American Jewish Woman's Place in the Promised Land, Their Spatial Distribution and Locational Decisions in Palestine, 1917–1939." In *Untold Stories: American Jewish Women in the Yishuv and Early State of Israel,* ed. Shulmit Reinharz and Mark A. Raider. Forthcoming.

———. "American Jewish Women and Palestine, Their Immigration, 1918–1939." In *Women in the Yishuv and the Early Years of the State of Israel* (in Hebrew), ed. Margalit Shilo, Galit Hazan-Rokem, and Ruth Kark. Jerusalem: Yad Izhak Ben-Zvi, in press.

———. "The Settlement of Prairie Jews in Palestine, 1917–1939," *International Journal of Canadian Studies* 16 (Fall 1997): 215–44.

Goell, Yohai. "Aliyah in the Zionism of an American Oleh: Judah L. Magnes." *American Jewish Historical Quarterly* 65 (1975–76): 99–120.

Goldberg, J. J., and Elliot King, eds. *Builders and Dreamers: Habonim Labor Zionist Youth in North America.* New York: Herzl Press, 1993.

Goldberg, Yona, and Natan Friedel, eds. *Hechalutz: Builders and Fighters.* New York: Hechalutz, 1947.

Goldscheider, Calvin. "American Aliya: Social and Demographic Perspectives." In *The Jew in American Society,* ed. Sklare, 335–84.

Gordon, Aaron David. *Selected Essays.* New York: League for Labor Palestine, 1938.

Gordon, Benjamin L. *New Judea: Jewish Life in Modern Palestine and Egypt.* Philadelphia, 1918; reprint, New York: Arno Press, 1977.

Goren, Arthur A. "A Two-Way Street: Visitors, Sojourners and Settlers from America to the Land of Israel." Lecture presented at the Field Study Course in Israel, "America and the Holy Land, 1620–1948," Institute of Contemporary Jewry and Rothberg School for Overseas Students, Hebrew University of Jerusalem, Jerusalem, 6 July 1988.

Bibliography

———, ed. *Dissenter in Zion, or: From the Writings of Judah L. Magnes.* Cambridge, Mass.: Harvard University Press, 1982.

Gottesman, Leo. *The Martyrs of Hebron: Personal Reminiscences of Some of the Men and Woman Who Offered up Their Lives during the Massacre of August 24, 1929, at Hebron, Palestine and of Some Who Were Spared.* New York, 1930; reprint, New York: Arno Press, 1977.

Graicer, Iris. "Cooperation between Private Capital and National Capital in the Development of Emek Zevulun" (in Hebrew). *Studies in the Geography of Eretz Israel* 13 (1993): 159–78.

Grand, Samuel. "A History of Zionist Youth Organizations in the United States from Their Inception to 1940." Ph.D. diss., Columbia University, 1958.

Grayevski, Pinchas Ben Zvi. *From the Archives of Jerusalem* (in Hebrew), vol. 7 (Jerusalem 1930).

Greenbaum, Y. "Problems of Aliyah" (in Hebrew). In *Aliyah, A Collection Regarding Aliyah,* vol. 2, 9–18. Jerusalem: Immigration Department of the Jewish Agency for Palestine, 1935.

Greenberg, Gershon. *The Holy Land in American Religious Thought, 1620–1948.* Lanham, Md.: University Press of America, 1994.

Grinstein, Hyman B. "Orthodox Judaism and Early Zionism in America." In *Early History of Zionism in America,* ed. Isidor S. Meyer, 219–27. New York, 1958; reprint, New York: Arno Press, 1977.

Gurevich, David. *Statistical Abstract of Palestine 1929.* Jerusalem: Keren Hayesod, 1930.

———. "Fifteen Years of Aliya to Eretz Israel" (in Hebrew). *Aliya: Collection on Aliya Matters.* vol. 2. 43–62. Jerusalem: Jewish Agency for Palestine, 1935.

———. *The Jewish Population of Jerusalem: A Demographic and Sociological Study of the Jewish Population and Its Component Communities, Based on the Jerusalem Jewish Census, September, 1939.* Jerusalem: Department of Statistics of the Jewish Agency for Palestine, 1940.

Gurevich, David, and Aaron Gertz. *Jewish Agricultural Settlement in Palestine (General Survey and Statistical Abstracts).* Jerusalem: Department of Statistics of the Jewish Agency for Palestine, 1938.

———. *Statistical Handbook of Jewish Palestine, 1947.* Jerusalem: Jewish Agency for Palestine, 1947.

Gurevich, David, Aaron Gertz, and Roberto Bachi, *The Jewish Population of Palestine: Immigration, Demographic Structure and Natural Growth* (in Hebrew). Jerusalem: Jewish Agency for Palestine, 1944.

Haber, Julius. *The Odyssey of an American Zionist: Fifty Years of Zionist History.* New York: Twayne, 1956.

Hacohen, Dvora, ed. *Ingathering of Exiles: Aliyah to the Land of Israel—Myth and Reality.* Jerusalem: Zalman Shazar Center for Jewish History, 1998.

Halamish, Aviva. "Immigration of Jewish 'Capitalists' to Palestine between the Two World Wars" (in Hebrew). In *Ingathering of Exiles,* ed. Hacohen, 193–232.

Halperin, Samuel. *The Political World of American Zionism.* Detroit: Wayne State University Press, 1961.

Halpern, Ben. "The Americanization of Zionism, 1880–1930." In *Solidarity and Kinship: Essays on American Zionism,* ed. Nathan M. Kaganoff, 56–87. Waltham, Mass.: American Jewish Historical Society, 1980.

———. *The American Jew: A Zionist Analysis.* New York: Schocken Books, 1983.

Handy, Robert T., ed. *The Holy Land in American Protestant Life, 1800–1948: A Documentary History.* New York: Arno Press, 1981.
Harpaz, Natan. "From Dream Houses to Box Houses: The Architectural Revolution of the 1930s in Tel Aviv" (in Hebrew). In *Eidan 3: Tel-Aviv in Its Beginning, 1909–1934,* ed. Mordechai Naor, 91–106. Jerusalem: Yad Izhak Ben-Zvi, 1984.
Harry, Myriam. *A Springtide in Palestine.* London: E. Benn, 1924.
Hayut, Yehuda. "The Founding of the Krayot in Haifa Bay" (in Hebrew). In *Haifa and Its Development, 1918–1948,* ed. Mordechai Naor and Yossi Ben-Artzi, 130–46. Jerusalem: Yad Izhak Ben-Zvi, 1989.
Hebrew University of Jerusalem, Yearbook 5690 (in Hebrew). Jerusalem: n.p., 1931.
Herbert, Gilbert, and Silvina Sosnovsky. *Bauhaus on the Carmel and the Crossroads of Empire, Architecture and Planning in Haifa during the British Mandate.* Jerusalem: Yad Izhak Ben-Zvi, 1993.
Herman, Simon N. *American Students in Israel.* Ithaca: Cornell University Press, 1970.
Herman, Victor. *Coming Out of the Ice: An Unexpected Life.* New York: Harcourt, Brace, Jovanovich, 1979.
Hertzberg, Arthur, *The Jews in America: Four Centuries of an Uneasy Encounter, A History.* New York: Simon and Schuster, 1989.
———, ed. *The Zionist Idea: A Historical Analysis and Reader.* New York: Atheneum, 1982.
Histadrut of Jewish Labor in Palestine, Department of Statistics and Information. *Labor Immigration, 1919–1947.* Tel Aviv: Histadrut of Jewish Labor in Palestine, March 1949.
Holmes, John Haynes. *Palestine To-day and To-morrow: A Gentile's Survey of Zionism.* New York, 1929; reprint, New York: Arno Press, 1977.
Hoofien, Sigfried. *Report of Mr. S. Hoofien to the Joint Distribution Committee of the American Funds for Jewish War Sufferers.* New York, 1918; reprint, New York: Arno Press, 1977.
Hope-Simpson, John. *Report on Immigration, Land, Settlement and Development.* London: H. M. Stationary Office, 1930.
Horgin, Pinhas, and Arieh Leib Goelman, eds. *Mizrachi Jubilee Collection in Honor of Twenty-five Years of the Mizrachi Organization in America, 5671–5696 (1911–1936)* (in English, Hebrew, and Yiddish). New York: Mizrachi Organization of America, 1936.
Horowitz, Aron. *Striking Roots: Reflections on Five Decades of Jewish Life.* Oakville, Ontario: Mosaic Press, 1979.
Hourani, Albert Habib. *Minorities in the Arab World.* London: Oxford University Press, 1947.
Howard, Ebenezer. *Garden Cities of To-Morrow.* London: Faber and Faber, 1974.
Hurwitz, Ariel, ed. *Against the Stream: Seven Decades of Hashomer Hatzair in North America.* Givat Haviva: Association of North American Shomrim in Israel and Yad Yaari, 1994.
Ir Yizrael—Afula Bat Kaf-Hay, 5685–5710/1925–1950 (City of the Jezreel—Afula at Twenty-Five, 5685–5710/1925–1950) (in Hebrew). Afula: n.p., 1950.
Jenkins, David. *Black Zion: The Return of Afro-Americans and West Indians to Africa.* London: Wildwood House, 1975.
Jubas, Harry Leib. "The Adjustment Process of Americans and Canadians in Israel and Their Integration into Israeli Society." Ph.D. diss., Michigan State University, 1974.
Kahn, Dorothy Ruth. *Spring Up, O Well.* London: Jonathan Cape, 1936.

Bibliography

Kann, Kenneth L. *Comrades and Chicken Ranchers: The Story of a California Jewish Community*. Ithaca and London: Cornell University Press, 1993.

Kaplan, Mordecai M. "A Program for the Reconstruction of Judaism." *Menorah Journal* 6 (4 August 1920): 181–93.

———. *Judaism as a Civilization: Toward a Reconstruction of American-Jewish Life*. New York: Reconstructionist Press, 1957.

Kark, Ruth. "Jaffa—the Social and Cultural Center of the New Jewish Settlement in Palestine." In *The Jerusalem Cathedra*, vol. 3, ed. Lee I. Levine, 215–32. Jerusalem: Yad Izhak Ben-Zvi; Detroit: Wayne State University Press, 1983.

———. "Changing Patterns of Land Ownership in Nineteenth Century Palestine: The European Influence." *Journal of Historical Geography* 10, no. 4 (1984): 357–84.

———. *Jaffa: A City in Evolution, 1799–1917*. Jerusalem: Yad Izhak Ben-Zvi, 1990.

———. *American Consuls in the Holy Land, 1832–1914*. Jerusalem: Magnes Press; Detroit: Wayne State University Press, 1994.

———, ed. *The Land that Became Israel: Studies in Historical Geography*. Jerusalem: Magnes Press; New Haven: Yale University Press, 1990.

———, and Michal Oren-Nordheim. "Colonial Cities in Palestine?: Jerusalem under the British Mandate." *Israel Affairs* 3 (Winter 1996): 50–94.

Kark, Ruth, and Tzvi Shiloni. "Renewal of the Settlement at Gezer" (in Hebrew). In *Sefer Zev Vilnay: Essays on the History, Archaeology and Lore of the Holy Land, Presented to Zev Vilnay*, ed. Eli Schiller, 331–43. Jerusalem: Ariel, 1984.

Katz, Yossi. "Achouzat Poria—The First Achouza in Eretz Israel" (in Hebrew). *Ofakim Be-Geographia* (Horizons: Studies in Geography) 4 (1979): 57–63.

———. "The *Ahuza* Project in Eretz Israel, 1908–1917" (in Hebrew). Master's thesis, Hebrew University of Jerusalem, 1979.

———. "The Development of Ahuzat Migdal, 1910–1921" (in Hebrew). *Cathedra* 42 (January 1987): 129–52.

———. *Jewish Settlement in the Hebron Mountains and the Etzion Bloc: From "Nahalat Herzog" to Gush Etzion* (in Hebrew). Ramat Gan: Bar-Ilan University, 1992.

———. *The "Business" of Settlement: Private Entrepreneurship in the Jewish Settlement of Palestine, 1900–1914*. Jerusalem: Magnes Press and Bar-Ilan University Press, 1994.

Katzman, Jacob. *Commitment: The Labor Zionist Life-Style In America—A Personal Memoir*. New York: Labor Zionist Letters, 1975.

Kaufman, Menahem. *An Ambiguous Partnership: Non-Zionists and Zionists in America, 1939–1948*. Jerusalem: Magnes Press; Detroit: Wayne State University Press, 1991.

Kazan, Judah Leib. *From New York to Raanana* (in Hebrew). Tel Aviv: M. Neuman, 1954.

Kisch, Frederick Hermann. *Palestine Diary*. London: Victor Gollancz, 1938.

Kleinman, Rachel, Yehoshua Ben-Arieh, and Dan Giladi. "The Beginnings of Netanya as an Agricultural Moshavah, 1928–1933" (in Hebrew). *The Netanya Book*, ed. Avshalom Shmueli and Moshe Brawer, 115–22. Tel Aviv: Am Oved, 1982.

Kluger, Binyamin. *Jerusalem: Neighborhoods Surrounding Her—The Neighborhoods outside the Walls in the Years 5620–5700 (1860–1940)* (in Hebrew). Jerusalem: n.p., 1979.

Knee, Stuart E. *The Concept of Zionist Dissent in the American Mind, 1917–1941*. New York: Robert Speller & Sons, 1979.

Kotzin, Daniel P. "An Attempt to Americanize the Yishuv: Judah L. Magnes in Mandatory Palestine." *Israel Studies* 5, no. 1 (2000): 1–23.

Kroyanker, David. *Jerusalem Architecture—Periods and Styles: The Period of the British Mandate 1918–1948* (in Hebrew). Jerusalem: Keter, 1989.

Lapide, Pinhas E. *A Century of U.S. Aliya.* Jerusalem: Association of Americans and Canadians in Israel, 1961.

Lestschinsky, Jacob. "Jewish Migration, 1840–1956." In *The Jews,* ed. Louis Finkelstein, vol. 2, 1536–96. Philadelphia: Jewish Publication Society of America, 1960.

Levin, Alexander Lee. *Vision: A Biography of Harry Friedenwald.* Philadelphia: Jewish Publication Society of America, 1964.

Levin, Marlin. *Balm in Gilead: The Story of Hadassah.* New York: Schocken Books, 1973.

Levin, Meyer. *In Search: An Autobiography.* New York: Horizon Press, 1950.

Levitas, Irving. "Reform Jews and Zionism, 1919–1921." *American Jewish Archives* 14 (April 1962): 3–19.

Liebes, Emanuel. "History of Moshav Beit Herut" (in Hebrew). Beit Herut: private publication, 1994.

Lindheim, Irma L. *Parallel Quest: A Search of a Person and a People.* New York: Thomas Yoseloff, 1962.

Linfield, Harry S. *The Jews in the United States, 1927: A Study of Their Number and Distribution.* New York: American Jewish Committee, 1929.

Lipsky, Louis. *Thirty Years of American Zionism.* New York: Nesher, 1927.

Lurie, Olga Rubinow. "Living Here in Palestine from 1920 to 1922, a Young Girl's Diary." *Moment* 11 (December 1986): 48–56.

Maimon, Ada. *Women Build a Land.* New York: Herzl Press, 1962.

Margalith, David. *Physicians: Forerunners of Modern Israel.* Tel Aviv: Jerusalem Academy of Medicine, 1973.

Martin, Ralph G. *Golda: A Biography.* New York: Ivy Books, 1988.

Melamed, Samuel M. "The Basis of Civilization." *The Reflex* 1 (January 1928): 1–10.

Mendes-Flohr, Paul R., and Jehuda Reinharz, eds. *The Jew in the Modern World: A Documentary History.* New York: Oxford University Press, 1980.

Metzer, Jacob. *National Capital for a National Home, 1919–1921* (in Hebrew). Jerusalem: Yad Izhak Ben-Zvi, 1979.

Metzker, Isaac, and Harry Golden, eds. *A Bintel Brief: Sixty Years of Letters from the Lower East Side to the Jewish Daily Forward.* New York: Schocken Books, 1971.

Meyer, Michael A. *Response to Modernity: A History of the Reform Movement in Judaism.* New York and Oxford: Oxford University Press, 1988.

Mills, Eric. *Census of Palestine, 1931.* 2 vols. Alexandria: Whitehead Morris, 1933.

Morahg, Ruhama, and Mordecai Morahg. *Toward Joy Profound.* Holon: M. and R. Project, 1990.

Morris, Yaakov. *Pioneers from the West.* Jerusalem: Youth and Hechalutz Department, World Zionist Organization, 1953.

———. *On the Soil of Israel: Americans and Canadians in Agriculture.* Tel Aviv: Association of Americans and Canadians in Israel, 1965.

Mossek, M. *Palestine Immigration Policy under Sir Herbert Samuel: British, Zionist and Arab Attitudes.* London: F. Cass, 1978.

Naor, Mordechai, ed. *The Pioneers of Herzliya: The Story of the First Settlers, 1924–1934* (in Hebrew). 3 vols. Herzlia: n.p., 1990.

Naor, Mordechai, Zeev Inbar, Zeev Segal, et al., eds. *Herzlia: Ha-Yovel Ha-rishon* (Herzlia: The First Jubilee) (in Hebrew). Herzlia and Tel Aviv: n.p., 1979.

Oren, Michal. "The Development of the Moshav Ovdim Idea." In *The Land that Became Israel,* ed. Kark, 215–32.

Bibliography

Orni, Efraim, and Elisha Efrat. *Geography of Israel.* Jerusalem: Israel Program for Scientific Translations, 1966.

Ostrowsky, Baruch. "Raanana—A Little American Town in Israel." *Land and Life* 12 (Fall 1949): 28–30.

Palestine, Government of. *Immigration Ordinances 1925–1926 and Regulations, Orders, etc., Made Thereunder.* Jerusalem, April 1926.

———. *Village Statistics.* Jerusalem, 1938.

Palestine, Government of, Office of Statistics. *Statistical Abstract of Palestine, 1942.* Jerusalem: Government Printing Press, 1942.

Palestine Office of the Zionist Organization. *Census of the Jews of Eretz Israel* (in Hebrew). 2 vols. Jaffa: 1918–19.

Parzen, Herbert. "Conservative Judaism and Zionism (1896–1922)." *Jewish Social Studies* 18 (October 1964): 235–64.

Paz, Yair. "Jewish Land Purchases in the Vicinity of Jerusalem in the years 1920–1932" (in Hebrew). Master's thesis, Hebrew University of Jerusalem, 1992.

Petersen, W. "A General Typology of Migration." In *Readings in the Sociology of Migration,* ed. Clifford J. Jansen, 49–68. Oxford: Pergamon Press, 1970.

Plessner, Yakir. *The Political Economy of Israel: From Ideology to Stagnation.* Albany: State University of New York Press, 1994.

Raider, Mark A. *The Emergence of American Zionism.* New York: New York University Press, 1998.

Ramat Gan Jubilee Book, 1921–1946 (in Hebrew). Ramat Gan: Local Council, 1946.

Reichman, Shalom. *From Foothold to Settled Territory: The Jewish Settlement, 1918–1948* (in Hebrew). Jerusalem: Yad Izhak Ben-Zvi, 1979.

Report of the Joint Palestine Survey Commission. London: Press Printers, 1928.

Revusky, Abraham. *Jews in Palestine.* London: P. S. King & Son, 1935.

Revutsky, Avraham [Abraham Revusky]. "Raanana, the American Colony." *Jubilee Volume of the Jewish National Fund,* 87–92. New York: Jewish National Fund, 1932.

Rodman, Samuel. "Ha-Gedud Ha-Ibri." In *Kadimah,* 15–29. New York: Federation of American Zionists, 1918; reprint, New York: Arno Press, 1977.

Rogel, Nakdimon. "Who Defended Tel Hai" (in Hebrew). *Kivunim* 38 (March 1990): 129–52.

Rosenblatt, Bernard A. *Social Zionism (Selected Essays).* New York: Public Publishing, 1919.

———. *Balfouria.* New York: Zionist Organization of America, 1920.

———. *Two Generations of Zionism: Historical Recollections of an American Zionist.* New York: Shengold Publishers, 1967.

Ruppin, Arthur. *Three Decades of Palestine: Speeches and Papers on the Upbuilding of the Jewish National Home.* Jerusalem: Schocken, 1936.

Safrai, Ze'ev. "The Influence of the Babylonian Talmud on the Attitude to Aliya" (in Hebrew). In *Ingathering of Exiles,* ed. Hacohen, 27–50.

Sampter, Jessie, ed. *A Guide to Zionism.* New York: Zionist Organization of America, 1920.

Samuel, Edwin. *Handbook of the Jewish Communal Villages in Palestine.* Jerusalem: Zionist Organization Youth Department, 1945.

———. *A Lifetime in Jerusalem: The Memoirs of the Second Viscount Samuel.* Jerusalem: Israel Universities Press, 1970.

Sandler, Bernard I. "Hoachoozo—Zionism in America and the Colonization of Palestine." *American Jewish Historical Quarterly* 65 (December 1974): 137–48.

———. "The Jews of America and the Resettlement of Palestine 1908–1934—Efforts and Achievements." Ph.D. diss., Bar Ilan University, 1978.

Sarna, Jonathan D. "The Myth of No Return: Jewish Return Migration to Eastern Europe, 1881–1914." *American Jewish History* 71 (December 1981): 256–68.

Schechter, Solomon. "Zionism—A Statement." In *Tradition and Change, The Development of Conservative Judaism,* ed. Mordecai Waxman, 457–66. New York: Burning Bush Press, 1958.

Schechtman, Joseph B. *Population Transfers in Asia.* New York: Hallsby Press, 1949.

Schmelz, U. O. "Modern Jerusalem's Demographic Evolution." *Jewish Population Studies,* vol. 20. Jerusalem: Institute of Contemporary Jewry, Hebrew University of Jerusalem, and Jerusalem Institute for Israel Studies, 1987.

Schoolman, Bertha. "3 American Pioneers in Israel." *Hadassah Newsletter* 36 (January 1956): 15.

Schwartz, Shulamith. "Americans in Palestine." In *Jewish Frontier Anthology, 1934–1944,* 341–48. New York: Jewish Frontier, 1945.

Scott, William A., and Ruth Scott. *Adaptation of Immigrants: Individual Differences and Determinants.* Oxford: Pergamon Press, 1989.

Shapiro, Yonathan. *Leadership of the American Zionist Organization 1897–1930.* Urbana: University of Illinois Press, 1971.

Shatzman, Vered. "Histadrut Bnai Binyamin—Yessuda Ve-peiluta, 1919–1929" (The Bnei Binyamin Organization—Its Founding and Its Activities) (in Hebrew). Master's thesis, Hebrew University of Jerusalem, 1989.

Sherman, C. Bezalel. "Immigration and Emigration: The Jewish Case." In *The Jew in American Society,* ed. Sklare, 53–55.

Shilo, Margalit. "On the Way to the Moshav: Ha-Ikar Hatzair, the 'American Group' in the Second Aliyah" (in Hebrew). *Cathedra* 25 (September 1982): 79–98.

Shilony, Zvi. *Jewish National Fund and Settlement in Eretz-Israel, 1903–1914* (in Hebrew). Jerusalem: Yad Izhak Ben-Zvi, 1990.

Shimoni, Gideon. *Jews and Zionism: The South African Experience (1910–1967).* Cape Town: Oxford University Press, 1980.

Shpiro, David H. *Aliya by Any Means: The History of Jewish "Illegal" Immigration into Eretz Israel under British Rule until the Thirties (1918–1937)* (in Hebrew). Tel Aviv: Am Oved, 1994.

Shumsky, Neil Larry. " 'Let No Man Stop to Plunder': American Hostility to Return Migration, 1890–1924." *Journal of American Ethnic History* 11, no. 2 (1992): 56–75.

Simon, Julius. *An American Corporation at Work in Palestine.* Tel Aviv: Palestine Publishing, 1939.

———. *Certain Days: Zionist Memoirs and Selected Papers.* Ed. and essay by Evyatar Friesel. Jerusalem: Israel Universities Press, 1971.

Sircon, Moshe. "Immigration to Israel, 1948–1953, Statistical Supplement." Jerusalem: *Falk Project for Economic Research in Israel and Central Bureau of Statistics,* Special Series No. 60, December 1957.

Sklare, Marshall. *America's Jews.* New York: Random House, 1971.

———, ed. *The Jew in American Society.* New York: Behrman House, 1974.

Sorin, Gerald. *A Time for Building: The Third Migration, 1880–1920.* Baltimore: John Hopkins University Press, 1992.

Bibliography

Stein, Kenneth W. *The Land Question in Palestine, 1917–1939*. Chapel Hill: University of North Carolina Press, 1984.

Stein, Leonard, ed. *The Letters and Papers of Chaim Weizmann*. 23 vols. Oxford: Oxford University Press, 1968.

Stein-Ashkenazy, Esther. "The Dispute within Revisionist Circles: The Aliyah of Beitar Members, Option or Obligation (1925–1935)" (in Hebrew). In *Ingathering of Exiles*, ed. Hacohen, 145–64.

Stern, Shimon. "The Development of Haifa's Urban Network, 1918–1947" (in Hebrew). Ph.D. diss., Hebrew University of Jerusalem, 1974.

Survey of Palestine Prepared in December 1945 and January 1946 for the Information of the Anglo-American Committee of Inquiry, A. 3 vols. Jerusalem: Government Printer, 1946.

Syrkin, Marie. *Golda Meir: Woman with a Cause*. London: Victor Gollancz, 1964.

———, ed. *Golda Meir Speaks Out*. London: Weidenfeld and Nicolson, 1973.

Szold, Henrietta. *Recent Jewish Progress in Palestine*. Reprint from *American Jewish Year Book 5676;* New York, Arno Press, 1977.

Anat Tal-Shir, "Latrun Battle 93" (in Hebrew) in *Seven Days: Friday Supplement to Yediot Achronot*, 21 May 1993.

Tartakover, Aryeh. "The Essence of Labor Zionism." In *Struggle for Tomorrow: Modern Political Ideologies of the Jewish People,* ed. Basil J. Vlavianos and Feliks Gross, 53–70. New York: Arts, 1954.

Teller, Judd L. "America's Two Zionist Traditions." *Commentary* 20 (October 1955): 343–52.

Teveth, Shabtai. *Ben-Gurion: The Burning Ground, 1886–1948*. Boston: Houghton Mifflin, 1987.

Tidhar, David. *Encyclopedia of the Pioneers of the Yishuv and Its Builders* (in Hebrew). 19 vols. Tel Aviv: Sifriat Rishonim, 1947–71.

Troen, S. Ilan. "Frontier Myths and the Applications in America and Israel." *Israel Studies* 5, no. 1 (2000): 301–29.

Tryster, Hillel. " 'The Land of Promise' (1935): A Case Study in Zionist Film Propaganda." *Historical Journal of Film, Radio and Television* 15, no. 2 (1995): 187–217.

Tzahor, Zeev. "David Ben Gurion's Attitude toward the Diaspora." *Judaism* 32 (Winter 1983): 9–22.

Urofsky, Melvin I. *American Zionism from Herzl to the Holocaust*. Garden City, N.Y.: Doubleday Anchor Press, 1975.

———. "Response [to Evyatar Friesel]." *American Jewish History* 75 (December 1985): 159–64.

Urofsky, Melvin I., and David W. Levy, eds. *Letters of Louis D. Brandeis*. 5 vols. Albany: State University of New York Press, 1971–78.

Vilnay, Zeev. *Jerusalem—Capital of Israel: The New City* (in Hebrew). Jerusalem: Achiavar, 1963.

———, ed. *Ariel Encyclopedia Le Yediat Eretz Israel* (in Hebrew). Tel Aviv: Am Oved-Tarbut veHinuch, 1968–80.

Waksman, Selman A. *Jacob G. Lipman*. New Brunswick, N.J.: Rutgers University Press, 1966.

Waldinger, Albert. "Abraham Cahan and Palestine." *Jewish Social Studies* 39, nos. 1–2 (Winter–Spring 1977): 75–92.

Wallace, Edwin Sherman. *Jerusalem the Holy*. New York: 1898; reprint, New York: Arno Press, 1977.

BIBLIOGRAPHY

Waxman, Chaim I. *American Aliyah: Portrait of an Innovative Migration Movement.* Detroit: Wayne State University Press 1989.

Waxman, Meyer. "The Mizrachi." In *Jewish Communal Register of New York City, 1917–1918,* 1350–58. New York: n.p., 1918.

Weisgal, Meyer. *Meyer Weisgal . . . So Far: An Autobiography.* London and Jerusalem: Weidenfeld and Nicolson, 1971.

West, Richard. *Back to Africa, A History of Sierra Leone and Liberia.* London: Jonathan Cape, 1970.

White, Paul E., and Robert I. Woods, eds. *The Geographical Impact of Migration.* New York and London: Longman, 1980.

Wischnitzer, Mark. *To Dwell in Safety: The Story of Jewish Migration since 1800.* Philadelphia: Jewish Publication Society of America, 1948.

Wise, Stephen S. *Challenging Years: The Autobiography of Stephen Wise.* New York: G. P. Putnam's Sons, 1949.

Zeiger, A. "Emma Lazarus and Pre-Herzlian Zionism." In *Early History of Zionism in America,* ed. Isidor S. Meyer, 77–108. New York: 1958; reprint, New York: Arno Press, 1977.

Zola, Gary L. "Reform Judaism's Pioneer Zionist: Maximilian Heller." *American Jewish History* 73 (June 1984): 375–97.

Index

Aaronovitch, Morris, 129
Aaronsohn, Aaron, 152
Abercrombie, Patrick, 224, 229, 236
Abrahamson, Louis, 307
Abu Shusha (Gezer), 167
Achva plan, 44
Acre, 151, 225
Afikim, Kibbutz, 62, 261, 263, 264, 270, 335
Africa Palestine Investments, 311
Afula, 69, 137, 138, 139, 143, 150, 154, 185, 188, 191, 195, 196, 205–6, 218–23, 228, 231, 232, 273, 312–15, 316, 325
Agranat, Aaron Joseph, 309
Agriculture (*see also* Livestock; Plantations; Poultry)
  Cereal, 150, 160, 172, 204, 205, 223, 255, 267, 270
  Fodder, 205, 216, 267, 270
  and Jews in the United States, 116
  Tobacco, 152–53, 172, 174, 215
  Vegetables, 152–53, 157, 172, 174, 200, 204, 216, 225, 267, 270, 322
Agronsky, Gershon, 54, 72, 85, 86, 136
Agudat Betar, 279
Agudat Netaim, 149, 185, 191, 242–43

Agudath Achim, Anshei America, 285
Agudath Israel, 39
Ahad Haam (Asher Zvi Ginzberg), 40
Ahuza Erez of New York, 186
Ahuza societies, 56, 112, 138, 149, 156–80, 186, 195, 239
Al Cos Te, 289
Alexandria, Egypt, 194
Aliyah. *See* Immigration to Palestine
Alper, Rabbi Michael, 42
America-Krit, 268–69
American Economic Committee for Palestine, 73, 74, 80–81, 253
American Ex Legionnaires Organization, 259
American Jewish Committee, 44–45
American Jewry, 37–57
  American-born, 32, 34
  Conservative, 39–40
  Eastern European origin, 30, 44, 47–49, 52, 106, 107
  German origin, 43, 47, 49
  Orthodox, 38–39
  Reconstructionist, 40
  Reform, 40–43, 49, 110
American Migdal Hotel Company (*see also* Migdal), 319

INDEX

American-Palestine Real Estate Agency, 186, 188, 219, 273, 277
American Palestine Settlers Association, 94–95, 259, 260
American Porcelain Tooth Manufacturing Company, 248, 299–302, 334
American School for Oriental Research, 109, 111
American Zion Commonwealth (AMZIC), 56, 69, 85, 112, 114–15, 127, 129, 133, 136, 138–43, 145, 147, 149, 151–54, 161, 163, 167, 169, 179, 181–233, 239, 243, 249, 256, 273–75, 290, 292–94, 303–6, 312–15, 317, 318, 335–36, 338
American Zionist Medical Unit, 53, 104, 337
America-Palestine Agency for Land Transactions, 306–7
America-Palestine Jewish Legion, 95
Amit, Irit, 192
Anglo-Palestine Bank (Anglo-Palestine Company), 131, 145, 161, 163, 167, 183, 286, 294, 310, 318
Anoka, Minnesota, 84
Antisemitism, 41, 44, 56, 88, 105–7, 116
Antonovsky, Aaron, 89–92, 97, 102, 104–5, 111
Arab riots
   of 1920, 64–65, 119
   of 1921, 65, 93, 121, 160, 323
   of 1929, 35, 51, 54, 65, 68, 94, 99, 163, 223, 288, 289, 310–11, 321
   of 1936–39, 66, 178
Arabs in Palestine, 52, 64–66, 136, 163, 164, 178, 193, 197, 209–10, 219, 231, 232, 234, 240, 257, 259, 289, 294, 310, 314
Arbeiter Ring (Workmen's Circle), 52
Arlosoroff, Chaim, 51, 61, 72–73, 84, 265
Armenians, 329–30
Aronson-Dushkin, Julia, 100, 201
Arsuf, 169
Ashinski, Aharon Mordechai, 279
Ashkelon, 192
Assimilation, 105, 116
Astoria, Long Island, New York, 98
Atlanta, Georgia. *See* Nahalat Atlanta
Atlantic City, New Jersey, 211, 225

Atlit, 152
Avihail, 137, 260, 262, 271, 335–36
Avukah, 50, 51

Babli, Eliezer, 187
Back-to-Africa movement, 328
Balfour, Lord Arthur James, 41, 181, 199, 200
Balfour Declaration, 35, 38, 41, 49, 65, 92, 199, 203, 329
Balfouria, 136, 137, 143, 152–53, 167, 181, 190–92, 194–207, 219, 226, 228, 231–32, 335–36
Baltimore, Maryland, 216, 242, 249
Baratz, Yosef, 82
Bar-David, Molly Lyons, 108, 254, 271
Bar-Ilan, Rabbi Meir (*see also* Berlin, Rabbi Meir), 62
Barclays Bank, 77, 132, 278
Baron de Hirsch Agricultural and Industrial School, Woodbine, New Jersey, 81, 258
Baron de Hirsch Fund, 258–59
Barsky, George, 286
Battir, 279
Bat Yam, 231, 296
Bayside Land Corporation, 227, 236, 238
Beer Sheva, 150, 193, 257
Beirut, 194
Beit Gan, 134
Beit Hagdudim Museum, Avihail, 19
Beit Shaan Valley, 230, 257–58, 268
Beit Shaarim, 230
Ben Ami, Oved, 189, 244
Benamy, M., 164
Ben-Avi, Ittamar, 68, 244, 277
Ben-Gurion, David, 58, 61, 72, 75–76, 96, 211
Ben Nachum, Dovid, 38, 68
Ben Shemen, 137
Bension, Dr. Ariel, 314
Bentov, Mordechai, 62
Bentwich, Norman, 154
Ben Yehuda, Eliezer, 68
Ben-Zvi, Yitzhak, 58, 75–76
Bergheim, Peter Melville, 167
Berkson, Dr. Isaac, 244
Berkson, Libby, 289

Index

Berlin, Rabbi Meir, 39, 50, 127, 278, 334
Berman, Isaac, 143, 189
Berman, Lee, 164
Berman, William, 63, 98–99
Bernstein, Aaron, 277
Bernstein, Dr. S., 24
Bernstein, Samuel, 277
Betar organization, 50
Bet Herut (*see also* Herut Bet), 254–55, 335
Bezalel School of Art and Crafts, Jerusalem, 131
Bialik, Chaim Nahman, 72, 85
Binenfeld, Zvi Arieh, 149, 249
Binyamina, 243, 261, 270
Binyan Hayishuv Company, 278
Birket Ramadan, 235
Biskind, Dr. Israel J., 54, 279
Bloom, Samuel Simon, 149, 248, 299–302, 334
Blumenfeld, Israel, 277
Blumenfeld, Zvi, 203, 205
Bnai Binyamin, 187, 189, 214, 216, 218, 243–46
Bnai Brak, 248
Bnai Zion Achuza of Hartford, 156, 170, 178–79, 186, 335
Borchov, Ber, 96
Boston, Massachusetts, 160, 186, 191, 217, 275, 279, 296, 308, 319
Bourskai Palestine Leather Factory, 298
Brandeis, Judge Louis D., 47–48, 49, 53–54, 60, 69, 71, 146, 183, 185, 190, 197, 200, 225, 227, 233, 253–54, 266, 279, 301
Brandeisia, 225
Brandeis-Mack group, 57, 279, 323, 336
Braun, Noe, 80
Brickner, Dov Natan, 323
British consulate, New York, 19, 80, 119, 129
Brodie, Israel B., 80
Bronx, New York, 77, 101, 235
Brooklyn, New York, 139, 156, 287, 297, 310
Brown, Michael, 72

Cahan, Abraham, 74

California, 64, 80, 84, 149–50, 156, 173, 225, 234, 236, 239
Carmel, El (Haifa), 65
Censuses
  of the Jewish Population in Haifa (1938), 26
  of Jewish Professionals (1922), 29, 31
  of Palestine (1922), 25, 161
  of Palestine (1931), 18, 25, 26, 134
  Census of the Jews of Eretz Israel, 18, 133, 157
  Jerusalem Jewish Census (1939), 27
Certificates
  Capitalist, 23, 24, 29, 77, 103, 124, 127–28, 333
  Labor Schedule (*Halutz*), 23, 29, 57, 118, 123–27
Charleston, South Carolina, 291
Chattanooga, Tennessee, 214, 297
Chavel, Rabbi Charles B., 39
Chazan, Nathan, 171
Chelsea, Massachusetts, 71
Chelsea, Michigan, 254
Chester, Pennsylvania, 181
Chicago, Illinois (*see also* Sarona), 75, 156, 165, 255, 298, 302
Chicago Ahuza, 164–66
Chicago Kollel, 280–81
Chipkin, Israel, 244
Cigarette manufacturing, 287, 297
Cincinnati, Ohio, 156
Citizenship
  American, 17–19, 26, 134, 136
  Palestinian, 26, 134, 311
Cleveland, Ohio, 54, 85, 87, 126, 156, 214, 255
Cleveland Ahuza No. 1, 187
Climer, Abraham, 77, 102
Cohen, Armond Emanuel, 42, 110
Cohen, Elias A., 84
Cohen, Erik, 272
Cohen, Moshe Ben Zeev, 275
Commissions of Enquiry: Shaw Commission, 1929, 123
Communism
  and communist ideology (*see also* socialism), 32, 52, 328–29
Consulate, Consular Agency. *See* United States

Co-operative Bank Bnai Binyamin, 243–44
Creamridge, New Jersey, 84
Cucuy, Asher, 204

Danish-American Company, 288–89
Darbeide, 224
Davidson, Gabriel, 116
Davis, E., 162
Davis, Moshe, 14–15, 109
Deedes, Sir Wyndham, 59
Degania A, Kibbutz, 62, 82, 264
Degania B, Kibbutz, 160, 261, 263, 264, 335
DeHaas, Jacob, 100, 179
Detroit, Michigan, 23, 68, 277, 329
Detroit Kvutza, 264
Dewey, John, 337
Diamant, David Naphtali, 298
Discharged and Demobilized Soldiers Association, 257–58
Dizengoff, Meir, 292, 296
Doukhan-Landau, Leah, 227
Dror, 96
Dual loyalty, 43–48
Dunkelman, Ben, 235
Dushkin, Alexander M., 83, 244, 337

Earlton, New York, 84
Eastman, Marcus, 249
Economic depression in Palestine, 1927–28, 22
Economic depression in the United States, 22, 23, 36, 51, 90, 101, 116, 245, 252, 331
Eder, David, 58
Eder, Edith Low, 108
Egypt, 194
Ein Ganim, 134
Ein Hai, 166
Ein Hamifratz, Kibbutz, 229
Ein Haoved, 262, 336
Ein Harod, Kibbutz, 133
Ein Hashofet, Kibbutz, 32, 83, 136, 261, 266–67, 335
Ein Shemer, Kibbutz, 261, 267
Ein Zeitim, 319–21
Einzelbauch, Rabbi Eliyahu, 309

Eisenberg, Aharon, 185, 242
Ekron, 134, 243
El Arish, 257
Elchanan, Rabbi Isaac, 98
El Haram, 168–69, 207–9, 211, 216, 217
Elkin, Eudice, 244
Ellington, Connecticut, 84
Emek Hefer, 111, 151, 166, 182, 252, 254, 260
Emigration from Palestine
  American Jewish, 25, 63, 106, 119, 175
  Jewish, 23, 25
Emigration from the United States
  American Jewish, 21–22, 68, 103, 106, 326–27
  General, 43–44
Epstein, Rabbi Moses Mordechai, 310
Eretz Israel—Land of Our Future, 75
Etkes, Perz Willard, 309
Ettinger, Jacob (Akiva), 69, 85, 158, 179–80, 204, 226, 247, 252–53, 257

Farband (Jewish National Workers' Alliance), 52
Farkas, Benjamin, 98
Far Rockaway, New York, 291
Federation of American Zionists. *See* Zionist Organization of America
Feingold, Henry L., 49
Feller, Isaac, 321–22
Fels, Mary, 146, 243, 277, 279
Felsenthal, Bernhard, 41
Fine, Israel, 216
Fineman, Irving, 109, 200
Finkelstein family, 159–60
Fish, Abraham and Sarah, 297
Fishman, Hertzel, 71, 92
Fishman, Shmuel, 92
Fishman family, 70–71, 92
Flag, American, 171, 181
Flaggtown, New Jersey, 83
Florida, 225
Forests, 152, 174, 230, 234, 245
Frankfurter, Professor Felix, 48
Freidman, Avraham, 246–47
Freidman, Menachem Mendel, 93, 287
Friedenwald, Dr. Harry, 242–43
Friedland, A. H., 85

Friedlander, Israel, 40, 47
Friedlander, Lillian, 289
Friedlander, Sam, 19, 246–47, 262
Frieman, Pinhas, 141
Furmansky, Moshe, 96

Gadera, 134
Galilee, 153, 164, 168
Gan Berakhah, Netanya, 244
Gan Hadar Beth, 238, 240
Gan Hadar Corporation, 76, 79, 238–40
Gan Haim, 234–27, 335, 336
Gan Haim Bet, 236, 336
Gan Haim Corporation, 234–36
Gan Hasharon, 254
Gan Rashel, 149, 154, 238–39
Gan Yavne, 92, 138–39, 166, 176–78, 180, 195
Garden cities, 195, 211
Garvey, Marcus, 328
Gaza, 192
Geddes, Sir Auckland, 60
Gelber, Sylva, 289
George, Henry, 146
Germany (*see also* Jews, Central European; Immigration to Palestine, Central European Jews), 36
Geula Company, 141–42, 185, 273, 294, 310
Geva, Kibbutz, 230
Ginnosar, Kibbutz, 261, 263, 335
Givat Brenner, Kibbutz, 261, 263, 335
Glikin, Moshe, 188, 318–19
Gluck, Dr. Nelson, 111, 289
Goell, Jacob, 94
Goell, Yohai, 91
Goldberg, Abraham, 141, 142
Goldberg, Nathan, 235
Goldman, Harry, 64, 160
Goldman, Simon, 157, 160, 166
Goldman family, 159
Goldscheider, Calvin, 17, 89–90
Goldsmith, Samuel A., 282
Goldstein, Dr. Israel, 269
Gordon, Aaron David, 96, 111
Gordon, Benjamin L., 75, 216
Gordon, S., 132
Gordonia, 96

Goren, Arieh, 100
Gottesman, Rabbi Leo, 98, 309
Gottheil, Richard J. H., 46
Government of Great Britain, 122, 130, 161
  Colonial Office, 122
Government of Palestine (including British military and civil administrations), 18, 25, 119, 122, 136, 163, 178, 182, 206
  Department of Immigration and Travel, 121–23, 126, 129, 131
  Department of Migration (Passport Control Department), 19, 120
  Department of Public Health, 120
  Department of Public Works, 101, 120, 309
  Department of Railways, 120
  Immigration ordinances, 118–26, 129–31
  Land Settlement Department, 238–39
  Legal Department, 258
Grand, Samuel, 83
Great Depression. *See* Economic depression in the United States
Greenblatt, Israel, 288
Grunhut, Moritz, 277
Guide to Zionism, 75
Gurevich, David, 19
Gush Ezion, 195

Habayit, 39
Haber, Julius, 171, 288, 298
Habonim, 50, 62, 65, 251, 255, 263, 270
Hachshara (training) farms, 82–84
Hadar, 261, 267
Hadassah, 51, 53, 54, 73, 100, 131, 248, 265, 277, 289, 311, 337
  Mount Scopus Medical Center, 277, 289
Hadassah Newsletter, 73
Hadera, 134, 150, 191, 195, 242–43, 261, 266–67, 277, 279
Hadoar, 71
Hagdud Haivri League, 259–60
Haifa, 17, 31, 26, 85, 97, 134, 135, 136, 139, 141, 192, 203, 219, 225, 267, 284, 302–9, 315, 325
  Bat Galim, 279

Haifa (*continued*)
  Carmelia, 306
  Central Carmel, 305, 308
  Hadar Hacarmel, 303–5, 308, 336
  Hod Hacarmel, 307
  Neve Shaanan, 305–6
  Port, 224–26, 232, 308
  Rom Hacarmel, 139, 306–7
  Western Carmel, 305, 336
Haifa Bay, 167, 186, 192, 194–96, 223–29, 232–33, 238, 252, 256
Haifa Bay Development Company, 224, 226–27
Haikar Hatzair, 50, 51, 80
Halperin, Hanoch, 163
Halpern, Ben, 106, 263
Halutz (pl. *Halutzim*), 30–32, 50, 52, 61, 63, 71, 76, 82, 86, 96, 108, 126, 138, 161, 251, 262, 270–71, 272, 331, 338
Hamara, 257
Hanita, 268
Hankin, Yehoshua, 143, 150–51, 193, 196, 206, 207, 210, 219, 252
Hanoteah, 187, 243–46
Har Canaan, 273, 319–21
Harpaz, Natan, 294
Harris, Herman, 215
Harris, Isaac, 186, 189, 308
Harry, Myriam, 106
Hartford, Connecticut (*see also* Bnai Zion Achuza of Hartford), 156, 301
Harzfeld, Avraham, 259, 269
Hashomer, 76
Hashomer Hatzair Organization of North America, 50–52, 62, 82–84, 90, 96, 126, 251, 263–70, 338
Hatzor, Kibbutz, 270
Health Services, 66, 100
Hebrew Union College, 42–43, 63, 110
Hebrew University of Jerusalem, The, 43, 91, 100, 109–11, 130, 136, 337
Hebron, 38, 98–99, 137, 249, 309–11
Hechalutz, 51, 62, 82, 96, 126, 264, 270
Hefzibah, 190, 242–43
Heizer, Oscar (*see also* United States consulate, Jerusalem), 131–32
Heliopolis, Egypt, 225
Heller, Rabbi Maximilian, 41
Herman, Simon N., 109

Herr, Aaron, 247, 262
Hershenov, Boris (Baruch), 277–78
Herut Aleph (*see also* Tzofit), 254
Herut Bet (*see also* Bet Herut), 254–55
Herut Gimmel, 254
Herut plan, 251–55, 271, 338
Herzl, Theodor, 46, 48, 225
Herzlia, 106, 136, 137, 138, 152, 154, 160, 168, 188, 189, 191, 195, 196, 207–18, 224, 226, 232, 238–39, 243, 293, 335
Hexter, Dr. Maurice, 265
Highstown, New Jersey, 84, 264
Hillman, A. M., 102
Histadrut (General Jewish Federation of Labor in Palestine), 133, 173, 187, 211, 300
Hoachoozo of St. Louis, 114, 157–63
Hoffman, Goldie, 64
Hoffman, Isidore B., 109
Holliday, Clifford, 229
Holy Land, 17, 28, 32, 35, 38–40, 69, 76, 97–98, 284, 321
Hope-Simpson, John, 222
Horovitz, David, 101
Hospitals, 211, 226, 312, 314
Hotels, 206, 211, 286, 297, 319
Hourani, Albert H., 329
Hovevei Zion, 49, 151, 157
Howard, Ebenezer, 315–17
Hula Valley, 230, 257, 269
Husseini, Musa Kasem Pasha el, 65
Hyman, Mrs. S. I., 279

Ibn Philistine, 66
Ilan (Applebaum), Ben-Zion, 62
Immigration to Palestine
  American Jews, 17–35, 44, 48–57, 60–61, 80, 92–93, 102, 106, 124, 126–29, 159, 203, 204, 217, 218, 235, 248, 309, 326–28, 330–40
  Arab attitudes toward, 64–66, 119, 121, 123
  Canadian Jews, 23, 64, 95, 176, 204, 281, 326, 338, 340
  Central European Jews, 19, 25, 36, 57, 124–25, 175, 204, 217, 303, 305, 330–33

Index

Eastern European Jews, 19, 25, 29, 39, 57, 63, 119, 123–25, 127, 129, 204, 214, 217, 222, 227, 229, 303, 309, 326, 330–32
Illegal immigration, 125
  Jews of other origins, 124, 216, 331–33, 339
  South African Jews, 326, 338–40
Immigration to the United States
  General, 43–44
  Jewish, 43–44, 92, 103, 157
Industry, 171, 174, 181, 211, 215, 216, 225, 236, 270, 286, 288, 312
Intercollegiate Zionist Association, 50, 51
Iraqi Petroleum Company, 227, 236
Israelite, Eliyahu, 157, 159, 161
Itin, Yehuda, 306

Jabotinsky, Vladmir, 50, 58, 72, 298
Jacobs, Aaron, 277
Jacobs, J. Jonas, 247
Jaffa (*see also* Tel Aviv), 18, 31, 38, 65, 121, 132, 133, 134, 136, 137, 189, 279, 284, 290–302
  Jewish Community Council of Jaffa, 104
Jarcho, Isaiah, 153, 160, 167–69, 171
Jedid, Count Selim, 308
Jelil, 168, 207, 209–10, 293
Jemmama. *See* Ruchama
Jenkins, David, 328
Jericho, 66, 257
Jerusalem, 18, 31, 27, 38, 109, 133, 134, 135–36, 139, 166, 175, 192, 273, 274–90, 317, 325
  Achvah neighborhood, 284–85
  Amos land, 274–75
  Bayit Vagan neighborhood, 279
  Beit Aharon neighborhood, 277
  Beit Hakerem neighborhood, 276–77, 279, 337
  Beit Yisrael neighborhood, 285
  Bukharian neighborhood, 288
  Business center, 274–75
  Garden of Antimos (Ben Yehuda St.), 274–75
  Givat Eliyahu neighborhood, 274–75
  Givat Shaul neighborhood, 279
  Kerem neighborhood, 285, 287
  Knesset Yisrael neighborhood, 285
  Mea Shearim neighborhood, 139, 285, 289
  Mekor Baruch neighborhood, 277–78
  Mekor Haim neighborhood, 275, 278
  Milner Quarter, 285
  Mizpeh Yerushalaim, 279
  Mount of Olives, 285
  Mount Scopus, 275, 277, 289
  Old City, 285
  Rehavia neighborhood, 274–75, 277, 279, 289–90
  Romema neighborhood, 277, 290
  Sanhedriah neighborhood, 278
  Shaare Hessed neighborhood, 277, 285
  Succat Shalom, 287
  Talpiot neighborhood, 274–77, 279, 289–90, 336
  Western Wall, 28
  Wittenburg neighborhood, 285
  Yemin Moshe, 285
Jerusalem-America Land Company, 186, 273, 277–78, 296, 307
Jewish Agency for Palestine (*see also* Palestine Zionist Executive), 18, 19, 25, 45, 100, 125–26, 134, 138, 260, 262, 337
  Colonization Department, 265
  Department of Commerce and Industry, 129, 289
  Department of Immigration, 19, 29
  Department of Statistics, 19
Jewish Agricultural Experiment Station, 152
Jewish Colonial Trust, 147, 183, 227
Jewish Colonization Association. *See* Palestine Jewish Colonization Association
Jewish Daily Forward, 73, 74, 107
Jewish Exponent (Philadelphia), 75
Jewish Farmer's Federation of Palestine, 187
"Jewish Homeland," 91, 92, 94–95, 109, 146, 327
Jewish Institute of Religion, 110
Jewish Legionnaires, 19, 54, 57–58, 59, 62, 65, 81, 86, 92–95, 118–19, 129,

INDEX

Jewish Legionnaires (*continued*)
    178, 201–203, 246–47, 251, 256–60, 262, 263, 271, 287
Jewish Legionnaire's Association, 19
Jewish National Fund (JNF), 51, 76, 138, 140–41, 144–48, 154–55, 162–63, 165, 169, 178, 182–83, 185, 186, 192, 194, 197, 207, 210, 219, 222–24, 226–27, 229–30, 233, 236, 238, 240, 242–45, 249, 251–71, 275, 279, 292–93, 319, 334
Jewish Theological Seminary of America, 40, 110
Jews
    Canadian, 38, 60, 95, 146, 156, 182, 234–35, 337, 340
    Central European, 29, 88, 126, 222
    Eastern European, 58, 77, 88, 106, 146, 222
    Middle Eastern and North African, 29, 216, 288
    Palestinian, 29, 35, 62–64
    South African, 60, 146, 182, 311, 338–40
Jezreel-Jaffa Company, 230
Jezreel Valley, 150, 167, 192, 194, 219, 223, 228–29, 232, 247, 312, 314, 325
Jiddah, 196, 228–29
Jidro, 192, 224
Joffe, Eliezer, 258, 337
Joint Distribution Committee, 281
Joint Palestine Survey Commission, 150, 152
Jordan. *See* Trans-Jordan
Jordan River, 95
Josephson, I. Z., 288
Judenfreund, Samuel, 167
Junior Hadassah, 50, 51

Kadooria, 314
Kadoorie, Sir Elly (Eliezer Silas), 286, 313–14
Kafrata, 196, 224, 227–28, 232
Kahn, Dorothy Ruth, 70, 96, 104–5, 139
Kallen, Deborah, 97, 337
Kamenetzky, Lewis Jack, 133, 263
Kanowitz, Isaac Meir, 302
Kansas City, Missouri, 278

Kaplan, Abraham, 164
Kaplan, Harry, 149
Kaplan, Rabbi Mordecai M., 40
Kaplan, Nathan D., 302
Kaplan, Pesach, 247
Kaplowitz, Joseph, 277
Karei Naaman, 229
Karkur, 164, 166, 248, 265
Kastina (Beer Tuvia), 157
Katz, Abraham David, 89–92, 97, 102, 104–5, 111
Katz, Yossi, 145
Katzman, Jacob, 71, 76
Katzmann, Boris, 54
Katznelson, Berl, 72
Kaufmann, Richard, 200, 210, 225, 229, 236, 305, 307, 312–13, 317, 323
Kazan, Judah Leib, 151, 153, 160, 167–69, 171, 288–89
Kehlman, Leopold, 167
Keren Hayesod, 76, 138, 145, 147, 161, 165, 185, 194, 227, 251–52, 260, 282, 298, 308, 314
Keren Hayishuv, 39
Kerr, Dr. Solomon, 77
Kesselman, Robert D., 54, 64, 101, 107, 136, 252, 276, 287, 336–37
Kfar Aaron, 243
Kfar Barka, 176
Kfar Bialik, 229
Kfar Blum, Kibbutz, 261, 263, 270, 335
Kfar Brandeis, 279
Kfar Gileadi, 257
Kfar Hasidim, 229
Kfar Hayeladim, 315
Kfar Hittim, 255
Kfar Ivri, 33, 319–21, 322
Kfar Malul, 167
Kfar Masaryk, Kibbutz, 229
Kfar Menachem, 136, 261, 269, 335
Kfar Saba, 168, 235, 243, 248, 335
Kfar Tavor, 134, 243
Kfar Vitkin, 111
Kfar Yehezkel, 165, 200, 315
Kfar Yehoshua, 230
Khirbaj-Khartia, 196, 224, 228–29
Khirbet Azun, 168, 179
Khirbet El Mansi, 265
King David Hotel, 286

418

Index

Kinneret, 50, 201, 264
Kiryat Bialik, 229
Kiryat Haim, 229, 238, 256
Kiryat Motzkin, 229
Kiryat Shmuel, 229
Kiryat Yam, 229, 236
Kisch, Colonel Frederick Herman, 121, 218
Klaiman, Israel, 282
Klei, Berl, 81
Klein, Rabbi Baruch M., 38
Klein, David, 279
Kligler, Israel, 64, 244, 289
Knesset Israel Yeshiva, Hebron, 63, 98–99, 309–10
Kollel America Tiffereth Yerushalaim, 23, 28, 38, 97–99, 136, 272, 274, 280–86, 289, 311, 338
Koller, Avraham Moshe, 253
Kook, Rabbi Dov, 315
Kordani, 225
Kornfeld, Alfred, 279
Kotler, Harry, 143, 186
Kupat Holim, 314
Kurdani, 224
Kushan (land title), 129, 154, 211, 218, 279, 294
Kuskus, 167, 196, 228, 230
Kvashnievsky, Ch., 298
Kvutzah (pl. Kvutzot), 163, 165, 202, 203, 239, 256, 264
Kvutzat Gordonia, Philadelphia, 82, 264
Kvutzat Schiller, 335

Labes, Emanuel, 111
Labor
  Arab, 157, 159, 244, 336
  Jewish, 157, 159, 173, 175, 178, 234–35, 239, 244, 336
Lamport, Samuel C., 149, 248, 277, 282
Land
  Purchases by American companies, 140–43
  Purchases by individual Americans, 69, 112, 114–15, 127, 138, 173
  Quality of, 148–54, 239
  Quantity of, 148–54
Land of Promise, 76

Land Registry (*tabu*), 196–97, 249
Landsberg, Alexander, 287–88
Landsman, Bertha, 100
Land Transfer Regulations, 1940, 66
Lapson, Judah, 84
Latrun, 249
Lauterbach, Rabbi Wolf, 311
Lavon, Zvi, 302
Lazarus, Emma, 44
League for Palestine Labor, 51
Leather processing, 297–98
Lebanon, 194
Legionnaires. *See* Jewish Legionnaires
Lehman, Judge Irving, 48
Lesser, Rabbi Abraham J. G., 38
Levensohn, Lotta, 100
Levin, Meyer, 234
Levin, Schmaryahu, 85
Levine, Melech, 258
Levine, Samuel, 119, 256
Levine, Shimon Zeev, 214, 218, 297, 315
Levontin, Zalman, 167
Levy, Dr. Isaac, 310
Lewin-Epstein, Eliyahu Zeev, 231
Lewin-Epstein, Levi, 231
Lewin-Epstein, Rehabiah, 80, 253
Lewinson family, 159
Lewisohn, Ludwig, 291
Liberty, New York, 84
Lifshitz, Shimon, 278
Lindheim, Irma L., 54, 100, 111, 251, 265–66, 334
Lipman, Jacob G., 191, 204
Lipman, Noah, 247
Lipsky, Louis, 74, 147, 161
Livestock, 157, 159, 160, 169, 172, 205, 216, 223, 225, 255, 267, 270, 322
Loewe, Zvi Arie, 285
Loewy, Joseph, 224, 308
London Conference, 182
Los Angeles, California, 275
Louis Marshall Colonization Fund, 260
Lowenstein, Leopold, 298

Maccabean, 46, 75
Machinery, American, 202, 265
Mack, Judge Julian W., 49, 80, 282
Magnes, Beatrice, 34

INDEX

Magnes, Judah, 34, 64, 91, 100, 154, 282, 289, 334, 336–37
Majdal, 196, 224, 227–28, 232
Malaria, 53, 203, 215, 252
Mandate for Palestine, Articles of, 124, 130–31
Manischewitz Matzo Factory, 284
Manor Textile Company, 230
Marshall, Judge Louis, 44–46, 168
Marshallia, 168
Masada, 51–52
Mead, Elwood, 149–50
Meir (Meyersohn), Golda, 62–63, 72, 80, 88, 263–64, 337
Melamed, Samuel L., 54
Melchett, Lord. *See* Mond, Sir Alfred
Memphis, Tennessee, 203, 205
Menahemia, 134
Menashe, Baron Felix de, 243
Menorah Palestine Building Corporation, 138, 143, 186, 189, 273, 296, 307
Merchavia, 62–63, 106, 111, 133, 134, 137, 197, 219, 228, 261, 263–65, 335
Meshek Company, 167, 219, 222, 224, 226, 230
Meshi Silk Factory, 129, 248, 298, 334
Mesuat Itzhak, 249
Meyersohn, Morris, 263–64
Michigan State College of Agriculture, 82, 264
Middle-class agriculturalist, 23, 32, 69–70, 244, 330–31, 338
Midrach Oz, 265
Migdal, 112, 114–15, 149, 273, 318–19, 323, 335
Migdal, Shoshana, 217
Migdal Corporation, 138, 170, 186–87, 318–19
Migdal Garden Villa, 188, 319
Mikveh Israel agricultural school, 258
Mills, Eric, 18
Milwaukee, Wisconsin, 263
Minneapolis, Minnesota, 106, 159, 255
Mirsky family, 106, 159
Mishmar Haemek, Kibbutz, 96, 111, 251, 261, 265–66, 335
Mishmar Hayam, 229
Miske, 235

Mizrachi Organization of America, 39, 50, 96, 126, 143, 159, 185, 249, 278, 309, 321–23
Mizrachi Organization of Poland, 209, 231
Model farm, 204
Mohilever, Rabbi Samuel, 49
Mohl, Emanuel, 54, 109, 179, 201, 252, 279, 336
Mond, Sir Alfred (Lord Melchett), 60–61, 168, 188, 235
Morahg, Ruhama and Mordecai, 36
Morgen Journal, 71

Naame, 270
Naan, Kibbutz, 261, 263, 335, 336
Naane, 79, 238–41
Nachalat Zion Company, 149, 319–21, 323
Nahalal, 230
Nahalat Atlanta, 114, 214
Nahalat Bayit, 278
Nahalat Itzhak, 149, 273, 322, 324
Nahalat Shivim, 149
Nahalat Yaakov, 229
Nahalin, 249
Naharaim, 109, 265
National Farm School, Bucks County, Pennsylvania, 83
Naturalization. *See* Citizenship
Negev, 108, 230, 257
Nes Ziona, 243, 248
Netanya, 149, 152, 187, 189, 195, 234, 244–46, 262, 335
Neumann, Emanuel, 238, 337
Neve Yaakov, 322–23
Newark, New Jersey, 77, 285
New Judea, 75
New Marbadia Carpet Company, 288
New Masses, 52
New Orleans, Louisiana, 291
New Palestine, 71–73
New York Achooza Aleph, 92, 114, 138–39, 141, 151–53, 160, 166–80, 186–87, 211, 253, 288, 306, 335–36
New York City, 39, 48, 53, 71, 75, 76, 85, 91, 98, 100–101, 104–5, 108, 109, 156, 166, 168, 171, 181, 191, 214,

Index

New York City (*continued*)
  224, 235, 238, 244, 255, 288, 298, 302, 309, 321
New York City Kehillah, 100
New York Herald Tribune, 73
New York Times, 46, 73–74
Nimrin, 231
Non-Partisan Conference to Consider Palestine Problems, 45
Nordau, Dr. Max, 225
Nordia, 139, 225–26
Norfolk, Virginia, 93, 287
Norman, Dr. Jacob P., 296
North Branch, New Jersey, 83
Novomeysky, Moshe, 287–88

Orenstein, Rabbi Itzhak Avigdor, 322–23
Orthodox American immigrants, 30, 38, 89, 272, 331, 338
Orthodox Jewish Congregational Union of America, 47
Ostend, 225
Ostrowsky, Baruch, 175–76
Ottoman regime, 194

Palestine and Near East Economic Magazine, 74, 248
Palestine Building Loan and Savings Association, 179, 279
Palestine Cooperative Company, 279, 318
Palestine Economic Corporation (PEC), 147, 227, 229, 236, 238, 286
Palestine Electric Corporation, 226, 265, 299, 303, 314
Palestine Exploration Fund, 153
Palestine Hotels, Ltd., 286
Palestine Jewish Colonization Association, 150, 157, 159, 160, 164–67, 187, 231, 243, 248, 252, 260, 310, 319–20
Palestine Knitting Works, 287–88
Palestine Land Development Company (PLDC), 85, 140–42, 150, 152–53, 162, 164, 166–69, 179, 188, 192, 196–97, 208–11, 224, 230, 273–75, 294, 303–5, 307–8
Palestine Mortgage and Credit Bank, 238
Palestine Pictorical, 76, 208

Palestine Securities Company, 286
Palestine Zionist Executive (*see also* Jewish Agency for Palestine), 18, 19, 98, 121, 123, 125–26, 129, 138, 161, 163, 165, 194, 206, 210, 218, 227, 297, 337
  Department of Agriculture and Settlement, 85, 158, 164, 200, 203–4
  Department of Colonization, 187
  Department of Immigration, 25
  Urban Settlement Department, 297
Pansak, Mordy, 296
Paper, Nahum, 150–51, 307
Pardes Hagdud, 149, 246–47, 259, 262, 335–36
Pardes Hannah, 243, 252
Paris Peace Conference, 41
Parks, 211
Passman, Charles, 127, 142–43, 188–89, 193, 205, 214, 222, 233, 293
Paterson, New Jersey, 298, 334
Pearlman, B., 288
Penn, Nibby, 255
Petah Tikvah, 134, 136–37, 151, 162, 243, 248, 284
Petaluma, California, 82, 264
Pevsner, Shmuel, 194, 308
Philadelphia, Pennsylvania, 75, 82, 156, 248, 288, 299, 323, 334
Pickman-Feinberg, Dr. Olga, 66, 131
Pierce, Asher, 235–36
Pittsburgh, Pennsylvania, 49, 156, 191, 277, 288
Plainfield, New Jersey, 84
Plantations
  Almond, 157, 159–61, 164, 166, 180
  Banana, 174, 216, 225
  Citrus, 76, 79, 151–54, 172–73, 175, 176, 178, 189, 215, 223, 225, 234–35, 238–40, 242–46, 248, 253–55, 260, 268, 294
  Olive, 152, 157, 164, 166, 180
Plumer, Lord, 300
Poale Agudath Israel, 39
Poale Zion of America (Jewish Socialist Labor Party), 36, 52, 54, 58, 61, 75, 81, 96, 106, 119, 126, 263
Poale Zion Youth. *See* Habonim
Pool, David de Sola, 137, 139, 247, 282

421

INDEX

Poria (*see also* St. Louis, Missouri; Hoachoozo of St. Louis), 64, 114, 134, 149, 157–63, 180, 193, 195, 318, 336
Poultry, 159, 160, 169, 172, 205, 216, 223, 255, 267, 270, 322
Press, Issy, 77
Pri Hadar, 238, 240
Professions and vocations of American immigrants
   Accountant and bookkeeper, 29–30, 34, 129, 337
   Administrator, 34
   Agricultural, 29–31, 53, 83, 236, 246
   Baker, 29
   Banker, 34
   Carpenter, 29, 58, 84, 104
   Clerk, 29, 93
   Commerce, 29
   Construction, 58, 59, 121
   Educator, 29, 31, 34, 93, 97, 302
   Electrician, 29
   Engineer, Architectural, 29, 31, 34, 53–54, 109, 171, 252, 309
   Insurance agent, 29
   Journalist and writer, 31, 34, 54, 129
   Laborer, 29, 30
   Legal, 31, 34, 93
   Machinist and mechanic, 29, 58, 84, 121, 129
   Medical (doctors, nurses, etc.), 29, 31, 34, 54, 100, 105, 129, 201–2, 309, 311
   Painter, 29
   Rabbi, 29, 34, 46, 97
   Shochet (ritual slaughterer), 29
   Social Work, 29, 34
   Stenographer, Secretary, 29, 100
   Student, 29, 63, 93, 98, 110–11, 130
   Tailor, 29, 58
Provisional Zionist Executive Committee on Zionist Affairs, 47

Raanana, 102, 137, 138, 156, 166–76, 179–80, 195, 211, 335
Rabalsky, Benjamin, 279
Rabalsky, Moses, 279
Rabalsky Group, 275
Rafiah, 164, 257
Raflowitz, Hyman, 190
Railroads, 203, 211, 219, 227, 236, 240, 279, 302, 314
Rama. *See* Sarona
Ramat David, Kibbutz, 261, 263, 270, 335
Ramat Gan, 129, 154, 248, 298–99
Ramat Hakovesh, 235
Ramat Rachel, 275
Ramat Yohanan, Kibbutz, 261, 264
Ramleh, 230
Ramot Meir, 79, 149, 154, 240, 336
Rehovot, 75, 86, 134, 150, 151, 185, 193, 210, 230, 238, 242
Reines, Rabbi Itzhak Yaakov, 322
Reisen, Simcha, 83
Revusky, Abraham, 62, 102, 156, 174–76, 235, 253, 267
Reyem, 238
Rishon Lezion, 134, 143, 189, 231, 243
Rivlin, Rabbi Yosef, 278
Robison, Sylvan, 194
Rockville, Connecticut, 84
Rodman, Samuel, 93
Rodovsky, Mr. [?], 297
Rokeach, Israel, 310
Roochwarg, Z., 84
Roosevelt, Theodore, 46
Rosenblatt, Judge Bernard, 56, 97, 146, 186, 189–90, 193, 197, 200–201, 207, 217, 219, 223, 227, 233, 292, 296, 305, 308, 311, 319, 334, 336–37
Rosenblatt, Louis, 286, 294, 296
Rosenbloom, Solomon, 277
Rosenstein, Morris, 133, 263
Rosh Pinnah, 243
Rosoff, Dr. Meyer L., 79, 238–42
Rothbort, Samuel, 77
Rothschild, Baron Edmond de, 152, 231
Rothschild, Lord Lionel Walter, 197
Rub-El-Nazra, 197
Rubenstein, H., 278
Rubinow, Dr. Isaac Max, 105, 201
Rubinow Lurie, Olga, 105
Ruchama, 166
Ruppin, Arthur, 63–64, 85, 140–41, 142, 149–50, 157, 160–62, 164, 166, 202, 207, 224, 274, 308

Rutenberg, Pinhas, 109, 226, 314

Sacks, Celia, 236
Sacks, Isaac, 102, 129, 149, 248, 298–99, 334
Sacks, Mendes, 236
Safed, 31, 38, 134, 136–37, 273, 284, 287, 311
Saletsky, Hannah, 206
Saletsky, Mordechai, 181, 205
Salit, Michael, 167, 277
Sampter, Jessie E., 75, 85–86, 100, 107–8
Samuel, Edwin, 289
Samuel, Sir Herbert, 93, 257, 292
Sandler, Bernard, 180
San Francisco, California, 102, 273–74, 279
Sapir, Asher, 262
Sarona (Rama), 114, 134, 149, 158, 164–66, 180, 195, 318, 336
Sarona (Templer colony near Jaffa), 167
Savannah, Georgia, 291
Schapira, Hermann, 145
Schechter, Solomon, 40
Schiff, Jacob, 48
Schmuckler, Rebecca, 51
Schneider, Rebecca, 273
Schoolman, Al P., 244
Schoolman, Bertha, 244
School of the Parents Education Association, Jerusalem, 97
Schools, 97, 174, 203, 211, 215
Schuldinger, Mr. [?], 189, 293
Schulman, Rabbi Samuel, 42–43
Schusheim, Rabbi Morris M., 244
Schwartz, Shmaya, 163
Schweizer, Peter, 142
Sedjera, 231, 242
Seligsburg, Alice L., 100, 201
Senator, Dr. Werner David, 265
Sereni, Enzo, 62, 126
Shaliah (pl. *shlichim*), 62, 126
Shamir, Pinhas, 164–65
Shankman, Mr. [?], 319–21
Shapira, Meir, 149, 248–49, 296
Shapiro, Nissel, 65
Shapiro, Yonathan, 56
Shapiro Tannery, 298

Sharf, Wolf (Zeev), 257
Sharon, plain of, 151, 164, 191, 207, 235, 245, 247–48
Shatz, Boris, 131
Shavei Zion, 49
Shaw Commission, 1929. *See* Commissions of Enquiry
Sheikh Munis, 210
Sheinkin, Menachem, 151–52, 293
Sheleg, Tamar, 108
Shifman, Samuel, 77
Shimoni, Gideon, 338–39
Shoolman, Max, 186, 189, 217, 235, 308
Shulman, Max, 165
Shunam, 196, 228
Sidney Ali, 168
Silver, Rabbi Abba Hillel, 319
Silverman, Ida M., 149, 248
Simons, H., 277
Singer, Abraham, 178
Single tax movement, 146
Skakolsky, Hirsh (Harris), 191, 243
Skupsky, Julius, 65
Sloan, Alexander K. (*see also* United States consulate, Jerusalem), 238
Slonim, M. J., 162
Smilansky, Moshe, 187, 245, 252
Smith, George Adam, 153
Socialism and socialist ideology, 32, 36, 48, 52
"Social Zionism," 97, 146, 190
Social Zionism, 97
Society of English and American Jews in Palestine, 249
Solel Boneh, 284, 286
Solomon, Eli, 205
Somerset, Pennsylvania, 77
Sorrenstein, Solomon, 282
Soskin, Zelig, 210
Spector, Abraham Aaron, 307
Sports clubs and facilities, 174, 211, 225
Springfield, Massachusetts, 156
St. Albans, Vermont, 70–71
St. Louis, Missouri (*see also* Hoachoozo of St. Louis; Poria), 156–57, 159–62
St. Paul, Minnesota, 307
Stein, Kenneth, 232
Stern, David, 150–51
Stone, Mr. [?], 297

Straus, Lina, 289
Straus, Nathan, 243–44, 275–77, 289
Straus, Nellie, 200–201
Strelsin, Moshe, 65
Sursock family, 188, 194, 196–97, 219, 224
Swan Lake, New York, 84
Synagogues, 174, 203, 211, 278, 281, 309
Syracuse, New York, 298
Syria, 95, 101, 258, 259
Syrkin, Marie, 88
Syrkin, Nachman, 44, 96
Szold, Henrietta, 64, 72, 100, 108, 109, 187, 201, 216, 225, 334, 337
Szold, Robert, 54, 80, 318

Tannenbaum, Israel, 277
Technion (Haifa), 109
Tel Adas, 167, 192, 194, 196–97
Tel Arad, 257
Tel Aviv (*see also* Jaffa), 31, 80, 104, 133–37, 141–43, 145, 162, 171–72, 175–76, 192, 210, 215, 249, 272, 273, 284, 290–302, 316, 325
   Borochov neighborhood, 142, 189, 292, 294–95
   Casino, 296
   Shapira neighborhood, 296
   Sheinkin neighborhood, 142, 293–95
Tel Aviv Bond Issue, 208, 292
Tel Aviv Development Company, 143, 294
Tel Aviv Town Council, 292–94
Tel Hadar, 238, 240
Tel Hai, 257
Tel Mond, 168, 252
Tel Raanan, 168
Thon, Dr. Jacob, 150, 194
Tiberias, 38, 134, 136, 137, 273, 284, 308, 311
Tiberias Hot Springs, 311
Tipat Halav, 100, 337
Tivon, 167, 196, 228, 230
Der Tog, 71
Toker, Jacob, 257
Topkis, Louis, 259, 298
Tourists
   American Jews, 19, 24, 125–26, 289

Visas and regulations, 124–25, 132
Towards Joy Profound, 87
Trachtenberg, Jacob, 247
Tractor, 160, 172, 202, 235
Trans-Jordan, 95, 150, 230, 258, 259
Tulsa, Oklahoma, 178
Tzahor, Zeev, 58
Tzofit, 254, 335

Um-es-Suf, 267
Um-Haled, 247
United Palestine Appeal, 194
United States, government of, 130, 161
United States Citizenship Act, 1907, 18, 26
United States Consular Agency, Haifa, 17
United States Consular Court, Jerusalem, 281–82
United States consulate, Jerusalem, 17, 26, 66, 93, 130–32, 190–91, 238, 280, 289, 301, 311
United States consulate general, Beirut, 17
United States Department of Agriculture, 152
United States Department of Interior, 150
United States Department of State, 18, 131, 191, 238
United States Navy, 58
University of Wisconsin, 51
Urban professionals, 34, 331, 338
Urofsky, Melvin I., 49
Ussishkin, Menachem, 68, 165, 207, 233, 269

Vineyards, 165, 174, 225
Visler, Leah, 132
Vitales, Harry, 252–53
Vulcanski, Yitzhak, 158, 210

Wadi Hawareth. *See* Emek Hefer
Wallace, Edwin Sherman (*see also* United States consulate, Jerusalem), 280
Warburg, Edward M., 46
Warburg, Felix, 46, 149, 288
Warburg, Otto, 140–41, 318
Washington, D.C., 47, 100
Water supply, 154, 160, 165, 167, 169,

Water supply (*continued*)
171, 174, 179, 200, 203, 206, 215, 222–23, 235, 239–40, 247, 314
Waxman, Chaim, 89–90
Weinshall, Dr. Abraham, 308
Weinstein, Solomon J., 187, 193, 224, 306, 321
Weitz, Joseph, 150–51, 169
Weizmann, Chaim, 45, 57–61, 146–47, 152, 162–63, 165, 185, 189, 192, 194, 199, 219, 223, 227, 235
What the American Zion Commonwealth Is Doing in Palestine, 76, 78
White Paper, Churchill (1922), 122
White Paper, MacDonald (1939), 66, 123
White, Zalman, 282
Wilmington, Delaware, 259, 298
Wilson, L., 85
Wilson, Samuel, 301–2
Wilson, President Woodrow, 41, 47
Winnipeg Ahuza Society, 210
Wise, Rabbi Stephen S., 42, 54, 111, 146, 166, 178
Women's training farm, Afula, 222
Woodbine, New Jersey. *See* Baron de Hirsch Agricultural and Industrial School
Worcester, Massachusetts, 156
World War I, 18, 92–93, 157, 164, 194, 231, 281, 318
World Zionist Organization, 57, 60, 72, 141, 150, 162, 182, 185, 219, 232, 299

Yakhin, 173, 175, 178, 187, 238–39, 248, 252–54
Yakir, [?], 164
Yavnieli, Shmuel, 257
Yeshiva University, 98
Yesod Hamaalah, 243
Dos Yiddishe Folk, 72–73
Yishuv. See Jews, Palestinian
Yizkor Book, 75
Young Judaea, 50–51, 248
Young Poale Zion. *See* Habonim

Zagrodsky, Dr. Melech, 162
Zarnuqa, 196, 230
Zeeland Memorandum, 146, 183
Zeff, Joseph, 48
Zelig, Haya Sarah, 323
Zichron Yaakov, 18, 134, 137, 243
Zionism, American, 39–42, 46–57, 73, 92, 96, 110, 116–17, 197
  Labor Zionism (*see also* Poale Zion of America), 36, 96
Zionist Commission for Palestine, 58, 59, 97, 119–21, 137, 201, 207, 256–57
Zionist Congresses, 46, 142, 145, 182, 192, 206, 219, 233, 259
Zionist Executive, London, 119, 126
Zionist Organization of America (ZOA, formerly Federation of American Zionists), 23, 48, 52–53, 59, 69, 72–73, 77, 119–20, 126, 141, 146, 161, 178–79, 183, 185–87, 193, 248, 252, 260, 278, 318
  Conventions of, 23, 146, 183, 186, 299
  Palestine Department, 23
  Palestine Service and Information Bureau, 29, 72, 77, 93, 98, 125–28
Zionist Organization of Canada, 59
Zionist Society of Engineers and Agriculturists, 53–54, 201
Zlotnick, Rabbi Yehuda Leib, 253
Zundelowitz, Rebecca, 260
Zur Shalom, 229